Fashion Patternmaking Techniques for Menswear

Antonio Donnanno

Fashion Patternmaking Techniques for Menswear

A Complete Reference Guide to Making Shirts, Trousers, Jackets, Coats, Cloaks, Knitwear and Underwear

HOAKI

HOAKI

Hoaki Books, S.L.
C/ Ausiàs March, 128
08013 Barcelona, Spain
T. 0034 935 952 283
F. 0034 932 654 883
info@hoaki.com
www.hoaki.com

hoakibooks

Fashion Patternmaking Techniques for Menswear
A Complete Reference Guide to Making Shirts, Trousers,
Jackets, Coats, Cloaks, Knitwear and Underwear

ISBN: 978-84-1065-025-1

Copyright © 2025 Hoaki Books, S.L.
Copyright © 2023 Ikon Editrice srl
Título original: *Il Sarto Prototipista Moderno*

Author: Antonio Donnanno
Translation: Katherine Kirby
Drawings: Elisabetta Drudi
Cover image: Gianni Pucci
Editor: Martina Panarello
Layout: Wendy Moreira
Cover design: Edu Vidiella

D.L: B 21401-2024
Printed in China

PREFACE

Giorgio Armani SS 1989

Emporio Armani

The tailor has freed himself. His evolution has been continuous and participatory: today he is endowed with unique personality and professionalism whose values are expressed by notable artistic sensibilities and a good degree of inventiveness. Clearly, for modern tailors who strive to reach high standards, the elementary, jumbled notes of the past can no longer suffice, nor can certain empirical forms (let alone superficial notions) satisfy their needs.

Today's tailors demand more culture, more knowledge of things, more detailed topics and an in-depth analysis of the technical reasons for working in one way rather than another. At the height of a degree of technical consciousness that has never been reached before, they feel the need for a rational and functional system for all purposes, be it technical or artistic. The professional awareness of tailors does not allow them to be outdated, especially when they know they can aspire to better tools and rely on better texts and aids. This is the very reason why I decided to create this new book, which will provide so much in the way of satisfaction, despite the sacrifice and extensive research it required.

In writing this text, I have covered the most fundamental topics, leaving out anything deemed unhelpful or unnecessary. In it, I illustrate every interesting aspect in the ongoing search for the best technical condition of the moment. It starts from a study of bodily conformation with the measurements of the normotype, and continues on to delve as far as possible into the correction of defects, studying the new technical concepts of our 'EURO' system.

Special attention will be paid to sample makers, an increasingly important professional figure in the menswear industry. This professional is responsible for making one or more prototypes, i.e. the sample garment that is then shaped, cut and sewn by hand by the tailor or seamstress, perfectly executing the designer's creation. This requires extensive patternmaking and tailoring expertise. The end result is not a test garment made from canvas, but a garment that necessarily has the same characteristics as the one that will be produced after approval by the designer and the technical department. They will mainly determine four aspects of the garment:

1) Does the final product respect the designer's original idea?
2) Is it in the right fabric for that specific garment?
3) Does the garment have the right fit for the company's target consumer?
4) Is it within the production cost budget?

Prototype tailors are not only responsible for making the prototype to be submitted to the stylist for approval: they must also make other prototypes based on pre-established measurements, to be given to the graphic designer for photographs to put in the catalogue.

I would like to thank all those who will make good use of this work of mine. My hope is, above all, that industry technicians, professional tailors, students and teachers will consider this book to be the best tool for finding solutions to their patternmaking and tailoring challenges.

TABLE OF CONTENTS

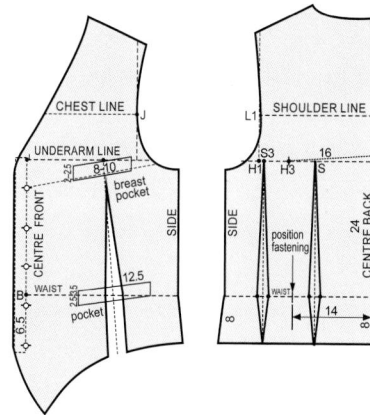

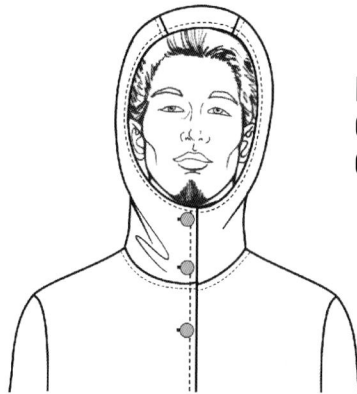

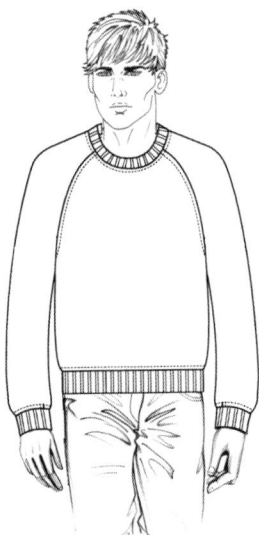

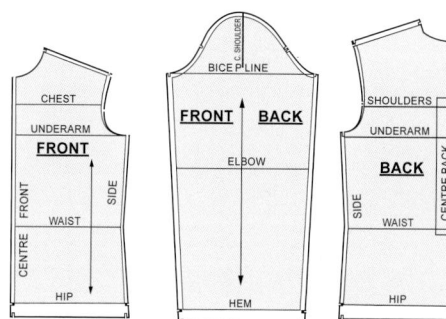

ACCESSORIES, EQUIPMENT
AND TAILORING CULTURE

Pavel Danilyuk from Pexels

PATTERNMAKING TOOLS

1. **WORK TABLE:** it should be large enough to make the patterns (110 x 200 cm / 43.3 x 78.8").
2. **DIGITISER:** makes it possible to acquire a real image of the paper pattern in a few moments and, thanks to a rapid processing system, vectorise it.
3. **PATTERN PAPER:** smooth and medium grain, in sheets or rolls, strong enough to withstand repeated use and to highlight the pattern well.
4. **MANILA BOARD:** useful for cutting out base patterns in all their components.
5. **CARBON PAPER:** used to trace certain parts of the pattern (facings, collars, sleeves, etc.).
6. **SCISSORS FOR PAPER:** useful for cutting out patterns, thereby sparing fabric scissors that would quickly become blunt.
7. **PENCILS WITH AN ERASER:** for drawing patterns.
8. **COLOURED PENCILS:** used to highlight details.
9. **RULERS: 80-100 cm or a yardstick**, useful for measuring and drawing straight lines on patterns. Rulers with a non-slip rubber base are ideal.
10. **LARGE L-SHAPED SQUARE (TAILOR'S SQUARE):** used for squaring corners or marking the grain of the weft.
11. **FRENCH CURVES:** useful for joining curved lines or shaped seams.
12. **LARGE COMPASSES:** for drawing arcs and circles.
13. **TRACING WHEEL:** necessary to trace the pattern from one layer of the pattern to the next, especially when drawing lapels. It is also used to mark assembly lines on the garment's lining, interfacing and lightweight, smooth fabric.
14. **WEIGHTS:** to hold the patterns in place during the first drawing phase.
15. **ADHESIVE TAPE:** holds paper patterns or pattern transformations to the table.
16. **LONG SEWING PINS:** used to secure the pattern on the fabric before cutting.
17. **PINCUSHIONS:** can be wrist, table or magnetic.
18. **PATTERN HOOKS:** very useful for hanging patterns whose individual parts have been tied together.
19. **PATTERN NOTCHERS:** used to mark notches or reference points on paperboard patterns.
20. **HOLE PUNCH:** to punch holes in cardboard patterns for hanging.
21. **PERFORATOR:** used to make reference holes in patterns, darts/pleats and pockets.
22. **HOLE PATTERN:** used to punch holes in cardboard and plastic patterns, with a diameter of 2 to 25 mm.
23. **CARDBOARD OR PLASTIC SHEARS:** useful for cutting industrialised cardboard or plastic patterns.
24. **SHEARS:** they can be up to 50 cm / 19.5" long and weigh up to 1 kg / 2.2 lb.

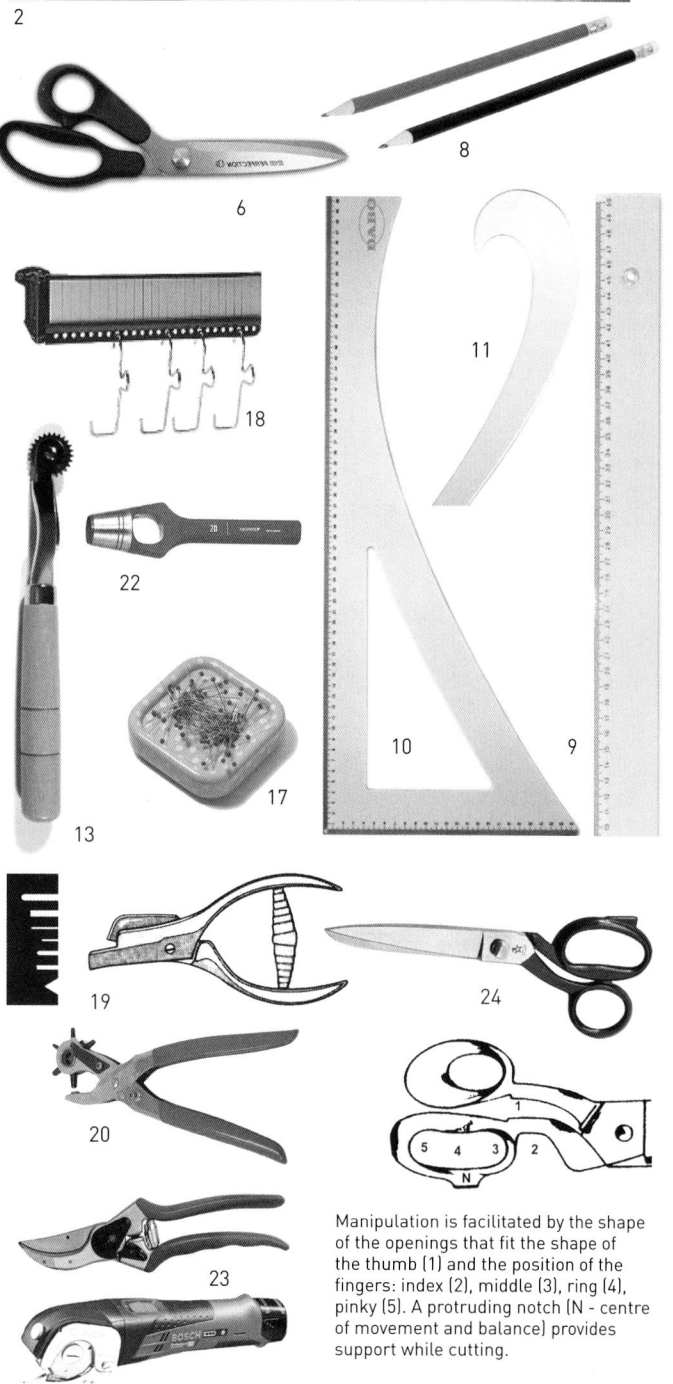

Manipulation is facilitated by the shape of the openings that fit the shape of the thumb (1) and the position of the fingers: index (2), middle (3), ring (4), pinky (5). A protruding notch (N - centre of movement and balance) provides support while cutting.

25. **MACHINIST'S SCISSORS:** about 12 cm / 4.7" long and with two points, these very sharp scissors are used for trimming and notching edges.

26. **PINKING SHEARS:** special scissors with a zig-zag blade, used to cut all types of fabrics so that they don't fray. They are also useful when you need to soften or lighten the edges of heat-seal interfacing.

27. **THREAD CLIPS:** special scissors used to trim over-hanging threads from basting, etc.

28. **BUTTONHOLE SCISSORS:** used to form buttonholes and eyelets, they have a screw that can be adjusted to the desired length.

29. **CUTTING TABLE:** consists of an iron frame, a tempered hardboard top and a chipboard sub-top. These tables are generally 110 to 200 cm / 43 to 79" wide and approx. 100 cm / 40" high, and can be equipped with fabric roll holders or spreading machines.

30. **THIMBLES:** in metal or bone, pitted with small grooves, to protect the middle finger while sewing. The one traditionally used by menswear tailors is open at the top, while the one for women is completely covered.

31. **MIRROR:** one or three-light. It's essential for all garment making processes, from the initial analysis of the client's figure to finishing the garment.

32. **MANNEQUIN:** useful in tailoring, as it reproduces the shape and contours of the figure, as well as chest, waist and hip measurements. It can be used to pin paper patterns, to check partially sewn garments and see if further changes are needed, and to finish and refine details such as the positioning of pockets and hem lines. Adjustable mannequins have mechanisms that allow individual areas of the chest, waist and hips to expanded or made smaller.

33. **TAILOR'S CHALK:** these pieces can be clay or wax, faint or bold, and come in assorted colours. Clay chalk is suitable for fabric with a smooth finish, while waxed chalk is suitable for rough fabrics. They're difficult to remove from fabric with a hard surface.

34. **CHALK SHARPENER:** a plastic or wooden tool with blades for sharpening tailor's chalk.

35. **HAND SEWING NEEDLES:** sizes and types vary depending on both the work to be done and the fabric to be sewn. The larger the number the finer the gauge.

36. **NEEDLES FOR SEWING MACHINES:** details on page 17.

37. **CHALK HEM MARKER:** a graduated metal rod inside which runs a container of powder chalk that is sprayed onto the garment by means of a rubber pump.

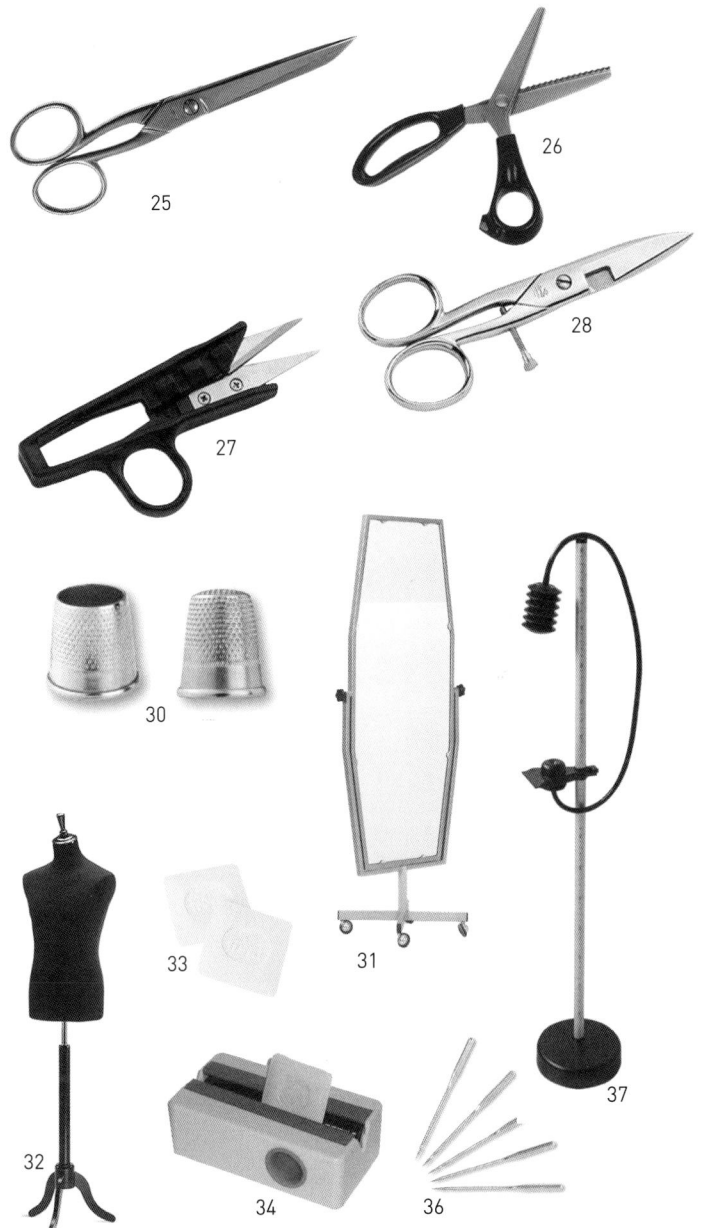

IRONING TOOLS

1) Irons
They can be with or without steam. Irons with a steam option make it possible to shrink fabrics without wetting them and to give shape to garments.

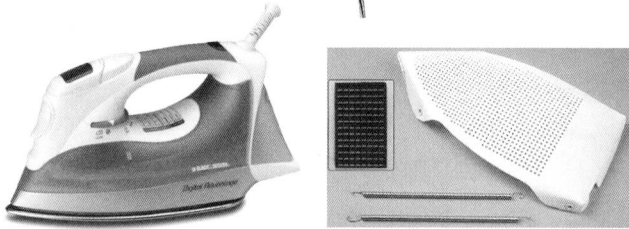

2) Steam press
Particularly useful in the application of heat-activated tape, steam presses make it possible to apply the interfacing over large areas or to group small parts together in a single ironing. The maximum exerted pressure is approximately 45 kg (100 lbs), which should be adjusted according to the recommendations of the cloth manufacturer.

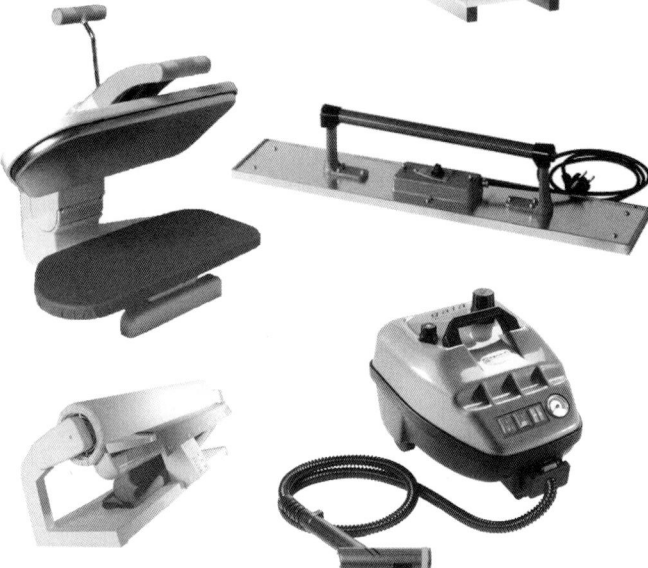

3) Ironing board or table
Padded wooden or metal mesh board in the shape of a semi-ellipse, mounted on a metal support or embedded inside a cabinet, used for ironing.

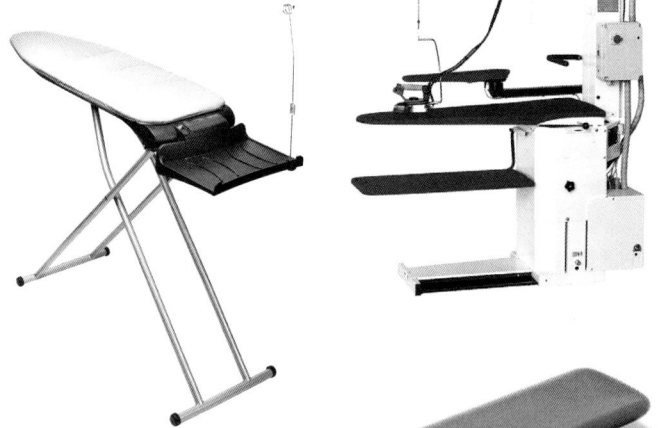

4) Sleeve ironing board
Small ironing board with two sides of different sizes, used for ironing sleeves and other very narrow openings.

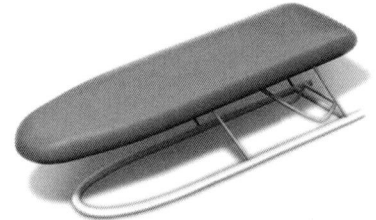

5) Tailor's ham
Oval-shaped, padded ironing accessory. Useful for ironing jacket breasts, pleats, sleeve puffs and shoulders.

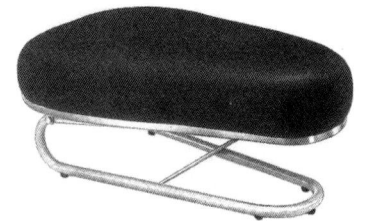

6) Velvet needle mat
A mat or board made of wood or other material, covered with very thin metal pins, used for ironing velvet, corduroy or fabrics with a raised motif.

7) Point presser
It is used to push out corners and to keep edges open for ironing.

8) Wooden clapper
Used to flatten seams, creases and enclosed edges while ironing.

Note on using irons
In tailoring, iron use must be calibrated. In other words, intelligently employed depending on the fabric to be used and the pattern to be executed.

The lighter the fabric, the less it 'obeys' the iron; the more delicate the fabric, the more the iron can damage it. You have to remember that, with a few rare exceptions, all the tight parts, all the wrinkles which the iron seems to fix by sheer thermal force, will eventually return.

SEWING MACHINES

A sewing machine is a mechanical or electromechanical apparatus used to join fabric or leather by means of a seam, by passing one or more threads made of cotton or other materials through a needle which moves alternately from top to bottom.

The most common sewing machine structure consists of a base from which an upright emerges, which, in addition to containing the moving parts of the needle bar and thread tension assembly, serves to support the arm. The opposite end of the horizontal arm is the sewing head, which holds the needle bar, presser foot and the parts that determine the tension of the upper thread. Below the machine bed are the parts used t determine the stitch (bobbin case and bobbins).

There are various models of sewing machines: they differ not only in the type of stitches created, but also in their structure, which consequently makes them suitable for different uses.

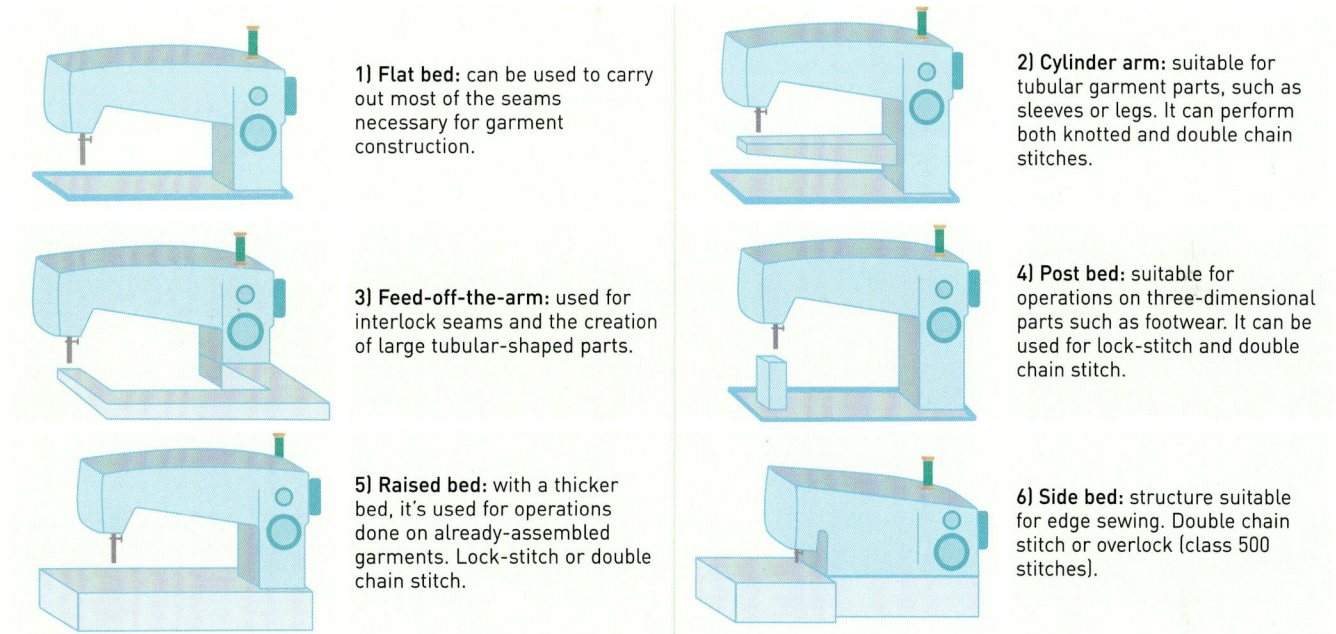

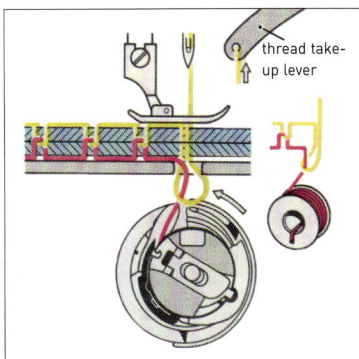

1) Flat bed: can be used to carry out most of the seams necessary for garment construction.

2) Cylinder arm: suitable for tubular garment parts, such as sleeves or legs. It can perform both knotted and double chain stitches.

3) Feed-off-the-arm: used for interlock seams and the creation of large tubular-shaped parts.

4) Post bed: suitable for operations on three-dimensional parts such as footwear. It can be used for lock-stitch and double chain stitch.

5) Raised bed: with a thicker bed, it's used for operations done on already-assembled garments. Lock-stitch or double chain stitch.

6) Side bed: structure suitable for edge sewing. Double chain stitch or overlock (class 500 stitches).

thread take-up lever

Thread-needle loop mechanism

SHUTTLES AND BOBBIN CASES FOR LOCKSTITCH

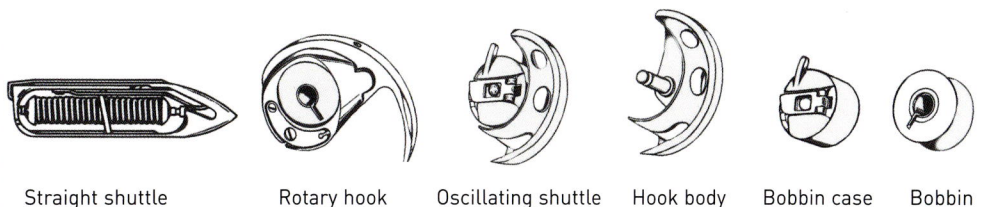

| Straight shuttle | Rotary hook | Oscillating shuttle | Hook body | Bobbin case | Bobbin |

HORIZONTAL ROTARY HOOK

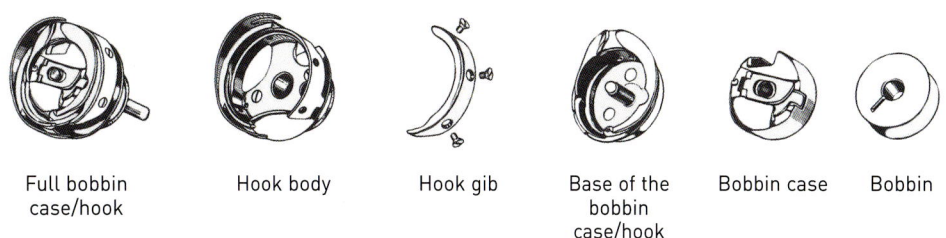

| Full bobbin case/hook | Hook body | Hook gib | Base of the bobbin case/hook | Bobbin case | Bobbin |

MACHINE-SEWN STITCHES

Stitches are units formed by thread in the production of seams and topstitching. A seam consists of a series of stitches joining two or more pieces of fabric. Stitching is a series of stitches incorporated onto a piece of fabric. It is used for embellishment (topstitching) and for finishing edges (hems). Seams are used to join pieces, while stitching is used to prepare pieces for joining and also includes trimmings and decorative finishes.

TYPES OF MACHINE-SEWN STITCHES

There are many different types of stitches that can be made by sewing machines. Here are some notes on the classification of stitch types taken from the United States Federal Standard No. 751. The listed stitches are divided into six classes.

Class 100. Simple chain stitch. This class of stitch shall be formed with one or more needle threads and has for its general characteristic interlooping. A loop or loops of thread or threads shall be passed through the material and secured by interlooping with succeeding loop or loops, after they are passed through the material, to form a stitch. The most frequently used type of stitch in this class is stitch 101, commonly called single-thread chain stitch. It's a type of stitch that can be easily undone and is therefore used for basting.

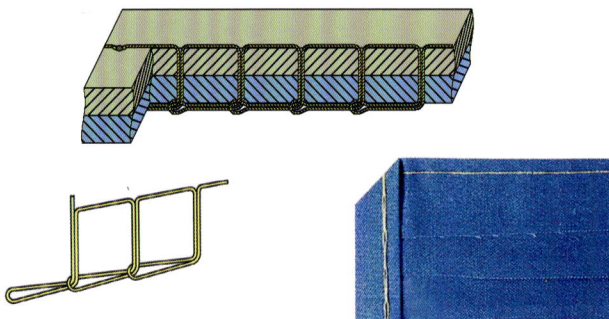

Class 200. Hand stitch. This class of stitch is formed by hand with one or more needle threads. Their general characteristic is that each thread passes through the material as a single line of thread. This results in an alternating succession of stitches made by the needle thread on both the upper and lower faces. These stitches are almost never created on industrial sewing machines.

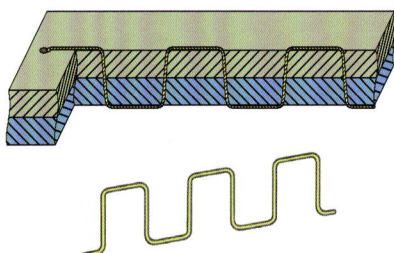

Class 300. Lockstitch. This class of stitch is formed by two or more groups of threads. Its main characteristic is the interlacing of the two groups: A) needle thread group; B) looper or bobbin thread.

Loops of group A are passed through the material where, thanks to a thread recovery unit, it is pulled into the fabric together with group B (looper or bobbin thread). Both faces of the fabric have a continuous succession of stitches, consisting of straight sections of thread. The most commonly used stitches belonging to the 300 class are stitch type 301, commonly referred to as a lock stitch and consisting of two threads, one carried by the needle and the other coming from a small bobbin placed on a special support under the needle plate, and stitch type 304, a lock stitch executed in a zig-zag pattern.

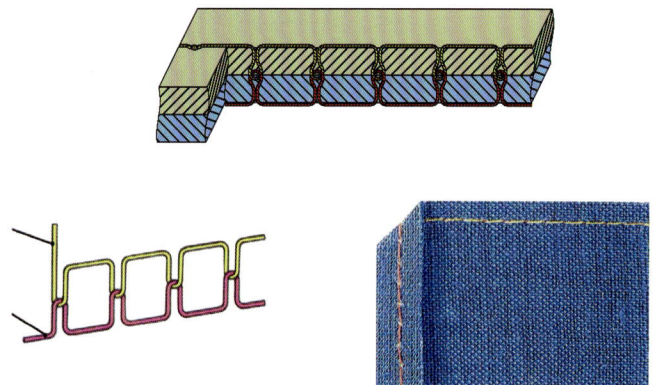

Class 400. Chain stitch. The stitch types belonging to this class are created by two thread groups: A) needle thread; B) bobbin thread. Their general characteristic is that the loops of the needle thread are formed when the needle passes through the fabric and are secured by interlacing and interlooping with the bobbin thread. This happens on the lower part (underside) of the fabric. The most commonly used stitches are: stitch type 401, commonly called multi-thread chain stitch; stitch type 404; stitch type 406, 2-needle coverseam; stitch type 407, 3-needle coverseam.

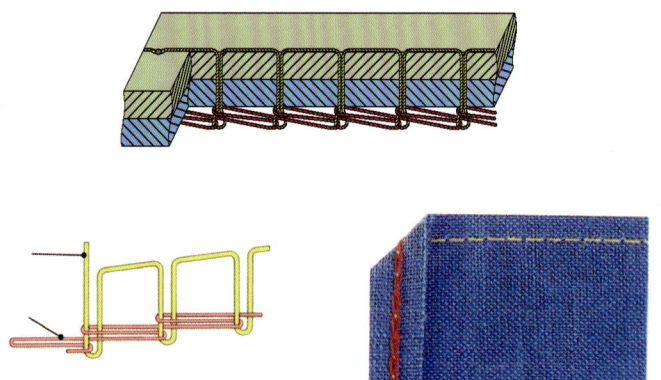

Class 500. Overedge (overlock) stitches. The types of points belonging to this class are formed by one or more groups of threads, namely: A) needle thread; B) looper thread; C) upper looper thread. In this stitch class, the loops of one thread group must pass over the edges of the fabric. This means that the thread can pass outside the fabric from under to over the edge. In other cases, the loops of two groups of threads may lace together, right on the edges of the assembled pieces of fabric. The most common stitch in this category is type 501, one-thread overlock (also called overedge). The stitching and covering of the cut edges of fabric is achieved with only the needle thread, which forms a loop in the lower part of the fabric. Through two blind loopers, it's brought out from below to the top, where it is interlooped with itself in the movement returning back to the lower side.

Stitch type 506. 2-needle and 4-thread overlock. The needle threads interloop, on the top and the bottom, both the covers due to the threads carried by the upper looper, which are interlaced on the edge of the fabric.

Stitch type 509. 2-needle, 3-thread overlock. Two needle threads interloop, on the top and bottom, the cover thread constituted by the lower looper thread, which an upper blind looper brings to the top of the fabric, making both needle threads able to interloop with it.

Stitch type 512. 2-needle, 4-thread overlock. Both needle threads are interlooped with the lower cover, while the upper cover is only interlooped by the right needle.

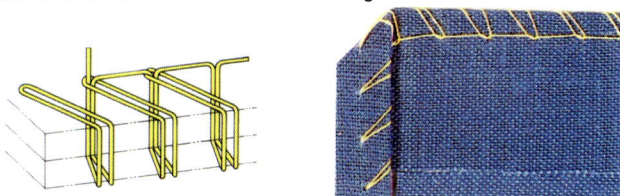

Stitch type 503. 2-thread overedge. In this stitch, loops of needle thread are passed through the fabric and brought to the edge, where they are interlooped with the looper thread. Loops of looper thread extend from the edge to the point of needle penetration.

Class 600. Covering chain stitch. The stitches in this class are formed by two or more groups of threads: A) needle threads; B) top cover threads; C) bottom looper threads.

A characteristic feature of the stitches belonging to this class is that the threads of groups B and C cover the upper and lower sides of the fabric.

Stitch type 602. 2-needle and 4-thread cover stitch with top cover.

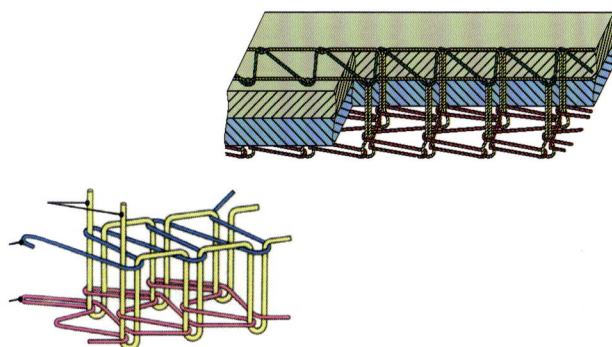

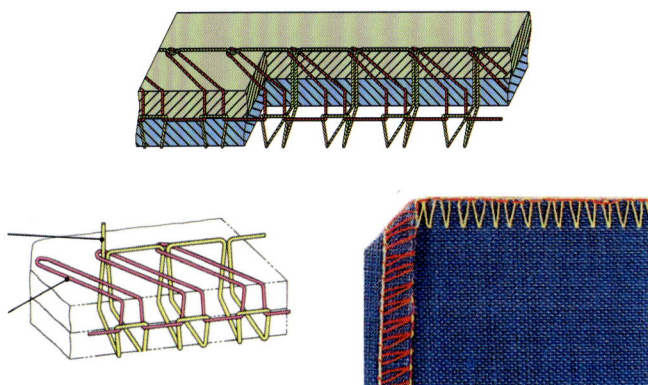

Stitch type 504. 3-thread overedge. Both loopers (looper and cover) are threaded and the lower one creates the stitches seen on the top of the fabric. The two groups of threads are interlooped together on the edge of the fabric and are in turn interlooped on the inside of the seam by the needle thread.

Stitch type 605. 3-needle, 5-thread cover stitch with top cover.

This process is mainly used for cut knit outerwear.

SEAM GUIDES AND PRESSER FEET

Seam guides enable sewing operations to be carried out quickly and optimally. Hemmers feed fabric in the direction of the needle in the correct position, thereby ensuring even seam distribution. The presser foot is attached to the presser bar and is pressed onto the fabric by the force of an adjustable spring, so that the fabric can be moved by the lower feed dog. Its shape and special features depend on the sewing operations to be done and the type of material used.

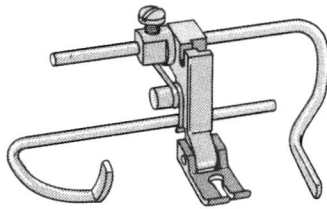

Adjustable hemmer to maintain fixed heights

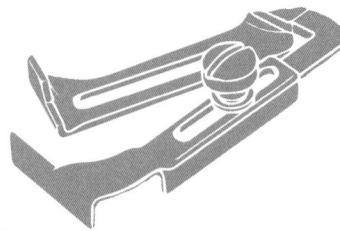

Hemmer foot

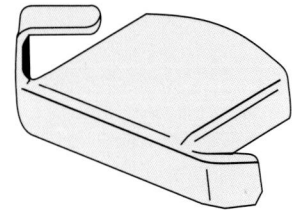

Magnetic guide

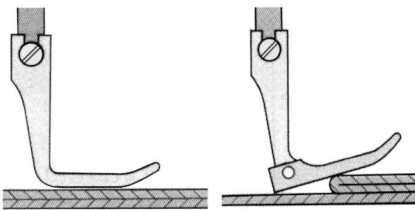

Fixed presser foot for seams without fabric thickness increases.

Articulated presser foot to pass over increases in fabric thickness.

Hemmer for turned edges.

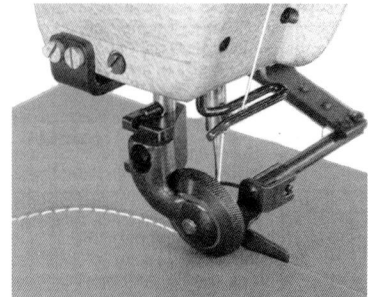

Roller foot and oscillating edge presser guide.

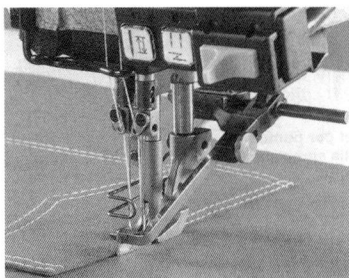

Levelling lever foot and edge guide.

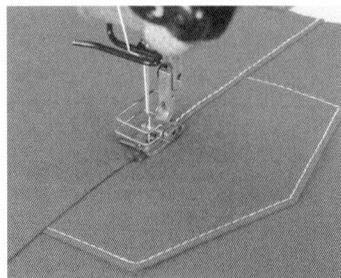

Compensating presser foot divided into two sections, with a guide for sewing hems 2 mm from the edge.

Guide with turned-up flat fell seams.

Guide for the application of bias tape.

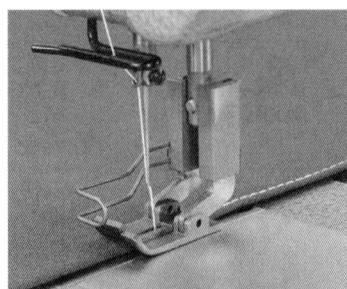

Compensating presser foot divided into two sections for sewing hems.

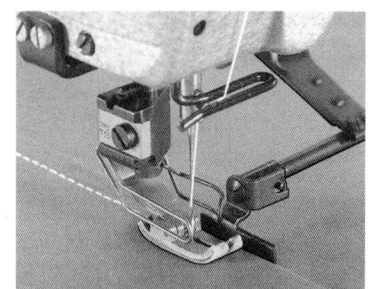

Teflon-coated presser foot.

SEWING MACHINE NEEDLES

There are different types of sewing machine needles, defined by DIN 5330. The needle to use should be chosen depending on the material to be sewn, the thread, and the type of stitch and seam to be made.

NEEDLE MEASUREMENTS

To do so, the metric unit 'Nm' is used, which corresponds to the diameter of the shaft just above the scarf, expressed in hundredths of a millimetre. In particular, we have 60 and 70 Nm for fine needles; 80 and 90 Nm for medium needles; and 110 and 120 Nm for thick needles.

NEEDLE POINTS

The different characteristics of materials to be sewn require needles with various tip types.

- **Conical points.** Sharp conical points (a) pass through the threads of fabric. They are used for blind stitching and for sewing fine, thin, compact fabrics. They are not suitable for knits. A normal conical point (b) moves the fabric threads to the sides without damaging them and is slightly rounded. This is the most versatile type of point. A truncated conical point (c) is very rounded and is used especially on button-attaching machines.

- **Rounded points.** Depending on their shape, they are divided into conical and spherical points and have different uses depending on the material to be sewn. Light ballpoints (a) are used for delicate fabrics. Medium (b) or blunt (c) ballpoint needles are used to sew elastic materials that contain rubber or elastomer threads. The threads are not pierced by the tip but only pushed aside.

- **Sharp points.** Used to sew leather, plastic materials, non-woven fabric and coated fabrics. They are subdivided and defined according to the position of the cutting part and their shape. In terms of positions, for example, there's a left-hand cut (b) for leather, while in terms of shapes, there are elongated (a), triangular and diamond-shaped points, just to name a few.

NEEDLE TYPES

1) **Leather needles.** These needles gently pierce leather without tearing it because they are wedge-shaped with sharp points. They are not suitable for synthetic (faux) suede. Sizes range from 90/14 to 110/18.

2) **Twin needles.** These needles are used for decorative stitching, topstitching and pintucking. They are composed of two needles mounted on a single shank. Sizes range from 80/12 to 90/14 with a width of 1.8 mm - 4 mm / 0.07 - 0.16". A 75/11 double needle for elastic seams is 4 mm / 0.16" in diameter.

3) **Triple needles.** These needles are designed for straight decorative stitching with fine thread, and they cannot be used on heavy fabrics or multiple layers. The needles are mounted very close together, on the same shank. Sizes range from 80/12 with a 2.5 mm / 0.10" diameter to 90/14 with a 3 mm / 0.12" diameter.

4) **Stretch needles.** These needles are designed to prevent skipped stitches on stretch fabrics. Sizes range from 75/11 to 90/14.

5) **Jeans needles.** These needles are used for sewing very densely woven or heavily starched fabrics. They do not warp because they have long, spherical points, stiff blades and thin eyes. Sizes range from 90/14 to 110/10.

6) **Topstitching needles.** They have a wide eye to be able to use thick thread and avoid skipped stitches or torn thread. Sizes range from 80/12 to 110/18.

7) **Wing needles.** These needles are designed for decorative hemstitches, as they separate threads to create a hole in dry fabrics such as linen. The blades are like two wings projecting from either side of the eye. Sizes range from 100/16 to 120/20.

8) **Twin wing needles.** These needles are used for decorative and/or special stitches. Two needles are mounted on the same shank: the universal needle makes a small hole and the wing needle performs the hemstitch. Only available in size 100/16.

9) **Self-threading needle.** These needles have a spiral inlet at the eye and are useful for those with poor eyesight. A diagonal opening that ends in the eye allows the thread to slide down the blade into place. Sizes range from 80/11 to 100/16.

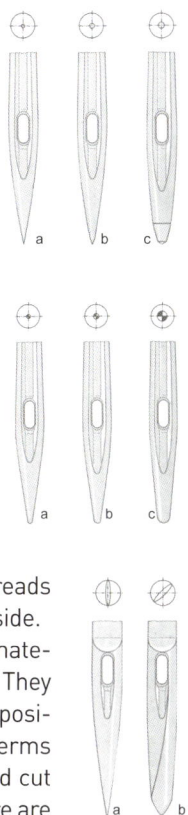

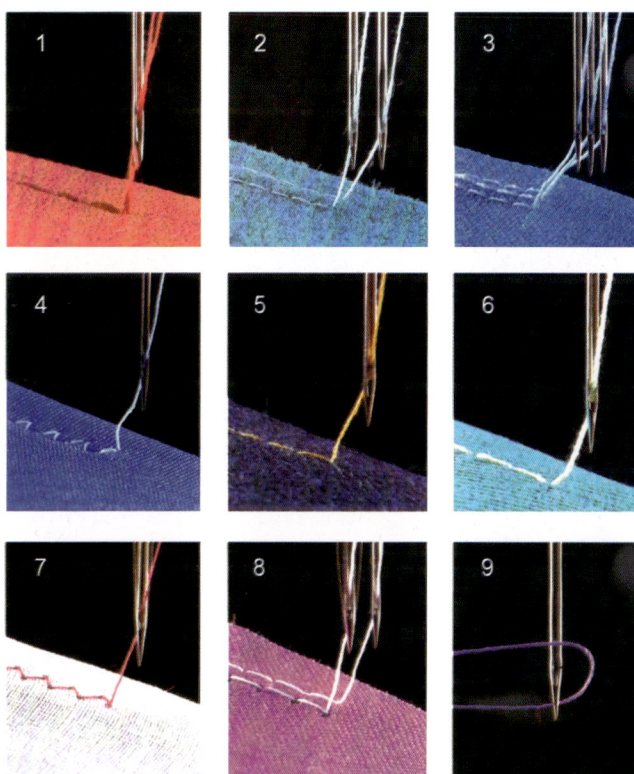

HAND SEWING NEEDLES AND THREADS

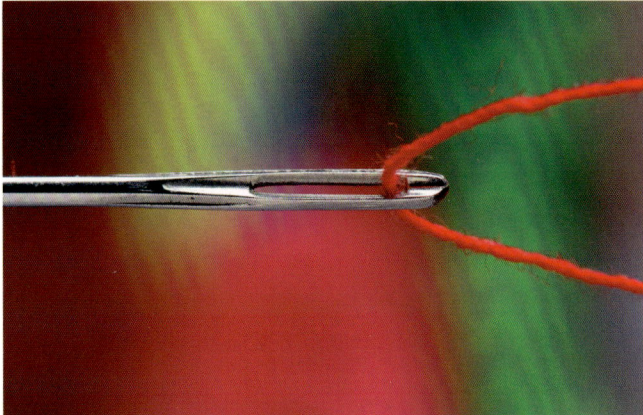

Depending on their use, hand sewing needles vary in length, diameter and in the shape of the point, which can even be curved in some cases (saddler's needles, mattress needles, etc.).

People often underestimate the importance of choosing the right needle and thread according to the type of fabric to be sewn, but it is important to remember that this step is crucial to a successful outcome.

CHOOSING THE RIGHT NEEDLES AND YARNS

The main rules to follow are:
1) sew lightweight fabrics with a fine needle and thread;
2) sew heavy fabrics with a sturdier needle and thread;
3) use the same thread for the needle and bobbin (except for embroidery);
4) change the needle from time to time;
5) if the seams are not even, check if the needle is blunt;
6) if stitches are being skipped, check if the needle is the right size;
7) in order to thread the needle faster, you should cut the thread diagonally without wetting it.

The same care must be taken with the threads to be used. In addition, it is possible that no. 30 cotton yarn does not correspond in thickness to no. 30 gauge polyester yarn, so it's always a good idea to check the yarn type before use.

When purchasing thread, the number indicating its thickness can be read on the label: as a rule, the higher the number, the thinner the yarn. For example, no. 80 cotton thread (which can be used for delicate fabrics such as lingerie and blouses) is much finer than no. 30 cotton thread (which is suitable for heavy cotton fabrics, workwear, upholstery, etc.).

WAXED THREAD

To coat and reinforce the thread used in hand stitching and to reduce the formation of knots and tangles, beeswax should be used: stitches made with waxed thread are more likely to stay in place. Waxed thread is sold in haberdashers, but can also be created directly using normal thread. To do so, run the thread over the piece of wax, iron it with a hot iron and remove the excess wax. Ironing makes the thread softer and easier to handle. However, waxed thread should not be used for temporary tacking; normal thread should be used instead.

The quality of the thread must be given due consideration when choosing a needle for a particular job. Good-quality thread (a) is smooth, even in thickness and flows well. Poor-quality thread (b), on the other hand, alternates between thin and thicker areas, which means it doesn't flow through fabric well, producing filaments and tangles. To check the quality of thread, examine it against fabric of a contrasting colour (light on dark and vice versa).

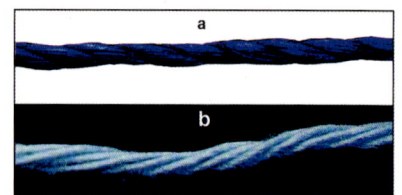

FABRIC		THREAD	NEEDLE
LIGHTWEIGHT FABRIC	Fine linen Georgette Tricot Wool Synthetic fabric	Silk no. 80-100 Cotton no. 80-100 Synthetic no. 80-100	65/9 75/11
MEDIUM WEIGHT FABRIC	Cotton Synthetic fabric Lightweight jersey Wool	Silk no. 50 Cotton no. 60-80 Synthetic no. 50 Cotton no. 50	75/11 90/14
HEAVYWEIGHT FABRIC	Denim jersey Heavyweight cotton Winter fabrics Upholstery Quilting	Silk no. 50 Cotton no. 40-50 Synthetic no. 40-50 Silk no. 30 Cotton no. 50	90/14 100/16

SEWING THREAD

The creation of a good-quality garment, especially if tailor-made, is closely linked to the characteristics of the yarns used to make it, which is why it is necessary to understand their qualities and thereby choose the best ones. According to European customs legislation, a yarn must fulfil three requirements to be considered 'sewing thread': 1) it must be put up on supports with a total weight of no more than 1000 g (yarn + support); 2) dressed for use as sewing thread; 3) it must have a final Z-twist.

Good yarn, to be defined as such, must have the following characteristics: 1) good sewability; 2) proven tear and abrasion resistance; 3) consistent flow through fabrics; 4) good resistance to acidic substances (e.g., sweat); 5) light and weather resistance; 6) seam brilliance; 7) high uniformity; 8) high heat resistance during the hemming process.

In addition, there are specific applications where yarn with flame-resistant characteristics or antistatic and water-repellent properties are required.

YARN FINENESS

An identifying characteristic of a given yarn is its density (or yarn count or yarn number), i.e., the conventional notation referring to fineness.

The International Organisation for Standardisation (ISO) identifies fineness via the tex system, which has the gram as the unit of weight for every 1000 metres of thread or yarn. For example, a tex 1 yarn means that 1000 of that yarn weighs 1 gram. DeciTex or dtex is used a lot as a submultiple: 1 tex = 10 dtex.

Other popular systems to measure fineness are as ratios between weight and length. Gauge measurements by weight, similar to the tex system, convey the weight of a material for a given length: the higher the number, the thicker the yarn, expressed in deniers (D). 1 denier is equivalent to 1/20 of a gram or 0.05 grams.

Gauge by length, on the other hand, inverts the ratio to be expressed as length per a given weight: the higher the number, the finer the yarn. This group includes the 'Number metric' system (Nm), which indicates the number of km (Nm x 1000) required to reach a weight of 1000 g.

There is also the English system. 'Number English' (Ne, NeC or ECC - English Cotton Count) indicates how many 840 yd (768 m) lengths of skein material there are per 1 lb (454 g) of yarn. For example, Ne 1 means that 1 hank of yarn of 768 meters weighs 454 grams. This fineness measurement is used for cotton, including in Italy.

One notable difference between polyamide and polyester yarns is that the latter have a higher specific weight, a thinner cross-section and are less fine than a polyamide yarn with the same reference number. This makes it possible to use thinner needles, which reduces the heating of the threads, resulting in better sealing as well as a more aesthetically pleasing seam.

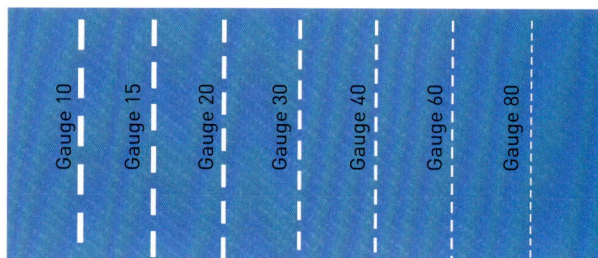

Various gauges compared

YARN TYPE	CHARACTERISTICS	USE
Twisted cotton sewing thread	High-quality, combed, brushed, twisted, gassed, mercerised, dyed and lubricated ringspun yarn. They are produced in a wide range of sizes.	Almost all sewing operations on cotton fabrics.
Twisted silk sewing thread	Twisted, dyed and lubricated silk filaments. 15 to 80 tex.	Buttonhole threads
Schappe silk sewing thread	Yarn processed and twisted according to the Schappe system, dyed and lubricated. 8 to 34 tex.	Almost all sewing operations on silk and cotton fabrics.
Twisted polyester sewing thread	Polyester staple yarn, dyed and lubricated. 8 to 34 tex.	Sewing on almost all fabrics.
Monofilament sewing thread	Generally made of polyester, these single filament threads are usually transparent. 70 to 850 D (100 and 8 tex).	Blind stitching.
Textured sewing threads	Filaments that are textured, dyed and lubricated, then coloured. 18 to 80 tex.	Finishing and trimming cut edges.
Core-spun yarn	High-quality sewing threads with a polyester thread core, covered with cotton. The polyester provides strength and the cotton serves as insulation to prevent the polyester from melting upon contact with the needle heated by friction. 7 to 35 tex.	Almost all seams, especially when the stitching speed is rather high.

BASIC FABRIC NOTIONS

Fabric is a flexible layer formed by one, two or more thread systems that are crossed and interwoven with each other in certain directions, depending on their weaves.

In everyday speech, the word 'textile' denotes a wide range of industrial or hand-made products with markedly different structural characteristics, but which at first glance might look quite similar. It is therefore important to create a fabric classification or codification system, not least so that there is a common language used across garment companies.

Fabrics are products that are made from fibres that undergo different types of processes. In particular, they can be made from:

- yarns, which can be turned into woven fabrics (cloth), knits, plaits, and openwork fabrics.
- fibres, from which non-woven fabrics (felt and needle-punched) are made.
- combinations, from which needlepunched, coated fabrics are made.

Fabric made from yarn

Woven fabric

Knitted fabric

Openwork fabric

Braided fabric

Non-woven fabric

Needlepunched

Felt

Combination fabric

Needlepunched fabric

Coated

The warp is the set of threads that form the length and direction of the fabric, stretched vertically on the loom between the two beams. The warp threads are usually more twisted and stronger than the weft threads. The latter is a complex of threads that are placed perpendicular to the warp, with which they are interwoven by means of bobbin-carrying shuttles. The weft forms the width of the fabric, which can vary from 70 cm to 150 cm / 0.77 to 1.64 yards, reaching, in bed linens, a width of 240 cm / 2.62 yards) and 300 cm / 3.28 yards for tulle. The selvedge is the lateral edging of the fabric. This sort of border can be of various widths, often characterised by a denser warp or warp threads in a different material. It prevents the fabric from fraying, but is also useful during finishing operations to keep the fabric taught.

FABRIC COMPOSITION ANALYSIS

For a tailor, knowledge of the fibres from which a fabric is made is important, both for possible allergies and to determine the best way to store and maintain the completed garment. The most effective way to distinguish natural from synthetic fibres is the 'flame test'. Take a piece of cloth and roll it up into a small ball, then burn it inside a small fireproof container.

- Cotton, linen, viscose and even rayon will burn with a glow, giving off the smell of burnt paper and leaving soft, grey ashes.
- Wool and silk burn slowly and char, retreating from the flame. They give off a smell of burnt hair or feathers and leave impalpable ashes.
- Polyester, nylon and other synthetics burn and melt only in the flame or very close to it. They give off a chemical smell and leave a hard ball instead of ashes.
- Acetate and acrylic burn and melt even after removal from the flame, leaving a hard ball. Acetate is identified by dipping the sample in acetone-based nail polish remover, which dissolves it.

HOW TO RECOGNISE THE 'RIGHT' AND 'WRONG' SIDES

It should always be remembered that, for all fabrics:
- The selvedge is always on the warp side.
- The warp is always stronger than the weft.

Alan de la Cruz from Unsplash

- The warp always has a higher thread count.
- The more twisted thread is generally the warp. In fuzzy fabrics, the pile wraps around the warp.
- In striped fabrics, the warp is parallel to the stripes.
- In checked fabrics, the print in the direction of the warp is never perfect, but slightly elongated.
- In pure silk fabrics, the warp threads are coupled and more twisted.
- On a bolt of fabric, the right is always inside the folded flap.
- Identifying lettering and numbers stamped on fabric can always be read from the wrong side: the right side has no such technical details of any kind, with rare exceptions.

- In sample bunches, the label is placed on the front (right side) of the fabric.
- In worsted cloth, the weave chord will be skewed to the right, while in woollen cloth it will be the opposite, i.e. skewed to the left.
- In printed fabrics, the pattern is, of course, sharper and more evident on the right side.

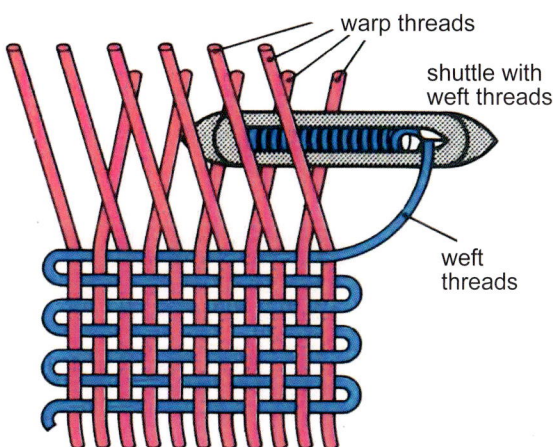

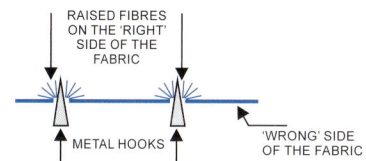

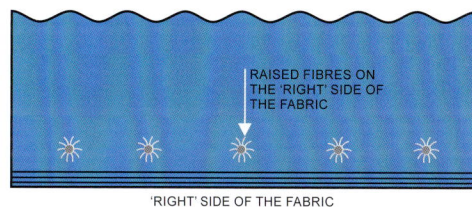

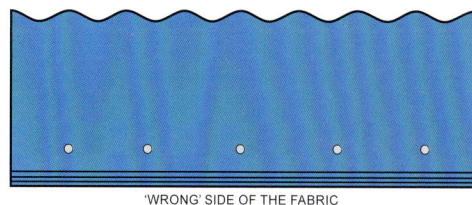

THE BODY-PATTERN RELATIONSHIP

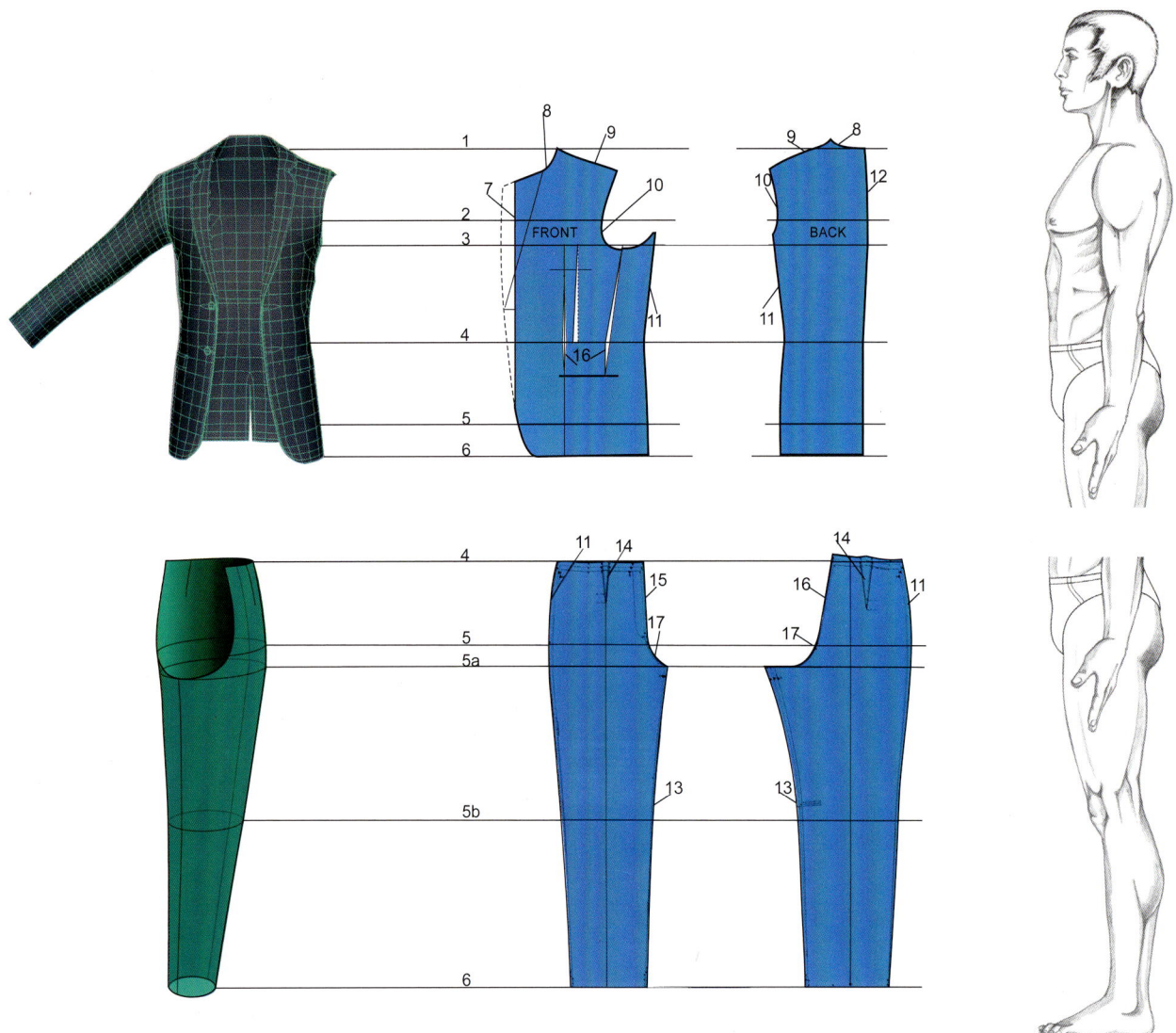

Each paper pattern is a two-dimensional map of the three-dimensional human body. It has straight and curved lines that correspond to the lines of the body with measurements or dimensions equal to those of the person, plus the basic ease and that of the pattern. Its modification consists of adding or removing space in all areas where the measurement is different from that of the body plus ease. The 'two-dimensional map' has the following reference lines.

1) Neck line: runs across the front and back neck.

2) Shoulder line: runs across the front and back shoulders.

3) Chest line: the torso at the height of the armpits.

4) Waist line: on the pattern with darts, it corresponds to the natural waist.

5) Hip line: corresponds to the fullest point of the pelvis, seen from the side.

5a) Crotch line: corresponds to the actual crotch.

5b) Knee line: corresponds to the actual knee.

6) Hem line: on the pattern it corresponds to the desired point according to the style, fashion and type of garment.

7) Centre-front line: on the pattern it corresponds to the actual centre front, to which the chosen closure (zip, buttons, lapels, etc.) is to be added.

8) Neckline: this is where the collar is added, or it can be trimmed with other details.

9) Shoulder seam: on the paper pattern, it corresponds to the actual shoulder.

10) Armscye or armhole: corresponds to the curve of the armpit, on which the sleeve crown (or cap) is to be sewn.

11) Side seam line: on the paper pattern, it goes from the under armsyce to the hem for the bodice and from the waist to the hem for trousers.

12) Centre back seam line: this seam runs from the neckline to the back hem, except for the slit in the centre.

13) Inner leg seam line (inseam): on the paper pattern, it runs from the curve of the crotch to the hem of the leg.

14) Darts and pleats: folds that fit the curves of the body.

15) Front crotch seam line: on the paper pattern, it goes from the waist and curves under the crotch area. It's curved at the front and back and is straight in the middle.

16) Seam line behind the curve of the body of the crotch: extends from the waist to the most prominent part of the buttocks. In this area, the seam is straight.

17) Crotch curve: on the paper pattern it corresponds to the curve of the body in the crotch area.

ANATOMY OF THE HUMAN BODY

While we have no illusions about converting the art of cutting into a science, we do think it is necessary to mention a few elementary notions of anatomy.

THE SKELETON

The skeleton constitutes the framework of the human body, indicating its proportions and characteristics. Bones can be long, flat, wide, short or irregular. The bones of the limbs are long and cylindrical. Wide, flat bones surround and protect the internal organs of the body. The most mobile parts of the body, the hands and feet, are made up of short bones. The skull is made up of irregular bones.

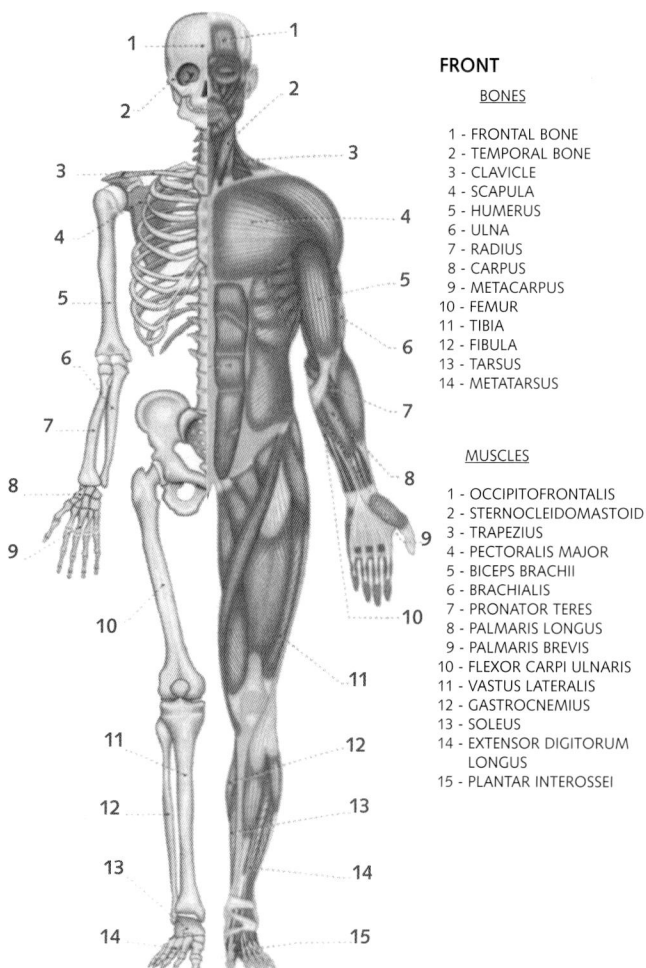

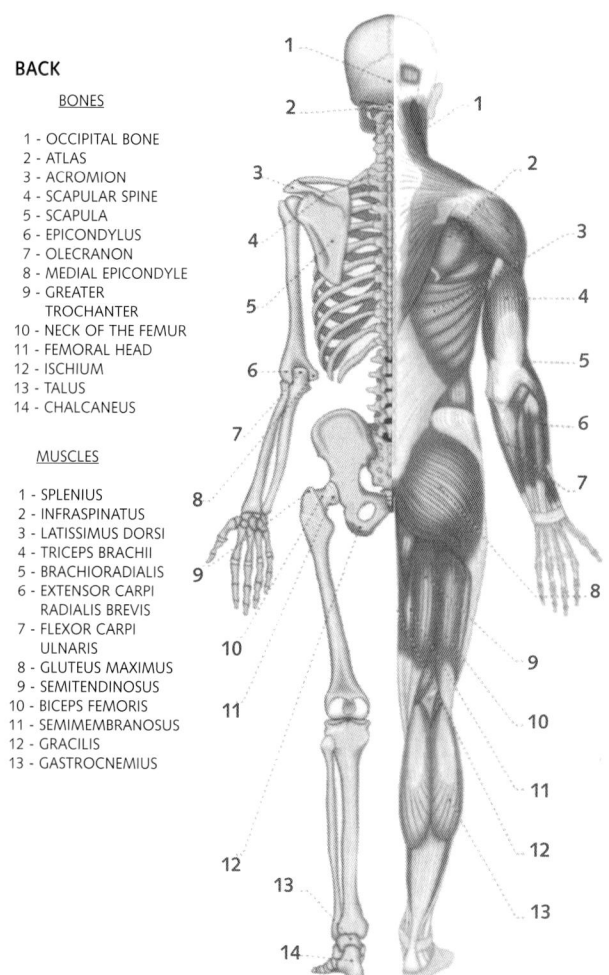

FRONT

BONES

1 - FRONTAL BONE
2 - TEMPORAL BONE
3 - CLAVICLE
4 - SCAPULA
5 - HUMERUS
6 - ULNA
7 - RADIUS
8 - CARPUS
9 - METACARPUS
10 - FEMUR
11 - TIBIA
12 - FIBULA
13 - TARSUS
14 - METATARSUS

MUSCLES

1 - OCCIPITOFRONTALIS
2 - STERNOCLEIDOMASTOID
3 - TRAPEZIUS
4 - PECTORALIS MAJOR
5 - BICEPS BRACHII
6 - BRACHIALIS
7 - PRONATOR TERES
8 - PALMARIS LONGUS
9 - PALMARIS BREVIS
10 - FLEXOR CARPI ULNARIS
11 - VASTUS LATERALIS
12 - GASTROCNEMIUS
13 - SOLEUS
14 - EXTENSOR DIGITORUM LONGUS
15 - PLANTAR INTEROSSEI

BACK

BONES

1 - OCCIPITAL BONE
2 - ATLAS
3 - ACROMION
4 - SCAPULAR SPINE
5 - SCAPULA
6 - EPICONDYLUS
7 - OLECRANON
8 - MEDIAL EPICONDYLE
9 - GREATER TROCHANTER
10 - NECK OF THE FEMUR
11 - FEMORAL HEAD
12 - ISCHIUM
13 - TALUS
14 - CHALCANEUS

MUSCLES

1 - SPLENIUS
2 - INFRASPINATUS
3 - LATISSIMUS DORSI
4 - TRICEPS BRACHII
5 - BRACHIORADIALIS
6 - EXTENSOR CARPI RADIALIS BREVIS
7 - FLEXOR CARPI ULNARIS
8 - GLUTEUS MAXIMUS
9 - SEMITENDINOSUS
10 - BICEPS FEMORIS
11 - SEMIMEMBRANOSUS
12 - GRACILIS
13 - GASTROCNEMIUS

MUSCLES

The bones in our body are moved by muscles. They have various shapes: long muscles are usually attached to the limbs, while wider muscles generally move the torso. Short muscles are fleshy and very powerful. Muscles contract, i.e. they become shorter and larger as their extremities move closer together.

ANTHROPOMETRY

Anthropometry (*anthropos* = man; *metron* = measure) is the science of measuring the human body as a whole or in its components, noting the similarities between them in particular.

ANTHROPOMETRY IN THE FIELD OF DIGITAL HUMAN MODELLING

A Digital Human Model (DHM) is a virtual mannequin based on advanced biomechanical models that is used to verify he physical interaction between man and product while using CAD platforms. This implies due attention to the anthropometric factor in these design support tools. If the goal is to analyse the dimensions of a specific anatomical structure in a virtual environment using software mannequins, the latter must ensure that the anthropometric data reported are true to the type being examined. Generally, the approach of simulation programs is based on two factors:
1) The choice of the most appropriate body type and gender.
2) The anthropometric sizing of the mannequin based on the *boundary case method*, choosing the anthropometric variable of greatest interest (only one measurement is selected, the computer program then is tasked with scaling all other body measurements proportionally).

On this page, we've highlighted some of the similarities between the most well-known anatomical structures in the study of fashion design, referring to a 'normotype', i.e. a body with well-proportioned measurements.

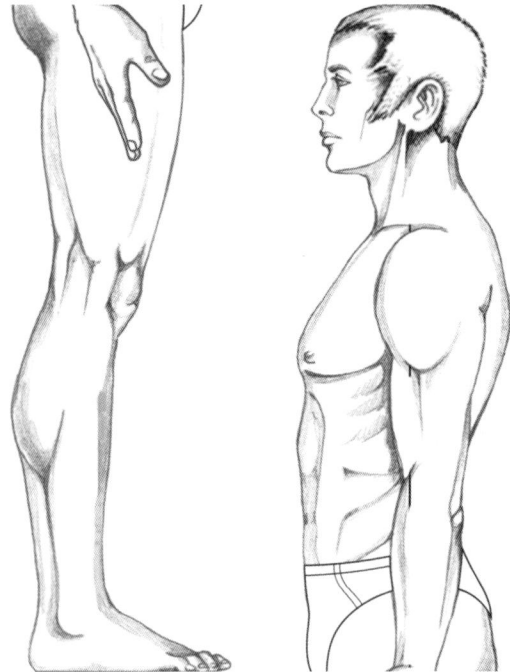

Half of the body is formed by the upper part, from the head to the groin, and the lower part, from the groin to the feet.

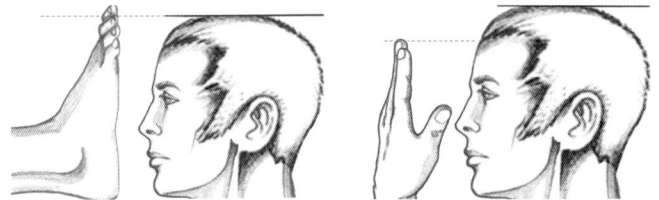

The length of the foot is slightly greater than the height of the head.

The length of the hand is equal to the height of the face.

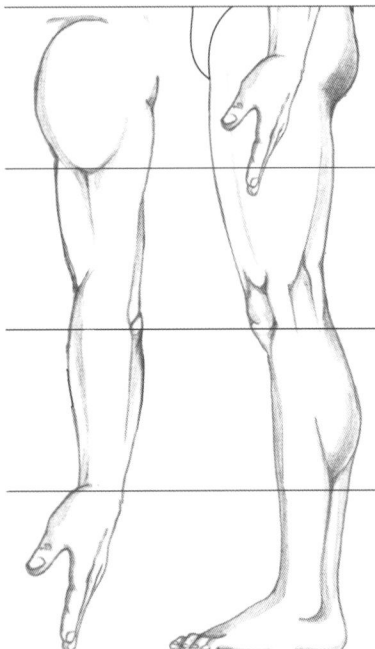

The total length of the leg and arm is about four units.

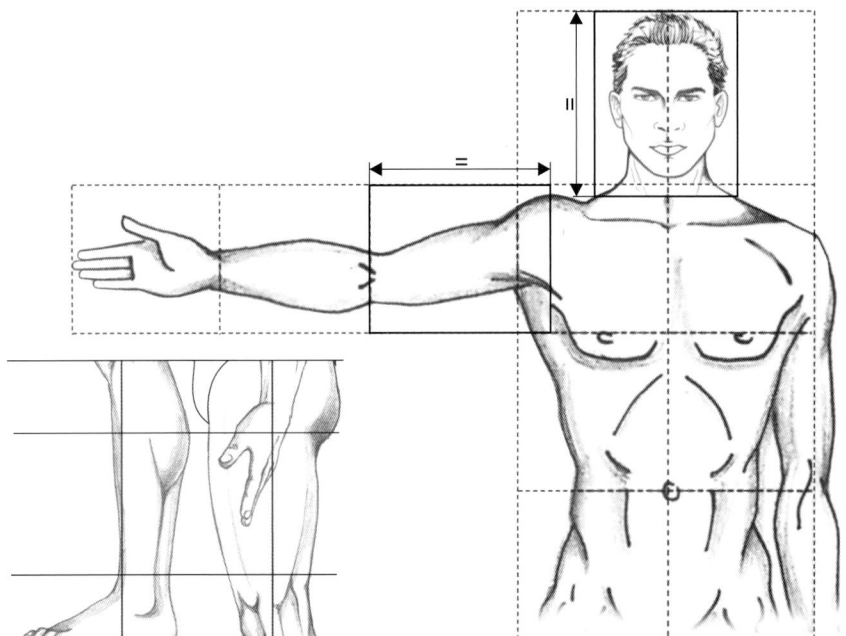

The length of the thighs is equal to the length of the lower leg including the foot.

The length of half the arm is equal to the head plus the neck.

ANALYSING MALE BODY TYPES

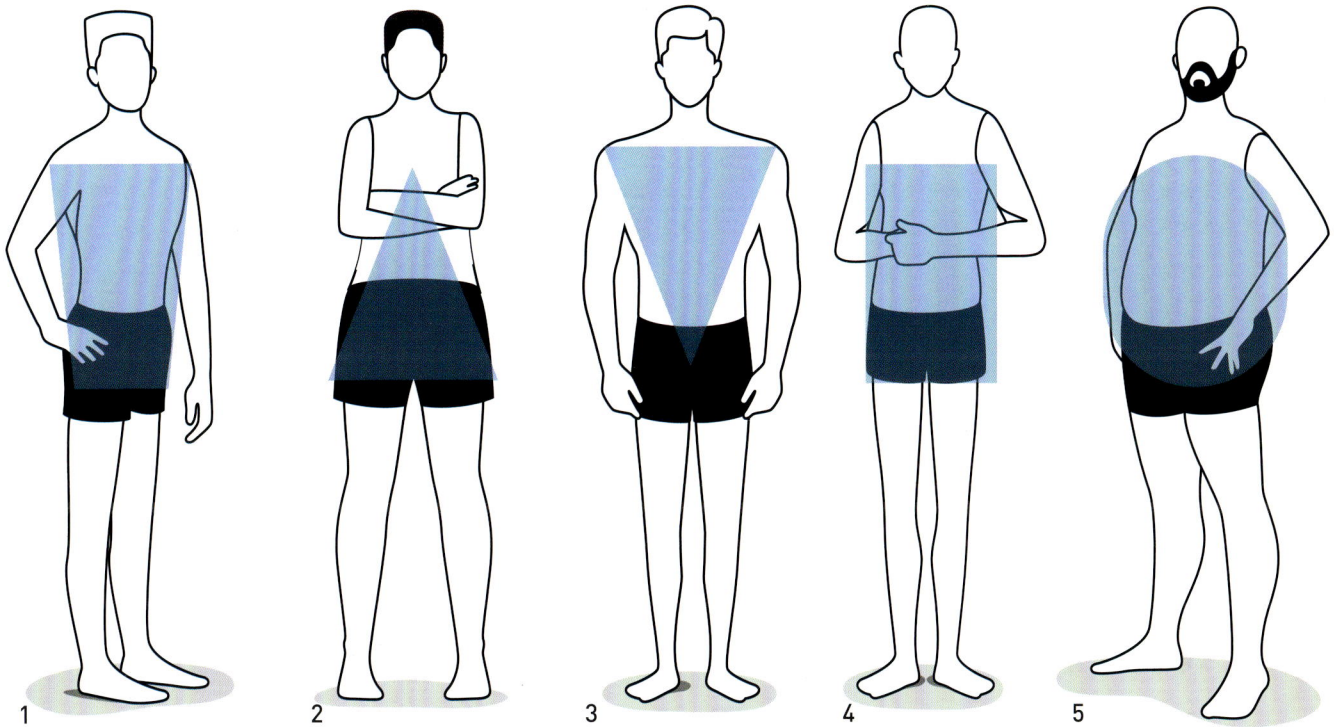

The first step in making a made-to-measure men's suit is to analyse the shape and proportions of the body of the person to be dressed, in order to find the cut that best enhances and complements the person's figure, the style and to deal with issues that may arise in the fit. This, together with the right fabric, pattern, details and alterations to the garment, will ensure a great fit, an optimal silhouette and a balanced, well-proportioned look.

1. TRAPEZOIDAL

This is the shape whose proportions align with the generic silhouette of the human body. The narrowest point of the torso is the waist, from which the figure widens to the shoulders, forming a trapezoid. Below the waist, the hips widen slightly and the legs are thicker at the thighs to gradually taper down to the ankle. This body shape is the one most often taken into account when creating garment patterns.

2. TRIANGLE-SHAPED

This form is characteristic of individuals who tend to store fat around their mid-sections, concentrated on the stomach, and less on the shoulders and hips. For those with this shape, garments should be designed to add details that draw attention to other parts of the body.

3. INVERTED TRIANGLE

Men with this shape have an athletic, muscular physique, with broad shoulders and a narrow waist. For these individuals, especially those who are very muscular, it can be difficult to find ready-made clothes that fit: the most suitable styles are those that fill out the hips to provide a more balanced look.

4. RECTANGLE-SHAPED

Men with rectangular torsos have shoulders and hips that are about as wide as the waist. The latter does not have a marked indentation and therefore the shape is rectangular overall. The most suitable styles are wide jackets that fit slide easily over the waistline, with small details such as slightly padded shoulders and a tapered waist.

5. OVAL-SHAPED

Men with this figure has a central torso that's wider than his waist and shoulders, and shorter legs and arms that widen at the central points. Clothing suitable for those with this conformation should help slim and frame the silhouette, minimising and camouflaging the shape of the abdomen.

PHYSICAL CONFORMATION

ABDOMEN SHAPES

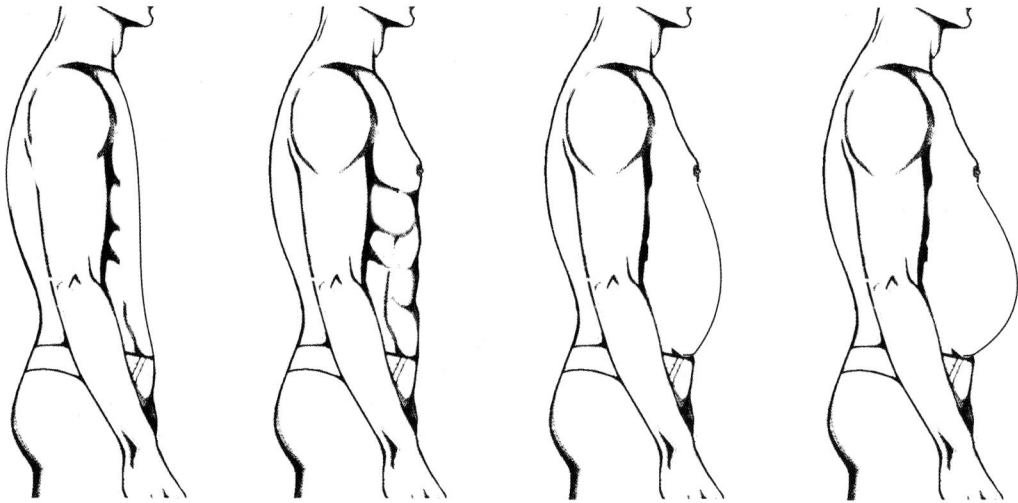

Flat　　　　　Regular　　　　　Prominent　　　　　Pot belly

GLUTE SHAPES

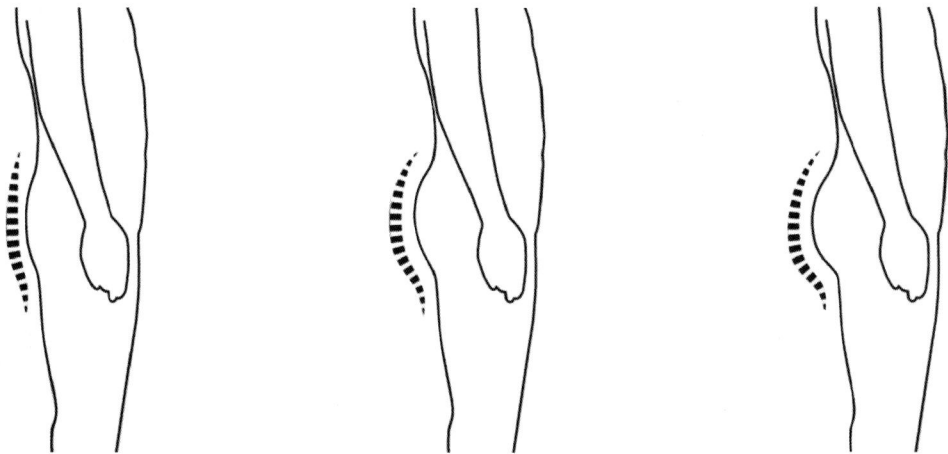

Flat　　　　　Regular　　　　　Protruding

LEG SHAPES

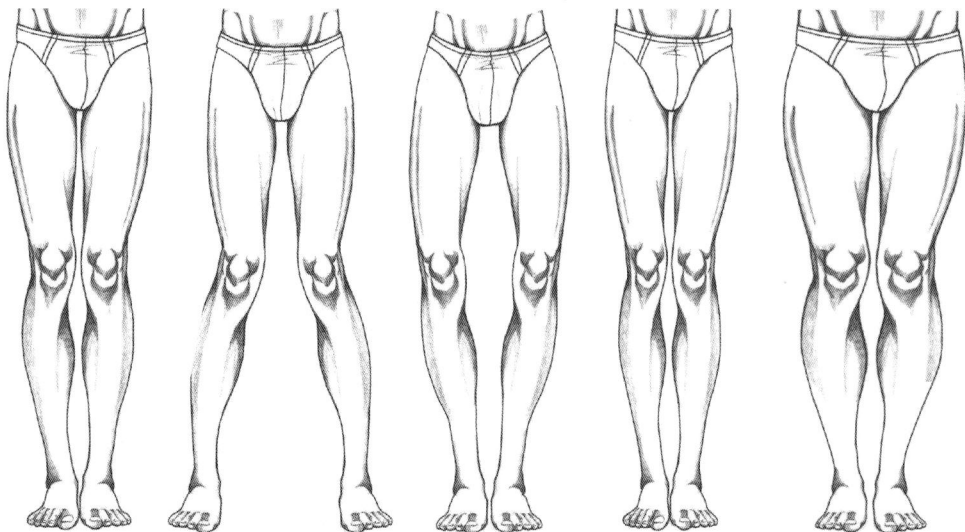

Regular　　　Knock knees　　　Bow legged　　　Skinny　　　Robust

MEASUREMENTS AND PROPORTIONS OF THE BODY

According to the canon of Polykleitos, the figure of the adult man is divided into seven and a half modules, where one module corresponds to the measurement of the head. The studies that have enabled us to prepare the comparative picture of the measurements and the relative ratios of our normotype therefore refer to the head. For the preparation, we took into account the requirements of posture and the way most people dress.

Let's take a look at all the proportional values of the other measurements calculated for an average height of 1.75 cm / 5.'9".

LENGTHS
- 0-1 - head length = height (175 cm) ÷ 7.5 = 23.3 cm / 9.17"
- 1-2 - armpit/shoulder = 175 ÷ 7.5 = 23.3 cm / 9.17"
- 1-3 - rear waist length = 175 ÷ 3.84 = 45.6 cm / 17.95"
- 1c-3b - front waist length = 175 ÷ 3.79 = 46.2 cm / 18.19"
- 3-3c - hip length = 175 ÷ 8.1 = 21.6 cm / 8.50"
- 3-4 - crotch length = 175 ÷ 6.8 = 25.7 cm / 10.12"
- A-B -shoulder grade = 175 ÷ 35.4 = 4.8 cm / 1.90"
- 3-5 - knee level = 175 ÷ 3 = 58.3 cm / 22.95"
- 3-7a - leg length = 175 ÷ 1.67 = 106 cm / 41.73"
- I-P - arm length = 175 ÷ 2.7 = 64.8 cm / 25.51"

WIDTHS
- L - chest semi-circumference = height (1.75) ÷ 3.64 = 48 cm / 18.90" (increases and decreases by 2 cm / 0.79" for every 5 cm / 1.97" of stature).
- M - waist semi-circumference = chest semi-circumference of chest (48 / 18.90") minus 1/12 chest semi-circumference = 44 cm / 17.32".
- N - hip semi-circumference = chest semi-circumference + 1/24 chest semi-circumference = 50 cm / 19.69".
- O - neck semi-cir. = 7/16 chest semi-cir. = 21 cm / 8.27".
- P - wrist = chest semi-cir. ÷ 2.4 = 20 cm / 7.87"
- G-H - biceps = 1/5 chest semi-cir. x 3.14 = 30.1 cm / 11.85".
- C-D - 1/2 rear chest sector = 2/5 chest semi-cir. = 19.2 cm / 7.56".
- E-B - back width (shoulder width) = 7/16 of semi-cir. chest (48 cm) = 21 cm / 8.27".

DEPTHS
- 1a-1b - upper back curve = 1/10 chest semi-cir. (48 cm) = 4.8 cm / 1.89".
- Rear torso cavity (scapula thickness) = 1 cm / 0.39".
- Size of buttocks = 1/24 chest semi-cir. = 2 cm / 0.79".
- F-3a - buttock protrusion = 2 cm / 0.79".
- I2 - humerus protrusion = 1 cm / 0.39".
- V - belly protrusion = 1/24 chest semi-cir. = 2 cm / 0.79" (at waist level).

MEASUREMENTS OF THE 1.75 M TALL NORMOTYPE (SUMMARY)
- Head length = 23.3 cm / 9.17"
- Underarm level = 23.3 cm / 9.17"
- Rear waist length = 45.6 cm / 17.95"

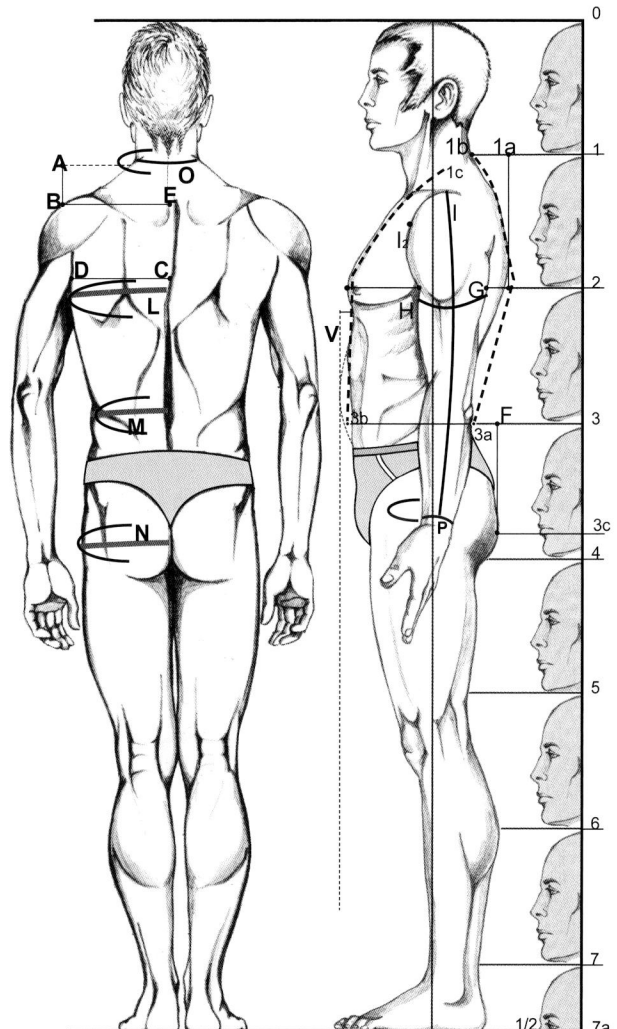

- Front waist length = 46.2 cm / 18.19"
- Hip length (from waist) = 21.6 cm / 8.50"
- Crotch length (from waist) = 25.7 cm / 10.12"
- Knee level (from waist) = 58.3 cm / 22.95"
- Leg length (from waist) = 106 cm / 41.73"
- Arm length (sleeve) = 64.8 cm / 25.51"
- Shoulder grade = 4.8 cm / 1.90"
- Neck semi-circumference = 21 cm / 8.27"
- Chest semi-circumference = 48 cm / 18.90"
- Waist semi-circumference = 44 cm / 17.32"
- Hip semi-circumference = 50 cm / 19.69"
- Arm circumference (biceps) = 31.1 cm / 12.24"
- Wrist circumference = 20 cm / 7.87"
- Upper thigh circumference = 50 cm / 19.69"
- Calf circumference = 37 cm / 14.57"
- 1/2 rear torso sector = 19.2 cm / 7.56"
- 1/2 front torso sector = 19.2 cm / 7.56"
- 1/2 shoulder width = 21 cm / 8.27"
- Upper back curve = 4.8 cm / 1.89"
- Rear torso cavity = 1 cm / 0.39"
- Buttock protrusion = 2 cm / 0.79"
- Humerus protrusion = 1 cm / 0.39"

HOW TO TAKE MEASUREMENTS

Before measuring, it's a good idea to tie an elastic band or ribbon around the waist and hips, at the most prominent point of the buttocks, without squeezing too tightly and taking care to position them straight and parallel to the floor. This will provide a reference point for more precise measurements.

LENGTHS

0) Height: means the total length of the body, i.e. from the top of the head to the floor. As shown here, the measurement is taken from the top of the body, then resting the tape measure at the nape of the neck and following the body to the hollow at the centre of the kidneys; from the level of the buttock, the tape drops straight down. Take the measurement all the way down to the ground, then deduct the height of the heel, or specify the point corresponding to the welt of the shoe.

1) Head length (or height): measured from the chin to the top of the head. This is the base unit of measurement for the Greek canon; it corresponds to a module in the measurement of the human body.

2) Underarm level: measured from the chin level to the axilla. It is equivalent to the head height and thus makes up the second module in the division of the body according to the Greek canon.

3) Neck to waist: place the tape measure at the most protruding bone at the base of the neck and measure to the waist (where a ribbon has been tied beforehand).

4) Front waist height (or length): measured from the highest point of the shoulder (where it attaches to the neck) to the waist.

5) Hip height: measure along the hip, starting from the tape at the waist to the most prominent point of the buttocks, where another ribbon or band should be placed.

6) Crotch height (to waist): this measurement can be taken in three ways: 1. seated on a flat surface, measure laterally from the waist, following the curve of the hip, to the surface; 2. using a right angle square, resting at the bottom of the groin and at the top of the belly, measure the precise height;

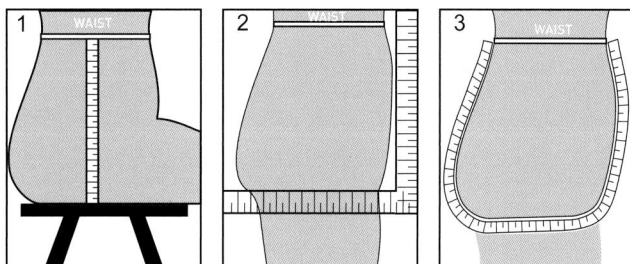

Crotch height measuring methods.

3. to get the total length of the crotch, rest the end of a tape measure on the centre of the front waist, pass it between the legs, going up to the centre of the rear waist while keeping the tape measure close to the body.

7) Waist to knee: this is measured from the waist to the knee, resting it on the outside of the leg.

8) Outer leg length from the waist: this is measured by placing the tape measure on the ribbon at the waist, near the most outer protrusion of the iliac bone, then extending it vertically, resting it on the leg, down to the ground if the person is barefoot, up to the top of the heel if he is wearing shoes. It is necessary to measure both legs to ensure a perfect final garment.

9) Inside leg (inseam) length: have the client stand with their legs slightly apart and measure from the highest point on the centre thigh (at crotch height) to the sole, at bare foot height, following the natural line of the inside leg and keeping the tape measure close to the body.

10) Shoulder grade: this is measured using a ruler placed at the base of the neck, at the point where the shoulder seam will be, keeping it perfectly horizontal. The measurement must be taken at the outer skeletal point of the body.

11) Diagonal shoulder length: measured from the base of the neck, where the seam will be, to the extreme edge of the shoulder joint.

12) Shoulder to elbow: from the point where the arm attaches to the body up to the elbow bone.

13) Sleeve length: with arms relaxed, measure the length in two steps: 1. from the outermost lateral point of the shoulder (approximately where the sleeve seam will go), measure to the elbow; 2. hold the tailor's tape in this position and continue measuring up to and including the wrist bone, following the lateral edge of the arm. This measurement should be taken on both arms just in case.

WIDTHS AND CIRCUMFERENCES

14) Neck circumference: measure around the neck, just below the Adam's apple, without squeezing.

15) Chest circumference: measure under the armpits and above the nipples. Make sure the tape measure is horizontally aligned and not tight and, while the arms are held at the sides and the client is breathing normally, take the measurement.

16) Waist circumference: measure at the height of the navel; ensure that the tape measure is aligned horizontally and that the client is not holding their breath.

16bis) Stomach circumference: measured about 5 cm / 1.97" above the navel.

16ter) Abdomen circumference: measure at about 5 cm / 1.97" below the navel, holding the tape measure horizontally.

17) Hip circumference: measure at the widest point, usually halfway up the buttocks, keeping the tape measure well aligned horizontally.

18) Back width: measure the distance from one arm to the other at the back, from the point where the sleeve seam will be applied.

19) Front chest: measure from one arm to the other at the front, where the sleeve seam will be applied.

height

1- head

curve of the back
27

21 armscye sector

2- neck to underarm

28 scapula depth (cavity)

31 belly protrusion

29 buttock protrusion

height nape to floor

height

0- height

20
18
15
3
6
16
5
17
crotch line
knee
7
8

humerus protrusion
30
14
19
11
10
15
16 bis
16
4
16 ter
17
crotch line
9

22
12
13
23

waist
24
25
26

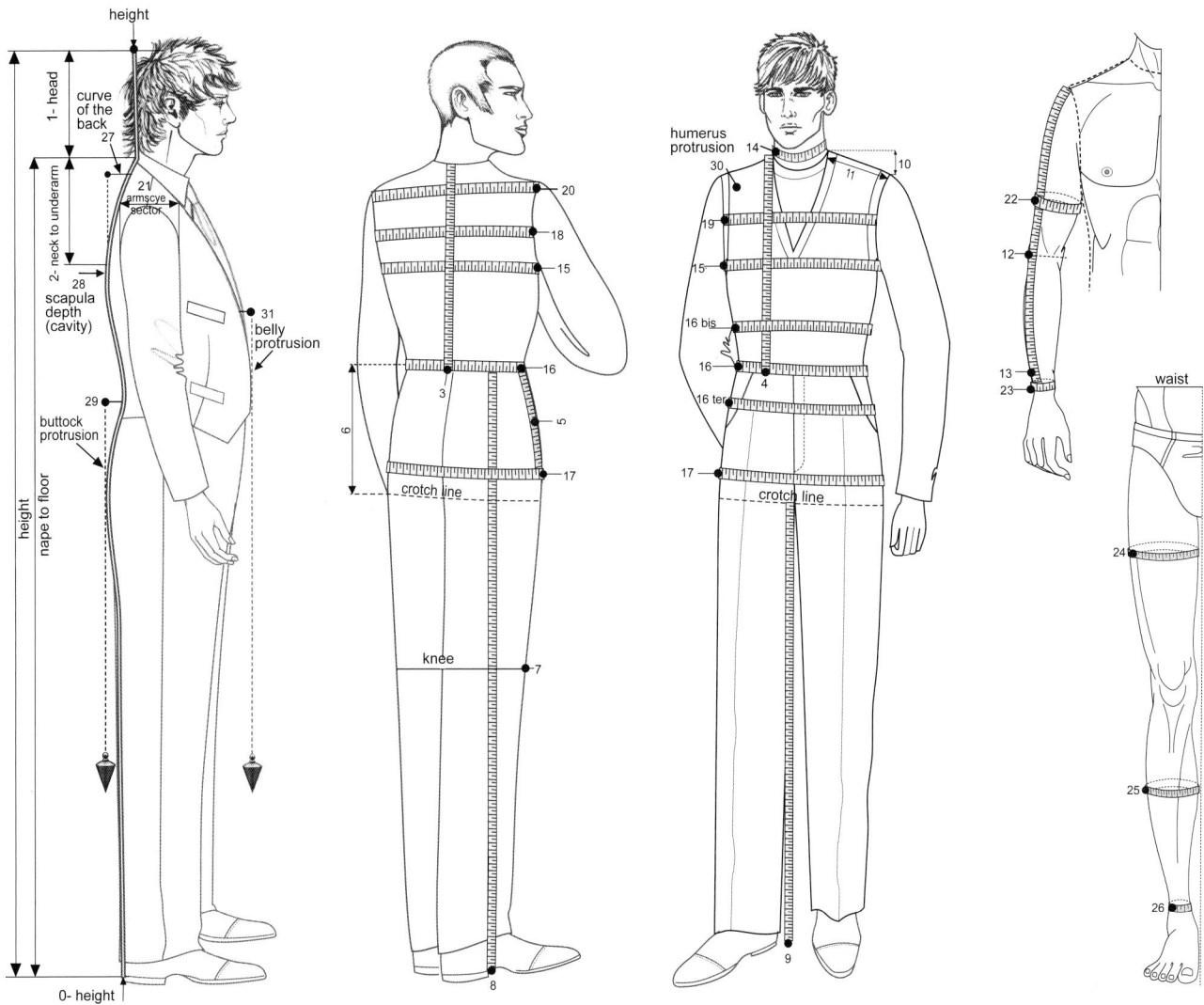

20) Back shoulder width: measure from the outermost lateral point of the left shoulder (where the sleeve seam will go) to the outermost lateral point of the right shoulder. The tape measure should not be held straight, but follow the natural curve of the back, passing along the most prominent bone under the neck.

21) Armhole sector: corresponds to 1/5 of the half-chest or the diameter of the circumference of the biceps.

22) Bicep circumference: with the client's arms relaxed and extended along their sides, measure the circumference of both biceps at the widest point, writing down only the larger of the two measurements.

23) Wrist circumference: measure just below the most protruding bone.

24) Upper thigh circumference: measure the circumference of both thighs just below the crotch and record the larger of the two values, making sure the tape measure is aligned horizontally.

25) Calf circumference: measure the circumference of both calves and enter the larger of the two values.

26) Ankle circumference: measure the circumference of both ankles and record the larger of the two values.

DEPTHS

27) Upper back curve: Place a ruler vertically on the centre back and measure the distance between the ruler and the body.

28) Rear torso cavity: from the middle of the back to the waist, place the ruler on the two shoulder blades and measure the depth of the central recess.

29) Buttock protrusion: measure by placing the ruler in the centre of the rear pelvis, taking the most protruding point of the buttocks as a reference, measuring the distance to the body to the waist level.

30) Protrusion of the humerus: this measurement is mostly created by the effect of the dip of the shoulder as seen on the anterior surface, resting the ruler on the humerus and at the base of the neck.

31) Belly protrusion: the measure to be noted is how much the belly protrudes in relation to the chest. A more technical use of the ruler is necessary to better see the distance at the armscye level. We know that if the person is in a resting position, the belly tends to protrude more. For this reason, always consider a centimetre less of belly protrusion.

FIT AND EASE

The fit, determined by the ease, is fundamental for every suit and thus for every tailored or industrial pattern. It must be carefully calculated and applied to ensure the suit is neither too tight nor too loose, so as not to ruin its line and silhouette. It's even more important when working on a tailored men's garment: the right ease ensures the suit will perfectly complement the person wearing it. If a suit or any other garment were to be sewn based only on the exact measurements taken from the body, the end result would be a garment that's difficult to wear, so tight that moving would be almost impossible.

On the other hand, the ease, i.e. the difference between the body's measurements and the final measurements of a suitably fitting garment, allows it to be made in the best possible way according to the style. It isn't a random value, but must be assessed by the tailor-patternmaker based on two different aspects: the line of the garment and how close-fitting it should be.

THE LINE OF THE GARMENT

The shape and style of a garment are two fundamental elements in calculating its ease. A good tailor, in fact, knows very well that there are different lines and grades of clothing that, when combined, create the right fit. There are three 'lines' when it comes to garments: 1) a simple (or straight) line; 2) a soft line (which follows the silhouette of the body); 3) and a curve-hugging line (which adheres to the body).

EASE

Another factor to be taken into account is how closely the garment fits the body, determined by ease levels, i.e.:

- zero, in direct contact with the skin, such as underwear and swimwear;
- one, clothes that are worn over underwear;
- two, garments worn over those in level one (such as jackets and waistcoats);
- three and four, for outerwear like capes and coats.

THE ROLE OF EASE

In order to move, breathe and live life comfortably and without limitations, other measurements must be add to those of the body in the three main portions (bust, waist and hips). Moreover, ease can be manipulated to change the silhouette or the general appearance and fit of the garment, i.e. those changes that make a jacket tight or loose-fitting. Furthermore, one must not forget the impact of fabric thickness on the fit of a garment: its texture and weight can make all the difference.

POSITIVE AND NEGATIVE EASE

A garment is said to have positive ease when the final measurements are larger than those of the body; conversely, it has negative ease when the final measurements are smaller than those of the body, such as when a stretch fabric or knit is used to make swimwear or underwear. Garments sewn with stiffer materials can be just as tight-fitting, but they have to be constructed with the right darts and various fastenings, such as zips, hooks and buttons.

GARMENT TYPES	Swimwear, bodysuits, leggings	Tops, bodices, waistcoats	Slim-fit jackets	Regular and deconstructed jackets	Classic jackets	Loose coats, parkas	Capes, padded jackets	Padded windcheaters
Chest circumference	-6 / -2 -2.36/-0.79"	0 / 8 0/3.15"	14 / 16 5.51/6.30"	18 / 20 7.09/7.87"	20 / 24 7.87/9.49"	24 / 28 9.49/11.02"	28 / 32 11.02/12.60"	32 / 36 12.60/14.17"
Waist circumference	-6 / -2 -2.36/-0.79"	0 / 6 0/2.36"	8 / 10 3.15/3.94"	12 / 14 4.72/5.51"	16 / 20 6.30/7.87"	-	-	-
Hip circumference	-6 / -2 -2.36/-0.79"	0 / 5 0/2"	14 / 16 5.51/6.30"	18 / 20 7.09/7.87"	20 / 24 7.87/9.49"	24 / 28 9.49/11.02"	28 / 32 11.02/12.60"	32 / 36 12.60/14.17"
Armscye sector	-1.5 / -0.5 -0.59/-0.20"	0 / 1 0/0.39"	1 / 1.5 0.39/0.59"	1.5 / 2 0.59/0.79"	2.5 / 5 1/2"	3.5 / 7 1.38/2.76"	4.5 / 8 1.47/3.15"	6 / 10 2.36/3.94"
Rear shoulder width	-1.5 / -0.5 -0.59/-0.20"	0 / 0.5 0/0.20"	1 / 1.5 0.39/0.59"	1.5 / 2 0.59/0.79"	2 / 3 0.79/1.18"	3.5 / 4 1.38/1.57"	4 / 5.5 1.47/2.17"	5.5 / 6 2.17/2.36"
Rear neck to waist	-	-	-	1 0.39"	2 0.79"	2 0.79"	2 0.79"	3 1.18"
Front neck to waist	-	-	-	1 0.39"	2 0.79"	2 0.79"	2 0.79"	3 1.18"

INDUSTRIAL SIZES

Sizes are expressed by conventional numbers that describe a person's measurements. As they are standardised, they cannot of course take into account the physical characteristics of every individual. Sizes may vary slightly between companies as there is no centralised classification system. As such, the numbers in our tables are to be considered approximate. The measurements below are without ease.

CLASSIC FIT CIRCUMFERENCE MEASUREMENTS (CM/IN)						
SIZE	XS	S	M	L	XL	XXL
Neck circumference	40 cm /15.75"	41/16.14"	42/16.54"	43/16.93"	44/17.32"	45/17.72"
Chest circumference	88/34.65"	92/36.22"	96/37.80"	100/39.37"	104/40.94"	108/42.52"
Waist circumference	80/31.50"	84/33.07"	88/34.65"	92/36.22"	96/37.80"	100/39.37"
Hip circumference	88 - 90 / 34.65-35.43"	92 - 94 / 6.22-37.00"	96 - 98 / 37.80-38.58"	100 - 102 / 39.37-40.16"	104 - 106 / 40.94-41.73"	108 - 110 / 42.52-43.31"
Rear shoulder width	40 cm /15.75"	41/16.14"	42/16.54"	43/16.93"	44/17.32"	45/17.72"
Armpit/shoulder sector width	12/4.72"	12.5/4.92"	13/5.12"	13.5/5.31"	14/5.51"	14.5/5.71"
Arm circumference	28.9/11.38"	30.1/11.85"	31.4/12.36"	32.6/12.83"	33.9/13.34"	35.2/13.86"
Shoulder grade	4.6/1.81"	4.8/1.90"	5/2"	5.2/2.04"	5.4/2.12"	5.6/2.20"
Rear shoulder length	15.6/6.14"	16.3/6.42"	17/6.69"	17.6/6.93"	18.3/7.20"	19/7.48"
Front shoulder length	14.6/5.75"	15.3/6.02"	16/6.30"	16.6/6.54"	17.3/6.81"	18/7.09"
LENGTH MEASUREMENTS (CM/IN)						
HEIGHT	167/5'6.5"	170/5'7"	175/5'9"	180/5'11"	185/6'1"	190/6'3"
Front neck to waist	44/17.32"	44.9/17.68"	46.2/18.19"	47.5/18.70"	48.8/19.21"	50.1/19.72"
Rear neck to waist	43.5/17.13"	44.3/17.44"	45.6/17.95"	46.9/18.46"	48.2/18.98"	49.5/19.49"
Armpit level (chest height)	22.3/8.78"	22.66/8.92"	23.33/9.19"	24/9.45"	24.66/9.71"	25.33/9.97"
Shoulder to elbow	30/11.81"	31/12.20"	32/12.60"	33/13"	34/13.39"	35/13.78"
Sleeve length	61/24.02"	62/24.41"	63/24.08"	64/25.20"	65/25.59"	66/25.98"
Waist to hip	18.6 - 20 / 7.32-7.87"	19 - 21 / 7.48-8.27"	20 - 21.6 / 7.87-8.05"	21 - 22.2 / 8.26-8.74"	21.6 - 22.8 / 8.50-8.98"	22 - 23.5 / 8.66-9.25"
Body rise	24.5/9.65"	25/9.84"	25.7/10.12"	26.5/10.43"	27.2/10.71"	27.9/10.98"
Waist to knee	59.6/23.46"	60.7/23.90"	62.5/24.61"	64.3/25.31"	66/25.98"	67.9/26.73"
Outer leg length	100/39.37"	101.8/40.09"	104.8/41.26"	107.8/42.44"	110.8/43.62"	113.8/44.80"
DEPTH MEASUREMENTS (CM/IN)						
Upper back curve	4.4/1.73"	4.6/1.81"	4.8/1.89"	5/2"	5.2/2.05"	5.4/2.13"
Buttock protrusion	0.9/0.35"	1/0.39"	1.1/0.43"	1.2/0.47"	1.3/0/51"	1.4/0.55"
Belly protrusion	1.9/0.75"	2 cm / 0.79"	2.1/0.83"	2.2/0.867"	2.3/0.91"	2.4/0.95"
Scapula protrusion	0.9/0.35"	1/0.39"	1/0.39"	1/0.39"	1.1/0.43"	1.2/0.47"
Head-from-humerus protrusion	0.5/0.20"	0.5/0.20"	0.6/0.24"	0.6/0.24"	0.7/0.28"	0.7/0.28"

MEASUREMENTS ON THE GARMENT AND THE PERSON

	MEASUREMENTS TAKEN FROM THE SHIRT	MEASUREMENTS TAKEN FROM THE BODY
COLLAR	Measure the width of the neck from the centre of the buttonhole to the centre of the button.	Measure the circumference of the neck at the point where the collar is buttoned, being sure to leave enough room by inserting a finger between the tape measure and the neck.
SHOULDERS	Measure from one end of the shoulder to the other, above the seam.	Take the shoulder width measurement from one armpit to the other, where the arm is connected to the torso, making sure not to extend into the armpit itself.
ARMS	Measure the length from the shoulder seam to the bottom of the sleeve, including the cuff.	Measure the length of the arm along the outer side, keeping it bent at 90 degrees, from the shoulder seam to the wrist bone.
CHEST	Measure the width from one end of the chest to the other, just below the armpit crease.	Measure the circumference at the widest point of the chest, with the client's arms hanging at the sides and keeping the tape measure slack.
WAIST	Measure the width from one side of the waist to the other.	Measure the circumference at navel height, holding the tape measure loosely.
WRIST	Measure the width from one end of the wrist to the other.	Measure the circumference while holding the centimetre tight.
LENGTH	Measure the length of the shirt from the neckline to the very end of the bottom hem.	Measure the back from the base of the neckline to below the buttocks, at the most prominent point.
HIPS	Measure the width by placing the tape measure on the bottom of the shirt, going from one side to the other.	Measure the circumference of the hips, holding the tape measure loosely.

TAILORING TERMINOLOGY

ARMSCYE
Lower part of the armhole of a shirt, suit, etc.

ASYMMETRICAL (PATTERN)
This is a pattern that has cuts, fastenings or motifs shifted to one side in relation to the centre front or centre back axis.

BIAS
Cutting on the bias means cutting the cloth diagonally in relation to its grain.

CLOSURE OR FASTENING
Fastenings open or close a garment, making them easier to put on and take off. They can be zips, buttons, clasps, hooks and toggles, Velcro or any other means of opening and closing an appropriately sized space.

COLLAR STAND
A strip of fabric under the collar of men's shirts.

COLLAR STAND
The part of the collar that rises from the neckline.

CONCEALED PLACKET
A placket in which a strip of fabric (a fly) conceals the buttoning on jackets, shirts, dresses, etc.

DART (OR TUCK)
A triangular fold added to patterns to give shape to the garment where there is a protrusion or curve in the body. Darts are wide on the seam line, where it removes excess fabric, and gradually narrow to a point corresponding to the protrusion or curve of the body. The size of the dart is proportional to the size of the protrusion. Its position, direction and location vary according to the pattern and conformation of the body.
They are generally divided into vertical darts and horizontal darts.
Vertical darts rise and fall from the shoulder to the chest; from the chest to the waist; from the neck to the shoulder blades; from the waist to the hips; from the elbow to the cuff of the sleeve.
Horizontal darts are those coming from the seams at the sides, centre front or centre back and those on the centre sleeve or elbow of the sleeve.

DRAWSTRING
A type of band (often at the waist) within which a freely moving cord has been placed.

FABRIC GRAIN
The direction that follows either the warp or weft of the fabric. On each pattern piece, an arrow should indicate how it should be placed in relation to the grain.

FACING
Facing finishes and supports fabric edges such as necklines, button fastenings and sleeve cuffs. They are placed on the inside of the garment, unless they are decorative.

FLAPS
Pieces of fabric applied to pocket openings.

FLARING
Widening of the bottom of trousers, sleeves, etc.

GATHERING
Gatherings are soft folds of fabric, gathered close together along the seam and oriented inwards towards the body.

GUSSET
A piece of fabric inserted into the underside of tight-fitting kimono sleeves to make arm movements easier.

INSET SLEEVE
A type of sleeve that is joined to the bodice along the entire perimeter of the upper arm/armpit.

KIMONO SLEEVE
A wide sleeve type without shoulder seams.

MOTIFS
Characteristics that distinguish various garments.

NECKLINE
Opening in the upper part of a t-shirt, shirt, blouse or jumper, making it possible to pull the garment over the head. The neckline can be of various lines: square, V-shaped, sweetheart, cowl, etc.

NOTCHES
Small cuts made on the contours of paperboard patterns with special scissors to indicate various reference and junction points.

PATTERN PLACEMENT
Setting the pattern perfectly straight along the grain line of the fabric, to obtain flawless garments.

PLEAT
A fold of fabric that is added to garments for practical reasons. Pleats can be: box pleats, knife pleats, loose pleats, inverted pleats, accordion, etc.

RAGLAN SLEEVE
A sleeve construction method in which the sleeve starts at the neckline with slanted seams reaching down to the armpits.

REINFORCEMENTS
Cloth or other material placed between the fabric and the lining of a garment to strengthen a part of it, or to support areas subjected to greater stress such as: openings, waistbands, pockets, collars, sleeves, cuffs, flaps, etc.

REVERS OR LAPEL
The folded over portion of the opening of a jacket, coat or overcoat. They come in various sizes and shapes: notched, peaked, shawl, etc.

SIZES
A numbering system used for clothing, corresponding to various measurements, proportions and heights.

UNDERSIDE OF A PLEAT
Inner part of a pleat.

VENT OR SLIT
Openings made in jackets or coats for various reasons (practical, aesthetic, fit).

YOKE
A seam placed horizontally along the front or back shoulder line of a shirt, jacket or overcoat.

SYMBOLS AND ABBREVIATIONS

When creating a pattern, each piece should be marked as it is completed. It is necessary to write down all indications that may be useful for the cutting and construction of the garment.

It is also very important to mark what pattern piece it is (bodice, front, yoke, back of the sleeve, cuff, sleeve). The straight of grain is indicated by a long line with an arrow at each end (◄───►) or by a line indicating the fold line along the grain. The fold is usually the centre front or centre back line.

A commonly used symbol replacing the words 'place on the fold of the fabric' consists of two right-angled arrows (▲___▲) pointing towards the fold line. The centre front and centre back lines can be marked 'CF' and 'CB'.

Reference notches are lines on adjacent pieces of a pattern that make it easier to align the seams of those pieces during construction, or are used as a guide for gathering, pleats, etc. These are transverse lines on the sewing outlines. A 3 mm / 0.12" cut is then made at the seam allowance of the fabric for each mark on the paper pattern.

It is a good practice to place notches wherever you think they might be useful. You can vary their number (single, double, triple) and their location for clarity.

SYMBOLS	
SYMBOL	**DESCRIPTION**
▲___▲	Part to be placed on the fold of the fabric, working in duplicate.
◄───►	Indicates how to align the pattern with the straight of grain.
– – – –	Modified pattern line or a seamline.
– –▽– –	Notches or indications to plumb or join.
◄●—●—●	Darts.
●———●	Centre line or fold line.
⌂	Pleats.
⊢——⊣ ✕	Placement symbols for eyelets and buttons.

ABBREVIATIONS	
S.G. = Straight of grain	**Ease** = Ease
Acr. = Across	**Dsc.** = Discard
Bi. = Bias	**C.Sh.** = Centre shoulder
C.F. = Centre front	**L.** = Length
C.B. = Centre back	**S.P.** = Shoulder point
Fcg. = Facings	**N.L.** = Neck line
Frt. = Front	**A.P.** = Armpit point
B.K. = Back	**Ovr.** = Overlap
Op. = Open	**Hip D.** = Hip division
Curl = Curl	**Ent. Fr.** = Entire front
Plm. = Plumb	**Ent. Bk.** = Entire back
Cl. = Close	**Cl. D.** = Closed dart

Place a notch at the point where the fastener will be placed and note any special instructions relating to the the zip or buttons.

Indicate style/ornamental details such as the placement of pockets.

Decorative stitching can be marked with a dotted line at the position where it will be executed. Because the pattern will be made without seam allowances, note that they must be added. Delete all unused lines on the finished pattern and write down any other instructions that might be useful, at any point in the process.

Be sure to write the name of the person or company for whom it was made, and also the date it was made.

Then store the pattern in a large envelope.

SHIRTS

MEN'S SHIRTS

Various types of shirts, with different shapes and prints, have risen and faded in popularity over the centuries. Until the end of the 19th century, a white shirt was a symbol of affluence: only the wealthiest people could afford to have their shirts washed frequently—and to have enough so that they could be changed often.

Striped shirts became fashionable in the late 19th century, though before that they weren't very popular and struggled to be part of classic city workwear. Checked shirts, on the other hand, continued to be seen as garments that were intended to camouflage possible stains.

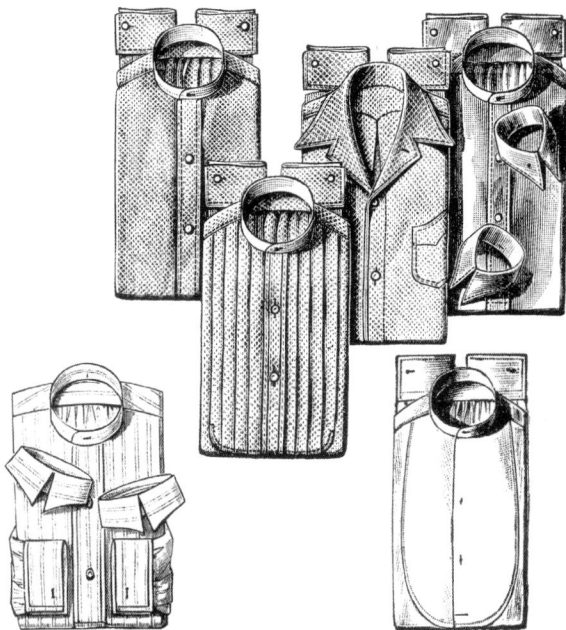

The shape of the shirt as we know it also came into existence in the late 19th century. Until 1871 (when the firm Brown, Davis & Co. of Aldermanbury in London, UK deposited the first style with a buttoning fastening on the front), shirts were pulled over the head. From the start, collars were given different shapes depending on the style of shirt, but the main distinction was mainly between a mandarin collar and a turndown collar.

Until the late 19th century, various versions fo the former dominated, but it was gradually replaced by the turndown version and, starting in the 1930s, it began to be worn only with dinner jackets or tailcoats. Both styles had a removable version that made it possible to wash just the collar, and not the rest of the shirt. Another advantage of the detachable collar was that a different collar shape could be worn with the same shirt, thus giving the impression that you owned many different shirts.

Since the end of WWI, collared shirts haven't undergone any major changes. In the 1960s, a chest pocket was added, replacing the now-vanished waistcoat, though classic shirts are still without it today.

TERMINOLOGY: PARTS OF A SHIRT

Even today, according to the shirt-making craftsmanship traditions, a fine-quality shirt must manufactured in a way that combines all the parts that have remained unchanged over time, parts that have precise terminology all of their own.

Before we learn how to construct a shirt, it is therefore necessary to know the names of most important parts of classic shirts, and to recognise, in detail, what determines their quality.

1. FRONT: the front part of a shirt, or rather the two parts that make it up, which also contains the front fastening with or without facing, a simple (French) or separate piece placket with concealed buttons, the chest pocket (optional), and any pleats, ruffles or other decorations.

2. BACK: the back of the torso, usually one piece of fabric without a central seam, made with or without a pleat, lateral darts, a central pleat or two side pleats.

3. CHEST POCKET: usually sewn on the left side of the front, it's found on more casual shirts with a button-down collar, and on work shirts.

4. PLACKET: a separate strip of fabric on the opening where the buttonholes are placed. It is mostly seen on casual button-front shirts, while formal and classic shirts do not have one.

5. CUFF: its shape varies according to the type of shirt. Formal shirt cuffs are always rounded or have the corners cut off. The slit (a sort of placket) that extends up from the cuff, where a button is always inserted in the middle, ends at the top with a small pointed seam called a 'fly'. The double, turned-up cuff, with holes for cuff links, is the most elegant, used for formal occasions.

6. SLEEVE PLACKET: opening along the sleeve that follows the cuff. It is usually closed by a button.

7. SIDES: lateral seams. the quality of a shirt's workmanship can easily be deduced from the seams along the sides. In fact, the higher the stitch density, the higher the quality: at least 8 or 9 stitches per centimetre (20 to 23 per inch) indicate an excellent-quality shirt.

8. HEM: the finish along the bottom of the shirt. It varies depending on the style.

8B. SHIRT TAIL: elongation of the hem at the back. Especially in elegant styles to be worn under suits, the shirt tail is necessary so that it does not come untucked at the back of the trousers.

9. BUTTONS AND BUTTONHOLES: buttons on high-quality shirts will be thick, i.e. 2 to 2.5 millimetres high, and made of various materials, although the most precious remains mother-of-pearl. The first and last buttonhole on the placket tell you a lot about the quality of the garment: they should be horizontal, as opposed to all the others which are vertical. This makes it easier to move when sitting down.

10. ARMHOLE OR ARMSCYE: point where the sleeve is inserted. Well-made shirts always have flat felled seams around the armholes.

11. REAR YOKE: parts of the shirt sewn on the upper part of the shoulders and armholes.

12. EPAULETTES: strips of fabric applied to the shoulders, present in military-style shirts.

13. YOKE: part of the shirt covering the rear shoulders. It comes in various shapes and can even be constructed separately from the rest of the shirt, with different, double or vertically cut fabric.

14. BACK AND PLEAT: parts at the back. Depending on the style, the back of the shirt may or may not have certain characteristics: smooth or with a central pleat, two side pleats, or with darts in the case of slim-fit shirts, so as to echo the shape of the body.

15. COLLAR: this part of the shirt often determines the degree of formality and style of the entire garment, because it is the most visible when wearing a jacket. The collars seen most often, however, are the straight point collar (with the two points slightly open), the spread collar (with the points more open), the buttondown collar (fastened to the shirt by small buttons), the mandarin collar, the stand-up collar, the Windsor, the full cutaway, and collars that extend into lapels.
In shirts, metal, bone or plastic stays are often inserted into the collar to help it stay flat and hold its shape.

16. COLLAR STAND: the part of the collar that touches the neck, hidden by the leaf (fall), useful for giving it shape and support.

17. HEM GUSSET: triangle of fabric sewn on lower edge of both side seams. It serves to reinforce the seam and prevent it from tearing.

18. DICKIE OR TUX FRONT: an elegant detail, found on formal shirts. In fact, shirts with this finish go well with tailcoats and dinner jackets, where the wingtip collar requires a dickie bow.

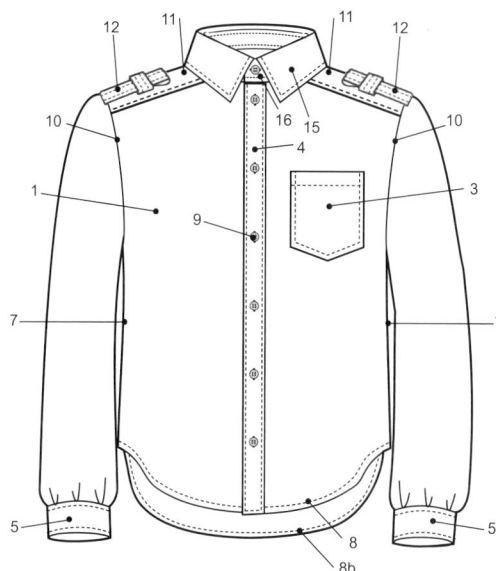

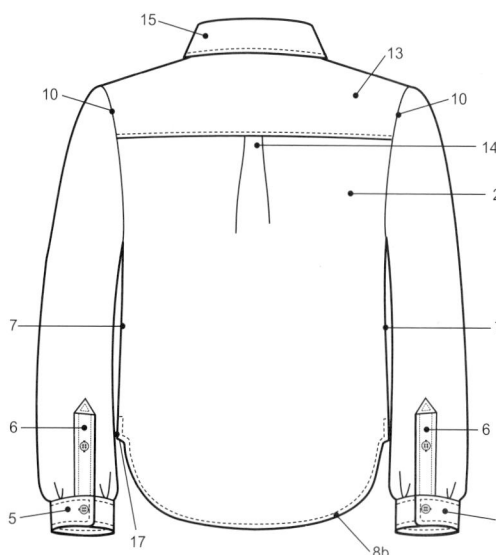

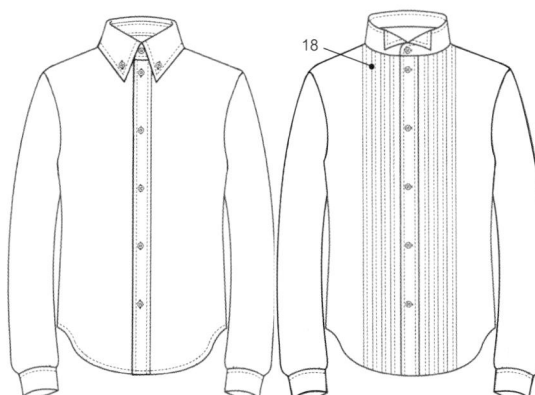

SHIRTING FABRICS

What makes a men's shirt of high quality and elegance is not only professional tailoring or a made-to-measure fit, which are important, but also the fabric, which determines its fineness and style. There are many different shirting fabrics available, and each of them creates a different type of garment, suitable for casual or formal occasions. Experts in this field know how to choose and use them.

Different fabric weaves, i.e. the way the horizontal and vertical threads are intertwined, create different tactile and optical effects. Below is a short and simple guide on how to use the most important fabrics for men's shirts and what the differences are.

1. POPLIN

Known and used in France as early as the 14th century, poplin is recognisable to the eye thanks to its stripes, while its handle is very compact. Its durability makes it useful and advantageous for shirts intended for everyday use. Despite these characteristics, it is also quite soft to the touch. Poplin is perfect for elegant tailored shirts worn in formal situations, and thus also as officewear. It's a must for men's shirts.

2. ZEPHYR

The lightness of this fabric is its main characteristic, so shirts made from zephyr have the advantage of being very breathable. It is therefore the perfect material for those who require significant breathability in their clothing or for those who like a certain level of comfort on all occasions, while still looking elegant outside in their free time.

3. OXFORD

The weave of this fabric creates the look of a tiny check. It has a heavier texture than the previous two fabrics and is suitable for more casual, typically youthful looks. In addition to leisure time, shirts made from this fabric can be worn in less formal work environments.

4. PINPOINT

This fabric is a sort of Oxford. Shirts made in pinpoint are incredibly durable and have a long life, constituting its main strengths. Even when washed frequently, shirts in this material deteriorate very little, meaning they are suitable for daily use, while remaining dressy enough for formal occasions.

5. TWILL

The main characteristic of this fabric is its weave: the threads are arranged diagonally in a particular style of weaving which creates oblique stripes. It's compact and has a thick handle. Twill is very easy and quick to iron and is therefore suitable for people who don't like to iron or who travel often. Moreover, once ironed, it stays crease free for a long time.

6. PIQUÉ

The special knit of piqué fabric creates its defining cellular texture, making it unique and perfect for those seeking sophisticated style. Given this characteristic, shirts made from this fabric are suitable for formal or ceremony wear, and also for very important business occasions.

7. END-ON-END (FIL-À-FIL)

Shirts made from fil-à-fil fabric are extremely light. Its weave makes it very distinctive: white threads are woven with coloured ones. The final effect is that of a striped or checked fabric. This detail makes end-on-end fabric shirts very versatile and suitable for all occasions.

8. DOBBY

This special fabric is characterised by geometric patterns. It has a fun and unique look that immediately catches the eye, with a slightly thick texture. Perfect for formal outfits or fashionable everyday looks.

9. JACQUARD

Shirts made from this fabric make outfits truly unique and original, thanks to its special, elaborate weave. Ideal for those who want a casual yet refined look without sacrificing details and modernity, jacquard gives shirts a youthful air while accenting the figure of the wearer.

Poplin

Zephyr

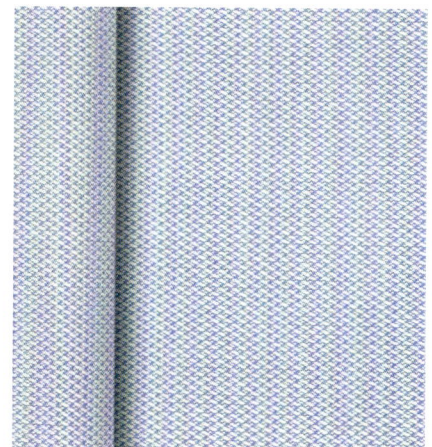

Oxford

Pinpoint

Twill

Piqué

End-to-end

Dobby

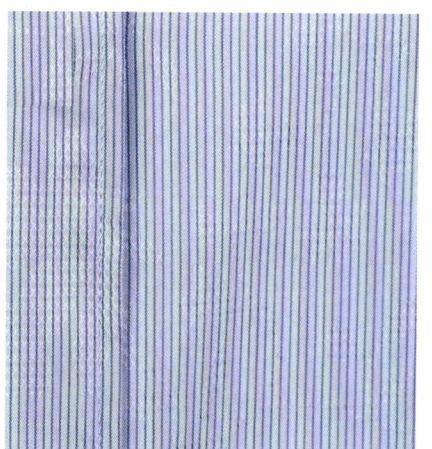

Jacquard

SHIRT TYPES AND FITS

CLASSIC SHIRTS

Classic shirts suit anyone who isn't influenced by the fashions of the moment, but who prefers timeless style, always paying attention to elegance and quality. Usually in white or light blue, plain colour or striped, they're versatile shirts that can be worn on any occasion. The most suitable collars are straight point and spread, preferably with removable stays. The front of classic shirts is either with or without a separate pieced placket for the buttons (standard placket v French placket), while the back is very elegant if plain, or with side darts in the case of a slim fit. The most becoming cuffs for this style of shirt are angled or rounded, both with one button.

CASUAL SHIRTS

Those who prefer an informal, sporty look can opt for shirts in checked, striped or plain-colour fabrics, enriched in some cases by contrast fabric inserts. These shirts are fully customisable in terms of fabrics, collars, cuffs, buttons and fit.

DANDY SHIRTS

Dandy style is synonymous with elegance, sophistication, originality and a touch of eccentricity. There are no set rules to define this garment, though a dandy-style shirt should attract attention due to its original fabric and cut.

DINNER JACKET SHIRTS

Worn on special occasions, shirts worn under dinner jackets can have either visible or covered buttoning. In addition, they have dickie at the front (additional fabric forming vertical pleats, extending to the waist, but preferably no further to avoid bulges which tucked into the trousers). The collars on this shirts can be classic, but it's best if they have short open points to make room for the bow tie, or if they're wing-tipped. In some cases, when opting for a more fashionable look, a mandarin collar can be applied. The cuffs are double to fit the cufflinks.

BUSINESS SHIRTS

These shirts are made to be worn for 10 to 12 hours (or more) per day, and thus in fabric that holds its shape without creasing. They are made from high-quality, double twisted 100% cotton yarn. These sorts of easy care fabrics are particularly comfortable, and impeccable, even after long hours at the office or travelling.

SHIRT FITS

The 'fit' indicates how snug or baggy it is, which is often determined by its shape. There are three types of fits to choose from, depending on the build of the wearer:
1) classic fit;
2) regular fit;
3) slim fit.

Classic fit

Classic fit shirts are characterised by:
1) comfortable ease;
2) a wide cut;
3) soft, roomy armholes;
4) an absence of seams and darts at the back.

Given these characteristics, classic-fit shirts are best suited to those with a robust build. Shirts with this fit are usually made in neutral tones (white or light colours) and are perfect to wear under a jacket. When in brighter shades, they also go quite well with sportier looks, paired with jeans.

Regular fit

Regular-fit shirts are halfway between classic and slim fits:
1) cut closer to the body than a classic fit, but more formal than a slim fit;
2) darts in the back;
3) the armhole is calibrated.

This hybrid nature makes regular-fit shirts suitable for those who seek comfort while wearing less classic styles. Regular-fit shirts are more elegant in classic colours, while they take on a vintage feel when in bright colours.

Slim fit

Slim-fit shirts:
1) are fitted at the sides of the body;
2) have narrow armholes;
3) darts at the back.

A waisted fit (nipped in at the waist) makes this style more suitable for those with a slim, lean physique. Unlike other shirts, in fact, a slim fit shirt is almost like a second skin. It's best suited to informal situations and is usually made in dark colours, patterns or stripes.

THE FIT OF A CUSTOM HAND-MADE SHIRT

The perfect fit is the main advantage of a made-to-measure shirt. Unlike ready-to-wear shirts, sartorial shirts fit comfortably, are perfect in length and width, and neither tighten at key points (collar, cuffs and waist) nor are they too loose. In addition, they guarantee unrestricted movement, allowing the arms to bend without the cuff rising too much. They ensure that all kinds of movements can be made without feeling too tight at the shoulders or chest. To achieve such a perfect fit, all the necessary measurements must be carefully taken. Another advantage of tailored shirts is the ability to personalise them by embroidering the client's initials, usually on the left side between the waist and chest, so that they are hidden when wearing a jacket.

Mohamad Khosravi Bua from Unsplash

Business shirt

Lynne Baltzer from Unsplash

Casual shirt

Mario Klassen from Unsplash

Dandy shirt

Dinner jacket shirt from Carnival

Dinner jacket shirt

Nimble Made from Unsplash

Informal shirts

Benjamin Rascoe from Unsplash

Office shirts

SIZE AND FIT COMBINED

Men's shirt sizes have always been one of the main dilemmas in the fashion industry. This is especially true in the field of custom-made shirts, so it is imperative that tailors know the size and fit of the perfect shirt in a given style.

READY-TO-WEAR SIZES

Most men's dress shirts sold in Italy are between sizes 38 and 48 (using the Italian system). These numbers indicate the circumference of the shirt collar in centimetres measured from the centre of the first button to the centre of its buttonhole. There is also a correspondence between the sizes in centimetres and the classic fit indicated by the letter abbreviations for t-shirt sizes (XS, S, M, L, XL, XXL, etc.). The following list will be quite useful (sizes are Italian):
- S: corresponds to size 38;
- M: between size 39 and size 40;
- L: between size 41 and size 42;
- XL: between size 43 and size 44;
- XXL: from size 45 upwards.

Obviously, the measurements are approximate and it must be remembered that shirt sizes can also be split, with the goal of offering a better fit. In fact, it is not unusual to find a size 41 and a 1/2 or a size 44 and 3/4.

AMERICAN / UK SIZES

American and UK sizes are measured in inches and Italian and EU sizes in centimetres. The conversion is quite easy and just involves a bit of multiplication, as one inch equals 2.54 cm. That means an ad hoc shirt size table can be quickly made.

The measurements in the following tables include ease, but are approximate because they may vary by brand and manufacturer.

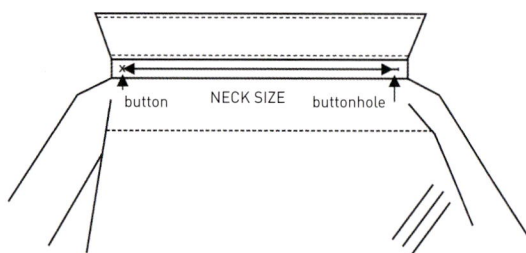

Neck (or collar) measurement.

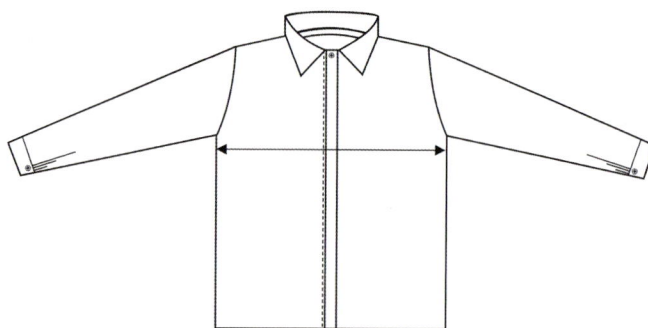

Chest circumference measurement.

CLASSIC FIT SHIRT MEASUREMENT CHART (cm/in)							
International size	Size in cm	Size in inches	Neck circ.	1/2 chest circ.	Sleeve length	Shirt length	1/2 waist circ.
S	37	14 ½	37 cm / 14 ½"	48 / 19"	63 / 24 ¾"	70 / 27 ½"	49 / 19 ⅓"
S	38	15	38 / 15"	50 / 19 ¾"	63 / 24 ¾"	71 / 28"	51 / 20"
M	39	15 ½	39 / 15 ½"	52 / 20 ½"	64 / 25 ¼"	72 / 28 ⅓"	53 / 20 ⅞"
M	40	15 ¾	40 / ¾"	54 / 21 ¼"	64 / 25 ¼"	73 / 28 ¾"	55 / 21 ⅓"
L	41	16	41 / 16"	56 / 22"	65 / 25 ½"	74 / 29 ¼"	57 / 22 ½"
L	42	16 ½	42 / 16 ½"	58 / 22 ¾"	65 / 25 ½"	75 / 29 ½"	59 / 23 ¼"
XL	43	17	43 / 17"	60 / 23 ½"	65 / 25 ½"	76 / 30"	61 / 24"
XL	44	17 ½	44 / 17 ½"	62 / 24 ½"	66 / 26"	77 / 30 ¼"	63 / 24 ¾"
XXL	45	18	45 / 18"	64 / 25 ¼"	66 / 26"	78 / 30 ¾"	65 / 25 ½"
XXL	46	18 ½	46 / 18 ½"	66 / 26"	66 / 26"	79 / 31"	67 / 26 ½"
3XL	47	19	47 / 19"	68 / 26 ¾"	66 / 26"	80 / 31 ½"	69 / 27 ¼"
3XL	48	19 ½	48 / 19 ½"	70 / 27 ½"	67 / 26 ½"	80 / 31 ½"	72 / 28 ¼"
4XL	49	20	49 / 20"	72 / 28 ⅓"	67 / 26 ½"	80 / 31 ½"	73 / 28 ¾"
4XL	50	20 ½	50 / 20 ½"	74 / 29 ¼"	67 / 26 ½"	80 / 31 ½"	75 / 29 ½"

REGULAR FIT SHIRT MEASUREMENT CHART cm/in							
International size	Size in cm	Size in inches	Neck circ.	1/2 chest circ.	Sleeve length	Shirt length	1/2 waist circ.
S	37	14 ½	37 cm / 14 ½"	46 / 18"	63 / 24 ¾"	70 / 27 ½"	46 / 18 ¼"
S	38	15	38 / 15"	48 / 19"	63 / 24 ¾"	71 / 28"	47 / 18 ½"
M	39	15 ½	39 / 15 ½"	50 / 19 ¾"	64 / 25 ¼"	72 / 28 ⅓"	48 / 19"
M	40	15 ¾	40 / 15 ¾"	52 / 20 ½"	64 / 25 ¼"	73 / 28 ¾"	50 / 19 ¾"
L	41	16	41 / 16"	56 / 22"	65 / 25 ⅔"	74 / 29 ¼"	52 / 20 ½"
L	42	16 ½	42 / 16 ½"	56 / 22"	65 / 25 ⅔"	75 / 29 ½"	54 / 21 ¼"
XL	43	17	43 / 17"	58 / 22 ¾"	65 / 25 ⅔"	76 / 30"	56 / 22"
XL	44	17 ½	44 / 17 ½"	60 / 23 ¾"	66 / 26"	77 / 30 ⅓"	58 / 23"
XXL	45	18	45 / 18"	62 / 24 ½"	66 / 26"	78 / 30 ¾"	60 / 23 ¾"
XXL	46	18 ½	46 / 18 ½"	64 / 24 ¾"	66 / 26"	79 / 31 ⅛"	62 / 24 ½"

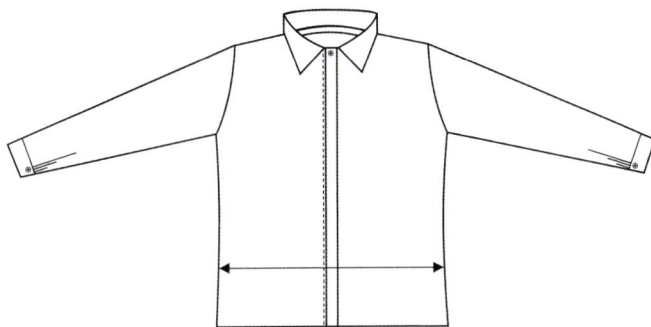

Waist circumference measurement.

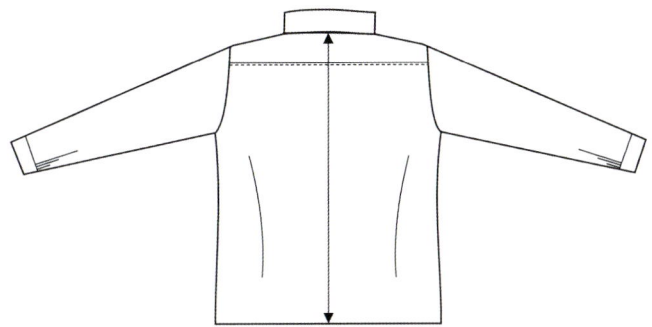

Shirt length measurement.

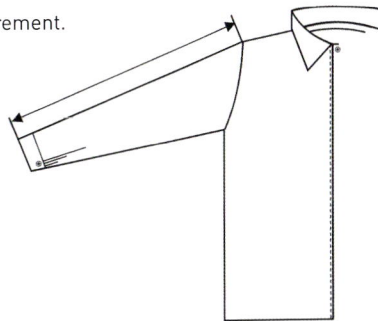

Sleeve length measurement.

The measurements in the tables on these pages include ease. However, they are indicative and may vary depending on the brand or manufacturer.

SLIM FIT SHIRT MEASUREMENT CHART cm/in							
International size	Size in cm	Size in inches	Neck circ.	1/2 chest circ.	Sleeve length	Shirt length	1/2 waist circ.
S	37	14 ½	37 cm / 14 ½"	45 / 17 ¾"	63 / 24 ¾"	70 / 27 ½"	41 / 16 ½"
S	38	15	38 / 15"	47 / 18 ½"	63 / 24 ¾"	71 / 28"	43 / 17"
M	39	15 ½	39 / 15 ½"	49 / 19 ⅓"	64 / 25 ¼"	72 / 28 ⅓"	45 / 17 ¾"
M	40	15 ¾	40 / 15 ¾"	51 / 20"	64 / 25 ¼"	73 / 28 ¾"	47 / 18 ½"
L	41	16	41 / 16"	53 / 20 ⅞"	65 / 25 ½"	74 / 29 ¼"	49 / 19 ¼"
L	42	16 ½	42 / 16 ½"	55 / 21 ¾"	65 / 25 ½"	75 / 29 ½"	51 / 20"
XL	43	17	43 / 17"	57 / 22 ½"	65 / 25 ½"	76 / 30"	53 / 20 ⅞"
XL	44	17 ½	44 / 17 ½"	59 / 23 ¼"	66 / 26"	77 / 30 ⅓"	55 / 21 ⅓"
XXL	45	18	45 / 18"	61 / 24"	66 / 26"	78 / 30 ¾"	59 / 23 ¼"
XXL	46	18 ½	46 / 18 ½"	63 / 24 ¾"	66 / 26"	79 / 31 ⅛"	59 / 23 ¼"

THE BASIC CLASSIC-FIT SHIRT

GENERAL NOTIONS

Shirts, especially custom-made ones, must be executed with a certain amount of ease, although not excessive, to allow ease of movement. The cuffs must fit snugly without slackening and must protrude from the jacket sleeve by approximately 1.5 cm / 0.59", while the volume of the sleeve above the cuff must be distributed with evenly spaced folds along the seam. The collar must also fit snugly around the neck, not tight but never too loose. In terms of its shape, it's always best to avoid those that are too high or too low. The most commonly used collars are the straight point collar (4-4.5 cm / 1.57-1.77" high), the Windsor collar and the buttondown collar.

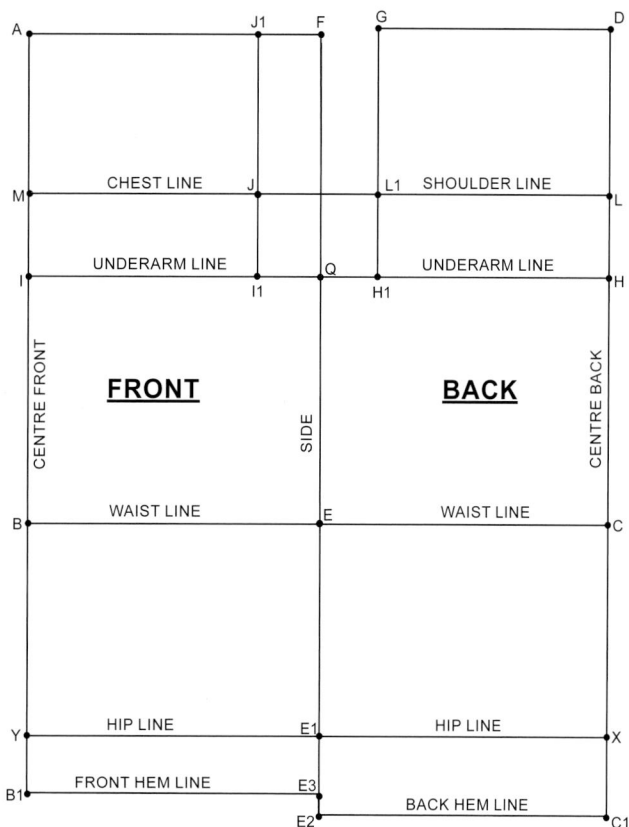

SIZE 48 MEASUREMENTS

- Height 175 cm / 5'9"
- Ease of the classic fit shirt = 20 cm / 7.87".
- Chest semi-circumference = 96 + 20 = 116 : 2 = 58 cm / 22.83"
- Waist semi-circumference = 88 + 20 = 108 ÷ 2 = 54 cm / 21.26"
- Hip semi-circumference = 96 + 20 = 116 ÷ 2 = 58 cm / 22.83"
- Neck semi-circumference = 42 ÷ 2 = 21 cm / 8.27"
- 1/2 shoulder width = 42 : 2 = 21 cm / 8.27"
- Front neck to waist 45.6 cm / 17.95"
- Rear neck to waist 46.2 cm / 18.19"

BASIC BLOCK CONSTRUCTION

Draw right angle A-B-C, with:
- A-B equal to the front neck-to-waist (e.g.: 45.6 cm / 17.95").
- B-C equal to semi-circumference of chest + ease for a classic fit shirt 20 cm / e.g.: 96 + 20 cm = 116 ÷ 2 = 58 cm / 22.83").

- C-D rear neck-to-waist (e.g.: 46.2 cm / 18.19").
- D-G = 1/2 shoulder width + 1 (e.g.: 42 ÷ 2 = 21 + 1 = 22 cm / 8.66").
- D-C1 total shirt length at the back (e.g. : 75 cm / 29.53").
- Draw C1-E2 (bottom rear).
- B-Y and C-X hip height (e.g: 20 cm / 7.87").
- Draw Y-X (hip line).
- Y-B1 as X-C1 minus 2 cm / 0.79".
- Draw B1-E3 (bottom front).
- D-H half of C-D . (e.g.: 46.2 ÷ 2 = 23.1 cm / 9.09").
- H-H1 as G-D (23 cm / 9.05").
- H1-G like D-H (23.1 cm / 9.09").
- Draw H1-G.
- Draw H-I like B-C = 58 cm / 22.83" (armpit level).
- B-E half of B-C (e.g: 58 ÷ 2 = 29).
- A-F as B-E.
- Draw F-E-E2 (side line).
- I-I1 like H-H1 minus 1 cm / 0.39" (23 - 1 = 22 cm / 8.66").
- H-L 1/3 of D-H (e.g.: 23.1 ÷ 3 = 7.7 cm / 3.03").
- I-M as H-L.

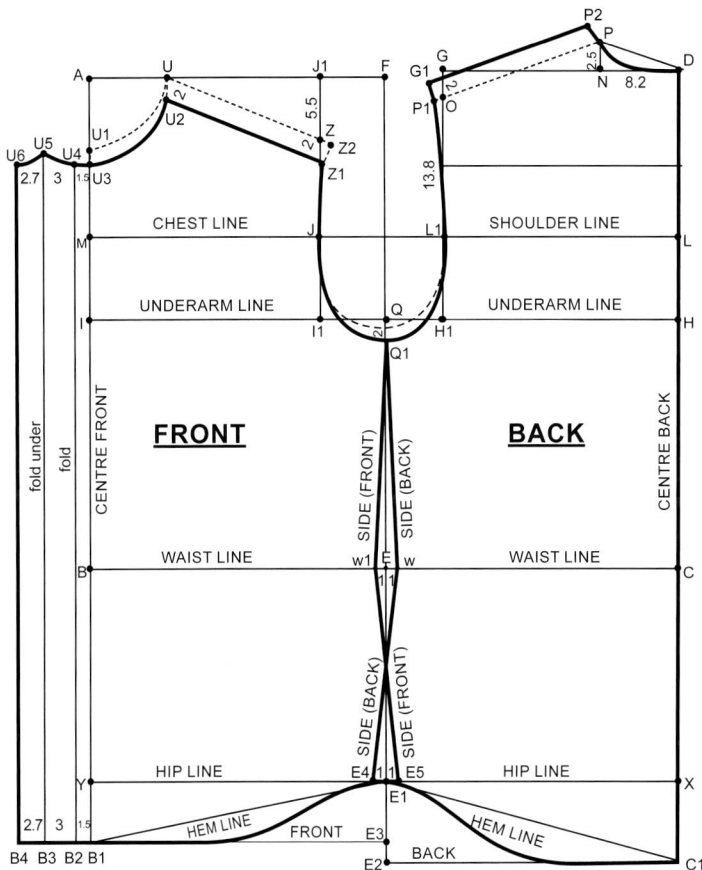

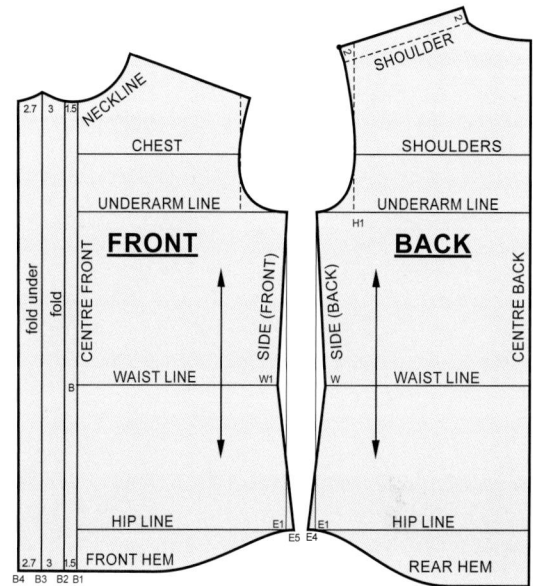

- Draw L-M parallel to H-I.
- Draw I1-J-J1 parallel to H1-L1-G.
- H1-I1 = H-I minus the sum of H-H1 + I-I1 = 13 cm / 5.12" (e.g.: 58 - (23 + 22) = 58 - 45 = 13 cm / 5.12") (armscye sector).

BACK

- G-O = 2.5 cm / 1".
- D-N 1/3 of D-G + 0.6 (e.g: 23 ÷ 3 = 7.6 + 0.6 = 8.2 cm / 3.23").
- N-P 2.5 cm / 1". Draw D-P.
- Draw P-O-P1 with the shoulder length measurement + 1 cm / 0.39".
- Q at half of H-I.
- Draw P1-L1-Q as in the figure.
- E-W 1.5 cm / 0.59" or as required.
- Draw guideline C1-E1.
- Draw the lower line as in the figure.

FRONT

- A-U 1/3 D-G at the back + 0.6 cm / 0.24" (e.g: 23 ÷ 3 = 7.6 + 0.6 = 8.2 cm / 3.23").
- Draw the arc U-U1.
- Lower U1 by 1 cm / 0.39".
- J1-Z = 5-5.5 cm / 1.97-2.16".
- Draw U-Z equal to P-P1 at the back
- Draw Z-J-Q as in the figure.
- U-U2 and Z-Z1 = 2-2.5 cm / 0.79-1".
- E-W1 as E-W.
- Draw guideline B1-E1.
- Draw the bottom line at the back as in the figure.
- Take up U-U2-Z2-Z1 and shift it onto the rear shoulder line P-P1 to bring the shoulder point forward.
- Complete the extension for the overlap and buttoning B1-B2 1.5 cm / 0.59"; B2-B3 3 cm / 1.18"; B3-B4 2.7 cm / 1.06" as shown.
- L1-P1 = H1-G minus H1-L1 minus G-O (e.g: 23.1 - 7.7 - 2.5 = 12.9 cm / 5.08").

CLASSIC-FIT SHIRT: BASIC SLEEVE

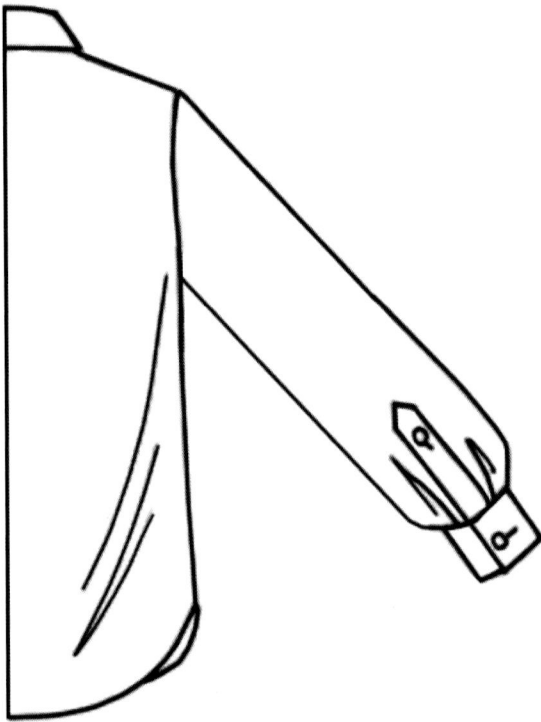

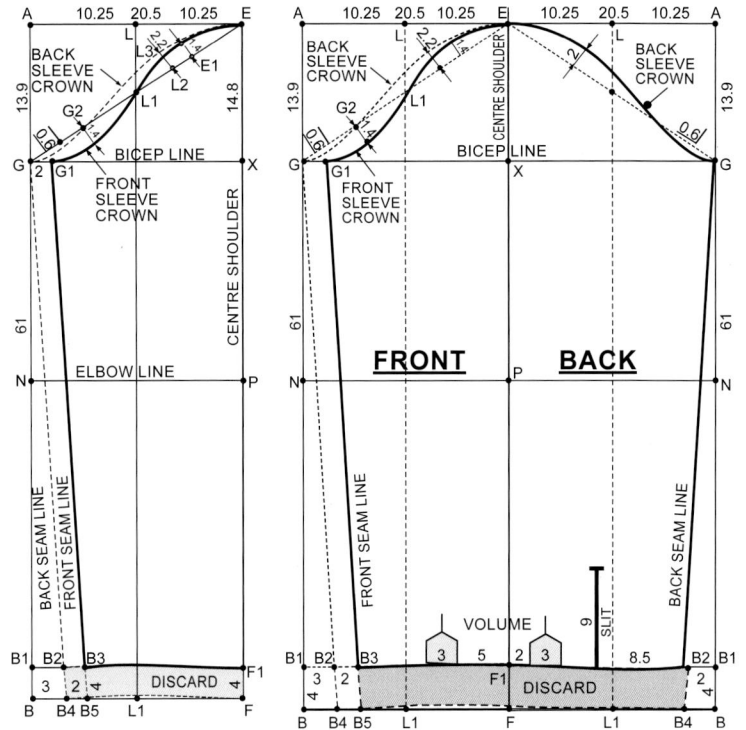

- Draw the rectangle A-B-E-F with:
- A-B = sleeve length (e.g: 65 cm / 25.59").
- A-E as the measurement of the bodice sector + 1/2 of the
  same sector (e.g: 13 + 6.5 + 1 = 20.5 cm / 8.07").
- A-G as L1-P1 of the torso block + 1 cm / 12.9 + 1 =
  13.9 cm / 5.47".
- E-X as A-G; draw G-X = bicep line.
- Join G-E with a diagonal line = guideline.
- A-N half of A-B + 2 = 65 : 2 = 32.5 + 2 = 34.5 cm / 13.58".
  Join N-P.
- A-L half of A-E = 20.5 : 2 = 10.25 cm / 4.03"
- B-L1 as A-L = 10.5 cm / 4.13". Draw L-L1.
- G-L1 half of G-E; E-E1 half of E-L1.
- E1-L2 1.3 cm / 0.51"; L2-L3 2 cm / 0.79".
- G-G2 half G-L1; G-G1 = 2 cm / 0.79".
- Draw the front crown E-L1-G1.
- Draw the back crown E-L3-G.

- B-B4 3 cm / 1.18" (or as desired).
- Draw dotted line G-B4 = rear seam line.
- B4-B5 as G-G1 2 cm / 0.79" = front seam line.
- Shorten the lower edge of the sleeves B-B1 and F-F1 by
  2.5-5 cm / 1-2" (or as desired) based on the height of the
  cuff (cuff height minus 2.5 cm / 1" for some volume in the
  sleeve).
- Narrow the bottom edge as desired.
- Draw B2-B3-F1 with a curved line.
- Draw B4-L1-F with a curved line.
- Take up the front and back sleeve and draw the full
  sleeve as in the picture.
- Draw the slit line at 8.5 cm / 3.35" from the back seam
  line for a length of approximately 7.5-10 cm / 2.95-3.94".
- Mark the folds which will add volume to the sleeve
  bottom, 2 cm / 0.79" each.

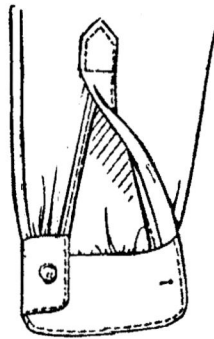

CUFF

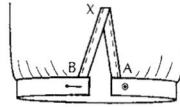

STRIP

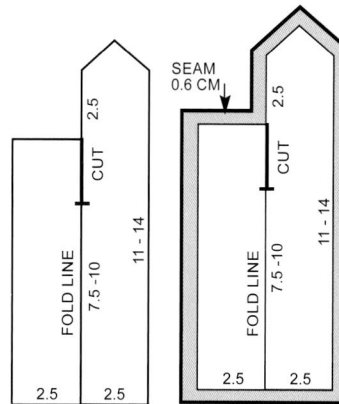

ENLARGE SLEEVE PLACKET

3	FOLD	
2.5	3	2.5

**ONE-PIECE STRIP
(2 PIECES)**

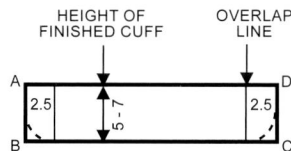

HEIGHT OF FINISHED CUFF · OVERLAP LINE

A · 2.5 · 5 - 7 · 2.5 · D
B · C

**PLAIN CUFF
(4 PIECES)**

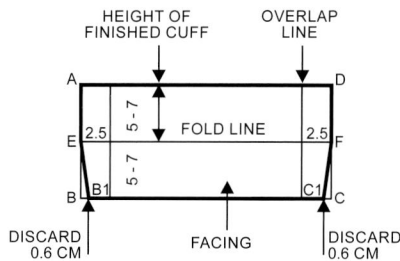

HEIGHT OF FINISHED CUFF · OVERLAP LINE

A · 5 - 7 · D
E · 2.5 · FOLD LINE · 2.5 · F
B · B1 · 5 - 7 · C1 · C
DISCARD 0.6 CM · FACING · DISCARD 0.6 CM

**ONE-PIECE CUFF
(2 PIECES)**

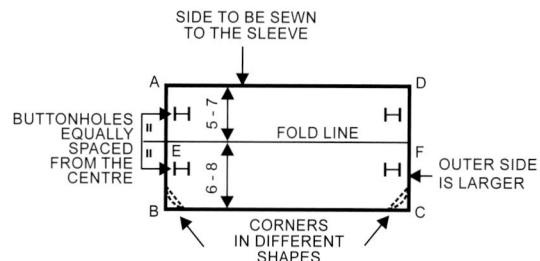

SIDE TO BE SEWN TO THE SLEEVE

A · 5 - 7 · D
BUTTONHOLES EQUALLY SPACED FROM THE CENTRE · E · 6 - 8 · FOLD LINE · F · OUTER SIDE IS LARGER
B · C
CORNERS IN DIFFERENT SHAPES

**DOUBLE CUFF
(4 PIECES)**

PLAIN CUFF

Draw the rectangle A-B-C-D with:
- A-B equal to the height of the desired cuff (e.g: 5-7 cm / 1.97-2.76").
- A-D equal to the measurement of the lower sleeve edge minus the folds + 5 cm / 1.97" for the fastening overlap (e.g: 26 cm / 10.24").

SINGLE-PIECE CUFF

Draw the rectangle A-B-C-D with:
- A-B equal to twice the height of the cuff.
- A-D equal to the measurement of the lower edge of the sleeve minus the fold space plus the width of the sleeve placket (e.g: 2.5 cm / 1").
- A-E half of A-B. Draw E-F.
- C-C1 and B-B1 = 0.6 cm / 0.24" (excess for the inner part).

DOUBLE CUFF

Draw the rectangle A-B-C-D with:
- A-B equal to twice the height of the cuff minus 1 cm / 0.39".

- A-D equal to the measurement of the lower sleeve edge minus the fold space plus 5 cm / 1.97" for the fastening.
- A-E half of A-B minus 1 cm / 0.39". Draw E-F.

EDGING AND SLEEVE PLACKET

A slit with a border is the most common system for shirts. The border is made from a strip of fabric twice the length of the slit and at least 3.5 cm / 1.38" wide, oriented on the straight of grain, that's folded and sewn to the sleeve.
For the slit, on the other hand, the pattern must be made first, as clearly illustrated in the figure.

Note:
The length of the sleeve crown must be greater than that of the armhole. The difference in length varies depending on the garment and the fabric. For men's shirts, the crown must be a maximum of 2 cm / 0.79" longer than the armhole on the bodice, except when using silk fabrics or for different volume requirements. For other garments, the values are generally: 1.5-3 cm / 0.59-1.18" for shirts; 3-4 cm / 1.18-1.57" for jackets; 5-7 cm / 1.97-2.76" for coats and jackets, except in the case of details, such as pleating, gathering, 'mappina' sleeves, etc. Before cutting the garment, it is essential to double-check the measurements of the crown and armhole, so as to avoid any unpleasant surprises.

CHECKING AND MODIFYING THE ARMHOLE

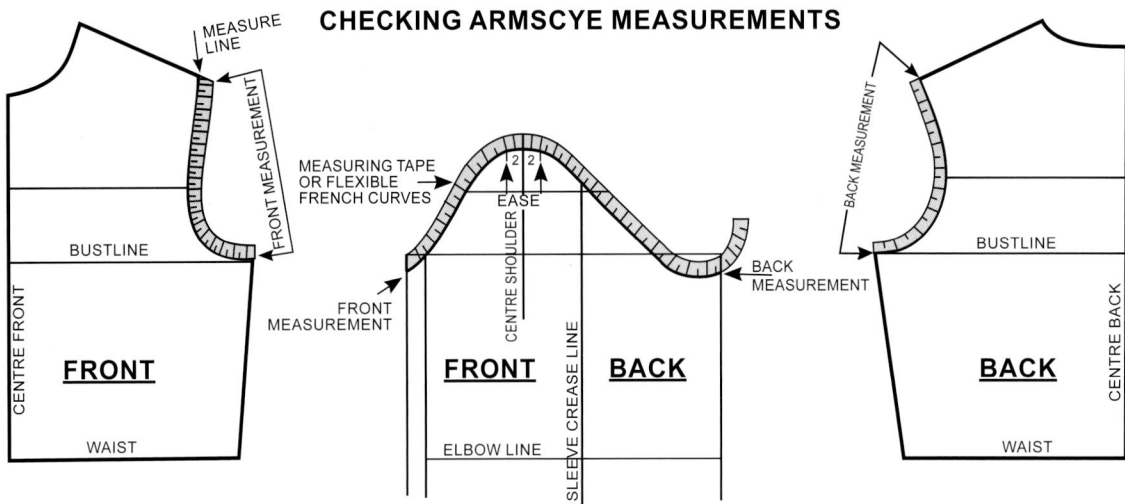

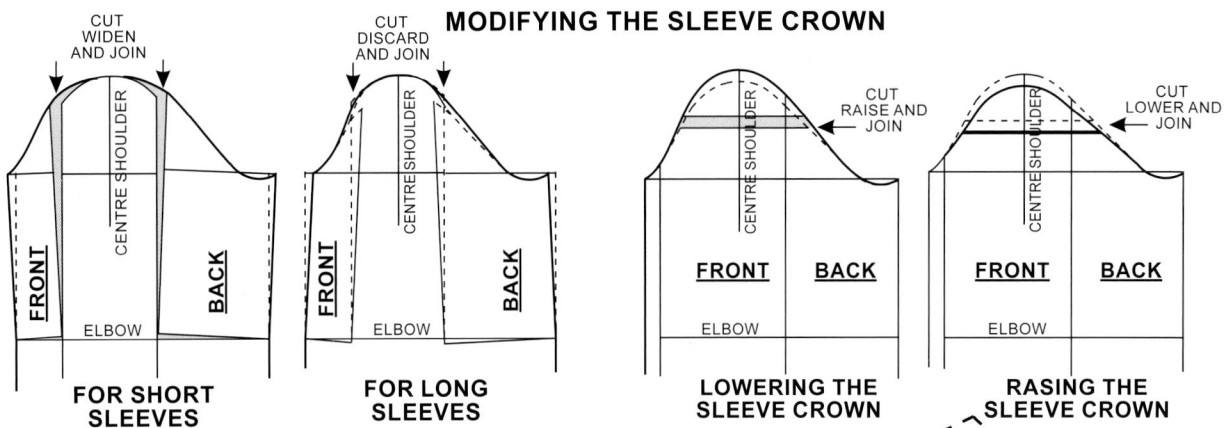

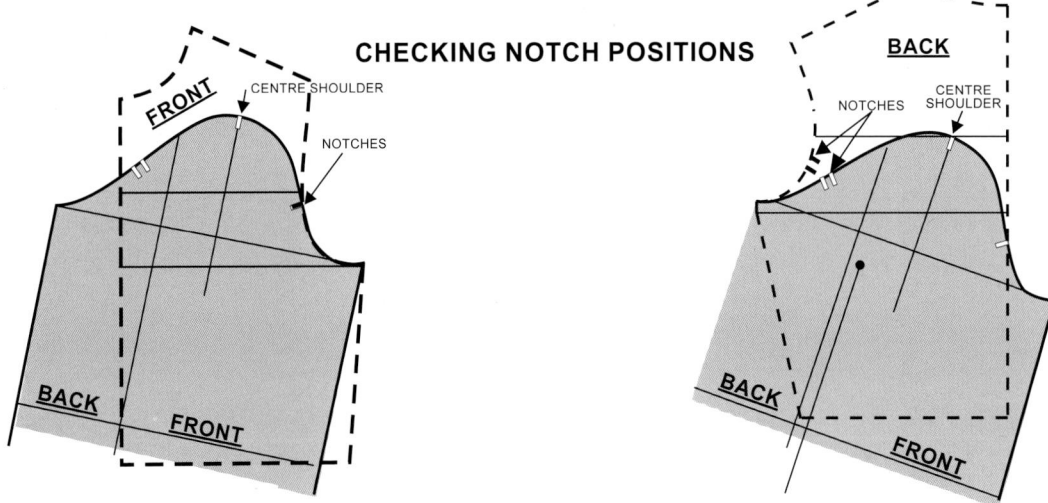

CHECKING ARMSCYE MEASUREMENTS

MEASURE LINE

MEASURING TAPE OR FLEXIBLE FRENCH CURVES

EASE

MEASURING TAPE OR FLEXIBLE FRENCH CURVES

FRONT MEASUREMENT

FRONT MEASUREMENT

BACK MEASUREMENT

BACK MEASUREMENT

CENTRE SHOULDER

SLEEVE CREASE LINE

BUSTLINE

CENTRE FRONT

FRONT

WAIST

FRONT

BACK

ELBOW LINE

BACK MEASUREMENT

BUSTLINE

BACK

CENTRE BACK

WAIST

MODIFYING THE SLEEVE CROWN

CUT WIDEN AND JOIN

CENTRE SHOULDER

FRONT

BACK

ELBOW

FOR SHORT SLEEVES

CUT DISCARD AND JOIN

CENTRESHOULDER

FRONT

BACK

ELBOW

FOR LONG SLEEVES

CENTRE SHOULDER

CUT RAISE AND JOIN

FRONT **BACK**

ELBOW

LOWERING THE SLEEVE CROWN

CENTRE SHOULDER

CUT LOWER AND JOIN

FRONT **BACK**

ELBOW

RASING THE SLEEVE CROWN

CHECKING NOTCH POSITIONS

FRONT

CENTRE SHOULDER

NOTCHES

BACK **FRONT**

BACK

NOTCHES

CENTRE SHOULDER

BACK

FRONT

A few checks and markings must be made to the base bodice block and the corresponding inset sleeve before moving onto the subsequent production stages (industrialization, positioning, cutting, etc.).

1. Check that the size of the crown or top of the sleeve is equal to the armhole of the bodice plus 2-4 cm / 0.79"-1.57" for the added room necessary for assembly and ease (the amount of extra material varies depending on the texture and type of fabric, the desired fit, and gathered details).

2. Check that the notches on the sleeve match those on the bodice, based on the position of the sleeve seam in relation to that of the side.

3. If the armscye on the sleeve is too long or too short compared to that of the bodice, or compared to that of the original pattern, modify as shown above.

SHIRT FACING

SHAPED FULL FACING

NOTCH EDGING EXTENSION
NOTCH CENTRE FRONT
SHAPED
STRAIGHT
STRAIGHT
CENTRE FRONT
CHEST LINE
BUSTLINE
FRONT
SIDE
WAIST LINE
7.5   7.5

FOLDED PART

SEPARATED FACING

EDGING EXTENSION
NOTCH CENTRE FRONT
CENTRE FRONT
CHEST LINE
BUSTLINE
FRONT
SIDE
WAIST LINE

CENTRE FRONT
EDGING EXTENSION
CENTRE FRONT
1.5 1.5
CHEST LINE
BUSTLINE
FRONT
SIDE
WAIST LINE
APPLIED PLACKET
1.2
PART TO FOLD
0.5
1.5 1.5

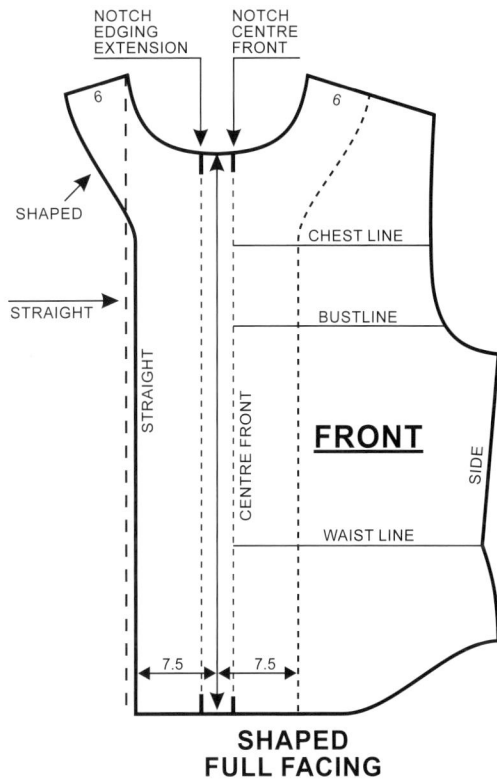

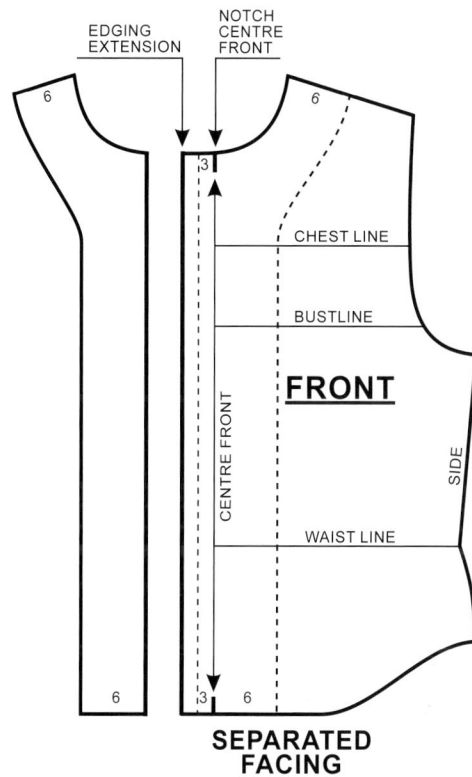

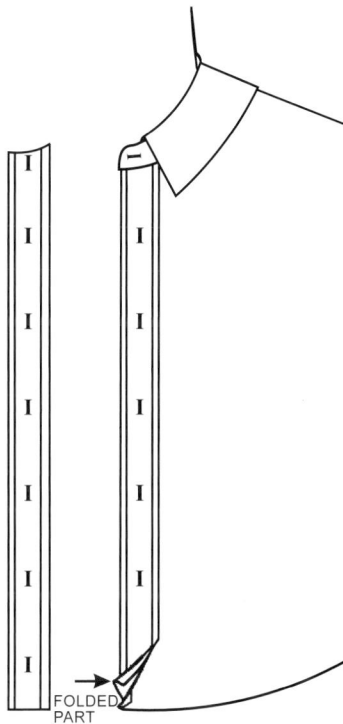

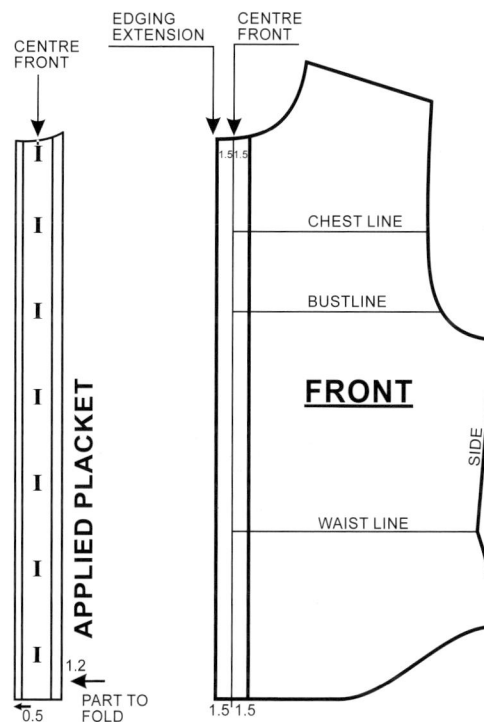

This type of facing is used for shirts with a casual collar.
- Draw the facing on the pattern with 6 cm / 2.36" on the shoulder line and 7.5 cm / 2.95" (6 + 1/2 cm extension) from the centre front line.
- Bring the outline of the facing over the centre front.

- Mark the notches and the straight of grain and join.
- Draw the facing on the pattern with 6 cm / 2.36" on the shoulder line and 6 cm / 2.36" from the centre front line.
- Take up the facing starting from the centre-front line.
- Mark the notches and the straight of grain and join.

REGULAR FIT MILITARY-STYLE SHIRT

SIZE 48 MEASUREMENTS

- Height = 175 cm / 5'9".
- Regular shirt fit = 16 cm / 6.30".
- Chest semi-circumference = 96 + 16 = 112 ÷ 2 = 56 cm / 22.05"
- Waist semi-circumference = 88 + 16 = 104 ÷ 2 = 52 cm / 20.47"
- Hip semi-circumference = 96 + 16 = 112 ÷ 2 = 56 cm / 22.05"
- Neck semi-circumference = 42 ÷ 2 = 21 cm / 8.27"
- 1/2 shoulder width = 44 + 1 = 45 : 2 = 22.5 cm / 8.86"
- Front neck to waist = 45.6 cm / 17.95".
- Rear neck to waist = 46.2 cm / 18.19".

BASIC BLOCK CONSTRUCTION

Draw a right angle A-B-C with:

- A-B equal to the front neck-to-waist (e.g.: 45.6 cm / 17.95").
- B-C equal to the semi-circumference of the chest + regular shirt ease 16 cm / 6.30" (e.g., 96 + 16 = 112 ÷ 2 = 56 cm / 22.05").
- C-D rear neck-to-waist (e.g.: 46.2 cm / 18.19").
- D-G = 1/2 shoulder width + 1 (e.g.: 44 +1 = 45 : 2 = 22.5 cm / 8.86").
- D-C1 total shirt length (e.g.: 75 cm / 29.53").
- Taper the sides Q-W-E1 and Q-W1 = 1.5 + 1.5 cm / 0.59" + 0.59".
- Draw C1-B1 (lower edge).
- B-Y and C-X hip height (e.g: 20 cm / 7.87").
- Draw Y-X (Hip Line)
- Y-B1 as X-C1.
- D-H half of C-D (e.g.: 46.2 ÷ 2 = 23.1 cm / 9.09").
- H-H1 as D-G = 22.5 cm / 8.86".
- H1-G as D-H = 23.1 cm / 9.09". Draw H1-G.
- Draw H-I as B-C = 56 cm / 22.05" (underarm level).
- B-E half of B-C (e.g.: 56 ÷ 2 = 28 cm / 11.02") A-F as B-E.
- Draw F-E-E2 (side line).
- I-I1 as H-H1 minus 1 cm / 0.39" (22.5 - 1 = 21.5 cm / 8.46").
- H-L 1/3 of D-H (e.g.: 23.1 ÷ 3 = 7.7 cm / 3.03"). I-M like H-L.
- Draw L-M parallel to H-I.
- Draw I1-J-J1 parallel to H1-L1-G.
- H1-I1 = H-I minus (H-H1 + I-I1), e.g. 56 - (22.5 + 21.5) = 56 - 44 = 12 cm / 4.72" (armscye sector).

BACK

- G-O = 2.5 cm / 1".
- D-N 1/3 of D-G + 0.5 cm / 0.20" (e.g: 22.5 ÷ 3 = 7.5 + 0.5 = 8 cm / 3.15").
- N-P = 2.5 cm / 1". Draw D-P as an outline.
- Draw P-O-P1 (shoulder length) + 1 cm / 0.79" (e.g. 17 cm / 6.69").
- Q at half of H-I.
- Draw P1-L1-Q as in the figure.
- E-W 1.5 cm / 0.59" or as required.
- Draw the lower line as in the figure.

FRONT

- A-U 1/3 of D-G at the back + 0.6 cm / 0.24" (e.g: 22.5 ÷ 3 = 7.6 + 0.6 = 8.2 cm / 3.23").

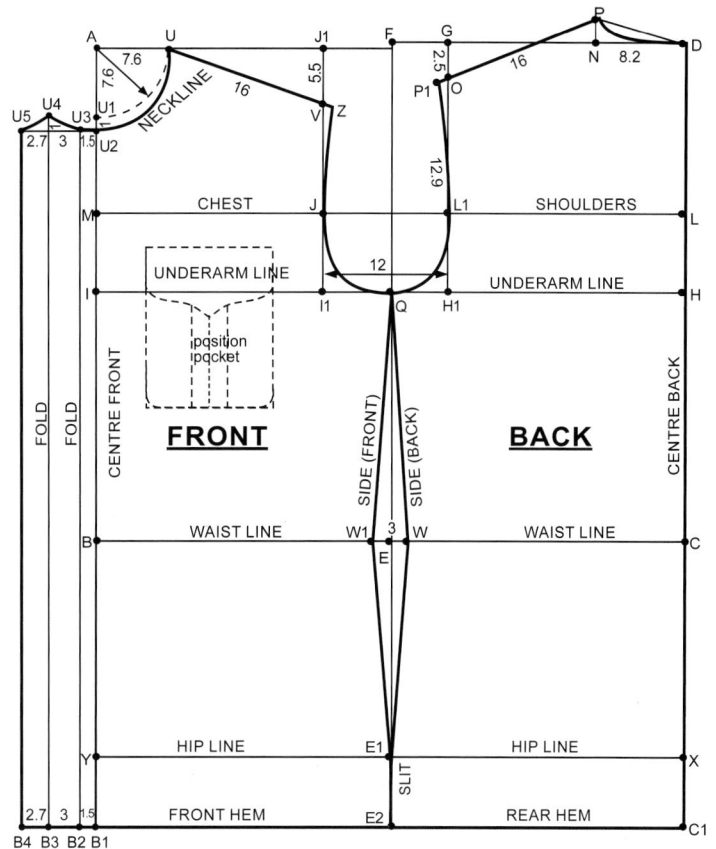

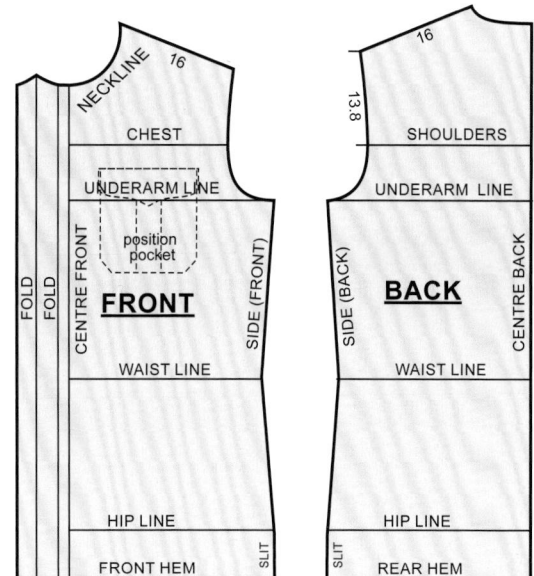

- Draw the arc U-U1.
- Lower U1 by 1 cm / 0.39".
- J1-Z 5-5.5 cm / 1.97-2.16".
- Draw U-Z equal to P-P1 at the back.
- Draw Z-J-Q as in the figure.
- E-W1 as E-W.
- Draw guideline B1-E1.
- Draw the rear lower line as in the figure.
- Carry out the extension for the overlap and buttoning: B1-B2 1.5 cm / 0.59"; B2-B3 3 cm / 1.18"; B3-B4 2.7 cm / 1.06" as shown.
- L1-P1 = H1-G minus H1-L1 minus G-O (e.g: 23.1 - 7.7 - 2.5 = 12.9 cm / 5.08").

CUFF

overlap line — 26 — overlap line
A — D
7
FOLD
E — F
2.5 — 2.5
7
B — C
draw the desired shape

A2 / A1 — 22.5 — F — D / D1
A
fold volume
guideline
B3 — 4 — D2
B2 — 3.5 — C1
B1 — 2
B — 22.5 — E — C
centre front — shoulder point — centre back

SHOULDER LOOP
2
6

STRAP
4
fold
4
16

FLAP
13.5
5

BREAST POCKET
13.5
fold fold
2 — 19
1.5 1.5

CENTRE FRONT — POINT SHOULDER — CENTRE BACK — POINT SHOULDER — CENTRE FRONT

FRONT pattern labels: A 9.5 19 9.5 E — BACK SLEEVE CROWN — 13.4 — L3 L2 E1 — G2 L1 — FRONT SLEEVE CROWN — BICEP LINE — G1 G — X — CENTRE SHOULDER — 63 — ELBOW LINE — N P — BACK SEAM LINE — FRONT SEAM LINE — B1 B2 B3 F1 — DISCARD — B B4 B5 L1 F

BACK pattern labels: A 9.5 19 9.5 E 9.5 19 9.5 A — BACK SLEEVE CROWN — 13.4 — FRONT — BACK — BICEP LINE — 63 — ELBOW LINE — VOLUME 9 — SLIT — DISCARD

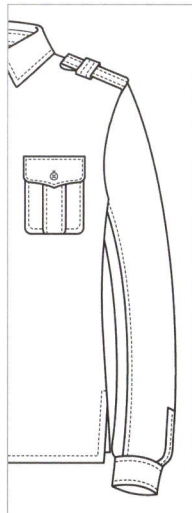

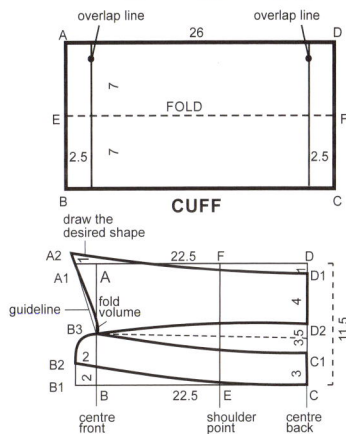

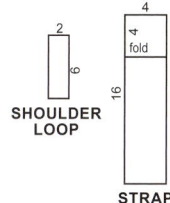

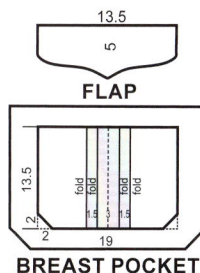

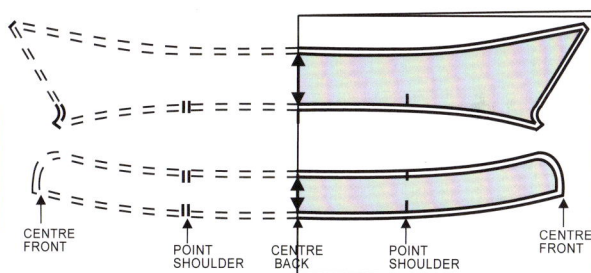

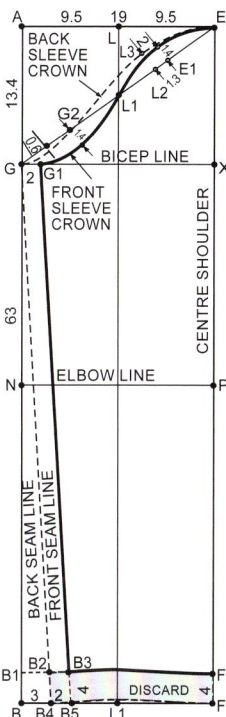

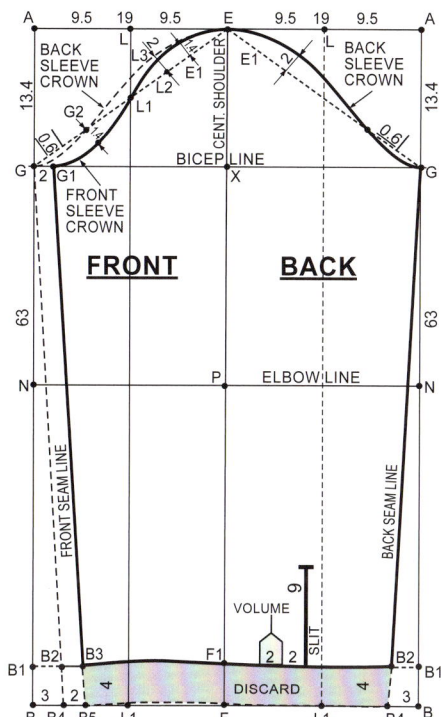

SLEEVE CONSTRUCTION
- Draw the rectangle A-B-E-F with:
- A-B = sleeve length (e.g: 65 cm / 25.59").
- A-E = measurement on the bodice block + 1/2 of the same + 1 cm / 0.59" (e.g.: 12 cm bodice armscye + 6 + 1 = 19 cm / 7.48").
- A-G = L1-P1 of the bodice + 0.5 cm / e.g. 12.9 + 0.5 = 13.4 cm / 5.28".
- E-X as A-G; draw G-X = bicep line.
- Join G-E with a diagonal line = guideline.
- A-N half of A-B + 2 cm / 0.79" (65 : 2 = 32.5 + 2 = 35 cm / 13.78". Join N-P.
- A-L half of A-E = 19 : 2 = 9.5 cm / 3.74"
- B-L1 as A-L = 8.5 cm / 3.54". Draw L-L1.
- G-L1 half of G-E. E-E1 half of E-L1.
- E1-L2 1.3 cm / 0.51". L2-L3 at 2 cm / 0.79".
- G-G2 half of G-L1. G-G1 = 2 cm / 0.79".
- Draw the front crown E-L1-G1.
- Draw the back crown E-L3-G.
- B-B4 = 3 cm / 1.18" (or as desired).
- Draw dotted line G-B4 (rear seam line).
- B4-B5 as G-G1 2 cm / 0.79" (front seam line).
- Shorten the lower edge of the sleeves B-B1 and F-F1 by 2.5-5 cm / 1-2"(or as desired) based on the height of the cuff (height of the cuff minus 2.5 cm / 1").
- Narrow the lower edge as desired (3 + 2 cm / 1.18" + 0.79").
- Draw B2-B3-F1 with a curved line.
- Draw B4-L1-F with a curved line.
- Take the sleeve of the front and back and trace the whole sleeve as in the figure.
- Draw the slit line of the sleeve placket at 8.5 cm / 3.35"

from the back seam line, for a length of approximately 7.5-10 cm / 2.95-3.94".
- Draw fold space markings for the width of the lower sleeve edge measuring 2 cm / 0.79" each.
- Tip: always check the sleeve crown measurement with the bodice armscye.

SINGLE-PIECE CUFF
Draw the rectangle A-B-C-D with:
- A-B equal to twice the height of the cuff.
- A-D equal to the measurement of the lower sleeve edge minus the fold space plus the width of the sleeve placket (e.g: 2.5 cm / 1").
- A-E half of A-B. Draw E-F.

COLLAR WITH SEPARATE STAND
Modify the front neckline as in the figure.
- Draw a rectangle A-B-C-D.
- A-B = collar height + stand + 4.5 cm / 1.77" (e.g: 4 + 3 + 4.5 = 11.5 cm / 4.53").
- B-C neckline as on the front and back bodice block. C-C1 = 3 cm / 1.18".
- C1-D2 = 3.5 cm / 1.38"; D2-D1 = 4 cm / 1.57"; B-B1 = 2-2.5 cm / 0.79-1".
- B-B3 = 4.75 cm; A-A1 = 3 cm / 1.18".
- Draw guideline B3-A1.
- C-E as the back neckline of the bodice.
- Connect the points as in the figure.

EPAULETTE AND LOOP
Draw two rectangles as shown in the figure.

BASIC SLIM FIT SHIRT

SIZE 48 MEASUREMENTS

- Height = 175 cm / 5'9".
- Slim fit shirt = 14 cm / 5.51".
- Chest semi-circumference = 96 + 14 = 110 ÷ 2 = 55 cm / 21.65".
- Waist semi-circumference = 88 + 14 = 102 ÷ 2 = 51 cm / 20.08".
- Hip semi-circumference = 100 + 14 = 114 ÷ 2 = 57 cm / 22.44".
- Neck semi-circumference = 42 ÷ 2 = 21 cm / 8.27"
- 1/2 shoulder width = 44 ÷ 2 = 22 cm / 8.66"
- Front neck to waist = 45.6 cm / 17.95".
- Rear neck to waist = 46.2 cm / 18.19".

BASIC BLOCK CONSTRUCTION

Draw the right angle A-B-C with

- A-B equal to the front neck-to-waist (e.g.: 45.6 cm / 17.95").
- B-C equal to semi-circumference of chest + ease for a 14 cm / 5.51" slim fit shirt (e.g. 96 + 14 = 110 : 2 = 55 cm / 21.65").
- C-D rear neck-to-waist (e.g.: 46.2 cm / 18.19").
- D-G shoulder width (e.g: 44 ÷ 2 = 22 cm / 8.66").
- D-C1 total shirt length (e.g.: 75 cm / 29.53").
- Draw the Q-W-E1 and Q-W1-E1 tapering (1.5 + 1.5 / 0.59" + 0.59").
- Draw C1-E2-B1 (lower edge).
- B-Y and C-X = waist to hip (e.g: 20 cm / 7.87").
- Draw Y-X (Hip Line).
- Y-B1 as X-C1.
- D-H half of C-D (e.g: 46.2 ÷ 2 = 23.1 cm / 9.09").
- H-H1 as D-G (22 cm / 8.66").
- Draw H1-G.
- Draw H-I as B-C = 55 cm / 21.65" (underarm level).
- B-E half B-C. (e.g: 55 ÷ 2 = 27.5 cm / 10.82").
- A-F as B-E.
- Draw F-E-E2 (side line).
- I-I1 as H-H1 minus 1 cm / 0.39" (22 - 1 = 21 cm / 8.27").
- Draw I1-J1 parallel to H1-G.
- H-L 1/3 of D-H (e.g.: 23.1 ÷ 3 = 7.7 cm / 3.03").
- Draw L-M parallel to H-I.
- H1-I1 = H-I minus (H-H1 + I-I1), e.g. 55 - (22 + 21) = 55 - 43 = 12 cm / 4.72" (armscye sector).
- H-S and X-S1 = 11 cm / 4.33".
- Draw the rear dart S-T1-S2 and S-T2-S2.

BACK

- G-O = 2.5 cm / 1".
- D-N 1/3 of D-G + 0.5 cm / 0.20" (e.g: 22.5 ÷ 3 = 7.5 + 0.5 = 8 cm / 3.15").
- N-P = 2.5 cm / 1". Draw D-P as an outline.
- Draw P-O-P1 with shoulder length measurement + 1 cm / 0.39" (e.g.: 17 cm / 6.69").
- Q in the middle of H-I.
- Draw P1-L1-Q as in the figure.
- E-W 1.5 cm / 0.59" or as required.
- Draw the lower line as in the figure.

FRONT

- A-U 1/3 of D-G + 0.6 cm / 0.24 (e.g: 22.5 ÷ 3 = 7.6 + 0.6 = 8.2 cm / 3.23").
- Draw the arc U-U1.
- Lower U1 by 1 cm / 0.39".
- J1-Z = 5-5.5 cm / 1.97-2.16".
- Draw U-Z equal to P-P1 at the back.
- Draw Z-J-Q as in the figure.
- E-W1 as E-W.
- Draw guideline B1-E1.
- Draw the rear lower line as in the figure.
- Carry out the extension for the overlap and buttoning: B1-B2 = 1.5 cm / 0.59"; B2-B3 = 3 cm / 1.18"; B3-B4 = 2.7 cm / 1.06".

FRONT **BACK**

COLLAR **CUFF**

- L1-P1 = H1-G minus H1-L1 minus G-O (e.g: 23.1 - 7.7 - 2.5 = 12.9 cm / 5.08").

SLEEVE CONSTRUCTION

- Draw the rectangle A-B-E-F with:
- A-B = sleeve length (e.g: 65 cm / 25.59").
- A-E as the measurement of the bodice sector + 1/2 of the same sector (e.g: 12 + 6 = 18 cm / 7.09").
- A-G as L1-P1 on the bodice = 12.9 cm / 5.08".
- E-X as A-G.
- Draw G-X = bicep line.
- Join G-E with a diagonal line = guideline.
- A-N half of A-B + 2 cm / 0.79" = 65 ÷ 2 = 32.5 + 2 = 34.5 cm / 13.58".
- Join N-P.
- A-L half of A-E = 18 ÷ 2 = 9 cm / 3.54"
- B-L1 as A-L = 9 cm / 3.54".
- Draw L-L1.
- G-L1 half of G-E.
- E-E1 half of E-L1.
- E1-L2 = 1.3 cm / 0.51"; L2-L3 = 2 cm / 0.79".
- G-G2 half of G-L1; G-G1 = 2 cm / 0.79".
- Draw the front crown E-L1-G1.
- Draw the back crown E-L3-G.
- B-B4 = 3 cm / 1.18" (or as desired).
- Draw dotted line G-B4 = rear seam line.
- B4-B5 as G-G1 = 2 cm / 0.79" (front seam line).
- Shorten the lower edge of the sleeves B-B1 and F-F1 by 2.5-5 cm / 1-2" (or as desired) based on the height of the cuff (height of the cuff minus 2.5 cm / 1" for a bit of margin).
- Narrow the lower edge as desired (3 + 2 cm / 1.18" + 0.79").
- Draw B2-B3-F1 with a curved line.
- Draw B4-L1-F with a curved line.
- Take up the front and back sleeve and draw the full sleeve as in the picture.
- Draw the line for the slit 8.5 cm / 3.35" from the back seam line, for a length of 7.5-10 cm / 2.95-3.94".
- Draw the fold space markings for the width of the lower edge of the sleeve as 2 cm / 0.79" each.

SINGLE-PIECE CUFF

Draw the rectangle A-B-C-D with:
- A-B equal to twice the height of the cuff.
- A-D equal to the lower sleeve edge minus the fold space, plus the width of the sleeve placket (e.g: 2.5 cm / 1").
- A-E half of A-B. Draw E-F.
- C-C1 and B-B1= 0.6 cm / 0.24" (excess for the inner part).

EDGING AND SLEEVE PLACKET: see explanations on page 47.

COLLAR WITH SEPARATE STAND

- Lower the neckline of the bodice front by 1.5-2 cm / 0.59-0.79".
- Draw a rectangle A-B-C-D.
- A-B = neck height + collar stand + 4.5 cm / 1.77" (e.g: 4 + 3 + 4.5 = 11.5 cm / 4.53".
- B-C bodice neckline on the front and back.
- C-C1 = 3 cm / 1.18"; C1-D2 = 3.5 cm / 1.38"; D2-D1 = 4 cm / 1.57"; B-B1 = 2-2.5 cm / 0.79-1".
- B-B3 = 4.75 cm; A-A1 = 3 cm / 1.18".
- Draw guideline B3-A1.
- C-E as the back neckline of the bodice.
- Connect the points as in the figure.

COLLARS

The collar is the most visible part of the shirt when wearing a jacket, which is why it's one of the most important details when it comes to the formality and style of the entire look. The main styles are:

- **Straight point:** this is the narrowest spread and the most traditional look. It's quite versatile, but more formal and should be worn with ties with small and medium knots. The narrow, elongated points of this look slim the face. The collar leaves are 7.5 cm / 2.95" long.
- **Semi-spread:** this is a classically styled collar, but with a less formal appearance. Compared to the straight point collar, it has a slightly larger width between the tips, but the leaves are still 7.5 cm / 2.95" long. It's ideal for those who love to wear ties.
- **Cutaway:** this collar has the shortest, most distant points. It gives the wearer modern, casual style, as its spread lets part of the collar stand peek out under the tie. The collar leaves are 7.5 cm / 2.95" long.
- **Spread:** this collar is somewhere between the cutaway and straight point collars, with a spread that's neither too wide nor too narrow. Like the cutaway, the leaves are 7.5 cm / 2.95" long.

- **Long button-down:** more sporty than the other collars, it was invented in the USA in the mid-1950s. Originally used only for sportswear, it is now worn in casual settings or in young or informal work environments. The leaves are particularly long: 9.5 cm / 3 3/4".
- **Short button down:** due to its short length, this collar has a particularly youthful appearance compared to the long version. The leaves in this case are 8 cm / 3.15" long.
- **Club:** refined and elegant, yet surprisingly versatile, this collar goes well with thin ties, worn open or with a pin. The leaves are 6.5 cm / 2.56" long.
- **Mandarin:** a collar with a unique and recognisable shape, suitable for all kinds of occasions. The height of this collar is 3.5 cm / 1.38".
- **Wing-tip collar or dinner jacket collar:** worn with particularly formal and elegant outfits, such as those for ceremonies and galas. The leaves are 5 cm / 2" long.

Almost all tailor-made collars have removable stays to keep the points sharp and prevent them from curving upward.

CLASSIC COLLARS

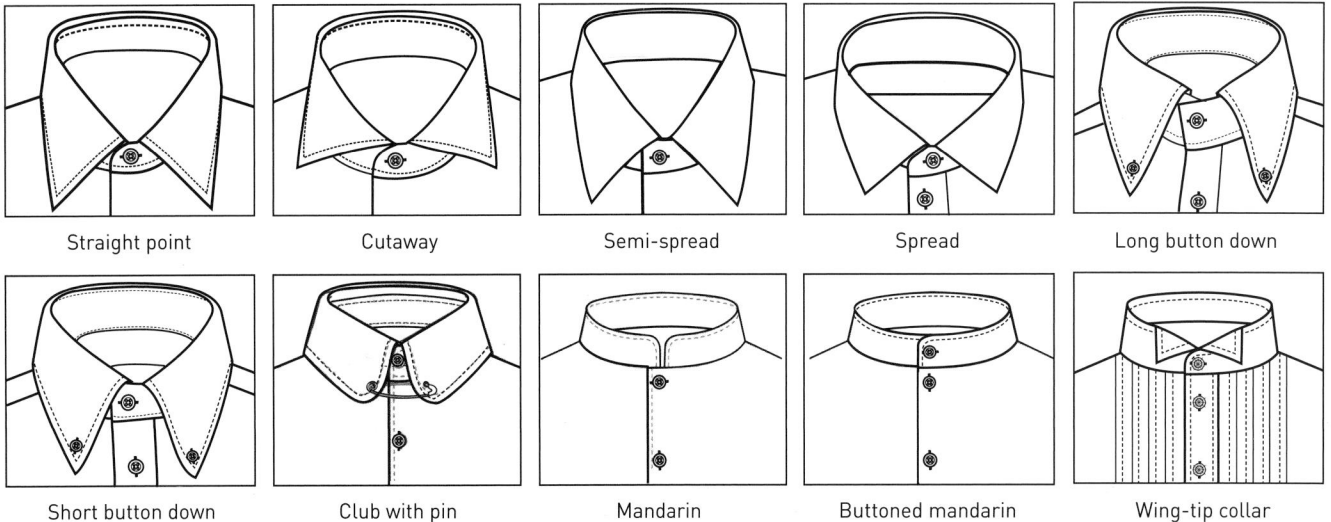

Straight point	Cutaway	Semi-spread	Spread	Long button down
Short button down	Club with pin	Mandarin	Buttoned mandarin	Wing-tip collar

SPORTY COLLARS

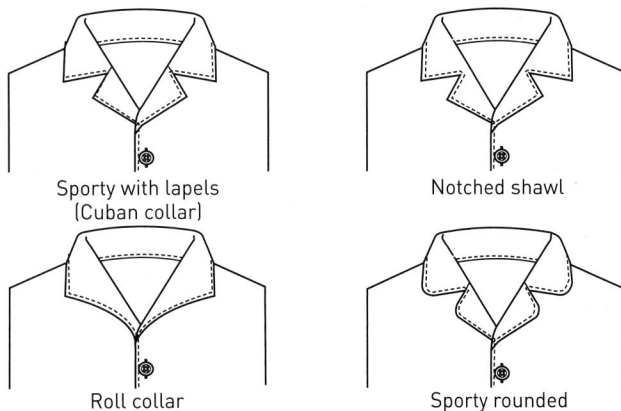

Sporty with lapels (Cuban collar)

Notched shawl

Roll collar

Sporty rounded

Classic collar

- Draw a rectangle A-B-C-D.
- A-B = leaf height + stand + 4.5 cm / 1.77"
  (e.g.: 4 + 3 = 7 + 4.5 = 11.5 cm / 4.53").
- B-C = 1/2 neckline as the front and back
  bodice (e.g: 21.5 cm / 8.46").
- C-C1 = 3 cm / 1.18".
- C1-D2 = 3.5 cm / 1.38".
- D2-D1 = 4 cm / 1.57".
- B-B1 = 2-2.5 cm / 0.79-1".
- B-B2 = 4.75 cm / 1.87".
- A-A1 = 3 cm / 1.18" or as desired.
- Draw guideline B2-A1.
- C-E as the rear neckline of the bodice.
- Draw E-F.
- Connect the points as in the figure.

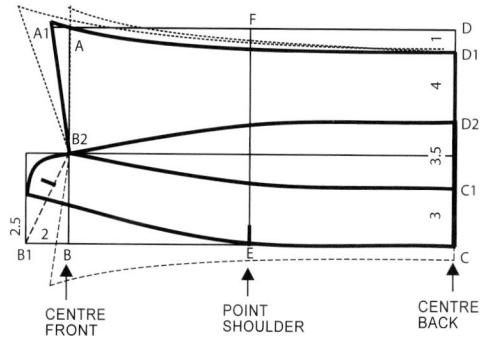

Mandarin collar

- Measure the neckline of the base block.
- Draw the rectangle A-B-C-D with:
- A-B equal to the height of the collar +
  2 cm / 0.79".
- B-C equal to ½ of the front and back
  base neckline + 1 cm / 0.39".
- B-B1 = 2 cm / 0.79".
- D-C1 = 2 cm / 0.79".
- C-E = rear neck measurement.
- C-C1 = collar height.
- A-A1 = 1 cm / 0.39".
- Join the points as in the figure.

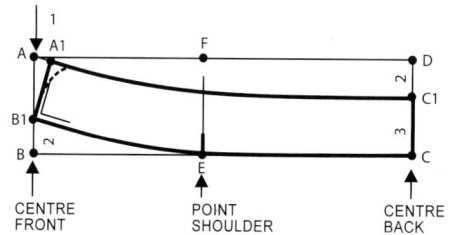

Wing-tip collar

- Measure the neckline of the base block.
- Draw the rectangle A-B-C-D with:
- A-B equal to the height of the collar +
  2 cm / 0.79".
- B-C equal to ½ of the front and back base
  neckline + 1 cm / 0.39".
- B-B1 = 2-2.5 cm / 0.79-1".
- B-B2 = 5 cm / 1.97".
- D-C1 = 2 cm / 0.79".
- C-E = rear neck measurement.
- C-C1 = collar height.
- A-A1 = 1 cm / 0.39".
- B2-A2 = fold height (3.5-4 cm / 1.38-1.57").
- Connect the points with lines as in
  the figure.

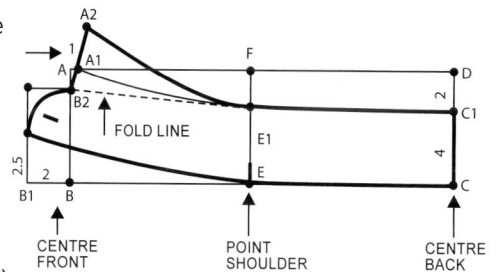

APPLICATION OF THE COLLAR TO A SHIRT WITH A COLLAR STAND

Collars are crucial in assessing the quality of a garment's construction. A well-made collar and neckline must not wrinkle or pull and must retain its shape and look even after washing. The points should be symmetrical and the edges should be smooth and flat. For collars of shirts in classic fabrics such as Oxford cloth or poplin, a very stiff, fusible cloth must be used to provide shape, support and stability. A collar with a collar stand is made up of two parts: the collar and an intermediate band (called the 'stand') placed between the neckline and the collar. In some garments, the stand is an extension of the collar, which saves a seam, although the creation method is the same for both versions.

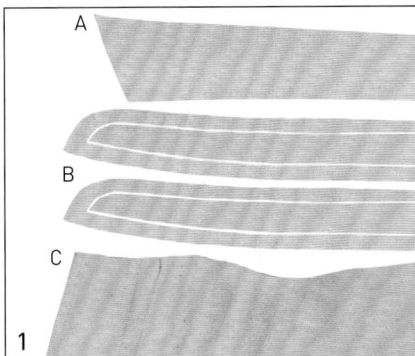

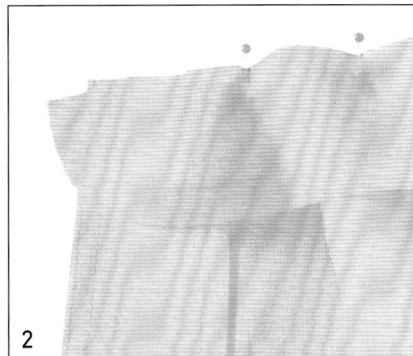

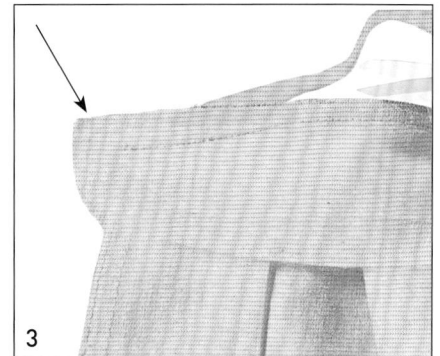

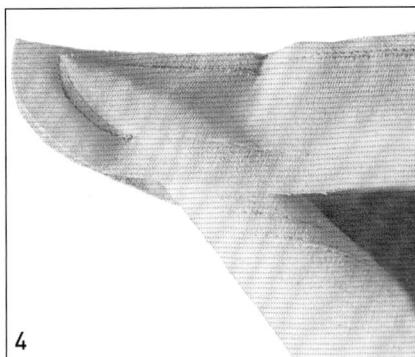

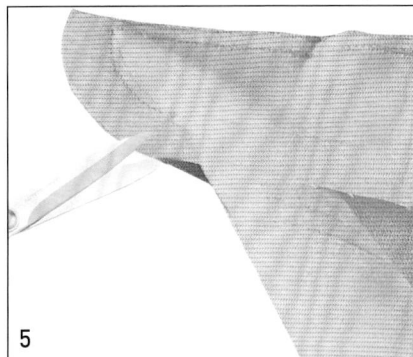

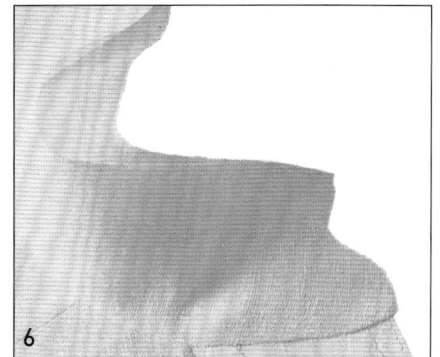

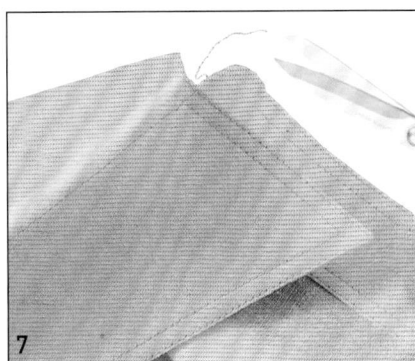

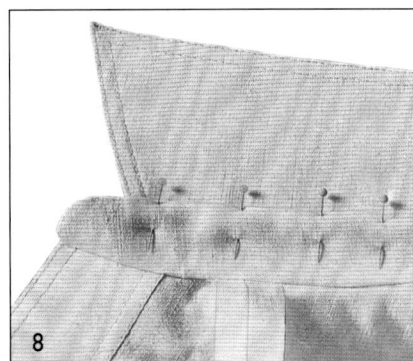

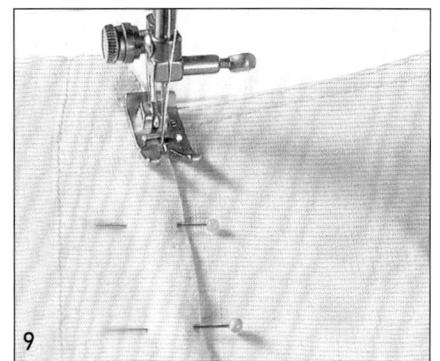

1) Topstitch the outer edge of the collar (A), apply interfacing to both parts of the stand (B) and finish the bodice (C).
2) Pin the parts of the collar stand by placing them right side against right side, with the shirt in between.
3) Sew the collar stand to the neckline, stopping 1.5 cm / 0.59" from the edges of the stand (arrow). Trimming and shifting the margins.
4) Roll up the two shirt front pieces away from the curvature of the collar stand, create the rounded part of the seam from the neckline side to the place where the collar stand is attached.
5) Cut to the mark, trim the margins along the curvature and make notches.
6) Turn the collar stand to the right side of the fabric.
7) Sew the collar on the right side of the outer stand with the undercollar close to the stand. Trim the seam allowances and iron the seam in the direction of the collar stand.
8) Iron the seam allowance of the inner collar stand downwards. Trim to 5 mm / 20". Pin the ironed edge of the collar stand so that it covers the seam line.
9) Topstitch around the stand through all layers of fabric.

SHIRT CUFFS

An often-underestimated detail, shirt cuffs come in many variations, suitable for the most diverse occasions. It is possible to divide cuff types into two macro categories: with cufflinks (more formal) or without cufflinks (less formal).
One further detail that differentiates cuffs is the shape of its corners, which may be straight, angled or round. This helps give the shirt a specific style: the straighter the corners are, the more casual the shirt is.
Tailor-made shirts also allow the width of the right or left cuff to be customised so that a watch can be worn more comfortably.

CUFF TYPES
- **Two vertical buttons**: the most casual cuff there is, only to be worn on purely informal occasions.
- **Two horizontal buttons**: also very sporty, this cuff style is very practical because you can adjust the button to your liking, especially when wearing a watch.
- **Angled single button**: the most common and classic type of cuff, and one of the most versatile. It's suitable for any occasion, from an aperitif to a party.
- **Double French (with cufflinks)**: this is one of the most elegant cuff styles there is. Compared to the styles listed above, this cuff is unique because it is twice as tall: when worn, it has to be folded over, until the double eyelets line up, so that the cufflinks can be inserted. The style of the cufflinks will partly determine how elegant the whole outfit is: fabric knots or steel cuff links, for instance, tend to make the look more casual, while gold, mother-of-pearl or other precious materials tend to make everything more sophisticated and formal.
- **Cocktail**: also called a Portofino cuff, casino cuff or Neapolitan cuff, this style is unique: the double button, a very casual element, is accompanied by a turn-over cuff, typical of the French cuff and therefore more elegant. However, this also makes it suitable to be worn with or without a jacket, preferably combined with a sporty tie.
- **French**: similar to the double French cuff, but with the height of a normal cuff, so without the flap and thus more practical to wear. This cuff falls into the category of the most elegant cuffs, worn on formal occasions, being part of the white tie dress code, i.e. worn under a tailcoat, or the black tie dress code, worn under a dinner jacket.

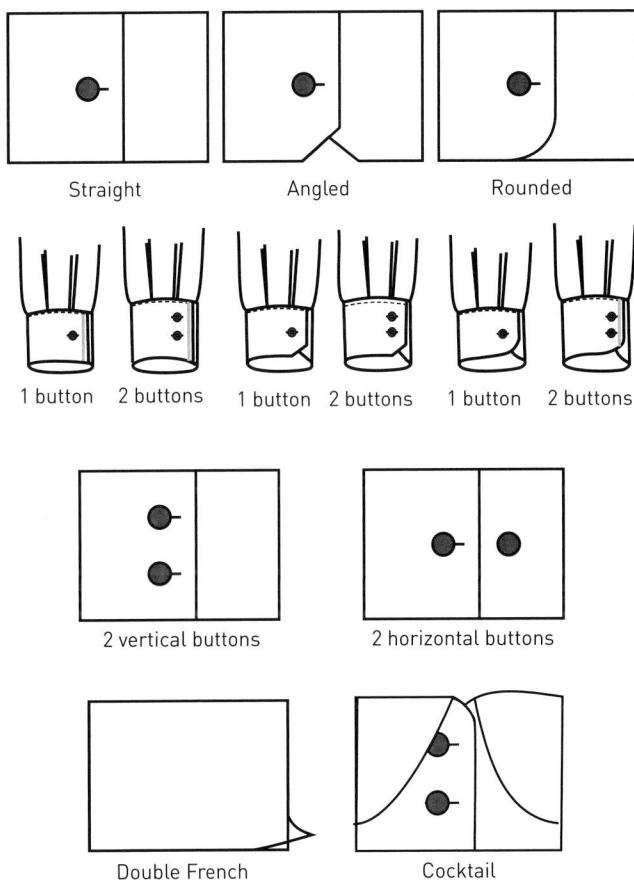

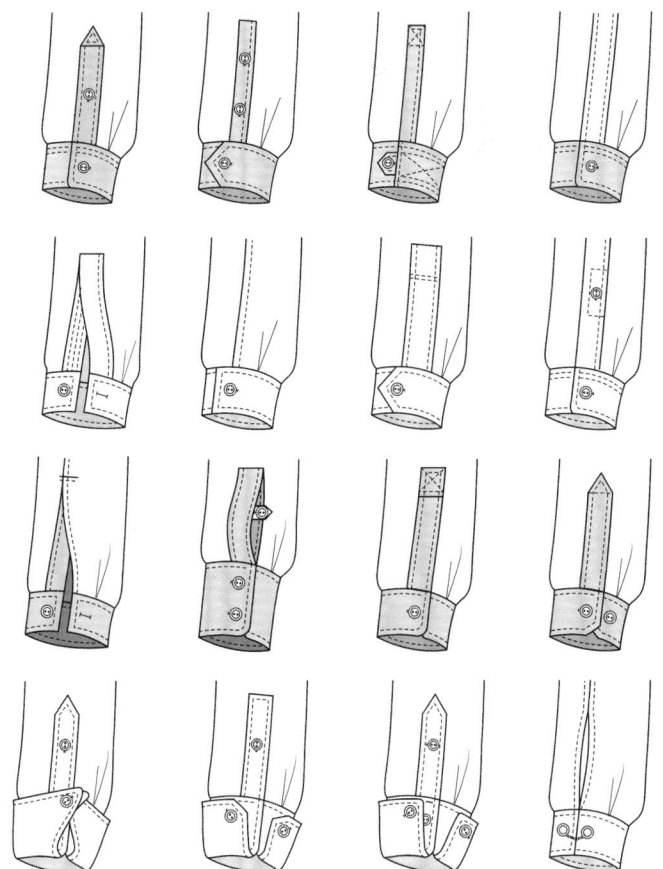

Straight

Angled

Rounded

1 button   2 buttons   1 button   2 buttons   1 button   2 buttons

2 vertical buttons

2 horizontal buttons

Double French

Cocktail

SHIRT SLEEVE OPENING WITH A SLEEVE PLACKET: METHOD 1

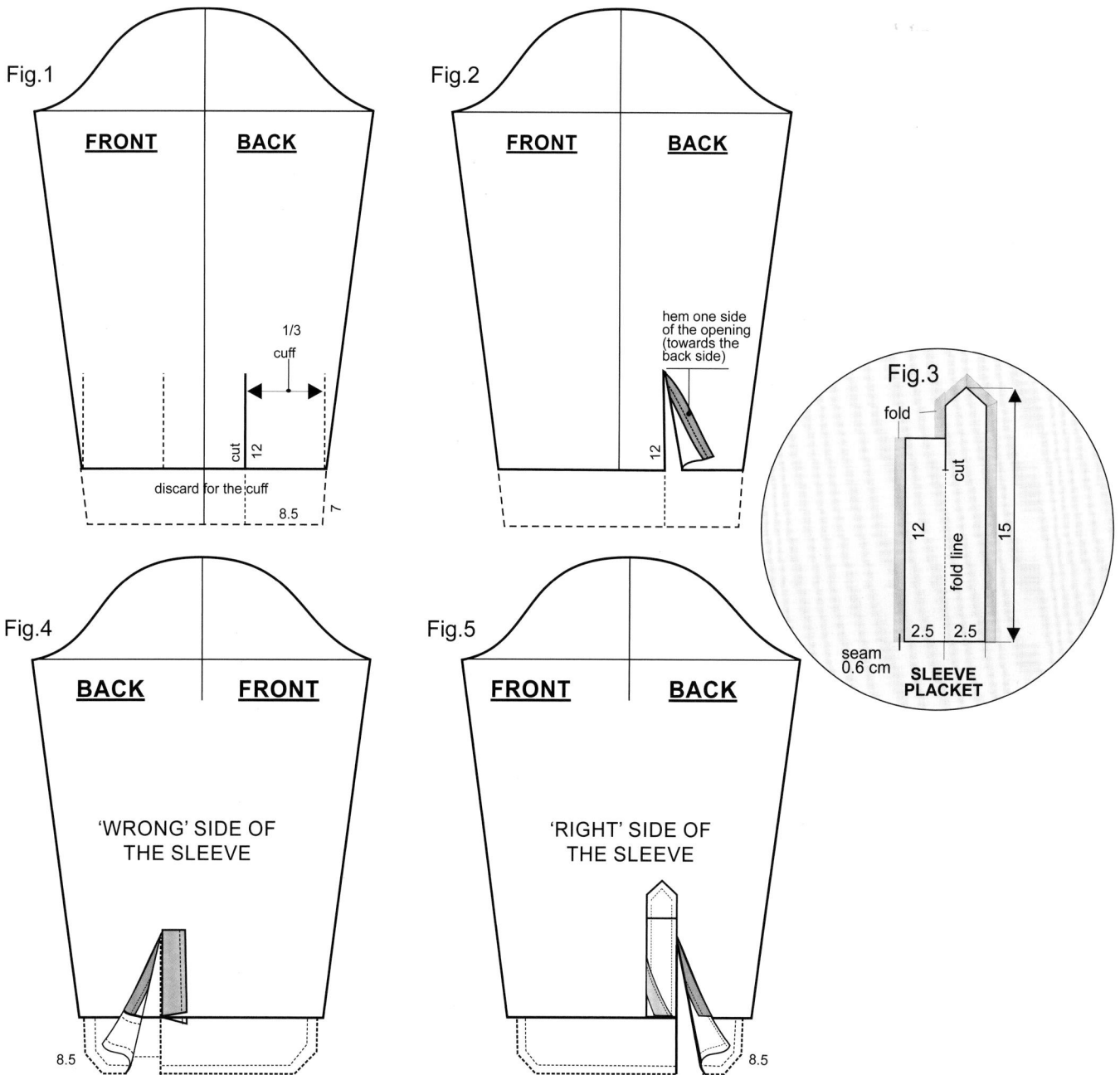

Fig.1

FRONT | **BACK**

1/3
cuff

cut
12

discard for the cuff

8.5 | 7

Fig.2

FRONT | **BACK**

hem one side
of the opening
(towards the
back side)

12

Fig.3

fold

cut

12 | fold line | 15

2.5 | 2.5

seam
0.6 cm

**SLEEVE
PLACKET**

Fig.4

BACK | **FRONT**

'WRONG' SIDE OF
THE SLEEVE

8.5

Fig.5

FRONT | **BACK**

'RIGHT' SIDE OF
THE SLEEVE

8.5

HOW TO TRIM SLEEVE SLITS

Sleeve plackets are openings on the lower edge of the sleeve which allow the cuff to overlap and button. The opening is placed in line with the elbow, at 1/3 of the width of the sleeve from the underarm seam line at the back. When the sleeve is worn, the opening is located just above the little finger (fig. 1). It is possible to trim the placket in three ways: with a fly, with a border or with a placket. The latter is the most common finish: this strip of fabric is applied to the lower edge of the sleeve before the cuff is attached, constructed as a continuous piece with the opening sewn and folded internally. In tailored shirts with simple cuffs, a button, which has both an aesthetic and practical function, is applied in the middle of the placket, whereas shirts with double French cuffs do not have a placket.

PLACKET APPLICATION

1) Make a cut at the bottom of the sleeve.
2) Prepare the fabric and sew according to the explanations below (the dark part indicates folded and ironed fabric):
- apply edging the left side of the cut (fig. 2);
- cut the slit leaving 6 mm / 0.24" for the seam allowances on the sides and top (fig. 3);
- fold and iron the placket;
- fold the other side of the placket and place it on the reverse side of the sleeve as in fig. 4;
- turn the sleeve over and sew the whole placket as shown in fig. 5.

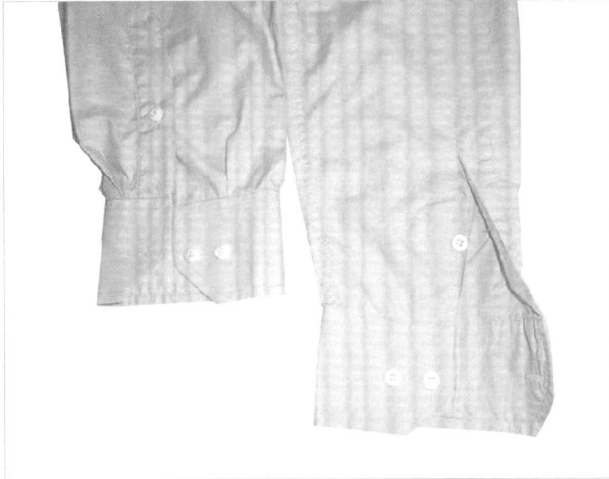

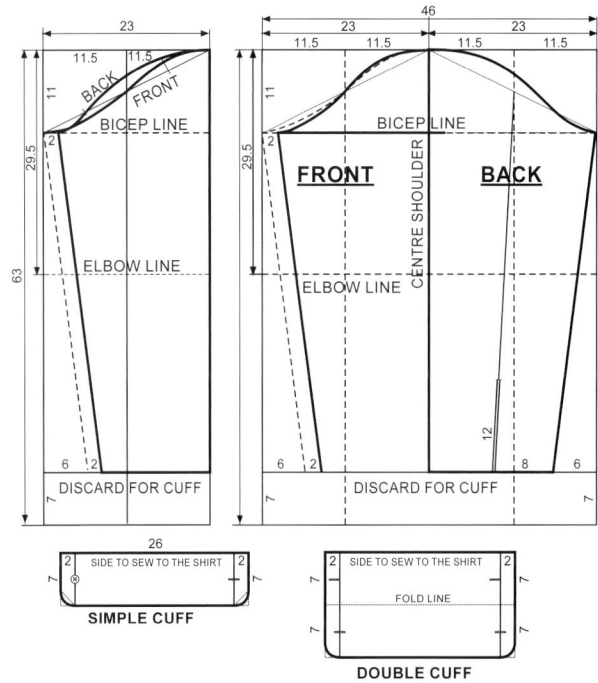

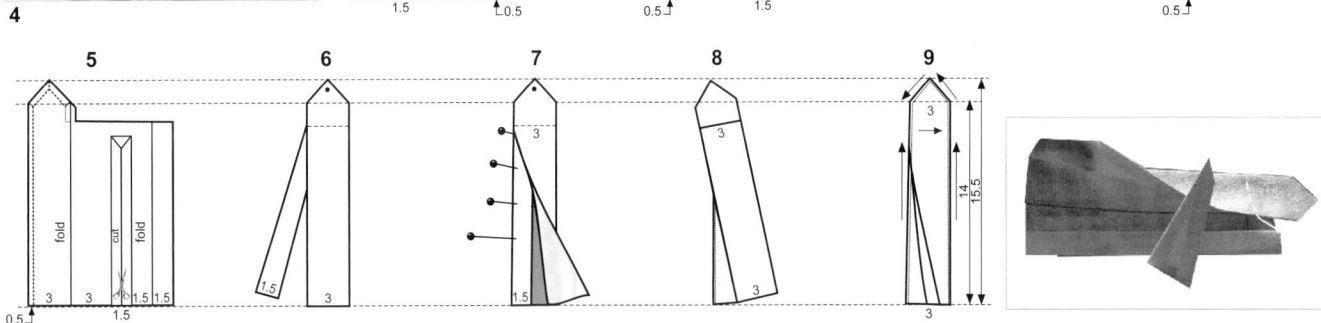

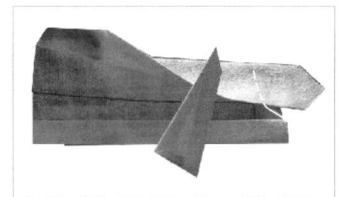

1) Fold 5 mm / 0.20" along the seam allowances downwards on both sides of the band. Mark the upper line of the sleeve opening with tacking.

2) Iron the sides of the band along the fold lines. The edges must align with the tacked opening mark.

3) Iron the two edges of the point downward also. Square the corners by folding the edges of the point first, followed by the lateral edges.

4) Match the marks on the placket band with those on the sleeve, placing the right side of the placket against the wrong side of the sleeve. Sew and then cut up to 5 mm / 0.20" from the point. Finally, make two small cuts in the corners.

5) Pull the band through the opening to the right face of the sleeve. Iron the seams towards the opening, then iron the triangle at the top of the band.

6) Pin the narrow edge of the band so that it covers the seam, then sew a seam along the inside edge of the band.

7) Fold the other side of the band so that it covers the seam and affix it with a few pins. Sew the outer fold of the overlap to the top of the opening.

8) Position the overlap so that the edges are flat and uniform.

9) Sew along the edges in the direction of the arrows, starting from the lowest edge, going around the point and then crosswise. Fasten the seam and check the opening.

CUFF OPENING WITH A FULL BAND

The first step in making the cuffs of a shirt is to apply interfacing to half of the single-piece wrist. The half of the cuff with interfacing goes on the outer side of the finished sleeve, while the half without interfacing will form the cuff. In two-piece cuffs, only one piece needs to have interfacing, which will also be placed on the outer side of the finished sleeve, while the other part will form the fly.

An 'opening with a full band' is a cut at the lower edge of the sleeve, finished with a strip of the same fabric, cut in the direction of the warp to give it greater stability. When the cuff is fastened, this band is hidden.

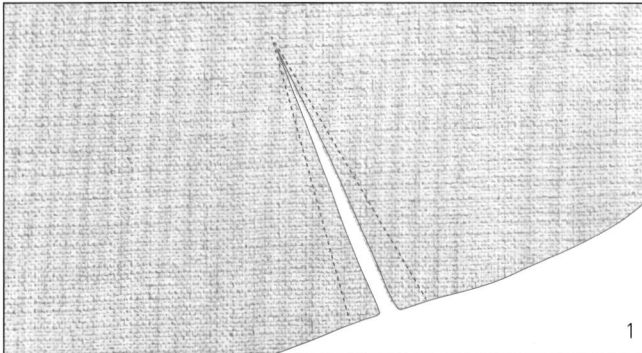

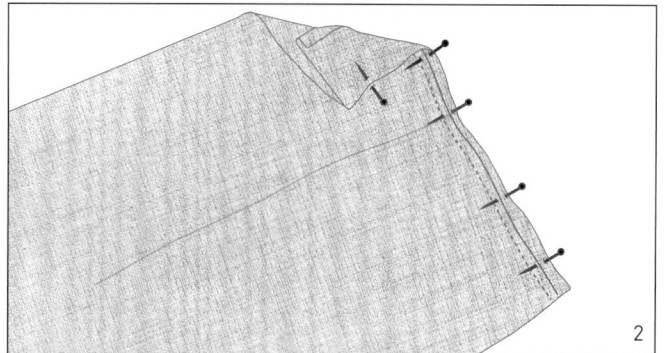

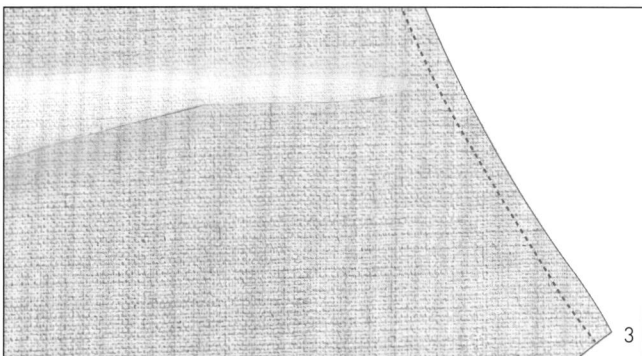

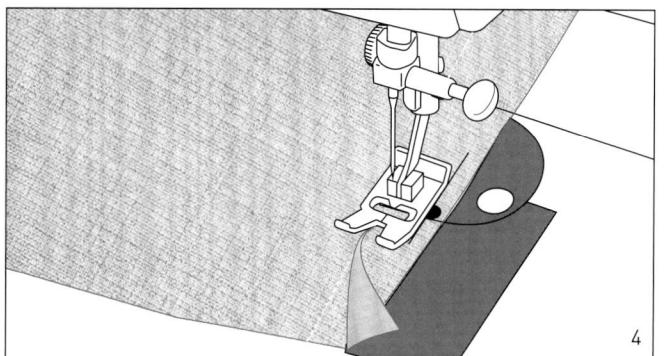

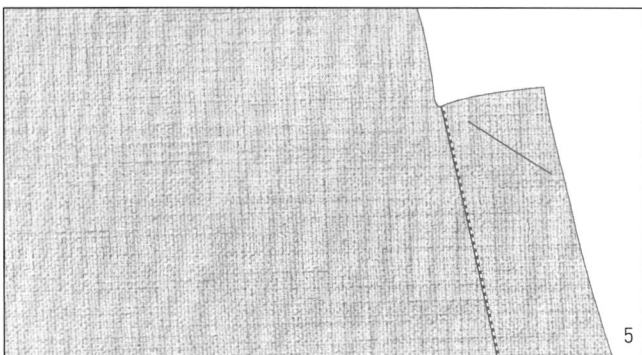

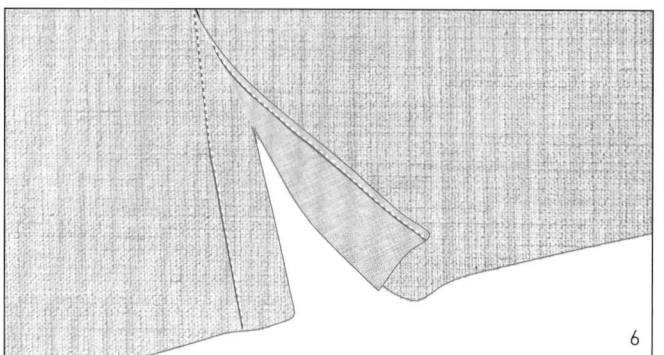

1) Mark the line for the opening at the wrist of the sleeve, then sew supporting seams at the sides of the opening and a crosswise stitch at the peak of the cut. Then cut along the line until that point.
2) At 5 mm / 0.20" from the strip of fabric, iron one edge downward, then pin the other edge to the opening with the right side of the fabric strip against the wrong side of the sleeve.
3) Using a presser foot, sew just along the sleeve support seam, leaving a 5 mm / 0.20" margin along the opening. The cut edges must align perfectly only at the end of the seam.
4) Bring the folded edge of the fabric strip over the seam, so that the fold barely covers the seam. Now create stitching along the edge, then iron.
5) Align the edges of the strip on the reverse side of the sleeve and sew diagonally from the top of the strip to keep it inside the sleeve once the cuff is completed.
6) Flatten the strip by ironing it over the edge of the opening that will be overlapped. Iron it underneath on the edge of the overlap, then apply the cuff.

APPLYING A CUFF TO A SLEEVE WITHOUT A PLACKET

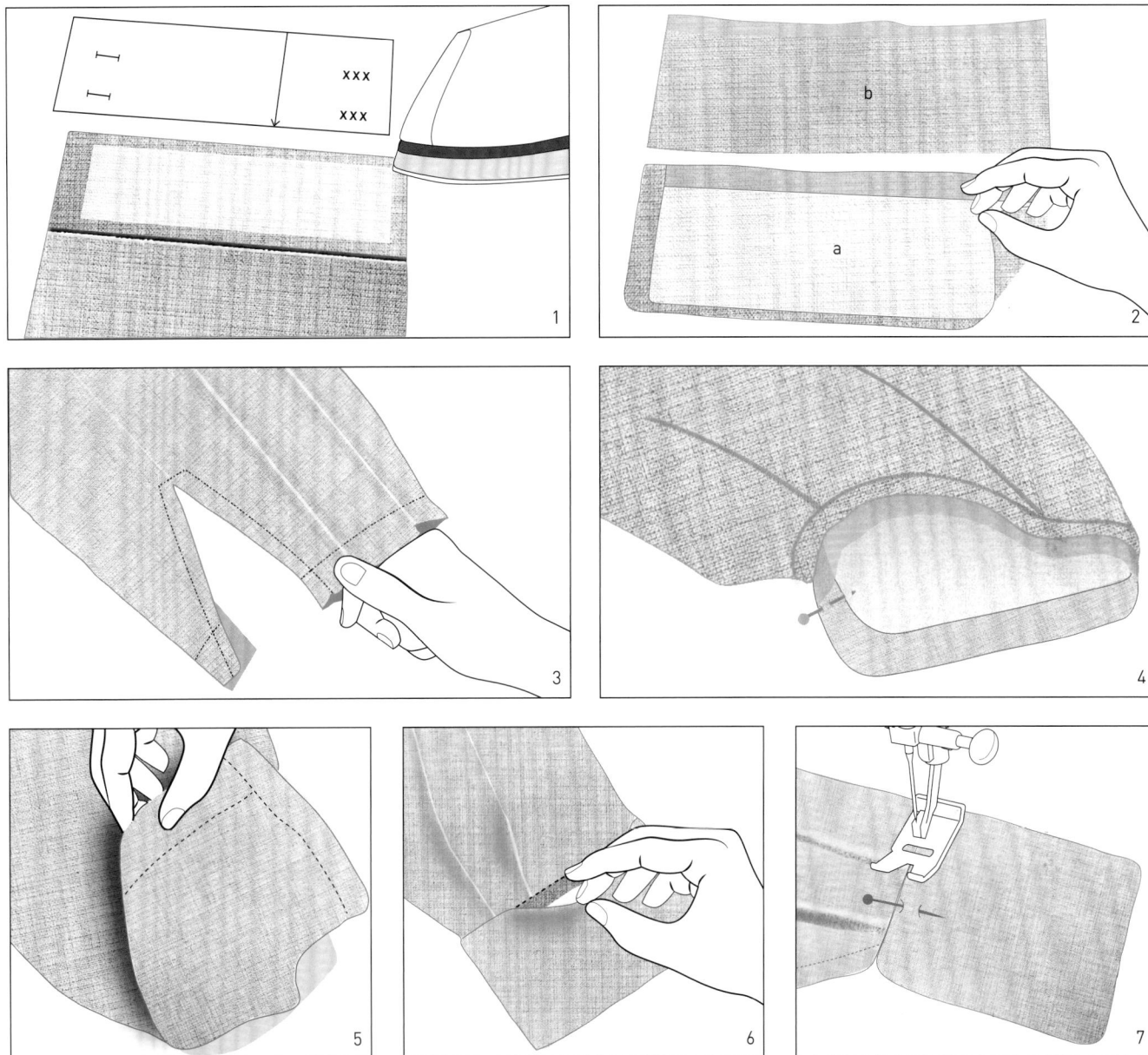

1) To create the exact shape of the fusible cloth, use the paper pattern of the cuff folded in half, eliminating the seam allowances. Then apply the cloth to the upper part of the cuff.

2) Iron by folding the seam allowances of the side with interfacing downward, then fold the cuff in half lengthwise, right sides together. Sew the ends by opening the ironed seam allowance. Cut and adjust the seam allowances (a) and turn the cuff to the 'right' side (b).

3) Pin the 'wrong' side of the sleeve and sew it to the side of the cuff without interfacing after having aligned all the marks. The ends of the cuff must be flush with the finished edges of the opening. Do not cut the seam allowances.

4) Wrap the part of the cuff without interfacing around the opening towards the front of the sleeve as far as possible. Align the 'right' side of the cuff to the 'right' side of the sleeve. Place a pin 2.5 cm / 1" from the sleeve opening.

5) Overlapping the first seam, sew each end of the cuff up to the pin so that the first row of stitches is not visible from the outside. Remove the seam allowance near the seam to avoid bulges.

6) Once turned right-side up, iron the cuff. The 'right' side of the cuff edge is sewn to the sleeve for approximately 2.5 cm / 1" near its opening.

7) Stitch along the edge on the cuff above the sleeve seam and a topstitch 5 mm / 0.20" from the edge of the cuff. Without topstitching, apply the cuff to the 'right' side of the sleeve, turn it inward and slip-stitch.

ATTACHING THE SLEEVE TO THE SHIRT

The 'flat method' and the 'no-gathering-seam method' are two of the ways that inset sleeves are sewn to shirts. However, the first method is certainly the most widely used when it comes to menswear. The advantage of this method is that it is less gathered than classic inset sleeves, because the sleeve is inserted before its seams or those of the side of the garment are made. For greater ease and a better fit, it is better to sew the sleeve and side seams before attaching the sleeve.

The markings previously made on the pattern help to position the inset sleeve correctly. In general, the gathering should be greater at the back of the sleeve than at the front. The extra length (usually 2-2.5 cm / 0.79-1") should not be left on the crown of the sleeve, but on the armscye, aligned with the centre of the sleeve.

The notches on the paper pattern indicate how to align the sleeve with the armhole: double notches are on the back of the sleeve and the back of the armscye, single notches indicate the front. The notches should be marked with a cut of approximately 5 mm / 0.20" inside the seam allowance.

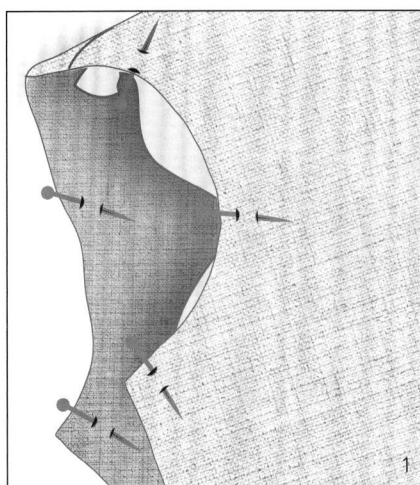

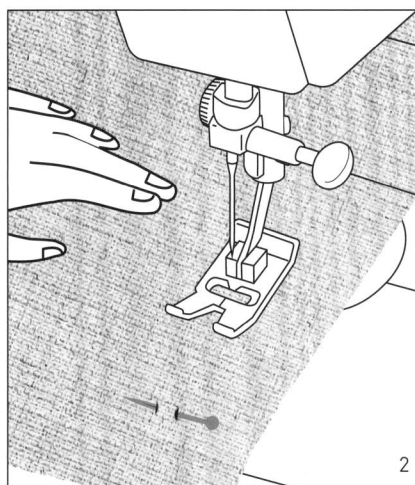

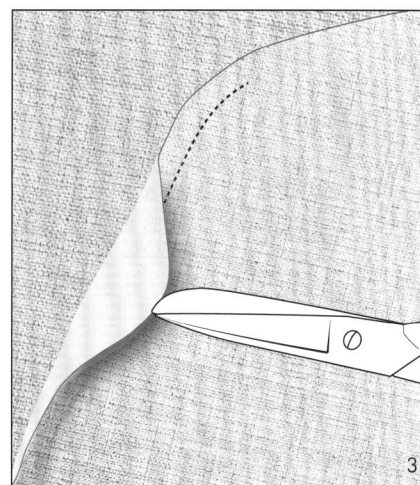

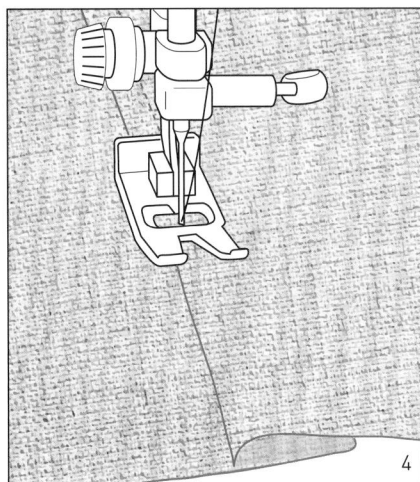

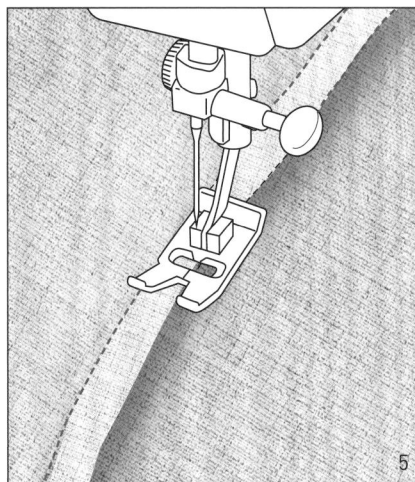

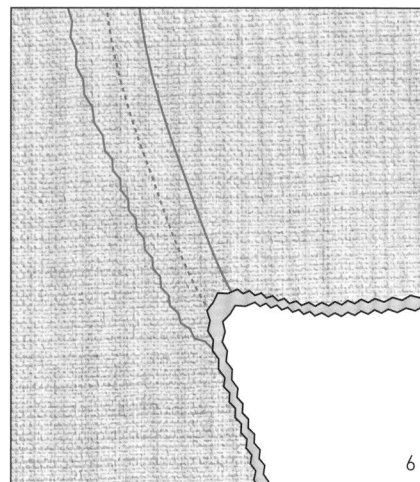

1) With the fabric right sides together, pin the sleeve to the armhole, aligning the notches and reference points. Insert the pins from the bodice side, taking care to carefully distribute the width of the sleeve crown evenly.

2) With the side of the bodice facing you, sew the sleeve to the armhole. Use the feed dog to facilitate the adaptation of the sleeve to the armscye.

3) Iron the seam far from the sleeve, then trim the seam allowance to approximately 5 mm / 0.20" to make a mock flat-felled seam.

4) Make the initial stitching on the right side of the bodice about 5 mm / 0.20" from the seam line.

5) Stitch along the edge of the seam line.

6) Join the sides of the shirt and the sleeve with pins to make a perfect continuous seam. Reinforce the underarm area with smaller stitches or apply the mock felled seam again using a special presser foot.

SHIRT WITH SHORT SLEEVES AND A SPORTY COLLAR

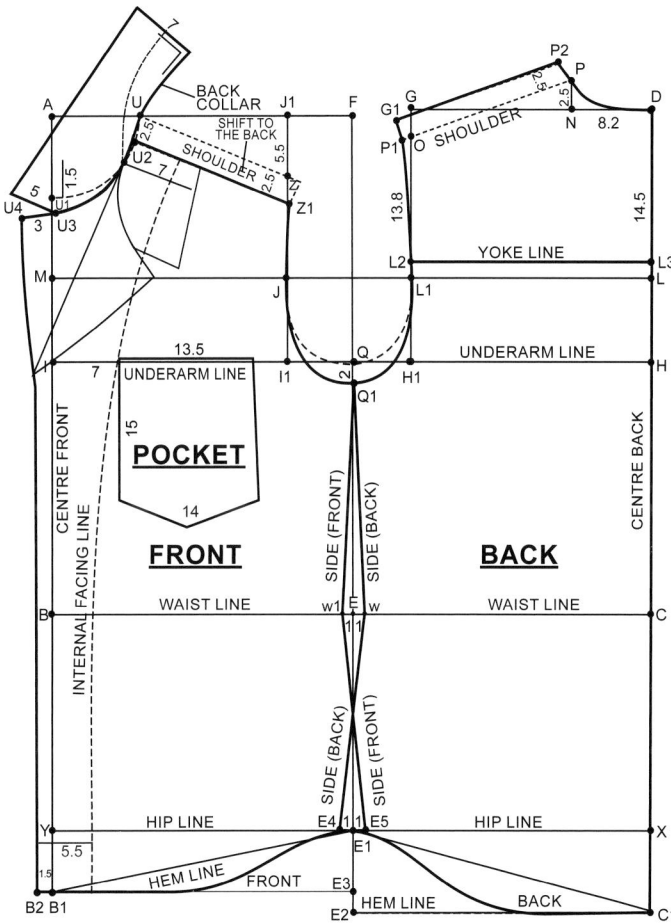

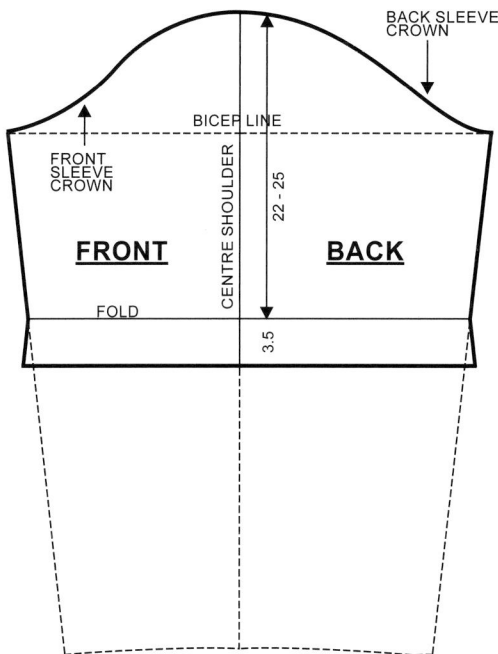

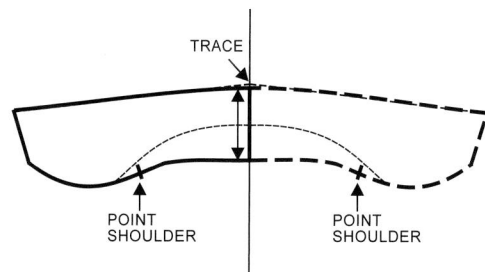

BACK COLLAR

SHIFT TO THE BACK

SHOULDER

POCKET

UNDERARM LINE

13.5

FRONT

CENTRE FRONT

INTERNAL FACING LINE

SIDE (FRONT)

SIDE (BACK)

BACK

CENTRE BACK

YOKE LINE

UNDERARM LINE

WAIST LINE

WAIST LINE

SIDE (BACK)

SIDE (FRONT)

HIP LINE

HIP LINE

HEM LINE

FRONT

HEM LINE

BACK

13.8

14.5

8.2

FRONT   **BACK**

BACK SLEEVE CROWN

BICEP LINE

FRONT SLEEVE CROWN

CENTRE SHOULDER

22 - 25

3.5

FOLD

TRACE

POINT SHOULDER

POINT SHOULDER

- Draw the base shirt block with the desired ease and fit.
- Carry out the transformations illustrated in the block.
- Make the sleeve base relative to the base of the shirt bodice with the same ease.

SHIRT WITH A FRONT PANEL

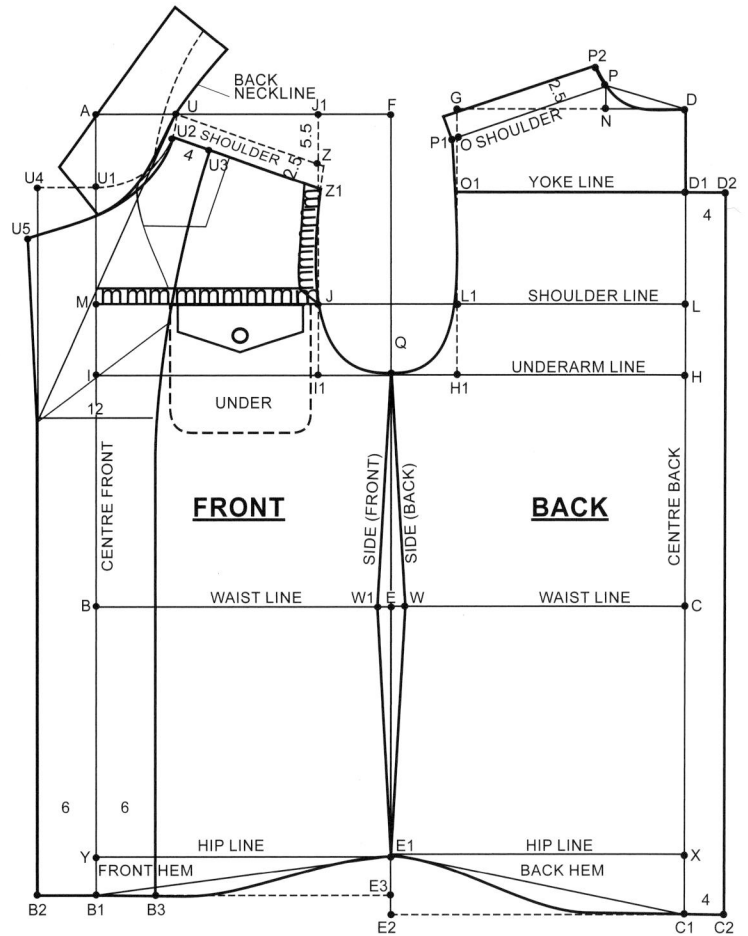

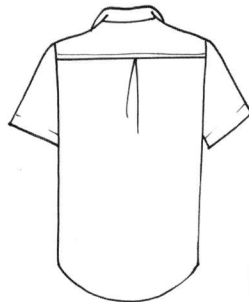

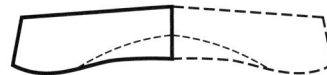

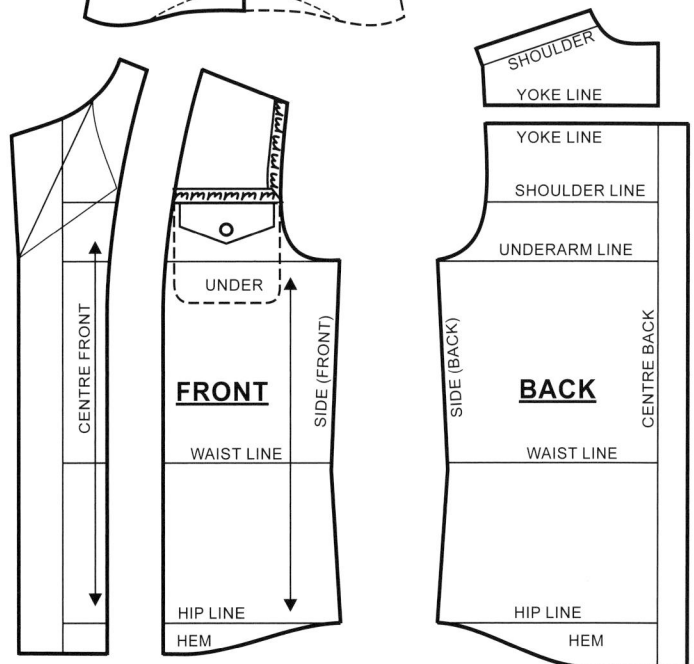

Labels on main pattern diagram:

BACK NECKLINE

A — U — J1 — F — G — P2 — P — D
U2 SHOULDER — P1 — O SHOULDER — N
U4 — U1 — 4 — U3 — Z — 5.5 — O1 — YOKE LINE — D1 D2
U5 — Z1 — 4
M — J — L1 — SHOULDER LINE — L
Q — UNDERARM LINE — H1 — H
I1 — I1
12 — UNDER
CENTRE FRONT
SIDE (FRONT)
SIDE (BACK)
CENTRE BACK

FRONT   **BACK**

B — WAIST LINE — W1 E W — WAIST LINE — C
6 — 6
Y — HIP LINE — E1 — HIP LINE — X
FRONT HEM — BACK HEM
B2 B1 B3 — E3 — E2 — C1 C2 — 4

Second set of pattern pieces (lower):

SHOULDER — YOKE LINE — YOKE LINE — SHOULDER LINE — UNDERARM LINE

CENTRE FRONT
FRONT — UNDER
SIDE (FRONT)
SIDE (BACK)
BACK
CENTRE BACK
WAIST LINE — WAIST LINE
HIP LINE — HIP LINE
HEM — HEM

- Draw the base shirt block with the desired ease and fit.
- Draw the yoke line behind O1-D1 at the desired height, as shown in the figure.
- Draw the extension of the centre back for the central fold D2-C2.
- Draw the extension of the centre front for the fastening overlap U1-U4.
- Draw the neckline U2-U5.
- Draw the front cut line U3-B3.
- Take up the pattern parts of the yoke, the cut and the bodice with another sheet of paper, affixing the reference marks and the straight of grain arrow.

SHIRT WITH A YOKE

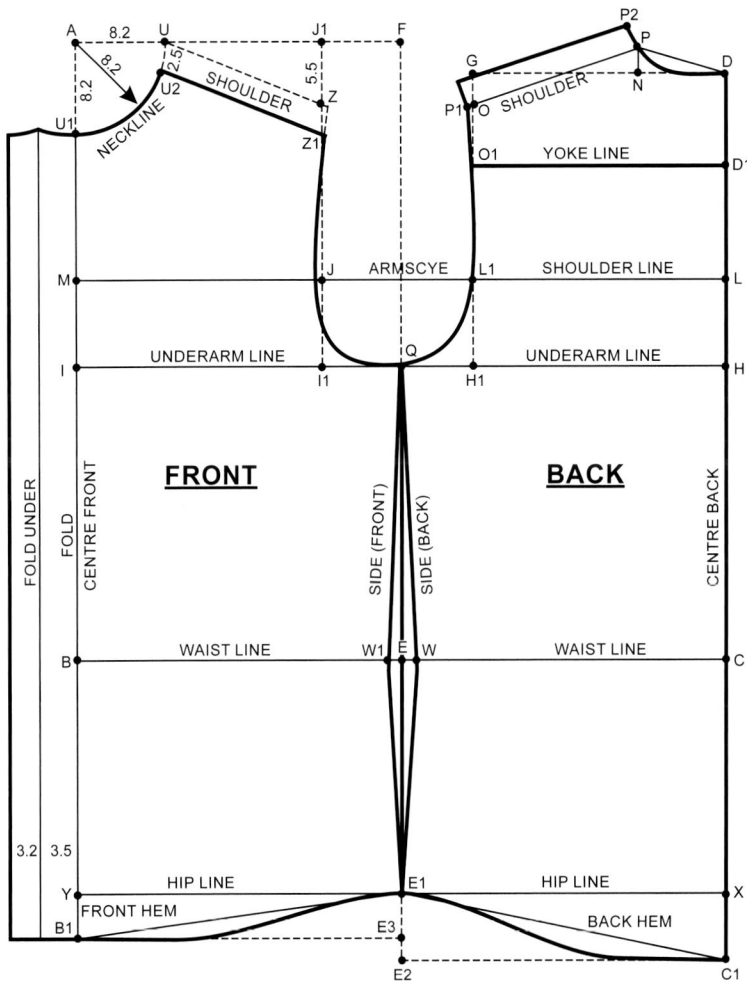

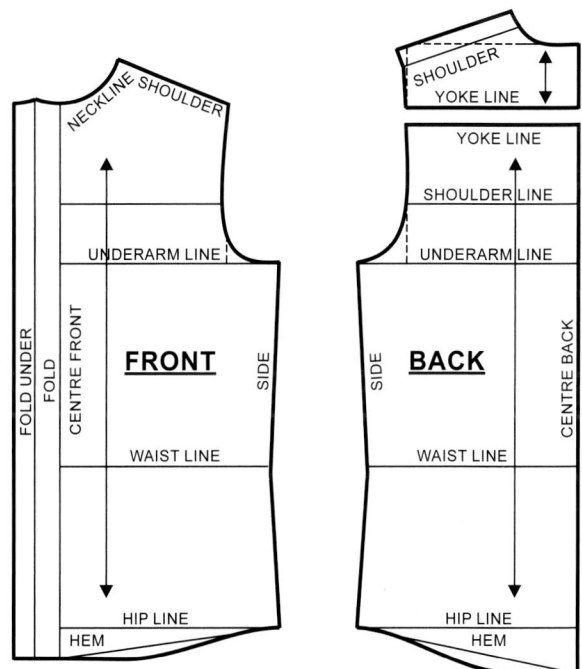

- Create the classic shirt base block.
- D-D1 = 8-10 cm / 3.15-3.94".
- Draw D1-O1 (Yoke Line).
- Cut and separate the parts.

SHIRT WITH A FRONT AND BACK YOKE

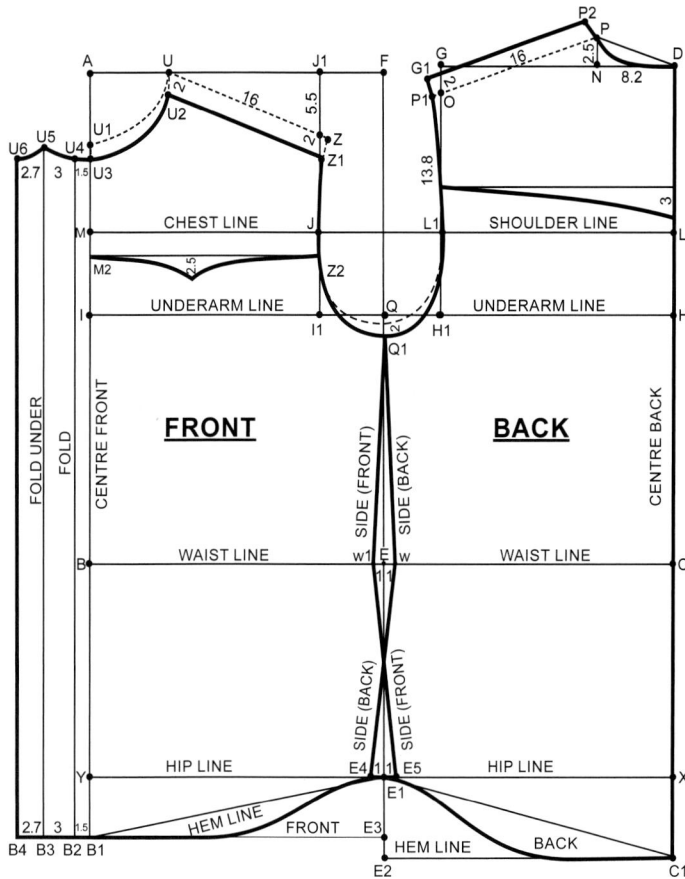

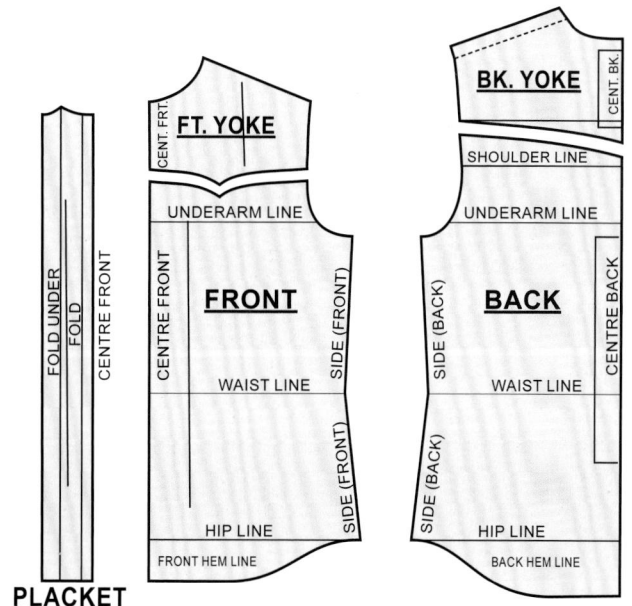

- Draw the base block for the shirt.
- Draw the front and back yoke lines with the desired height and shape, as shown in the figure.
- Take up the pattern parts of the yoke and bodice with another sheet of paper, affixing the reference marks and the straight of grain arrow.

ASSEMBLING THE YOKE ON THE SHIRT

On a shirt, and generally on all garments, the yoke is the part that covers the upper back, just above the shoulder blades. The yoke can also extend to the front, so its paper pattern shows the position of the shoulders at the neckline and armscyes. All marks must be transferred to the fabric after cutting, so that the collar and sleeves can be aligned properly. It's important that the warp runs parallel to the rear seam of the yoke, ensuring the stability of the fabric at the point where the shirt is most subject to stress. Above the shoulders, fabric on the bias helps it naturally fit the body. The lining of the yoke is cut from the same paper pattern. After being sewn, the raw edges of the yoke are enclosed in the front and back seams.

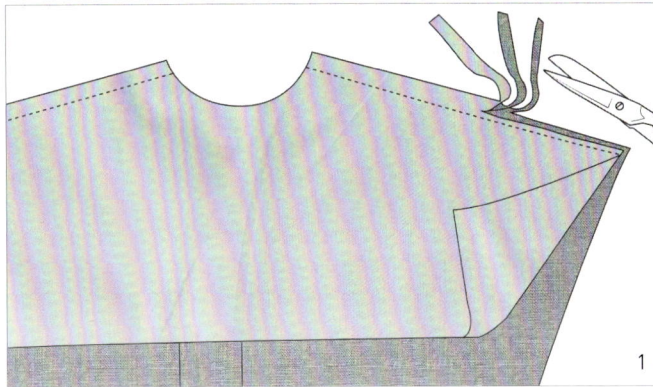

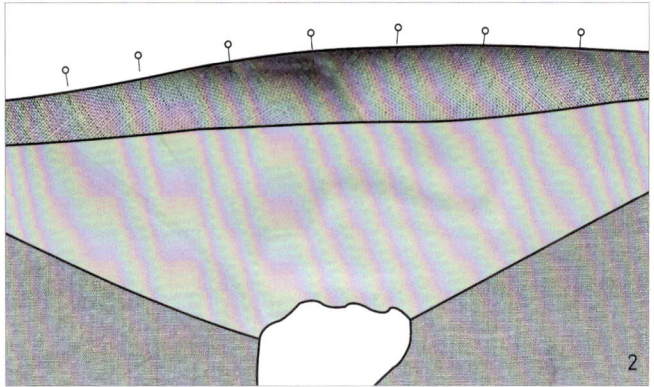

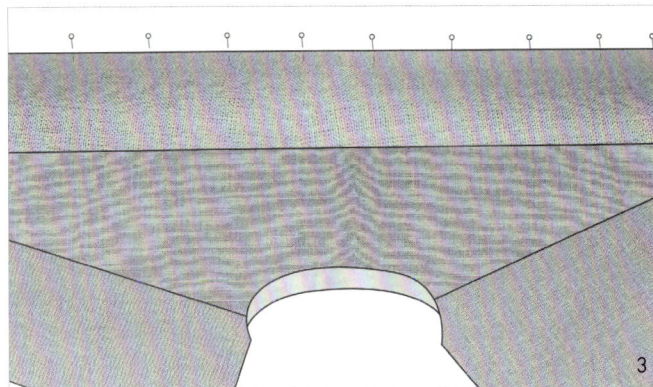

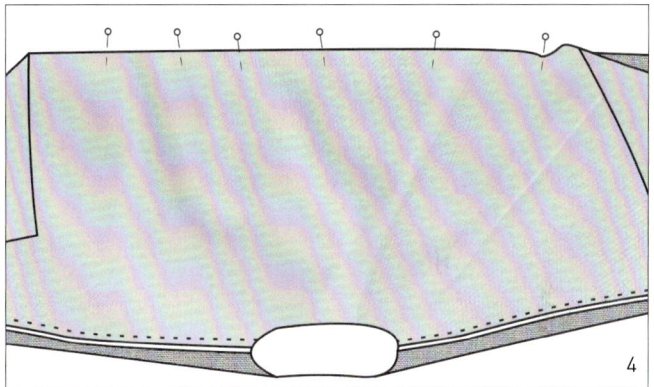

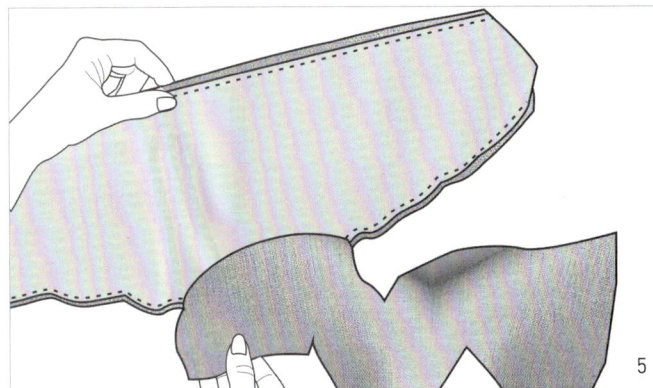

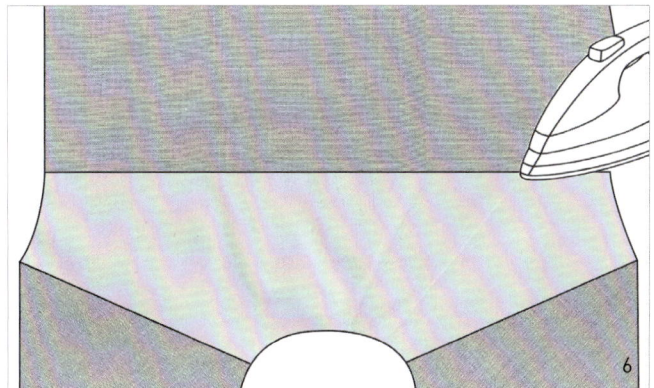

1) Start by sewing the yoke and its lining to the two front panels. The yoke and lining should be placed right sides together, with the shirt front in between. Trim and adjust the margins.
2) Pin the back of the shirt to the yoke, right sides together, leaving the lining of the yoke free.
3) Roll the back of the shirt up to the yoke seam with pins and the front up to the shoulder seams.

4) Shift the lining over the rolled front and back, aligning the seam of the lining with that of the pinned yoke. Sew, trim and adjust the seam allowances.
5) Pull out all parts of the shirt from the neck opening. The yoke will have the 'right' side out.
6) Flatten the shoulder and yoke seams and iron.

ASYMMETRICAL SHIRT

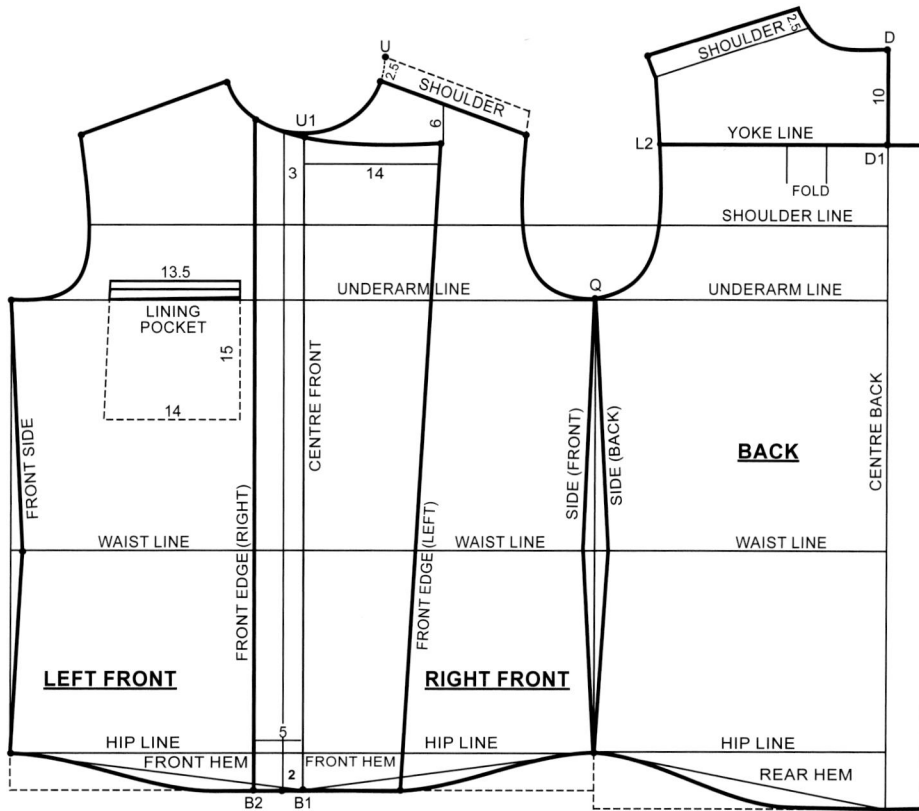

- Draw the shirt base block with the desired fit and ease.
- Apply the transformations as illustrated in the figure, with the yoke at the back and the asymmetrical fastening at the front.
- Take up the front right, the front left and the back.
- Separate the back yoke.
- Draw the mandarin collar.
- Use the sleeve pattern relative to the chosen fit.

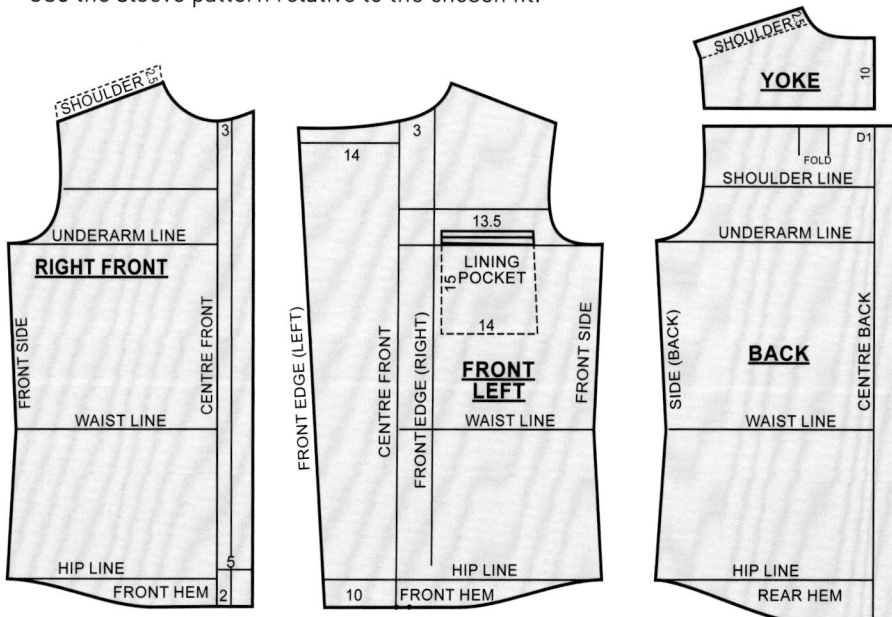

KIMONO SHIRT

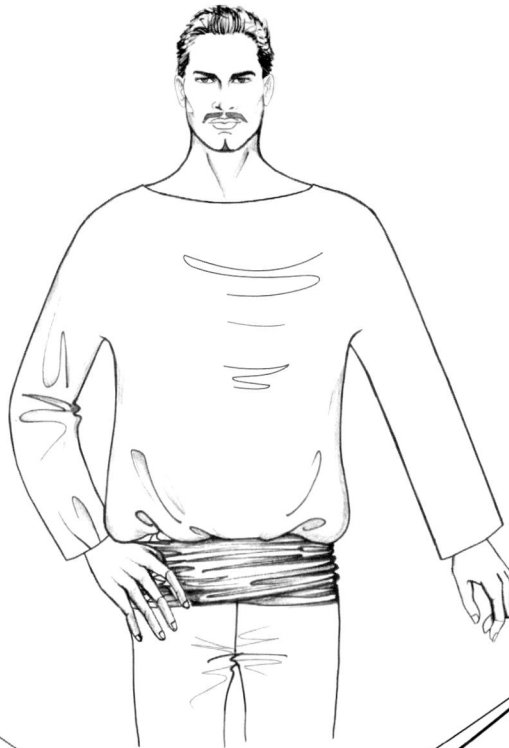

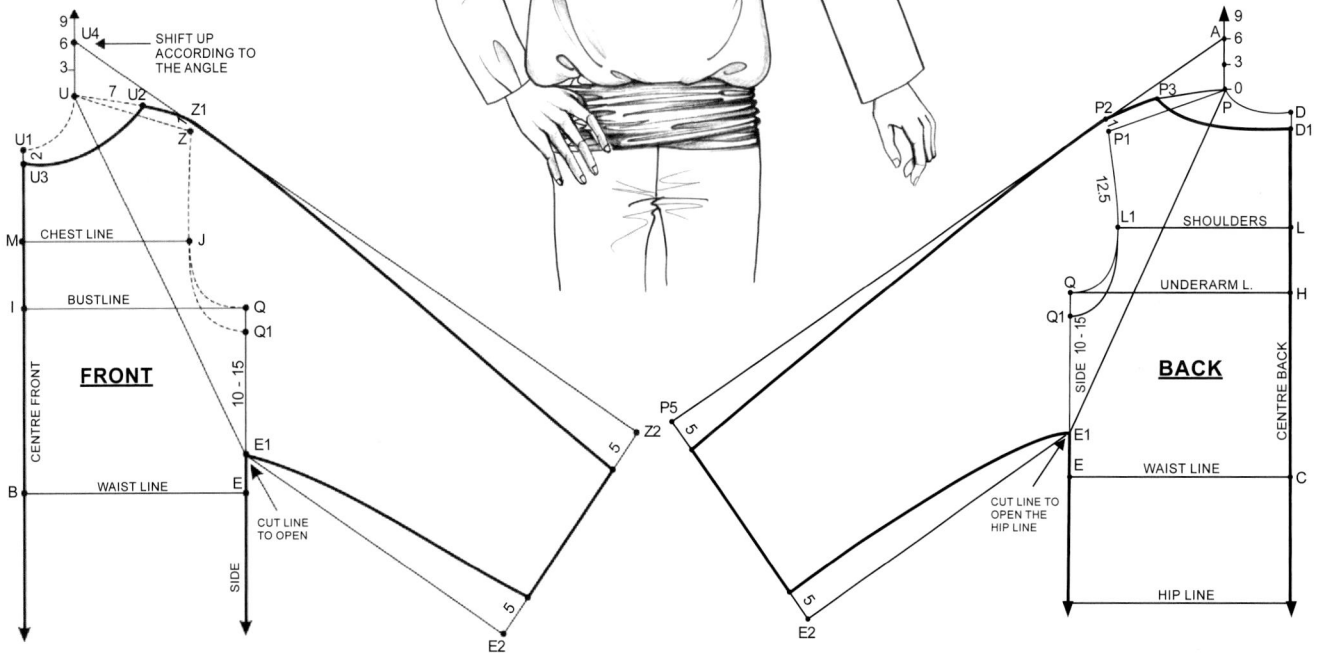

SCALE 1:10

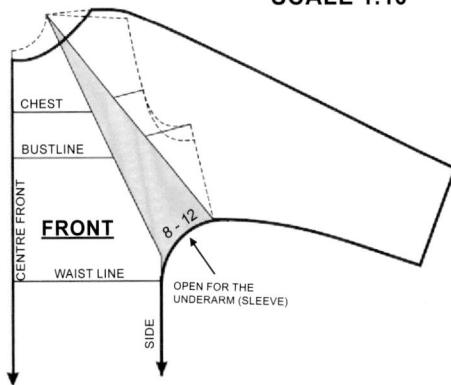

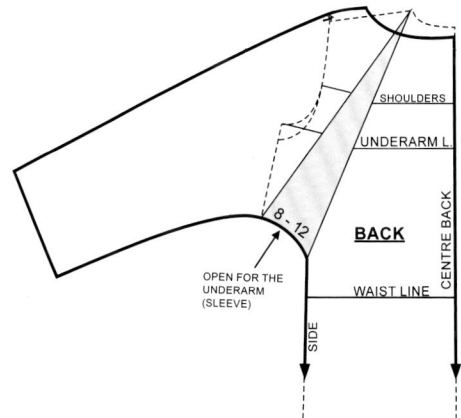

- Draw the base of the shirt bodice with the desired fit.
- From the first point of the neckline, draw a vertical line with a height of 3-12 cm / 1.18-4.72", depending on the desired angle.
- From this point, draw a straight line that passes 1 cm / 0.39" from the second shoulder point and continue along the length of the sleeve.
- From U at the front and P at the back, draw a diagonal line to the side line at 10-15 cm / 3.94-5.91" from Q, depending on how deep you want it to be.

- Draw E1-E2 parallel to Z1-Z2 for the front and P2-P5 for the back.
- Create the desired width of the lower edge of the sleeve.
- To create the width in the underarm, cut along diagonal line E1-U at the front and E1-P at the back and open as desired.
- Smoothly join the outlines.

SHIRT WITH LATERAL PANELS
SLIM FIT BASE BLACK - 12 CM / 4.72" EASE

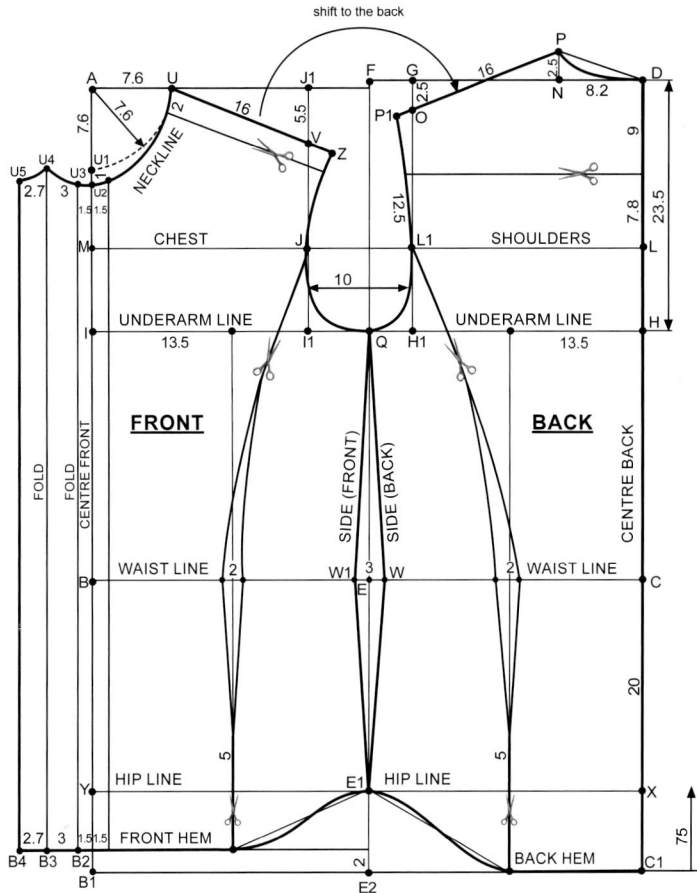

shift to the back

FRONT

BACK

NECKLINE

CHEST

SHOULDERS

UNDERARM LINE

UNDERARM LINE

FOLD

FOLD

CENTRE FRONT

SIDE (FRONT)

SIDE (BACK)

CENTRE BACK

WAIST LINE

WAIST LINE

HIP LINE

HIP LINE

FRONT HEM

BACK HEM

FRONT **BACK**

DISCARD FOR THE CUFF

shoulder

fold

NECKLINE

CHEST

UNDERARM LINE

FOLD

FOLD

CENTRE FRONT

SIDE (FRONT)

FRONT

WAIST LINE

WAIST LINE

HIP LINE

FRONT HEM

SHOULDERS

UNDERARM LINE

SIDE (BACK)

BACK

CENTRE BACK

WAIST LINE

WAIST LINE

HIP LINE

BACK HEM

- Create the shirt base block with a slim fit (12 cm / 4.72") or as desired.
- Transform as shown in the figure, based on the measurements.

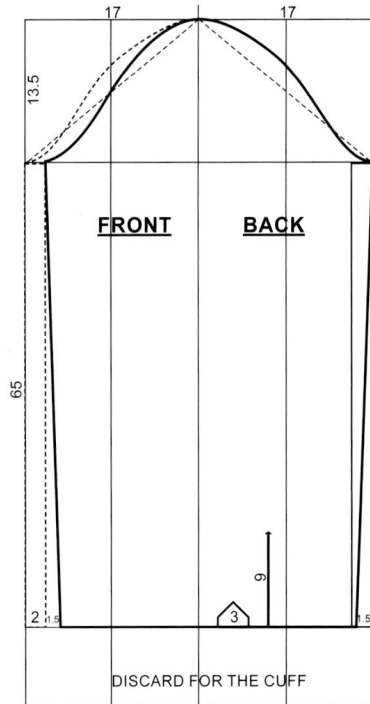

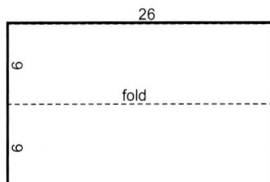

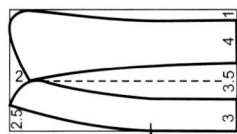

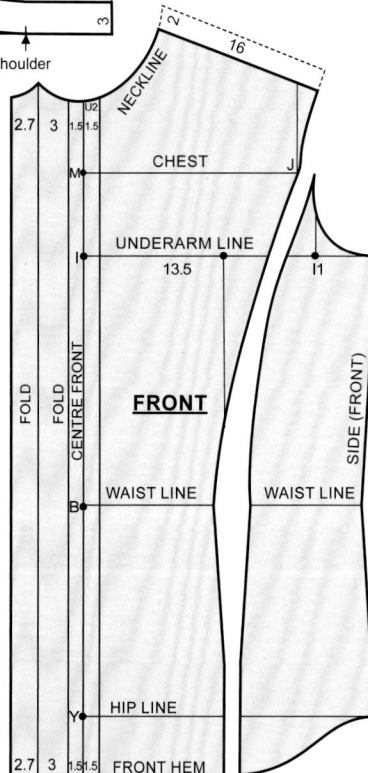

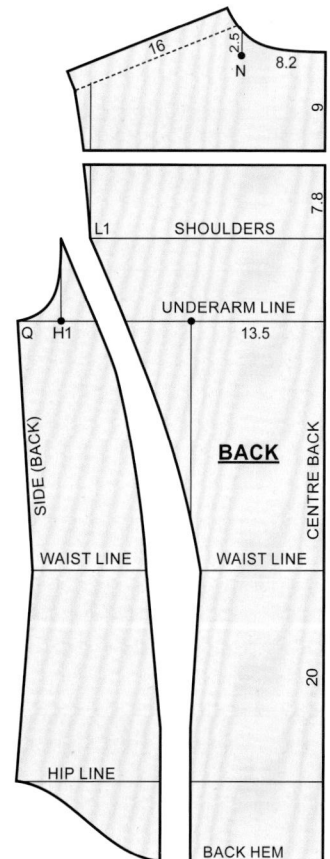

RELAXED KIMONO BASE BLOCK - LONG SLEEVE

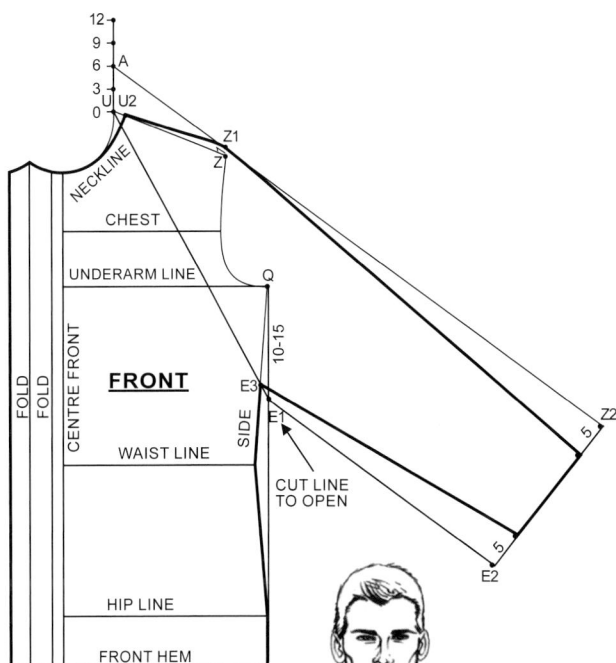

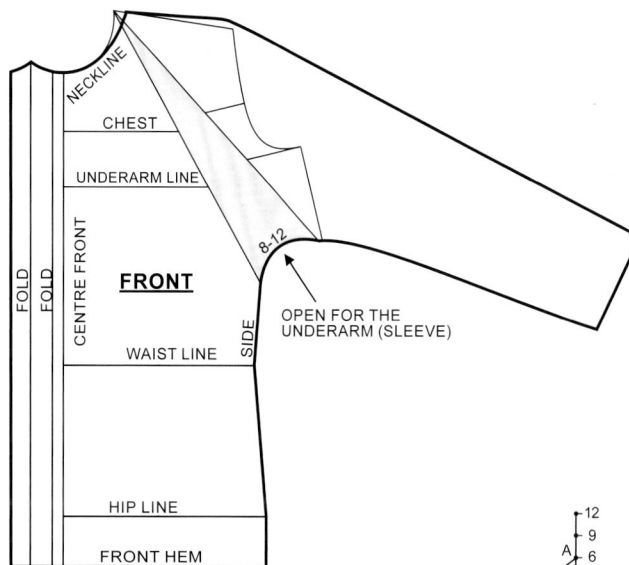

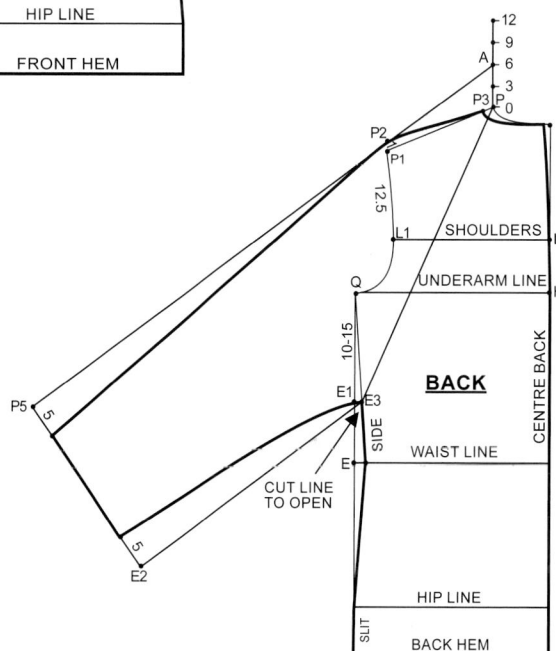

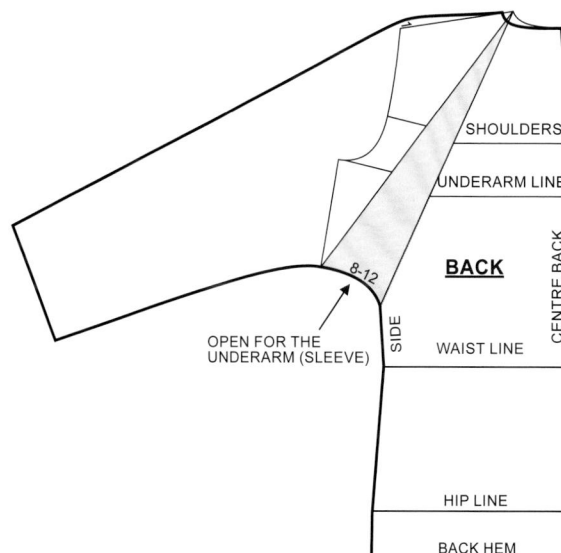

FRONT

12
9
6
3
A
U U2
0
Z1
Z
NECKLINE
CHEST
UNDERARM LINE
Q
FOLD
FOLD
CENTRE FRONT
FRONT
SIDE
10-15
E3
E1
WAIST LINE
CUT LINE TO OPEN
HIP LINE
FRONT HEM
Z2
5
5
E2

FRONT (opened)

NECKLINE
CHEST
UNDERARM LINE
FOLD
FOLD
CENTRE FRONT
FRONT
SIDE
8-12
OPEN FOR THE UNDERARM (SLEEVE)
WAIST LINE
HIP LINE
FRONT HEM

BACK

12
9
A
6
3
P3 P
0
P2
P1
12.5
L1
SHOULDERS
L
Q
UNDERARM LINE
H
P5
5
10-15
E1 E3
SIDE
CENTRE BACK
BACK
E
WAIST LINE
CUT LINE TO OPEN
5
E2
HIP LINE
SLIT
BACK HEM

BACK (opened)

SHOULDERS
UNDERARM LINE
8-12
SIDE
CENTRE BACK
BACK
OPEN FOR THE UNDERARM (SLEEVE)
WAIST LINE
HIP LINE
BACK HEM

- Draw the base block of the bodice or shirt with the desired measurements or size and a suitable fit.
- From the first point of the neckline U, draw a vertical line with a height of 3 to 12 cm / 1.18-4.72", depending on the desired angle.
- From this point, draw a straight line passing 1 cm / 0.39" from the second shoulder point (Z1 at the front and P2 at the back) and continue along the length of the sleeve.
- From U at the front and P at the back, draw a diagonal line to the side line 10-15 cm / 3.94-5.91" from Q, depending on the desired sleeve fit.
- Draw E1-E2 parallel to Z1-Z2 at the front and P2-P5 at the back.
- Draw the desired width of the lower sleeve edge.
- For a deeper armscye, cut along the diagonal line E1-U at the front and E1-P at the back and open as desired.
- Smoothly join the outlines.

SHIRT WITH RAGLAN SLEEVES

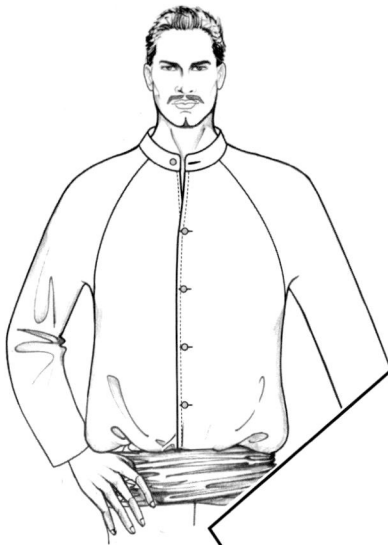

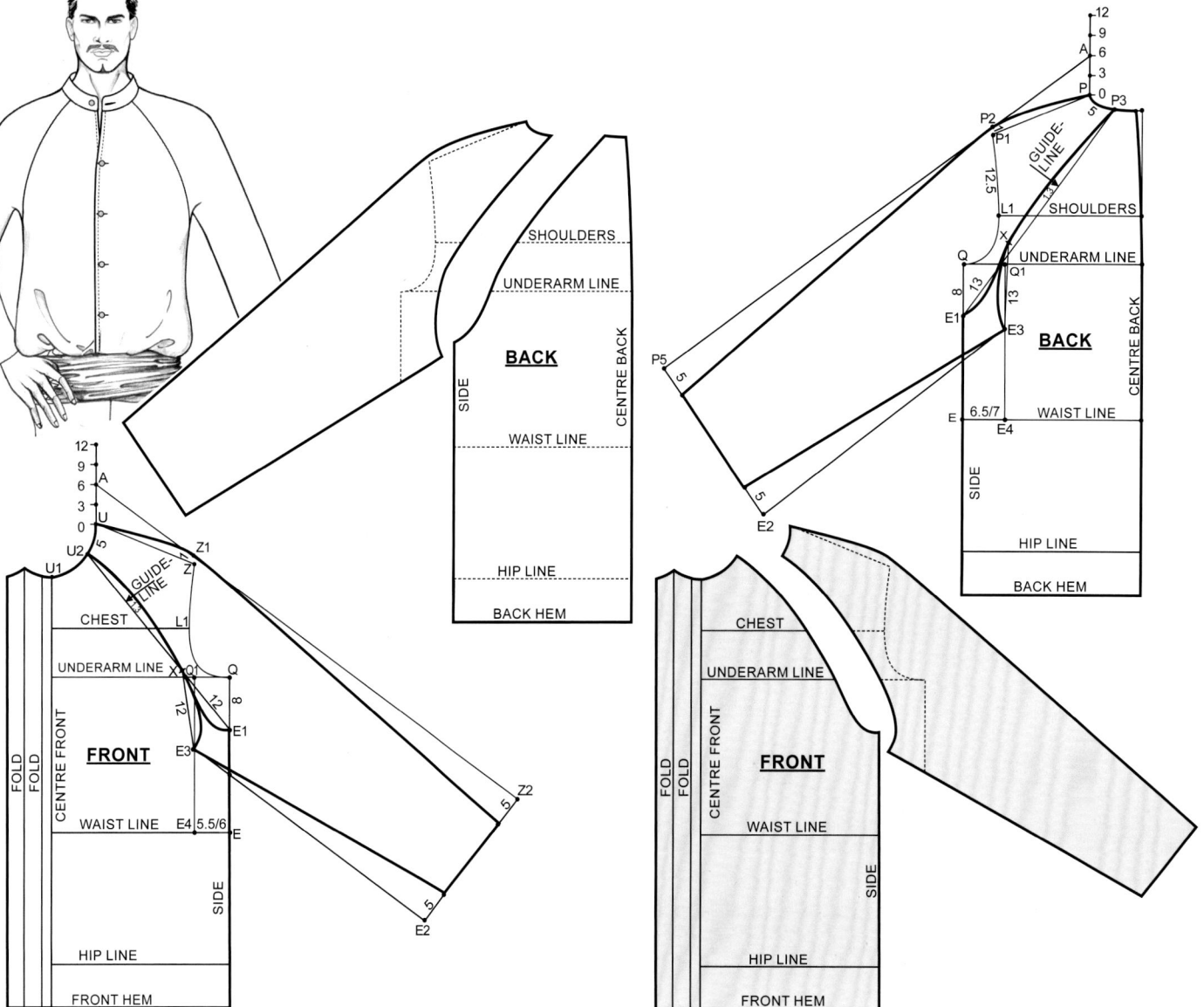

- Draw the base block of the bodice or shirt in the desired size or fit with suitable ease.
- Separate the back half from the front half.

BACK

- Draw vertical line P-A in the length required to create the desired angle of the sleeve.
- Draw a straight line A-P5 (passing through P2 at 1 cm / 0.39" from point P1) with P2-P5 equal to the sleeve length taken from the centre of the shoulder.
- Q-E1 = 5-8 cm / 1.97-3.15" depending on the desired armscye depth.
- E-E4 = 6.5 cm / 2.56". Draw vertical line E4-Q1.
- P-P3 = 3-6 cm / 1.18-2.36" Draw guideline P3-E1.
- E1-X towards P3 = 13 cm / 5.12" for where the curves meet.
- Draw the outline of E1-Q1-P3.
- Draw X-E3 as X-E1.
- Draw E3-E2 parallel to P2-P5.
- Adjust the lower edge of the sleeve according to the pattern.
- Smoothly trace the outer and inner lines of the sleeve and bodice.
- Take up the sleeve and bodice with precision.

FRONT

- Draw vertical line U-A in the length required to create the desired angle of the sleeve.
- Draw a straight line A-Z2 (passing through Z1 at 1 cm / 0.39" from point Z), with Z1-Z2 equal to the sleeve length taken from the centre shoulder; same for the back.
- Q-E1 = 5-8 cm / 1.97-3.15" depending on the depth of the armscye.
- E-E4 = 6.5-7 cm / 2.56-2.76".
- Draw vertical line E4-Q1.
- U-U2 = 3-6 cm / 1.18-2.36". Draw guideline U2-E1.
- E1-X towards U2 = 13 cm / 5.12" for where the curves meet.
- Draw the curved line E1-X-U2.
- Draw X-E3 as X-E1.
- Draw E2-E3 parallel to Z1-Z2, in the same measurement as E2-E3 at the back minus 1 cm / 0.39".
- Adjust the lower edge of the sleeve according to the pattern.
- Smoothly trace the outer and inner lines of the sleeve and bodice.
- Carefully transfer the sleeve and bodice on another sheet of paper.

RAGLAN SLEEVE ON AN INSET SLEEVE

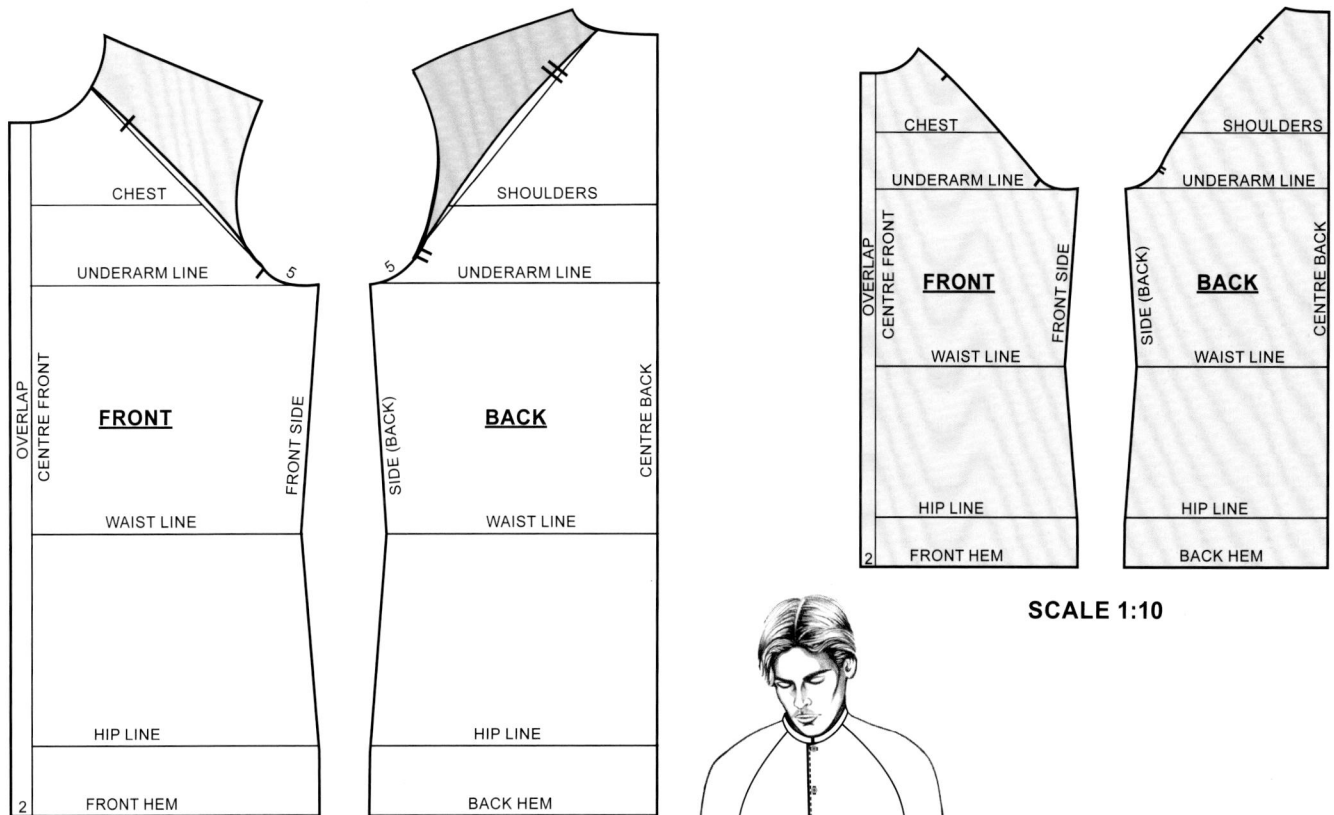

CHEST

UNDERARM LINE

OVERLAP
CENTRE FRONT

FRONT

FRONT SIDE

WAIST LINE

HIP LINE

2 FRONT HEM

SHOULDERS

UNDERARM LINE

SIDE (BACK)

BACK

CENTRE BACK

WAIST LINE

HIP LINE

BACK HEM

CHEST

UNDERARM LINE

OVERLAP
CENTRE FRONT

FRONT

FRONT SIDE

WAIST LINE

HIP LINE

2 FRONT HEM

SHOULDERS

UNDERARM LINE

SIDE (BACK)

BACK

CENTRE BACK

WAIST LINE

HIP LINE

BACK HEM

SCALE 1:10

This type of raglan sleeve is more suitable for garments made of stretch fabrics or jersey, as it fits closer to the body. It is less suitable for stiff fabrics and roomy sleeves, unless a modification is made to widen it appropriately.

CONSTRUCTION

- Draw the base block of the shirt bodice with appropriate measurements and ease.
- Draw the line of the raglan sleeve from the armscye to the neck, in the desired shape or according to the pattern, and add the notches.
- Draw the base of the inset sleeve with the desired ease and length.
- Take the two parts of the raglan sleeve drawn on the bodice and place them on the sleeve, keeping them shifted from the centre of the sleeve by 1.5 cm / 0.59" and raised by 1 cm / 0.39" to remove some of the softness of the inset sleeve.
- Join the lines smoothly, as shown in the picture, and check that the length of the armscye is the same as that of the bodice.
- Gently join the points that meet the raglan sleeve.

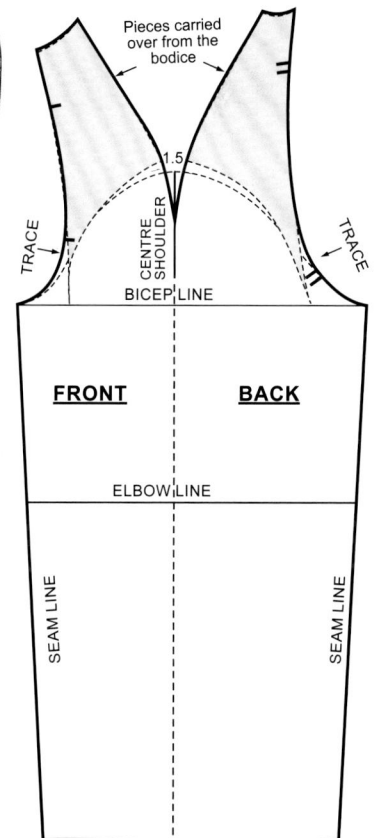

Pieces carried over from the bodice

1.5

TRACE

TRACE

CENTRE SHOULDER

BICEP LINE

FRONT

BACK

ELBOW LINE

SEAM LINE

SEAM LINE

SADDLE RAGLAN SLEEVE

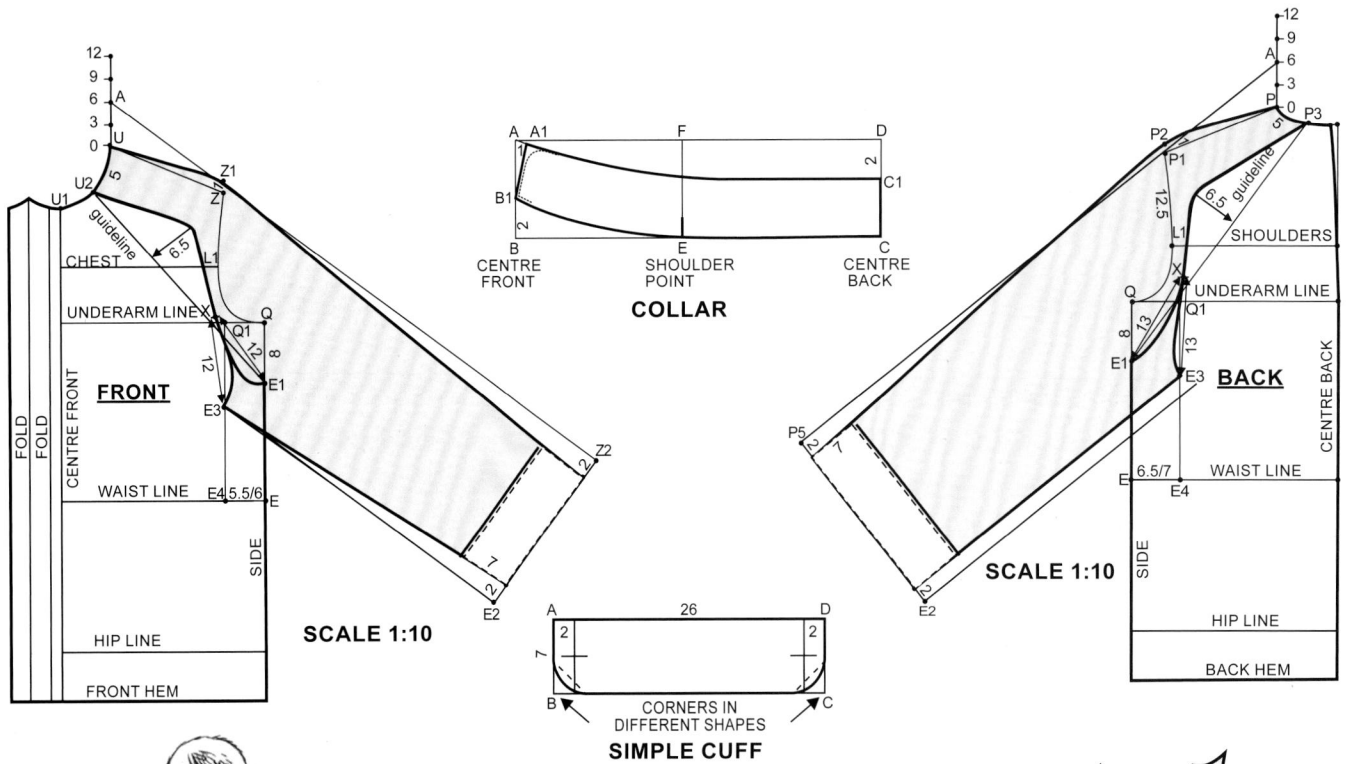

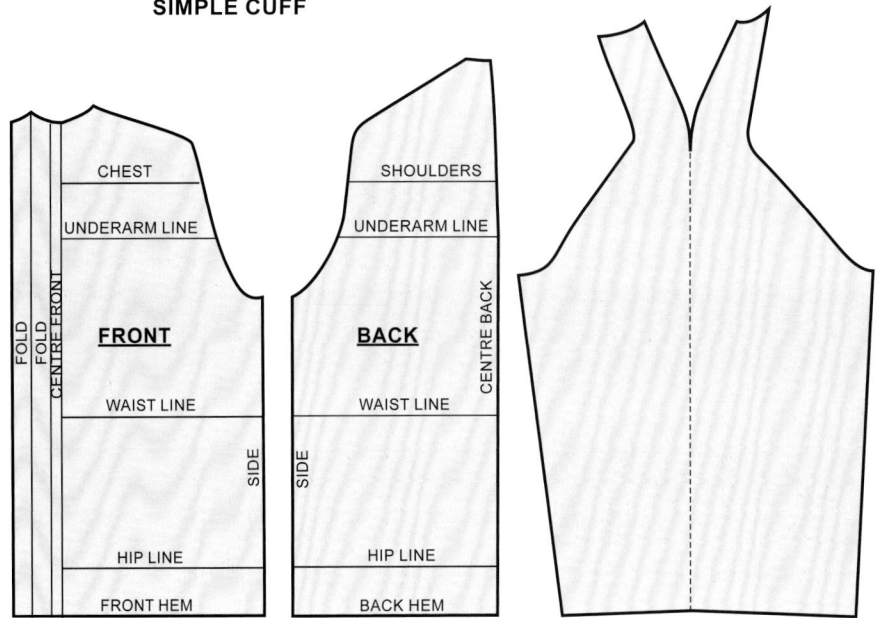

FRONT

COLLAR

SIMPLE CUFF

BACK

SCALE 1:10

CORNERS IN DIFFERENT SHAPES

FRONT

BACK

BASE BLOCK

The pattern for this type of sleeve is to be executed starting from the construction of the raglan sleeve on the previous page, varying the way it is attached to the bodice, which must faithfully reflect the shape drawn on the pattern.

COLLAR

- Measure the front and back neckline of the bodice block.
- Draw the rectangle A-B-C-D with:
- A-B equal to the height of the collar + 2 cm / 0.79".
- B-C equal to base neckline front and back +1 cm / 0.39".
- B-B1 = 2 cm / 0.79".
- D-C1 = 2 cm / 0.79".

- C-E = back neckline measurement (e.g.: C-E): 8 cm / 3.15".
- C-C1 = collar height.
- A-A1 = 1 cm / 0.39".
- Join the points with lines in the image.

SIMPLE CUFF

- Draw the rectangle A-B-C-D with:
- A-B equal to the height of the cuff offset from the sleeve = 7 cm / 2.76".
- B-C equal to the circumference of the wrist + 2 cm / 0.79" of ease + 2 cm / 0.79" per side for the fastening overlap (e.g.: wrist 20 cm + 2 = 22 + 4 = 26 cm / 10.24").

DINNER JACKET SHIRT WITH PLEATS
REGULAR FIT SHIRT BASE BLOCK 16 CM / 6.30"

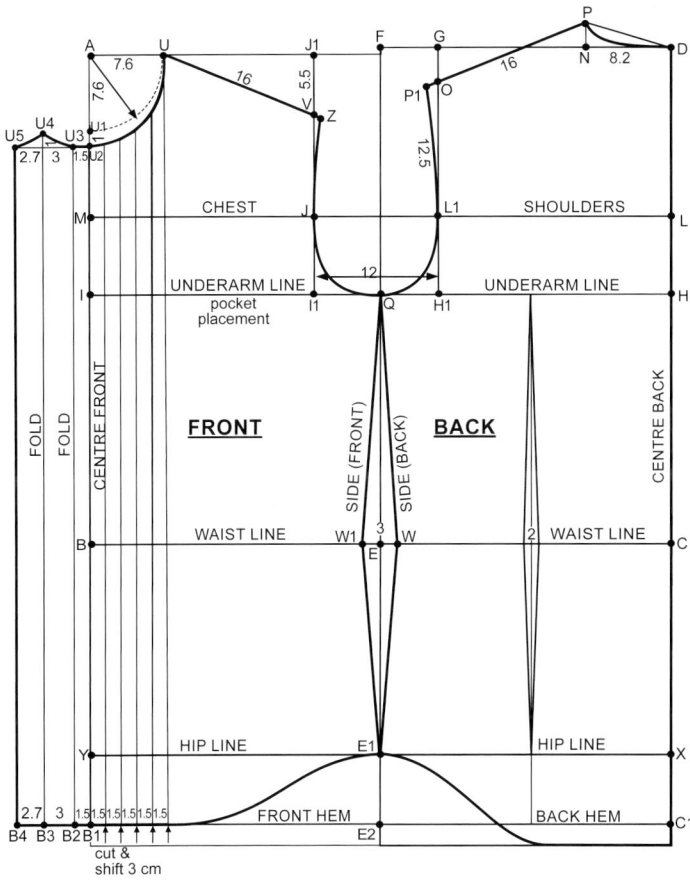

Top pattern diagram

Labels and measurements:

A — 7.6 — U — 16 — J1 — <5.5 — F — G — 16 — P — N — 8.2 — D

7.6

U4 — U3 — J1 — P1 — O — Z

U5 — 2.7 — 3 — 1.5 U2 — 12.5

M — CHEST — J — L1 — SHOULDERS — L

I — UNDERARM LINE — 12 — Q — UNDERARM LINE — H
pocket placement — I1 — H1

FOLD — FOLD — CENTRE FRONT — FRONT — SIDE (FRONT) — SIDE (BACK) — BACK — CENTRE BACK

B — WAIST LINE — W1 — 3 — W — 2 — WAIST LINE — C
E

Y — HIP LINE — E1 — HIP LINE — X

FRONT HEM — E2 — BACK HEM — C1

2.7 — 3 — 1.5 1.5 1.5 1.5 1.5 — B4 B3 B2 B1
cut & shift 3 cm

Bottom-left pattern diagram

2.7 — 3 — 16 — V — O — 16

M — CHEST — J — L1 SHOULDERS

I — UNDERARM LINE — UNDERARM LINE
pocket placement — I1 — Q — H1

FOLD — FOLD — CENTRE FRONT — SIDE (FRONT) — SIDE (BACK) — CENTRE BACK

B — WAIST LINE — W1 — W — 2 WAIST LINE

FRONT — BACK

Y — HIP LINE — E1 — HIP LINE
HEM — BACK HEM

2.7 — 3 — 1.5 1.5 — 1.5 — 1.5

- Create the shirt base block with regular fit ease of 16 cm / 6.30" or as desired.
- Transform as shown in the figure, based on the measurements.
- Create the inset sleeve as explained on the previous pages.

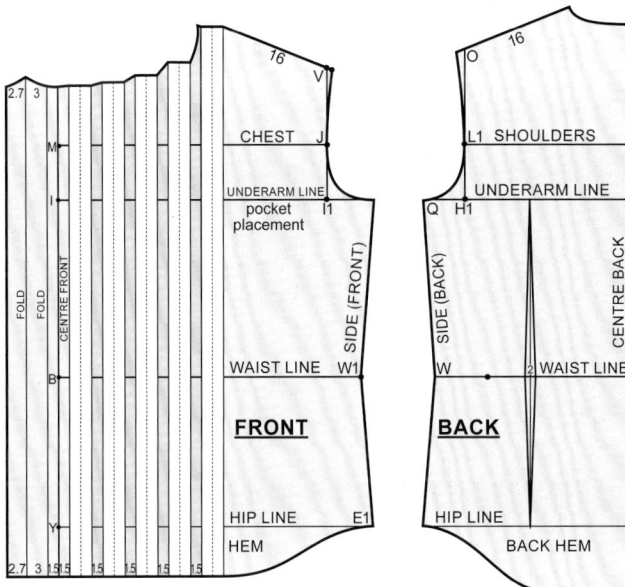

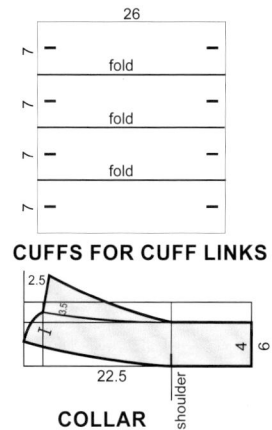

CUFFS FOR CUFF LINKS

26
7 — fold
7 — fold
7 — fold
7

COLLAR

2.5
3.5
7
22.5 — shoulder — 4 — 6

SHIRT WITH RUFFLES AT THE FRONT AND CUFFS

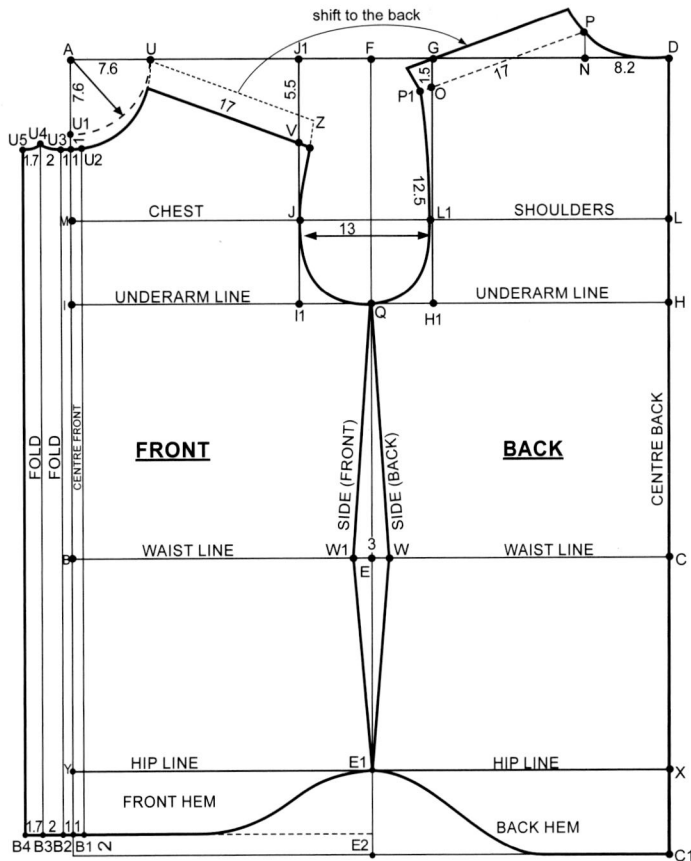

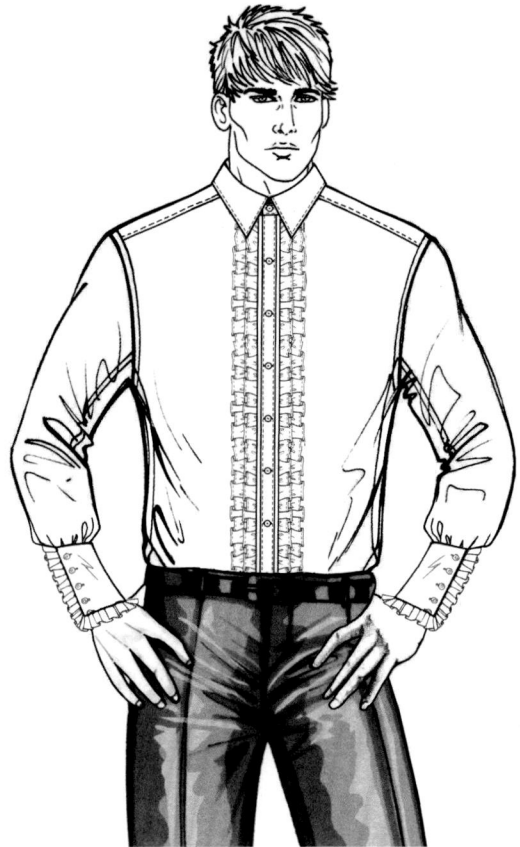

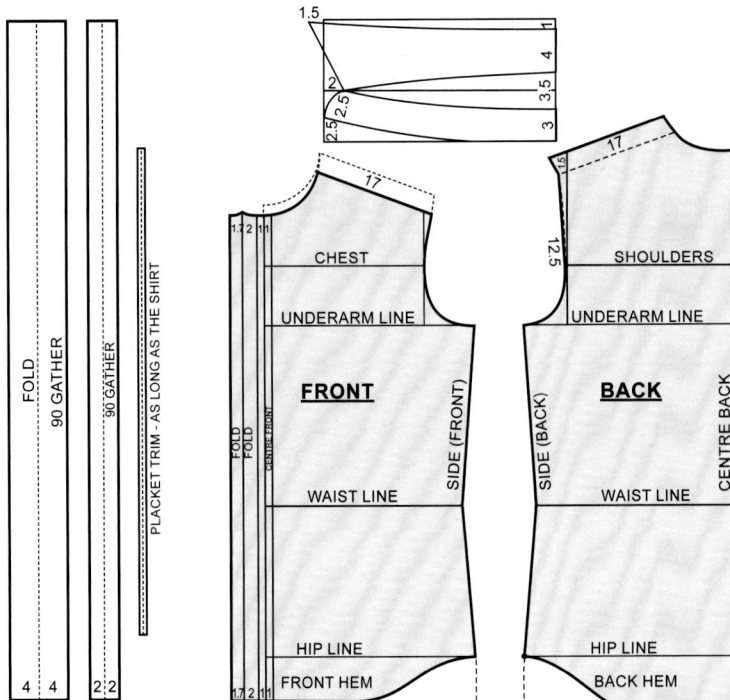

FRONT RUFFLES

RUFFLES CUFF

COLLAR WITH A STAND

CUFF

- Draw the base block of the shirt with classic-fit ease of 20 cm / 7.87" or as desired.
- Transform as shown in the figure, based on the measurements.
- Create the strips to make the front ruffles.
- Create the sleeve and cuff with ruffles as shown in the figure.

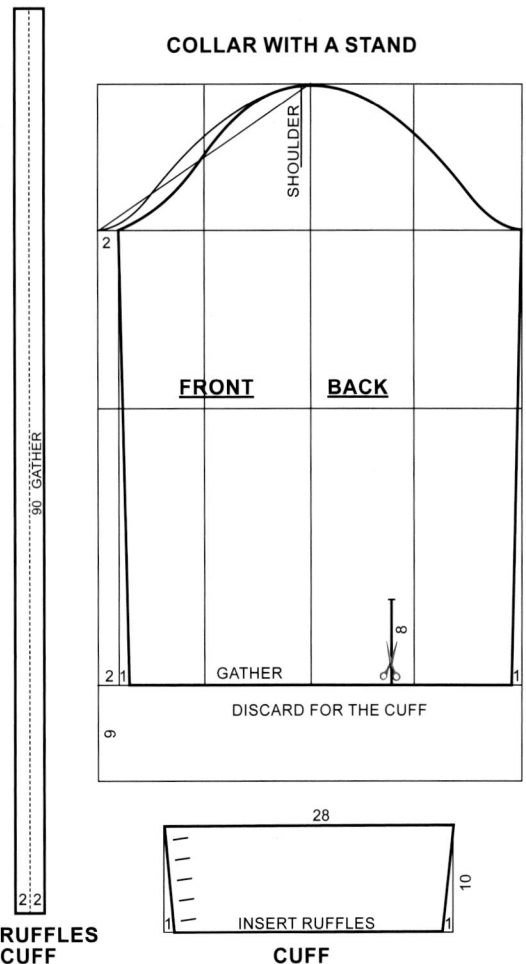

TROUSERS

TROUSERS WITH AND WITHOUT PLEATS

The upper part of a man's trousers must be professionally constructed: it mustn't be too tight or too loose, as both issues interfere with comfort and movement. It is therefore convenient to measure the crotch, hips and waist carefully and construct this area very precisely.

Throughout the history of fashion, men's trousers have come with pleats; the version without them became popular no earlier than the mid-20th century. They have recently come back into fashion, as slim, close-fitting lines have given way to larger proportions and silhouettes. Physical conformation and personal style are the key criteria for deciding whether to opt for trousers with or without pleats.

Trousers with two pleats.

Single or double darts

Generally speaking, pleats create the necessary slack to prevent fabric from pulling excessively and ruining the silhouette. A single pleat is useful to ensure a comfortable fit, while double pleats not only lend more sophistication to a look, they also ensure additional comfort in the crotch area. Double pleats can be backward facing (reverse pleats) or front facing.

Without pleats

Trousers without pleats have a slim (and thus tighter) fit. The style they bring to the silhouette is quite different from their predecessors: essential and devoid of aesthetic whims. They are best worn high-waisted and with a tapered leg. Tailored construction makes them suitable for even the most robust physiques, although the absence of darts still tends to emphasise the abdomen.

Trousers with a pleat.

Trousers without pleats.

POPULAR MEN'S TROUSER MODELS

CLASSIC TROUSERS   TROUSERS WITH TURN-UP CUFFS   JEANS   JODHPURS   SHORTS   TRACKSUIT TROUSERS

PATTERN TERMINOLOGY

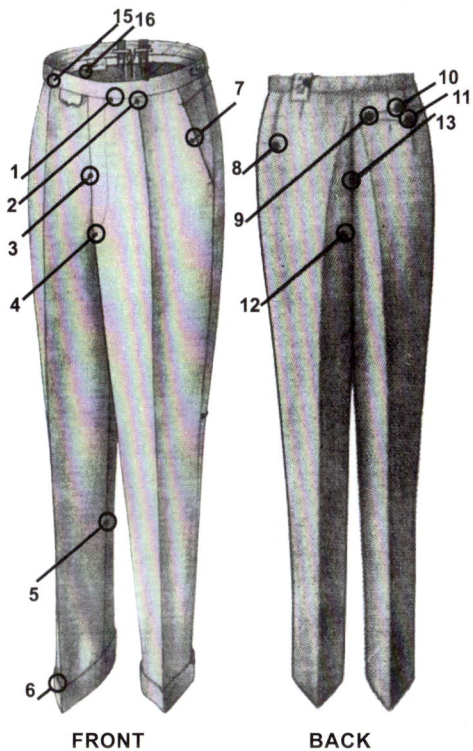

FRONT **BACK**

TOTAL CROTCH LENGTH

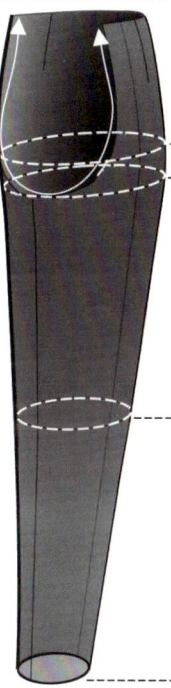

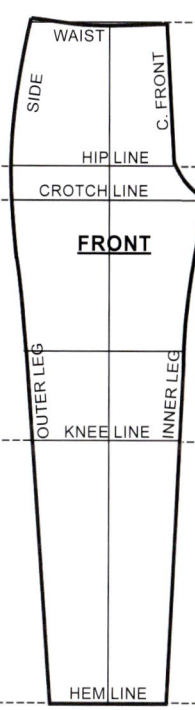

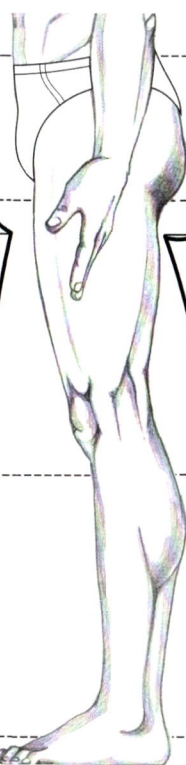

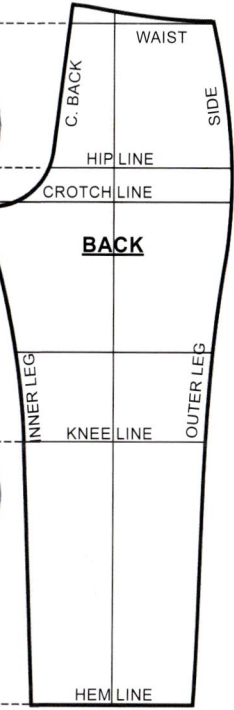

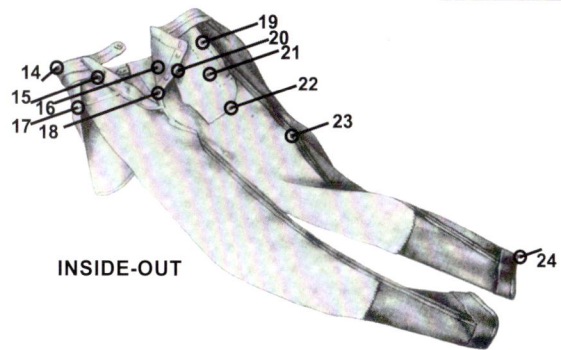

WAIST

SIDE

C. FRONT

HIP LINE

CROTCH LINE

FRONT

OUTER LEG

INNER LEG

KNEE LINE

HEM LINE

WAIST

C. BACK

SIDE

HIP LINE

CROTCH LINE

BACK

INNER LEG

OUTER LEG

KNEE LINE

HEM LINE

INSIDE-OUT

1) Waistband
2) Front pleat
3) Flap/fly
4) Front crotch
5) Inner leg seam (inseam)
6) Cuff
7) Front pocket
8) Rear dart
9) Rear pocket bar
10) Rear pocket
11) Rear pocket flap
12 and 13) Rear crotch
14) Waistband lining
15) Buttonholes (if any)
16) Pocket lining stitches
17) Pocket lining
18) Buttons or zip
19 and 21) Pocket lining
20) Placket for zips or buttons.
21 and 22) Lining
23) Side seam
24) Kick tape
25 and 26) Hem

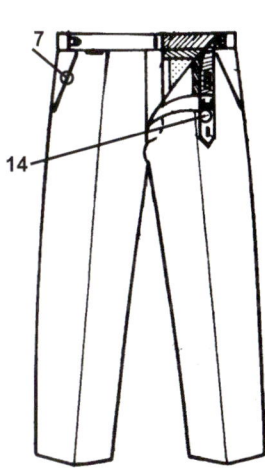

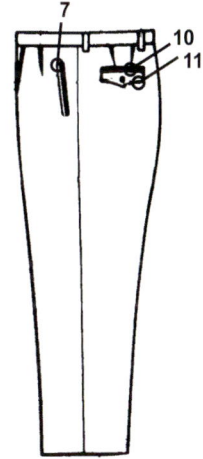

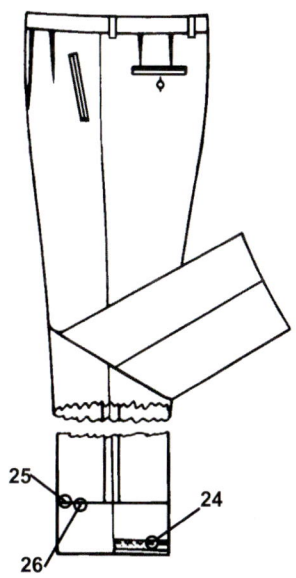

TROUSER LENGTHS

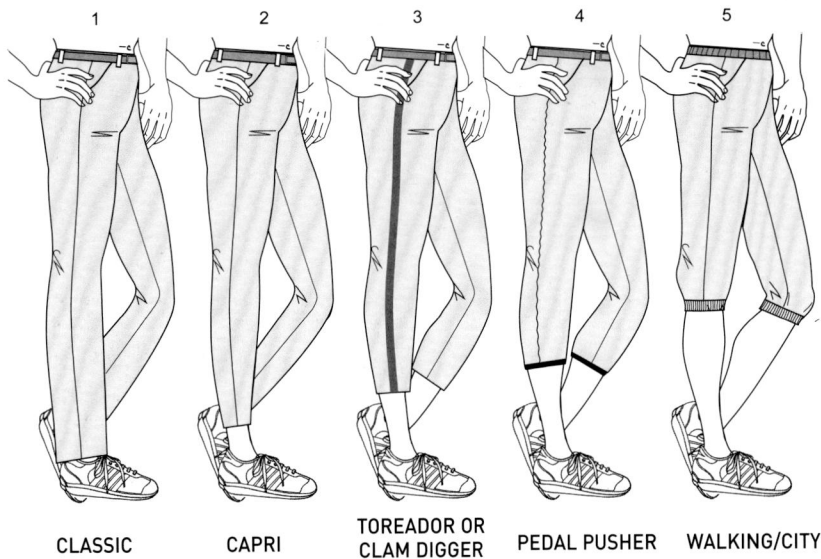

1	2	3	4	5
CLASSIC	CAPRI	TOREADOR OR CLAM DIGGER	PEDAL PUSHER	WALKING/CITY

1) Classic trousers: mid-heel length, with or without turn-up cuffs.
2) Capri trousers: 3-4 cm / 1.18-1.57" from the malleolus.
3) Toreador or clam digger: just below the calf.
4) Pedal pushers or deck: below the knee.
5) Walking/city shorts to knickerbockers: just below the knee.
6) Bermuda shorts: just above the knee.
7) Military shorts: between the knee and the thigh.
8) Jamaica shorts (Jams): halfway between the knee and crotch.
9) Tennis shorts and classic shorts: about 6-10 cm / 2.36-3.94" from the crotch.
10) Hot pants/ short shorts: beginning of the thigh.

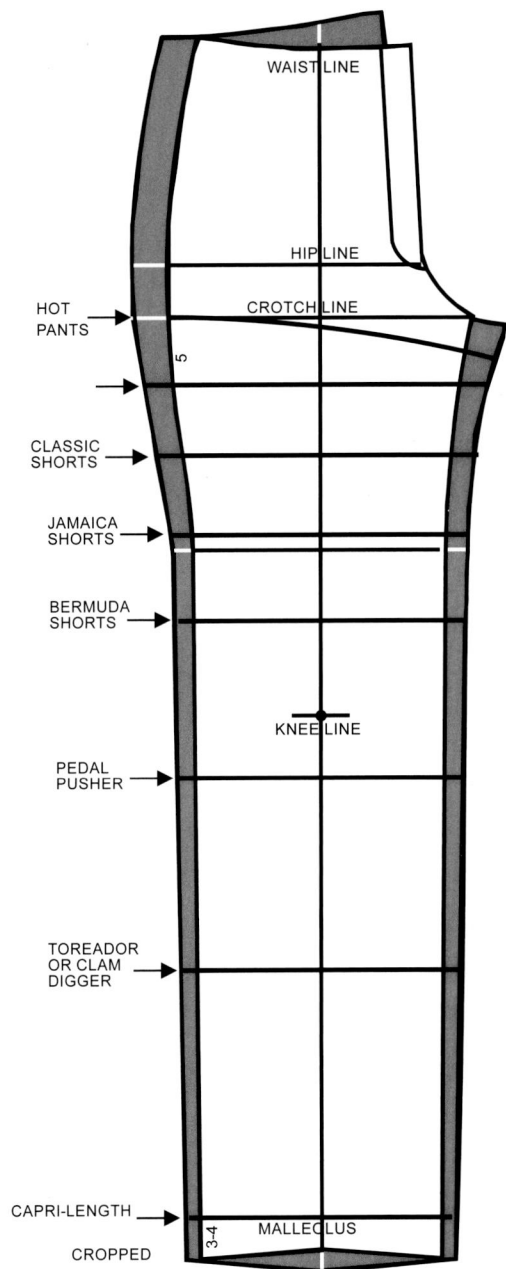

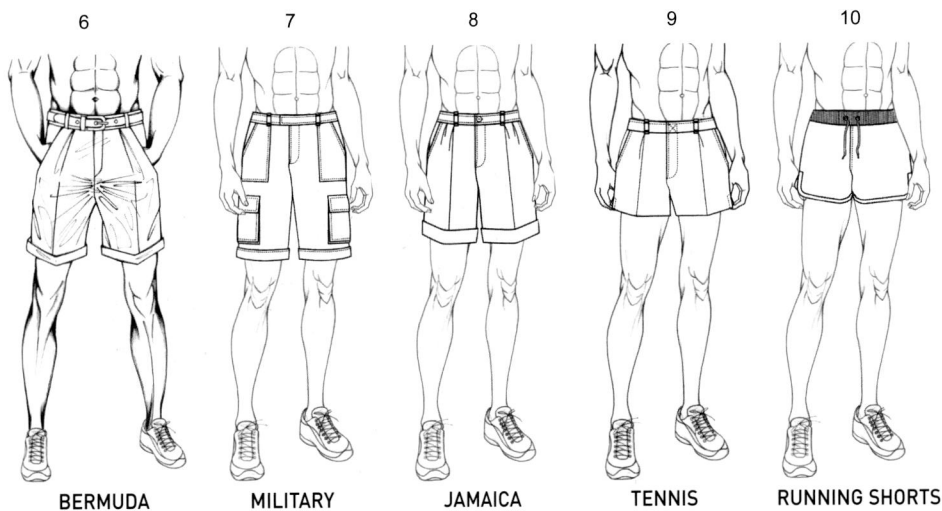

6	7	8	9	10
BERMUDA	MILITARY	JAMAICA	TENNIS	RUNNING SHORTS

TROUSER MEASUREMENTS

Trousers measurements must be taken over the underwear normally worn by the client, standing in a natural position, with the body's weight evenly distributed over both feet.

To start, tie an elastic band or ribbon around the waist, not too tight, to serve as a reference point from which to take the measurements. For greater precision, an additional reference point can be added around the pelvis, at the most prominent point of the buttocks.

Measurements should be taken with a tape measure, keeping it close to the body, but not too tight. For circumference measurements, it should be kept parallel to the floor; for length measurements, perpendicular to the floor. The ease for the desired fit should be added later, depending on the garment type.

WAIST CIRCUMFERENCE
Measure the circumference at the thinnest point of the waist, keeping the tape measure neither too loose nor too tight.

HIP CIRCUMFERENCE
Measure at the most prominent point of the hips and buttocks, holding the tape measure perfectly parallel to the floor.

LEG CIRCUMFERENCES
Depending on the type of trouser, the measurements to take are:
- Upper thigh circumference.
- Mid-thigh circumference.
- Knee circumference.
- Calf circumference.
- Ankle circumference.

WAIST TO HIP
Measure from the hollow of the waist, where the webbing is, to the most prominent part of the pelvis.

WAIST TO KNEE
Measure from waist to knee.

WAIST TO ANKLE
Measure from the waist to almost below the lower ankle bone (malleolus).

BODY RISE
This measurement can be taken in two ways:
1) Using a right angle square, resting on the groin at the lower end and on the stomach at the upper end, measure the precise height.
2) While sitting on a flat surface, measure from one side of the waist downwards, following the curve of the hip, to the floor.

TOTAL CROTCH LENGTH
Place the end of the tape measure on the centre of the waist at the front and extend it between the legs, going up to the centre of the waist at the back, keeping the tape measure close to the body.

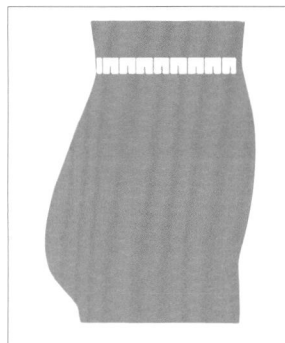

WAIST CIRCUMFERENCE

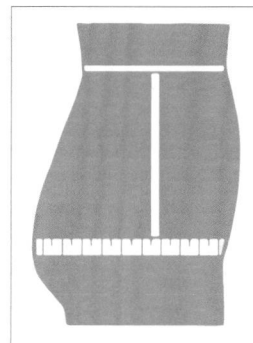

HIP CIRCUMFERENCE

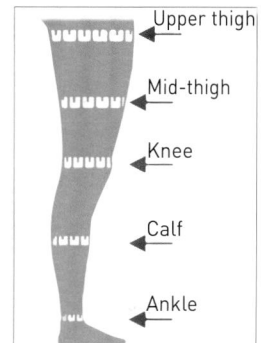

LEG CIRCUMFERENCE

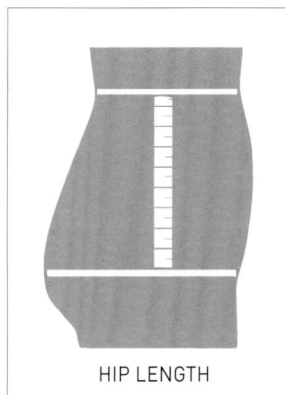

HIP LENGTH

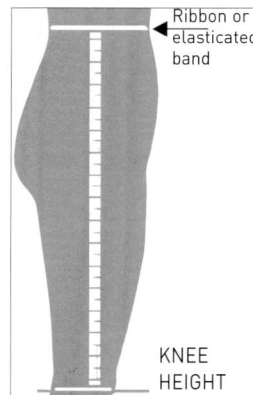

KNEE HEIGHT

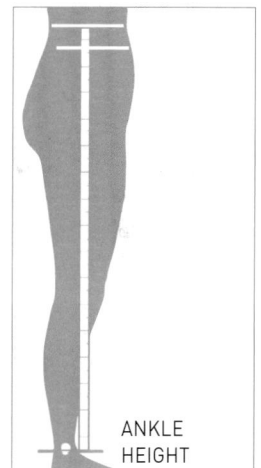

ANKLE HEIGHT

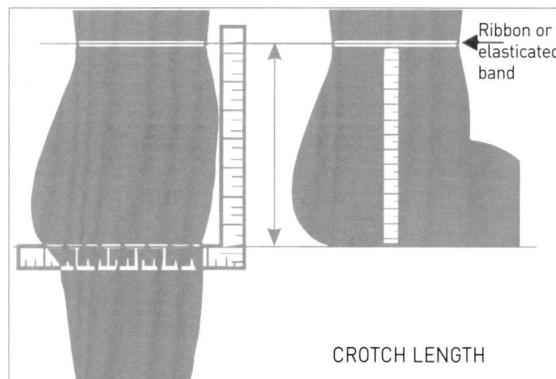

CROTCH LENGTH

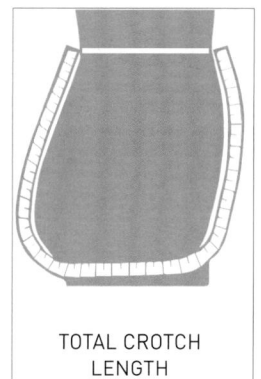

TOTAL CROTCH LENGTH

TROUSER BASE BLOCK

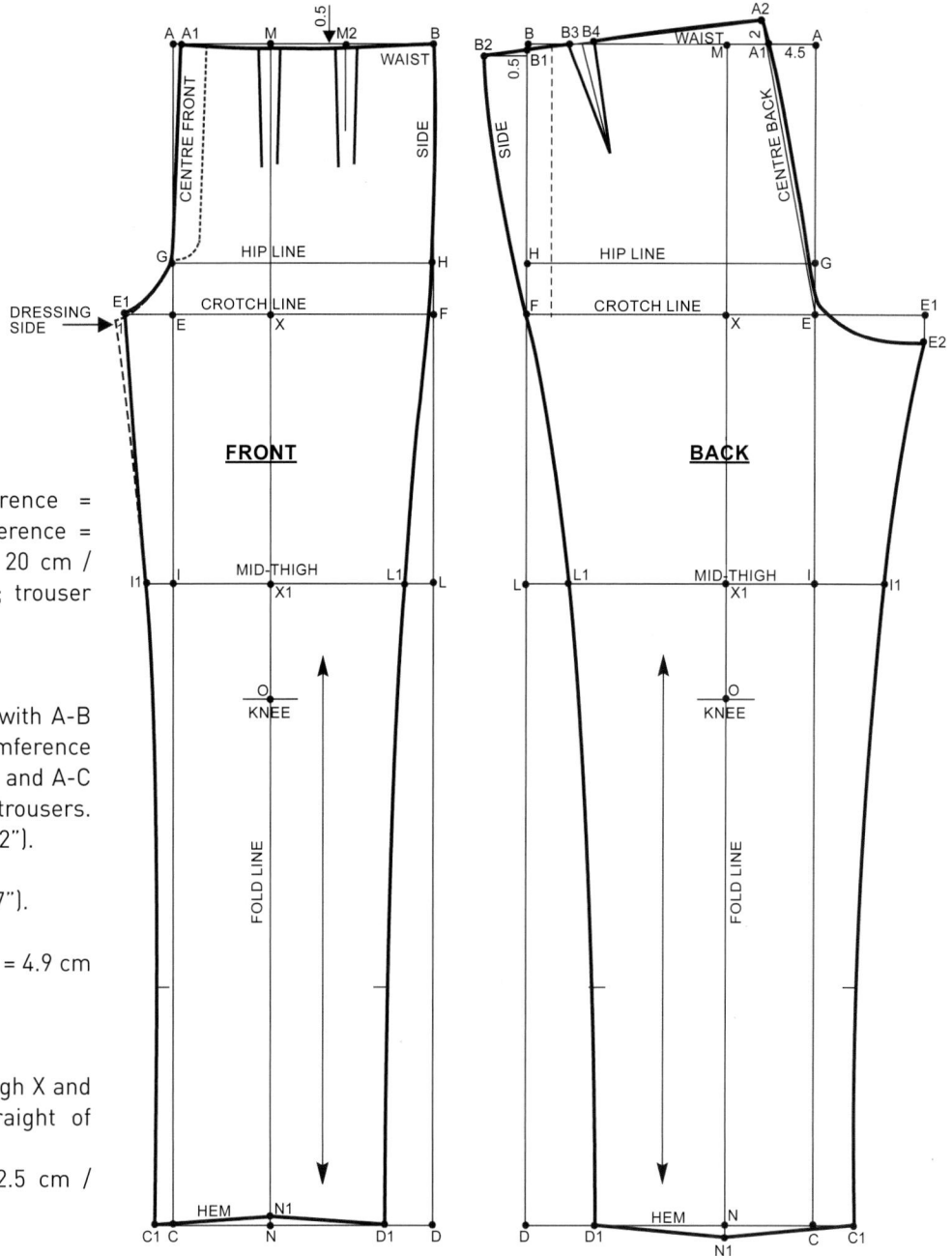

Measurements: hip circumference = 98 cm / 38.58"; waist circumference = 88 cm / 34.65"; waist to hip = 20 cm / 7.87"; rise = 25.7 cm / 10.12"; trouser length = 105 cm / 41.34".

Front

- Draw the rectangle A-B-C-D, with A-B equal to 1/4 of the hip circumference (e.g.: 98 ÷ 4 = 24.5 cm / 9.65") and A-C equal to the total length of the trousers.
- A-E = body rise (25.7 cm / 10.12").
- B-F as A-E. Draw E-F.
- A-G = waist to hip (20 cm / 7.87").
- Draw G-H (Hip Line).
- E-E1 = 1/5 of E-F (e.g: 24.5 ÷ 5 = 4.9 cm / 1.93").
- E-I as A-E. Draw I-L.
- X in the middle of E1-F.
- Draw M-N with crossing through X and write 'Crease Line' and 'Straight of Grain'.
- M-O = waist to knee (e.g: 62.5 cm / 24.61").
- M-M2 = 6 cm / 2.36".
- Draw the dart or pleat with the necessary depth and width.
- X1-L1 = 12.5 cm / 4.92".
- X1-I1 as X1-L1 (thigh).
- N-N1 = 1.5 cm / 0.59".
- N-C1 = 11 cm / 4.33" (or as desired).
- N-D1 as N-C1.
- Draw C1-N1-D1 (lower edge).
- Draw E1-G-A1 with a curved line.
- Draw E1-I1-C1 smoothly.
- Draw B-A1 smoothly and write 'Waist'.
- Smoothly connect B-H-L1-D1.

Back

- Draw the rectangle A-B-C-D with A-B = 1/4 hip circumference + 2 cm / 0.79" (e.g.: 98 ÷ 4 = 24.5 + 2 = 26.5 cm / 10.43") and A-C equal to the total length of the trousers (e.g.: 105 cm / 41.34").

- A-E = body rise (25.7 cm / 10.12").
- B-F as A-E. Draw E-F.
- A-G = waist to hip (20 cm / 7.87").
- Draw G-H (hip line).
- E-E1 = 1/3 of E-F + 1.5 cm / 0.59" (e.g.: 26.5 ÷ 3 = 8.83 + 1.5 = 10.3 cm / 4.06").
- E1-E2 = 2 cm / 0.79".
- E-I as A-E.
- Draw I-L.
- X in the middle of E1-F.
- Draw M-N crossing through X and write 'Crease Line'.
- M-O = waist to knee (e.g: 62.5 cm / 24.61").
- A-A1 = 4.5 cm / 1.77".
- A1-A2 = 2-3.5 cm / 0.79-1.38".

(according to the client's conformation).
- B-B1 = 0.5 cm / 0.79".
- Draw A2-B2 through B1, measuring A-B (Waist).
- B2-B3 = 1/3 of A2-B2.
- Pleats and darts with width and depth as required.
- X1-L1 = 14 cm / 4.92".
- X1-I1 as X1-L1 (Thigh).
- N1-C1 = 12 cm / 4.72".
- N1-D1 = 12 cm / 4.72".
- N-N1 = 1.5 cm / 0.59".
- Draw C-N1-D1 (Lower edge).
- Draw E2-E-A2 (Centre Back).
- Draw E2-I1-C1 (Inside Leg).
- Draw B3-F-L1-D (Side).

MODIFICATION OF THE FRONT DRESSING 'LEFT' OR 'RIGHT'

The side one dresses on refers to the extra material provided to a part of the front of men's trousers to accommodate the male anatomy.

How much fabric varies in relation to the top part of the trousers: if they are tight-fitting, more ease is required because the back forces the front to follow the body and emphasise the difference in shape, whereas if the groin area is wider, just a bit may suffice and, in some cases, may even be unnecessary, especially in industrial contexts.

In tight-fitting and made-to-measure trousers with fitted groins, a width of 1 to 1.5 cm / 0.39 to 0.59" is required.

There are various ways to make this modification to the basic block. There are two common methods.

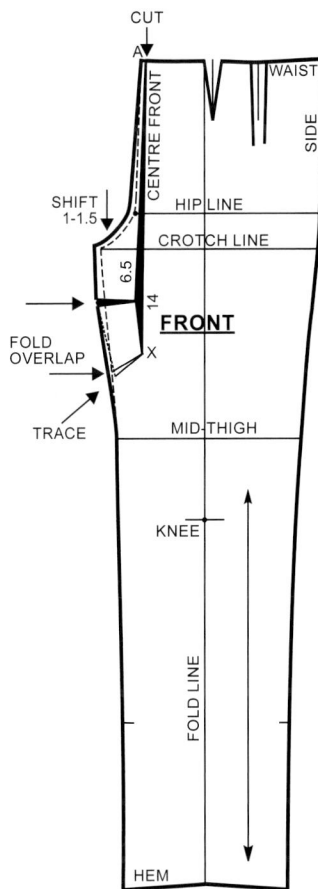

METHOD 1

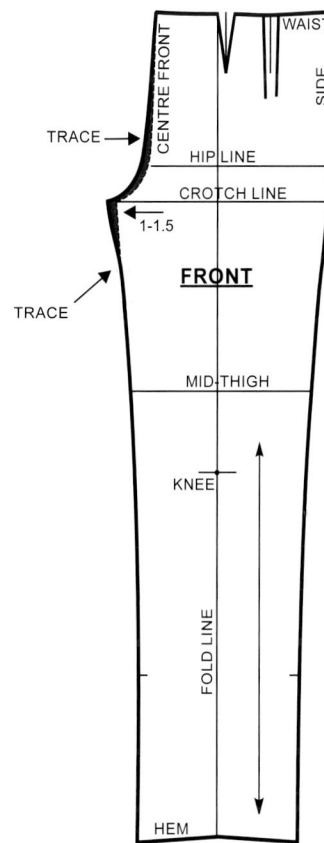

METHOD 2

Method 1

This method is the most common. Three cuts are to be made: one vertical cut parallel to the centre front; one horizontal cut 6.5 cm / 2.56" from the crotch line, and one 14 cm / 5.51" from the crotch line. Cut along the lines and create added volume by rotating the two pattern pieces on fulcrums A and X until the desired size is reached. Then smoothly unite the outlines.

Method 2

This method is much simpler, though less precise than the previous one.

It can be achieved by a parallel widening of the centre front up to the crotch line, obtaining the necessary breadth for the dressing side of the groin, then connecting to the under-leg. Alternatively, the increase can be created by drawing the part freehand or with the help of a French curve.

CREATING THE CENTRAL CREASE LINE

A central crease on the front of the trouser leg is about more than aesthetics: it helps make it easier to move and thus more comfortable. In fact, it justifies greater volume at the knee thanks to the room created down the front of the leg. There are three ways to create it. The first is the most common and the most in-line with the values illustrated; the second is designed to maintain the breadth of the knee and the third is advisable for trousers designed for heftier men, because it helps keep the front balanced.

For this last pleat, one can't speak of proportions, but it is important that it is closed and well composed—although it may be more appropriate to make it minimal for people with a larger waist and more accentuated for people with a thinner waist.

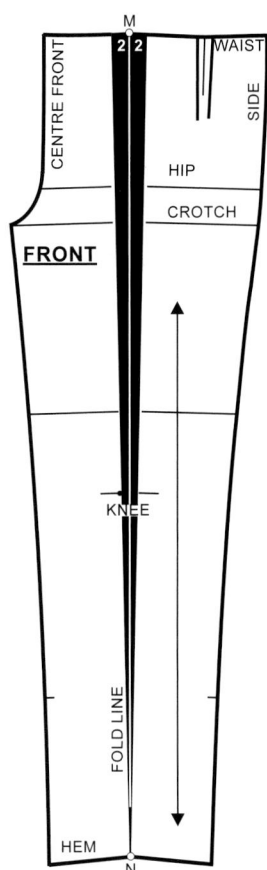

METHOD 1

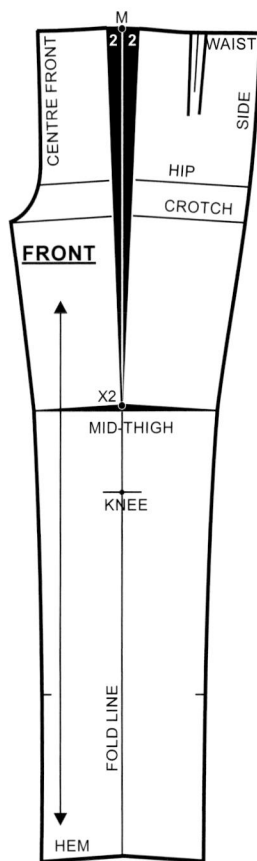

METHOD 2

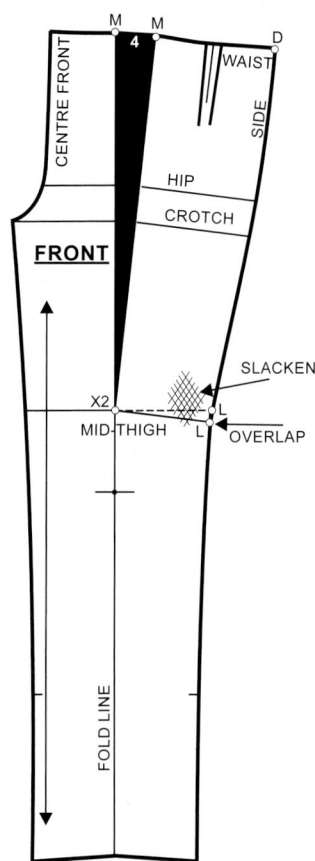

METHOD 3

TECHNIQUES

Method 1
- Draw the front of the trousers with the desired measurements and ease.
- Cut along pleat line M-N.
- Open 2 cm / 0.79" on one side and 2 cm / 0.79" on the other.

Method 2
- Draw the front block of the trousers.
- Cut along the pleat line to point X2.
- Open 2 cm / 0.79" from one side and 2 cm / 0.79" from the other.

Method 3
- Draw the front of the trousers.
- Slash along the fold line to point X2.
- Slash along line L-X2.
- Pivot the M-D-L pattern part 4 cm / 1.57" using X2 as the fulcrum, making it overlap at point L.
- When assembling the garment, you will need to slacken the outside of the leg at knee level with an iron.

TROUSERS WITH REAR DART AND A FRONT PLEAT

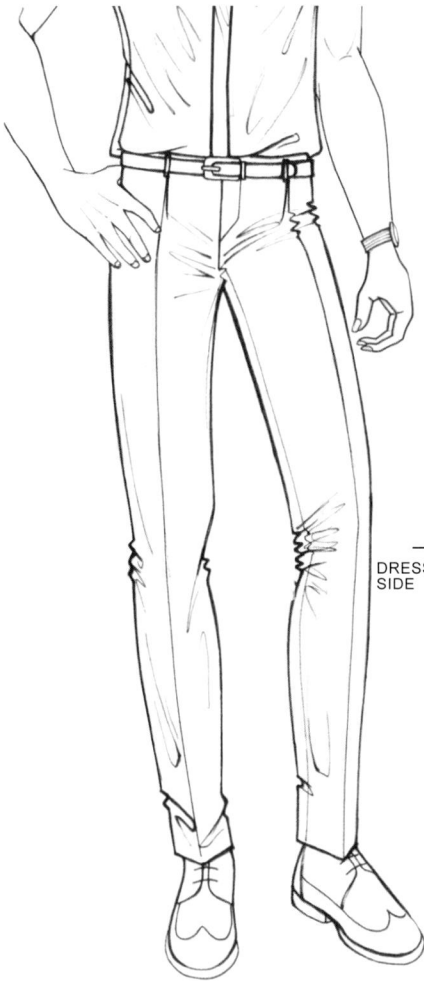

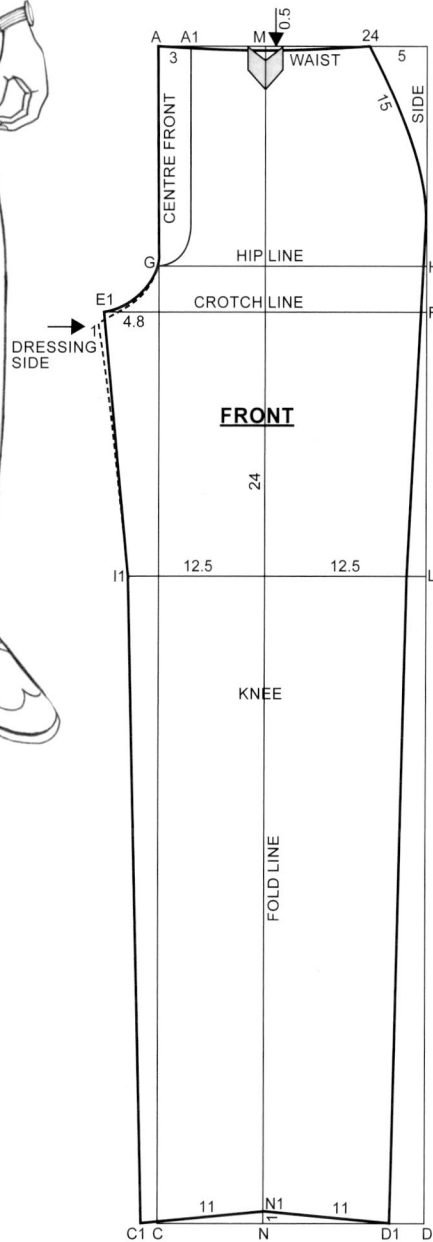

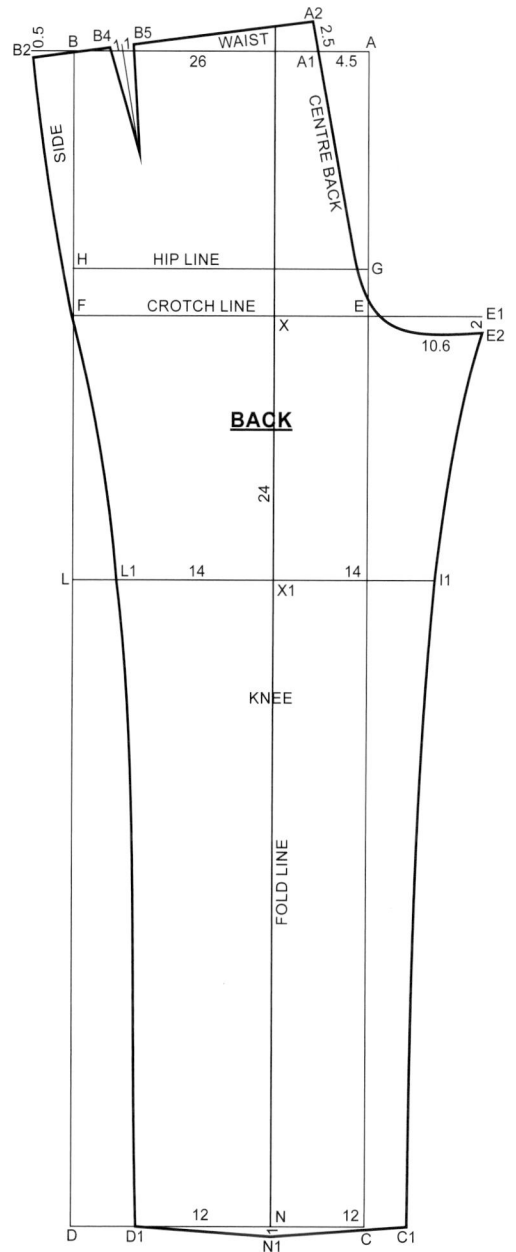

FRONT

A · A1 · M 0.5 · 24
3 · WAIST · 5
CENTRE FRONT · 15 · SIDE
G · HIP LINE · H
E1 · CROTCH LINE · F
4.8
DRESSING SIDE
24
I1 · 12.5 · 12.5 · L
KNEE
FOLD LINE
11 · N1 · 11
C1 C · N · D1 D

BACK

B2 0.5 · B · B4 · B5 · WAIST · A2 2.5 · A
11 · 26 · A1 · 4.5
SIDE · CENTRE BACK
H · HIP LINE · G
F · CROTCH LINE · E · E1 2
X · 10.6 · E2
24
L · L1 · 14 · X1 · 14 · I1
KNEE
FOLD LINE
12 · N · 12
D · D1 · N1 · C · C1

- Draw the base blocks with pleats and darts in the desired size and fit.
- Discard at the hips and create the dart at the back as in the figure.
- Leave 3 cm / 1.18" slack on the front pleat line to create the crease.

Note:
Unstitched decorative pleats or 'trouser pleats' incorporate the shaping quality of the pleat plus added width, and are usually found on the front.

CIGARETTE TROUSERS WITHOUT DARTS/PLEATS

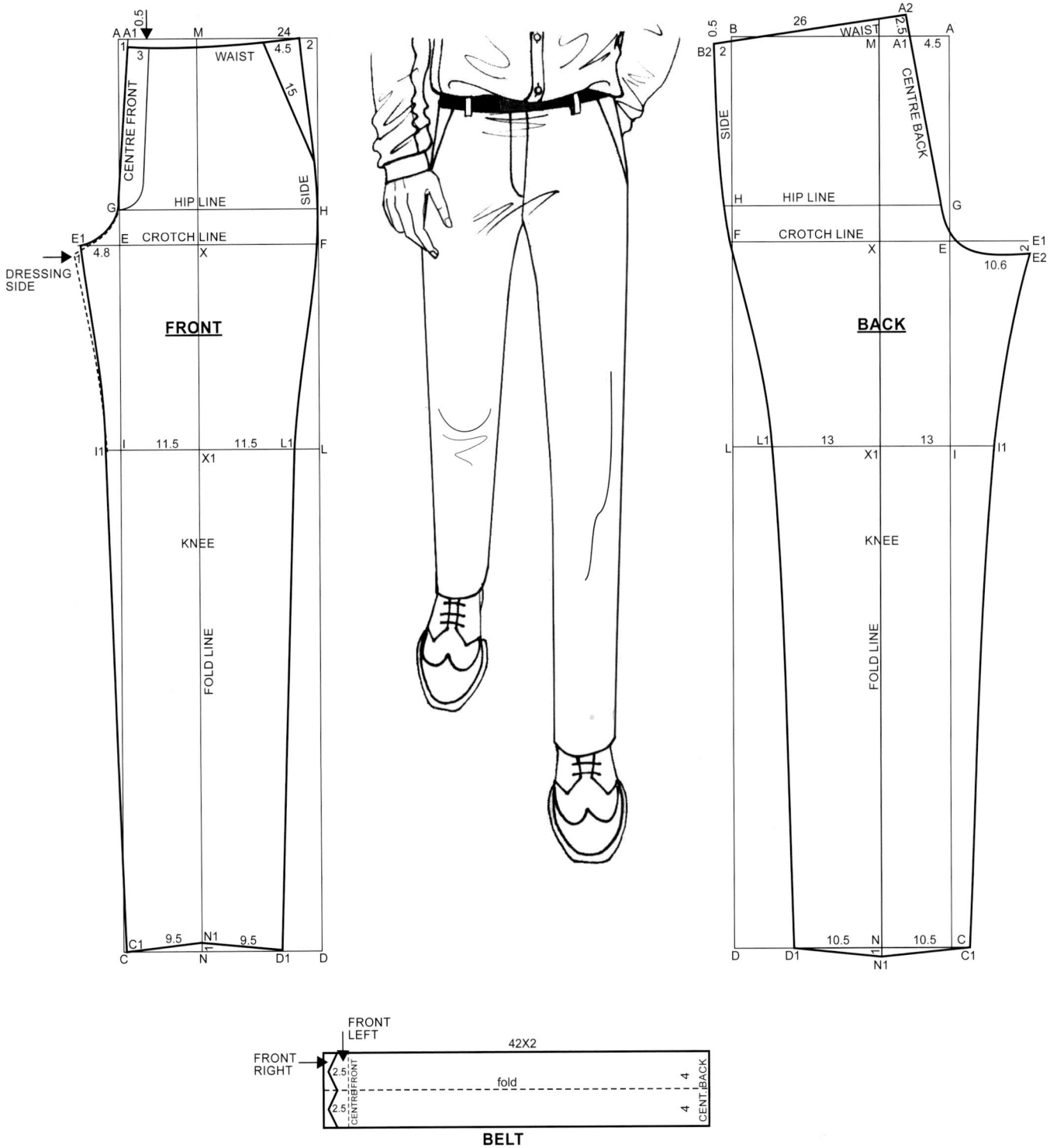

FRONT

CENTRE FRONT

WAIST

HIP LINE

CROTCH LINE

SIDE

DRESSING SIDE

KNEE

FOLD LINE

A A1 0.5
M 24 2
1 3 4.5
15
G H
E1 E
4.8
X F
I1 I 11.5 11.5 L1 L
X1
C1 9.5 N1 9.5 D
C N D1

BACK

SIDE

WAIST

CENTRE BACK

HIP LINE

CROTCH LINE

KNEE

FOLD LINE

0.5 B 26 A2 A
B2 2 M 2.5 A1 4.5
H G
F E E1
X 10.6 E2
L L1 13 13 I I1
X1
D D1 10.5 N 10.5 C C1
N1

BELT

FRONT LEFT

FRONT RIGHT

CENTRE FRONT

42X2

fold

CENT. BACK

2.5
2.5
4
4

- Create the trouser base blocks without pleats in the measurements and fit as in the chart.

- Adjust the bottom of the leg to the desired size, as shown in the figure.

JEANS BASE BLOCK

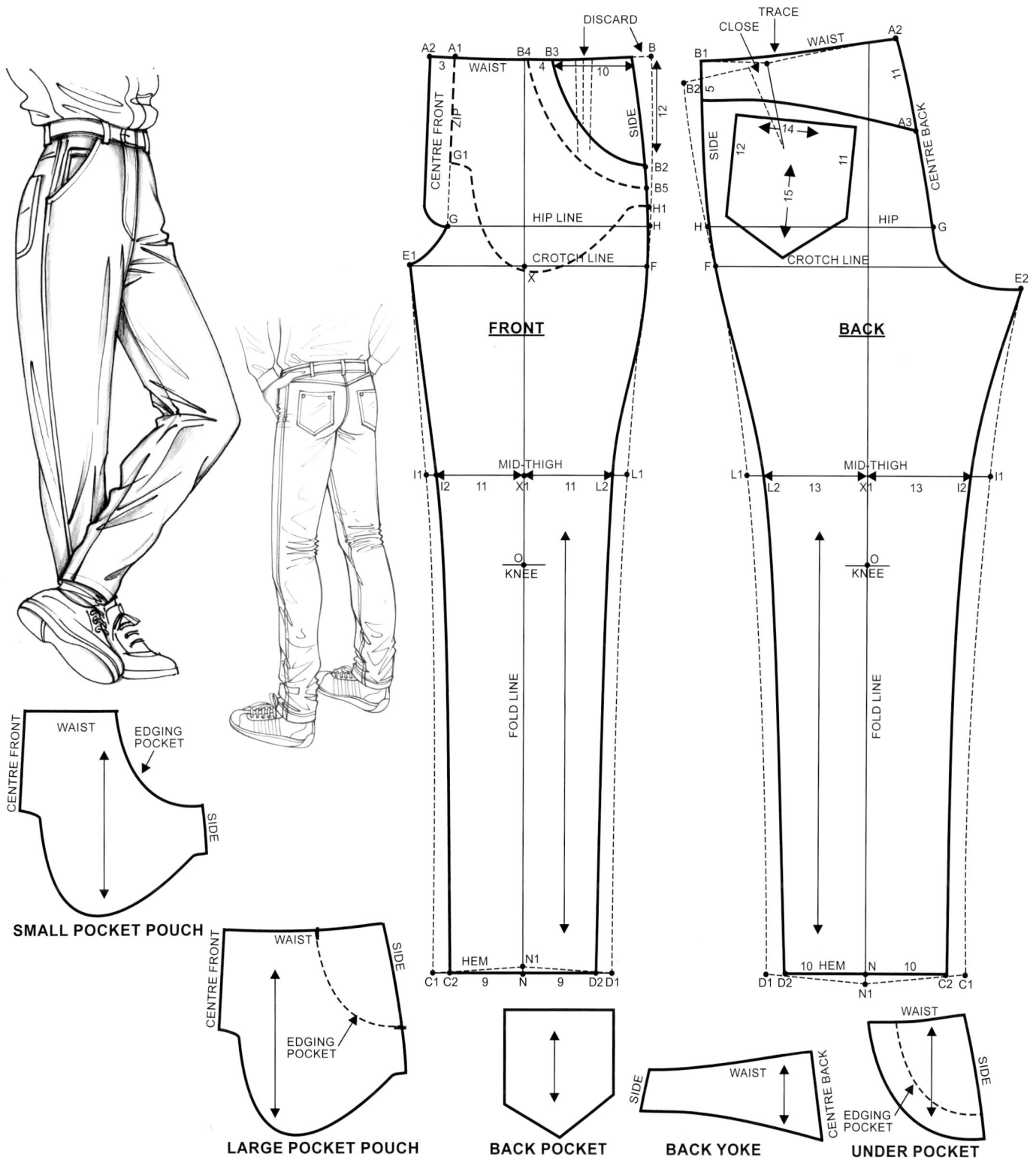

SMALL POCKET POUCH

LARGE POCKET POUCH

BACK POCKET

BACK YOKE

UNDER POCKET

FRONT

BACK

- Draw the trouser base block.
- Remove the darts and pleats at the hip.
- Taper from I1 and L1 on both the back and the front by 1.5-2 cm / 0.59-0.79".
- Draw points C2 and D2 in the measure desired (the back should always be 2 cm / 0.79" wider).
- Connect E1-I2-C2 and F-L2-D2 at the front.
- Connect E2-I2-D2 and F-L2-C2 at the back.
- Make the yoke A2-A3-B2-B1 in the desired measurements.

- Draw the rear pocket with the desired measurements and shape.
- Draw front pocket B2-B3 in the desired shape.
- Draw the flap B4-B5 approximately 4 cm / 1.57" from the edge of the pocket.
- Draw the large pocket pouch A1-G1-X-H1-B onto which the fabric under pocket piece will be sewn.
- Draw the smaller pocket pouch (which will be sewn to the pocket edge) A1-G1-X-H1-B5-B4.

TROUSERS WITH TURN-UP CUFFS

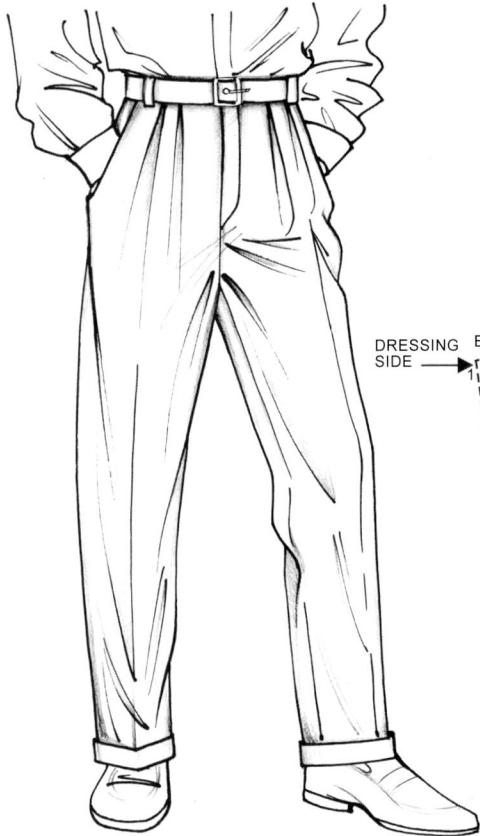

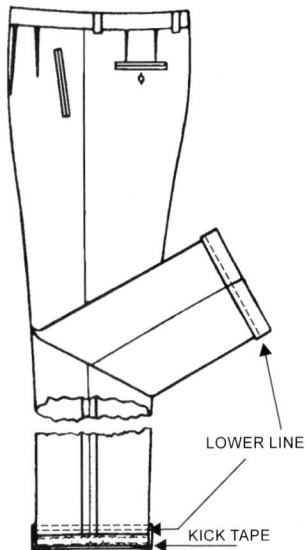

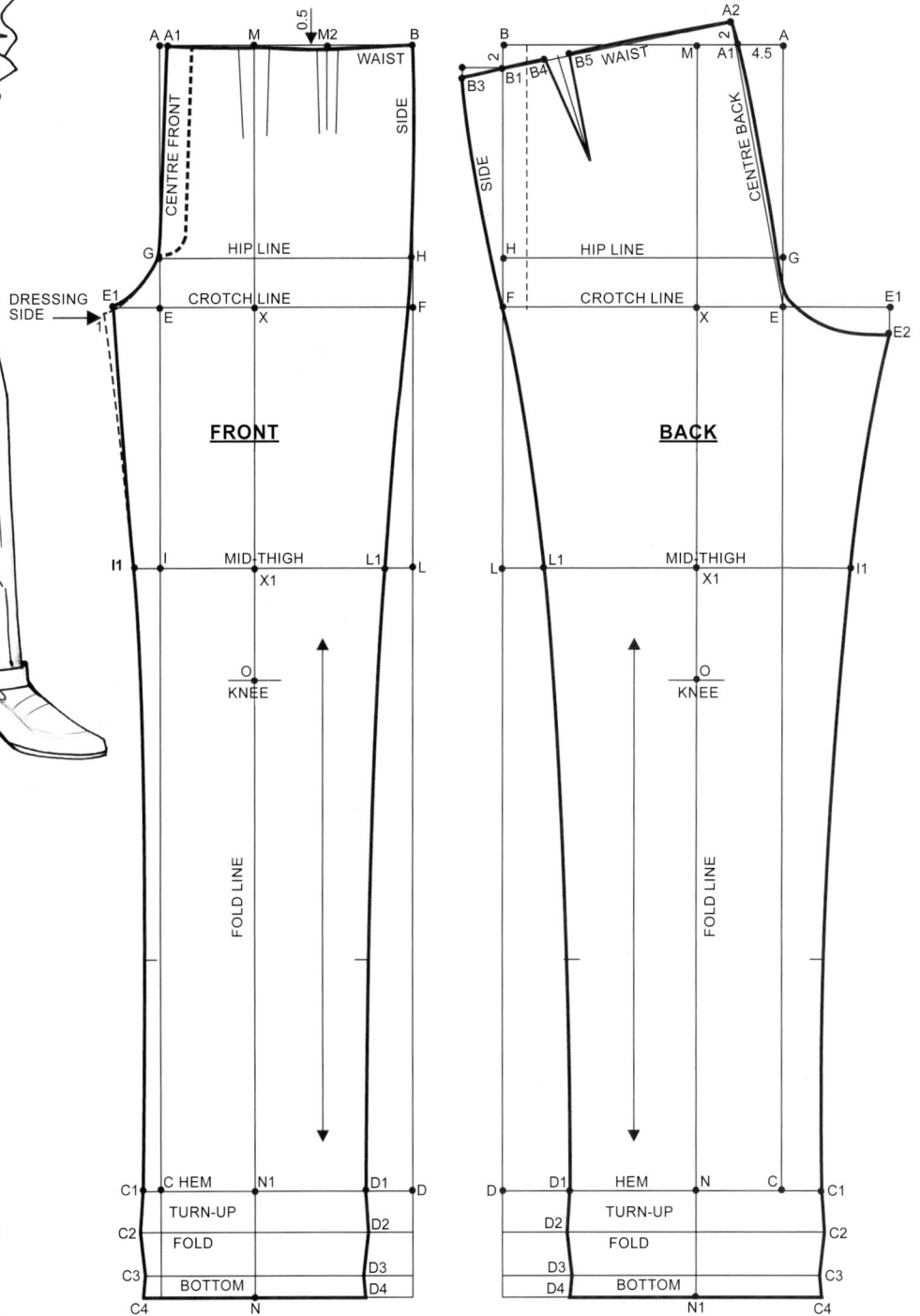

FRONT

CENTRE FRONT

DRESSING SIDE →

WAIST

SIDE

HIP LINE

CROTCH LINE

MID THIGH

KNEE

FOLD LINE

HEM

TURN-UP

FOLD

BOTTOM

BACK

SIDE

WAIST

CENTRE BACK

HIP LINE

CROTCH LINE

MID THIGH

KNEE

FOLD LINE

HEM

TURN-UP

FOLD

BOTTOM

LOWER LINE

KICK TAPE

Trouser cuffs are created by lengthening the front and back by 3 to 5 cm / 1.18-2", depending on the desired style. Establish the length of the trousers before adding the cuffs, using the base pattern as a guide.

- Draw the base block of the trousers with or without pleats and darts.
- C1-C2 = desired height of the finished cuffs (4 cm / 1.57").
- Draw C2-D2.

- C2-C3 is the fold line, same distance as C1-C2.
- Draw C3-D3.
- C3-C4 inner hem = 1/2 of C2-C3.
- Draw C4-D4.
- Join points C1-C2-C3-C4 and points D1-D2-D3- D4 with lines angled in opposite directions as the previous ones, so that they adhere well when folded.

CLASSIC MILITARY TROUSERS
WITH BELLOWS POCKETS

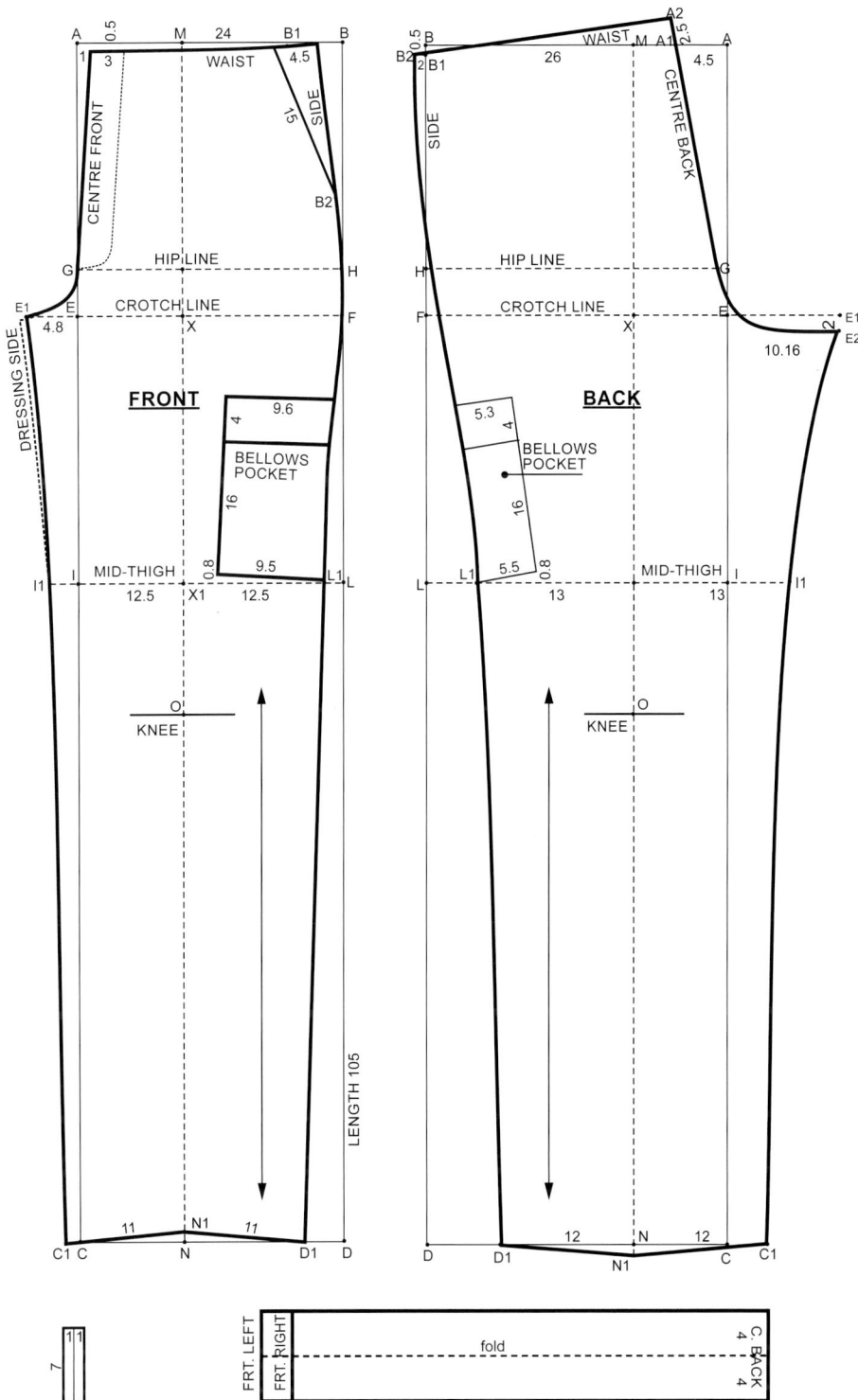

FRONT

| A | 0.5 | M | 24 | B1 | B |
| 1 | 3 | | WAIST | | 4.5 |

CENTRE FRONT
WAIST
SIDE
15
B2

HIP LINE
G — H

CROTCH LINE
E1 E
4.8
X F

DRESSING SIDE

9.6
4
BELLOWS POCKET
16
0.8
9.5
L1 L

MID-THIGH
I1 I
12.5 X1 12.5

O
KNEE

LENGTH 105

11 N1 11
C1 C N D1 D

BACK

| B | 0.5 | A2 | 2.5 | | |
| B2 B1 | 26 | WAIST | M A1 | 4.5 | A |

SIDE
CENTRE BACK

HIP LINE
H — G

CROTCH LINE
F X E
2 E1
10.16 E2

5.3
4
BELLOWS POCKET
16
L1 5.5 0.8
L

MID-THIGH
13 13 I1 I

O
KNEE

12 N 12
D D1 N1 C C1

BELLOWS POCKET

1 1 15 1 1
16
1 1

fold 4
POCKET FLAP 4

7 1 1

FRT. LEFT
FRT. RIGHT
fold
C. BACK 4
4

- Create the trouser base without pleats in the appropriate size and fit.
- Draw the outline of the bellows pocket on the side.
- Make the pattern of the bellows pocket and the flap, as in the figure.

- Create the pattern of the trouser waistband according to the waist circumference.
- Make the loops for the belt (5 pieces) to later attach them to the waistband.

PARACHUTE TROUSERS

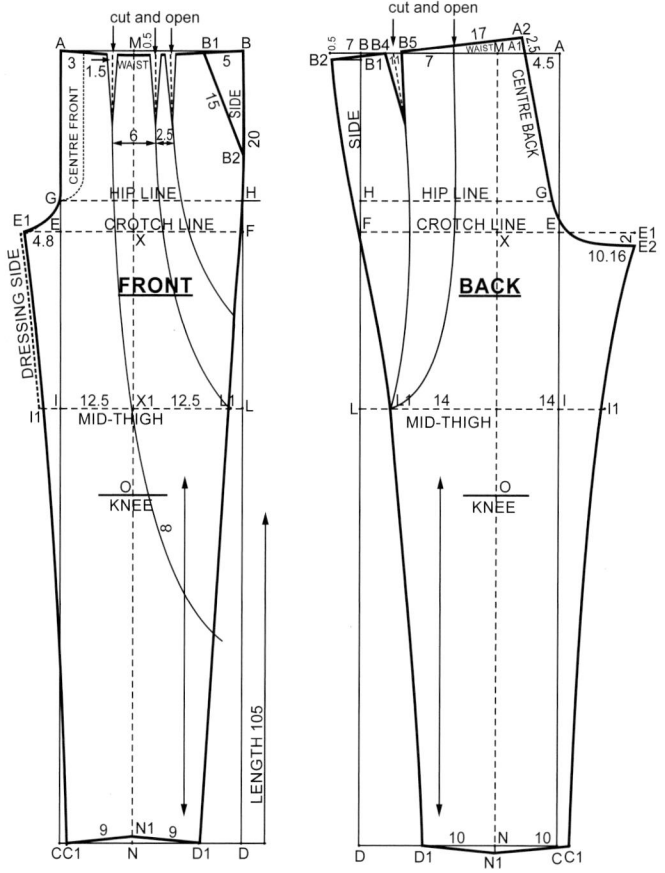

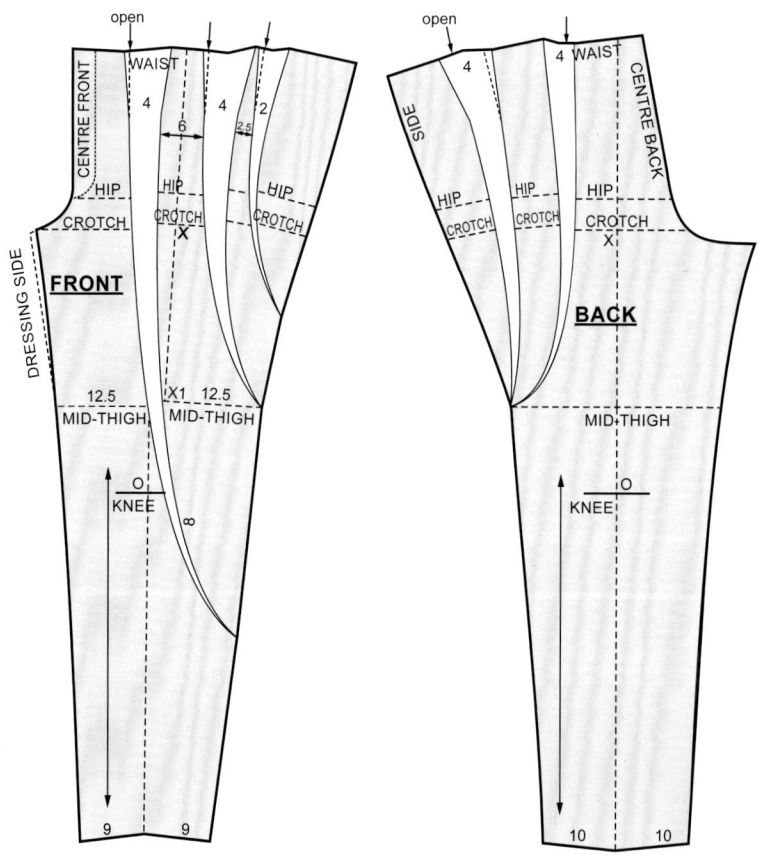

- Create the trouser base blocks with pleats in the appropriate measurements and fit.
- Draw the cut lines as shown in the figure.
- Cut and open as illustrated.

FLARES

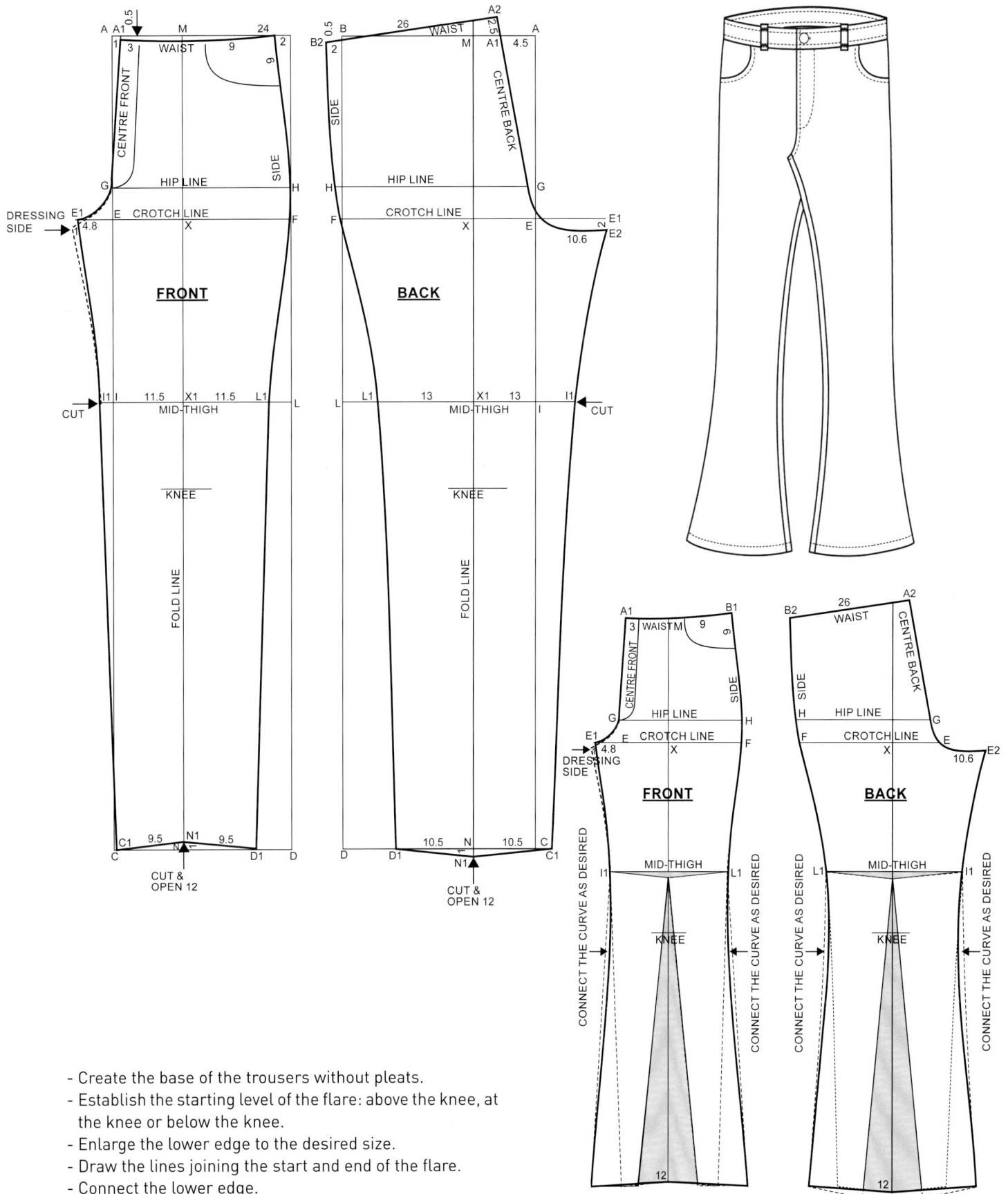

FRONT

BACK

FRONT

BACK

- Create the base of the trousers without pleats.
- Establish the starting level of the flare: above the knee, at the knee or below the knee.
- Enlarge the lower edge to the desired size.
- Draw the lines joining the start and end of the flare.
- Connect the lower edge.

KNEE BREECHES

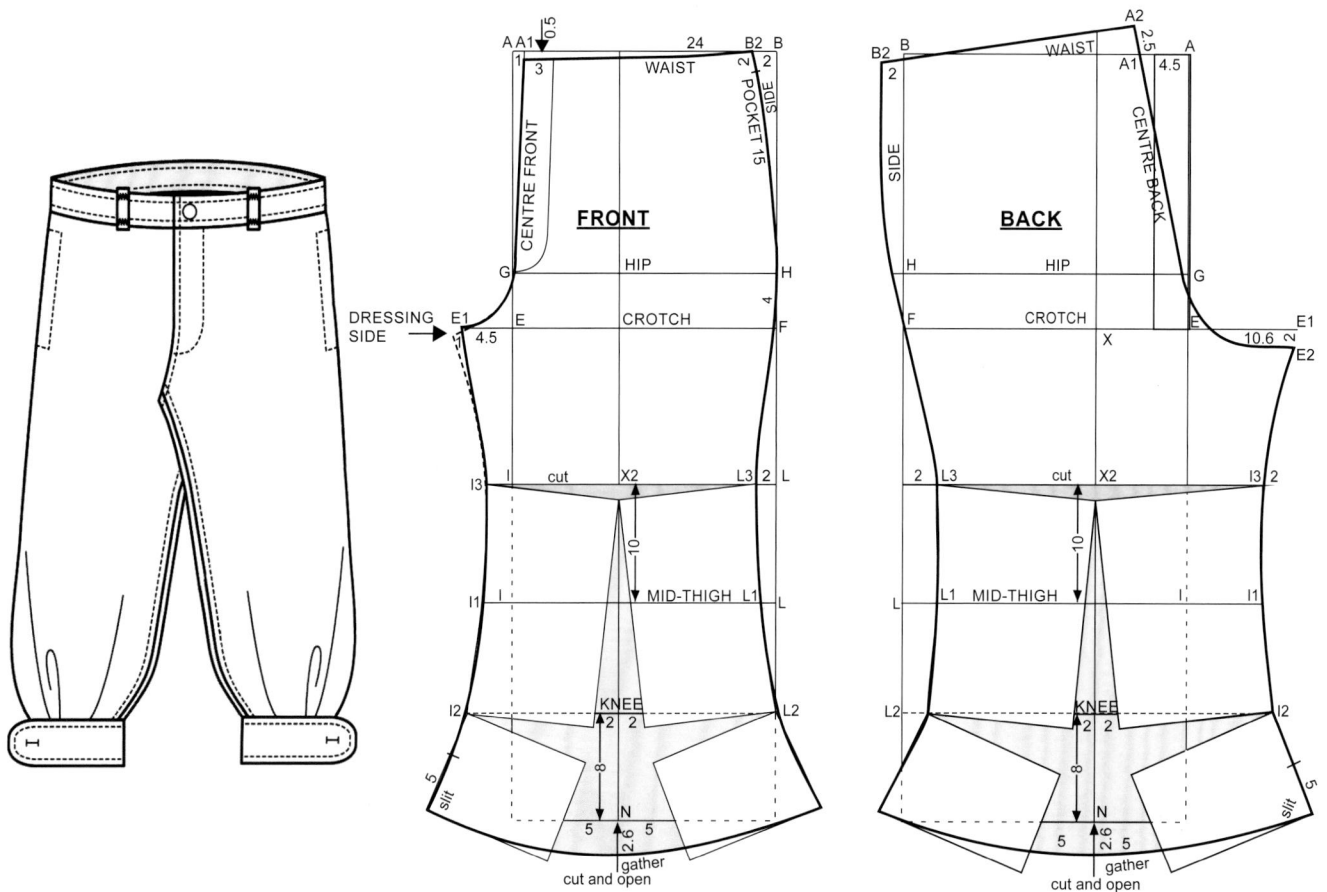

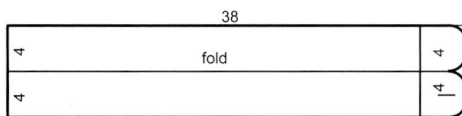

FASTENING STRAP ALONG THE HEM

BELT LOOP X5

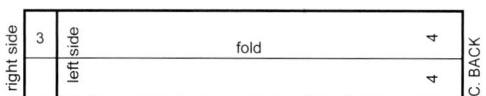

WAISTBAND

- Draw the base pattern of the trousers with pleats using custom measurements or those in the chart.
- Carry over the length at 6-8 cm / 2.36-3.15" from the knee line.
- Shift up the bottom 1 cm / 0.39" on each side, on both the back and the front.
- Approximately 10 cm / 3.94" from the mid-thigh line (2x crotch depth), upwards and 8-10 cm / 3.15"-3.94" from the bottom line downwards draw I2-L2 and I3-L3.

- Cut the fold line N to X2 and the lines I2-L2 and I3-L3. Open as shown and mark the opening.
- Measure the circumference of the underside of the knee, add the buttonhole and button extension of 3-4 cm / 1.18-1.57" and draw the band that goes along the lower edge.
- Create the waistband and belt loops.

KNICKERBOCKERS

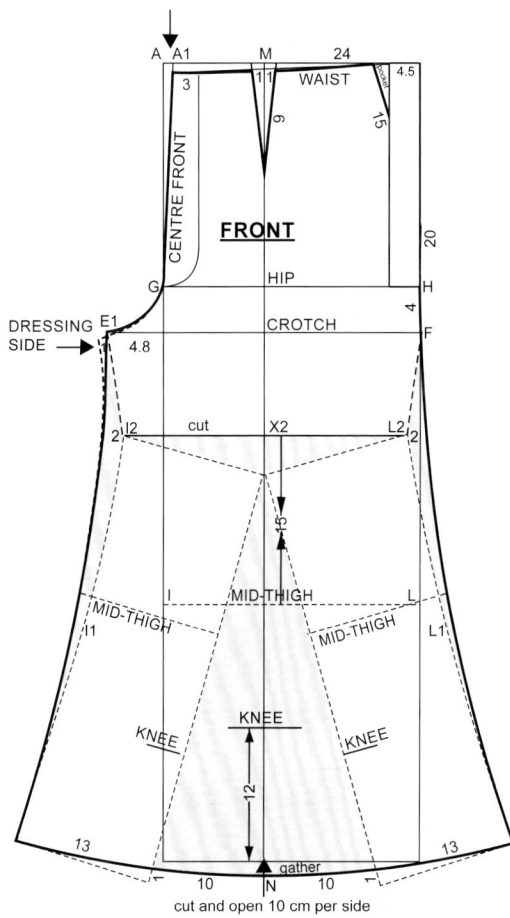

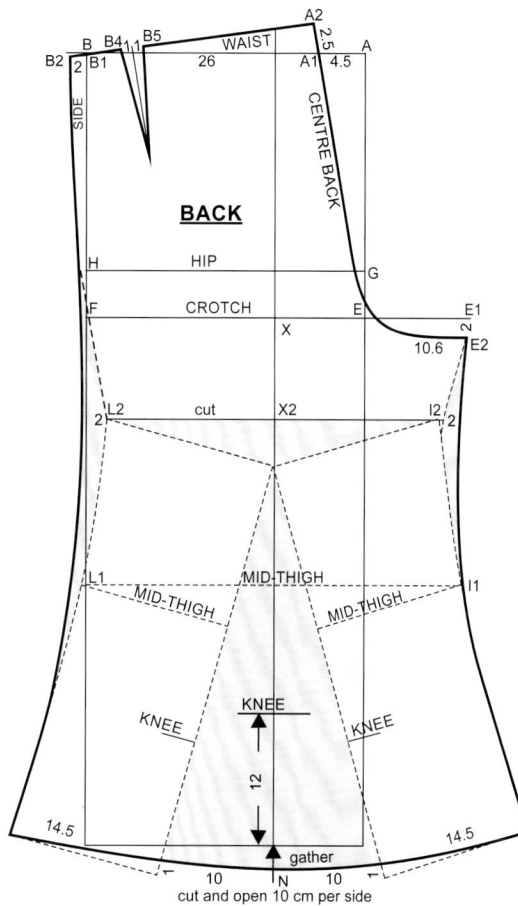

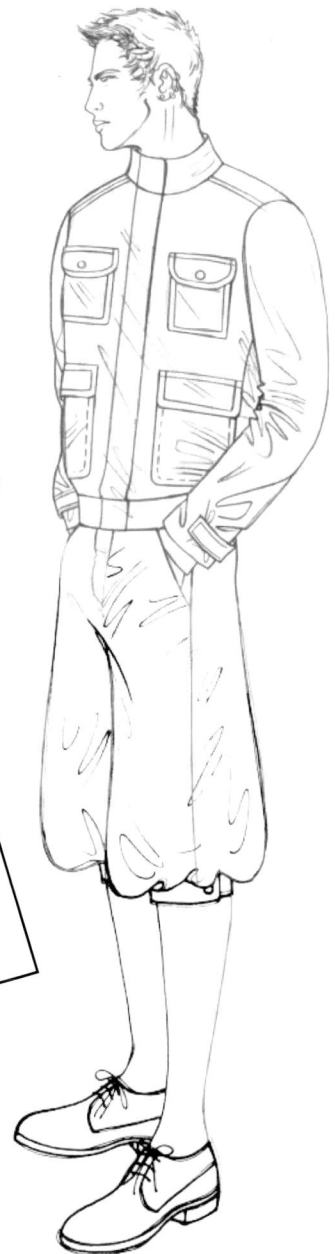

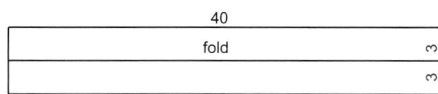

STRAP AT THE HEM

BELT LOOP

BELT

- Draw the base pattern for trousers with or without pleats using custom measurements or those in the chart.
- Bring the length to 10-12 cm / 3.94-4.72" from the knee line.
- Open the bottom 1 cm / 0.39" on each side, on both the back and the front.
- Draw I2-E2 approximately 15 cm / 5.91" from the mid-thigh line (2x crotch depth), moving upwards.

- Cut the fold line from N to X2 and line I2-L2, and open 10 cm / 3.94" at the lower edge, as in the figure, and gather.
- Measure the circumference of the underside of the knee, add the buttonhole and button extension by 3-4 cm / 1.18-1.57" and trace the band along the lower edge of the trousers.
- Create the waistband and belt loops.

JECKERSON TROUSERS WITH PATCHES

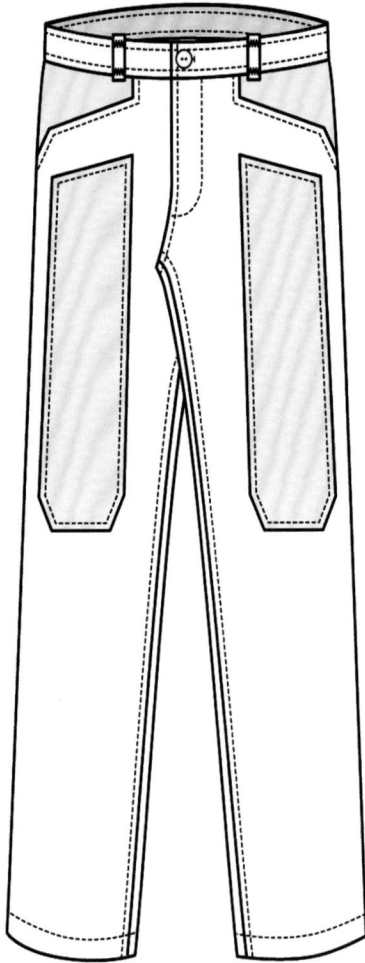

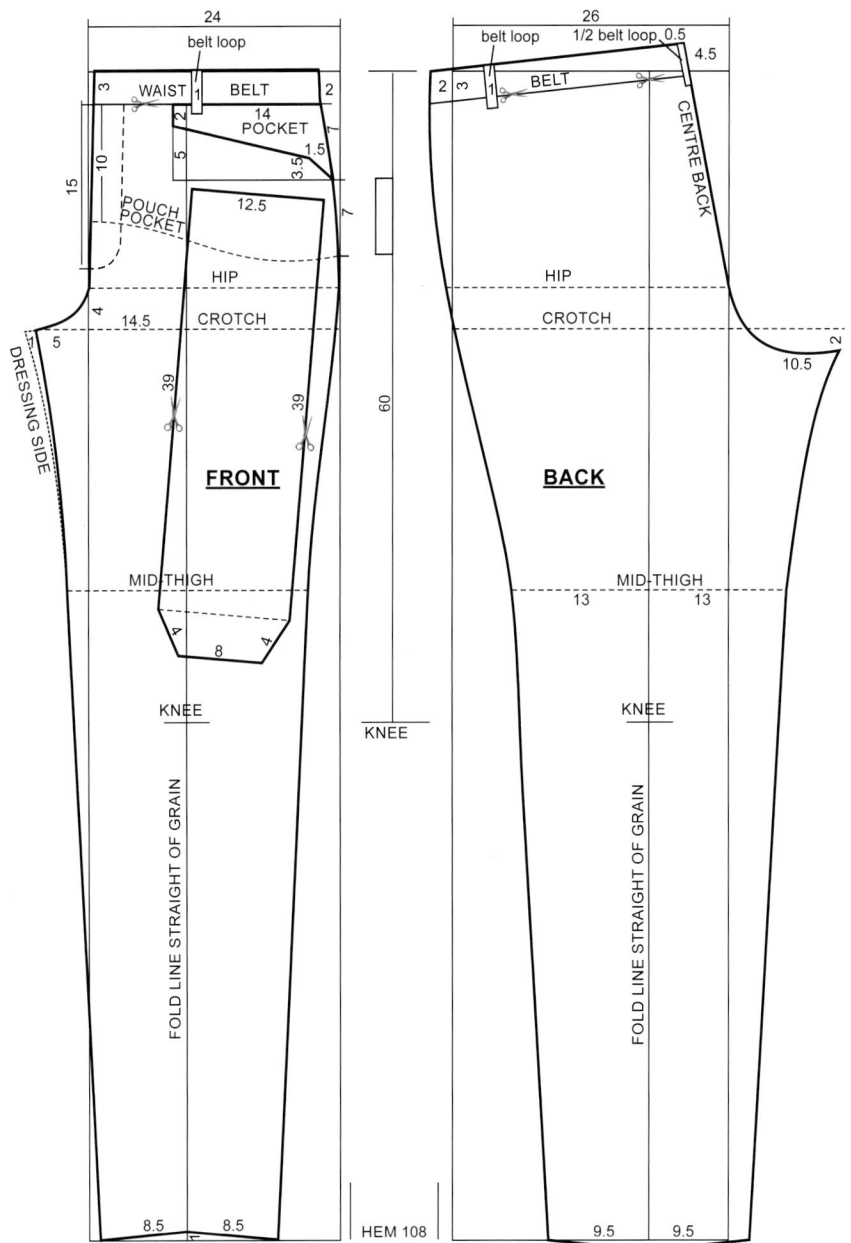

FRONT

BACK

belt loop · WAIST · BELT · POCKET · POUCH POCKET · HIP · CROTCH · DRESSING SIDE · MID-THIGH · KNEE · FOLD LINE STRAIGHT OF GRAIN · HEM 108

belt loop · 1/2 belt loop · BELT · CENTRE BACK · HIP · CROTCH · MID-THIGH · KNEE · FOLD LINE STRAIGHT OF GRAIN

24 · 14 · 3 · 1 · 2 · 5 · 1.5 · 3.5 · 12.5 · 15 · 10 · 7 · 4 · 14.5 · 5 · 39 · 39 · 8 · 60

26 · 0.5 · 4.5 · 2 · 3 · 1 · 10.5 · 2 · 13 · 13 · 9.5 · 9.5 · 8.5 · 8.5

- Create the base pattern for trousers with the ease of skinny jeans (2-4 cm / 0.79-1.57") and transform as in the figure.

JODHPURS

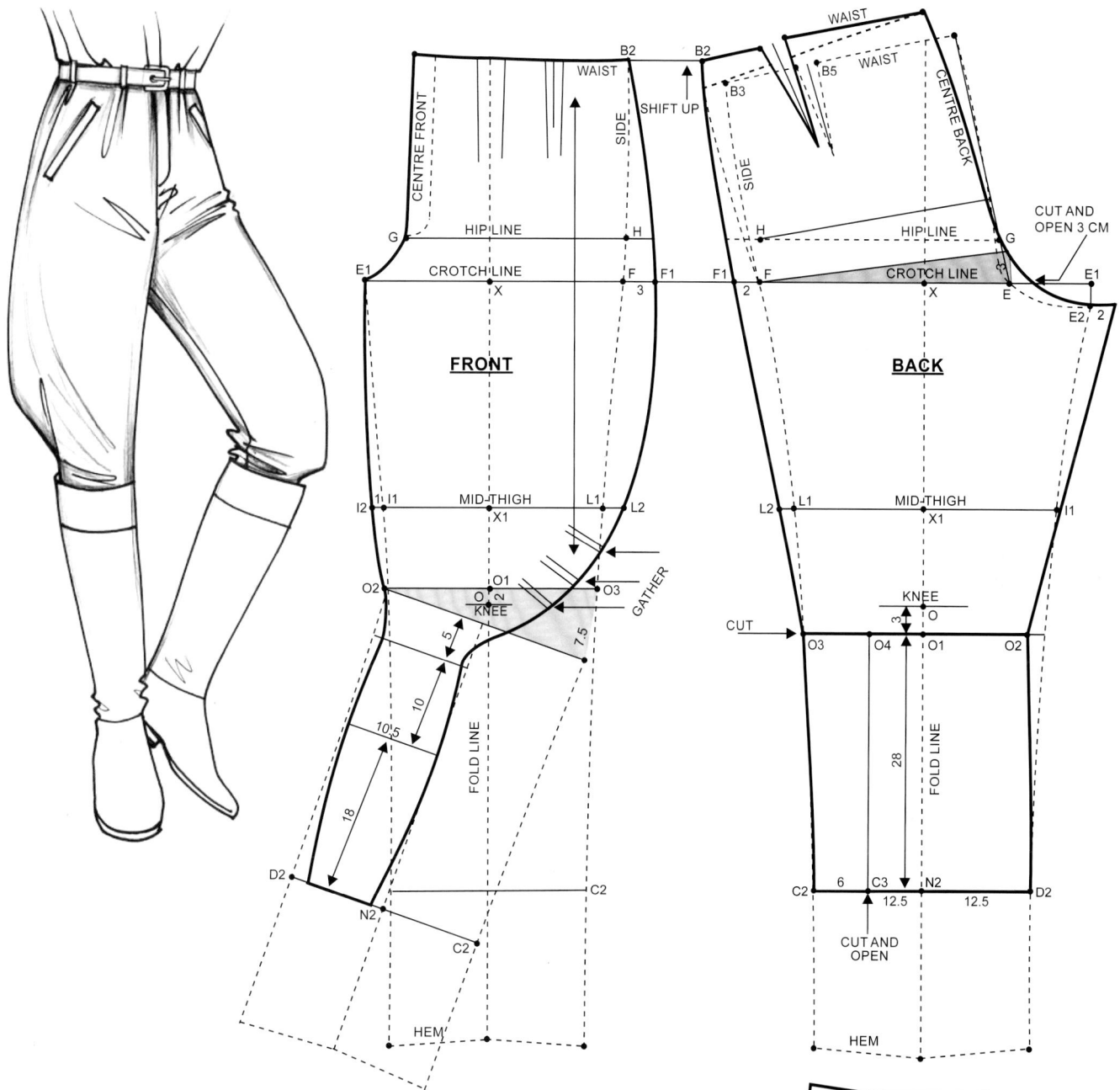

- Draw the base pattern for classic trousers.

Front

- Draw the line O2-O3 2 cm / 0.79" from the knee line, cut and open to 7-7.5 cm / 2.76-2.95" by pivoting on point O2.
- Draw the side and lower leg as in the figure.

Back

- Cut along line E-F and rotate the top part by 3 cm / 1.18", pivoting on point F.
- F-F1 = 2 cm / 0.79". Draw F1-B2 in the same length as F1-B2 on the front.
- Draw the side and lower leg as in the figure.
- Draw the line O2-O3 3 cm / 1.18" below the knee line and cut O2-O3-C2-D2.
- Cut along C3-O4 and widen the lower edge by 3 cm / 1.18".

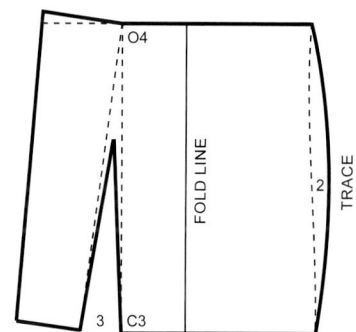

DROP CROTCH TROUSERS

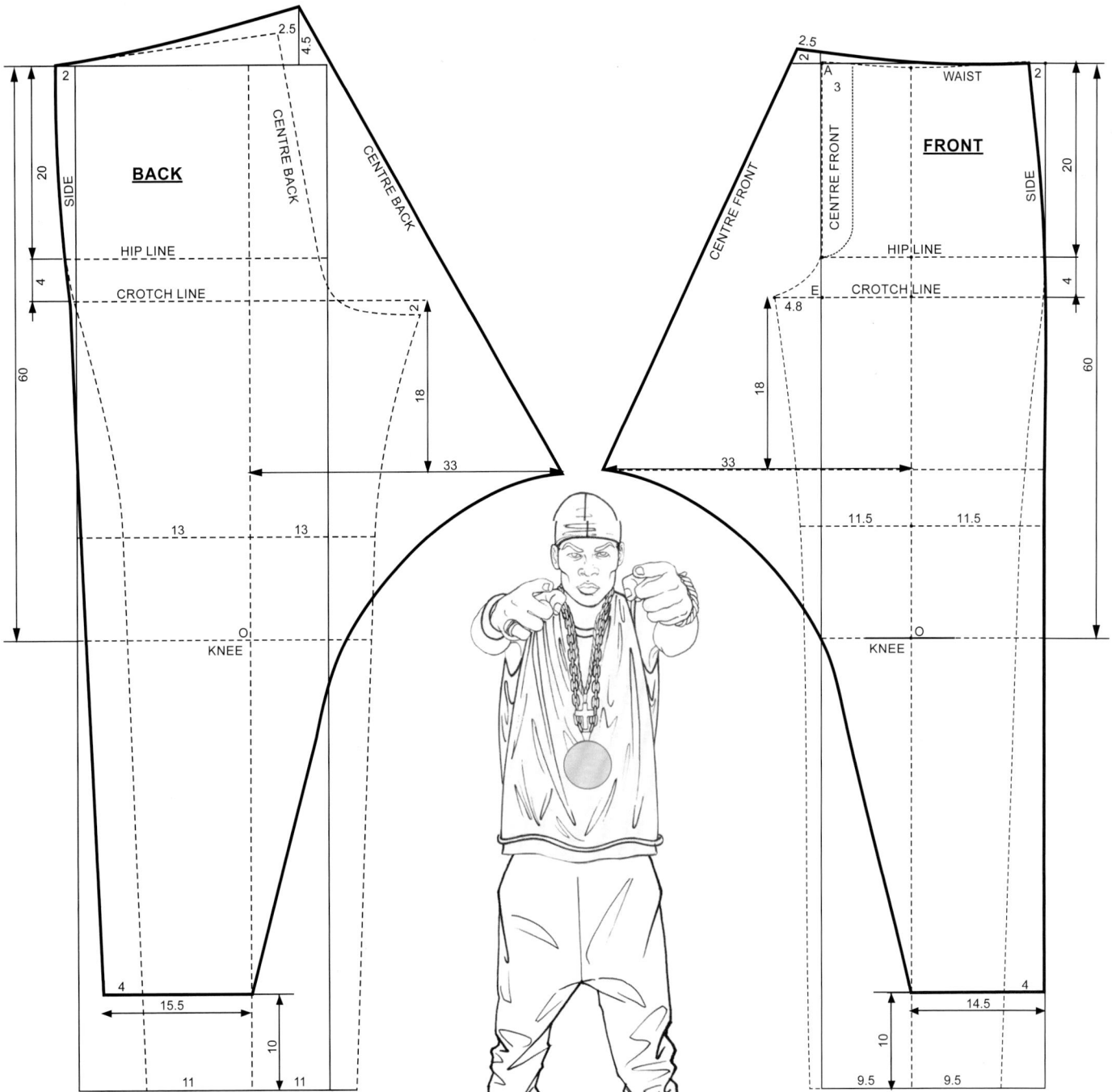

BACK

CENTRE BACK

CENTRE BACK

SIDE

2

20

4

60

2.5

4.5

HIP LINE

CROTCH LINE

2

18

33

13   13

O

KNEE

4

15.5

10

11   11

FRONT

CENTRE FRONT

CENTRE FRONT

SIDE

2.5

2

A

3

WAIST

2

20

4

60

E

4.8

HIP LINE

CROTCH LINE

18

33

11.5   11.5

O

KNEE

4

14.5

10

9.5   9.5

Create the base pattern for trousers without darts in the desired size and fit and transform as shown in the figure.

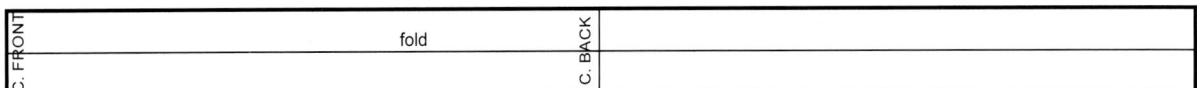

C. FRONT

fold

C. BACK

WAISTBAND WITH A DRAWSTRING - INSERT LACES OR CORD 1.5 M

THAI FISHERMAN TROUSERS

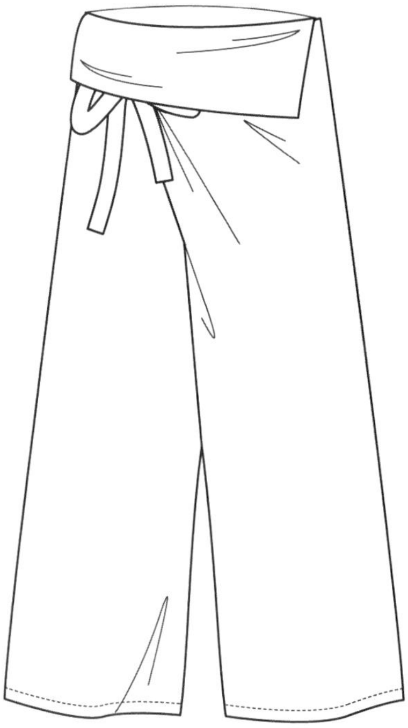

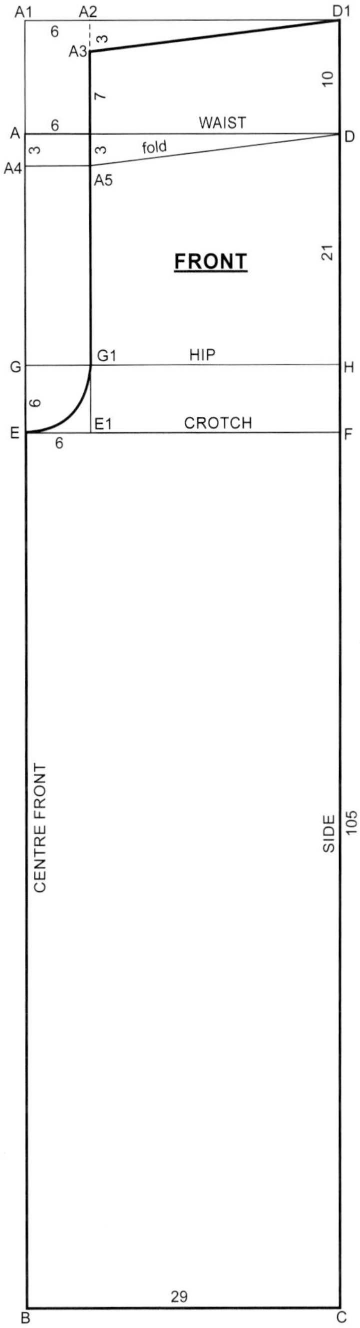
A1
A2
D1
6
3
A3
7
10
A
6
WAIST
D
3
3
fold
A4
A5
FRONT
21
G
G1
HIP
H
6
E
E1
CROTCH
F
6
CENTRE FRONT
SIDE
105
29
B
C

A1
A2
D1
7
3
D2
10
7
A
A3
WAIST
D
fold
3
D3
BACK
G
G1
HIP
H
6
E
E1
CROTCH
F
7
SIDE
CENTRE BACK
108
33
B
C

Front

Draw the rectangle A-B-C-D with:

- A-D = 1/4 of the hip circumference + 4-6 cm / 1.57-2.36"(e.g.: 96 ÷ 4 = 24 + 5 = 29 cm / 11.42").
- A-B = desired trouser length (e.g: 105 cm / 41.34").
- A-A1 = 10 cm / 3.94"; D-D1 as A-A1.
- Draw the rectangle A-A1-D1-D.
- A-G = waist to hip (e.g: 21 cm / 8.27"); draw G-H.
- A-E = crotch depth + 2 cm / 0.79" (e.g.: 24 + 2 = 26 cm / 10.24").
- E-E1 = 6 cm / 2.36"; A1-A2 = 6 cm / 2.36"; draw E1-A2.
- A2-A3 = 3 cm / 1.18"; draw A3-D1.
- A-A4 = 3 cm / 1.18"; draw A4-A5-D.
- Draw G1-E with a curved line.

Back

Draw the rectangle A-B-C-D with:

- A-D = 1/4 of the hip circumference + 8-10 cm / 3.15-3.94"(e.g.: 96 ÷ 4 = 24 + 9 = 33 cm / 12.99").
- A-B = front length + 3 cm / 1.18"(e.g.: 105 + 3 = 108 cm / 42.52").
- A-A1 = 10 cm / 3.94"; D-D1 as A-A1.
- Draw the rectangle A-A1-D1-D.
- A-G = waist to hip (e.g: 21 cm / 8.27"); draw G-H.
- A-E = crotch depth + 2 cm / 0.79" (e.g.: 24 + 2 = 26 cm / 10.24").
- E-E1 = 7 cm / 2.76"; A1-A2 = 7 cm / 2.76"; draw E1-A2.
- D1-D2 = 3 cm / 1.18"; draw A2-D2.
- D-D3 = 3 cm / 1.18"; draw A3-D3.
- Draw G1-E with a curved line.

SCOTTISH KILT

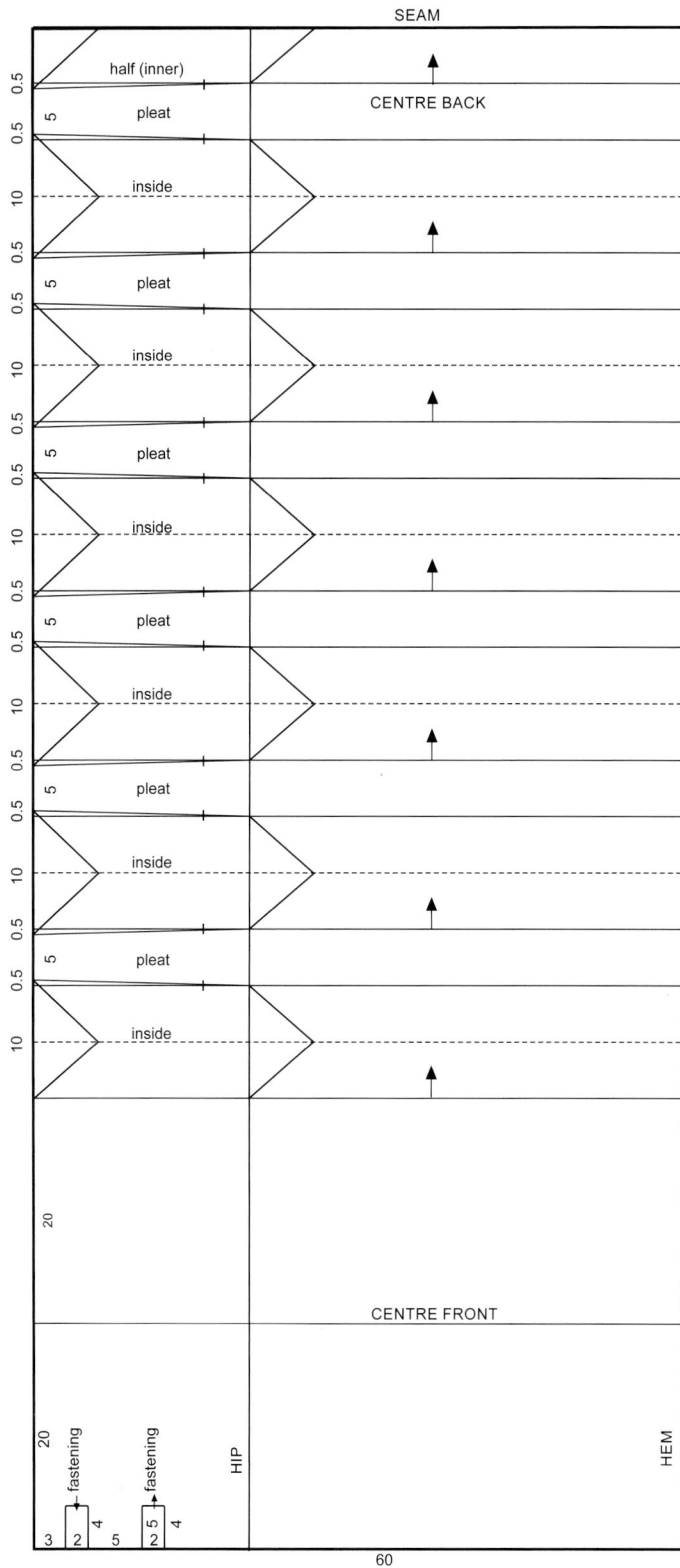

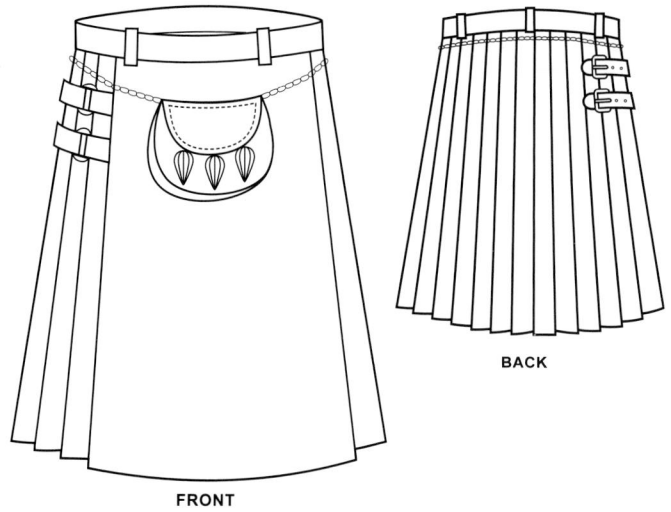

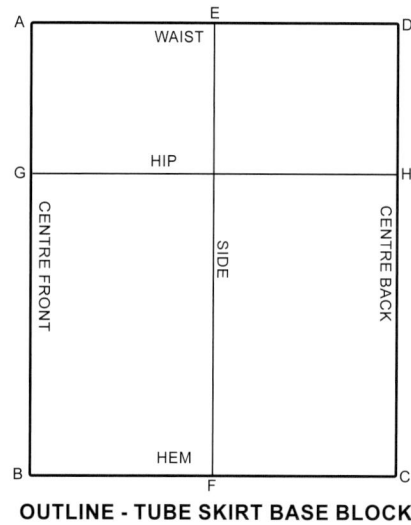

FRONT

BACK

OUTLINE - TUBE SKIRT BASE BLOCK

- Make the tube skirt base (rectangle A-B-C-D, with A-D = hip circumference + 2 cm / 0.79"; A-B = desired height; A-G = hip length).
- Add 20 cm / 7.87" to the front for the overlap.
- Divide half of the skirt into equal parts, starting with one part as wide as the overlap flap and continuing with 5 cm / 2" folds.
- Divide the width of the 5 cm / 1.97" pleats (based on the difference between hip circumference and waist circumference) in equal parts according to the number of folds and make them all the same length (14 cm / 5.51").
- Cut the pleat strips and glue them onto another sheet of paper, spacing them at a distance that's double that of the pleat (10 cm / 3.94").
- Finish with half an inverted pleat, to be sewn with the other half.

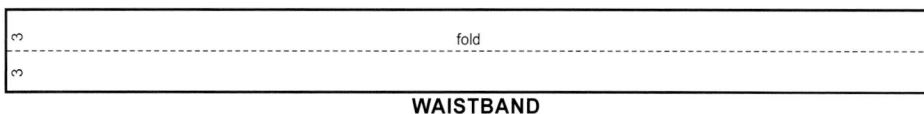

WAISTBAND

MORNING DRESS TROUSERS

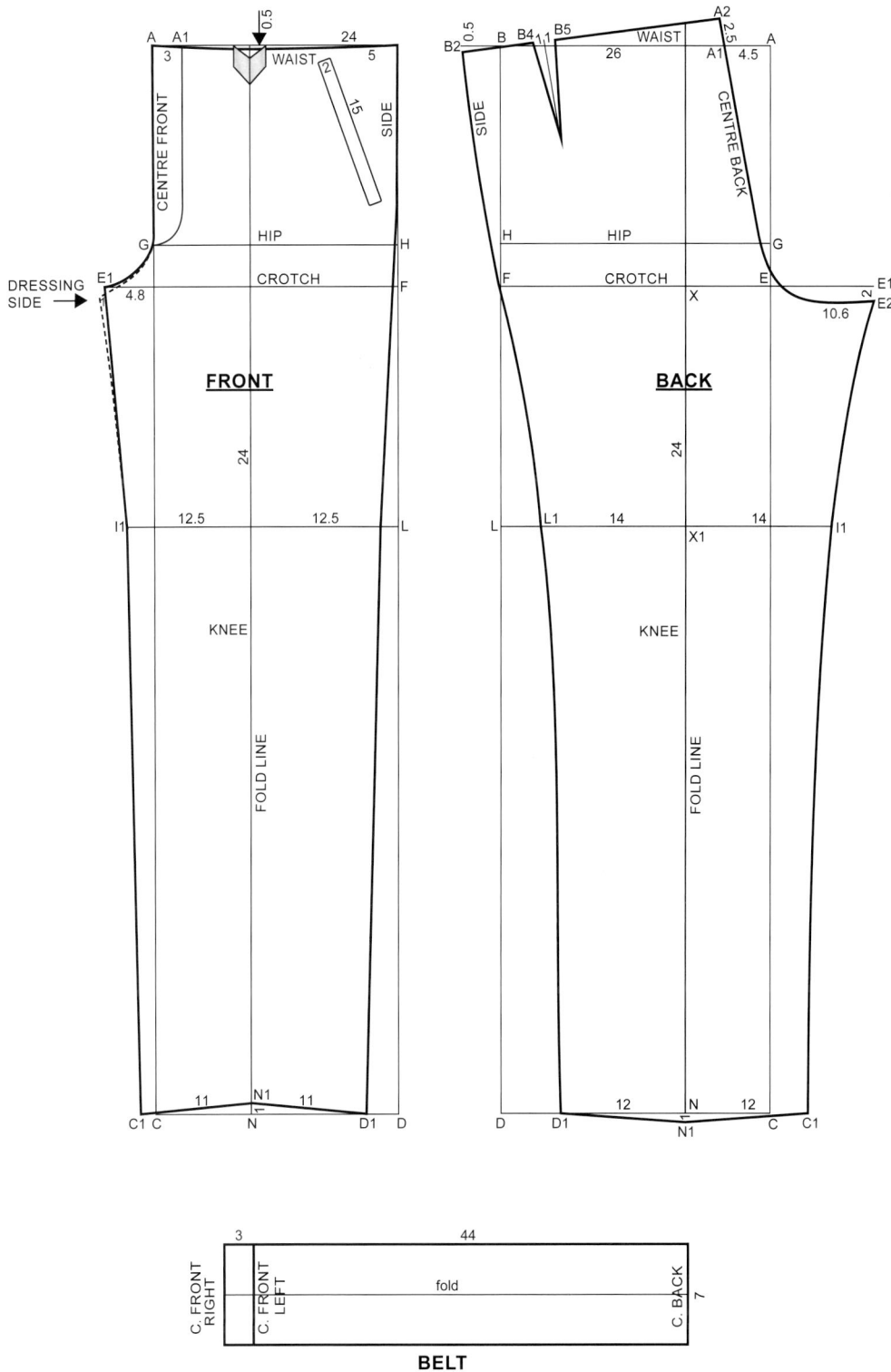

FRONT

CENTRE FRONT

SIDE

A A1 3 | 0.5 | WAIST 2 | 24 | 5

15

DRESSING SIDE →

G | HIP | H

E1 | CROTCH | F

4.8

24

I1 | 12.5 | 12.5 | L

KNEE

FOLD LINE

C1 C | 11 | N1 | 11 | D1 D

N

BACK

SIDE

CENTRE BACK

B2 0.5 | B | B4 1.1 | B5 | WAIST | A2 2.5 | A
26 | A1 4.5

H | HIP | G

F | CROTCH | E
X | E1 2 | E2
10.6

24

L | L1 | 14 | 14 | I1
X1

KNEE

FOLD LINE

D | D1 | 12 | N | 12 | C C1
N1

BELT

C. FRONT RIGHT | C. FRONT LEFT | 3 | 44 | fold | C. BACK 7

Morning dress trousers are created using a straight-shaped base with the darts pointing inwards. They are made of Cheviot wool with fine stripes in two shades of grey, tapered, without cuffs or belt loops.

- Make the base blocks for trousers with a single pleat in the desired measurements and appropriate fit.
- Draw the waistband using the waist circumference measurement.

BLACK TIE TROUSERS

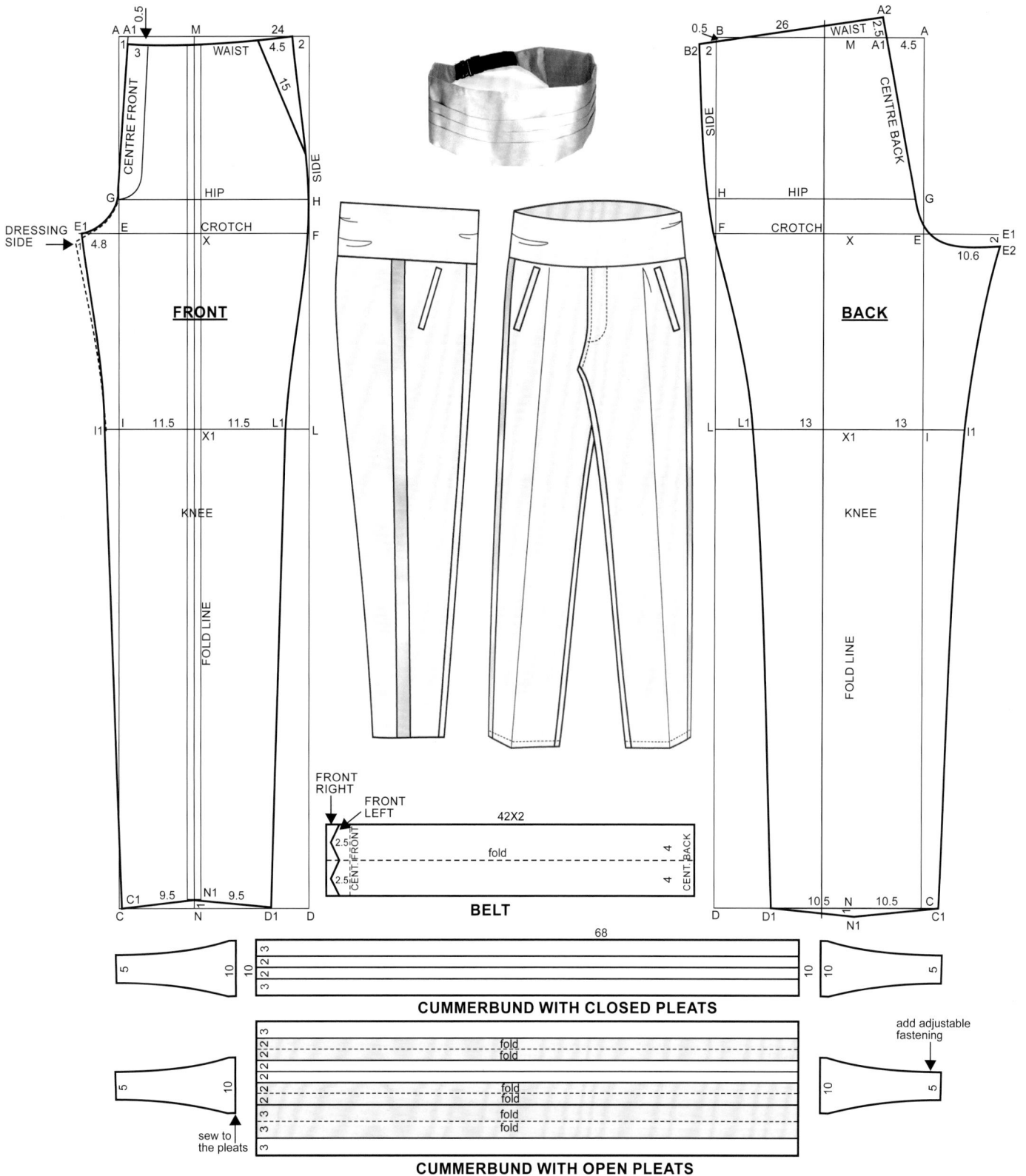

FRONT

A A1 0.5
M
24
1 3
WAIT
4.5 2
CENTRE FRONT
15
SIDE
G
HIP
H
DRESSING SIDE →
E1
E
CROTCH
X
F
4.8

FRONT

I1 I
11.5
X1
11.5
L1
L

KNEE

FOLD LINE

C1 9.5
N1
9.5
D1 D
C
N

BACK

0.5 B
26
WAIST
A2
A1
2.5
A
B2 2
M
4.5
SIDE
CENTRE BACK
H
HIP
G
F
CROTCH
X
E
E1
10.6
E2

BACK

L
L1
13
X1
13
I
I1

KNEE

FOLD LINE

D D1
10.5
N
10.5
C1
C
N1

BELT

FRONT RIGHT
FRONT LEFT
42X2
2.5
CENT. FRONT
fold
4
2.5
4
CENT. BACK

CUMMERBUND WITH CLOSED PLEATS

5
10
3
2
2
3
68
10
10
5

CUMMERBUND WITH OPEN PLEATS

5
10
3
2
2
2
2
3
3
fold
fold
fold
fold
fold
fold
add adjustable fastening
10
5

sew to the pleats

These trousers should be in the exact same fabric as the dinner jacket, in the exact same colour. They have a classic straight cut, without darts and without cuffs. The special feature of this model is a thin stripe of black silk that runs down the outer seams on both legs, from waist to hem. The cummerbund completes the look, although it is not often worn today, especially among young people.

Create the pattern for trousers without darts as on the previous pages, in the appropriate measurements.

SHORTS

FRONT

BACK

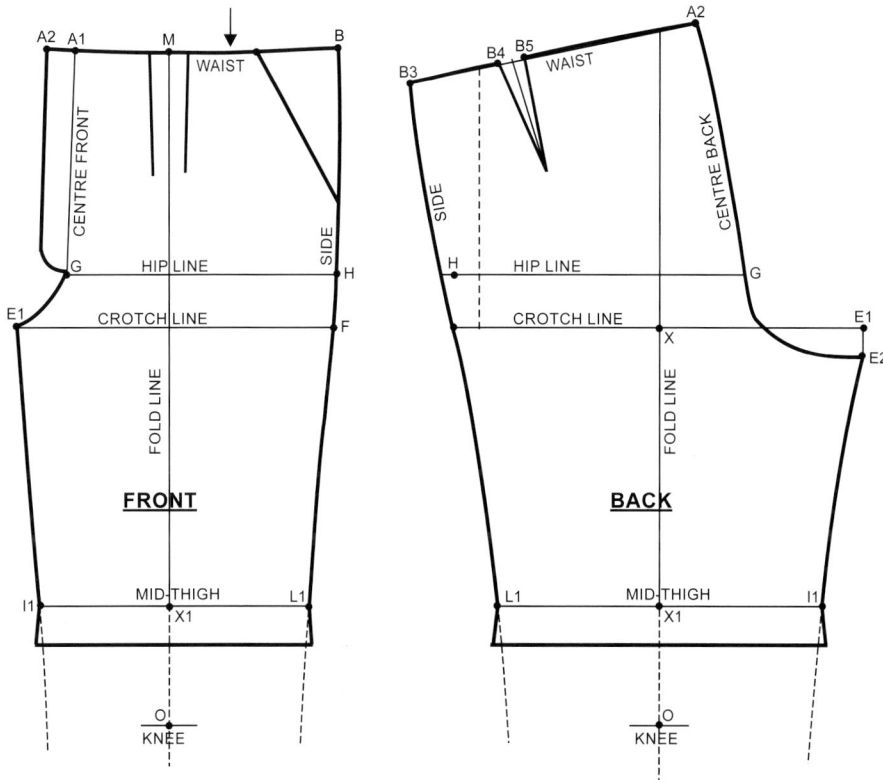

- Draw the trouser base blocks with appropriate measurements and ease.
- Create the desired length.
- Draw the extension for the cuff.

WIDE-LEG SHORTS

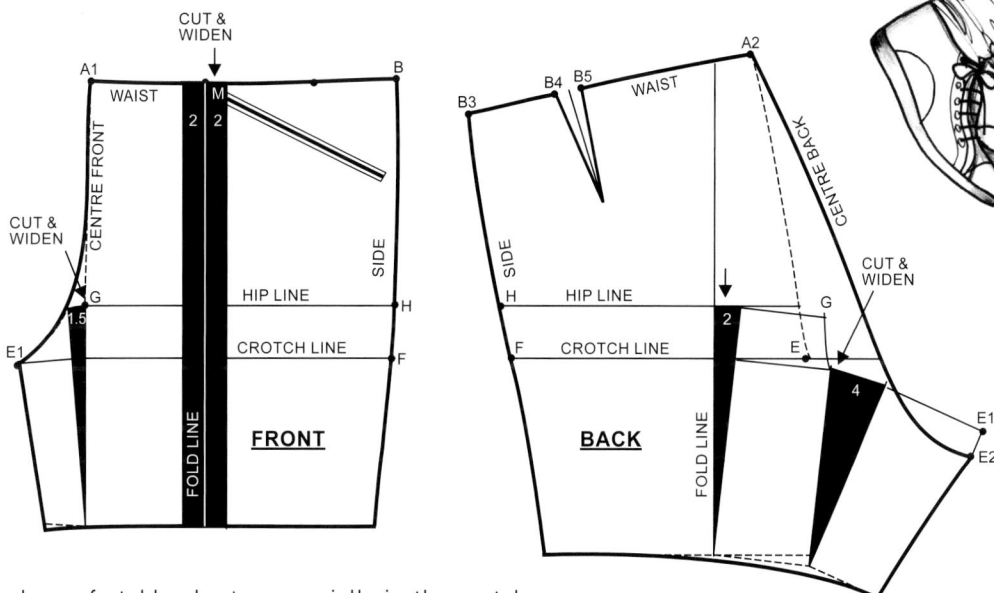

FRONT

BACK

For relaxed, comfortable shorts, especially in the crotch, transform the pattern as shown in the figure.

CARGO SHORTS

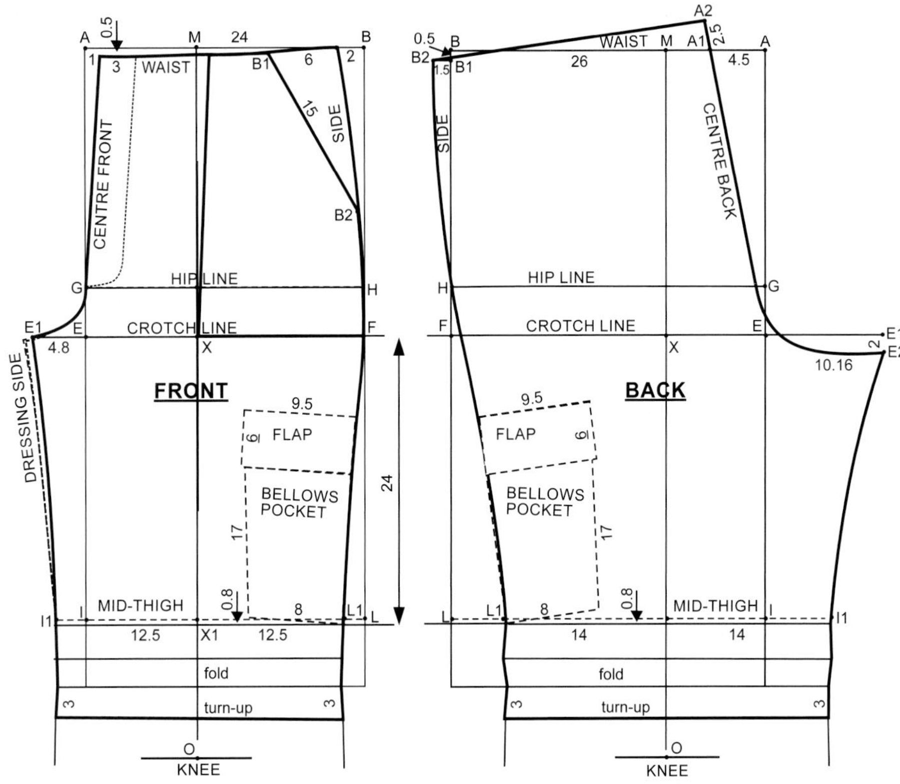

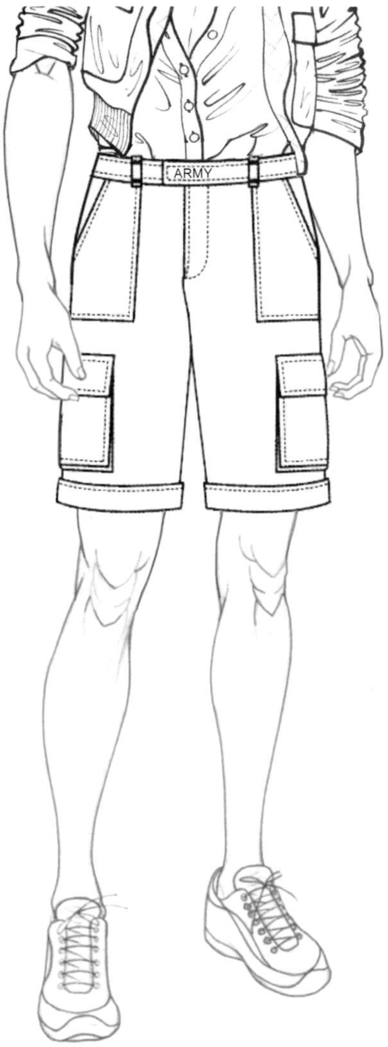

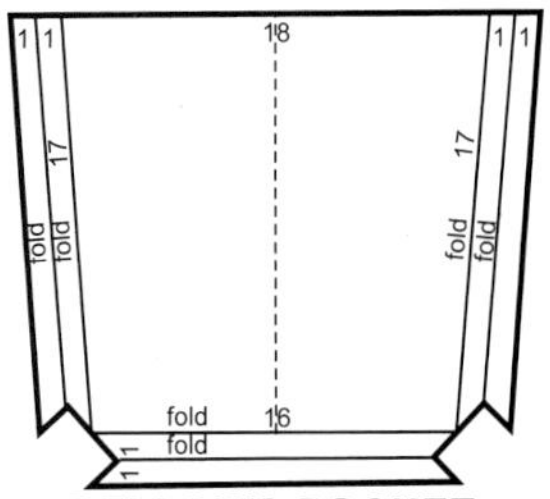

FRONT

CENTRE FRONT

WAIST

SIDE

DRESSING SIDE

HIP LINE

CROTCH LINE

MID-THIGH

fold

turn-up

KNEE

A 0.5 · M 24 · B
1 3 WAIST · B1 6 2
15 SIDE
B2
G · HIP LINE · H
E1 E · CROTCH LINE · F
4.8 · X
9.5
6 FLAP
17 BELLOWS POCKET
24
0.8
I1 I · MID-THIGH · L1 L
12.5 · X1 · 12.5
O · KNEE

BACK

CENTRE BACK

HIP LINE

CROTCH LINE

MID-THIGH

fold

turn-up

KNEE

0.5 B · WAIST M A1 2.5 · A
B2 1.5 B1 26 4.5
SIDE
H · HIP LINE · G
F · CROTCH LINE · E · E1
X · 10.16 · E2
9.5
FLAP 6
BELLOWS POCKET
17
0.8
L L1 · 8 · MID-THIGH · I · I1
14 · 14
O

BELLOWS POCKET

18
17
fold fold
fold
18
1 1 · 1 1

POCKET

5
23.5
11
19

27.6	
2	fold
3	28

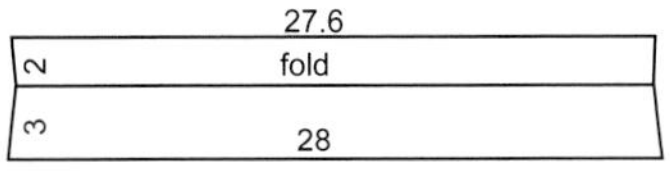

cuff to trim the turn-up - back

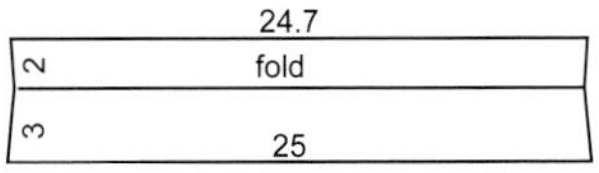

24.7	
2	fold
3	25

cuff to trim the turn-up - front

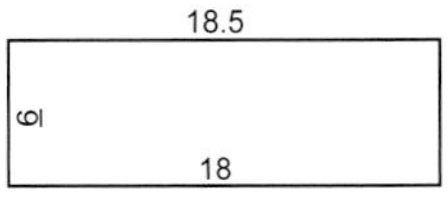

POCKET FLAP

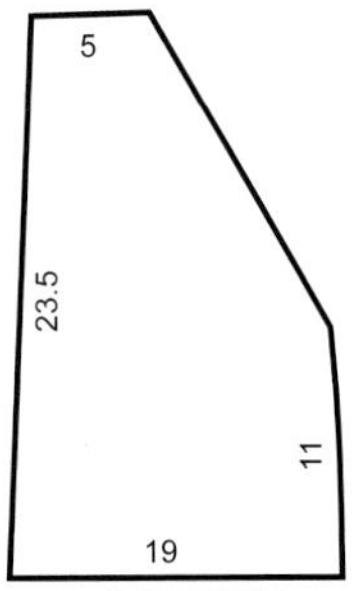

18.5
6
18

BELT

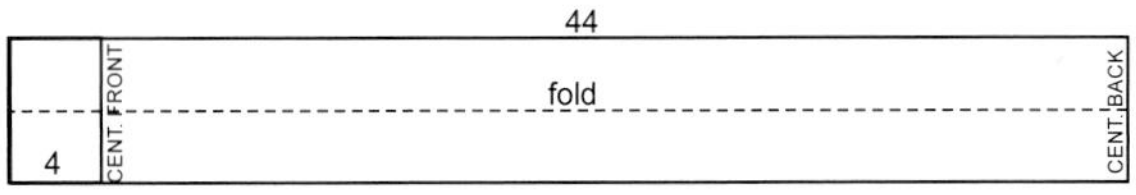

44
CENT. FRONT · fold · CENT. BACK
4

- Draw the base pattern of the trousers without pleats in the desired length and appropriate fit.
- Mark the position of the patch pocket on the front.
- Create the pattern of the bellows pocket and the flap as shown in the figure.

- Create the trouser waistband pattern according to the waist circumference.
- Make the leather belt loops (5 pieces) which will be attached to the waistband.

TENNIS SHORTS

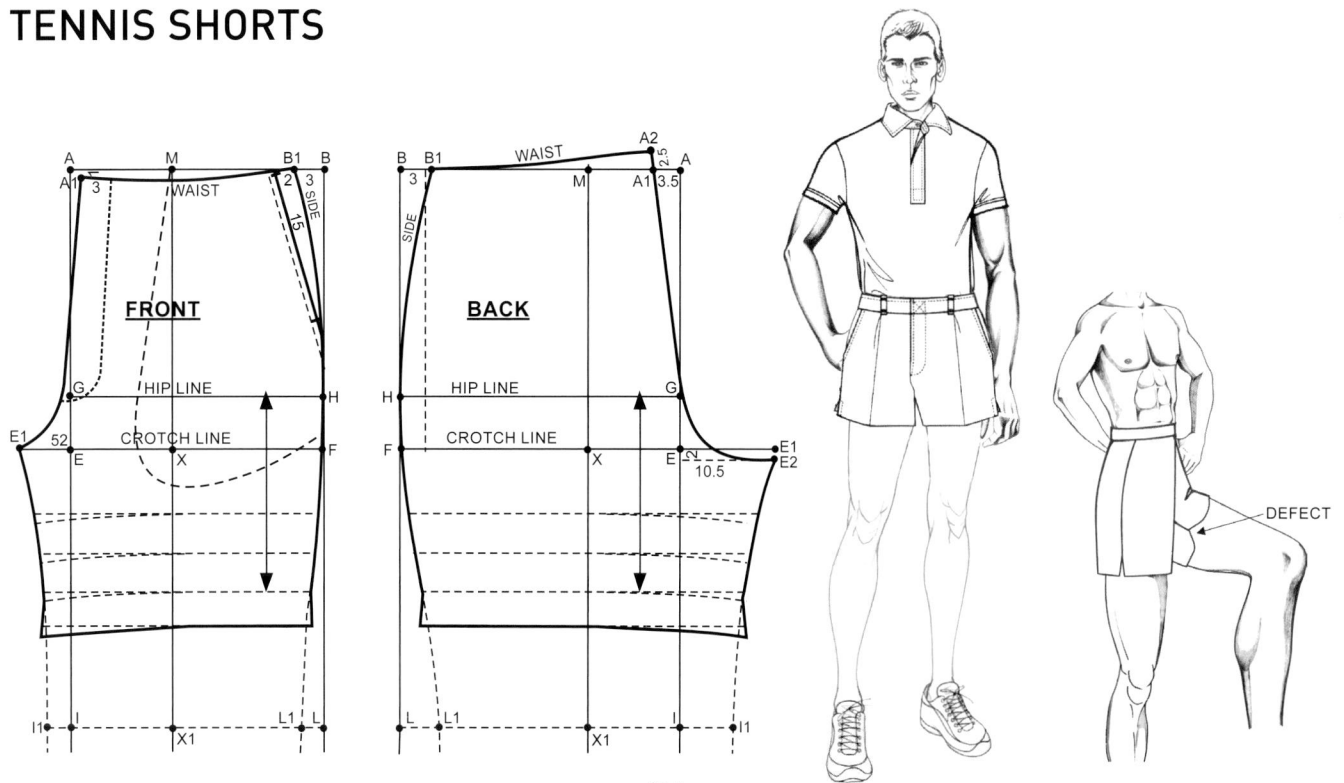

- Create the trouser base without pleats in the length desired.
- At the lower edge of the inner front and back leg, draw in by 0.6 cm / 0.24" and lower it by 1 cm / 0.39".
- At the lower edge of the outer front and back legs, draw in by 1 cm / 0.39".
- Add the extension for the hem and connect smoothly with the curves.

Note:
To prevent a hollow forming on the inside of the leg of the shorts, 1 cm / 0.39" should be added to the lower edge of the inside leg. This causes the hem to meet the curved area of the inner seam at an angle closer to a right angle (as shown in the pattern).

JOGGERS
WITH A SINGLE SEAM

- Draw the rectangle A-B-C-D with A-B equal to the trouser length + 6 cm / 2.36" and A-D as the hip circumference measurement + 6 cm / 2.36".
- A-V = half of A-D. Draw V-Z.
- Place the trouser base pattern in this rectangle, on the crotch guideline, keeping the side lines separated by 3 cm / 1.18" per part from the line.
- V-Z and the rear waistline 3-3.5 cm / 1.18-1.38" from A-D.
- Extend the lines of the centre front and the centre back to line A-D.
- Z-B1 = front hem measurement + 3 cm.
- Z-C1 = back hem measurement + 3 cm for volume.
- Join E-B1 and E1-C1.

NOTE:
The pattern can be positioned whole, or with the back and front split into two parts if a lateral seam is needed for zips or other purposes.

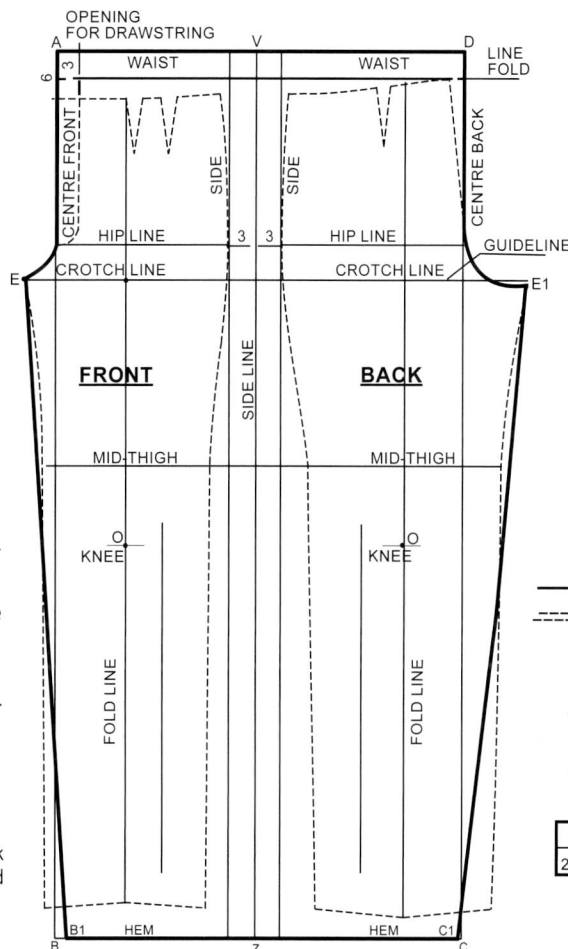

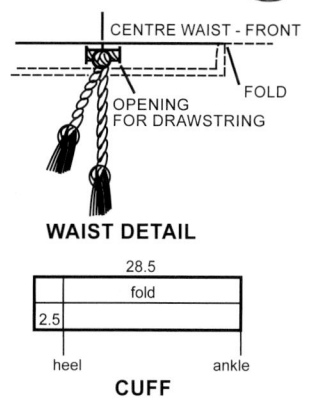

WAIST DETAIL

CUFF

FULL JUMPSUIT BASE BLOCK

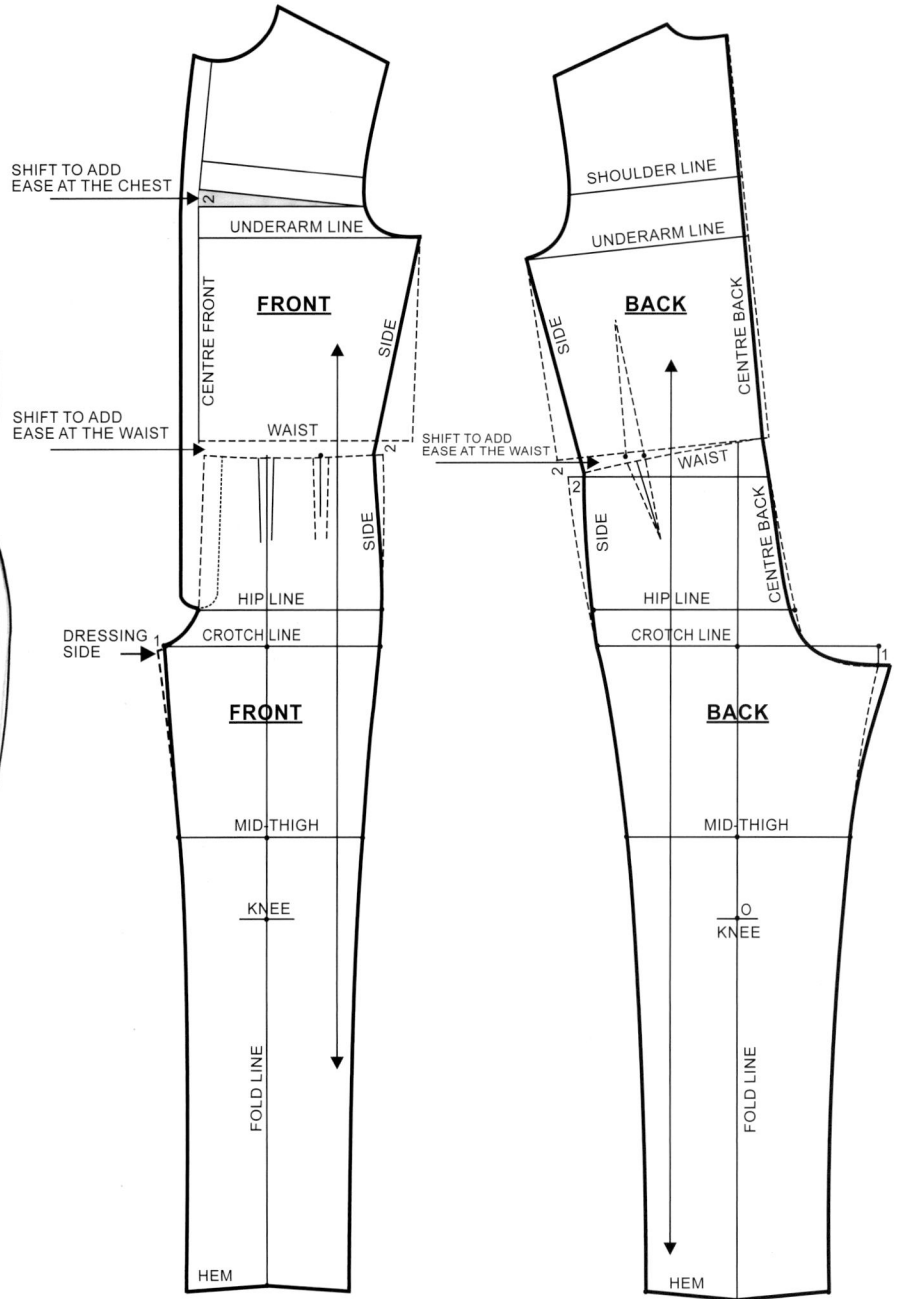

SHIFT TO ADD
EASE AT THE CHEST

UNDERARM LINE

CENTRE FRONT

FRONT

SIDE

SHIFT TO ADD
EASE AT THE WAIST

WAIST

SIDE

DRESSING
SIDE

HIP LINE

CROTCH LINE

FRONT

MID-THIGH

KNEE

FOLD LINE

HEM

SHOULDER LINE

UNDERARM LINE

SIDE

BACK

CENTRE BACK

SHIFT TO ADD
EASE AT THE WAIST

WAIST

SIDE

CENTRE BACK

HIP LINE

CROTCH LINE

BACK

MID-THIGH

KNEE

FOLD LINE

HEM

- Draw the base pattern for trousers in the desired measurements and fit.
- Create the bodice base block in the same fit as the trousers.
- Join the front and back of the top to the front and back of the trousers, keeping them 2 cm / 0.79" apart at the waistline of the centre back and 2 cm / 0.79" at the top of the centre front to allow for movement, as shown in the figure.

- Eliminate the darts of both the top and the trousers and reduce the hip excess as required by the style of the garment.
- Make the fastening extension 2-2.5 cm / 0.79-1".
- Join all front and side lines.

SHORT JUMPSUIT

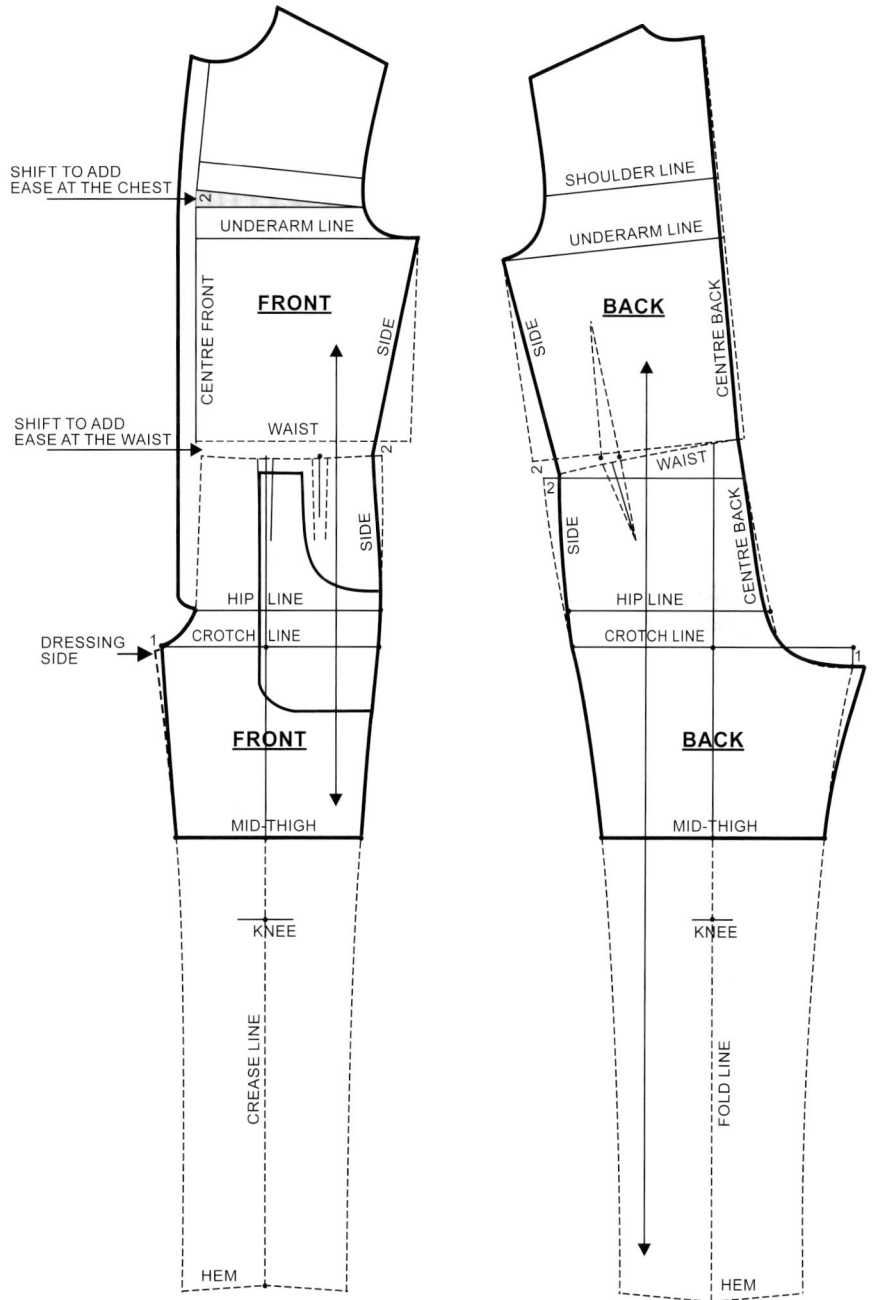

SHIFT TO ADD
EASE AT THE CHEST

UNDERARM LINE

SHOULDER LINE

UNDERARM LINE

CENTRE FRONT

FRONT

SIDE

SIDE

BACK

CENTRE BACK

SHIFT TO ADD
EASE AT THE WAIST

WAIST

SIDE

WAIST

SIDE

CENTRE BACK

DRESSING
SIDE

HIP LINE

CROTCH LINE

HIP LINE

CROTCH LINE

FRONT

BACK

MID-THIGH

MID-THIGH

KNEE

KNEE

CREASE LINE

FOLD LINE

HEM

HEM

- Draw the base block of the full jumpsuit.
- Draw the desired hemline of the leg.
- Discard the part below the hemline.
- Smoothly create the outline.

ADAPTING TROUSERS TO DIFFERENT BODY TYPES

Anterior pelvic tilt

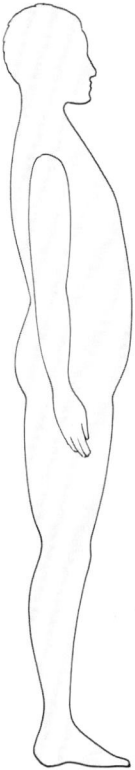

This posture is very difficult to work with because it initially results from the stiffening or tightening of the leg from the ankle upwards, so the pelvis is forced to tilt forward to restore balance.

- Point E = add 1 cm / 0.39".
- Point G = open by 2 cm / 0.79".
- Point H = subsequent opening.
- Point I = add 0.5 cm / 0.20".
- Point D = decrease by 2 cm / 0.79".
- Crotch = add 2 cm / 0.79".

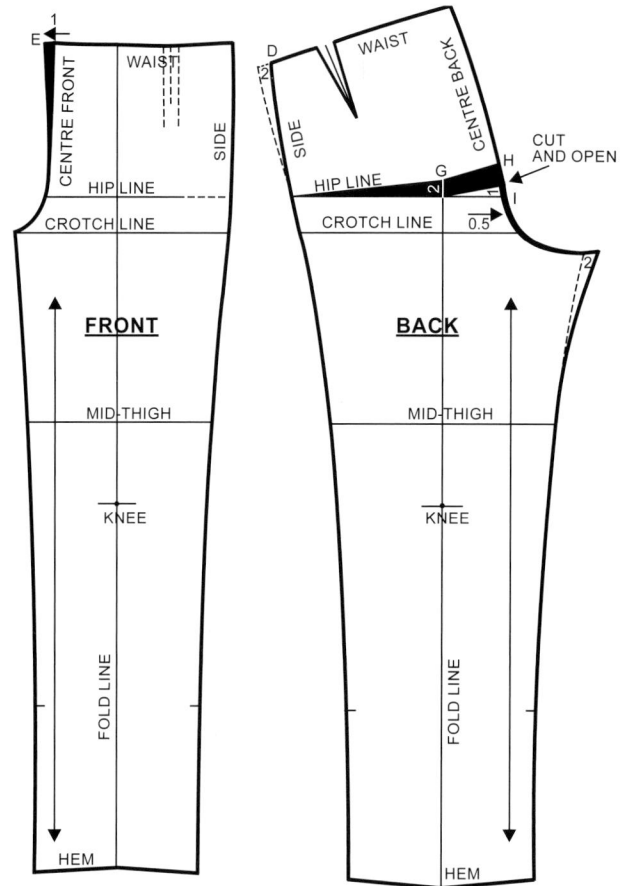

Forward shifted pelvis (sway back)

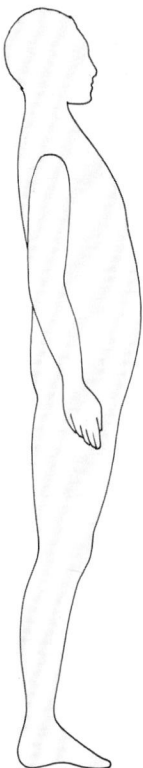

This posture is typical of obese people, whose pelvis is shifted forward in order to balance their weight.

- Point A = add 0.5 cm / 0.20".
- Point B = add 1 cm / 0.39".
- Point C = discard 1 cm / 0.39".
- Point D = add 1 cm / 0.39".
- Point E = add 1 cm / 0.39".
- Point F = overlap by 2 cm / 0.79".
- Point G = add 1 cm / 0.39".
- Point H = overlap by 1.5 cm / 0.59".
- Point I = overlap by 2 cm / 0.79".
- Point L = overlap.
- Point N = decrease by 0.5 cm / 0.20".
- Point O = shift down by 0.5 cm / 0.20".

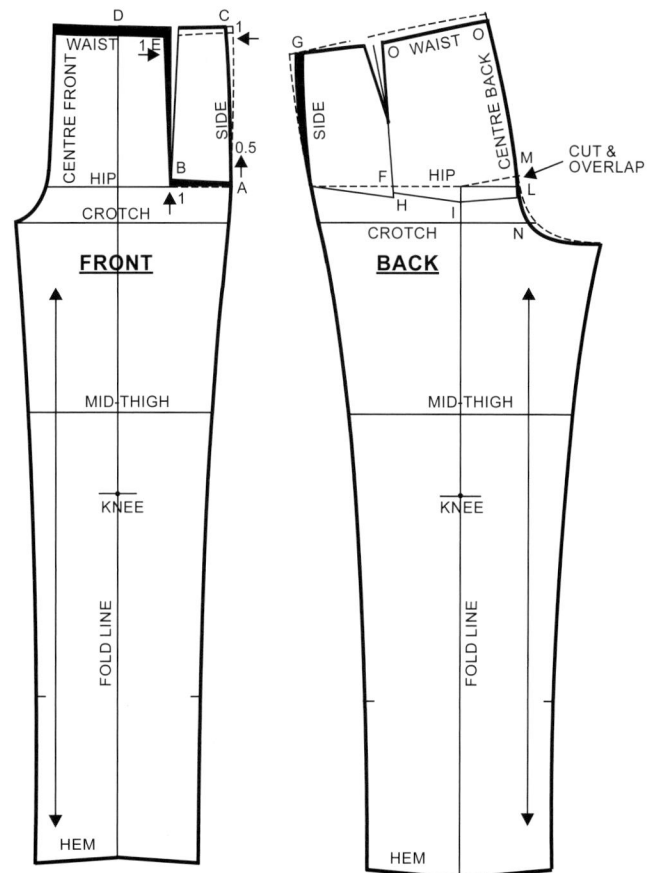

Narrow hips and protruding buttocks

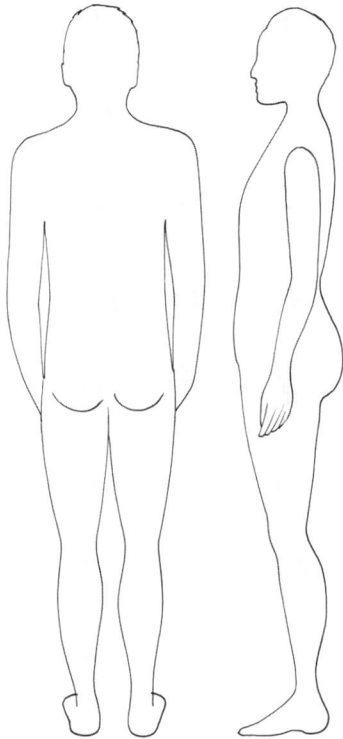

Characteristics
- Hips narrower by 1 cm / 0.39.
- Buttocks protruding by 2 cm / 0.79".

Correction
- Point A = add 1 cm / 0.39".
- Point B = decrease by 1 cm / 0.39".
- Point C = decrease by 2 cm / 0.79".
- Point D = add 2 cm / 0.79".
- Point E = subsequent shifts.
- Point F = add 0.5 cm / 0.20". Increase the point of biforcation by 2 cm / 0.79".

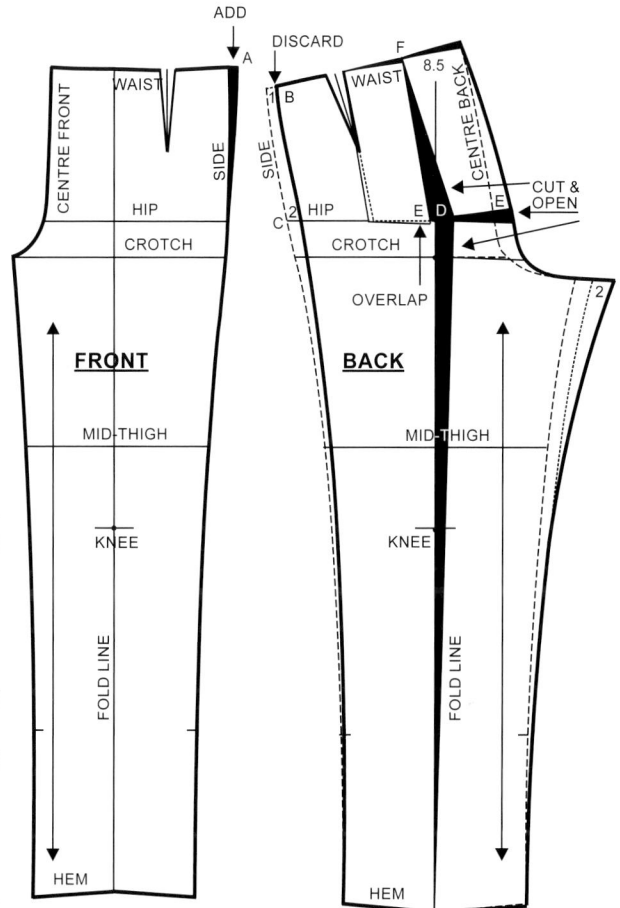

Wide hips and flat buttocks

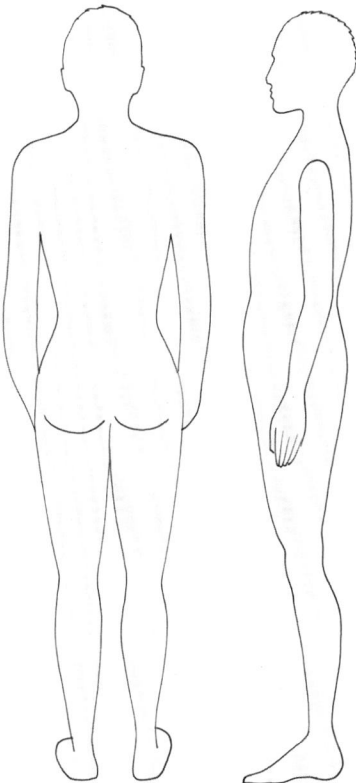

Characteristics
- Hips wider by 1 cm / 0.39".
- Buttocks reduced by 2 cm / 0.79".

Correction
- Point A = decrease by 1 cm / 0.39".
- Point B = add 1 cm / 0.39".
- Point C = add 2 cm / 0.79".
- Point D = add 1 cm / 0.39".
- Point E = overlap by 2 cm / 0.79".
- Point F = overlap.
- Point G = lower by 0.5 cm / 0.20".

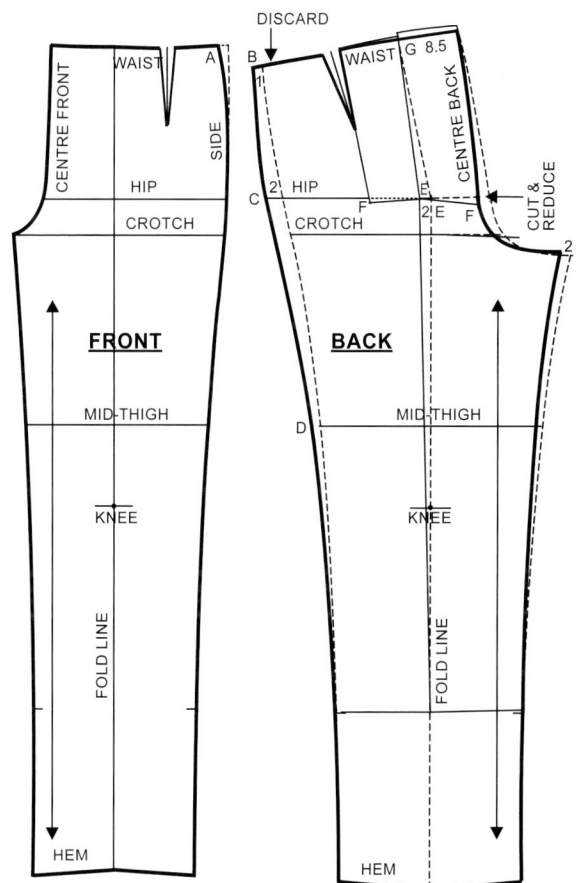

Asymmetrical hips

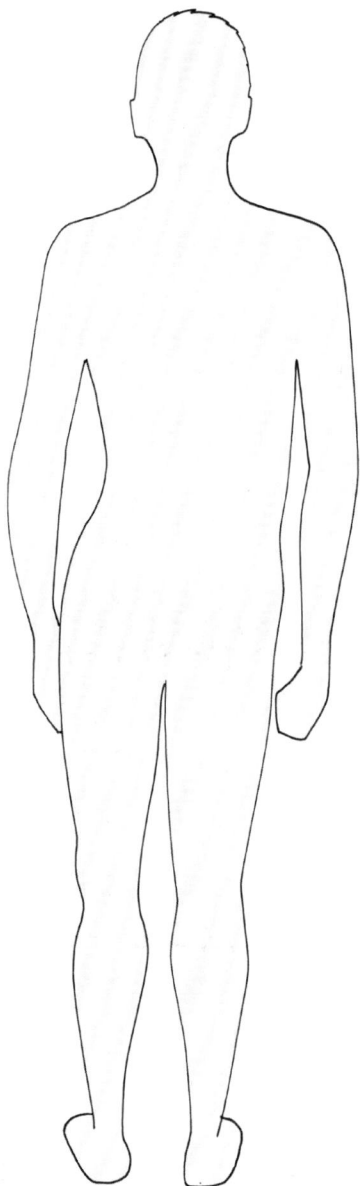

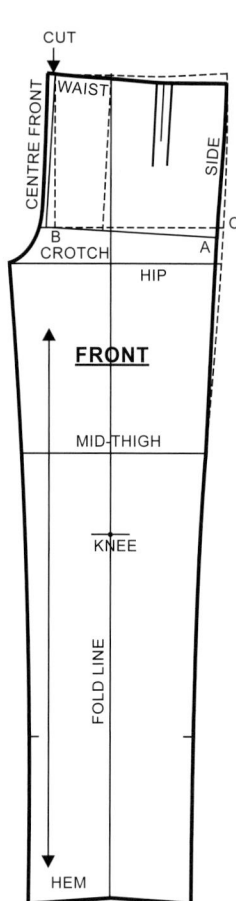

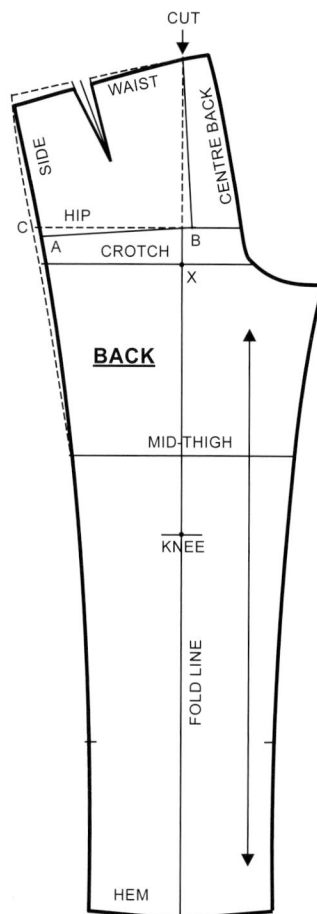

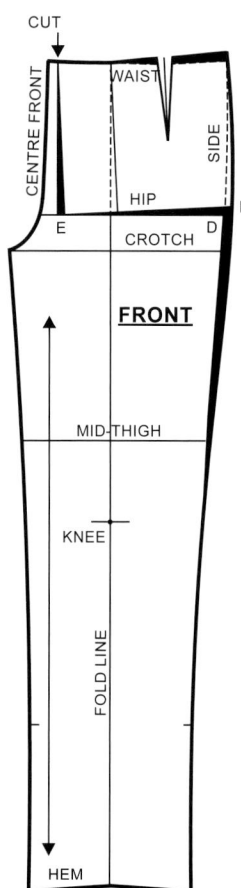

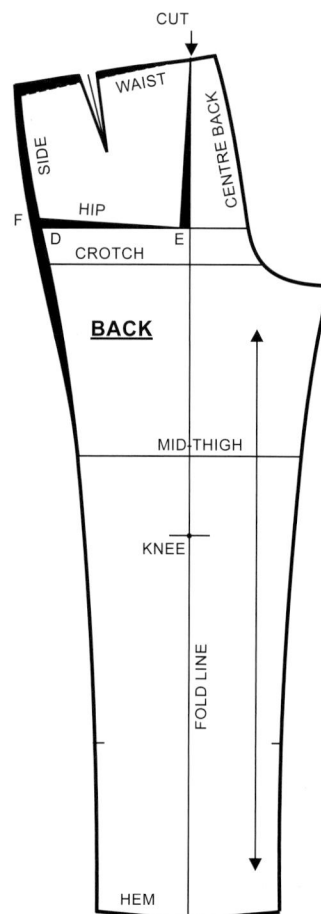

An uneven pelvis results in a high hip and a low hip in equal measure, so that the upper edge must be dropped on the low side and raised on the high side.

Low side
- Point A = overlap by 1 cm / 0.39" on point C.
- Point B = overlap.

High side
- Point D = open by 1 cm / 0.39".
- Point E = subsequent opening.

108

SARTORIAL TROUSER CONSTRUCTION

After drawing and adjusting the pattern as necessary, you can move on to the final assembly or construction phase. The tailoring techniques we will see herein refer to classic trousers. Before you create the final seams, one of the two threads of each basting stitch must be pulled out. Cut the basting of the crotch seam and anywhere else you will add a pattern detail, such as a slant pocket. Before the basting is removed, check that the changes made to the seam allowances are clearly marked. Other bastings (darts, folds, side seams and inner seams) can remain and be used as seam guides. Iron the seam lines that cross one another. In addition, use the ironing ham to iron curved areas and the sleeve ironing board or the padded roll for straight seams. To flatten a seam or dart without over ironing, it helps to hold them down with a wooden clapper until the fabric has cooled.

Below is a potential sequence for trouser construction; however, it is only a suggestion. Construction sequences may vary from one tailor's shop to another.

1) Finish the edges around the perimeter with an overedge seam or bias tape.
2) Sew and iron the darts.
3) Sew along the edges of the pleats (if desired).
4) Sew the slant pockets.
5) Attach the fastening with a placket.
6) Tack the partial lining at knee height.
7) Sew the inner seams.
8) Sew the side seams.
9) Sew the pockets set into the seam.
10) Sew the crotch.
11) Sew the lining.
12) Attach waistband.
13) Attach the fasteners on the waistband.
14) Sew the hem of the trousers.
15) Sew the hem of the lining.
16) Remove the basting and clean.
17) Final ironing of the legs and crotch.
18) Final ironing of the hips.

FINISHING EDGES WITH AN OVEREDGE STITCH

Finishing the seam margins of the front and back is a detail that will reveal the quality of the garment and the refinement of the tailor, along with the final stitching and ironing of darts. If the darts are loose, a seam isn't necessary. All you will need to do is leave the tacking in place until the waistband is added.

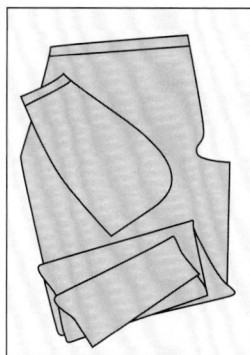

HOW TO SEW AND IRON PLEATS

1) Sew close to the basting, from the widest part to the tip, making the last 4 or 5 stitches on the pleat; shorten the stitches for 2.5 cm / 1" on the wide part and about 1 cm / 0.39" on the point. Leave thread ends of about 10 cm / 3.94" at the bottom.
2) Knot the ends of the thread, inserting a pin in the point to bring the knot as close as possible to the fabric. Cut the thread at 1 cm / 0.39".
3) Remove the tacking and other loose stitches. Iron the pleat flat on both sides to inset the stitches.
4) Place the dart over the ironing ham, reverse side up, pressing it towards the centre front or back. Flatten it with the wooden clapper.
5) Iron the dart from the front of the fabric, protecting it: press it towards the centre front or back with the ironing cloth or by using a protective plate on the iron.

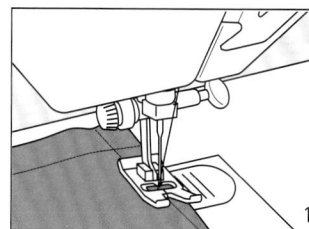

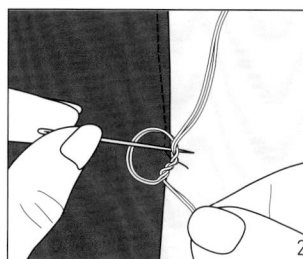

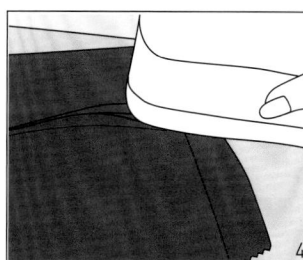

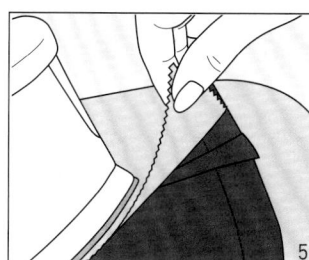

SLANT POCKETS

Slant pockets start from the outer seam at an angle of about 30 degrees and end at the waist. Often seen on classically styled trousers (so often that they are sometimes called 'trouser pockets'), they consist of two pieces: the facing and the pouch with a border. The facing is usually cut from the lining fabric to reduce bulk. Often the pattern relative to the pocket also includes a pocket support, which is an extension of the facing up to the centre front seam. This support holds the pocket in place and keeps the front of the trousers smooth. The finished pocket opening will be slightly longer than the marked position line, so that it can adapt to the curve of the body. The opening must be supported to prevent it from drooping.

SEAM ALLOWANCES
AND MARKS FOR IRONING

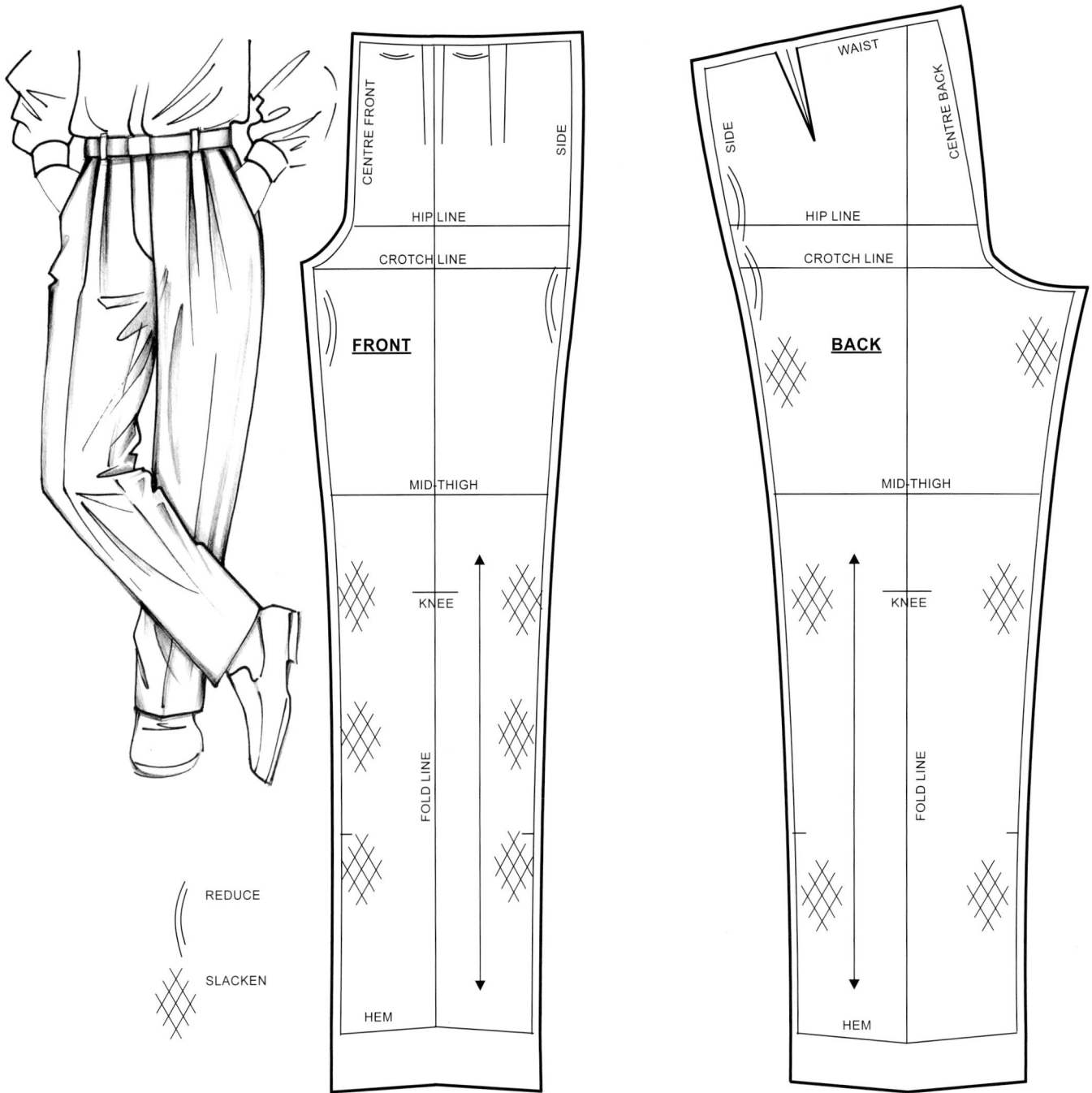

CENTRE FRONT

SIDE

HIP LINE

CROTCH LINE

FRONT

MID-THIGH

KNEE

FOLD LINE

HEM

REDUCE

SLACKEN

WAIST

SIDE

CENTRE BACK

HIP LINE

CROTCH LINE

BACK

MID-THIGH

KNEE

FOLD LINE

HEM

Trouser patterns do not have seam allowances, so they must be added directly onto the fabric (for tailor-made garments) or onto the paper pattern (for industrial tailoring, before sizing).

They must run parallel to the lines of the pattern and they may vary, depending on its different parts, the garment type, the fabric, and the processes that will be used.

In general, seam allowances are marked as such:
- Waist 1.3 cm / 0.51".

- Inner leg = 1.3 cm / 0.51".
- Outer leg and hip = 1.7-2.5 cm / 0.67-1".
- Crotch = 1.3 cm / 0.51".
- Fly for zip = 2-2.5 cm / 0.79-1".
- Hem = 2.5-6 cm / 1-2.36" or as desired.
- Centre back = 2.5-3.5 cm / 1-1.38" for potential changes.

The figure also shows all the instructions on how to iron the fabric and give it the right shape.

Ironing, as it pertains to the work of a tailor, is a fairly complex process, but one that all professional tailor should know. The iron is used to shape the fabric, creating indestructible shapes and preventing the design of the fabric from suffering. The pattern on the previous page shows the conventional markings that serve as a guide for where to iron.

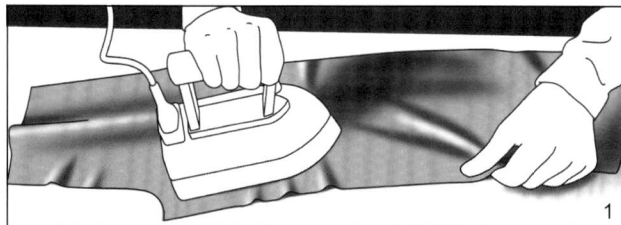

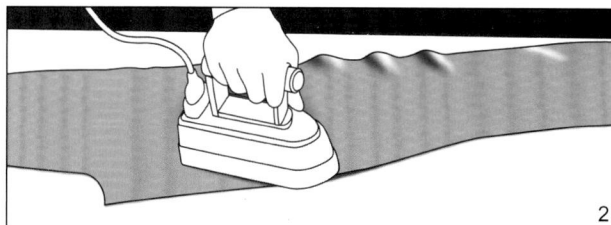

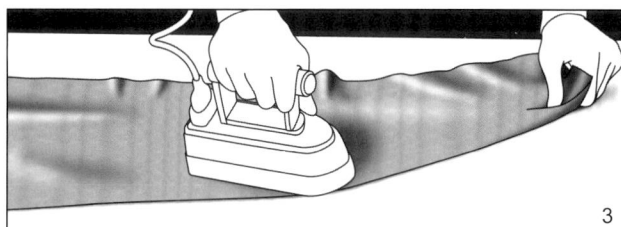

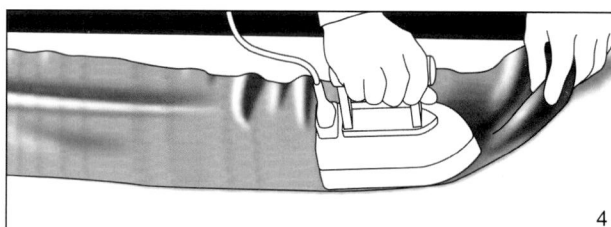

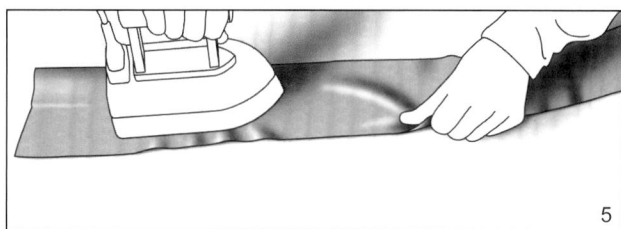

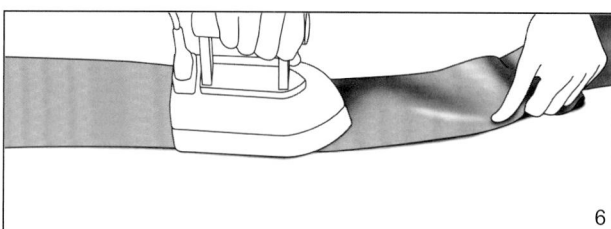

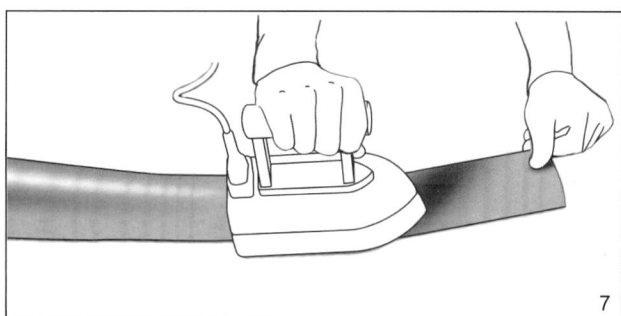

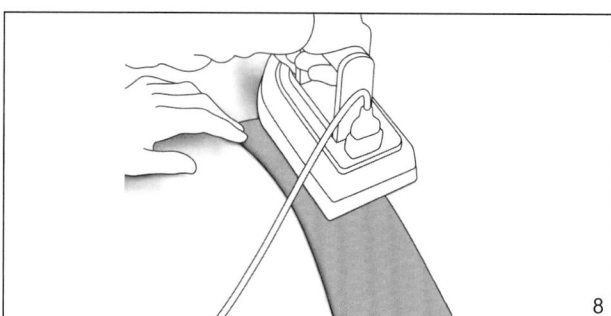

FRONT

1) Place the iron on the inner side of the front while the left hand, converging, prepares to slacken the knee of the garment.
2) Bring the iron towards the outside, forcing it a bit, as the left hand pulls the fabric away, moving it towards the side to facilitate the effort.
3) Continue with the iron towards the lower edge, while the left hand, forcing it with the thumb, determines how much fabric is lifted off the workbench.
4) Continue with the iron towards the lower edge to completely relax the part. The left hand should always determine how and where the fabric is shifted. Repeat on the hip.

5) With the front folded, proceed with the iron from above to accentuate the effects. Start with a slight indentation, while the left hand prepares to pull at the knee.
6) Continue along the edge of the front from the knee to the lower edge, continuously forcing the fabric a bit.
7) Move the iron towards the lower edge, continuing to force the fabric while controlling it with the left hand.
8) Once you reach the lower edge, the left hand still contains the effect, creating the final stretching and settling of the two parts with the iron.

IRONING TECHNIQUES 2

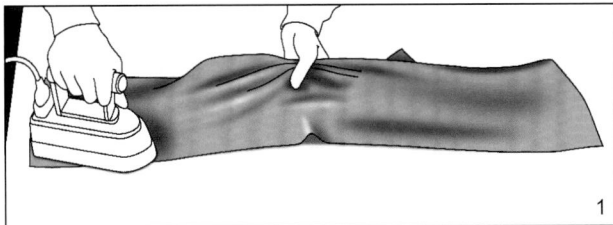

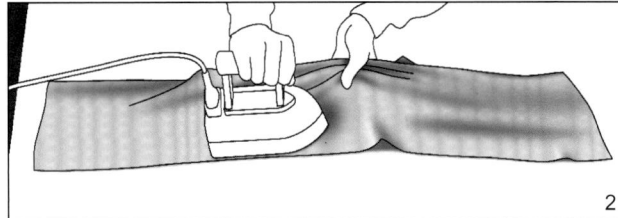

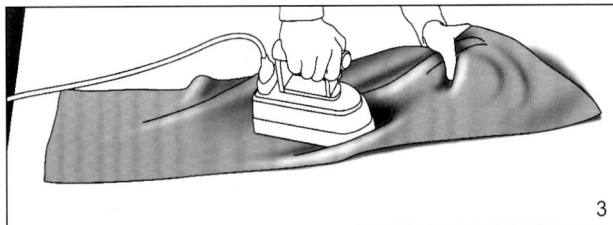

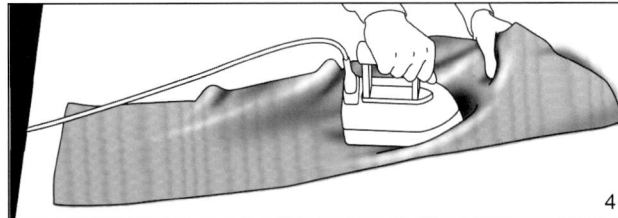

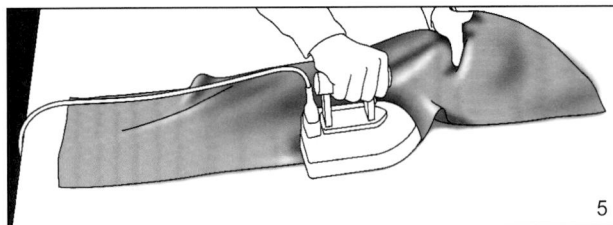

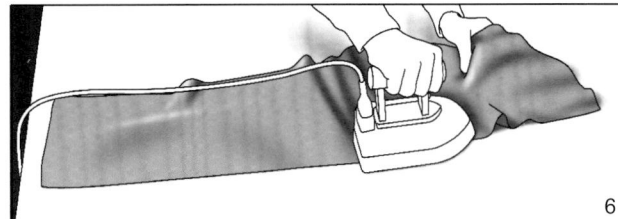

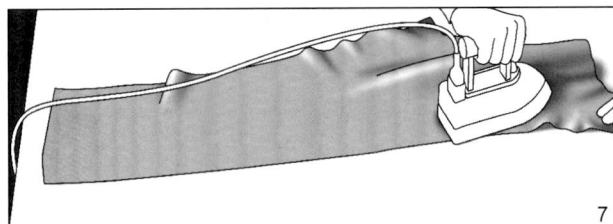

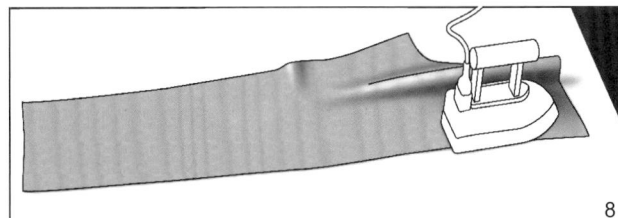

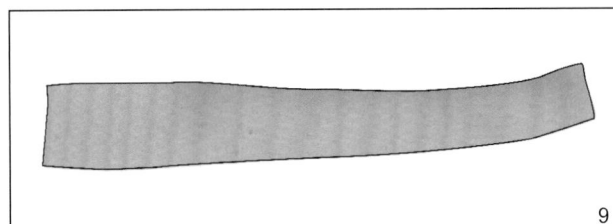

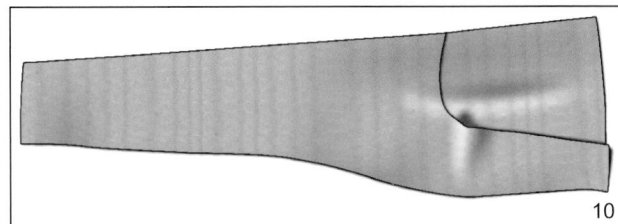

BACK

1) Place the iron on the lower side of the hip and use your left hand to hold the fabric taught at the calf, so that it slackens at the ankle.

2) Continue with the iron up to the calf line, as you move the left hand further up, exerting pressure on the fabric to loosen the knee.

3) Having reached the knee with the iron, rotate it, extend the tip towards the hip and push firmly above the knee. As you do, use the left hand to control the work at the buttocks.

4) Keeping the left hand on the buttock point, proceed with the iron toward the crotch level, at about 10 cm / 3.94"), the area most subject to stretching.

5) After the lower part of the hip has been worked, the iron has reached the ideal position from which to complete the slackening of the groin.

6) At this point, guided by the left hand, which firmly pulls the fabric, the iron is pushed upwards to stretch out and pass over the crotch level.

7) Iron upwards to return, while using the left hand to make the fabric come together appropriately. Check slackened fabric on the inner side.

8) Remove the iron and let rest to set the fabric.

9-10) Repeat the process on the inside, as you did for the front, slightly accentuating the effect. Slacken the upper portion of the groin too.

LOW-RISE TROUSERS

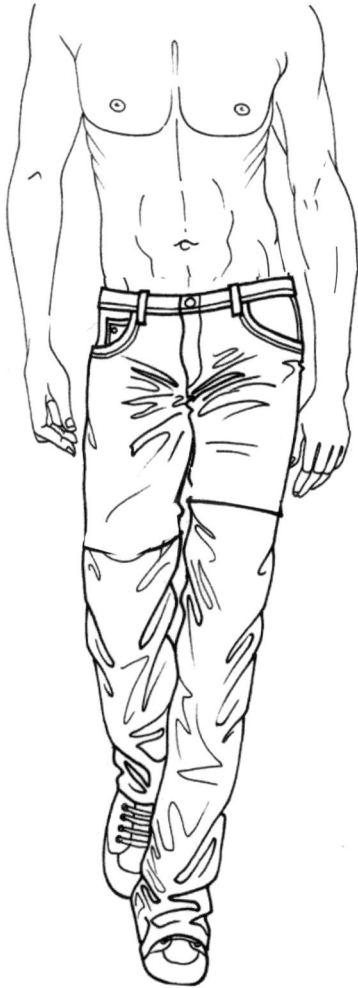

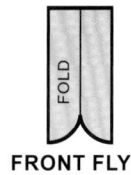

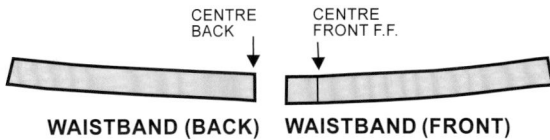

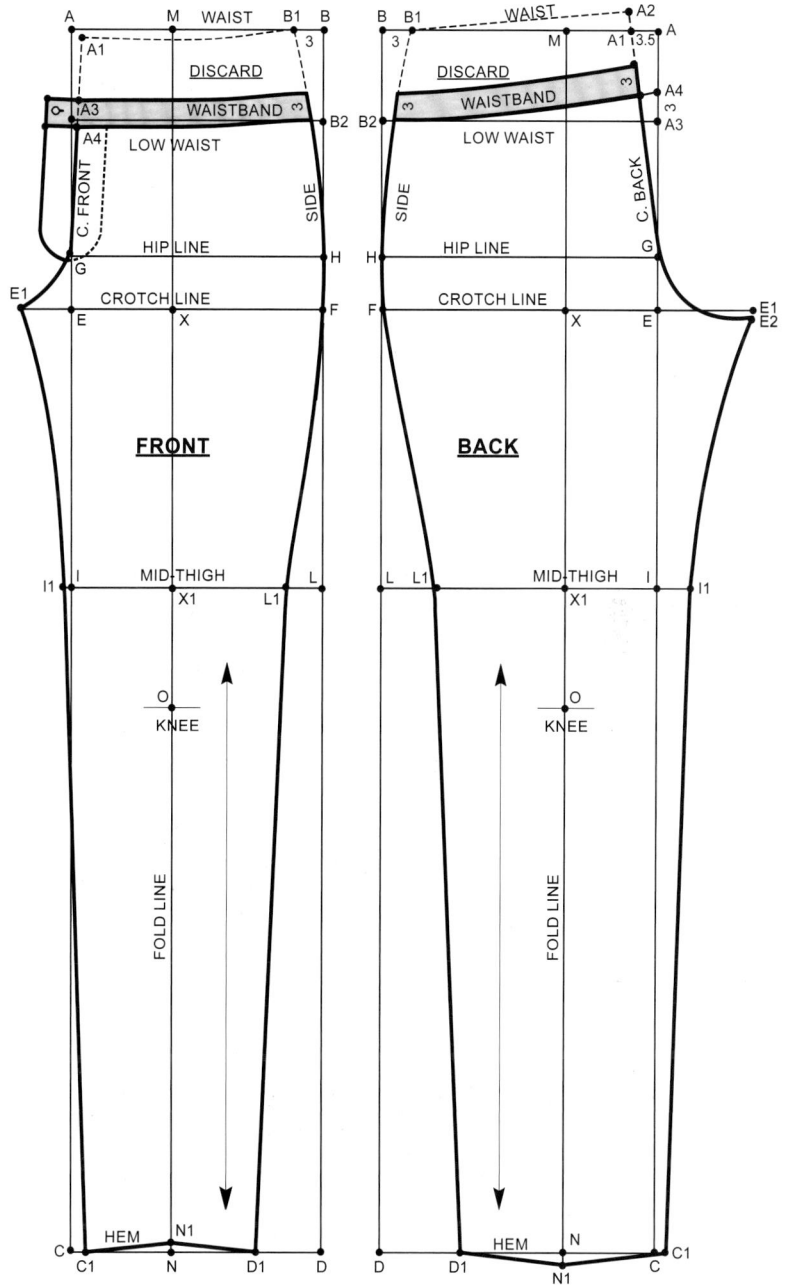

FRONT FLY

WAISTBAND (BACK)   **WAISTBAND (FRONT)**

CENTRE BACK   CENTRE FRONT F.F.

FRONT

BACK

Measurements

- Hip circumference = 96 cm / 37.80" + ease 2-4 cm / 0.79-1.57".
- Waist circumference = 88 cm / 34.65" + ease 1-2 cm / 0.39-0.79".
- Waist to hip = 20 cm / 7.87".
- Crotch depth = 24 cm / 9.45".
- Trouser length = 105 cm / 41.34" (or as desired).
- Upper thigh circ. (e.g.: 50 cm / 19.69").

Procedure

- Draw the base block for the trousers without darts.
- Lower the waistline of the front and back A-A3 by 5-8 cm / 2-3.15" or as desired, depending on the pattern, and mark the line.

- Draw the low-rise waistline A3-B2 at the front and back.
- Raise the rear centre A3-A4 by 1.5 cm / 0.59" + 1.5 cm / 0.59" for the proper drape.
- Lower A3-A4 at the front by 0.5 cm / 0.20".
- Draw the waistband parallel to the waistline, in the height desired (e.g: 3 cm / 1.18").
- Take up the parts of the waistline at the front and back and extend the front waistline by 3 cm / 1.18" for the button.

HIGH-RISE TROUSERS

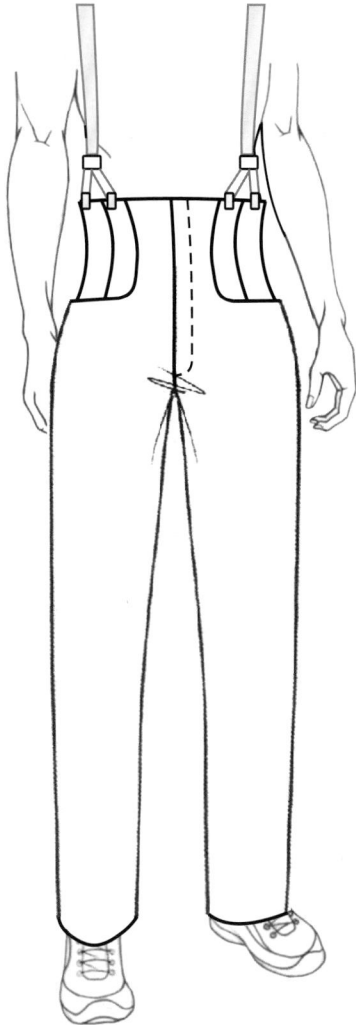

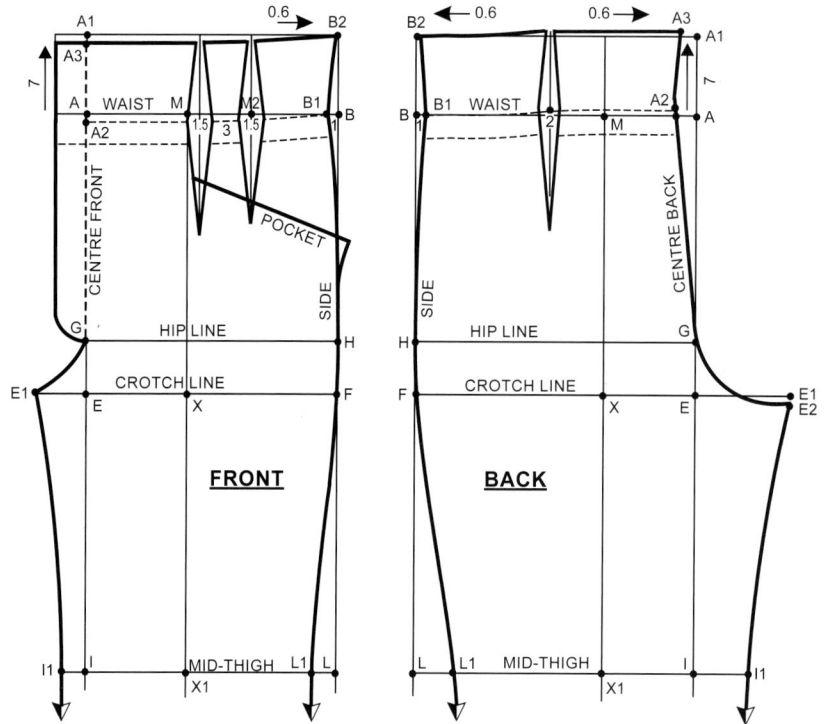

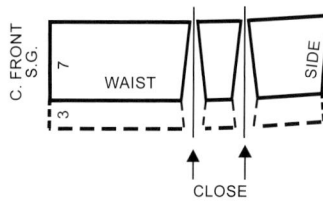

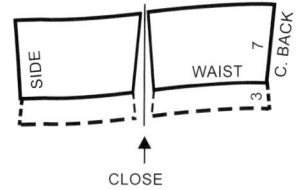

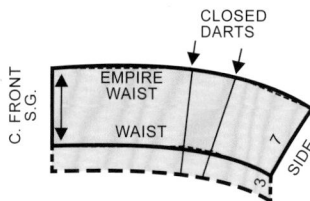

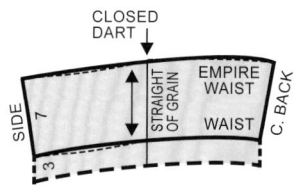

FRONT

BACK

FRONT FLY

INNER WAISTBAND LINING

Measurements
- Hip circumference = 96 cm / 37.80" + ease 2-4 cm / 0.79-1.57".
- Waist circumference = 88 cm / 34.65" + ease 1-2 cm / 0.39-0.79".
- Waist to hip = 20 cm / 7.87".
- Crotch depth = 24 cm / 9.45".
- Trouser length = 105 cm / 41.34" (or as desired).

Procedure
- Draw the base block of the trousers with darts.
- Raise the front and back waistline A-A1 by 5-7 cm / 2-2.76" or as desired, according to the pattern, and mark point A3.

- Reduce the rise of the centre A1-A2 to 0.5 cm / 0.20".
- Draw the front and back upper waistline A3-B2, adding 1.2 cm / 0.47" at the back and 0.6 cm / 0.24" at the front (or with custom measurements).
- Extend the centre lines of the darts and create double darts (mirror the darts in the opposite direction) at the front and back.
- Take up the waistline extension including 3 cm / 1.13" below the waistline, to create the internal facing.
- Close the darts and smoothly trace the outline.

114

POCKETS

No matter the garment, pockets are considered important style details: they can be practical or simply decorative. It's a good idea to make them with the utmost care, as they will give the garment a tailored look.

If they serve a practical purpose, they must be positioned at the right height relative to the hands and be simple in their construction. When they are meant to define the look and style of a garment, their shape, position and finishing should make them attractive and decorative.

To make them, it is advisable to use a strong, firm fabric that does not fray, such as silesia, a special cotton lining with a glossy finish. Alternatively, a diagonal weave fabric in cotton or heavyweight materials, or another strong lining cloth can be used. The pocket selected will depend on the type of garment, its style and the fabric used. In particular, it's best to sew patch pockets before assembling the other parts of the garment.

Pocket types

There are four general kinds of pockets: patch pockets, set-in pockets, slant pockets, and besom pockets.

Patch pockets are made of fabric pieces that are sewn onto the face of the garments.

Set-in pockets are concealed, blending in with the side seam of the trousers (i.e., they are 'set into' the seam).

Slant pockets are openings made diagonally from the waist to the sides of the trousers.

Besom pockets are much like a slit in the fabric; they are usually finished and trimmed by a folded fabric border (a welt or jet), and can be completed with a flap.

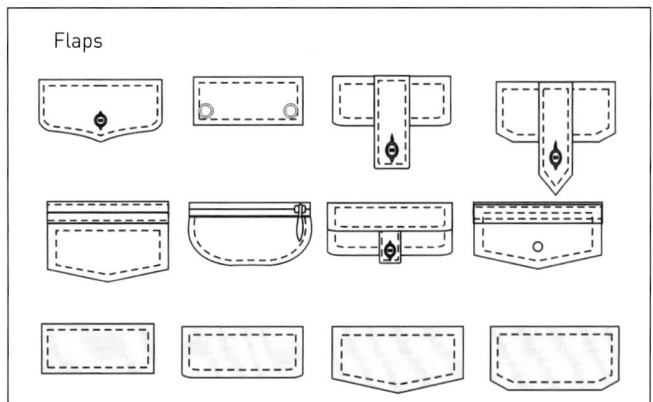

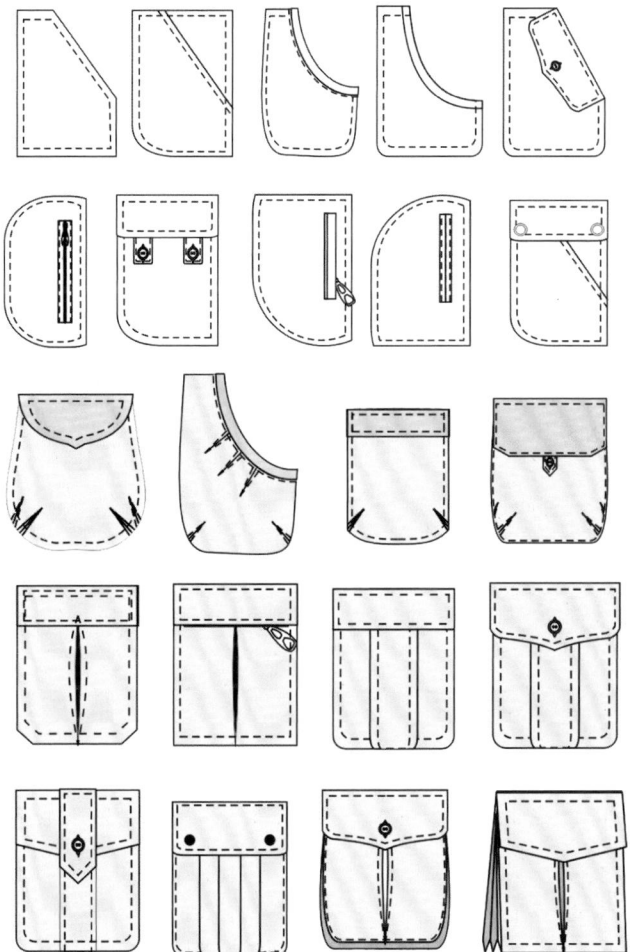

Flaps

POCKET CONSTRUCTION

Patch pocket

1) Trim the upper edge of the pocket and fold the hem on the outside. Pull the edges of the hem 3 mm (0.12") beyond the pocket, so that the seams tend inwards. Stitch along the seam allowance line indicated by the pattern, cut the corners diagonally and trim the allowances.

2) Turn the hem to the front of the fabric, using a suitable tool to push out the corners. Iron below the seam allowances on the sides and lower edge.

3) Fold the edges diagonally in relation to the lower corners so that the folds line up. Iron the diagonal folds, then trim the seam allowances to 5 mm / 0.20".

4) Iron the seam allowances again so that two 45-degree angles are formed; cut away the remaining seam allowances. Stitch along the edges or topstitch.

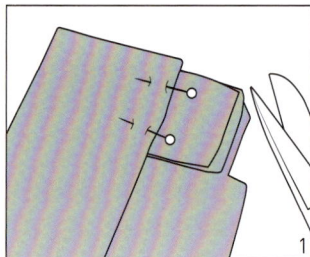

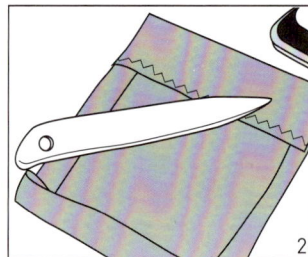

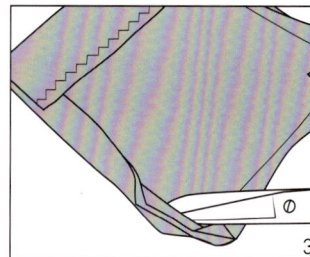

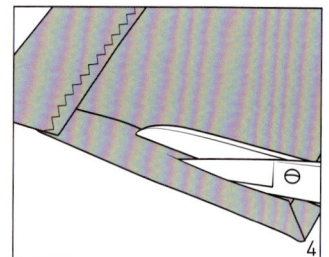

Set-in pocket

1) Sew a piece of tape on the reverse side of the trousers, in the edge of the pocket extension on the front of the garment. Sew the pockets onto the front and back extensions, trim the edges to 5 mm (0.20"), then sew them using a zig-zag stitch. Iron them in the direction of the pockets.

2) Pin the front to the back and close the pocket opening with basting. Sew the pocket and garment above and below the pocket opening, using short reinforcement stitches and a backstitch at the opening.

3) Create a seam around the pocket, finishing laterally. Make two cuts above and below the extension at the back of the garment only, so that the seam can be opened with the iron.

4) Open the seam of the garment above and below the two pocket cuts and iron the pocket towards the front of the garment. Trim the cut edges of the pocket together and remove the basting stitches.

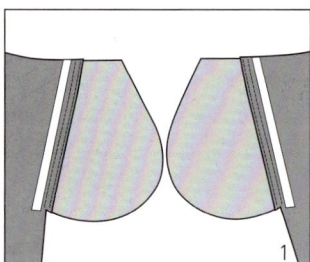

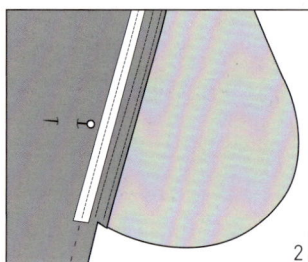

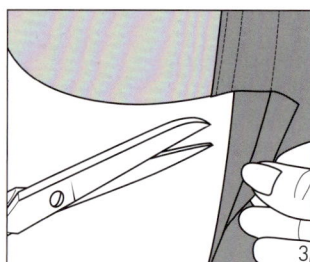

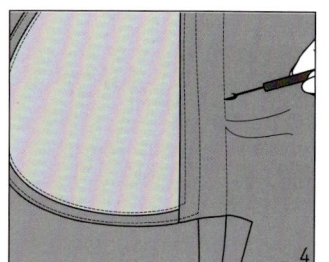

Welt (jetted) pocket

Before starting, it is important to carefully check the position of the pocket and double-check it after you've cut the opening. The instructions on this page create 12.5 cm / 4.92" pockets. For double-welt pockets, cut the two strips of fabric as long as the width of the finished pocket + 4 cm / 1.57", with a height of 2.5 cm / 1". For folded-hem pockets, cut the border as wide as the pocket width by adding 1 cm / 0.39" and calculate a height equal to twice the finished height plus 2.5 cm / 1".

Procedure

1) Reinforce the back of the pocket with a piece of fusible tape cut with pinking shears. Prior to application, remove all but one of the loose stitches in the pocket.
2) Using chalk and a ruler, mark the position of the pocket on the front face of the trouser fabric, carrying over the centre line and the two end lines. Alternatively, create basting.
3) Cut two strips 2.5 cm / 1" high and 16 cm / 6.30" long on the straight of grain.
4) For each pocket, make two 16 x 19 cm / 6.30-7.48" lining rectangles.
5) Prepare a strip of fabric for each pocket 5 cm / 2" high and 16 cm / 6.30" long: this piece will serve as an internal support. Place the strip on the 'right' side of one of the lining pieces, aligning the upper edges. Baste 5 mm (0.20") from the upper edge and sew the lower edge to the lining with a medium-width zig-zag seam.
6) Iron the two strips several times with steam, while holding them taut to remove the elasticity from the fabric and eliminate all creases.
7) Fold the strips lengthwise, wrong side to wrong side, and iron them. Machine baste 5 mm (0.20") from the fold, to be used as a guide. Trim the margins to 5 mm (0.20") from the seam.
8) Place the two borders on the front with the cut edges touching, along the centre line of the pocket. The seams of the borders must be 1 cm / 0.39" above and below this line. Affix the borders with pins and mark (on the borders) the two lines at the ends of the opening.
9) Sew the seams on the 'right' side of the fabric, along the two bastings, using a 1.5 cm / 0.59" long stitch. Check the seam on the 'wrong' side and correct it in case of flaws. Iron before cutting the opening.

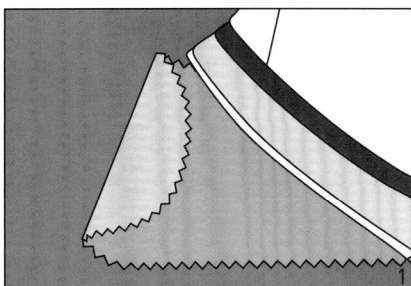

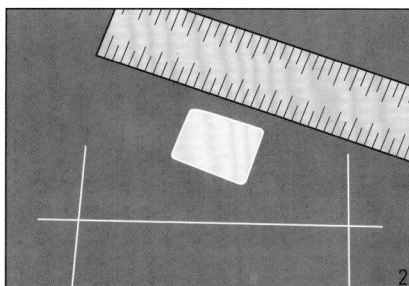

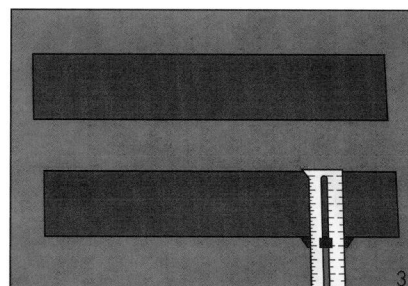

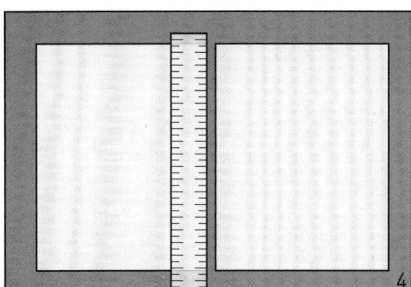

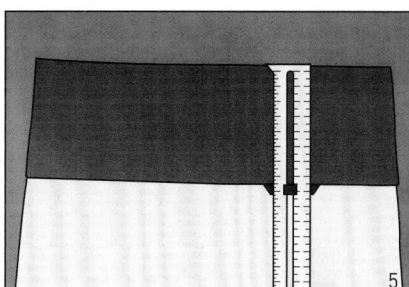

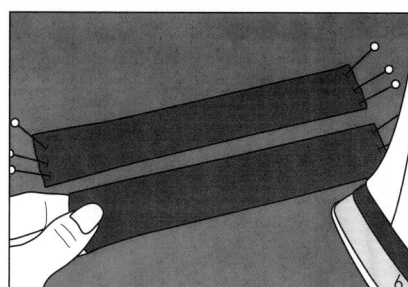

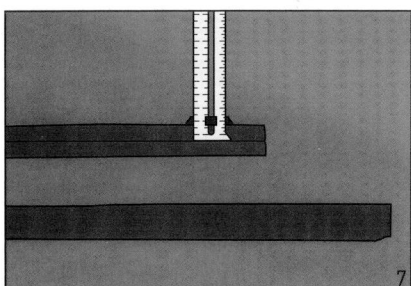

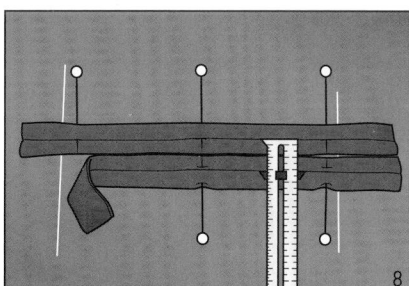

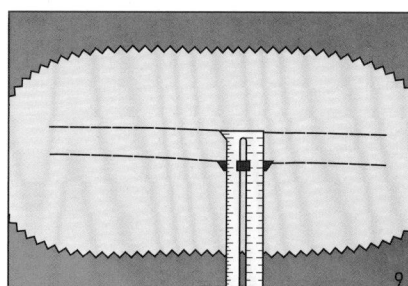

10) Cut the pocket opening from the reverse side and stop 1 cm / 0.39" from each end without cutting the welts. Then make two diagonal cuts up to the last stitch of the two seams. It's best to apply anti-fraying liquid to the edges if using a loosely woven or thin fabric.

11) Fold the welts inward, arranging them smoothly on the opening so that they are straight and even. Baste the two edges together diagonally by hand, then iron.

Applying the lining

12) Cut the lining according to the pattern and place it over the two welts, aligning its edge with the lower edge of the pocket.

13) Sew along the previous seam with the lining side down. Then fold the lining downward and iron.

14) For the pocket on the jacket, sew the lining/support piece against the welt and following the previous seam. The lower edges of the lining are not even.

15) Fold the garment to cover the welts and machine baste the base of the triangles. Check the ends on the 'right' side to see if the seam is straight and the corners are well-affixed.

16) Sew the two lining pieces together with a seam allowance of 1.5 cm / 0.59"; create the seam on the triangles, passing over them several times for added reinforcement, and round off the bottom corners. Iron on and cut out the outer edges of the lining with pinking shears.

17) Sew in the groove of the upper welt, staying on the 'right' face of the garment and using the presser foot to hinge and attach the lining to the welts. Be sure to sew through all the layers.

18) Iron the pocket lining to flatten it.

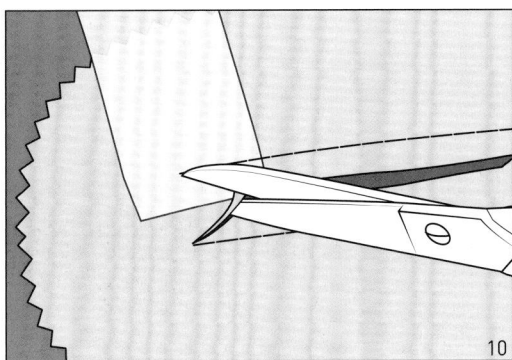

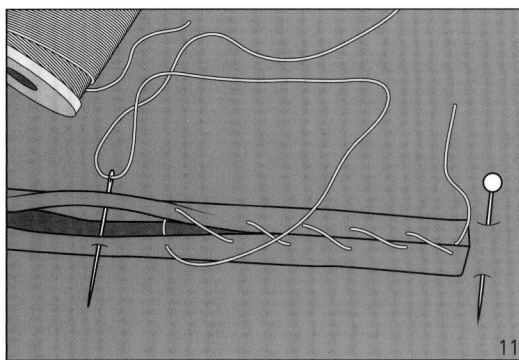

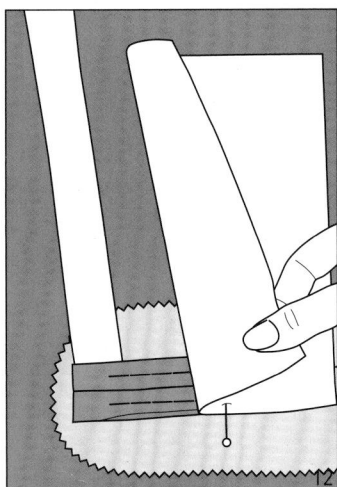

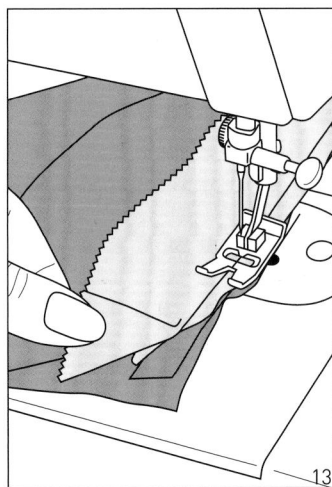

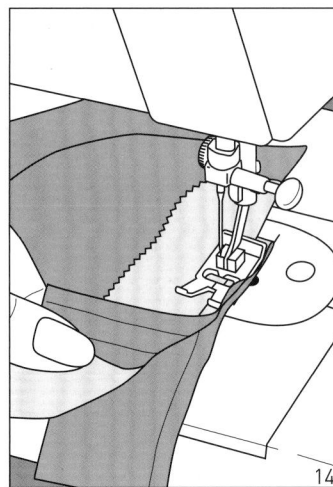

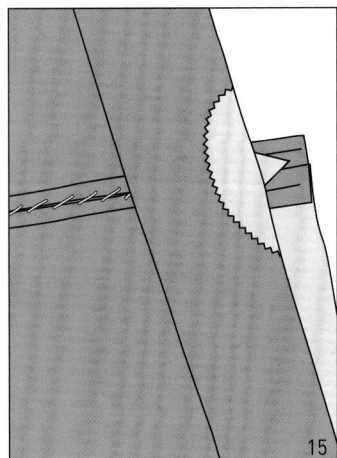

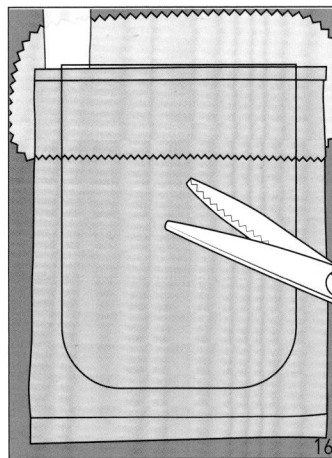

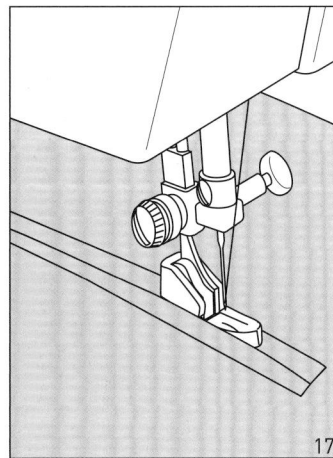

Slant pockets

Without added support

1) Cut a piece of tape or ribbon as long as the pocket opening. Use the front of the pattern as a guide.

2) Place the pocket facing on the front of the trousers, right sides together, aligning the opening. Centre the tape on the seam line, on the 'wrong' side of the front, and pin it.

3) Sew at 1.5 cm / 0.59", with the ribbon upwards and the lining on the feed dog. Shift the seam allowances.

4) Iron the seam allowances towards the pocket facing and fold and flatten them 3 mm / 0.12" from the seam.

5) Fold the facing inwards. Steam iron, flattening the edge with the wooden clapper. Topstitch the edge to finish it.

6) Place the pocket with the strip on the ironing ham, with the 'wrong' side facing upwards. Place the front over it, aligning the marks and seams, pin the side and waist and close the opening with hand basting.

7) Pin the pocket facing to the pocket with the strip and sew around the outer seam allowance. Finish the seam allowance. Finally, use the sewing machine to baste the pocket at the waist and hip.

With additional support

8) Follow points 1 to 6 above, then pin the pocket facing to the pocket with the strip and sew all around. On the overlap side of the placket, trim the support along the centre-front line, but be careful not to trim it on the side that will be overlapped.

9) Use a sewing machine to baste the edges of the pocket at the waist and hip about 1 cm / 0.39" from the centre-front line. The front edge of the support will be take up in the seam when the zip is attached and will thus remain in place.

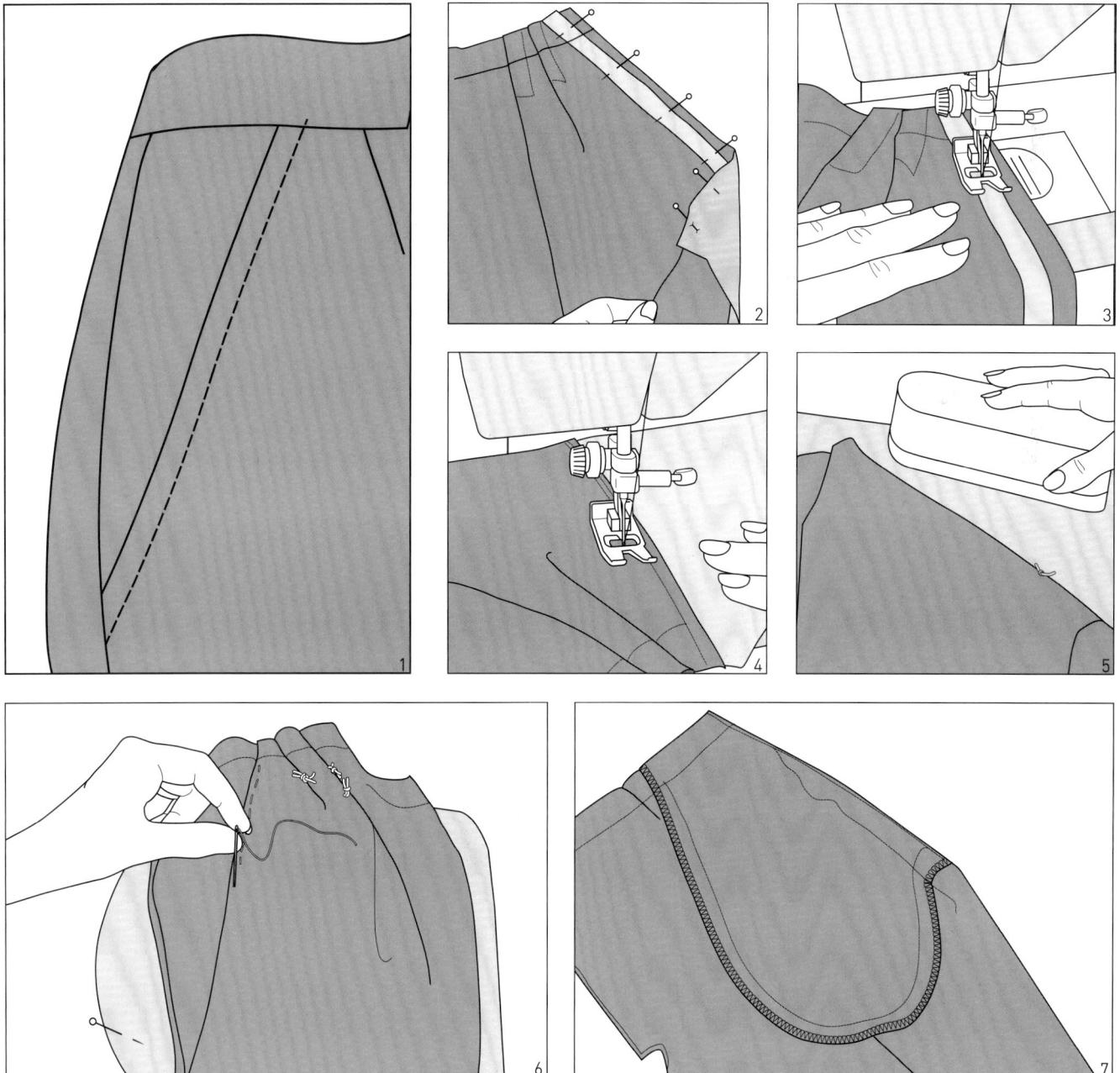

SEAMS: INNER, OUTER AND THE CROTCH

1) Sew the seams on the inner and outer leg with a normal stitch length. Trim the seam allowances to 1.5 cm / 0.59" and finish them. Remove the basting and iron the seams. Trim the seam allowance of the waist to 1.5 cm / 0.59".

2) Pin or baste the crotch seam. Cut a piece of tape or lining selvedge as long as the seam, centre it on the seam and sew from the centre back, as close as possible to the base of the opening.

3) Sew the curve of the crotch again, close to the previous seam. Trim the seam allowance of the curve to 1 cm / 0.39" and trim the margins. Open the centre back seam with the iron, above the curve of the crotch.

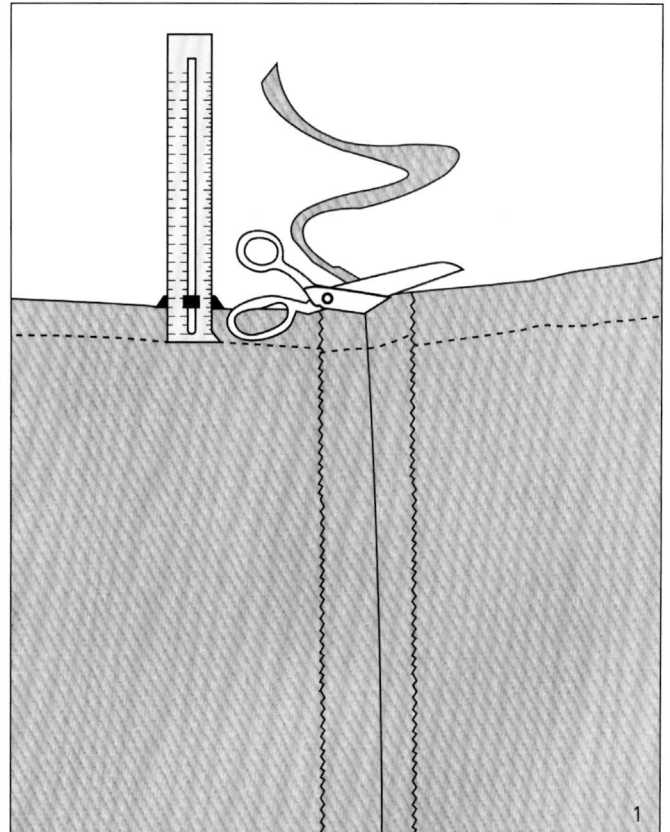

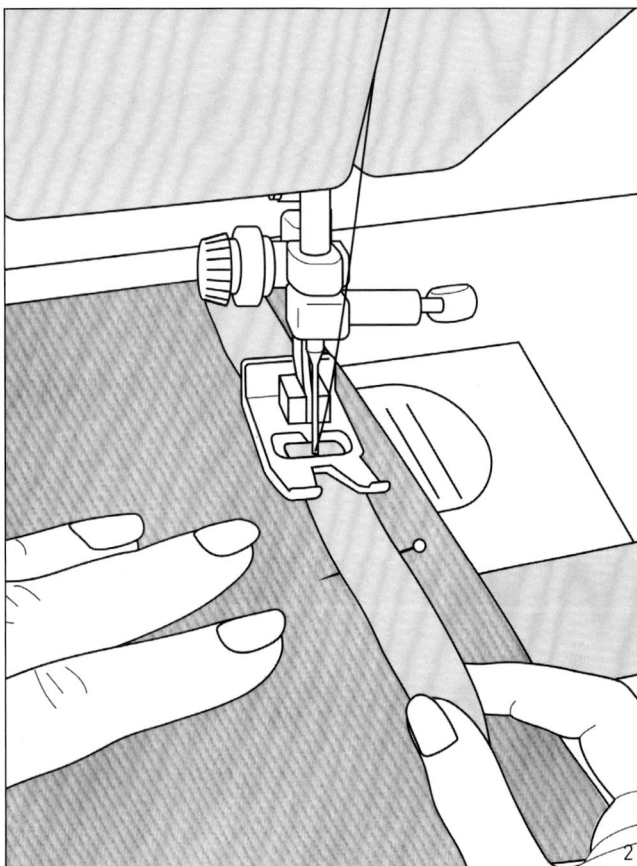

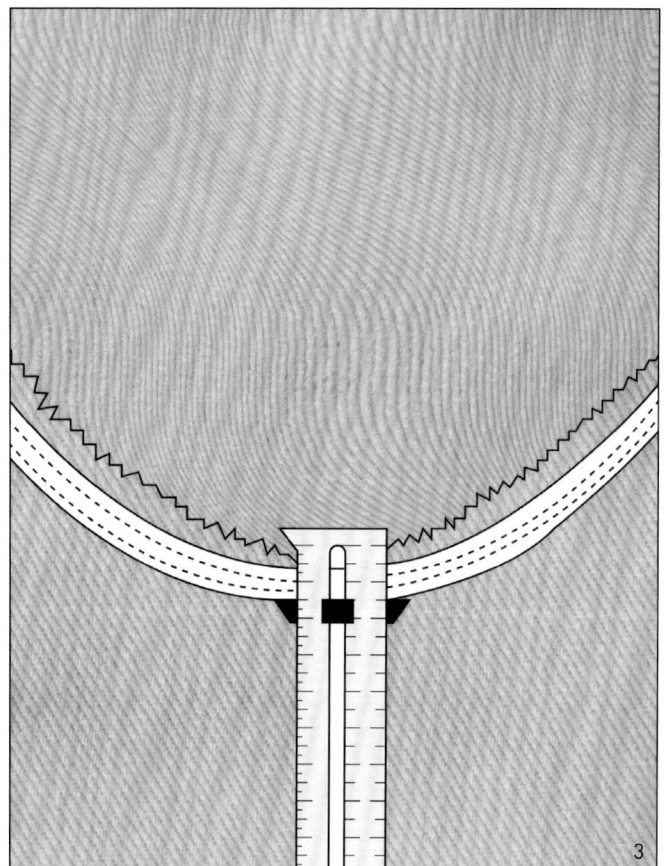

HOW TO LINE TROUSERS

Cut the lining material using the trouser pattern, leaving seam allowances of 1.5 cm / 0.59". Before cutting the lining, fold the pattern along the hem line. The lower cut edge of the lining must correspond to the hem line of the trousers. If the pattern has slant pockets, pin the pocket with the strip of fabric to the front piece, aligning the line marked for the pocket with the diagonal line of the opening. Use this piece for the front of the lining. If the lining has pockets inserted in the side seam, remove the pocket extension. If the garment has a front opening with a fly, eliminate the fly, leaving 1.5 cm / 0.59" of seam allowance. If the pattern has deep pleats at the waist, you can reduce the width by cutting the pattern along the fold and overlapping it, thereby creating a smaller pleat. The lining can be sewn with a traditional sewing machine or with an overlocker. It is only attached to the trousers at the waist, so it can be shifted out of the way when ironing the trousers.

Lining trousers that have a fly

1) Cut the lining, mark the darts, creases and the base of the opening. 'Right' sides together, align the lines of the darts and pleats on the waistband; fold them in the opposite direction of the trouser lines.

2) Baste the darts and creases on the waistband. Iron the darts on the top only.

3) Fold and iron on the wrong side, from the upper edge down to 2.5 cm / 1" below the marking at the base of the opening. Fold down the cut edge to align it with the dart and iron. Sew along the edges of the second dart. Make a small cut below the seam.

4) Sew the lateral, inside and crotch seams in a normal stitch length; the opening should be slightly longer than that of the trousers. Trim the seam allowances and open the seam with the iron.

5) Sew the curve of the crotch once more over the previous seam; trim the curve. Finish the edges and iron.

6) Stuff the lining into the trousers, wrong sides together, and pin it to the seams. Let the pleats go in order to align the edge of the lining with that of the zip, then re-stitch them. Baste the waistline. Hem the lining after having hemmed the trousers.

Lining the knee in unlined trousers

1) Mark the front of the paper pattern 12.5 cm / 4.92" above and below the knee line; use the pattern as a guide to cut the lining following the contour of the trousers in the knee area. Finish the lining with multiple zig-zag stitching.

2) Place the lining on the 'wrong side' of the trousers in front, on the knee area. Baste it on the lateral and inside seams. It is incorporated into the leg seams during construction and remains free at the top and bottom.

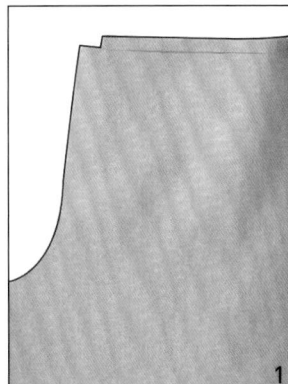

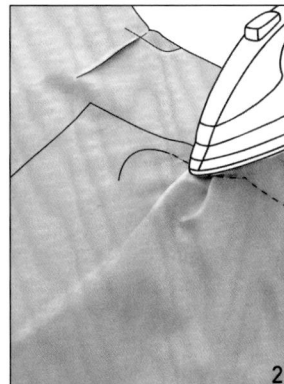

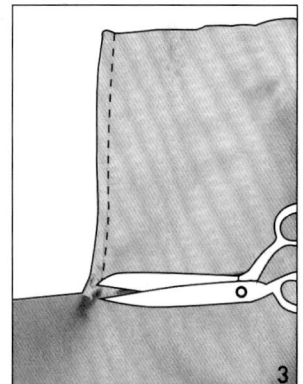

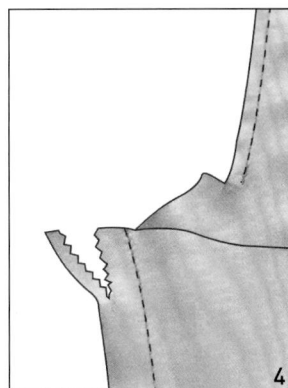

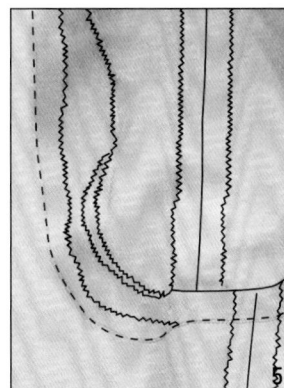

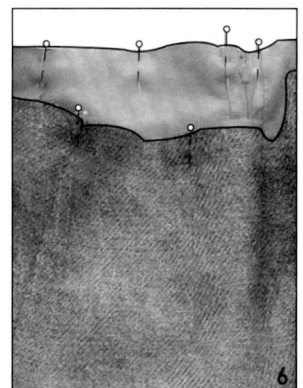

FLY FASTENINGS AND FINISHES

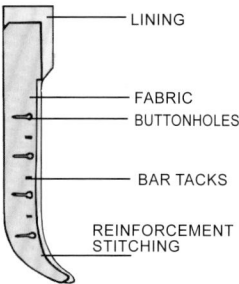

LINING

FABRIC
BUTTONHOLES

BAR TACKS

REINFORCEMENT
STITCHING

BUTTONHOLE FLY

PROCEDURE FOR A BUTTON FLY

1. Join the lining to the fabric with: flat felled seams, visible stitching with the lining inside-out or with direct reinforced stitching.
2. Turn over and iron the lining with an iron using the steam function.
3. Create the eyelets on the fly (or tab) using a sewing machine.
4. Reinforcement seam with edging.
5. Overcast the edges. 6. Tape for fastenings. 7. Turn inside out. 8. Sew button fly to the garment. 10. Sew the bar tacks. 11. Reinforcement stitching.

Procedure for the button fly

1. Overcast and corresponding section of the forequarter. 2. Join the lining at the flap, turning and ironing. 3-4. Sew the fly to the trousers. 5. Add buttons. 6. Close the end of the waistband. 7. Apply lining with the end closure at the waistband. 8. Turn the waistband end over. 9. Turn the fly lining and waistband edge over. 10. Close the lining and button fastening.

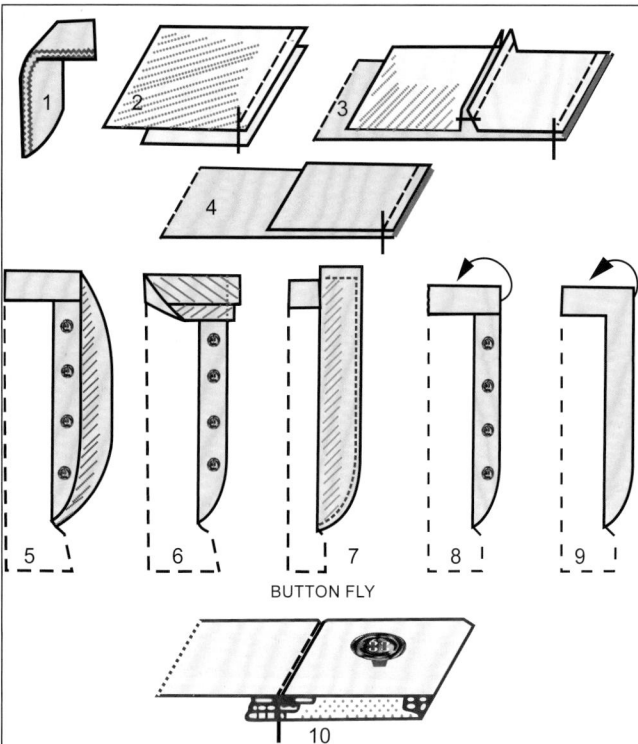

BUTTON FLY

Zip fly

Having completed the fly with overlap from left to right, place it on a zip in the right length, i.e. on average 18-23 cm / 7.09-9.06" and in any case 2.5-5 cm / 1-2" longer than the finished opening. The zip must be closed and face down on the facing of the side to be overlapped, with the tape on the centre front and the bottom stop 3 mm (0.12") above the base of the opening.

Application: A) Pin the outer zip tape to the facing and, using the presser foot for zips, sew it to the facing only. B) Fold the facing over on the side that will be overlapped and machine baste close to the fold. C) Align all the centre-front marks on the upper edge and pin them. Also pin the other side of the zip to the overlap facing only, on the reverse side. Sew the zip while keeping the facing shifted away from the trousers. D) Create a seam on the front of the trousers at 3 cm / 1.18" from the central fold, ending at 3 points behind on the central fold. Remove the basting. E) Open the zip, fold the counter-flap in half lengthwise, finish the edges, place it under the zip, on the side that will be overlapped, with the top edges aligned and the folded edge approximately 2.5 cm / 1" from the spiral. Sew close to the fold, through all the layers, and remove the basting. F) Make a supporting seam across both sides of the zip at the top, with the zip open, and trim them. Cut away the seam allowances of the crotch below the facing of the fly up to 5 mm / 0.20" from the seam. Close the zip and, from the reverse side, attach the lower edge of the counter-flap to the facing of the overlap; from the 'right' side of the fabric, sew a bar tack at the base of the zip opening.

Gusset and finishes

Gusset: 1. Half-moon overcasting of the gusset. 2. Folding and ironing of the gusset triangles. 3. Joining of the gusset pieces. 4. Application of the gusset to the trousers.

GUSSET

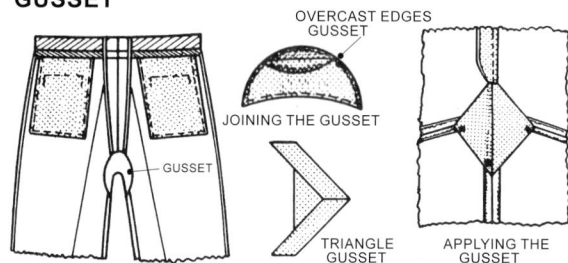

OVERCAST EDGES
GUSSET

JOINING THE GUSSET

GUSSET

TRIANGLE
GUSSET

APPLYING THE
GUSSET

Finishes: 1. Industrial finishing of waistband seam margins. 2. Manual finishing of waistband seam margins. 3. Flap stopper at the lower end of the crotch. 4. Special stitch on the left flap using a Columbia P100 sewing machine or similar.

FINISHES

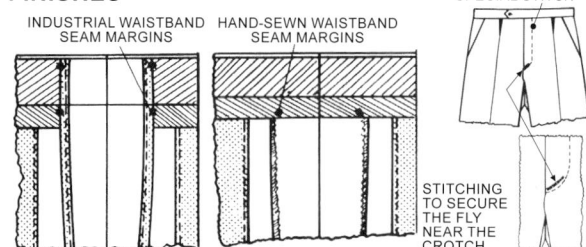

INDUSTRIAL WAISTBAND
SEAM MARGINS

HAND-SEWN WAISTBAND
SEAM MARGINS

SPECIAL STITCH

STITCHING
TO SECURE
THE FLY
NEAR THE
CROTCH

TROUSER CONSTRUCTION

Steps and sequences

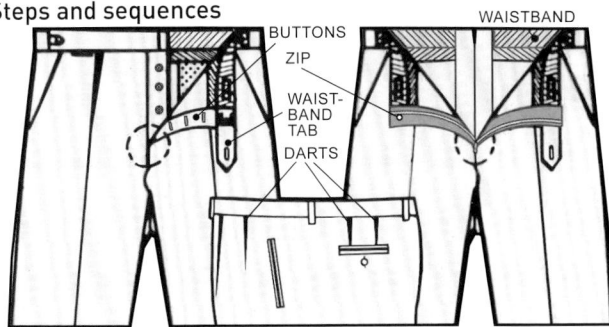

Steps and sequences
1) Finish the darts. 2) Construction of the belt loops. 3) Tailor-made and pre-made waistbands.

Darts

As you work, the darts remain flat. The wide part of the triangle that makes them is at the waistband and the points extend down to the widest part of the hips, ending at least 3 cm / 1.18" above the hip line.

On trousers, darts should be placed on the front and back quarters. On the front they can be open (1) or closed (2). Rear darts (3) are usually longer than those at the front. After basting them to the required size, they should be machine-sewn: match the last 4 or 5 stitches at the bottom of the fold; shorten the wide part at the top by 2.5 cm / 1" and the lower part at the point by 1 cm / 0.39", leaving about 10 cm / 3.94" of extra thread for knotting and trimming. Iron them from the reverse side folded towards the centre front and centre back (4), without over ironing, holding them down with a wooden clapper until they cool. Then iron them on the 'right' side, protecting the fabric with an ironing cloth.

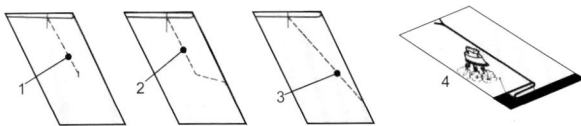

Belt loops

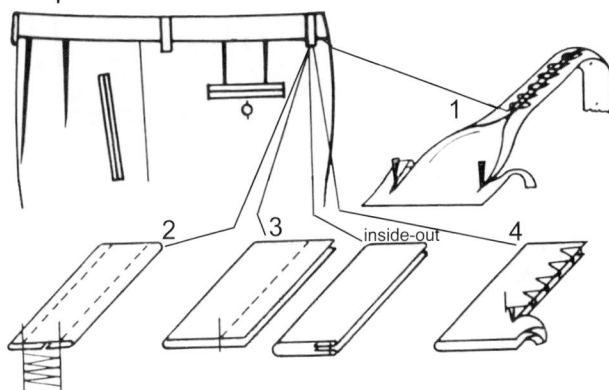

1) Belt loop construction with blindstitching. 2) Belt loop construction with two needles. 3) Belt loop construction with straight stitching (in three steps: 3b stitching, turning inside-out and ironing). 4) Belt-loop construction with overcasting (in two steps: overcasting and ironing).

Tailor-made and industrial waistbands

Waistbands are generally made of the same fabric as the trousers. They complement and finish trousers by marking the waistline and giving the figure an elegant look. It is the last thing to be applied, after having sewn the front to the back, the zip or button attachment, and after the lining has been applied. Some companies produce pre-assembled waistbands for the garment industry.

How to make sartorial waistbands

1) Cut the fabric on the straight of grain, i.e. perpendicular to the selvedge.

2) The length of the fabric waistband is equal to the waist circumference + 4-5 cm / 1.57-1.97" to allow for the overlapping tab for a button, a hook and an eyelet.

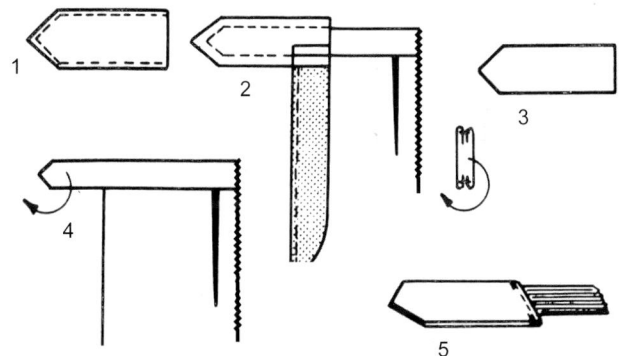

1) Union of tensioner side strap (side adjustor) pieces. 2) Sewing of the waistband tab with a sewing machine. 3-4) Reversing of the side straps and waistband tab. 5) Sewing of the elastic to the tensioner side straps.

Classic trouser hook

Trouser hooks are produced by fastening manufacturers in materials such as brass, iron and stainless steel. They still have a important role in elegant clothing. In particular, trousers with a classic cut are almost always finished with a concealed hook: if so, the metal elements are what make the difference. An experienced hand, when examining the workmanship of classic or elegant trousers, will immediately check the presence of this accessory, as well as its quality.

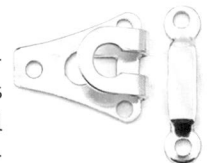

WORK PLAN

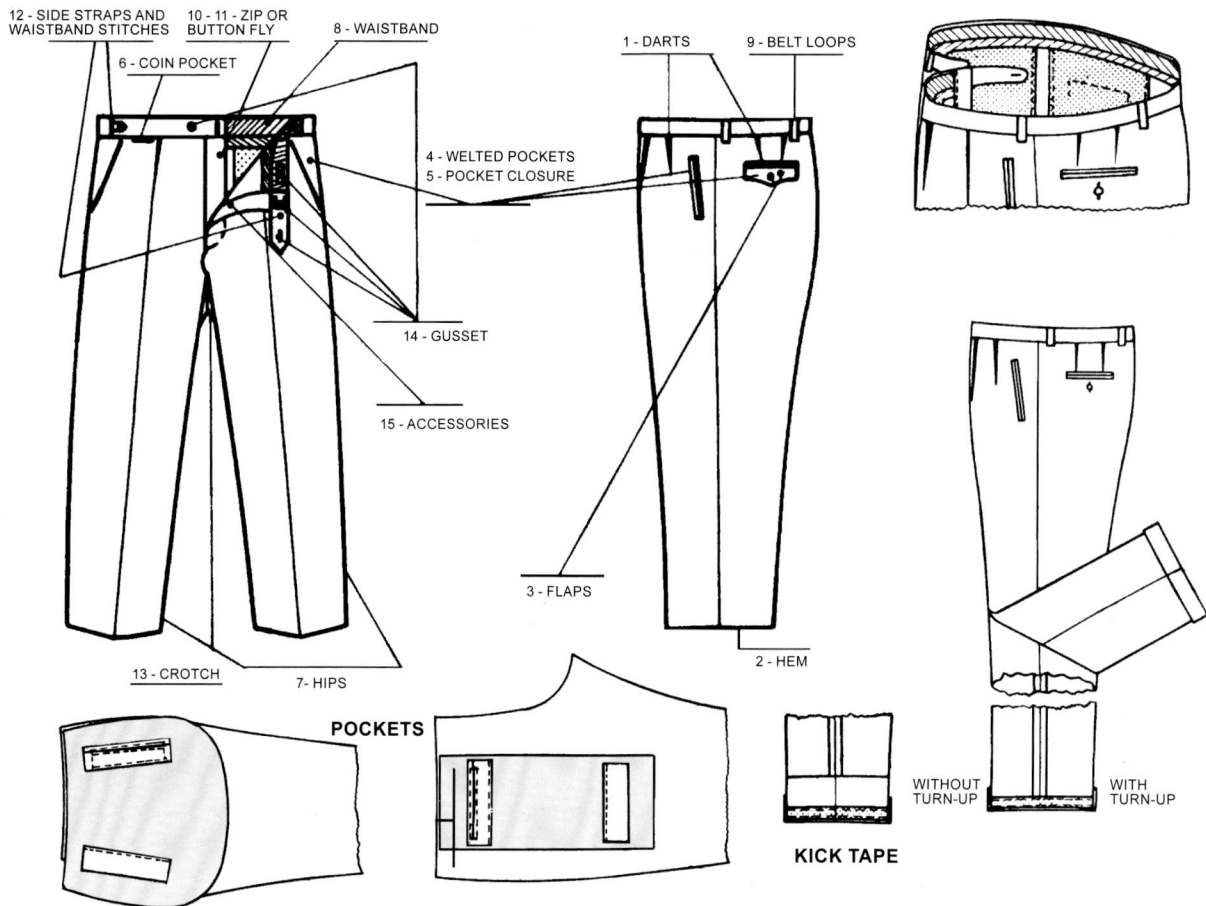

12 - SIDE STRAPS AND WAISTBAND STITCHES
10 - 11 - ZIP OR BUTTON FLY
8 - WAISTBAND
6 - COIN POCKET
1 - DARTS
9 - BELT LOOPS
4 - WELTED POCKETS
5 - POCKET CLOSURE
14 - GUSSET
15 - ACCESSORIES
3 - FLAPS
2 - HEM
13 - CROTCH
7 - HIPS
POCKETS
WITHOUT TURN-UP
WITH TURN-UP
KICK TAPE

1) Darts and pleats: - Sew open darts on the front parts - Sew closed darts on the front parts - sew darts on the back parts - iron.

2) Hem: - Overcast the bottom edges of the parts - Apply the kick tape to the back parts or all round with two rows of stitching, with the side seams already done. Trousers with turn-up cuffs, closed hem at kick tape - Blindstitch hems - Basting of cuffs - Affixing of cuffs.

3) Flaps: - Application of the lining to the pocket flap - Turn flaps out - Iron the flaps - Overcast stitching on the edge of the pocket facing - Application of facing to the pocket lining - Turn out - Iron edging - Prior application of the button to the pocket flap, avoiding the lining.

4) Welted pockets: - Sew the pockets with two edges - Sew pockets with two edges and insertion of flaps - Cut at the 4 corners - Turn edges out - Sew welting - Sew front pocket welting - Sew front pocket edging - Sew front pocket - Sew ends of front pocket welting on facing - Fasten front pockets.

5) Closing the pockets: - Fasten the pocket edging - Sew the outline exten-sion - Close the pockets - Turn pockets out - Close pockets with reinforced stitching - Fixing of flap to pocket trim.

6) Small pocket: - Sew lining on facing - Sew lining on rear pocket trouser side - Cut size of small pocket - Close small pocket lining - Turn out.

7) Sides: - Join the sides and close the legs - Iron - Open seams.

8) Waistband: - Preparation of bias tapes for linings and reinforcements - Creasing of bias tapes - Sewing with rigid tongue for invisible fastening, 2 lining tapes, 1 reinforcement - Folding and ironing of the lining - Application of the pre-made ribbon to the waistband - Joining of the waistband to the trousers - Opening - Ironing of the waistband seams - Anchoring of the pocket linings to the waistband - Invisible stitching - Waistband reinforcement seams.

9) Belt loops: - Sew the loops - Turn out - Ironing of belt loops - Bar-tacking of belt loops.

10) Zip fly and hook and eye fastening: - Joining of lining to the eyelet flap fabric - Construction of zip or eyelet fastening on the fly - Application of the second lining on the fly - Application of the fly to the garment - Bar-tacking - Fly reinforcement seams.

11) Zip fly and button fastening: - Overcast stitching on the facing and the area corresponding to the rear trouser pocket - Join the lining to the facing - Apply facing to trousers - Close waistband ending - Turn out lining, fly and waistband tab.

12) Side straps and waistband point: - Join pieces of adjustable waistband tabs - Sew waistband point seam - Turn out waistband tabs and waistband point - Sew elastic and adjustable waistband tabs.

13) Crotch: - Overcast stitch the back section at the crotch - Trim back sections at the crotch - Sew the seam - Press seams open - Close fly at the start of the crotch.

14) Gusset: - Overcast stitch the gusset pieces - Fold - Press gusset pieces - Join at seam - Attach gusset - Finish waistband seam margins.

15) Accessories: - Make eyelets - Sew on buttons - Sew on labels - Attach hook and bar set to the waistband.

FORMAL JACKETS

HISTORICAL BACKGROUND

The jacket is the upper part of men's clothing. The ancient Romans wore a fitted, decorated doublet called a *synthesis* or *vestis cenatoria*, imported from the East. This garment could be the ancestor of the jacket, having undergone various transformations over the centuries of course. In the Middle Ages, when the needle, called 'silky iron', was imported from China, craftsmen developed new techniques to join various pieces of fabric cut to shape, to make close-fitting garments. Up until then, all garments had been draped. The only men's jacket from this era that has survived up to today is kept in Lyon, France.

Then, in the 1100s there were: the *cotte d'armes*, the *gambeson* (also aketon, padded jack, etc.), a kind of padded waistcoat, and the *pourpoint* or *gipon*, a type of jacket. By 1350, the jacket had already reached perfection, extending a palm below the hips and a disc-like sleeve attachment that fitted into the bodice with many seams. Garments with many buttons were highly prized.

In 1358 in France it was called a *jacque*. Made of low-quality fabric, it was worn by the less well-off.

Towards the first half of the 1800s, the *frock coat* appeared in England, which was similar to the tailcoat in terms of aesthetics and line. At the same time, the redingote jacket and the paletot shared the honour of dressing stylish men of that era. From 1860 onwards, the jacket was straight-cut, hip-length and single-breasted with 3-4 buttons. Later, in the early 1900s, the chest pocket appeared on the left side and, as time went on, the lines of the jacket were gradually modified according to the fashions of the era.

Today, single-breasted jackets can be three-button or two-button with a lapel breakline at the waist or hip height. Double-breasted styles can have six or four buttons. The shapes of the lapels near the collar, both in the single-breasted and double-breasted styles, truly vary. They can be notched, peaked, shawl, etc. The pockets can be: patch, welted (jetted), with inserted flaps, etc. The length varies according to the dictates of fashion and according to the occasion on which it is worn. Jackets can have a vent at the centre back, two side vents, a small box pleat, or be entirely without them.

1450 *1500* *1540* *1585* *1650* *1690*

1745 *1778* *1792* *1793* *1796* *1800*

1807 *1818* *1843* *1862* *1920* *1928*

SELECTING THE FABRIC

The first, incredibly important step in creating a custom-made suit is the choice of fabric: plain or patterned, wool, silk or cotton, soft or crisp. The possibilities are practically endless. There are three aspects to consider when choosing fabric: appearance, feel (called the hand or handle), and weight.

1) The first decision, based on visual appearance, concerns the choice between plain or patterned fabrics. The two most commonly used colours for jackets are grey and blue, the former being more suitable for daytime and the latter for evening wear. Neutrals and soft colours, i.e. beige and light grey tones, are particularly sophisticated and go well with just about everything. They can also be used for high-end clothes. Turning to fabrics with prints, current trends favour micro-effects and minute, almost invisible motifs, in addition to glen plaid and other checks. On the other hand, stripes are less common, and they remain associated with managers.

2) The fabric must be pleasant to touch; a winter jacket should have a warm, woolly, soft hand, while a summer jacket will have a dry, cool hand.

3) The linear weight per metre is between 220 and 300 grams (7.76-10.58 oz) for summery fabrics and between 280 and 400 grams (9.87-14.11 oz) for winter fabrics.

In general, wool is the most suitable fibre for clothes in every season: for spring-summer it will be blended with silk, cotton or linen, while for autumn-winter, a cashmere or flannel blend is preferred, the latter being a very comfortable fabric suitable both for suits and for jackets or trousers worn on their own. There are two types of flannel: the woollen kind, made with a coarser yarn, has a warmer, sportier look; while the worsted one has a finer texture, making it more elegant.

Knowing how to choose the fabric of the jacket according to the occasion is essential. For the office, grey or blue grisaille is ideal, a classic material that can be worn in all seasons. For the evening, one can opt for mohair, a fabric with a beautiful sheen. In this case, the standard colour is blue.

Cheviot

Pinstripes

Flannel

Grisaille

Tweed

Glen plaid

Bird's eye

Corduroy

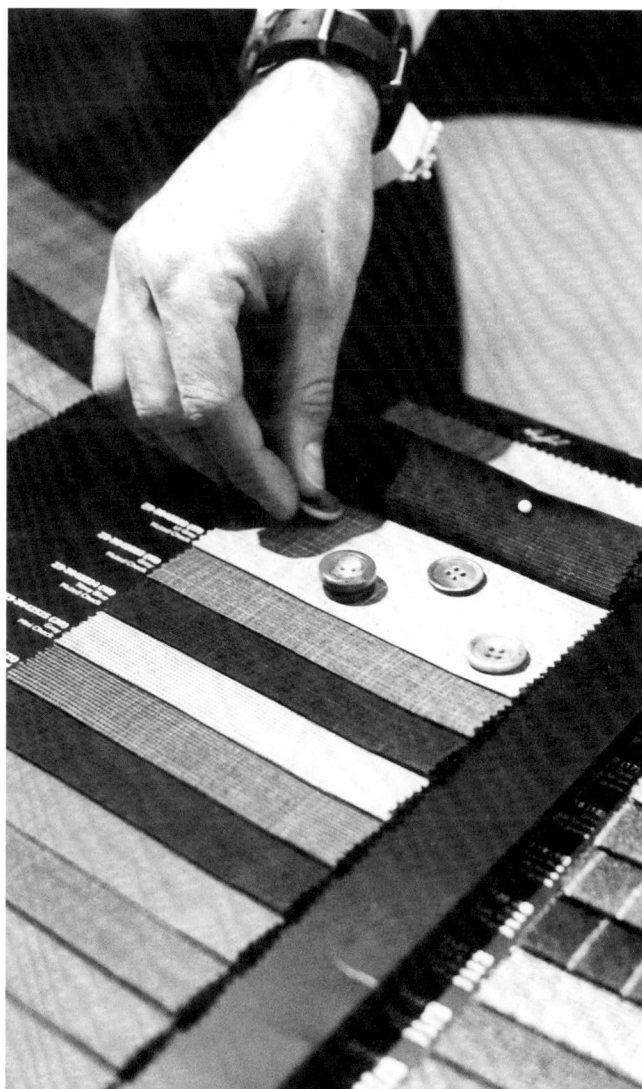

LININGS

A lining is a special type of fabric applied to the inside of many kinds of garments and accessories of various kinds. It is a functional part of the garment and it is used to improve fit and comfort: it allows the body to slide easily within the garment, but it is also used to conceal the complex structure of a garment or accessory, to support the silhouette, and to add insulation.

Winter jackets are almost always lined, but summer jackets can be partly lined, particularly at the shoulders to make them more comfortable to wear. Trousers are generally lined from the waistband down to the calf, but in the case of particularly rough woollen fabrics, the lining should reach the knee. Linings that are slightly smaller than the garment itself are more comfortable. In jackets, coats and mackintoshes, however, the outside layer of the garment should not be affected in any way by taut lining, which is why the torso and sleeve linings of these garments are normally created in measurements that are slightly larger than the garment itself.

The textile fibres used for the lining are almost exclusively artificial (acetate, viscose, cupro) and synthetic (polyester, polyamide), as a smooth material that slides over the body and other garments is required. However, they can also be made of cotton and wool or wool blends in smooth or worsted versions to decorate the garment or to make it warmer. Materials that aren't slippery should only be used for the torso and not for the sleeves.

Technical characteristics

In order to meet the needs of the wearer, the lining must resist ripping, wear and tear, and the stitching that it will be subjected to; it must have dimensional stability when exposed to steam (shrinkage due to ironing) and colour fastness. In addition, the fabric used must have a good thickness and weight.

Product characteristics

The way linings 'behave' when being worked is of particular importance. Special care must be taken when selecting materials to ensure that they meet the requirements of industrial workability on the one hand and suitability for consumer use on the other. The main product-related characteristics are: 1) appearance; 2) few defects; 3) uniformity of colour; 4) the hand; 5) fraying; 6) ease of care; 7) ease of crease removal; 8) smooth enough to slip on and off, but not too slippery; 9) the 'squareness of regular weaves (straight of grain); 10) regular selvedges; 11) ability to fold for half-height linings.

Advantages of linings

Linings make garments more valuable, and buyers tend to prefer lined garments during the purchase stage, even if it means a higher cost. Another positive aspect is the 'air-conditioning' effect: the layer of air between the outer fabric and lining increases comfort in all seasons. Moreover, it helps sweat evaporate, keeping it off the body.

In general, a lined garment holds its shape and looks good, as a nice lining, with pleasing patterns and colours, makes any garment more attractive and up-to-date. Moreover, quality linings help to prevent, or at least delay, the wear and tear of garments.

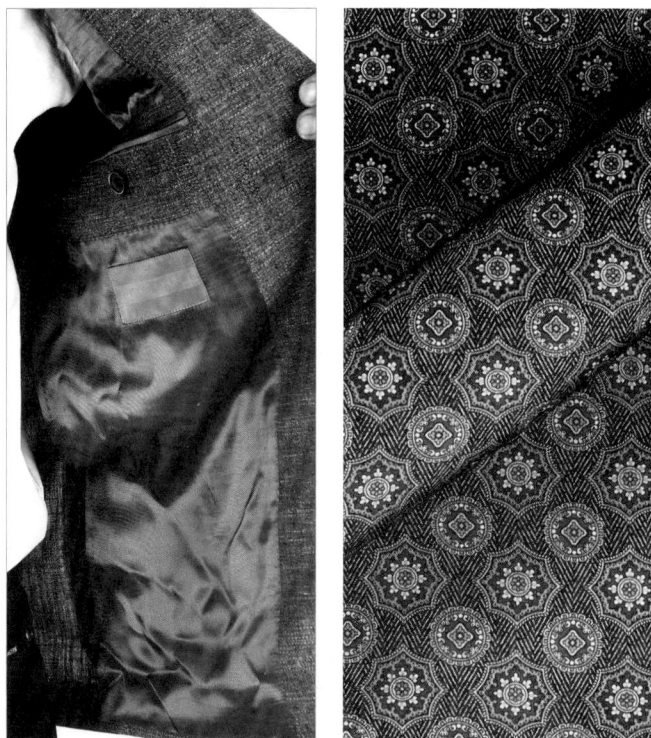

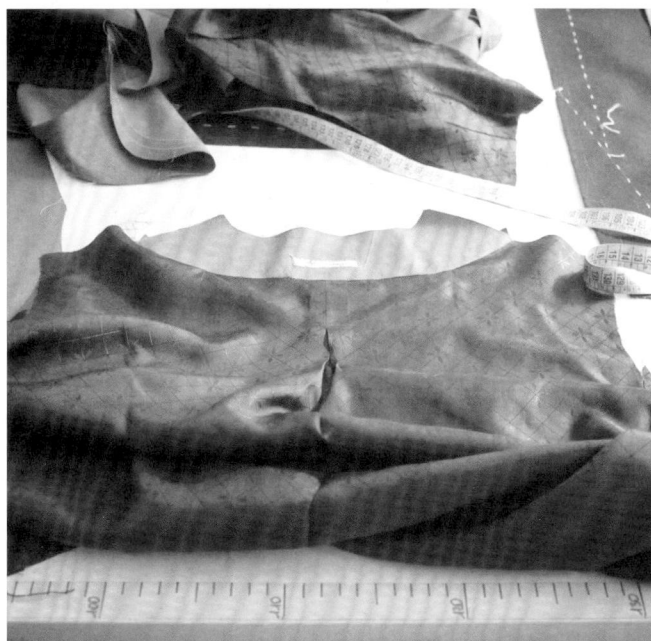

JACKET MEASUREMENTS, FIT AND EASE

The measurements for making a jacket are the same as those used for a shirt, namely: neck circumference; chest circumference; hip circumference; rear shoulder width; front chest width; rear neck to waist; front neck to waist; hip length; total jacket length.

Jacket fits are also similar to those of the shirt, namely: classic fit, slim fit, and regular fit.

Classic-fit jackets are comfortable, with a chest circumference of 20-24 cm / 7.87-9.45".

Slim-fit jackets are cut close to the body, with a chest circumference of 14-16 cm / 5.51-6.30". The addition of darts at the back and front help shape the garment for a perfect fit.

Regular-fit jackets have a chest circumference of 18-20 cm / 7.09-7.87" and are somewhere between classic and slim fit.

These sorts of standardised fits do not apply to tailor-made jackets because the person's measurements have to be taken in order to make the pattern. Before this step, be sure to check that the person is wearing their usual undergarments, a shirt or t-shirt, and that they aren't wearing baggy clothing, which could create inaccurate measurements. In addition, it is useful to tie a piece of ribbon or string around the waist and hips to give yourself a precise reference point while measuring.

Measurements must be noted on a special form, together with any particular physical characteristics and conformations of the client, in order to make appropriate adjustments to the base pattern and avoid mistakes and improperly fitting elements.

All measurements must be carefully checked on the completed pattern before nesting and cutting the fabric.

MEASUREMENTS FOR A CLASSIC FIT COAT - 38" CHEST CIRCUMFERENCE				
DESCRIPTION	CM	1/2 EASE (CM)	IN	1/2 EASE (IN)
Height	175	/	68.90	/
1/2 neck circumference	21	0.5	8.27	0.20
1/2 chest circumference	48	10-12	18.90	3.94-4.72
1/2 waist circumference	44	8-10	17.32	3.15-3.94
1/2 hip circumference	48-49	10-12	18.90-19.29	3.94-4.72
1/2 rear shoulder width	21	1-2	8.27	0.39-0.79
Bicep circumference	31.1	2-3	12.32	0.79-1.18
Rear neck to waist	45.6	2	17.95	0.79
Front neck to waist	46.2	2	18.19	0.79
Waist to hip	21.6	/	8.50	/
Sleeve length	64.8	/	25.51	/
Belly protrusion	2	/	0.79	/
Upper back curve	4.8	/	1.89	/

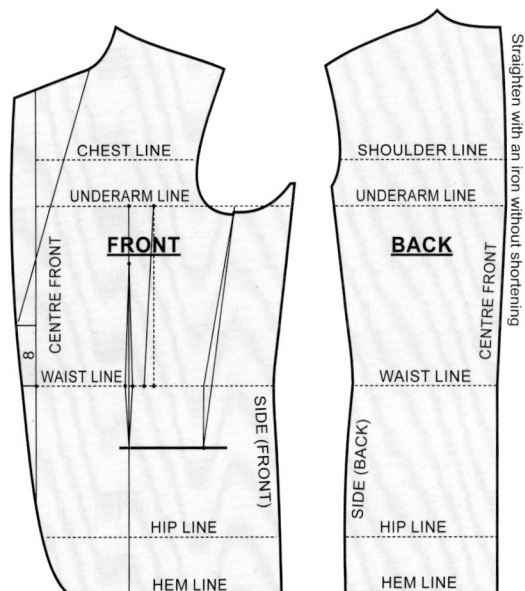

CLASSIC AND FORMAL JACKET STYLES

Classic men's jackets can be single- or double-breasted. Single-breasted jackets can have four buttons with a lapel breakpoint above the chest, three buttons with a breakpoint just below the chest, two buttons with a breakpoint at the waist or hip, or one button with a breakpoint at the waist. Double-breasted styles can have four or six buttons.

There are different shapes that define the top of the lapels in both the single-breasted and double-breasted styles.

The pockets can be: patch, welted (jetted), flap, etc.

The length of the jacket varies according to the style of the moment and according to the occasions on which it is worn. Jackets can have a vent at the centre back, two side vents, a small box pleat, or be entirely without them.

Dinner jackets (called tuxedos in the United States) are worn on formal occasions in the evenings, and are usually made of silk or wool woven fabric. They consist of a single or double-breasted jacket, often black, but also white, blue, burgundy or purple, usually with lapels of various shapes in a different type of fabric, such as satin.

They are worn with black trousers with a silk band down the outside of the leg.

The Spencer is a type of long-sleeved jacket for men and women that comes down to the waist. It was adopted by military officers, with prominent frog fasteners, and became popular as women's fashion in the early 1800s. Spencers can have single or double-breasted buttoning, various collars, and lapels with contrasting satin fabric, like the dinner jacket.

Morning dress is formal day attire in England; it usually includes a black 'morning coat' with wide, long tails that start at the front and striped trousers in grey and black. A light-coloured, pearl grey or white waistcoat generally accompanies the suit. Morning dress was at its peak in the early 1900s.

The tailcoat (or dress coat) is a distinctive and elegant formal coat. This jacket is short at the front and long at the back (the skirt), which is divided into two rounded tails. It is worn with trousers in the same colour as the jacket with two shiny bands that run down the outside of the legs. It is also paired with a white dress shirt, a pique-knit bib and a waistcoat.

SINGLE-BREASTED JACKETS

four buttons   three buttons   two buttons   one button

DOUBLE-BREASTED JACKETS

six buttons   six buttons, closed   four buttons

DINNER JACKETS (TUXEDOS)

single-breasted, square shawl lapels   single-breasted, pointed shawl lapels   single-breasted pointed (peak) lapels   double-breasted, wide shawl lapels

Tailcoat   Morning coat   Spencer

INTERFACING

Every expert in the industry knows the importance of the interfacing in jacket construction, and what fine-quality interfacing can mean in the context of workmanship: simpler working processes, a jacket that holds its shape, and its benefits for the fabric.

However, interfacing cannot be cut like the fabric nor can they be worked together. From the front panel in fabric, you will have to create a pattern for the interfacing that has effects that adapt well to the line of the jacket in advance, in order to simplify the sewing process.

The most apt comparison to convey the importance of the interfacing in the construction of a jacket is that with the foundations of a house: both require special attention and good technical preparation.

The interfacing that we propose below is a well-suited to modern lines and, with the proper adjustments, to all types of fabric. Due to the matching of the rigidity of the fabric and to that of its lining, all you need to do is deepen the folds at the sides of the waist: this will result in a greater opening of the darts and allow the peak to increase.

Pattern construction

Reproduce the shape of the front on paper, stopping laterally at the underarm and at the waist level. The connecting pieces for the pocket and the side panel will be applied later, i.e. when the interfacing is attached to the fabric. Dividing the pattern at 1/3 of the shoulder (e.g: 16 ÷ 3 = 5.3 cm / 2.09"), directed towards the point corresponding to the most protruding part of the chest (X).

Make a 0.5 cm / 0.20" long opening at the level reached, with its fulcrum and point on the lapel. The resulting opening on the shoulder will allow for a small rotation of 0.5 cm / 0.20" as an outlet for the neckline and a 1 cm / 0.39" increase on the back side, for the expected drape.

Make a guideline for the tuck, running parallel to the lapel breakpoint and on it, at the waistline, shape the base dart measuring 1 cm / 0.39".

Make a waist dart of approximately 4.8 cm / 1.89" (1/10 of the semi-chest) by creating two folds on the armscye, as shown in the figure. On the back side of the dart, make a slight curve. The interfacing will be supplemented by a 0.7 cm / 0.28" loose dart at pocket level to create the roundness of the belly and an opening at the level of the humerus. The inner fabric will give balance and shape to the jacket so that, after the try-on and fitting session, it will fit the body perfectly.

Over time, the cloth will further adapt to the wearer, without losing the initial shape given by the tailor. Obviously, a jacket with interfacing requires many hours of work as well as skill and experience, which is why it is the most expensive jacket on the market, regardless of the fabric used.

Jackets with interfacing fit close to the body and drape perfectly on the figure. A test of the quality of the interfacing work done is to have the wearer raise their arms: the jacket should remain on the body and only the sleeves should rise.

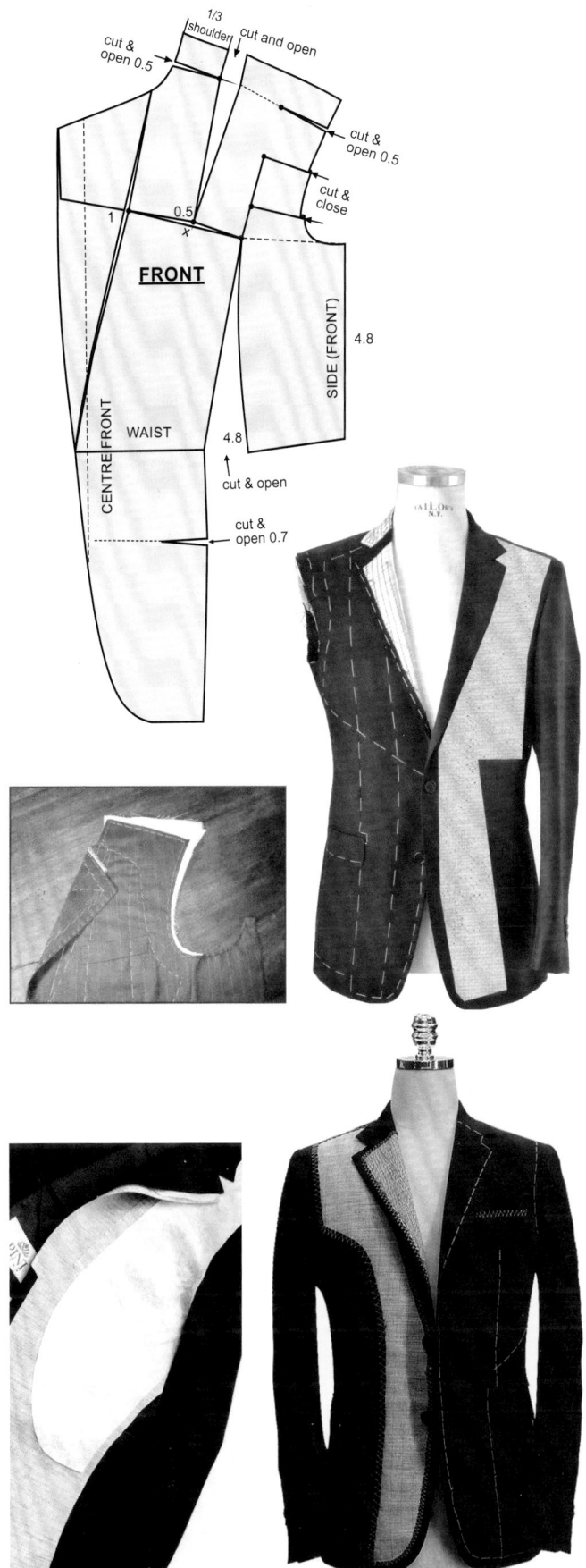

CHECKED AND STRIPED JACKETS

Checks, plaids and stripes are particularly challenging when it comes to their placement, as the stripes and checks need to be aligned properly. Fabrics such as herringbone, houndstooth and others with woven patterns also require careful alignment because they have repeating prints that create stripes or colour blocks. Randomly scattered motifs, however, should not be aligned.

The following notes refer to the cutting of a pattern for checked fabric, but apply equally well to striped fabric. In this case, you need only consider the positioning of the vertical or horizontal stripes, depending on the direction of the stripes in the fabric. With these fabrics, it's convenient to choose a simple pattern, one that has relatively few seams and details such as shaped seams or side panels, darts or horizontal tucks, unless special stylistic choices are made.

Choosing simple patterns will help maintain the continuity of the print on the fabric. Indeed, it is nearly impossible to align the print along all the garment's seams, yet too many mismatched edges can create an eyesore. Try to avoid horizontal or diagonal darts in the bodice of jackets with a check print. If you absolutely must add them, the side seams should line up below the dart and not above it. If the curvature of the sleeve at elbow height is created by a dart, the two pieces along the vertical seam must be aligned above the dart, but they will not match below it.

Here are a few useful tips for these types of fabrics:

1) Making a mock garment is certainly good practice, as it can be very helpful to establishing the length of the hemmed garment and to making the main adjustments before cutting the fabric.

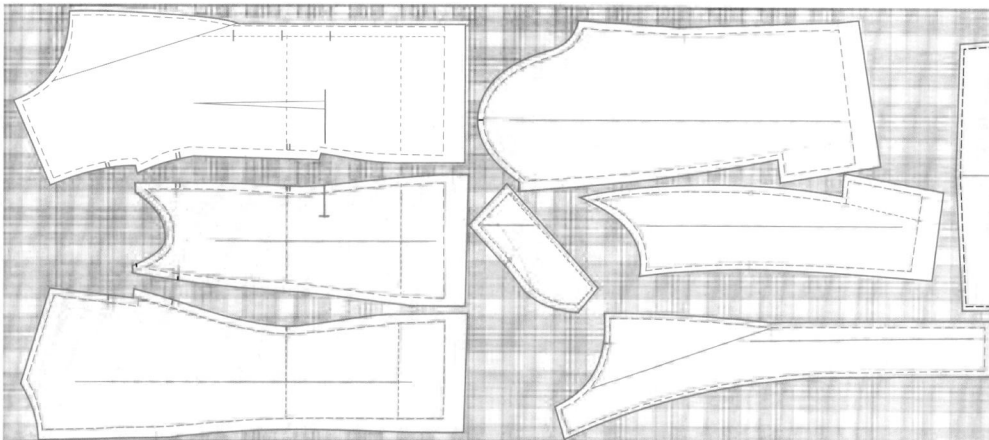

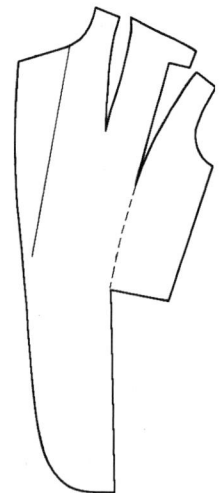

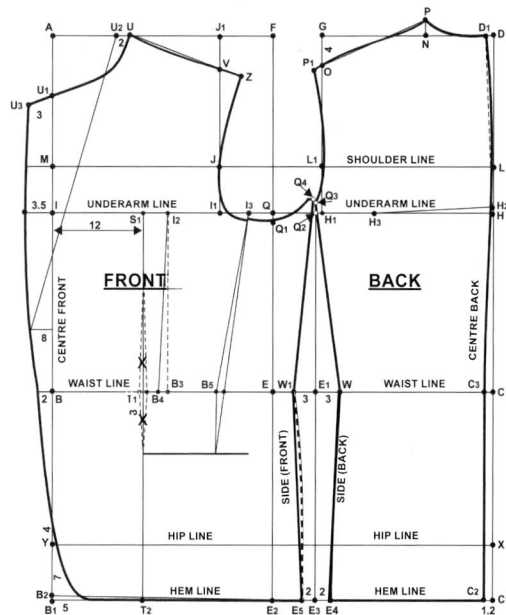

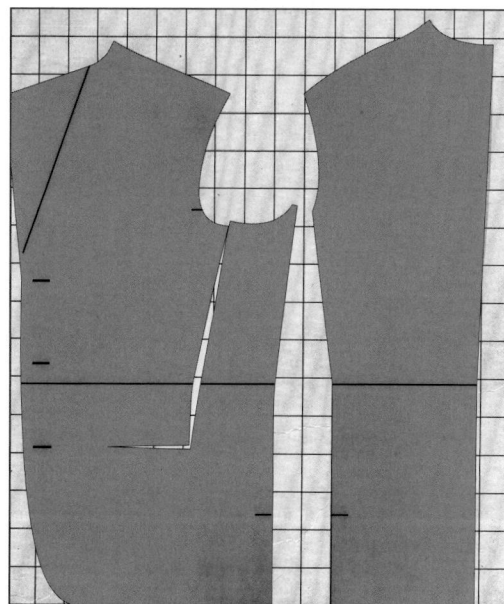

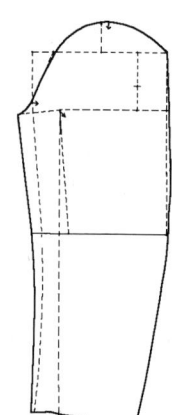

Note:

For glen plaid, a rather thick interfacing should be used, emphasising the hollow of the waist and providing greater support to the side, making sure the lengths of the waist converge perfectly. The paper pattern is created by closing the regular dart, through shifting, and creating a horizontal dart. Taking advantage of the unique opening, we give the sleeve a flare for the humerus ridge by increasing the part by 0.5 cm / 0.20". In addition, the pattern will be less round in the back, evenness in the lines in the hips, and squared in its effects. An outline with a straight hip from the waist to the lower hem and a horizontal parallel line on the same lower edge. The front usually does not have a central dart, which is optional anyway.

2) Before nesting and cutting the pieces, determine the position of the stripes within the garment and where they should fall on the bodice.

3) Avoid placing a dominant horizontal line or group of lines at chest height. To this end, see how the fabric looks by draping it from the shoulder to the hem.

4) Some check garments are better balanced if the hem line coincides with the underside of a dominant crossline in the fabric. However, you can also draw attention away from the hem, placing it between two dominant stripes, depending on your preference.

5) Place the dominant vertical stripes/lines at the centre front and back or position the pattern so that the centre line of the front is halfway between two dominant vertical stripes.

6) Position the upper part of the sleeve in the same way, using the shoulder point as a guide in centring the sleeve on or between the dominant vertical stripes.

7) Checks may also not line up along the shoulder seam, at the seam joining the upper part of the collar to the lapel, and at the rear notch of the armscye in inset sleeves.

8) Pockets, cuffs and pocket flaps should be cut after the first test run because they may have to be repositioned.

Execution

1) Lay each piece on the open fabric in a single layer, starting with the front. Place its centre edge on or between two vertical lines. Check the position of the horizontal lines on the chest, waist and hem. Cut the single layer of the front of the jacket then remove the pattern.

2) Turn the piece over and use it to cut out the other half of the front.

Then cut the front facing with matching cross lines on the front edge. The seam line of the lapel should follow the dominant vertical line, while the facing on the inner placket may not be entirely on the straight of grain.

3) Place the centre back seam on or between two dominant vertical lines, as for the front. Lay the paper pattern on the fabric, lining up the notches (arrows) of the front and back pieces on the same place along the seam line.

4) Cut around the edges of the back piece, then mark the upper and lower limits of the fold line. Remove the paper pattern and fold the fabric, aligning the checks. Cut around the other half, then cut out the upper part of the collar to be aligned with the centre back.

5) Centre the sleeve on or between the dominant vertical lines.

Place the pattern on the fabric by aligning the checks with those on the jacket at the notch (arrow) along the seam line. It is not necessary to match the checks on the rear notch. Cut one sleeve and use it to make the second.

6) Place the pocket pattern on the garment during the first try-on and draw the position of the lines of the motif on it to ensure they line up perfectly. Then place the pattern on the fabric, aligning the marks, and cut.

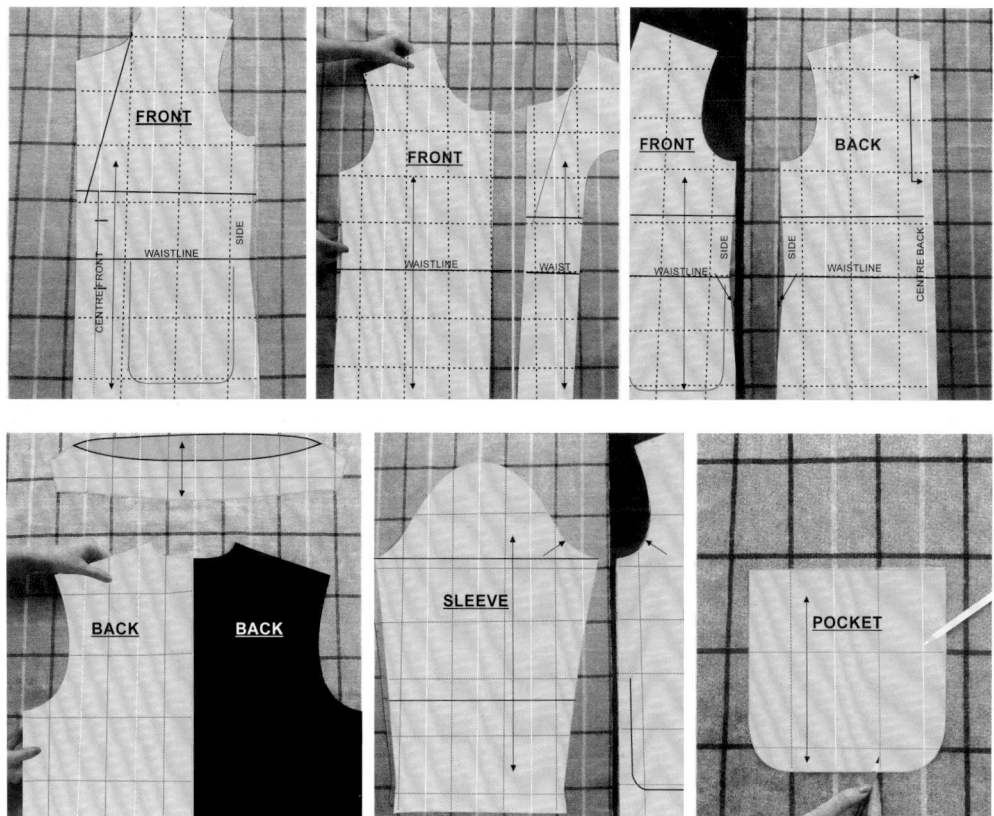

BASE JACKET - CLASSIC FIT

CHEST EASE - 24 CM / 9 ½"

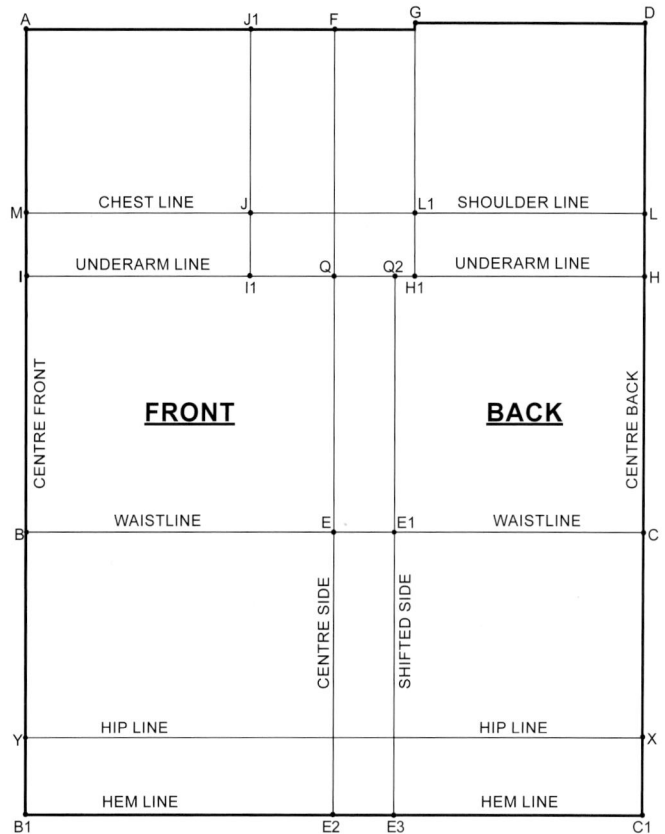

Size 16 UK measurements

- Height = 175 cm / 5'9".
- Chest semi-cir. = 96 + 20 = 116 : 2 = 58 cm / 22.83"
- Waist semi-cir. = 88 + 20 = 108 ÷ 2 = 54 cm / 21.26"
- Hip semi-cir. = 96 + 20 = 116 ÷ 2 = 58 cm / 22.83"
- Neck semi-circumference = 42 ÷ 2 = 21 cm / 8.27"
- 1/2 shoulder width = 42 ÷ 2 = 21 cm / 8.27"
- Front neck to waist = 45.6+ 2= 47.6 cm / 18.74".
- Rear neck to waist = 48.2 cm + 2 = 48.2 cm / 18.98".
- Draw right angle A-B-C, with:
- A-B = front neck-to-waist + ease of 2 cm / 0.79") e.g.: 45.6 + 2 = 47.6 cm / 18.74").
- B-C = chest semi-circumference + 20 cm ease (7.87") (e.g: 96 + 20 = 116 ÷ 2 = 58 cm / 22.83").
- C-D rear neck-to-waist + 2 cm / 0.79" ease (e.g.: 46.2 + 2 = 48.2 cm / 18.98").
- D-C1 = jacket length (e.g: 75 cm / 29.53").
- Join D-C1 and write 'Centre back'.
- B-B1 as C-C1 (26.8 cm / 10.55").
- Join A-B1 and write 'Centre front'.
- B1-C1 as B-C. Join B1-C1 and write 'Lower edge' or 'Hem'.
- B-E half of B-C.
- B1-E2 as B-E.

- A-F as B-E.
- Join F-E2 and write 'Centre side'.
- D-H half of D-C+ 0.5 cm / 0.20" (e.g: 48.2 ÷ 2 = 24.1 + 0.5 = 24.6 cm / 9.69").
- H-I like B-C = 58 cm / 22.83" (armpit level).
- E2-E3 = 6 cm / 2.36".
- Q-Q2 as E2-E3 (6 cm / 2.36").
- Join Q2-E3 (shifted side).
- B-Y and C-X = waist to hip (e.g: 20-21.5 cm / 7.87-8.46").
- Draw Y-X and write 'Hip line'.
- D-G = shoulder width + ease divided by 2 (e.g: 42 + 2.5 = 44.5 ÷ 2 = 22.25 cm / 8.76").
- H-L = 1/4 of D-H (e.g.: 24.6 ÷ 4 = 6.15 cm / 2.42").
- Draw L-M and write 'Shoulder line' (L-L1) and 'Chest line' (M-J).
- H-H1 as D-G (e.g: 22.25 cm / 8.76").
- Draw G-L1-H1.
- I-I1 = D-G minus 0.5 cm / 0.20" at the back (e.g: 22.25- 0.5 = 21.75 cm / 8.56").
- A-J1 like I-I1.
- Draw I1-J1 parallel to G-H1.
- I1-H1 = H-I minus (I-I1 + H-H1), (e.g: 58 - (21.75 + 22.25) = 58 - 44 = 14 cm 5.51") (armscye or underarm sector).

Back

- H-H3 = 16 cm / 6.30" (e.g.: 1/3 chest semi-circumference = 48 ÷ 3 = 16 cm / 6.30").
- H-H2 = 0.6 cm / 0.24".
- Create the right angle H3-H2-D.
- Draw H2-D1 as H-D with a curve.
- G-O = 4 cm / 1.57".
- D1-N = 1/3 of D-G + 1 / 0.39" (e.g: 22.25 ÷ 3 = 7.41+ 1 = 8.41 cm / 3.31").
- N-P = 2.3 cm / 0.91". Draw the outline D1-P.
- P-P1 = shoulder length + 1 cm / 0.39" (e.g.: 1/3 chest semi-circumference + 1 cm / 0.39" = 48 ÷ 3 = 16 - 1 = 17 cm / 6.69").
- Draw the outline P-P1 passing through O.
- Q2-Q3 = 2.5 cm / 1".
- Draw the armhole P1-L1-Q3 smoothly.
- E1-W = 3 cm / 1.18".
- C-C3 = 1.2-1.7 cm / 0.47-0.66".
- C1-C2 as C-C3 = 1.2-1.7 cm / 0.47-0.66".
- Draw the centre back line D1-L-H-C3-C2.
- E3-E4 = 2 cm / 0.79".
- Draw the side line Q3-W-E4.
- Make the slit as shown in the figure, with a length of 20 cm / 7.87" or as desired.
- L1-P1 = H1-G minus H1-L1 minus G-O (e.g: 24.6 - 6.15 - 4 = 14.45 cm / 5.69").

Front

- A-U = half of A-J1 minus 0.5 cm / 0.20" (e.g.: 21.5 ÷ 2 = 10.75 - 0.5 = 10.25 cm / 4.04").
- A-U1 = 8 cm / 3.15".
- U-U2 = 2 cm / 0.79".
- Draw the breakline up to the desired height (e.g: 8 cm / 3.15" from the waist).
- J1-V = 4 cm / 1.57".
- U-Z as P-P1 at the rear minus 1 cm / 0.39".
- Draw the outline U-Z , passing through V.
- Q-Q1 = 2 cm / 0.79".
- Q2-Q4 = 3 cm / 1.18".
- Draw the armhole Z-J-Q1-Q4 smoothly.
- E1-W1 = 3 cm / 1.18".
- E3-E5 = 2 cm / 0.79".
- Draw the side line Q4-W1-E5.
- U1-U3 = 3-3.5 cm / 1.18-1.38".
- Draw the lapel outline as shown in the figure.
- I-S = 12 cm / 4.72"; S-S1 = 9.5 cm / 3.74"; T-T1 = 8 cm / 3.15".
- T- B = 12 cm / 4.72"; B5-B6 = 8 cm / 3.15".
- Draw the dart in a suitable measurement, as in the figure.
- Draw the dart I3-B6 as in the figure.

Note:
The waist darts and the excess at the side are proportionate to the desired difference between the hips and the waist, which is to be distributed proportionally on the waist dart line and the hip line, plus the creation of a small 1.5 cm / 0.59" dart with vertices on the armscye and pocket lines.

135

BASE JACKET SLEEVE

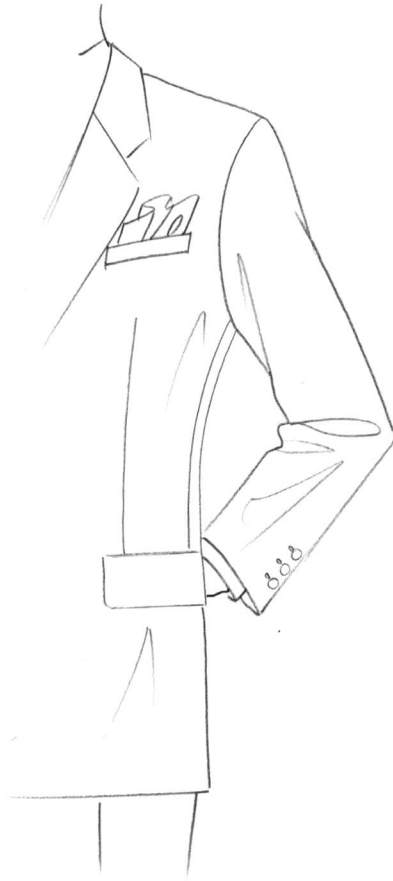

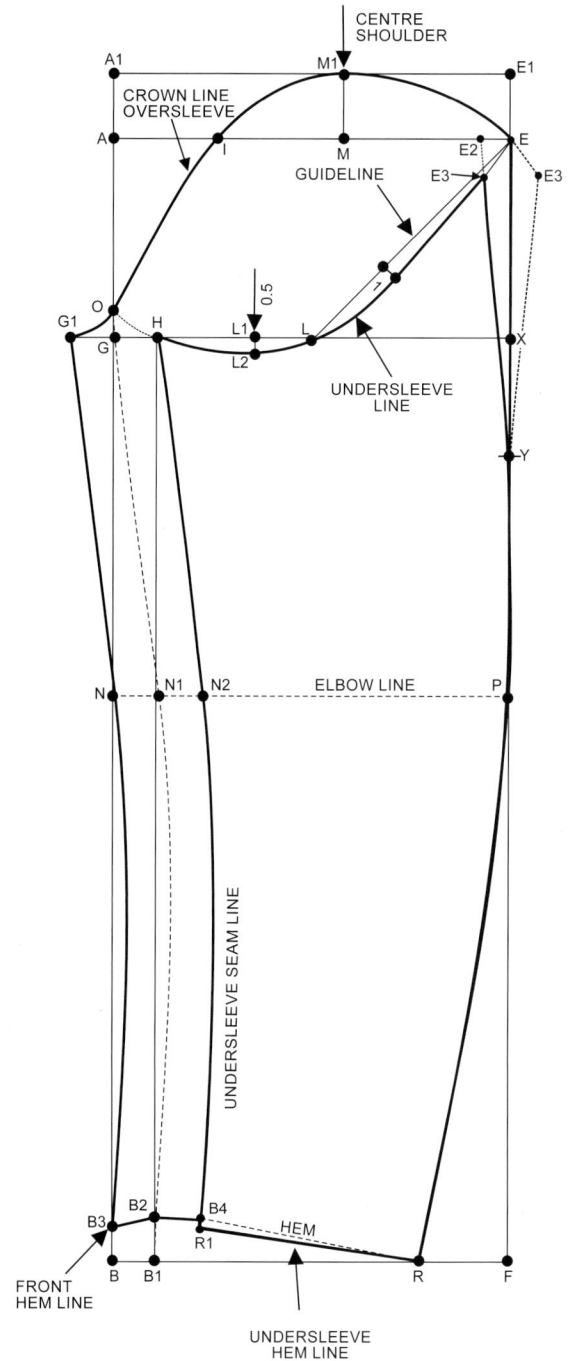

Measurements
- Bicep circumference 29 cm / 11.42".
- Arm length 62 cm / 24.41".

On the left side of a sheet of pattern paper draw the rectangle A-G-X-E with:
- A-E like base jacket armscye sector + 1/2 sector + 1 cm / 0.39" (e.g.: 14 + 7 = 21 + 1 = 22 cm / 8.66").
- A-G as measurement L1-P1 minus 1 cm / 0.39" of the base of the rear torso (in this case, 13.45 cm / 5.29".
- A-A1 = 1/3 of A-G (e.g: 11 ÷ 3 = 3.6 cm / 1.42").
- E-E1 like A-A1.
- Draw A-A1-E-E1
- A1-B = sleeve length + 1 cm / 0.39" (e.g.: 62 + 1 = 63 cm / 24.80").
- A1-N (elbow) = half of A1-B + 0.5 cm / 0.20" (e.g.: 63 ÷ 2 = 31.5 + 0.5 = 32 cm / 12.60").
- A-M = 1/2 of A-E + 1 cm / 0.39" (e.g: 22.75 ÷ 2 = 11.4 + 1 = 12.4 cm / 4.88").
- Draw M-M1 (Centre shoulder).
- A-I = 1/4 of A-E (e.g: 22.75 ÷ 4 = 5.7 cm / 2.24").
- G-H = 2.5 cm / 1".
- Draw H-B1 parallel to A-B.
- X-L = 1/2 of G-X (e.g.: 22.75 ÷ 2 = 11.37 cm / 4.48").

- Draw guideline E-L.
- L-L1 = 1/2 of H-L.
- L1-L2 = 0.5 cm / 0.20".
- G-O = 1.5 cm / 0.59".
- G-G1 = 2.5 cm / 1".
- E-E2 = 2 cm / 0.79".
- E-E3 = 3 cm / 1.18".
- Smoothly draw the front sleeve crown E-M1-I-O-G1.
- Smoothly draw the rear sleeve crown E-E3-L-L2-H-O.
- B1-B2 = 2 cm / 0.79".
- B3-B2 and N-N1 = 2.5 cm / 1".
- B4-R1 = 0.5 cm / 0.20".
- Connect with curved line R-P-E3 and R1-N2-H (Undersleeve).

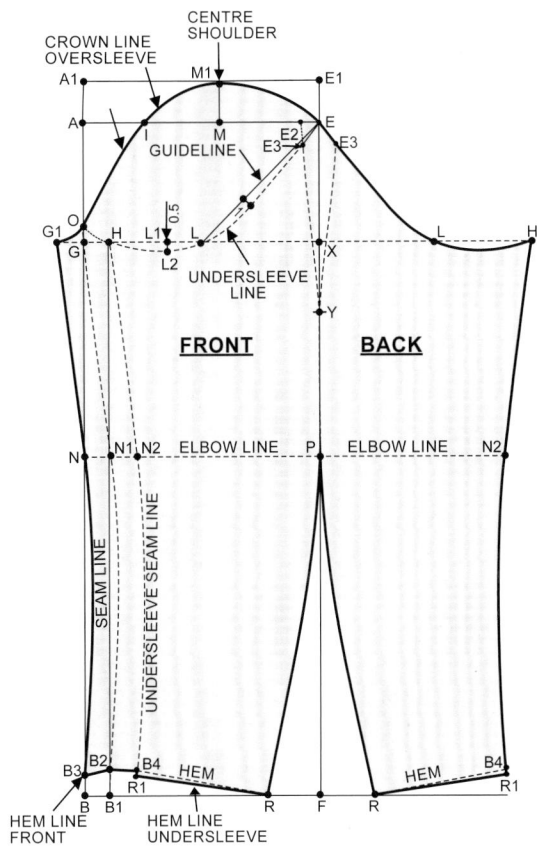

JOINED SLEEVE (diagram)

CROWN LINE OVERSLEEVE — CENTRE SHOULDER

A1　M1　E1
A　I　M　E　E2　E3
GUIDELINE
O　G1　G　H　L1　0.5　L　L2　X　E2　E3
UNDERSLEEVE LINE
FRONT　**BACK**
L　H
Y
N　N1　N2　ELBOW LINE　P　ELBOW LINE　N2
SEAM LINE　UNDERSLEEVE SEAM LINE
B3　B2　B4　HEM　HEM　B4
B　B1　R1　R　F　R　R1
HEM LINE FRONT　HEM LINE UNDERSLEEVE

JOINED SLEEVE

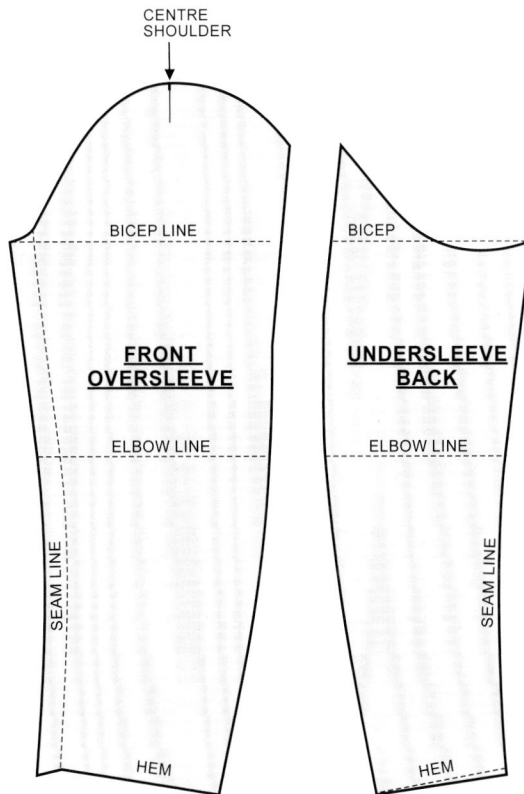

SLEEVE IN TWO PIECES (diagram)

CENTRE SHOULDER
BICEP LINE　BICEP
FRONT OVERSLEEVE　**UNDERSLEEVE BACK**
ELBOW LINE
SEAM LINE　SEAM LINE
HEM　HEM

SLEEVE IN TWO PIECES

Joined sleeve

Copy the undersleeve E2-Y-P-R-R1-H-E2, position it on E-F as illustrated in the figure and gracefully connect with the sleeve crown line. Always carefully double-check the total sleeve crown measurement, which must be greater than the measurement of the jacket armscye by a variable amount depending on the ease and the type of fabric used.

Sleeve assembly and construction

On a jacket, the sleeve is the first sign of good tailoring. There are different schools of thought as to the line of the sleeve crown. The classic system offers a gather-free sleeve, with a well-rounded, more or less ample crown. Then there is the Neapolitan system, which is well known and loved all over the world, with the 'mappina' (gathered) sleeve crown.

On the following pages, we will take a closer look at sleeve construction.

Drape

It is possible to see the drope of jacket sleeves and overcoats even while they're on a hanger: the sleeve should fall without folds and be turned slightly forward as if there were an arm inside. If that's the case, the sleeve is perfectly plumb. However, if it turns in on itself and tends towards the rear of the garment, its drape is imperfect and will make arm movements uncomfortable when worn. This defect cannot be corrected once the garment is made; it is a pattern error, unless it is enough to simply move the centre of the sleeve.

BASE JACKET - SLIM FIT

EASE 14 CM / 5 ½"

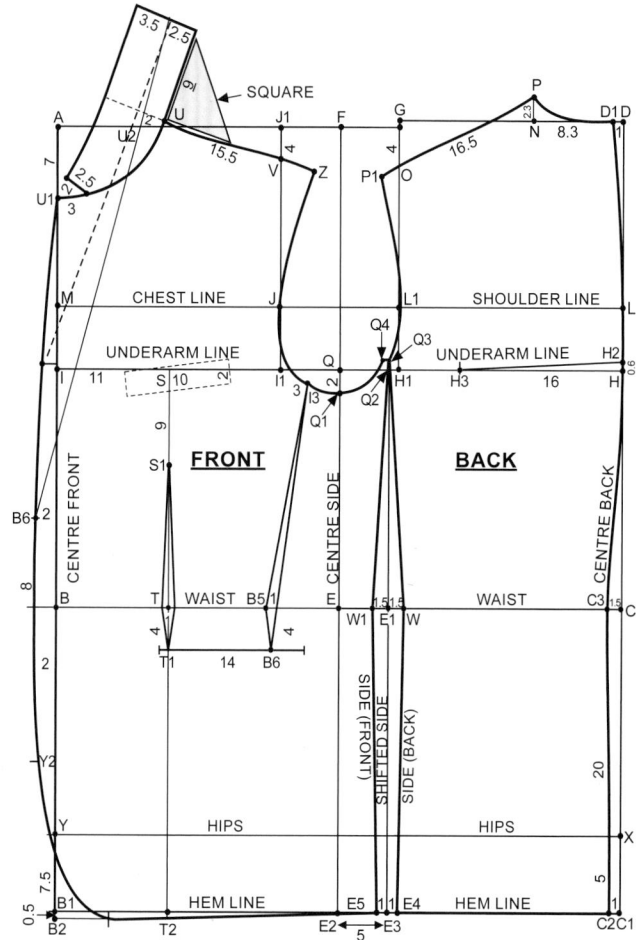

Size 16 UK measurements
- Height = 175 cm / 5'9".
- Chest semi-cir. = 96 + 14 = 110 ÷ 2 = 55 cm / 21.65"
- Waist semi-cir. = 88 + 14 = 102 ÷ 2 = 51 cm / 20.08"
- Hip semi-cir. = 100 + 14 = 114 ÷ 2 = 57 cm / 22.44"
- Neck semi-cir. = 42 ÷ 2 = 21 cm / 8.27"
- 1/2 shoulder width = 42 + 1.5 = 43.5 ÷ 2 = 21.75 cm / 8.56"
- Front neck to waist = 45.6 cm / 17.95".
- Rear neck to waist = 46.2 cm / 18.19".
- Draw right angle A-B-C, with:
- A-B = front neck-to-waist (e.g: 45.6 cm / 17.95").
- B-C = chest semi-circumference + 14 cm / 5.51") ease for slim fit (e.g: 96 + 14 = 110 : 2 = 55 cm / 21.65").
- D-C = rear neck to waist (e.g.: 46.2 cm / 18.19").
- D-C1 = jacket length (e.g: 75 cm / 29.53").
- Write 'Centre back'.
- B-B1 as C-C1 (28.8 cm / 11.34").
- Join A-B1 and write 'Centre front'.
- B1-C1 as B-C (55 cm / 21.65"). Join B1-C1 and write 'Lower edge' or 'Hem'.
- B-E half of B-C (27.5 cm / 10.83").
- B1-E2 as B- E (27.5 cm / 10.83").

- A-F like B-E (27.5 cm / 10.83").
- Join F-E2 (centre side).
- D-H half of D-C+ 0.5 cm / 0.20") (e.g: 46.2 ÷ 2 = 23.1 + 0.5 = 23.6 cm / 9.29").
- H-I like B-C = 55 cm / 21.65" (armpit level).
- E2-E3 = 5 cm / 2".
- Q-Q2 like E2-E3.   - Join Q2-E3: Shifted side.
- B-Y and C-X = waist to hip (e.g: 20-21.5 cm / 7.87-8.46").
- Draw Y-X and write 'Hip line'.
- D-G = half shoulder width + ease (e.g.: 42 + 1.5 = 43.4 ÷ 2 = 21.75 cm / 8.56").
- H-L = 1/4 of D-H (e.g.: 23.6 ÷ 4 = 5.9 cm / 2.32").
- Draw L-M and write 'Shoulder line' (L-L1) and 'Chest line' (M-J).
- H-H1 like D-G (e.g.: 21.75 cm / 8.56").
- Draw G-H1.
- I-I1 as D-G - 0.5 cm / 0.20" at the back (e.g: 21.75- 0.5 = 21.25 cm / 8.37").
- A-J1 as I-I1 (21.25 cm / 8.37").
- Draw I1-J1 parallel to G-H1.
- I1-H1 = H-I minus (I-I1 + H-H1) = 11.5 cm / 4.53" (e.g: 55 - (21.25 + 22.25) = 11.5 cm / 4.53" (armscye sector).

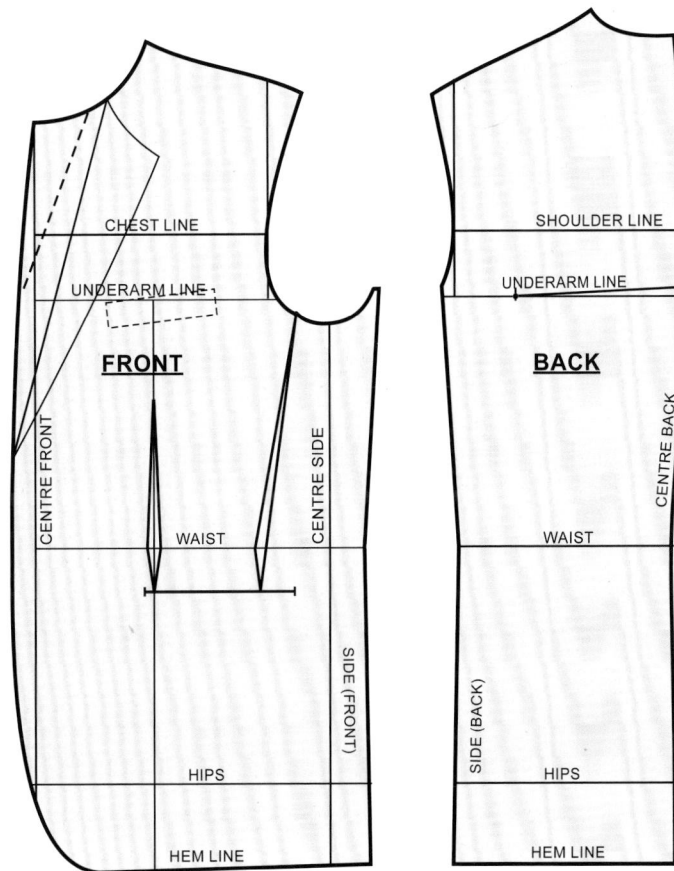

Diagram labels:

FRONT — CHEST LINE, UNDERARM LINE, CENTRE FRONT, WAIST, CENTRE SIDE, SIDE (FRONT), HIPS, HEM LINE

BACK — SHOULDER LINE, UNDERARM LINE, CENTRE BACK, WAIST, SIDE (BACK), HIPS, HEM LINE

COLLAR — C. BACK, 3.5, 2.5, 9 back collar, 2.5

BACK

- H-H3 = 16 cm / 6.30" (1/3 chest semi-circumference = 48 ÷ 3 = 16 cm / 6.30").
- H-H2 = 0.6 cm / 0.24".
- Create the right angle H3-H2-D1.
- Draw H2-D1 as H-D with a curve.
- G-O = 4-4.8 cm / 1.57-1.89".
- D1-N = 1/3 of D-G + 1 cm / 0.20" (e.g: 21.75 ÷ 3 = 7.25 + 1 = 8.25 cm / 3.25").
- N-P = 2.3 cm / 0.91".
- Draw the outline D1-P.
- P-P1 = shoulder length + 0.5 cm / 0.20" (e.g.: 1/3 chest circumference + 0.5 cm = 48 ÷ 3 = 16 + 0.5 = 16.5 cm /6.50").
- Draw the outline P-P1passing through O.
- L1-P1 = 12.7 cm / 5" (measurement for A-G sleeve).
- Q2-Q3 = 2.5 cm / 1".
- Draw the armhole P1-L1-Q3 smoothly.
- E1-W = 1.5 cm / 0.59".
- C-C3 = 1.2-1.7 cm / 0.47-0.66".   - C1-C2 like C-C3.
- Draw the centre back line D1-L-H-C3-C2.
- E3-E4 = 2 cm / 0.79".
- Draw the vent line (if any) with a height of 23 cm / 9.06" or as desired.

FRONT

- A-U half of A-J1 minus 0.5 cm / 0.20" (e.g.: 21.25 - 0.5 = 20.75 ÷ 2 = 10.3 cm / 4.06").
- A-U1 = 8 cm / 3.15". U-U2 = 2 cm / 0.79".
- Draw the breakline up to the desired height (e.g: 8 cm / 3.15" from the waist). J1-V = 4 cm / 1.57".
- U-Z as P-P1 at the rear minus 1 cm / 16.5 - 1 = 15.5 cm / 6.10".
- Draw the outline U-Z passing through V.
- Q-Q1 = 2 cm / 0.79".
- Q3-Q4 = 1 cm / 0.39".
- Carefully draw the armscye Z-J-Q1-Q4.
- E1-W1 = 1.5 cm / 0.59"; E3-E5 = 1 cm / 0.39" smoothly.
- Draw the side line Q4-W1-E5.
- Draw the lapel outline as shown in the figure.
- I-S = 11 cm / 4.33"; S-S1 = 9.5 cm / 3.74"; T-T1 = 8 cm / 3.15".
- Draw the dart as in the figure.
- T-B = 9 cm / 3.54".
- B5-B6 = 4 cm / 1.57".
- Draw the dart I3-B6 as in the figure.
- Make the collar, pocket and chest pocket as clearly illustrated.
- L1-P1 = H1-G minus H1-L1 minus G-O (e.g.: 23.6 - 5.9 - 4 = 13.7 cm / 5.39").

BASE JACKET SLEEVE - SLIM FIT

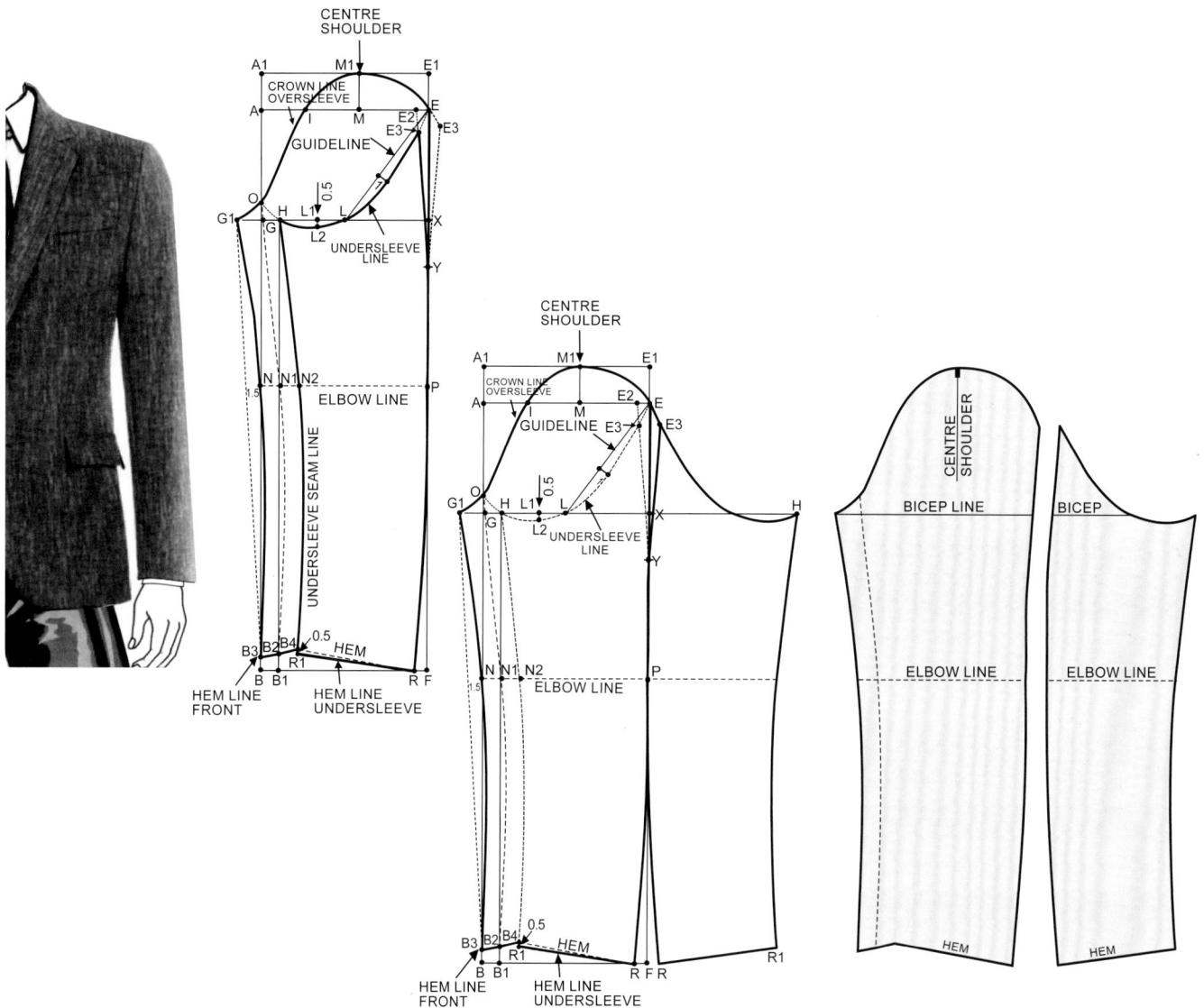

Measurements

- Bicep circumference = 29-30 cm / 11.42-11.81".
- Arm length = 62 cm / 24.41".

On the left side of a sheet of pattern paper draw the rectangle A-G-X-E with:

- A-E as base jacket sector + 1/2 sector + 1 cm / 0.39" (e.g.: 11.5 + 5.75 + 1 = 18.2 cm / 7.17".
- A-G equal to L1-P1 minus 1 cm / 0.39" on the rear torso base (e.g.: 13.7- 1 cm = 12.7 cm / 5").
- A-A1 = 1/3 of A-G (e.g: 12 ÷ 3 = 4 cm / 1.57").
- E-E1 like A-A1. Draw A-A1-E-E1.
- A1-B = sleeve length + 1 cm / 0.39" (e.g.: 62 + 1 = 63 cm / 24.80").
- A1-N (elbow) half of A1-B + 0.5 cm / 0.20" (e.g.: 65 ÷ 2 = 32.5 + 1 = 33.5 cm / 13.19").
- A-M = 1/2 A-E + 1 cm / 0.39" (e.g: 17 ÷ 2 = 8.5 + 1 = 9.5 cm / 3").
- Draw M-M1 (Centre shoulder).

- A-I = 1/4 of A-E (e.g: 17 ÷ 4 = 4.25 cm / 1.67").
- G-H = 2.5 cm / 1".
- Draw H-B1 parallel to A-B with a curve.
- X-L half of G-X (e.g.: 22.75 ÷ 2 = 11.37 cm / 4.48").
- Draw guideline E-L.
- L-L1 half of H-L.
- L1-L2 = 0.5 cm / 0.20".
- G-O = 1.5 cm / 0.59".
- G-G1 = 2.5 cm / 1".
- E-E2 = 2 cm / 0.79".
- E-E3 = 3 cm / 1.18".
- Smoothly draw the front sleeve crown E-M1-I-O-G1.
- Smoothly draw the rear sleeve crown E-E3-L-L2-H-O.
- B1-B2 = 2 cm / 0.79".
- B3-B2 and N-N1 = 2.5 cm / 1".
- B4-R1 = 0.5 cm / 0.20".
- Connect R-P-E3 and R1-N2-H with curved lines (under-sleeve).

140

LAPEL TYPES

Also called revers, the term 'lapel' refers to the folded part of the front neckline which is found below the collar.

It is one of the most important details of men's jackets, capable of radically changing the style and character of the garment. Depending on the customer's wishes and the tailor's way of doing things, it can be more or less substantial, padded with horsehair cloth, or more lightweight, reinforced only with thin cloth.

The notch

A small but crucial detail of the jacket is the notch, i.e., the small slit separating the collar from the lapel. Obviously, the shape of this element depends directly on the lapel chosen, although the 'classic' one forms an angle of less than 90° and is most often used for both tailored and industrial jackets.

Classic lapels (step or notched)

This type of lapel is the most common when it comes to jackets. In this case the notch is rather large and determines the placement and shape of the lapels: they form a right angle pointing laterally, towards the shoulder.

Pointed (or peak) lapels

This style is most commonly used to make double-breasted jackets, but is also seen on very formal suits such as morning coats or tailcoats. In contrast to the previous style, this type of lapel is formed by a very small notch that creates a lapel with the points oriented upwards, creating an optical effect that emphasises the width of the shoulders and chest.

Shawl (or roll) lapels

Less common but certainly more distinctive than the others, the shawl lapel, also called a roll collar, is certainly the most distinctive. It is commonly found on dinner jackets and robes: it has a rounded shape and does not have a notch. In this case, therefore, the lapel is a simple segment that starts at the collar and ends below the chest. The lapel and collar are thus made up of a single strip of fabric.

Length and width of lapels

There is no fixed, universal rule on this subject, but everything varies according to different styles and schools of thought. Traditional Neapolitan tailoring, for example, has always opted for wider lapels, while many other schools of tailoring prefer more proportionate, narrower lapels.

In general, however, the customer will be inclined to choose between classic, pointed or shawl lapels mainly according to the use and occasion on which the jacket will be worn, while the length and width of the lapel will be determined mainly by personal taste. A particular type of men's jacket, entirely without lapels, became popular during the 1960s: today it is echoed on sportier, more casual styles. Jackets

without lapels or with very short lapels are mainly worn on informal occasions and we generally see them on double-breasted jackets with four or more buttons.

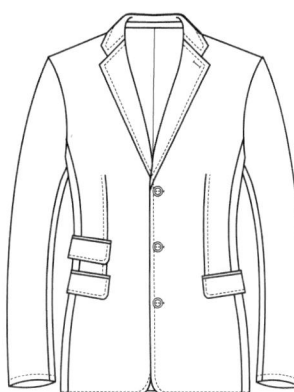

Step, single-breasted.

Step, double-breasted.

Pointed, single-breasted.

Pointed, double-breasted.

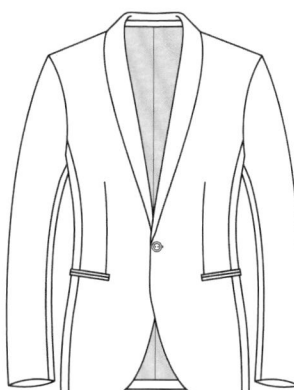

Shawl, single-breasted.

Shawl, double-breasted.

FASTENINGS AND LAPELS

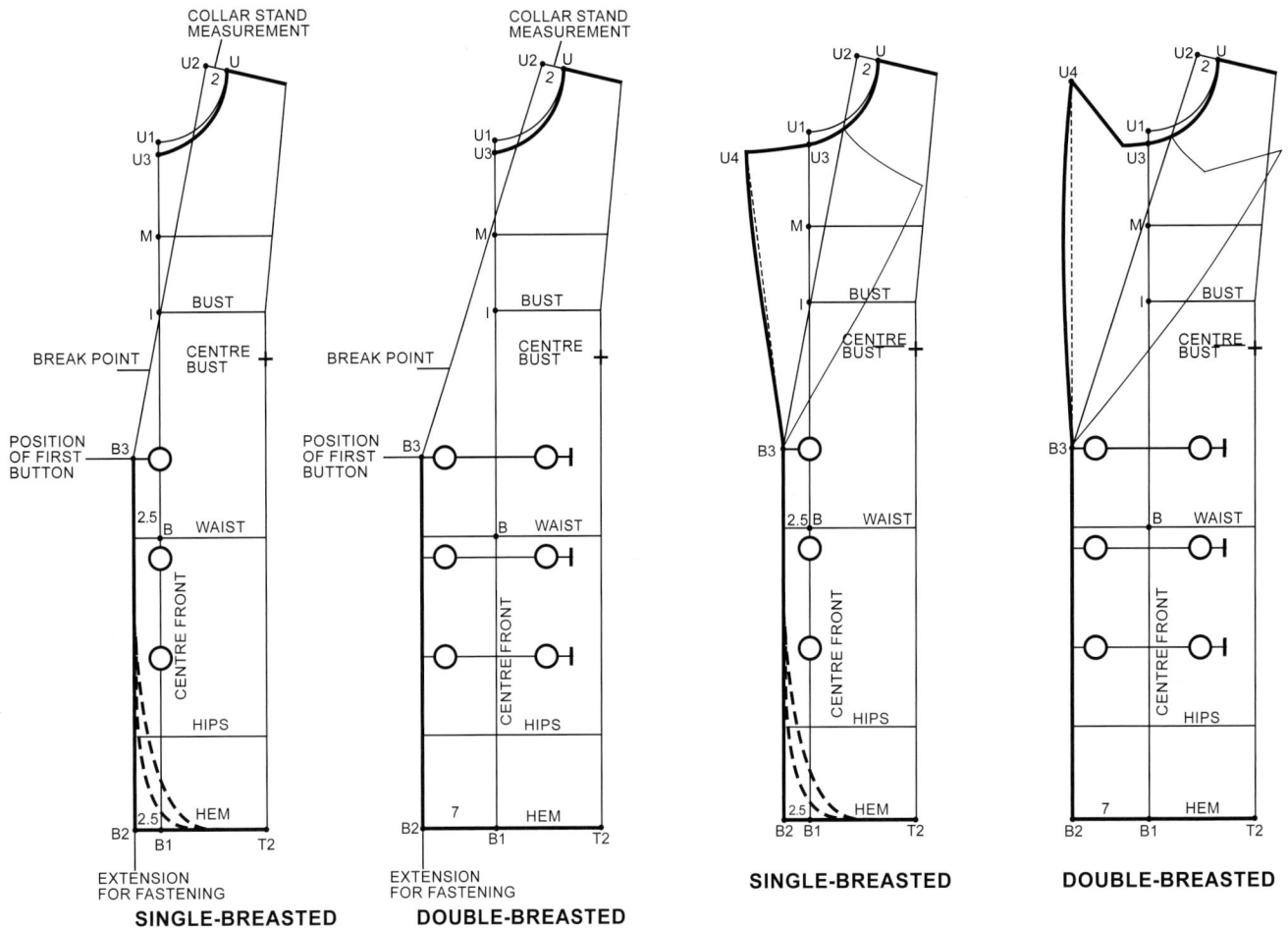

The fastening refers to the overlapping of the two parts of the front. There are two types as far as jackets are concerned:
1) single-breasted, which is the simpler of the two; and
2) double-breasted, the more complex option.
The measurements of the overlap may vary depending on the pattern, the type of garment and its style.

Single-breasted jackets

For single-breasted jackets, the overlap of the two front pieces ranges from 2.5 cm to 3 cm / 1-1.18". For coats and overcoats, the overlap is between 4 cm and 5 cm / 1.57-2".

Execution

- Extend the centre front B1-B2 by 2.5 cm / 1" and shape the lower edge as desired.
- Mark the position of the first button on overlap line B3, at the desired height, according to the figure.
- From U on the collar, extend the shoulder line by 2-2.5 cm / 0.79-1", depending on the height of the collar stand.
- Draw the breakline (or fold) U2-B3.

Double-breasted jackets

For double-breasted jacket and coat patterns, the overlap of the two front pieces is 7-8 cm / 2.76-3.15".

Execution

- Extend the centre front B1-B2 by 7-8 cm / 2.76-3.15".
- Mark the position of the first button on overlap line B3 at the desired height, according to the figure.
- From U on the collar, extend the shoulder line by 2-2.5 cm / 0.79-1", depending on the height of the collar.
- Draw the breakline U2-B3.

Lapels (or revers)

Lapels are flaps that extend from the front panels of the jacket, being an integral part of them. Lapels can come in different shapes and widths, depending on the pattern and style of the garment, so no measurements are marked on the base.

Execution

- Lower point U1 as desired, according to the position and length of the collar and the shape of the lapel.
- Draw the extension of the collar U4 with the desired measurements.
- Join U4 to B3, smoothly adjusting the shape.
- To check that the lapel corresponds to the pattern and has the correct width and position, after having constructed the outer part, fold it along the breakline and make the necessary corrections (if any).

BOLERO

FRONT

CENTRE FRONT

9 · 7 · 4 · 15.5 · 4 · 4 · 4

CHEST LINE

UNDERARM LINE

10

6

WAISTLINE

SIDE (FRONT)

BACK

15.5 · 8.5 · 1 · 2.5

SHOULDER LINE

UNDERARM LINE
16

SIDE (BACK)

CENTRE BACK

WAISTLINE

4 · 4 · 3 · 3 · 6 · 1.5

53

FRONT

4

CHEST LINE

UNDERARM LINE

SIDE (FRONT)

4

4

BACK

SHOULDER LINE

UNDERARM LINE
16

SIDE (BACK)

CENTRE BACK

4 · 4

CENTRE
SHOULDER

BALANCED
CENTRE
SHOULDER

A1 · M1 · E1

8.5 · 1 · 4 · E2

A · 3.5 · M · E3 · E

12

OVERSLEEVE

O · 7.5 · BICEP · X

G1 · 2.5 · G · 2.5 · H · L2 · L

UNDERSLEEVE

N · N1 · N2 · ELBOW · P

61

B3 · 2.5 · 2.5 · B4 · 9 · 1 F

B2 · R1

B · B1 · 15 · R

HEM LINE
FRONT

HEM LINE
UNDERSLEEVE

CENTRE SHOULDER

BICEP LINE
17.5

OVERSLEEVE

ELBOW
15.5

2.5 · 9

BICEP
12.5

UNDERSLEEVE

ELBOW
11

9

Measurements: size 16 UK (as in the chart).
Chest ease = 14 cm / 5 ½".

Note:
The sleeve cap is 2.5 cm / 1" larger than the armhole measurement of
the bodice.

THREE-BUTTON SINGLE BREASTED JACKET

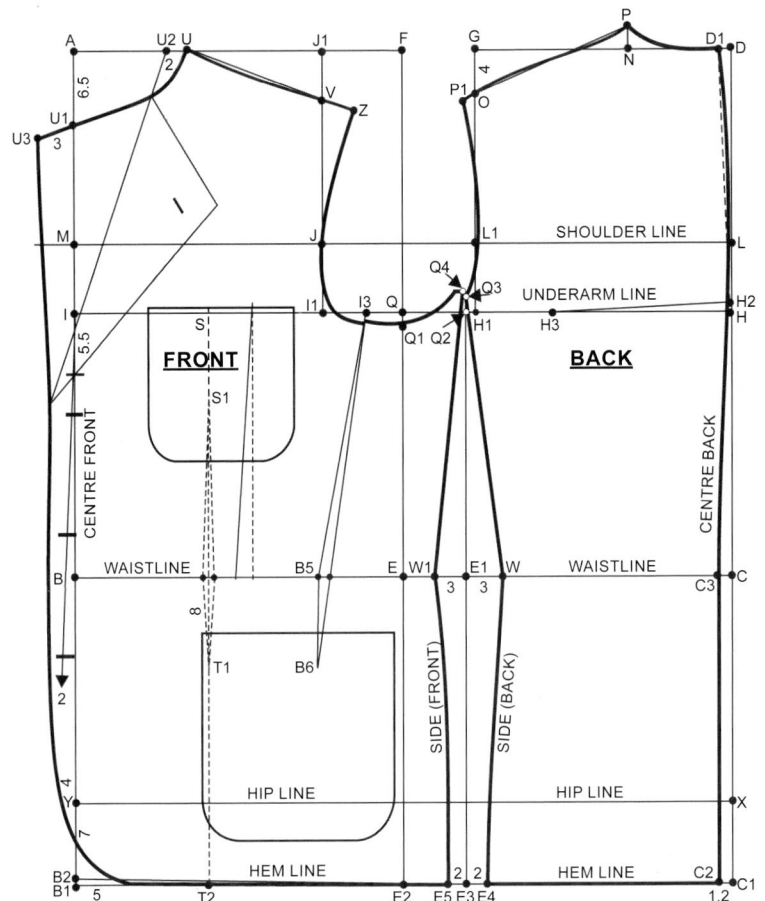

- Draw the jacket base block with the appropriate measurements and ease.
- Make the breakline for the lapel 5-5.5 cm / 2-2.17" from the armpit level line.
- A-U1 = 6.5 cm / 2.56".
- Draw the overlap and lapel line according to the new measurements.
- Draw the patch pockets as in the figure.

When making this jacket, it's a good idea to specify how far the client's belly protrudes, so as not to end up with an imprecise overlap.

Placement of the pattern is also important. Indeed, extra care must be taken while arranging the front pieces on the fabric, ensuring that the selvedge is perfectly parallel to the edge of the pattern, from the waistline to the armscye level. It would be problematic if one neglected this suggested placement technique, especially when it comes to striped fabric. The figure must be in harmony with all the aesthetic details of the style. Note that after placing the button corresponding to the pocket level, the others follow at a distance equal to the width of the pocket.

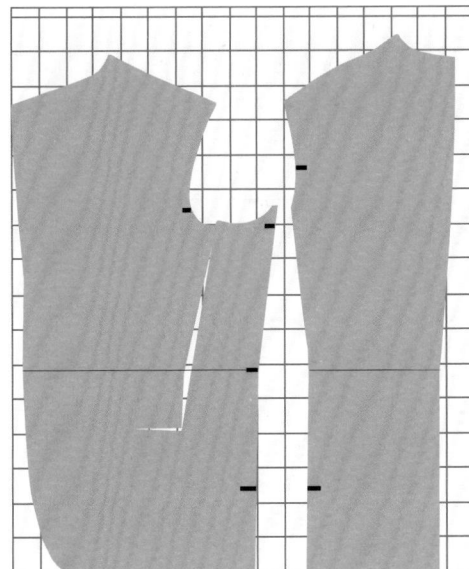

Glen plaid is suitable for this style but, to allow the print to line up at the salient parts of the jacket, it is best to use a rather thick interfacing to emphasise the hollow at the waist and to give greater support to the lateral pieces, making the lengths converge perfectly at the waist. The paper pattern is created by closing the regular dart, shifting it to create a horizontal one. The central dart should be eliminated so as to maintain the flow of the print. The back should be less round and the hips should have a straight line.

DECONSTRUCTED JACKET BASE - REGULAR FIT

EASE 18 CM / 7 1/8"

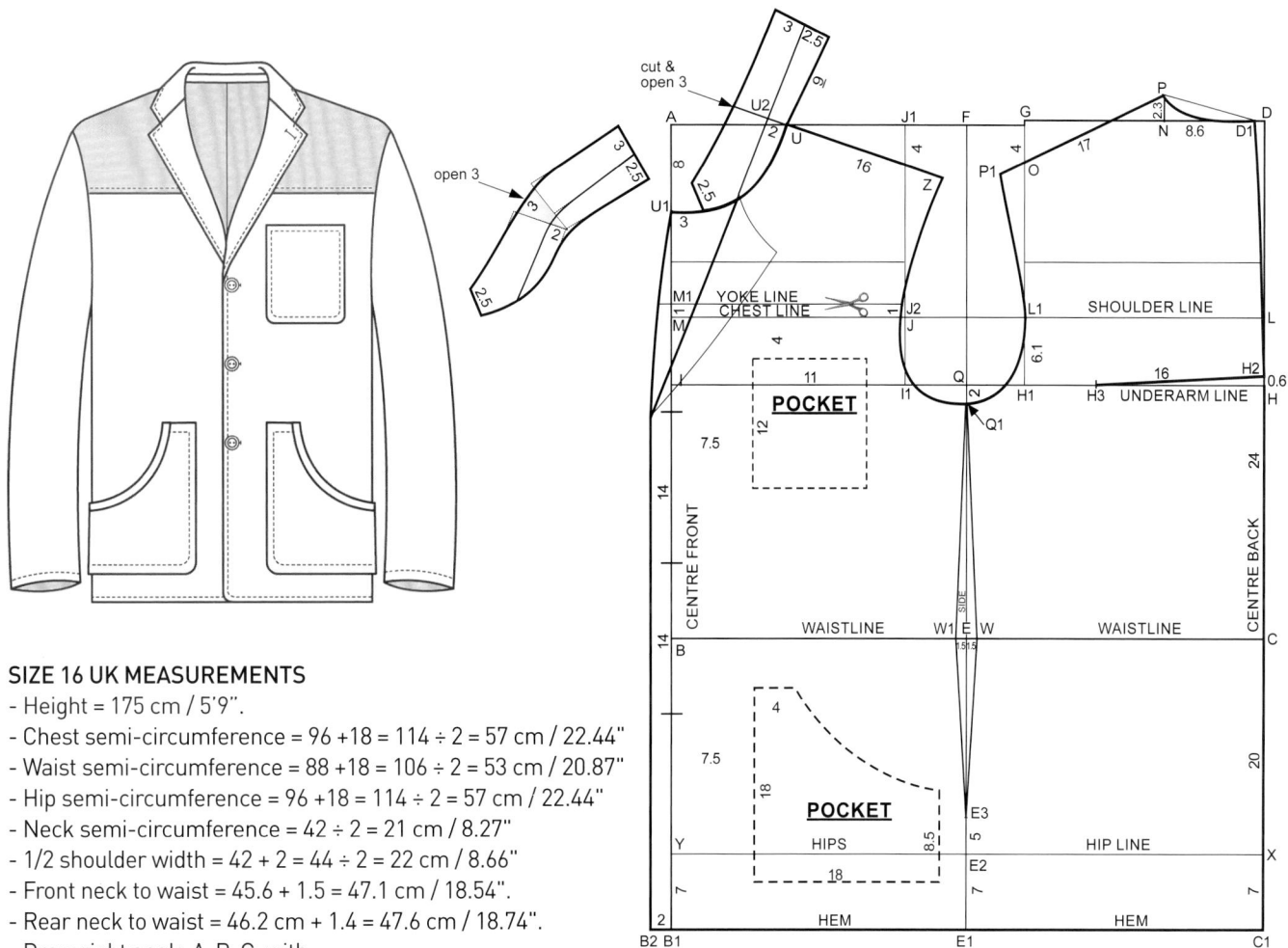

SIZE 16 UK MEASUREMENTS

- Height = 175 cm / 5'9".
- Chest semi-circumference = 96 +18 = 114 ÷ 2 = 57 cm / 22.44"
- Waist semi-circumference = 88 +18 = 106 ÷ 2 = 53 cm / 20.87"
- Hip semi-circumference = 96 +18 = 114 ÷ 2 = 57 cm / 22.44"
- Neck semi-circumference = 42 ÷ 2 = 21 cm / 8.27"
- 1/2 shoulder width = 42 + 2 = 44 ÷ 2 = 22 cm / 8.66"
- Front neck to waist = 45.6 + 1.5 = 47.1 cm / 18.54".
- Rear neck to waist = 46.2 cm + 1.4 = 47.6 cm / 18.74".
- Draw right angle A-B-C, with:
- A-B = front neck-to waist + ease (e.g.: 45.6 + 1.5 = 47.1 cm / 18.54").
- B-C = chest semi-circumference + ease (e.g.: 96 + 18 = 114 ÷ 2 = 57 cm / 22.44")
- D-C = rear neck to waist + ease (e.g.: 46.2 + 1.4 = 47.6 cm / 18.74").
- D-C1 = jacket length (e.g: 75 cm / 29.53").
- Join D-C1 and write 'Centre back'.
- B-B1 as C-C1 = 27.4 cm / 10.79".
- Join A-B1 and write 'Centre front'.
- B1-C1 as B-C. Join B1-C1 and write 'Lower edge'.
- B-E half of B-C; B1-E1 as B-E; A-F as B-E.
- Join F-E1 (side).
- D-H half of C-D + 0.5 cm / 0.20"(e.g: 47.6 ÷ 2 = 23.8 + 0.5 = 24.3 cm / 9.57").
- H-I as B-C = 57 cm / 22.44" (underarm level).
- B-Y and C-X = waist to hip (e.g: 20 cm / 7.87").
- Draw Y-X and write 'Hip line'.
- D-G = half shoulder width + ease ÷ 2 (e.g: 42 + 2 = 44 ÷ 2 = 22 cm / 8.66").
- H-L = 1/4 of D-H (e.g.: 24.3 ÷ 4 = 6 cm / 2.36").
- Draw L-M and write 'Shoulder line' and 'Chest line'.
- H-H1 like D-G (e.g: 22 cm / 8.66"). Draw G-H1.
- I-I1 as D-G - 0.5 cm / 0.20" at the back (e.g: 22 - 0.5 = 21.5 cm / 8.46").
- A-J1 as I-I1 (21.5 cm / 8.46"). Draw I1-J1 parallel to G-H1.
- I1-H1 = H-I minus I-I1 + H-H1 (e.g: 57 - 43.5 (22+ 21.5) = 13.5 cm / 5.31" (armscye or underarm sector).

BACK

- H-H3 = 16 cm / 6.30"; H-H2 = 0.6 cm / 0.24".
- Create the right angle H3-H2-D1.
- Draw H2-D1 like H-D with a curve.
- G-O = 4 cm / 1.57"; D1-N = 1/3 of D-G + 1 cm / 0.39" (e.g: 23 ÷ 3 = 7.66 + 1 = 8.66 cm / 3.41".
- N-P = 2.3 cm / 0.91". Draw the outline D1-P.
- P-P1 = shoulder length + 1 cm / 0.79" (e.g.: 16 + 1 = 17 cm / 6.69").
- Draw the outline P-P1 passing through O; Q-Q1, 2 cm / 0.79".
- Smoothly draw the armhole P1-L1-Q.
- E-W = 1.5 cm / 0.59"; E-W1 = 1.5 cm / 0.59"; E2-E3 = 5 cm / 1".
- L1-P1 = H1-G minus H1-L1 minus G-O.

FRONT

- A-U half of A-J1 minus 0.5 cm / 0.20" (e.g.: 23 ÷ 2 = 11.5 - 0.5 = 11 cm / 4.33".
- A-U1 = 8 cm / 3.15"; U-U2 = 2 cm / 0.79".
- Draw the breakline up to the desired height (e.g: 8 cm / 3.15" from the waist). J1-V = 4 cm / 1.57".
- U-Z as P-P1 at the rear minus 1 cm / 0.39" (1/3 chest semi-circumference = 48 ÷ 3 = 16 cm / 6.30").
- Draw the outline U-Z passing through V; Q-Q1= 2 cm / 0.79".
- Draw the armhole Z-J-Q1 smoothly; E-W1= 1.5 cm / 0.59".
- Draw the side line Q1-W1-E1; B1-B2 = 2 cm / 0.79".
- Draw the outline B2-U1 smoothly.

COLLAR

Make the collar as clearly illustrated in the figure.

DECONSTRUCTED JACKET

Also called unstructured, these are garments whose excessive rigidity has been removed from their structure, thus re-inventing the jacket in terms of volumes and further developing the concept of luxury in men's fashion. This 'relaxed' style was created in opposition to the idea of formality, and its design and fit adapt perfectly to the body in a mix of elegance and comfort. Deconstructed jackets come in different shapes, fabrics and cuts that make them suitable for even the most formal occasions. In cashmere, merino wool, silk or linen, with tailored details on the inside, deconstructed jackets today are a new way to conceive of elegance, revisited with an original and modern twist. Giorgio Armani first came up with the idea for this innovative jacket in the late 1970s/early 1980s, a real revolution in fashion as it was considered a unisex of garment.

DIFFERENCES WITH BLAZERS

Men's deconstructed jackets can be classified as refined sportswear garments designed to be more casual than blazers. It differs from the latter precisely because it is more casual in character, a sign of the transition to comfortable fits made in a tailored manner, just as the blazer did in the past with respect to formal jackets. Since it has no shoulder pads or lining, its main strength is its essential nature, the very thing that makes it a *must* for anyone who wants to wear jackets all-year round, even in summer, or for those who prefer a garment that adapts to their shoulders and body shape. Deconstructed jackets are ideal worn with a pullover jumper (sweater) or button-down shirt, with jeans or casual trousers, for a refined but not too formal everyday look. They combine some features of the classic elegant menswear jacket with those of casual style, a truly classy item in the contemporary man's wardrobe.

LININGS AND TRIM

Deconstructed jackets are usually only partially lined, making them cooler and lighter than fully lined jackets. As a result, all the seams and edges of the facing, now visible due to the absence of the lining, must be finished with appropriate edging to prevent fraying and to give the garment a pleasing appearance on the inside as well.
So, what follows is a primer on how to finish deconstructed jackets internally.

Before placing the pattern and cutting the fabric, it is a good idea to finish all seam allowances before sewing, so that it can be done more easily. In addition, it is necessary to leave an extra 2-2.5 cm / 0.79-1" allowance in order to be able to finish the seams later.
There are three ways to finish the seams:
1) Stitching in the folds for light to medium weight fabrics.
2) Overlock stitching with an overlocker.
3) and 4) A border, sewing a strip of bias rayon on the allowance at 2.5-3 mm (0.1-0.12") from the cut edge. Fold the

strip and place it on the edge on the 'wrong' side, sew in the groove of the previous seam and trim 5 mm (0.20") from the seam.

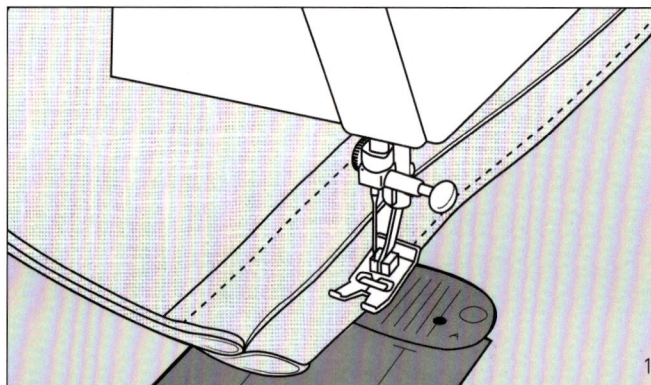

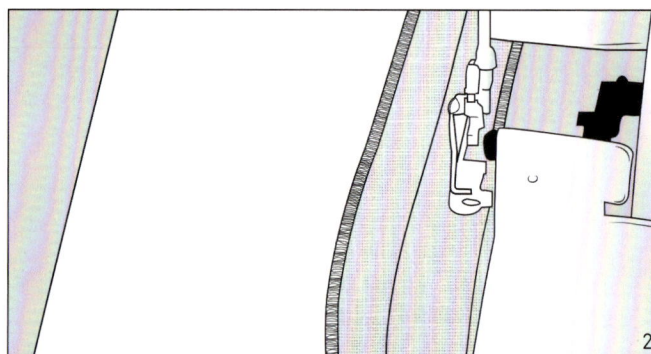

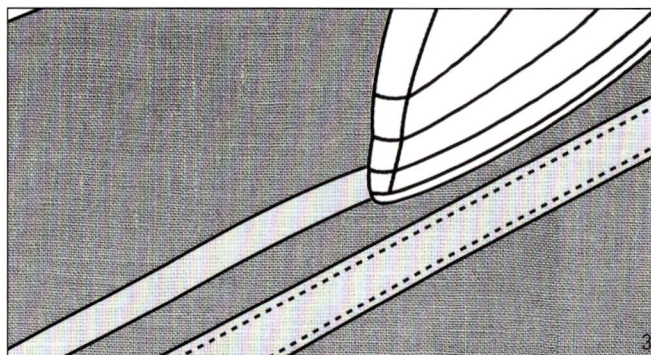

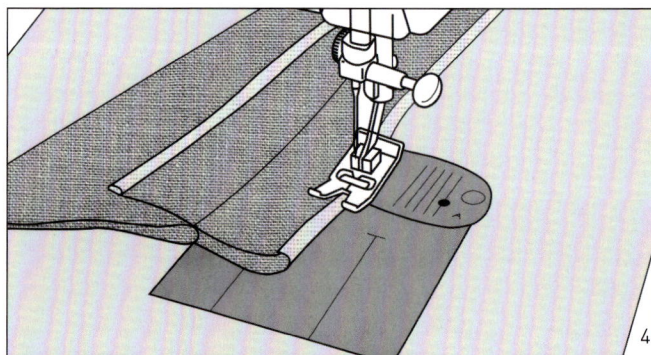

APPLYING PARTIAL LINING

1) First make a supporting seam on the neckline and shoulders of the back lining, previously cut with the pattern. Fold the hem twice for 5 mm (0.20") and topstitch it.

2) Finish the inside edge of the facing so that it's the same as the lining and sew the side seams of the front facing and the back lining, right sides together, then iron the edges towards the back.

3) Make small cuts along the neckline of the lining, pin it to the collar, shoulders and armholes, sew it with a slip stitch, and baste the armhole.

4) Sew the lateral edges of the lining and the fabric together; sew the lower edge of the placket facing along the hem fold. Finally, sew and hem the sleeve linings.

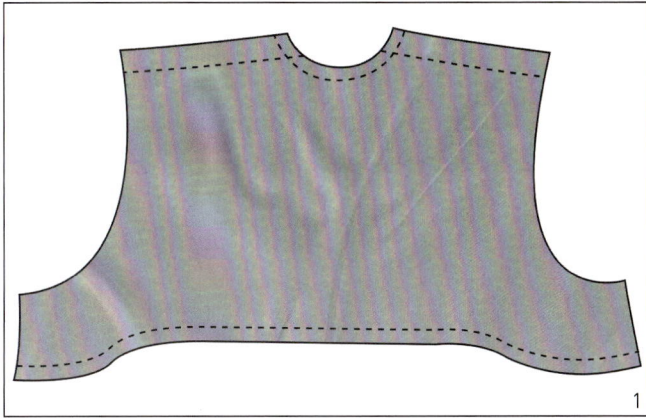

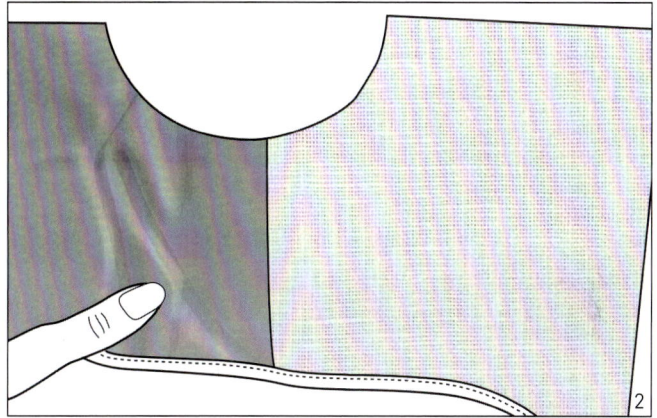

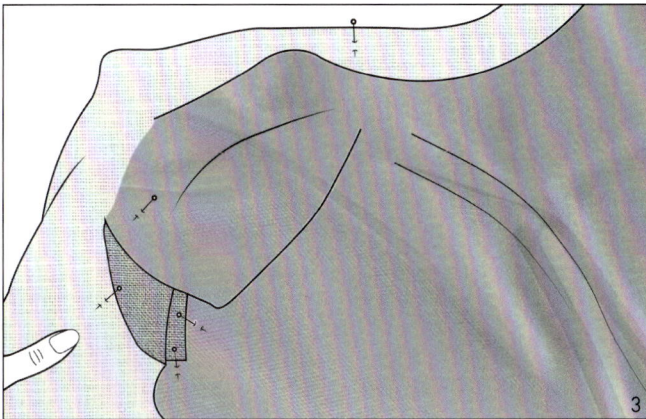

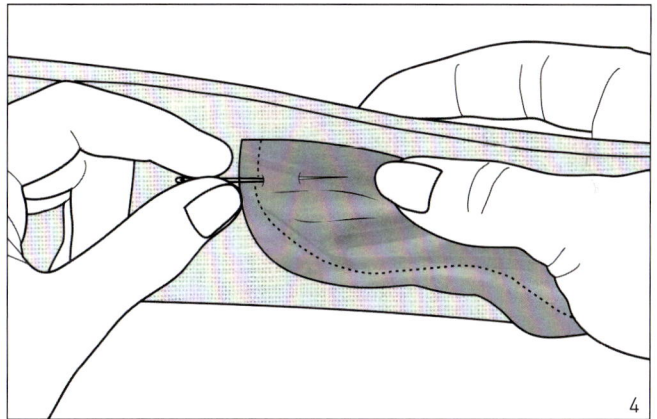

LOOSE DECONSTRUCTED JACKET WITH A YOKE

EASE 18 CM / 7 1/8"

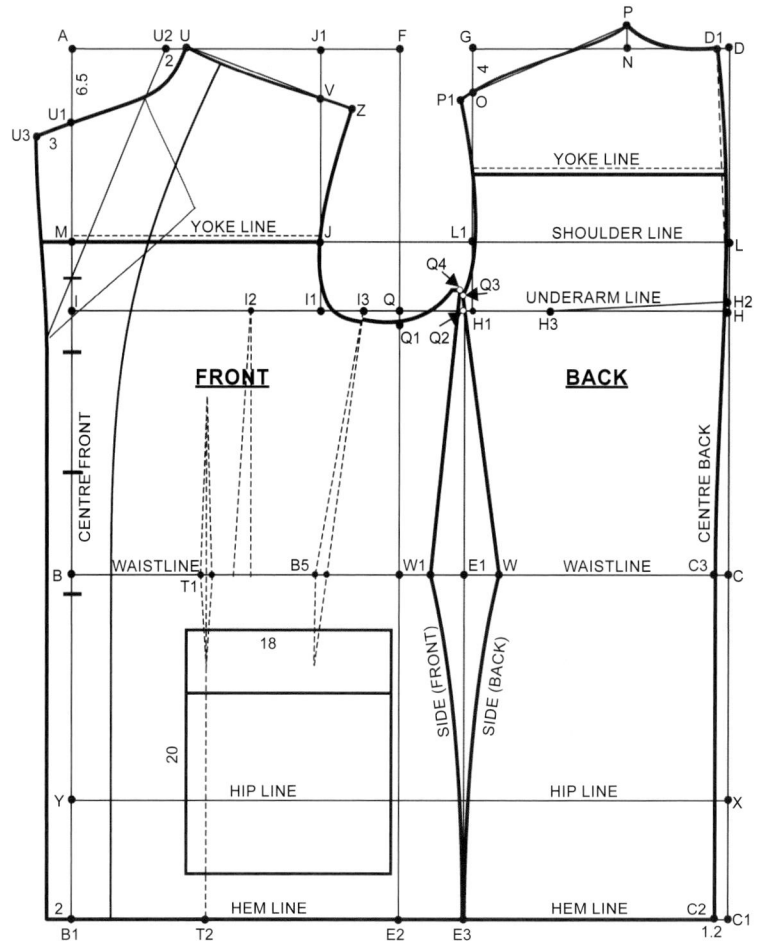

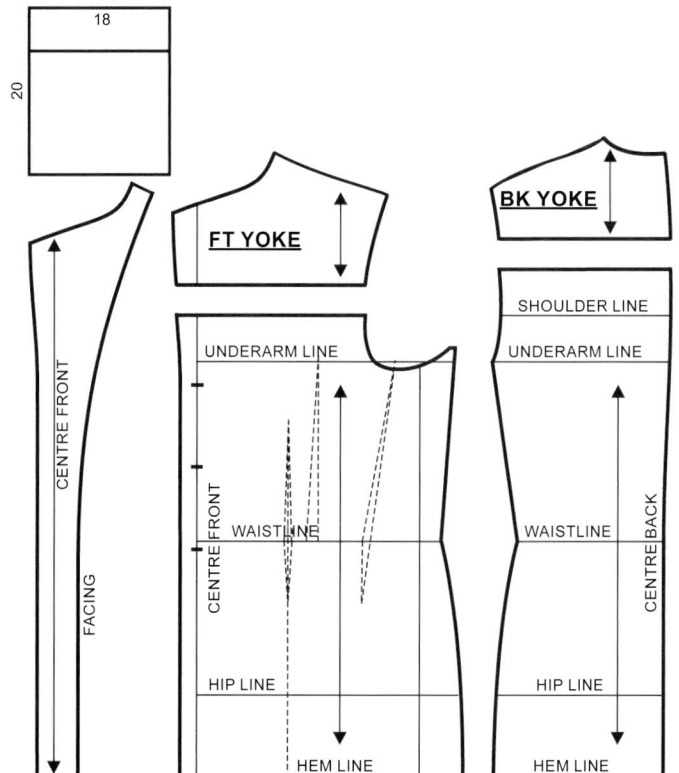

- Draw the deconstructed jacket base with 18 cm / 7.09" ease.
- Eliminate the darts and reduce the waist tapering to create the desired fit.
- Draw the breakline (or fold) in the desired position.
- Draw the front and back yoke lines at the desired height.
- Draw the pocket
- Draw the facing.
- Take up all parts of the pattern.

DECONSTRUCTED SAFARI JACKET

EASE 18 CM / 7 1/8"

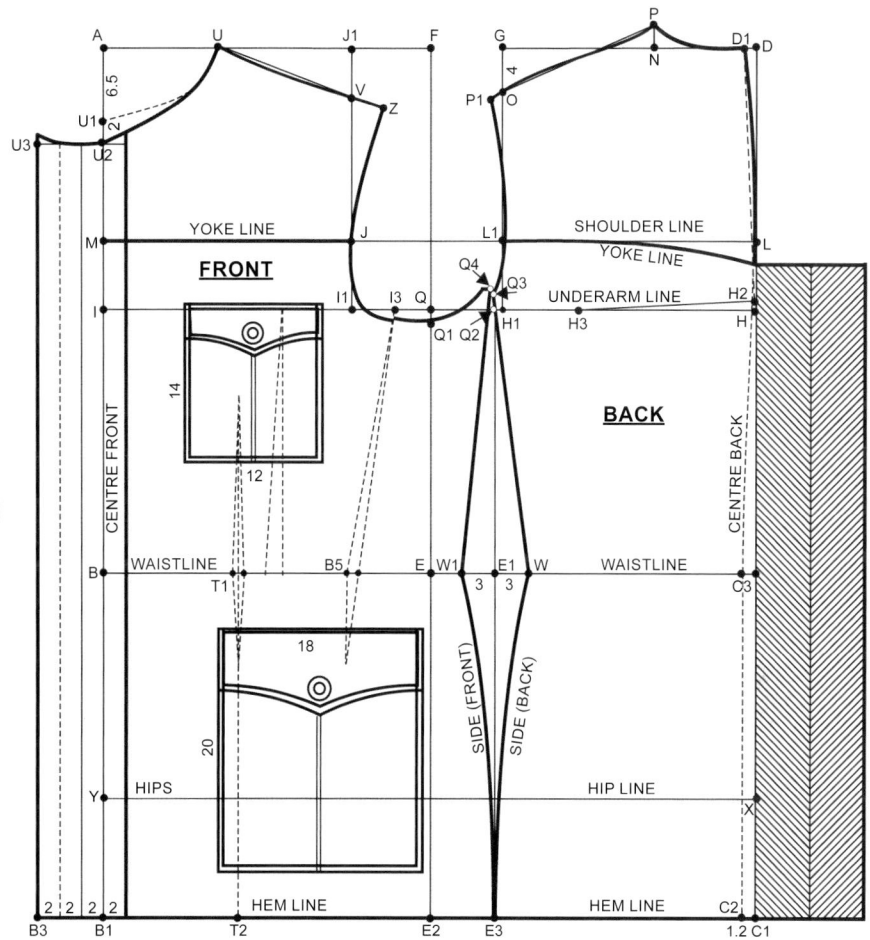

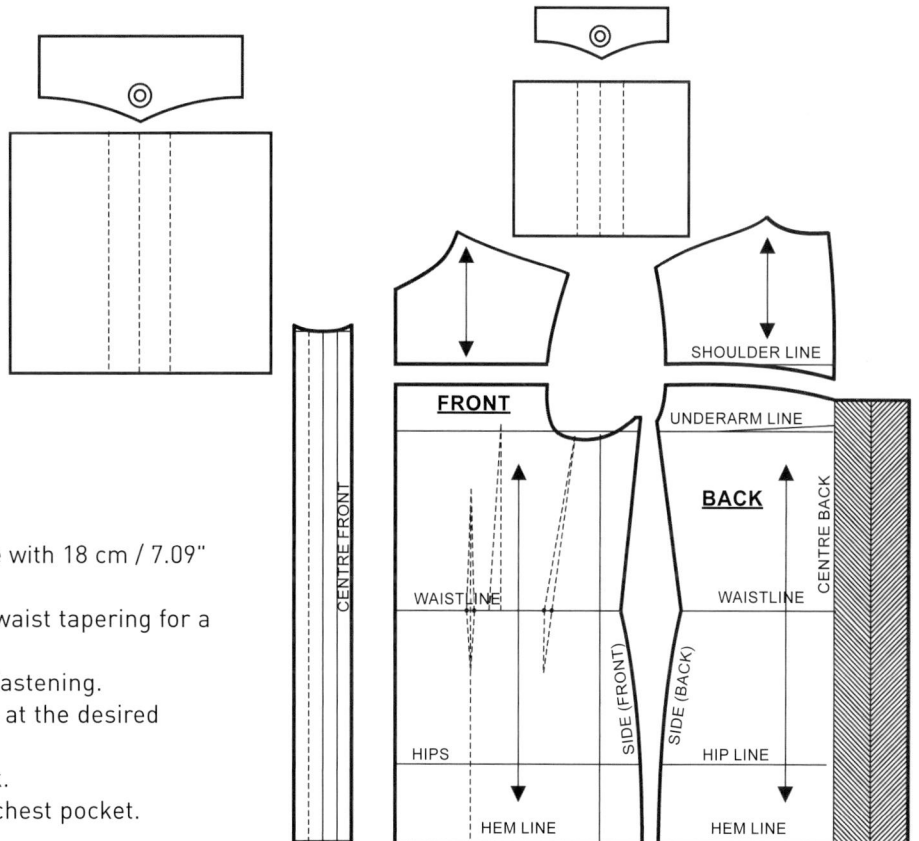

- Draw the deconstructed jacket base with 18 cm / 7.09" ease.
- Eliminate the dart and reduce the waist tapering for a looser fit.
- Draw the extension for the button fastening.
- Draw the front and back yoke lines at the desired height, in the desired shape.
- Draw the inverted pleat at the back.
- Draw the front hip pocket and the chest pocket.
- Take up all parts of the pattern.

DECONSTRUCTED NORFOLK JACKET

EASE 18 CM / 7 1/8"

COLLAR

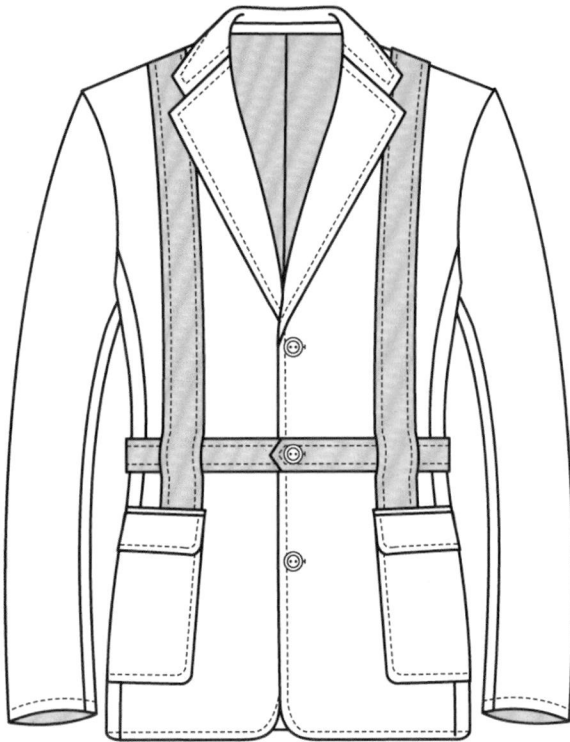

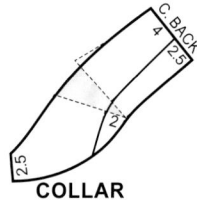

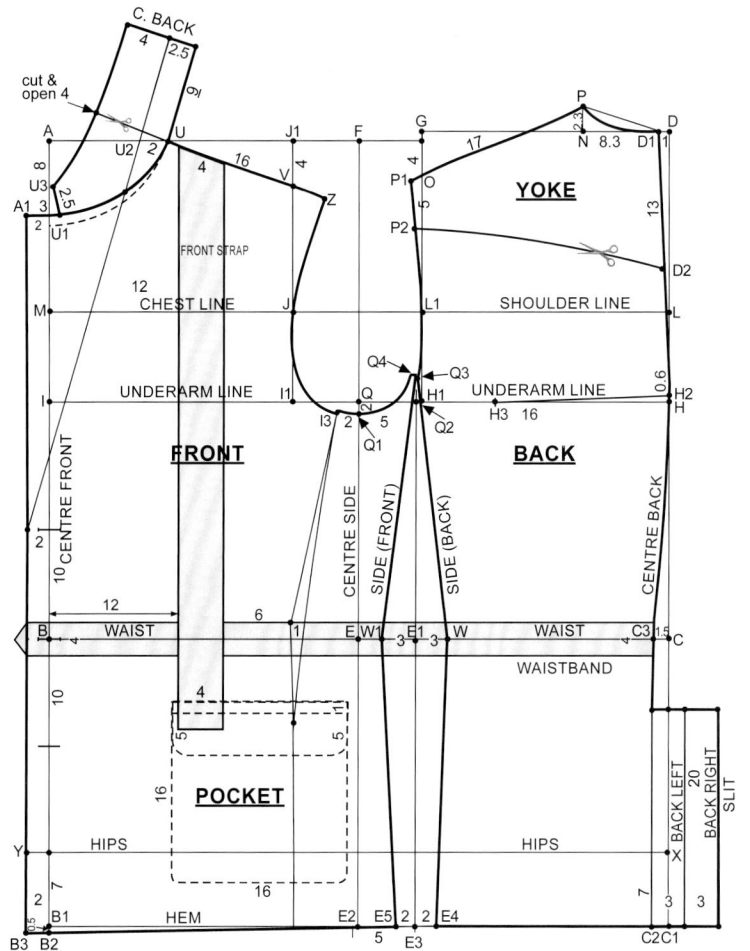

Size 16 UK measurements

- Height = 175 cm / 5'9".
- Chest semi-cir. = 96 +18 = 114 ÷ 2 = 57 cm / 22.44"
- Waist semi-cir. = 88 +18 = 106 ÷ 2 = 53 cm / 20.87"
- Hip semi-cir. = 96 +18 = 114 ÷ 2 = 57 cm / 22.44"
- Neck semi-cir. = 42 ÷ 2 = 21 cm / 8.27"
- 1/2 shoulder width = 42 + 2 = 44 ÷ 2 = 22 cm / 8.66"
- Front neck to waist = 45.6 + 1 = 46.6 cm / 18.35".
- Rear neck to waist = 46.2 cm + 1 = 47.2 cm / 18.58".
- Draw the right angle A-B-C, with:
- A-B = front neck to waist + ease (e.g.: 45.6 + 1 = 46.6 cm / 18.35").
- B-C = chest semi-circumference + ease (e.g: 96 + 18 = 114 ÷ 2 = 57 cm / 22.44"
- D-C as A-B + 0.6 cm / 0.24".
- D-C1 = jacket length (e.g: 75 cm / 29.53").
- Join D-C1 and write 'Centre back'.
- B-B1 like C-C1. Join A-B1 and write 'Centre front'.
- B1-C1 as B-C. Join B1-C1 and write 'Hem'.
- B-E half of B-C. B1-E2 as B-E.
- A-F like B-E. Join F-E2 and write 'Centre side'.
- D-H half of D-C + 0.5 cm / 0.20" (e.g: 48 ÷ 2 = 24 + 0.5 = 24.5 cm / 9.65").

- H-I parallel to B-C, write 'Armpit level'.
- E2-E3 = 5 cm / 2".
- Q-Q2 like E2-E3.
- Join Q2-E3 and write 'Shifted side'.
- B-Y and C-X = waist to hip (e.g: 20 cm / 7.87").
- Draw Y-X and write 'Hip line'.
- D-G = (shoulder width + ease) ÷ 2 (e.g.: 42 + 2 = 44 ÷ 2 = 22 cm / 8.66").
- H-L = 1/4 of D-H (e.g.: 24.5 ÷ 4 = 6.12 cm / 2.41").
- Draw L-M and write 'Shoulder line' and 'Chest line'.
- H-H1 like D-G (e.g: 22 cm / 8.66").
- Draw G-H1.
- I-I1 as D-G - 0.5 cm / 0.20" at the back (e.g: 22 - 0.5 = 21.5 cm / 8.46").
- A-J1 as I-I1 (21.5 cm / 8.46").
- Draw I1-J1 parallel to G-H1.
- I1-H1 = H-I minus I-I1 + H-H1 [e.g: 57 - 43.5 (22 + 21.5) = 13.5 cm / 5.31" = armscye or armhole sector].
- L1-P1 = H1-G minus H1-L1 minus G-O (e.g: 24.5 - 6.12 - 4 = 14.38 cm / 5.66").

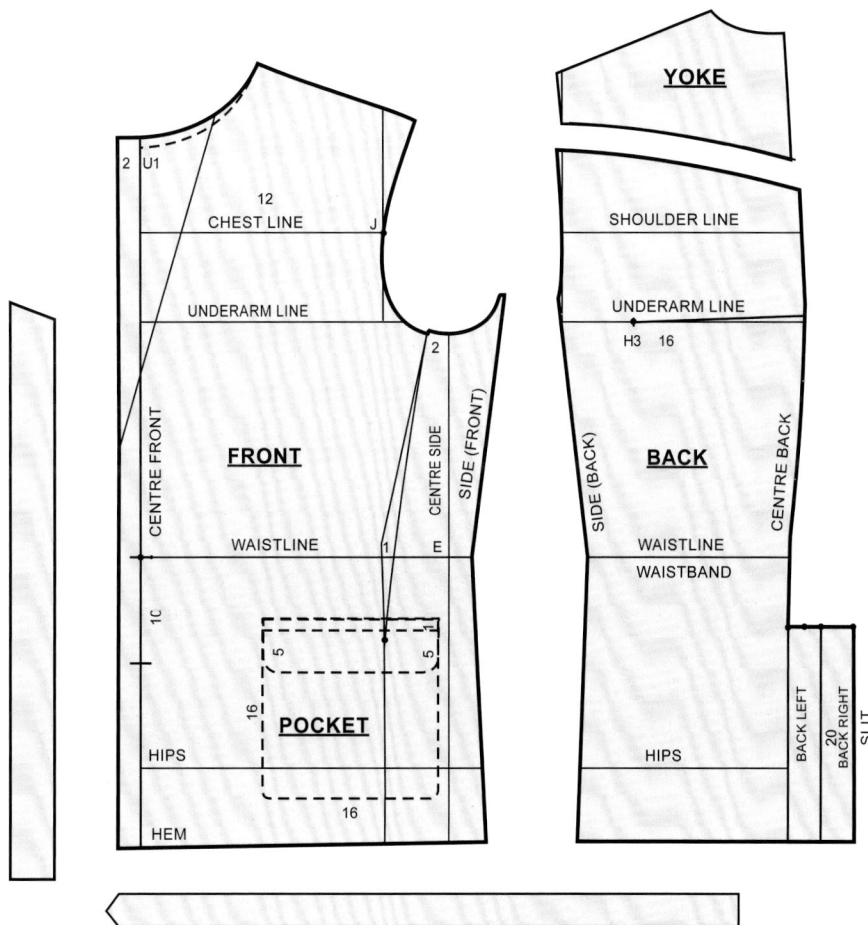

YOKE

SHOULDER LINE

UNDERARM LINE

H3 16

SIDE (BACK)

BACK

CENTRE BACK

WAISTLINE

WAISTBAND

BACK LEFT

20 BACK RIGHT

SLIT

HIPS

2 U1

12

CHEST LINE J

UNDERARM LINE

2

CENTRE FRONT

FRONT

CENTRE SIDE

SIDE (FRONT)

WAISTLINE 1 E

1C

5

5

16 **POCKET**

HIPS

16

HEM

BACK

- H-H3 = 16 cm / 6.30".
- H-H2 = 0.6 cm / 0.24".
- Create the right angle H3-H2-D1.
- Draw H2-D1 like H-D with a curve.
- G-O = 4-4.8 cm / 1.57-1.89".
- D1-N = 1/3 of D-G + 1 cm / 0.20" (e.g: 23 ÷ 3 = 7.66 + 1 = 8.66 cm / 3.41").
- N-P = 2.3 cm / 0.91". Draw the outline D1-P.
- P-P1 = shoulder length + 1 cm / 0.79" (e.g.: 1/3 chest semi-circumference + 1 cm / 0.39" = 48 ÷ 3 = 16 + 1 = 17 cm / 6.69").
- Draw the outline P-P1 passing through O.
- D-D2 = 13 cm / 5.12".
- P1-P2 = 5 cm / 2". Draw The Yoke line.
- Q2-Q3 = 2.5 cm / 1".
- Draw the armhole P1-L1-Q3 smoothly.
- E1-W = 3 cm / 1.18".
- C-C3 = 1.2-1.7 cm / 0.47-0.66".
- C1-C2 like C-C3.
- Draw the centre back line D1-L-H-C3-C2.
- E3-E4 = 2 cm / 0.79".
- Draw the side line Q3-W-E4.
- Create the vent as shown in the figure.

FRONT

- A-U half of A-J1 minus 0.5 cm / 0.20" (e.g.: 21.5 ÷ 2= 10.75 - 0.5= 10.25 cm / 4.04").
- A-U1 = 8 cm / 3.15".
- U-U2 = 2 cm / 0.79".
- Draw the breakline up to the desired height (e.g: 10 cm / 3.94" from the waist).
- J1-V = 4 cm / 1.57".
- U-Z as P-P1 at the rear minus 1 cm / 0.39" (1/3 chest semi-circumference = 48 ÷ 3 = 16 cm / 6.30").
- Draw the outline U-Z passing through V.
- Q-Q1 = 2 cm / 0.79".
- Q2-Q4 = 3 cm / 1.18".
- Draw the armhole Z-J-Q1-Q4 smoothly.
- E1-W1 = 3 cm / 1.18".
- E3-E5 = 2 cm / 0.79".
- Draw the side line Q4-W1-E5.
- A1-U3 = 3-3.5 cm / 1.18-1.38". Draw the lapel outline as shown in the figure.
- Make the collar, pocket, belt and vertical motifs as clearly illustrated.

NORFOLK JACKET - BASE SLEEVE

OVERSLEEVE

OVERSLEEVE **UNDERSLEEVE**

OVERSLEEVE **UNDERSLEEVE**

FRONT STRAP
50.5
4   4

POCKET
5   5
16
16

WAISTBAND
59
3

YOKE

FRONT **BACK**

MEASUREMENTS

- Bicep circumference = 29 cm / 11.42".
- Arm length = 62 cm / 24.41".

On the left side of a sheet of pattern paper draw the rectangle A-G-X-E with:

- A-E as base jacket sector + 1/2 sector + 1 cm / 0.39" (e.g.: 11.5 + 5.75 = 17.25 + 1 = 18.25 cm / 7.19").
- A-G as L1-P1 minus 1 cm / 0.39" of the base of the rear torso (in this case, 13.4 - 1 = 12.4 cm / 4.88").
- A-A1 = 1/3 of A-G (e.g: 12.4 ÷ 3 = 4 cm / 1.57").
- E-E1 like A-A1.
- Draw A-A1-E-E1.
- A1-B sleeve l. + 1 cm / 0.39" (e.g.: 62 + 1 = 63 cm / 24.80").
- A1-N half of A1-B + 0.5 cm / 0.20" (e.g.: 63 ÷ 2 = 31.5 + 0.5 = 32 cm / 12.60").

- A-M = 1/2 A-E + 1 cm / 0.39" (e.g: 18.25 ÷ 2 = 9.1 + 1 cm / 0.39" = 10.1 cm / 3.98").
- Draw M-M1 (Centre shoulder).
- A-I = 1/4 of A-E (e.g: 18.25 ÷ 4 = 5.7 cm / 2.24").
- G-H = 2.5 cm / 1".
- Draw H-B1 parallel to A-B.
- X-L half of G-X (e.g.: 18.25 ÷ 2 = 9.12 cm / 3.59").
- Draw guideline E- L
- L-L1 half of H-L.
- L1-L2 = 0.5 cm / 0.20"; G-O = 1.5 cm / 0.59".
- G-G1 = 2.5 cm / 1"; E-E2 = 2 cm / 0.79"; E-E3 = 3 cm / 1.18".
- Smoothly draw the front sleeve crown E-M1-I-O-G1.
- Smoothly draw the rear sleeve crown E-E3-L-L2-H-O.
- B1-B2 = 2 cm / 0.79"; B3-B2 and N-N1 = 2.5 cm / 1"; B4-R1 = 0.5 cm / 0.20".
- Connect with curved line R-P-E3 and R1-N2-H (Undersleeve).

NEAPOLITAN JACKET

Famous around the globe for its high quality, Neapolitan tailored jackets possess unique characteristics that make them practical to wear but also elegant and refined.

CHARACTERISTICS AND WORKMANSHIP
Neapolitan jackets are categorised as a deconstructed jacket, but its details lie in its tailoring.

1. The fabric of the sleeve is inserted below the shoulder, so that the seam is similar to that of a shirt.

2. The fit of the sleeve is narrower than normal. It's also shorter to allow for more of the shirt cuff to be seen.

3. The size of the sleeve crown is approximately 10 cm / 3.94" wider than the armhole of the bodice: this will create what is known as the 'mappina' effect, i.e. gathering along the upper part of the sleeve, which also helps ensure more comfortable arm movements.

4. The shoulders are soft and flowing, being finished with little or no padding.

5. Neapolitan tailored jackets are made with very wide lapels (8-10 cm / 3.15-3.94") with a very high notch to create a more elongated look.

6. Neapolitan jackets are traditionally single-breasted with two buttons, but the three-roll-two is very fashionable today.

7. Being a sportswear jacket, the lining is only applied to half of the jacket at the back, finished throughout, and left unattached along the lower edge of the lining.

8. The pocket is called 'a barchetta' in Italian because it is cut with a pronounced upper angle to resemble the outline of a 'little boat'.

9. The back of the jacket is shorter than normal tailored jackets. There are three vents: one on each side (up to 30 cm / 11.81 long) and one in the middle.

Stacked or "waterfall" buttons

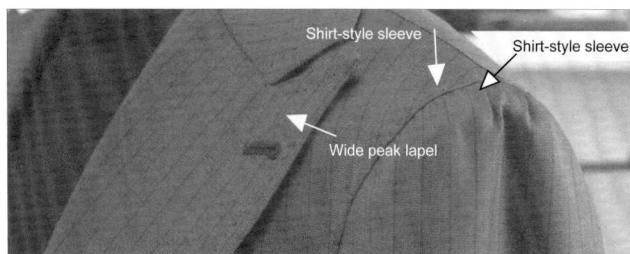

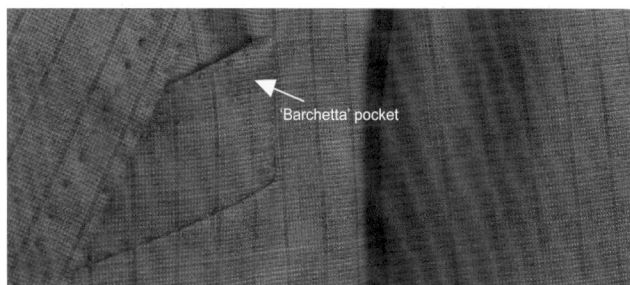

Shirt-style sleeve

Shirt-style sleeve

Wide peak lapel

'Barchetta' pocket

DECONSTRUCTED NEAPOLITAN JACKET

EASE 18 CM / 7 1/8"

COLLAR

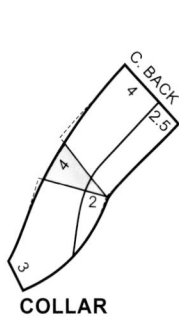

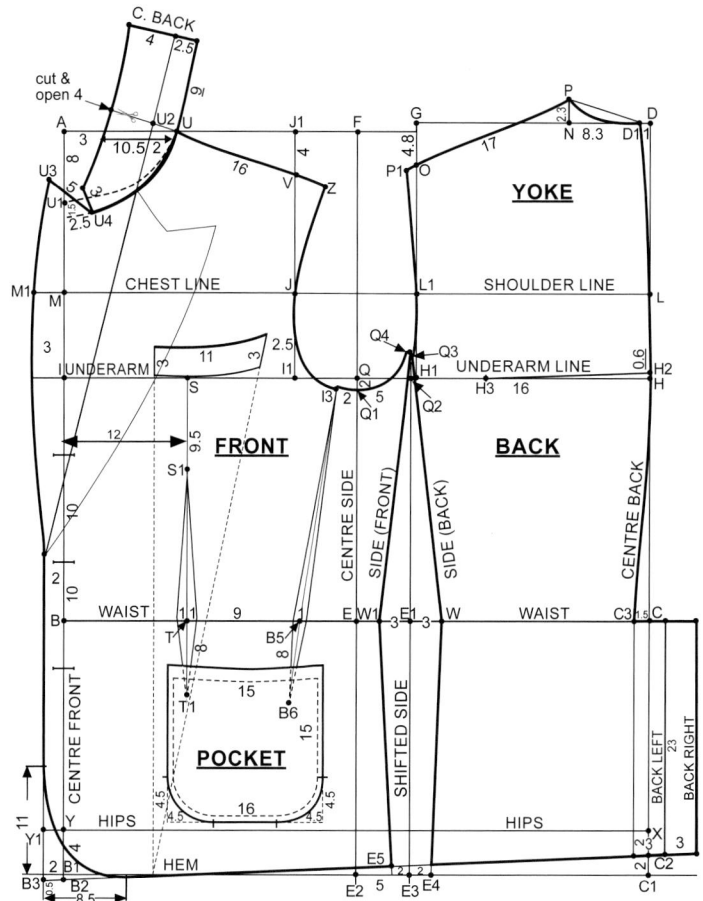

SIZE 16 UK MEASUREMENTS

- Height = 175 cm / 5'9".
- Chest semi-cir. = 96 +18 = 114 ÷ 2 = 57 cm / 22.44"
- Waist semi-cir. = 88 +18 = 106 ÷ 2 = 53 cm / 20.87"
- Hip semi-cir. = 96 +18 = 114 ÷ 2 = 57 cm / 22.44"
- Neck semi-cir. = 42 ÷ 2 = 21 cm / 8.27"
- 1/2 shoulder width = 42 + 2 = 44 ÷ 2 = 22 cm / 8.66"
- Front neck to waist = 45.6 + 1 = 46.6 cm / 18.35".
- Rear neck to waist = 46.2 cm + 1 = 47.2 cm / 18.58".

Draw right angle A-B-C, with:

- A-B = front neck to waist + jacket ease (e.g.: 45.6 + 1 = 46.1 cm / 18.15").
- B-C = chest semi-circumference + ease (e.g: 96 + 18 = 114 ÷ 2 = 57 cm / 22.44")
- D-C = rear neck to waist + jacket ease (e.g: 46.2 + 1 = 47.2 cm / 18.58").
- D-C1 = jacket length (e.g: 75 cm / 29.53").
- Join D-C1 and write 'Centre back'.
- C1-C = D-C1 minus C-D (e.g: 75 - 47.2 = 27.8 cm / 10.94").
- B-B1 as C1-C = 27.8 cm / 10.94".
- Join A-B1 and write 'Centre front'.
- B-E half of B-C.
- B1-E2 as B-E.
- A-F as B-E.

- Join F-E2 (centre side).
- D-H half of C-D + 0.5 cm / 0.20" (e.g: 47.2 ÷ 2 = 23.6 + 0.5 = 24.1 cm / 9.49").
- H-I as B-C = 57 cm / 22.44" (armpit level).
- E2-E3 = 5 cm / 2".
- Q-Q2 like E2-E3.
- Join Q2-E3 (shifted side).
- B-Y and C-X = waist to hip (e.g: 20 cm / 7.87").
- Draw Y-X and write 'Hip line'.
- D-G = (shoulder width + ease) ÷ 2 (e.g.: 42 + 2 = 44 ÷ 2 = 22 cm / 8.66").
- H-L = 1/4 of D-H (e.g.: 24.3 ÷ 4 = 6 cm / 2.36").
- Draw L-M and write 'Shoulder line' and 'Chest line'.
- H-H1 like D-G (e.g: 22 cm / 8.66").
- Draw G-H1.
- I-I1 as D-G minus 0.5 cm / 0.20" at the back (e.g: 22 - 0.5 = 21.5 cm / 8.46").
- A-J1 as I-I1 (e.g: 21.5 cm / 8.46").
- Draw I1-J1 parallel to G-H1.
- I1-H1 = H-I minus I-I1 + H-H1 (e.g: 57 - (21.5 + 22) = 13.5 cm / 5.31" (armscye or underarm sector).
- B1-C1 as B-C.
- Join B1-C1.
- B1-B2 = 0.5 cm / 0.20"; C1-C2 = 2 cm / 0.79".
- Smoothly draw B2-C2 and write 'Lower edge' or 'Hem'.
- L1-P1 = H1-G minus H1-L1 minus G-O= 13.3 cm / 5.24".

POCKET BREAST POCKET

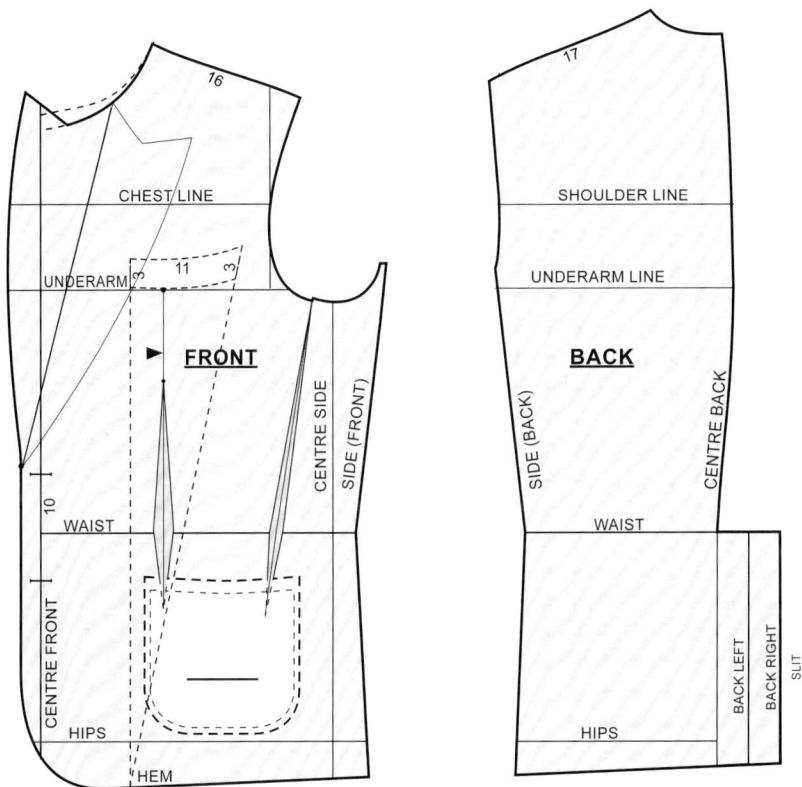

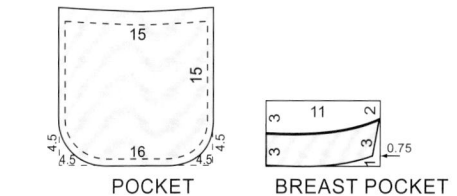

Formal Neapolitan jackets have a left chest pocket shaped like a boat, called a 'barchetta' pocket.

BACK

- H-H3 = 16 cm / 6.30" (1/3 chest semi-circumference = 48 ÷ 3 = 16 cm).
- H-H2 = 0.6 cm / 0.24".
- Create the right angle H3-H2-D1.
- Draw H2-D1 like H-D with a curve.
- G-O = 4-4.8 cm / 1.57-1.89".
- D1-N = 1/3 of D-G + 1 cm / 0.20" (e.g: 23 ÷ 3 = 7.66 + 1 = 8.66 cm / 3.41").
- N-P = 2.3 cm / 0.91". Draw the curved line D-P.
- P-P1 = shoulder length + 1 cm / 0.39" (1/3 chest semi-circumference + 1 = 48 ÷ 3 = 16 + 1 = 17 cm / 6.69").
- Draw the outline P-P1 passing through O.
- Q2-Q3 = 2.5 cm / 1".
- Draw the armhole P1-L1-Q3 smoothly.
- E1-W = 3 cm / 1.18".
- C-C3 = 1.2-1.7 cm / 0.47-0.67". - C1-C2 like C-C3.
- Draw the centre back line D1- L-H-C3-C2.
- E3-E4 = 2 cm / 0.79".
- Draw the side line Q3-W-E4.
- Make the slit as shown in the figure, with a length of 18-23 cm / 7.09-9.06" or as desired.

FRONT

- A-U = half of A-J1 minus 0.5 cm / 0.20" (e.g.: 21.5 ÷ 2= 10.75 - 0.5 = 10.25 cm / 4.03").
- A-U1 = 8 cm / 3.15". U-U2 = 2 cm / 0.79".
- Draw the breakline up to the desired height (e.g: 10 cm / 3.94" from the waist).
- J1-V = 4 cm / 1.57".
- U-Z as P-P1 at the rear minus 1 cm / 0.39" (1/3 chest semi-circumference = 48 ÷ 3 = 16 cm / 6.30").
- Draw the outline U-Z passing through V.
- Q-Q1 = 2 cm / 0.79". - Q2-Q4 = 3 cm / 1.18".
- Draw the armhole Z-J-Q1-Q4 smoothly.
- E1-W1 = 3 cm / 1.18"; E3-E5 = 2 cm / 0.79".
- Draw the side line Q4-W1-E5.
- A1-U3 = 3-3.5 cm / 1.18-1.38". Draw the lapel outline as shown in the figure.
- I-S = 12 cm / 4.72"; S-S1 = 9.5 cm / 3.74"; T-T1 = 8 cm / 3.15".
- Draw the dart as in the figure.
- T- B = 9 cm / 3.54"; B5-B6 = 8 cm / 3.15".
- Draw the dart I3-B6 as in the figure.
- Make the collar, pocket and chest pocket as illustrated.

NEAPOLITAN JACKET - SLEEVE

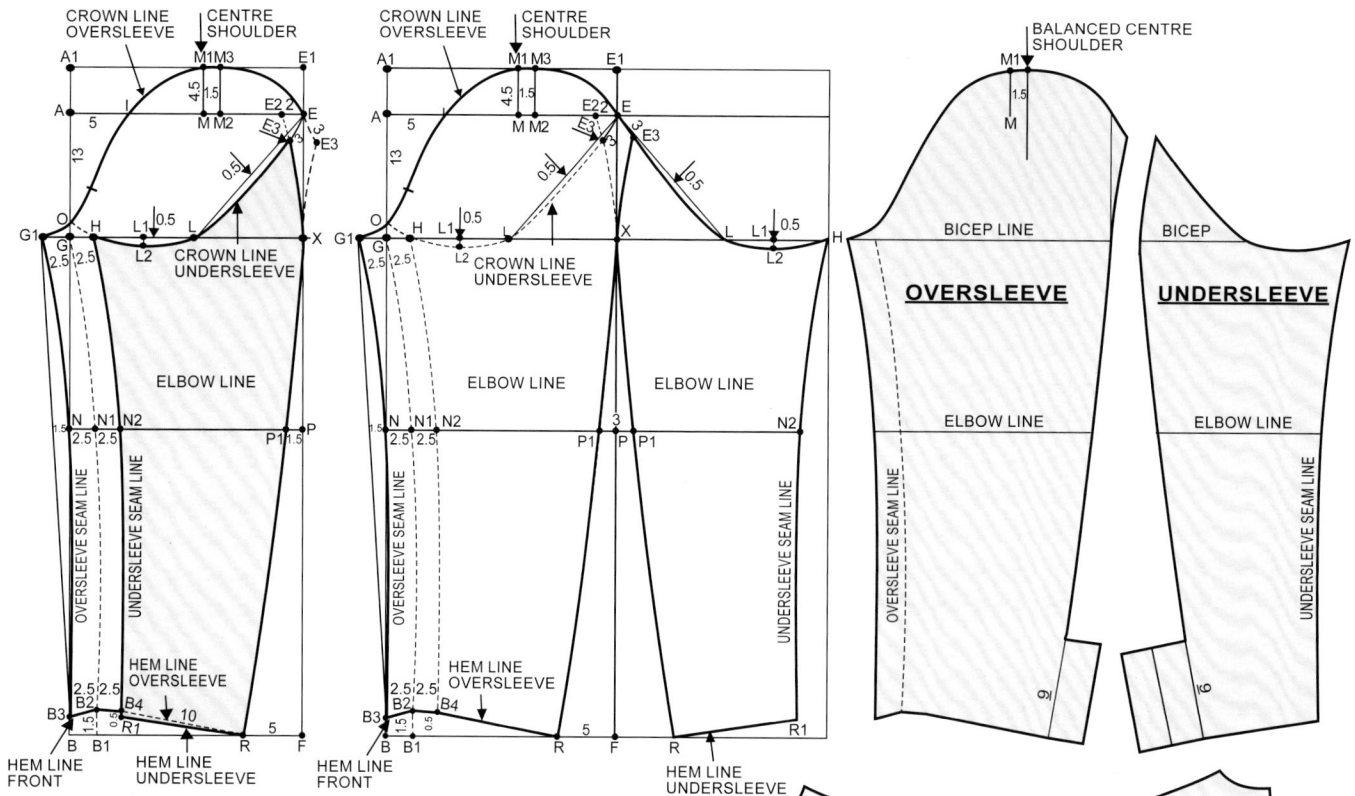

MAPPINA SLEEVE
(gathered detail on Neapolitan jackets)

POCKET

MEASUREMENTS

- Bicep circumference = 29-31 cm / 11.42-12.20".
- Arm length = 62 cm / 24.41".

On the left side of a sheet of pattern paper draw the rectangle A-G-X-E with:

- A-E= base jacket sector + 1/2 sector + 2.5 cm / 1" (e.g.: 13.5 + 6.75 = 20.25 + 2.5 = 22.75 cm / 8.96").
- A-G the same length as L1-P1 minus 1 cm / 0.39" of the rear torso base (in this case, 13.5 cm / 5.31").
- A-A1 = 1/3 of A-G (e.g: 13.5 ÷ 3 = 4.5 cm / 1.77").
- E-E1 as A-A1. Draw A-A1-E-E1.
- A1-B = sleeve length + 1 cm / 0.39" (e.g.: 62 + 1 = 63 cm / 24.80").
- A1-N (elbow) half of A1-B + 0.5 cm / 0.20" (e.g.: 63 ÷ 2 = 31.5 + 0.5 = 32 cm / 12.60").
- A-M = 1/2 A-E + 1 cm / 0.39" (e.g: 19.75 ÷ 2 = 9.87 + 1 = 10.87 cm / 4.28").
- M-M1 = centre shoulder; M-M2 = shift of 1.5 cm / 0.59" from M-M1 for drape.
- M2-M3 = new sleeve centre to make sure it is balanced and drapes properly.
- A-I = 1/4 of A-E (e.g: 19.75 ÷ 4 = 4.93 cm / 1.94").
- G-H = 2.5 cm / 1".

- Draw H-N2-B4 with a curved line.
- G-X as A-E; X-L half of G-X.
- Draw guideline E-L.
- L-L1 half of H-L; L1-L2 = 0.5 cm / 0.20"; G-O = 1.5 cm / 0.59"; G-G1 = 2.5 cm / 1"; E-E2 = 2 cm / 0.79"; E-E3 = 3 cm / 1.18".
- Smoothly draw the crown of the oversleeve E-M1-I-O-G1.
- Smoothly draw the armscye of the undersleeve E-E3-L-L2- H.
- B1-B2 = 2 cm / 0.79"; B3-B2 and N-N1 = 2.5 cm / 1"; B4-R1 = 0.5 cm / 0.20".
- Connect R-P1-E3 and R1-N2-H with curved lines.
- Take the undersleeve and position it next to the oversleeve and gracefully join the sleeve lines following the curse.

156

BACK WITH A VENT AND/OR BOX PLEAT

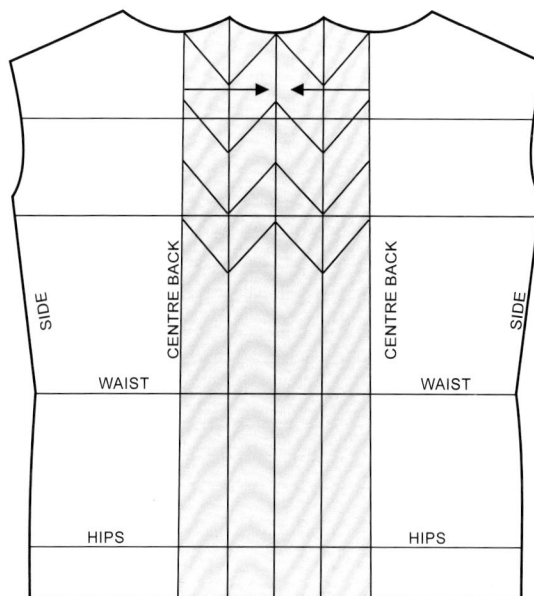

A box pleat is used to enlarge a specific part of a garment. It is created by inserting a flat box pleat, usually along a seam. It can be closed, when sewn on top and bottom (as in the figure), or open, when sewn on one end only.

BACK WITH A HALF-BELT AND YOKE

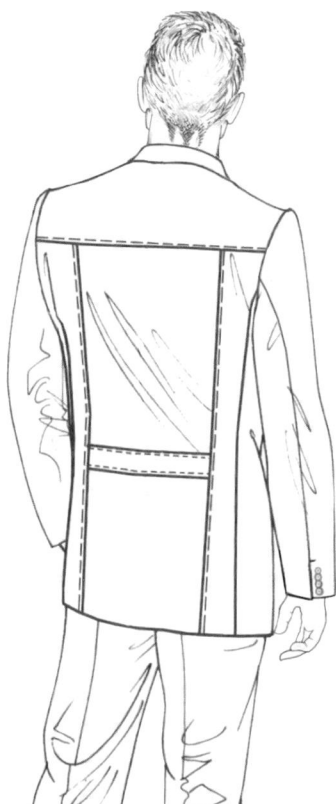

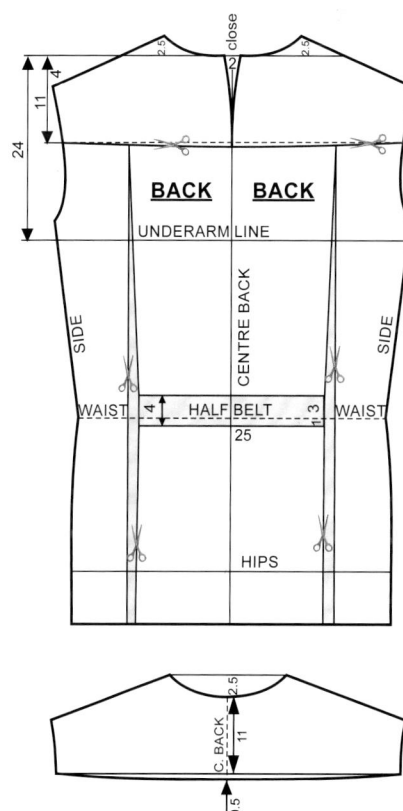

BASE DOUBLE-BREASTED JACKET

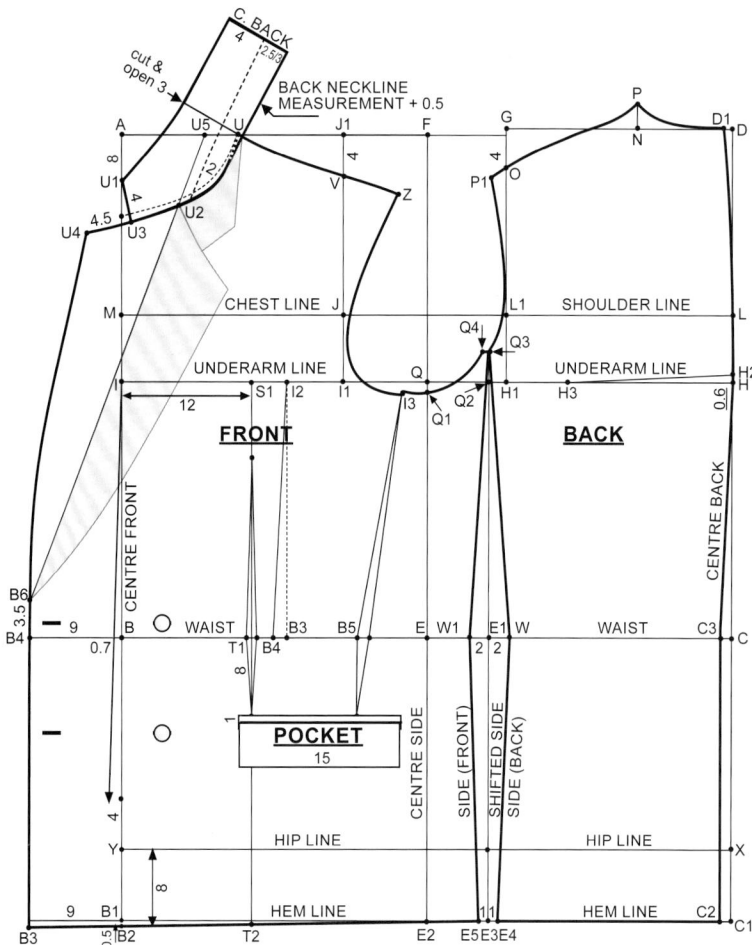

- Draw the base block of the jacket with the desired size, length and ease (classic fit, regular fit or slim fit).
- Extend the front centre overlap B2-B3 and B-B4 by 9 cm / 3.54".
- U1-U3 = 4-4.5 cm / 1.57-1.77"; U3-U4 = 4.5-5.5 cm / 1.57-2.17".
- Join B3-B4-U4 as in the figure.
- Join the split line from U2 to B6 at 3.5 cm / 1.38" or so from the waistline (or otherwise, depending on the pattern).
- For the rest, follow the indications on the diagram, already explained on the previous pages.

Application of a horizontal dart on a double-breasted base block

The shape of any double-breasted jacket is decisively influenced by the protrusion of the lower belly.

Its size, which leads it to largely exceed the outline of the body, and shape do not allow the tailor to work on the edge of the front. For this reason, we've decided to illustrate the geometric version of the horizontal dart, applied to a regular double-breasted jacket base.

We should mention right away that it's a pattern that takes some effort, though it remains functional and attentive to detail. Alternatively, there's always the option to draw a regular base block front with a suitable overlap, i.e. approx. 9 cm / 3.54", and then apply the horizontal dart to it, measuring 0.5 cm / 0.20", using the classic procedure. However, the trunk of a double-breasted jacket really shouldn't be too

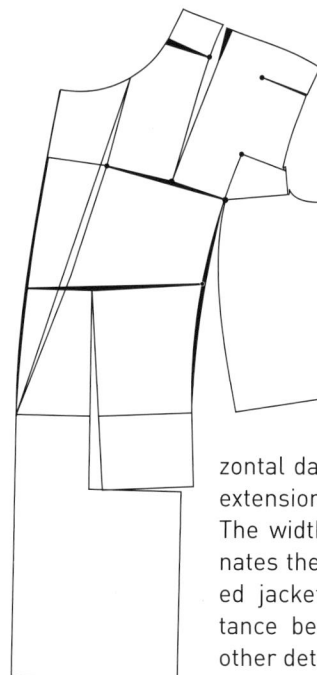

'globe-like', in order to help the front where it culminates due to the crossing and overlapping of the lapels. The top and sides of the pattern presented here are identical to the single-breasted style, but it has an additional horizontal dart, created by a 0.5 cm / 0.20" extension unloaded on the pocket level. The width of the breast pocket coordinates the proportions of double-breasted jackets also, determining the distance between the buttons and many other details.

Note:
To keep things balanced, the back of the double-breasted jacket must be 0.5 cm / 0.20" longer when measured from the lower edge. As a result, the waist and hips will be lowered by the same amount. In addition, the front side of the underarm dart must undergo marked slackening.

DOUBLE-BREASTED JACKET WITH FOUR BUTTONS AND PEAK LAPELS

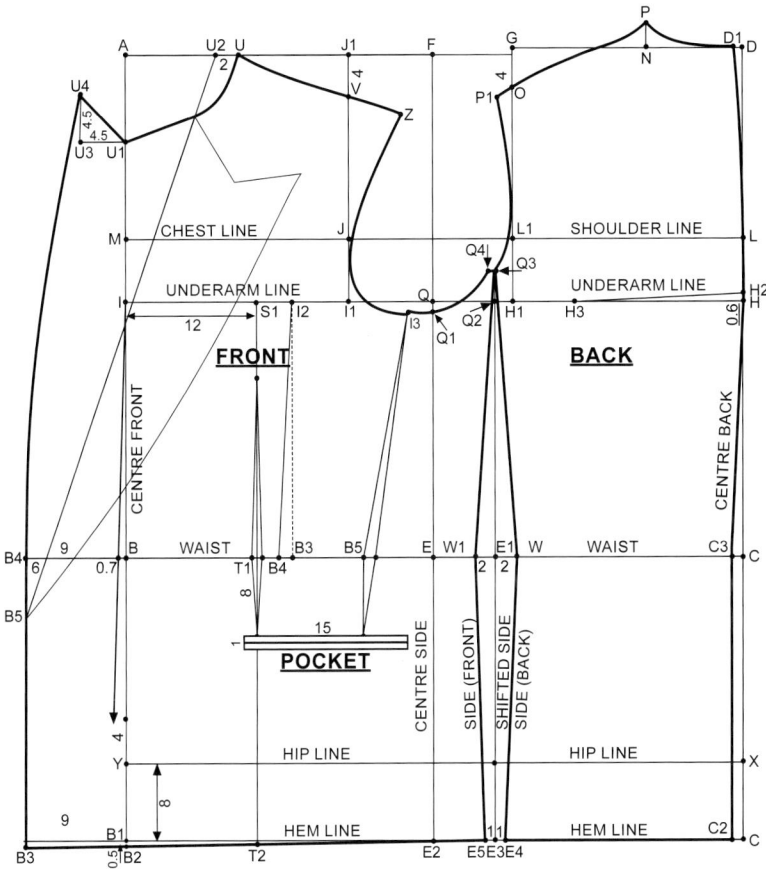

- Draw the base of the jacket with the desired measurements, length and ease.
- Extend the front centre overlap B2- B3 and B-B4 by 9 cm / 3.54".
- U1-U3 = 4.5 cm / 1.77"; U3-U4 = 4.5-5.5 cm / 1.77-2.17".
- Join B3-B4-U4 as in the figure.
- Join the breakline from U2 to B5 about 6 cm / 2.36" from the waistline.
- For the rest, follow the indications in the diagram, already explained on the previous pages.

DOUBLE-BREASTED JACKET WITH SIX BUTTONS AND PEAK LAPELS

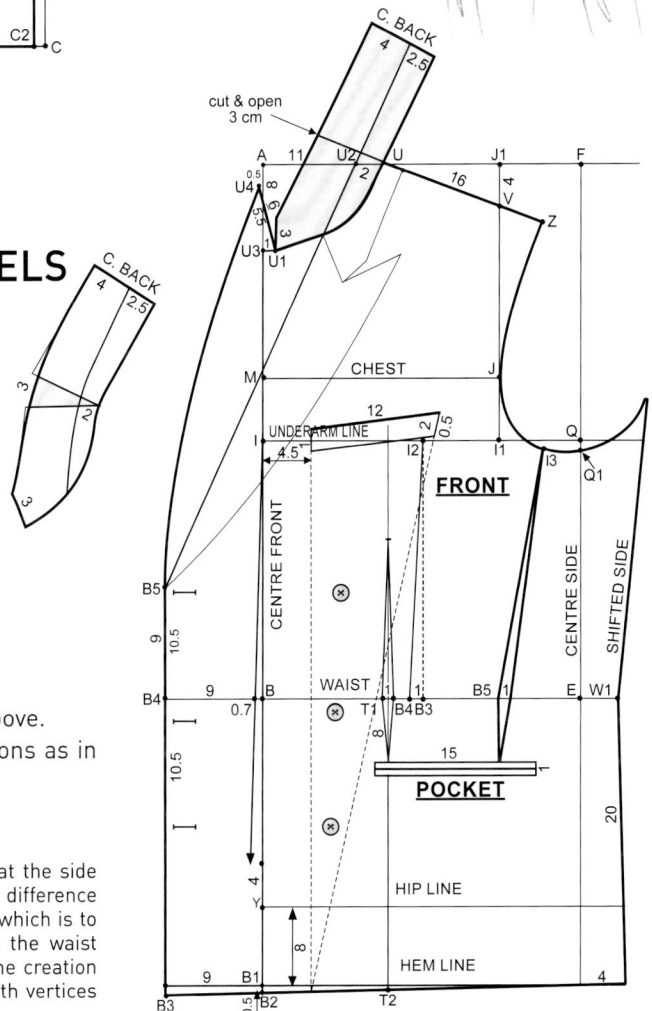

- Follow the directions as above.
- Mark the eyelets and buttons as in the figure.

Note:
The waist darts and the excess at the side are proportionate to the desired difference between the hips and the waist, which is to be distributed proportionally on the waist dart line and the hip line, plus the creation of a small 1.5 cm / 0.59" dart with vertices on the armscye and pocket lines.

NAVY BLAZER

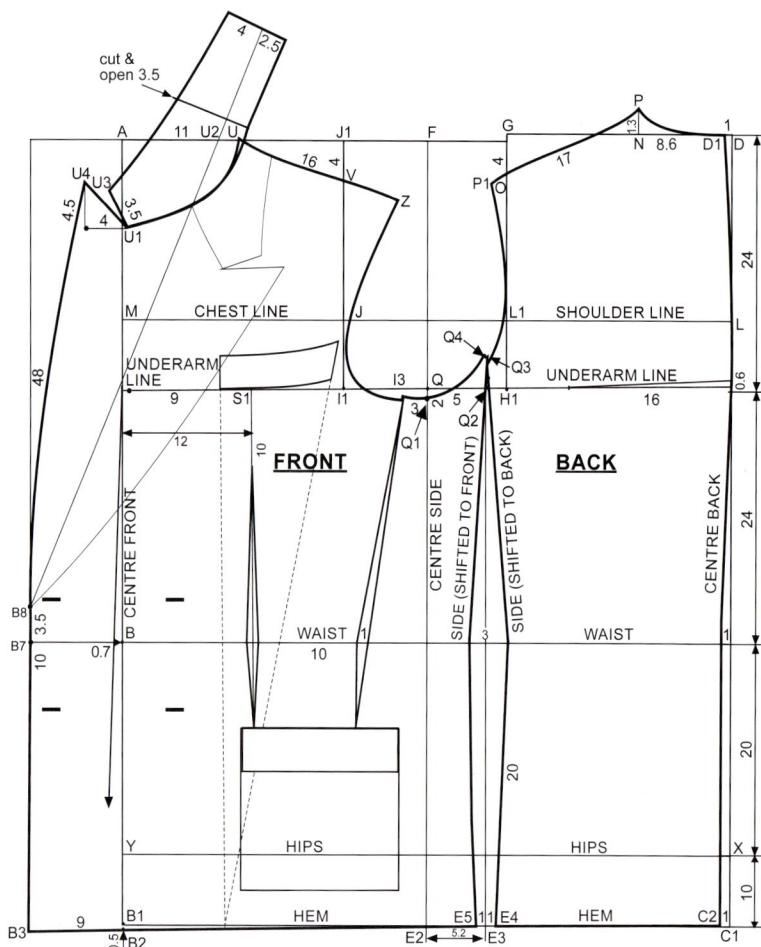

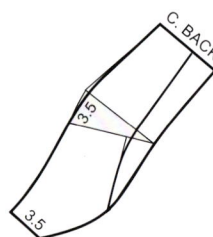

The navy blazer is a dark blue double-breasted jacket with gold buttons, generally made of serge, hopsack, flannel and lambswool for winter, and cool wool or linen for summer.

- Draw the base block of the jacket with the appropriate size and ease (18 cm / 7.09") and the desired overall length, as clearly shown in the figure.
- Extend the front centre overlap B2-B3 and B-B7 by 9 cm / 3.54").
- U1-U3 = 3.5 cm / 1.38"; U1-U4 = 5.5 cm / 2.17".
- Join B3-B7-B8-U4 as in the figure.
- Join the breakline from U2 to B8 at 3.5 cm / 1.38" or so from the waistline (or otherwise, depending on the pattern).
- Mark the eyelets and buttons as in the figure.
- Mark the pocket and chest pocket.
- Divide the front from the back.

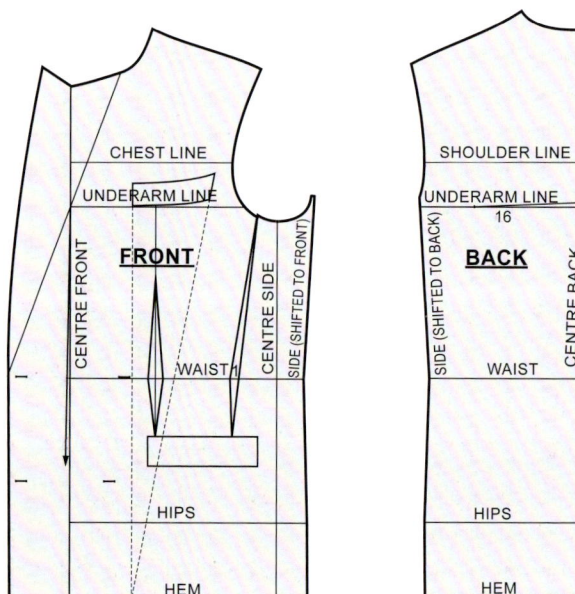

SLEEVE FOR THE DOUBLE-BREASTED NAVY BLAZER

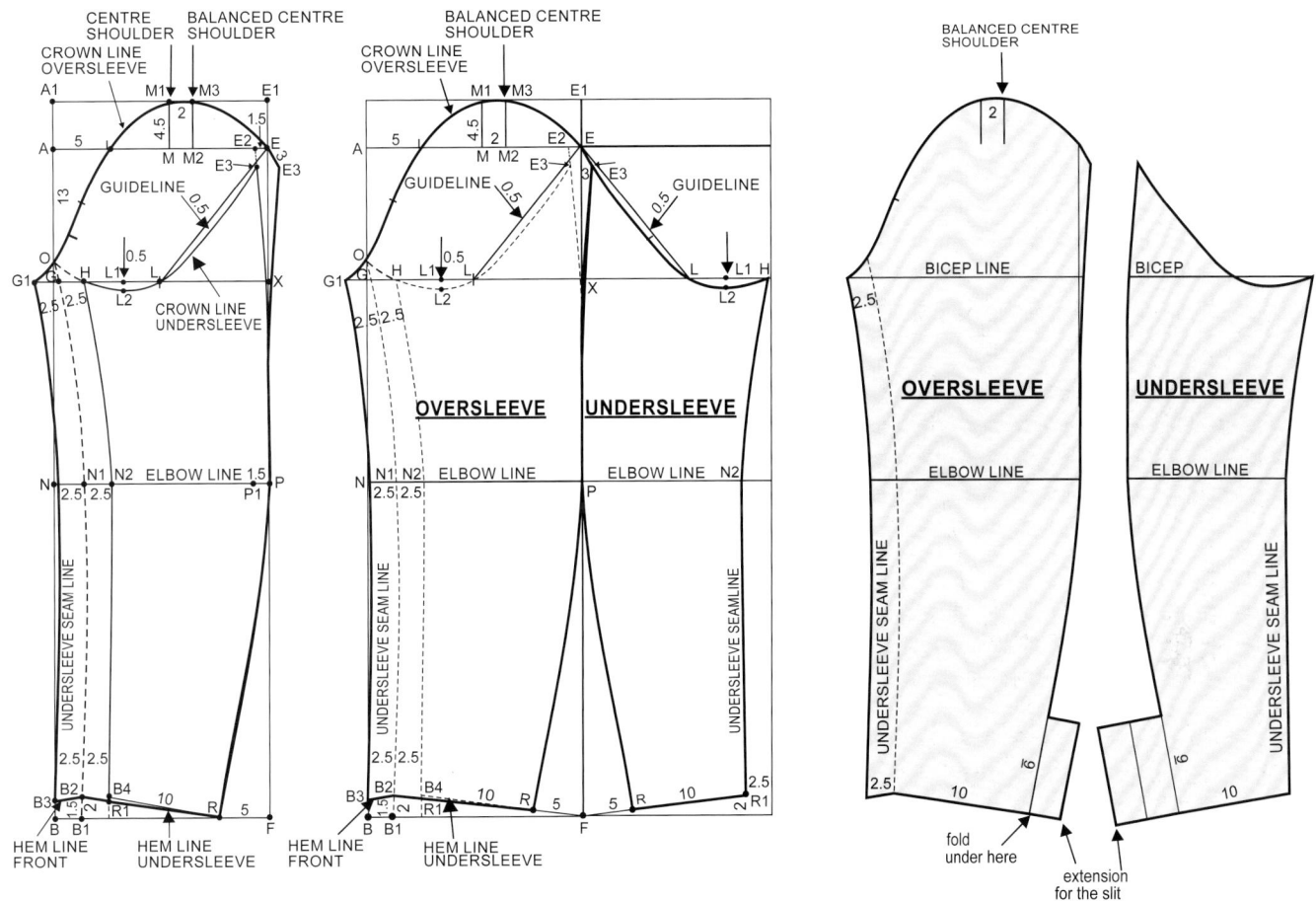

MEASUREMENTS

- Bicep circumference = 29-31 cm / 11.42-12.20".
- Arm length = 62 cm / 24.41".

On the left side of a sheet of pattern paper draw the rectangle A-G-X-E with:

- A-E= base jacket sector + 1/2 sector + 1 cm / 0.39" (e.g.: 12.5 + 6.25 = 18.75 + 1 = 19.75 cm / 7.76").
- A-G the same length as L1-P1 on the rear torso base block minus 1 cm / 0.39" (in this case, 13.5 cm / 5.31").
- A-A1 = 1/3 of A-G (e.g.: 13.5 ÷ 3 = 4.5 cm / 1.77").
- E-E1 like A-A1. Draw A-A1-E-E1.
- A1-B = sleeve length + 1 cm / 0.39" (e.g.: 62 + 1 = 63 cm / 24.80").
- A1-N (elbow) half of A1-B + 0.5 cm / 0.20" (e.g.: 63 ÷ 2 = 31.5 + 0.5 = 32 cm / 12.60").
- A-M = 1/2 A-E + 1 cm / 0.39" (e.g.: 19.75 ÷ 2 = 9.87 + 1 = 10.87 cm / 4.28").
- From M-M1 (centre shoulder), shift 2 cm / 0.79" for the right drape (M-M2).
- M2-M3 new centre sleeve to make sure it is balanced and drapes properly.

- A-I = 1/4 of A-E (e.g.: 19.75 ÷ 4 = 4.93 cm / 1.94").
- G-H = 2.5 cm / 1".
- Draw H-N2-R1 with a curved line.
- G-X as A-E.
- X-L half of G-X (e.g.: 19.75 ÷ 2 = 9.87 cm / 3.88").
- Draw guideline E-L.
- L-L1 half of H-L.
- L1-L2 = 0.5 cm / 0.20".
- G-O = 1.5 cm / 0.59".
- G-G1 = 2.5 cm / 1".
- E-E2 = 1.5 cm / 0.59".
- E-E3 = 3 cm / 1.18".
- Smoothly draw the oversleeve crown E-M1-I-O-G1.
- Smoothly draw the underarm armscye E-E3-L-L2-H-O.
- B1-B2 = 2 cm / 0.79".
- B3-B2 and N-N1 = 2.5 cm / 1".
- B4-R1 = 0.5 cm / 0.20".
- Connect R-P1-E3 and R1-N2-H with curved lines (undersleeve).
- Take the undersleeve, position it next to the oversleeve and smoothly join the sleeve lines, as in the figure.

SINGLE-BREASTED DINNER JACKET WITH PEAK LAPELS

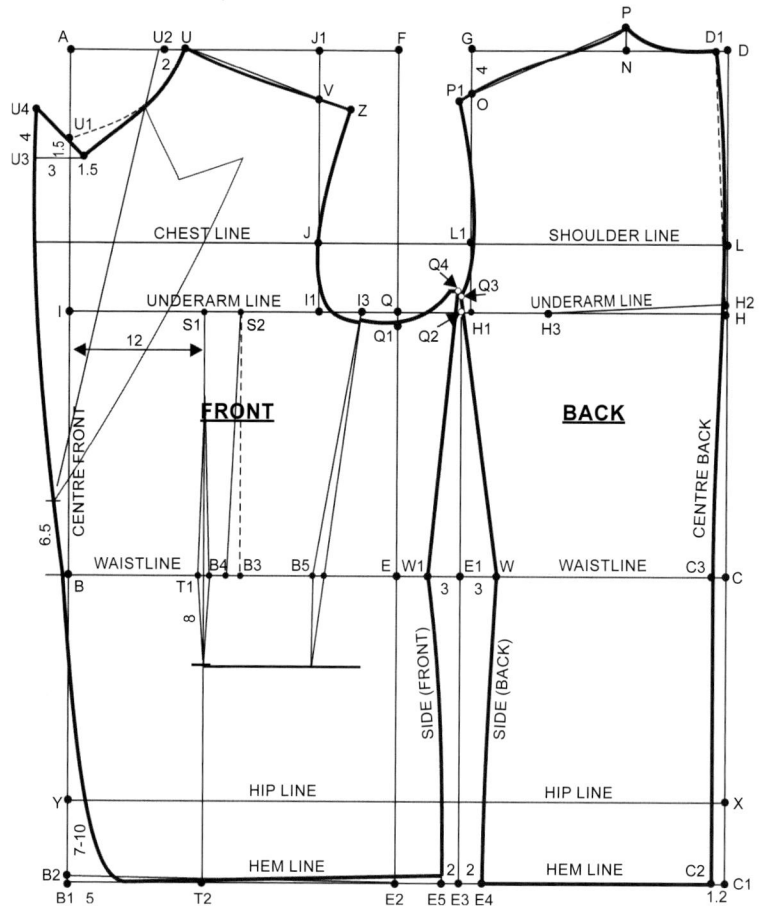

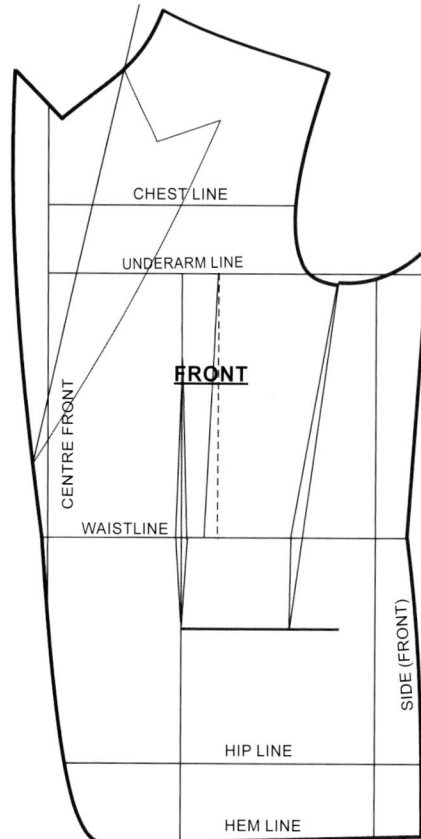

The dinner jacket is a special jacket, but from a patterning point of view, it does not differ much from a regular jacket. If there are any special details in the pattern, it's solely due to the fact that it requires a lot of stability in the neckline, together with a lot of waist movement, which cannot be low. Dinner jackets are usually made of rigid fabric and this type of garment almost always has a pointed lapel or a shawl collar.

To execute this pattern, refer to the outlines clearly illustrated in the figure.

ROLL COLLAR DINNER JACKET

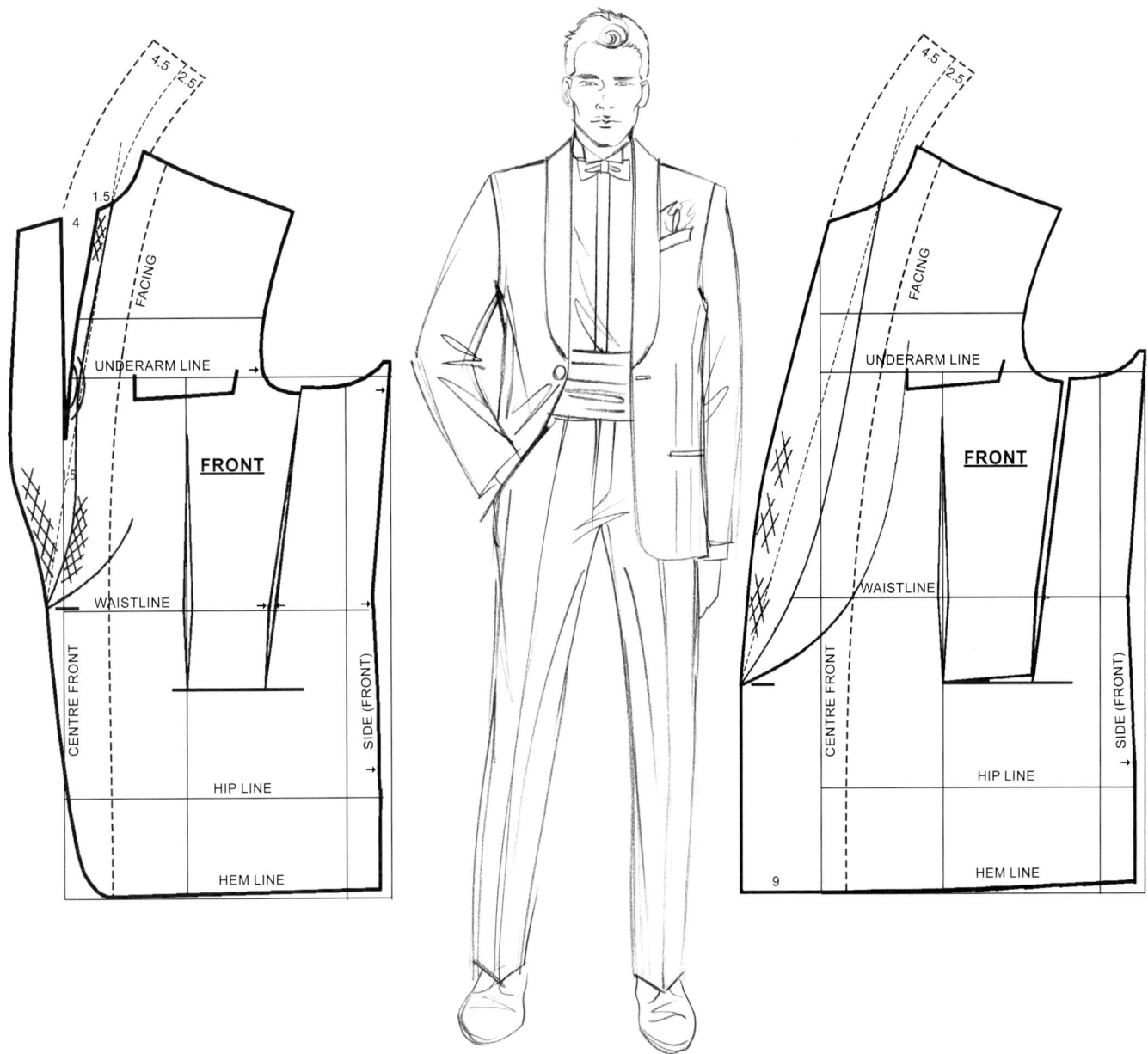

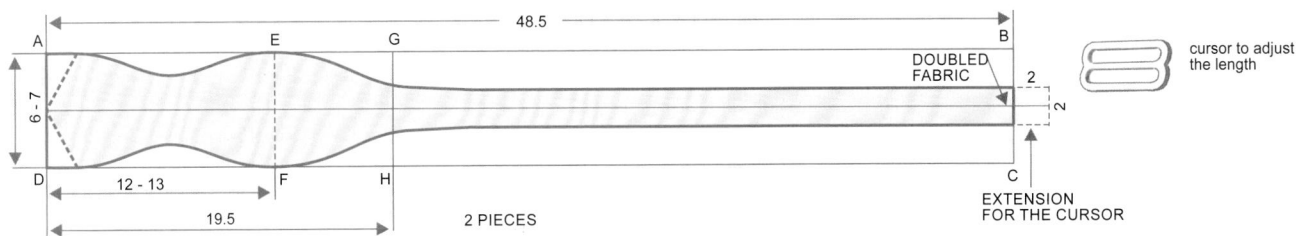

SINGLE-BREASTED DINNER JACKET

In order to create the shawl lapel, you must first smoothly shape the breakline by created an accentuated ridge at the waistline level (indentation sector).

Place the back side of the dart parallel to the breakline (distance 1.5 cm / 0.59"). The depth of the dart will be 4 cm / 1.57".

The side is a straight line and duly reduced to adapt to the curve that will take place at the rear. The lapels of this dinner jacket must be slackened at the points indicated in the figure.

DOUBLE-BREASTED DINNER JACKET

This style differs from the previous one in the length of the lapel and the greater curved effect.

It is made by creating the basic dinner jacket pattern, turning it into a double-breasted garment.

FULL EVENING DRESS

Full evening dress (or tails, or "white tie") is a suit for extra special ceremonies or occasions.

In particular, a regular base block in a regular or slim fit should be used for this style of jacket.

The lapel is pointed and is covered with textured or smooth silk fabric, or satin.

As a rule, it is not possible to button a tailcoat, as the waist-coat (single or double-breasted, strictly in white pique fabric) worn underneath must be visible.

- Draw the base block of the jacket with peaked lapels.
- Extend the centre back by the desired length to create C-C1 (e.g.: 60-65 cm / 23.62-25.59" from the waist line).
- Draw the lower hemline C1-B1.
- B-T1 = 19 cm / 7.48".
- B-B2 = 17.5 cm / 6.89".
- B2-B3 = 5.5 cm / 2.17".
- B5-B6 = 8 cm / 3.15".

- Draw the curved dart at the front B7-I2-B8.
- C3-C6 = 6.5 cm / 2.56".
- X-E3 = 25 cm / 9.84".
- E2-E3 = 6 cm / 2.36".
- E3-E4 = 5 cm / 2".
- Draw the dart E4-W1-Q2-W.
- C2-C9 at the back = 8 cm / 3.15".
- Draw the side panel line L2-C6-C9.
- Draw the skirt (tail) I2-B8-C10-C8-C7-L2.
- Draw the back vent C2-C3-C4-C5.
- Draw the back L2-C6-C8-C10-C5-C4-C3-D1-P-P1-L2.
- Adjust the pattern as illustrated.

FRONT diagram labels:
- cut & open 3.5
- 4 | 2.5
- 6
- 16
- 3.5
- 6
- 3 | 1.5
- CENTRE FRONT
- CHEST LINE
- M
- UNDERARM LINE
- 2.5
- 5.5
- B3
- **FRONT**
- WAIST
- 7

SIDE diagram labels:
- SHOULDERS
- UNDERARM LINE
- **SIDE**
- SIDE
- SHIFTED SIDE
- WAIST
- HIP LINE
- **TAIL**

BACK diagram labels:
- 17
- **BACK**
- SHOULDER LINE
- UNDERARM LINE
- WAIST
- 7
- CENTRE BACK
- HIPS
- 10
- 1.5 | 1.5

Sleeve diagram labels:
- CROWN LINE OVERSLEEVE
- CENTRE SHOULDER
- BALANCED CENTRE SHOULDER
- A1
- M1
- M3
- E1
- A
- 5
- I
- 4.5
- 2
- 1.5
- M
- M2
- E2
- E3
- E3
- E3
- 13.5
- GUIDELINE
- 0.5
- O
- 0.5
- H
- L1
- L
- X
- G1
- G1
- B2.5
- L2
- UNDERSLEEVE LINE
- 2
- N1
- N2
- ELBOW LINE
- 1.5
- N
- 2.5
- 2.5
- P1
- P
- UNDERSLEEVE SEAM LINE
- 2.5 | 2.5
- B3
- B2
- B4
- 10
- R
- 5
- B
- B1
- 1.5
- 2
- R1
- R
- F
- HEM LINE FRONT
- HEM LINE UNDERSLEEVE

OVERSLEEVE diagram labels:
- BALANCED CENTRE SHOULDER
- 2
- BICEP LINE
- 2.5
- **OVERSLEEVE**
- ELBOW LINE
- UNDERSLEEVE SEAM LINE
- 2.5
- 10
- 6
- fold under here

UNDERSLEEVE diagram labels:
- BICEP
- **UNDERSLEEVE**
- ELBOW LINE
- UNDERSLEEVE SEAM LINE
- 6
- 10
- extension for the slit

Collar diagram labels:
- C. BACK
- 4 | 2.5
- 2.5
- 6
- 3.5

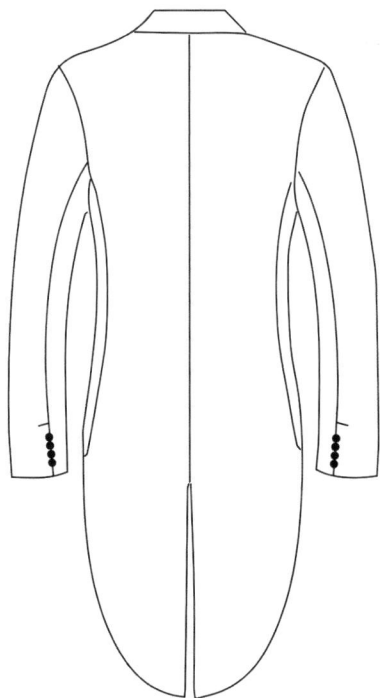

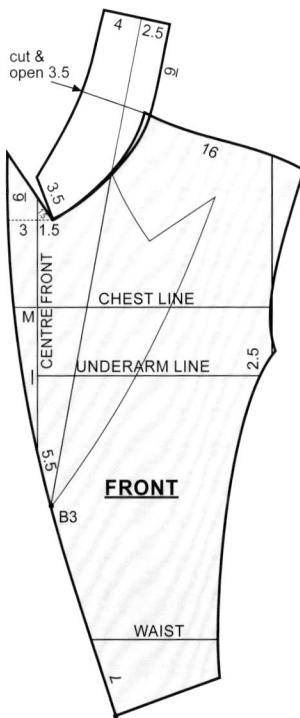

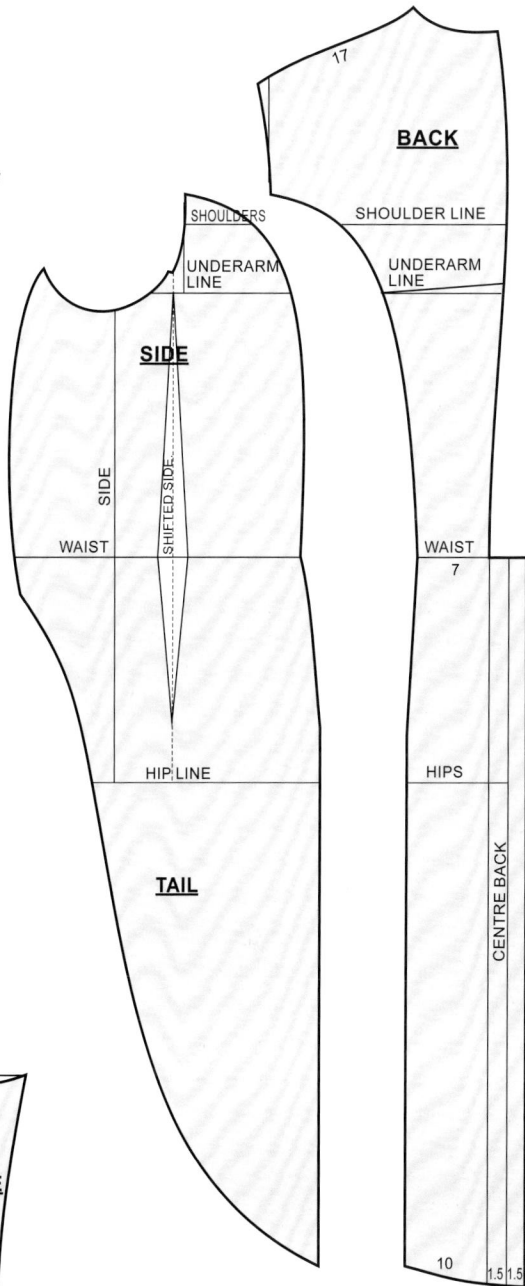

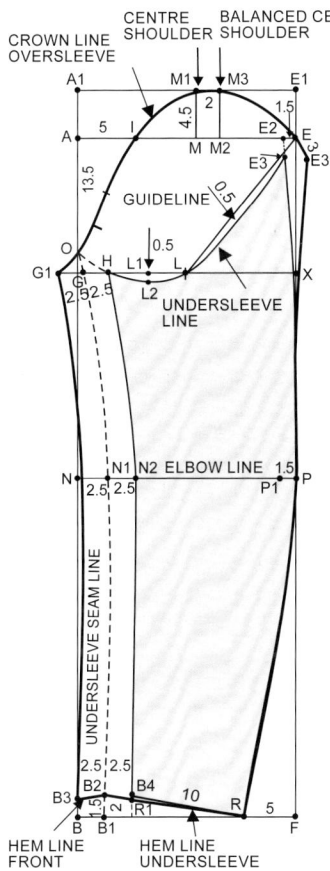

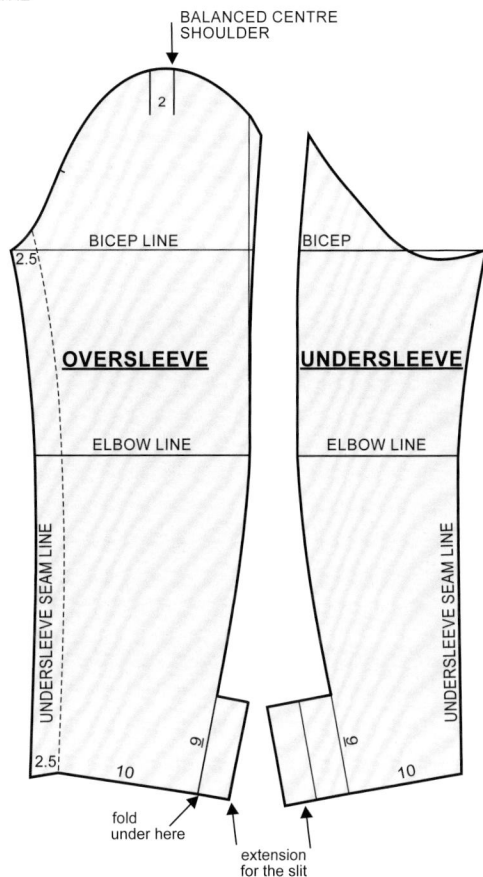

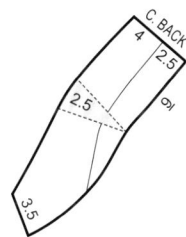

EXPLANATION OF THE SLEEVE AND COLLAR ON THE PREVIOUS PAGES

The diagram labels (pattern construction):

CHEST LINE — **SHOULDER LINE**

UNDERARM LINE — **UNDERARM LINE**

FRONT — **BACK**

CENTRE FRONT — **CENTRE BACK**

SIDE (FRONT) — **SIDE (BACK)**

WAIST — **WAIST**

HIP LINE — **HIP LINE**

TAIL

HEM LINE

Points and measurements: A, U2, U, J1, F, G, P, D1, D, U4, U1, V, Z, P1, O, N, U3, 4, 1.5, 3, 1.5, 2, 4, L2, L1, L, SHOULDER LINE, Q4, Q3, H2, H, I, I1, I3, Q, H1, H3, 12, S1, I2, I4, 3.5, Q1, Q2, 2, 6, S2, 9.5, B, 3, E, W1, 3, 3, W, C8, C7, 3, C3, C, C4, 5.5, B7, B8, E1, 5.5, W2, C6, 6.5, B5, B6, 9.5, 7.5, 15, Y, 4, HIP LINE, 2, 6, HIP LINE, X, T2, E2, E3, 11.5, E5, E4, 6, 6, 10, 1.5, 1.2, C5, B1, C10, C9, C2, C1

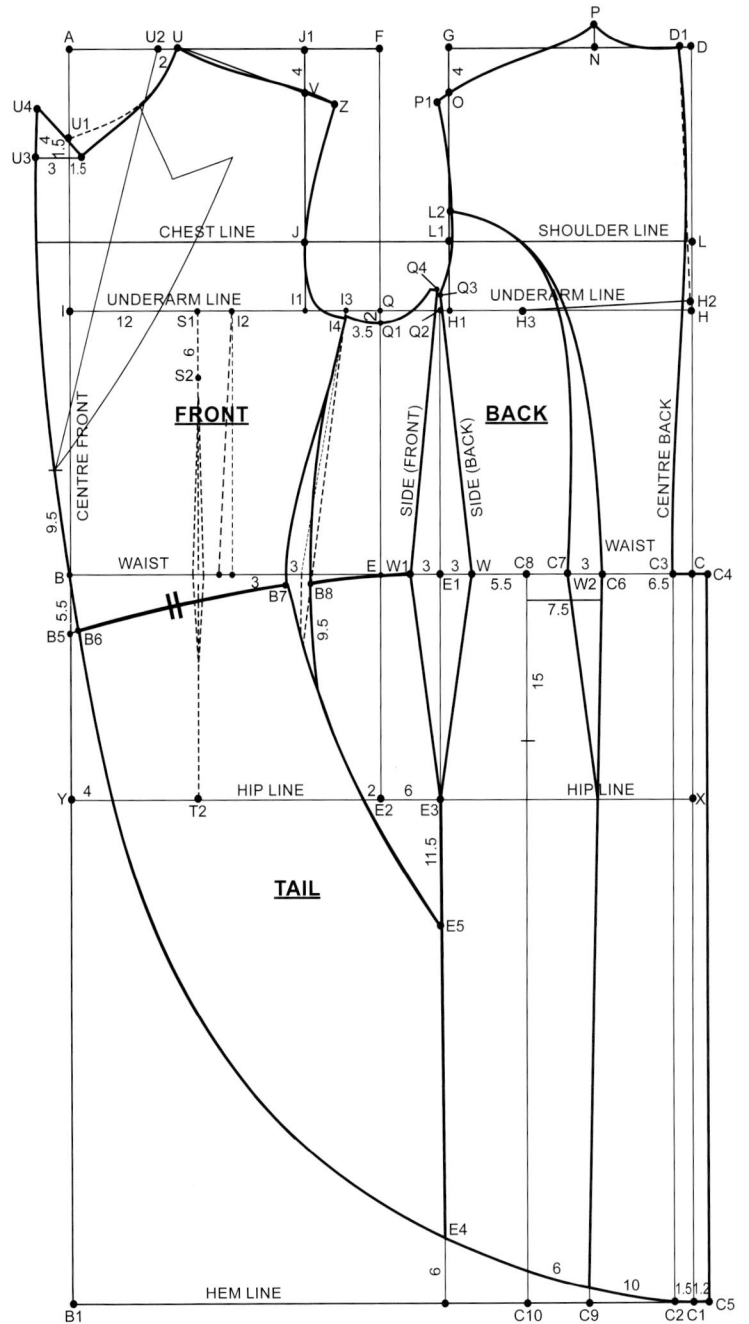

Morning dress is composed of three pieces: a jacket, trousers and a waistcoat.

The jacket's long tails are constructed in such a way that, starting from the single button at the front, they descend towards the back, forming a swallow tail curve. The base block used for the construction of the jacket is regular with appropriate measurements and fit, and with peak lapels.

It is single-breasted, in black or smoky grey, with a single button fastening and a pocket on the left chest. This jacket is worn with tapered trousers without turn-up cuffs made of the same light, thin striped fabric, a pearl grey or cream waistcoat and a silver, pearl grey, black or white silk tie. The shirt should be white or ivory, with concealed buttons, cuffs with buttonholes for cufflinks and a stiff collar.

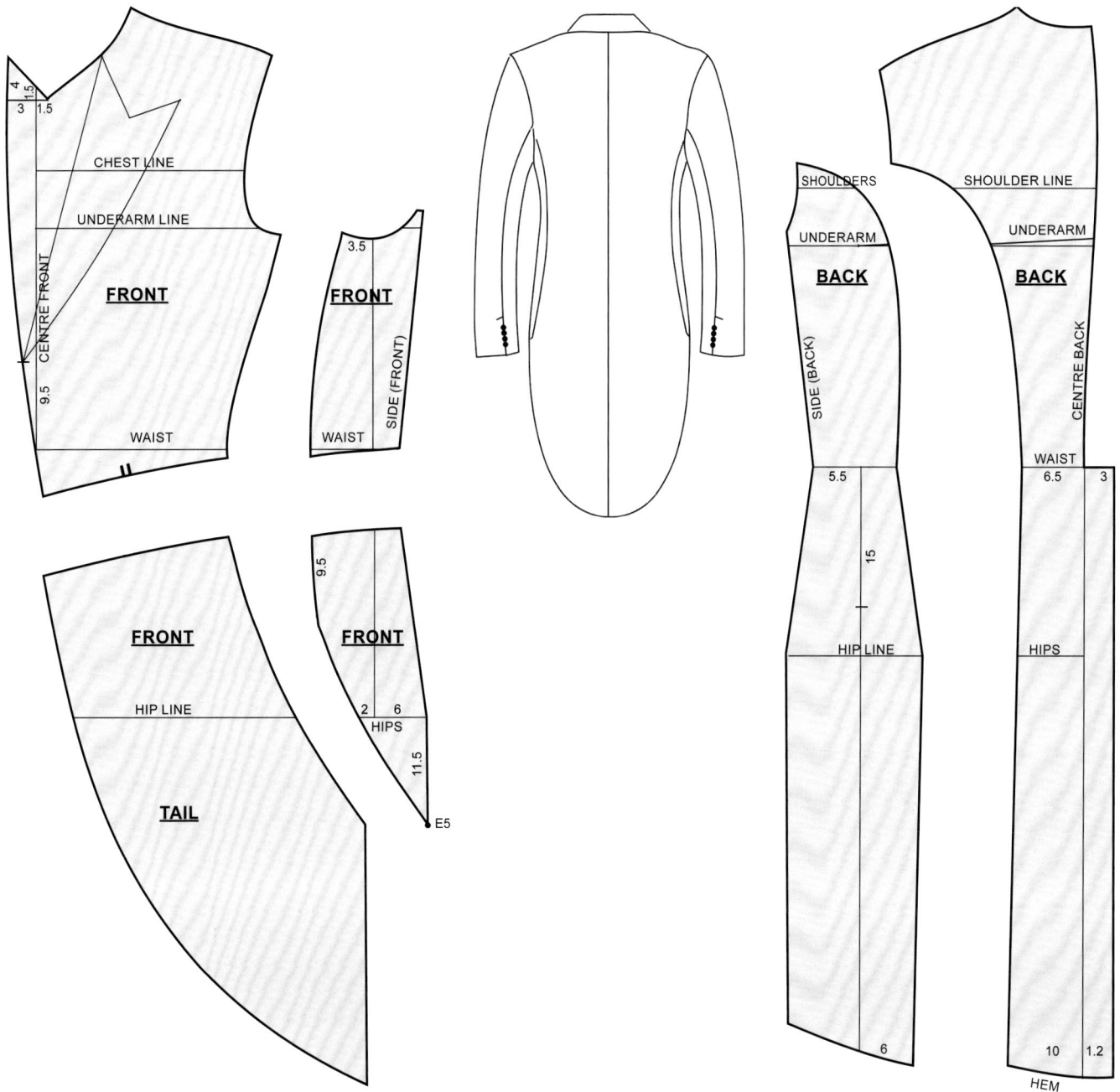

Labels within diagrams:

FRONT (top left)
- CHEST LINE
- UNDERARM LINE
- CENTRE FRONT
- WAIST
- 4, 1.5, 3, 1.5
- 9.5

FRONT / SIDE (FRONT)
- 3.5
- WAIST

FRONT / TAIL
- HIP LINE

FRONT
- 9.5
- HIPS
- 2, 6
- 11.5
- E5

BACK / SIDE (BACK)
- SHOULDERS
- UNDERARM
- 5.5
- 15
- HIP LINE
- 6

BACK / CENTRE BACK
- SHOULDER LINE
- UNDERARM
- WAIST
- 6.5, 3
- HIPS
- 10, 1.2
- HEM

- Draw the base block of the jacket with peaked lapels.
- Extend the centre back C-C1 as desired (e.g.: 60-65 cm / 23.62-25.59" from the waist line).
- Draw the lower hemline C1-B1.
- B-B5 = 5.5 cm / 2.17". Draw B5-B7 and B8-W1 with a curved line.
- C1-C9 at the back = 10 cm / 3.94".

- Draw the side panel line L2-C7-C9-E4-E3-W-Q4.
- Draw the side panel Q4-W1-E3-E5-B8-I4.
- Draw the back vent C2-C3-C4-C5.
- Draw the dart at the front B7-E5-B8-I4
- Draw the lines of the tail B6-E4-E5-B7.
- Form a dart in the fold at point B7 of 1-1.5 cm / 0.39-0.59".

SPENCER JACKET

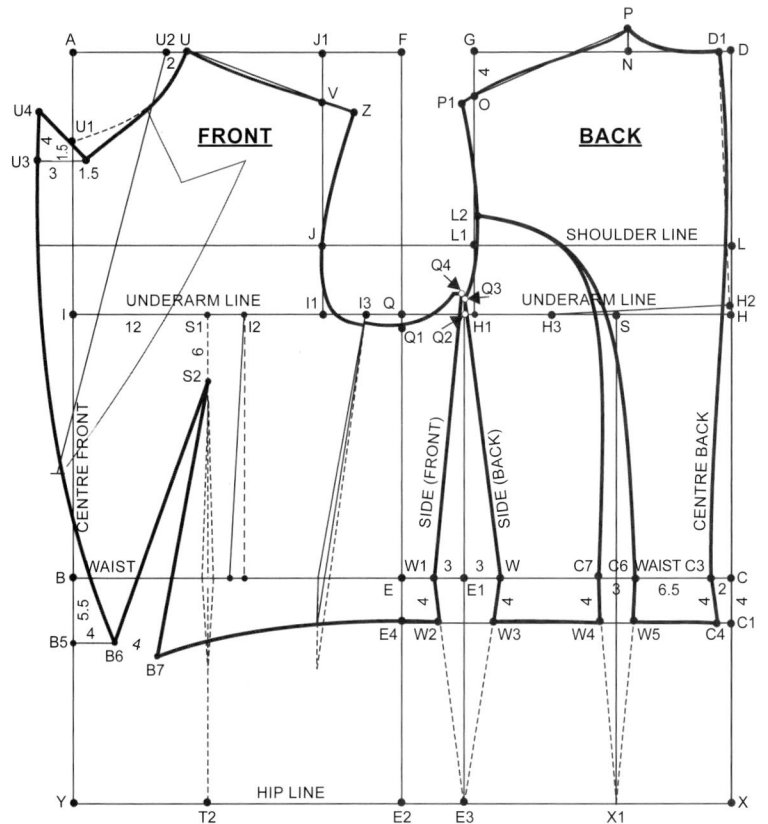

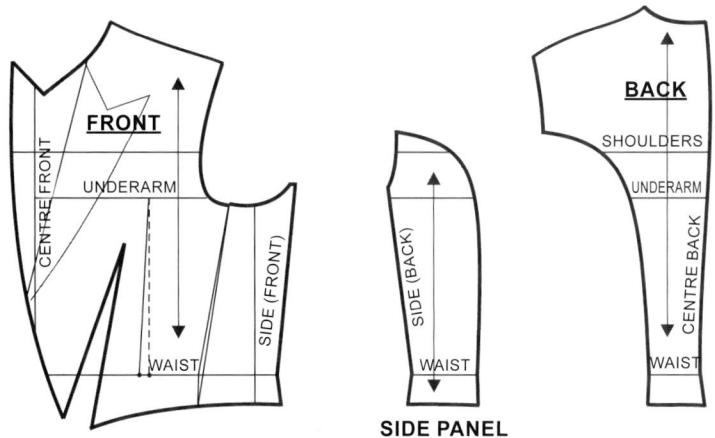

The Spencer is a short jacket that recalls the upper part of full evening dress, and is therefore quite elegant. Today, it is mainly worn by young people as non-traditional wedding wear.
This jacket extends 4-5 cm / 1.57-2" below the waist and is quite fitted. It should be worn with trousers in a contrasting classic colour: black, white, cream, etc.
For making the pattern to the Spencer, it is necessary to refer to the evening dress jacket, since the lines are essentially thesame in the upper part.

- Draw the base block of the jacket with peaked lapels.
- Extend the centre back C-C1 by 3.5-5 cm / 1.38-2".

- E-E4 like C-C1. Draw C1-E4.
- B-B5 = 4.5-5.5 cm / 1.77-2.17". B5-B6 = 4 cm / 1.57".
- Draw the dart at the front B6-S2-B7.
- B6-S2 equal to B7-S2.
- C-C3 = 2 cm / 0.79". Draw the centre back line.
- H-S = 10.5 cm / 4.13". Draw S-X1.
- Calculate the width of the darts and the side tapering.
- Draw the lines of the side panels L2-C6-W5 and L2-C7-W4.
- Draw the lines of the side on the back piece Q3-W-W3.
- Draw the lines of the side on the front piece Q4-W1-W2.
- Draw a curved line B7-E4-W2.
- Join W3-W4 and W5-C4.

JACKETS WITH BACK VENTS

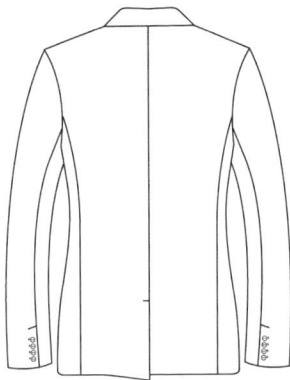

Vent in centre back

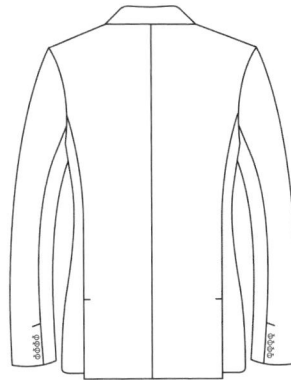

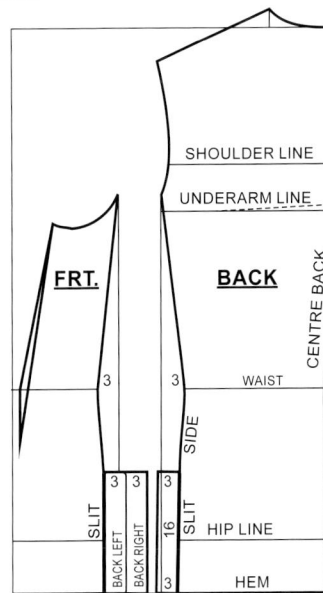

Lateral vents

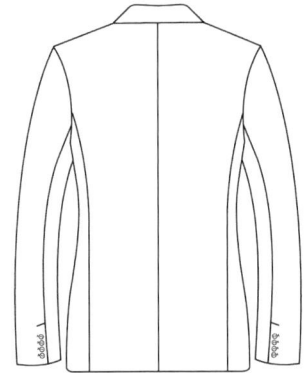

Without vents

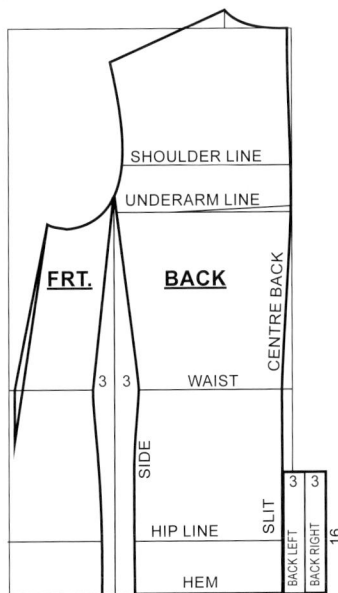

Vent in centre back

Slit in the side panel

The slits, called 'vents', at the back of the jacket are an important detail to be crafted carefully and professionally.

They originally had a functional purpose: while riding a horse, they allowed the rider to move more freely when the jacket was buttoned in front.

Today, the need to be free to move arises whenever one has to sit with the jacket buttoned. In addition, the vents make it easier to access the trouser pockets.

VENT TYPES

Jackets can have a vent at the centre back, two lateral vents, or have none at all.

The centre vent became very popular in America in the 1950s. Today, jackets with a single vent are the most common type in industrial manufacturing because they are cheaper and easier to make. In particular, classic blazers have a single vent. Jackets with two lateral vents, considered to be English in their style, combine functionality and aesthetics: the slits are usually placed near the trouser pockets, making it easy to slip the hand into them. They also help to visually slim the figure, as they run vertically along the body at the sides of the back panel.

Jackets without vents, which originated in Italy, create a simple, clean line and look more elegant than the others, albeit at the expense of functionality. In fact, vent-less jackets tend to bunch up when you put your hands in the trouser pockets and they tend to crease when you sit down without undoing the front button. This style of jacket best enhances a slender physique with broad shoulders. It is often used in formal wear, such as a dinner jacket.

In general, it's a good idea to choose the type of vent according to when the jacket will be worn and the client's personal style. Certainly jackets with vents will be more comfortable, although less elegant.

IRONING AND SEAM ALLOWANCES FOR JACKETS

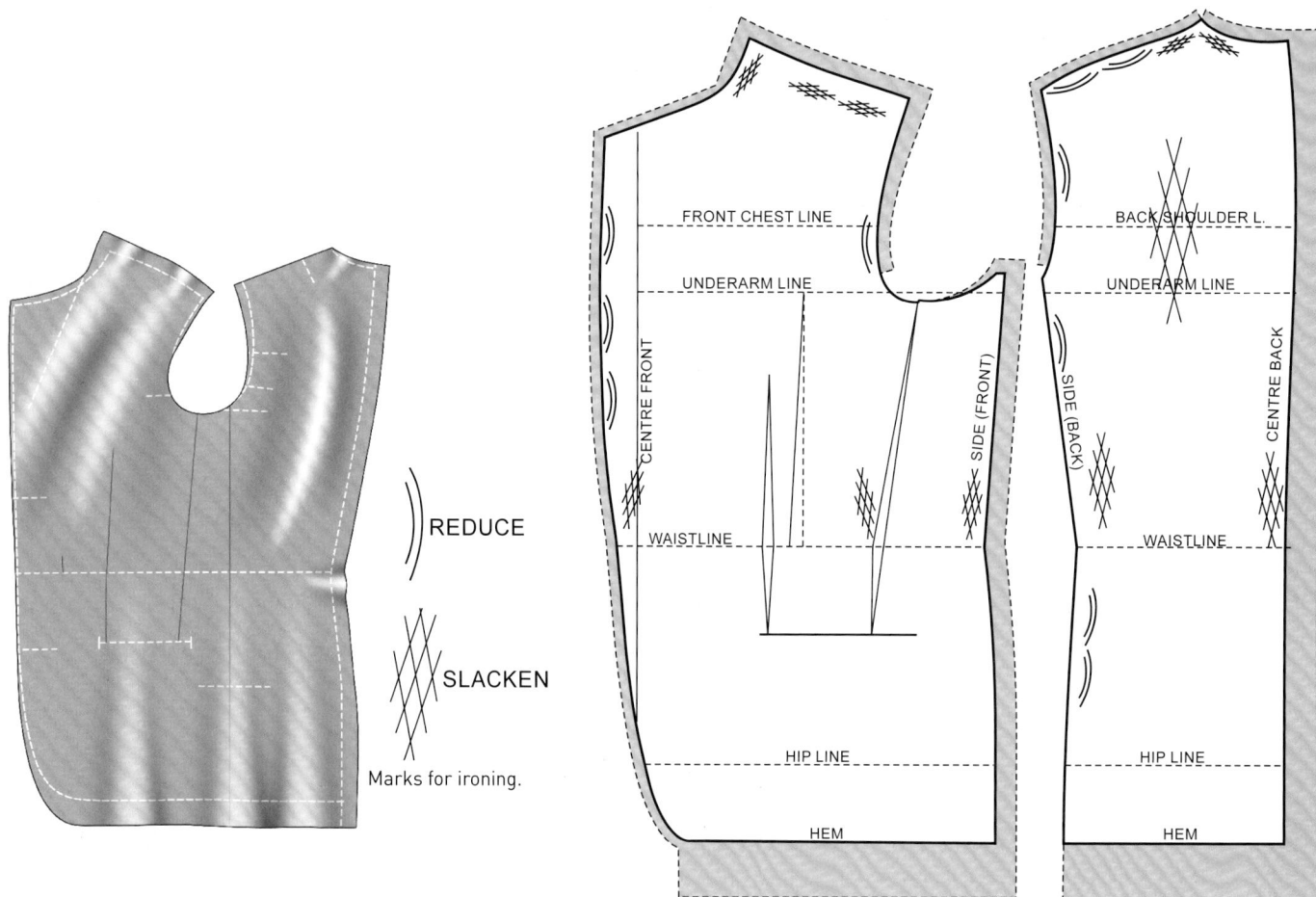

))REDUCE

XX SLACKEN

Marks for ironing.

FRONT CHEST LINE

UNDERARM LINE

CENTRE FRONT

SIDE (FRONT)

WAISTLINE

HIP LINE

HEM

BACK SHOULDER L.

UNDERARM LINE

SIDE (BACK)

CENTRE BACK

WAISTLINE

HIP LINE

HEM

Illustrative graphic of how to iron and jacket seam allowances.

SEAM ALLOWANCES

The seam allowances are parallel to the edge lines.
The margin at the back shoulder is optional and, in any case, means that you must sew below the 0.6 cm / 0.24" demarcation line.

IRONING

For jackets, it's best to rectify the shoulder line from the neckline to the humerus. In general, you'll need to gather the slack and extend and slacken the neckline, flatten and adjust the darts and give the right shape to the hip and waist.

Ironing is necessary to shape the fabric, creating indestructible forms and preventing the design of the fabric from being altered. Knowledge of this technique is indispensable for a professional tailor, as it will make the garment perfect and soften the effects of a dip in the body while respecting the design.

FRONT

1) Shoulders: with the left hand, pick up a length of fabric at the elbow to create tension at the shoulder.
2) Shoulder and neckline: use the iron to continue and stretch the shoulder, while shifting the position, you'll also slacken the neckline.

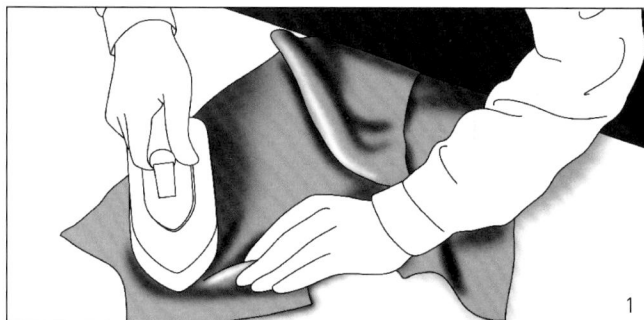

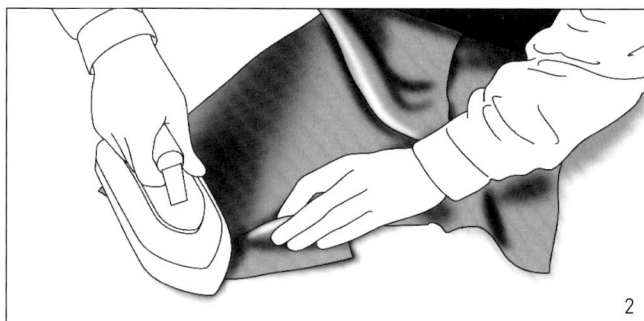

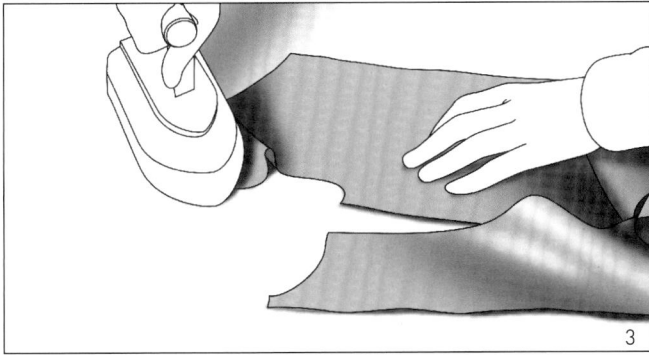

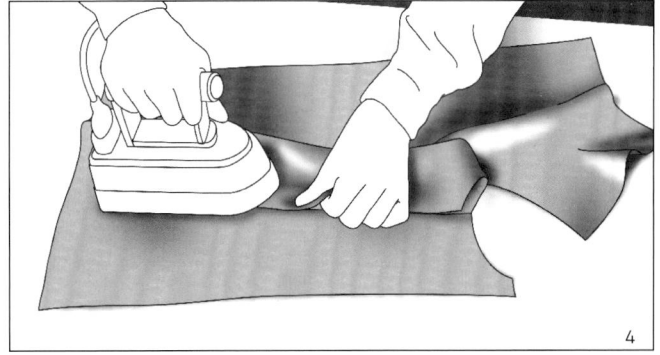

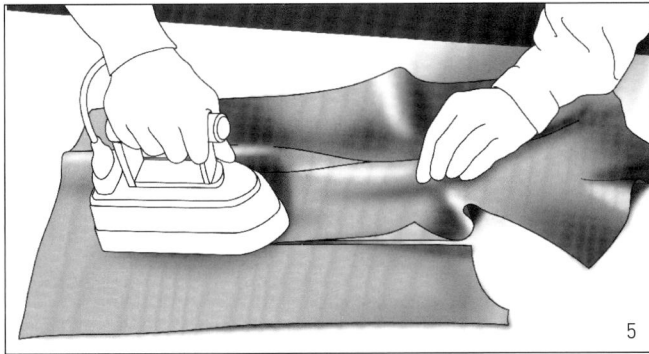

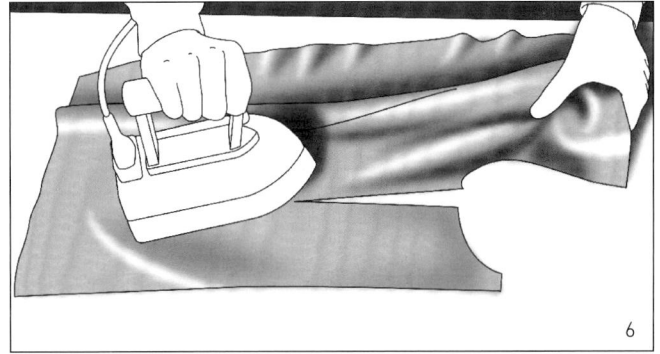

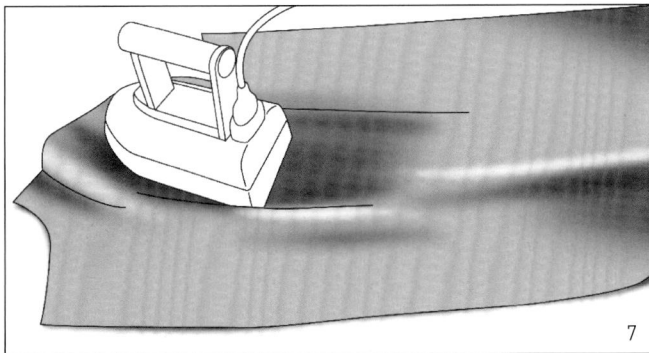

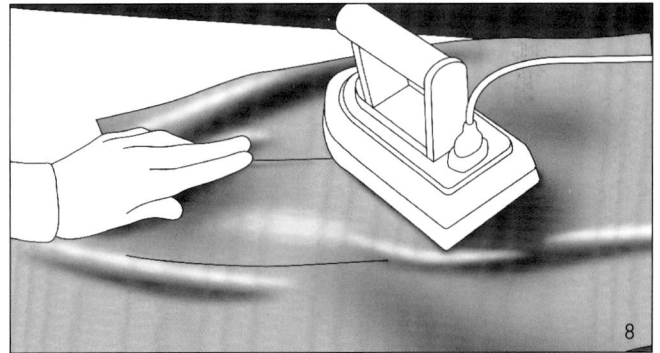

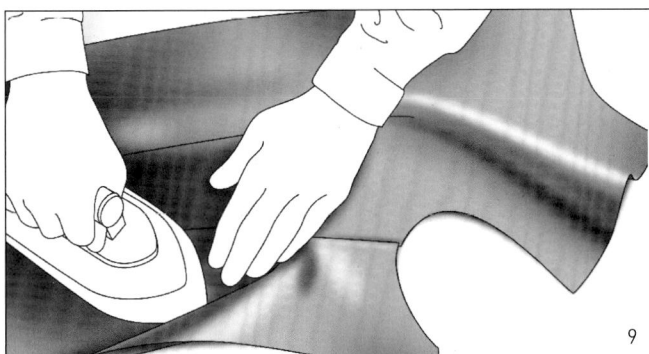

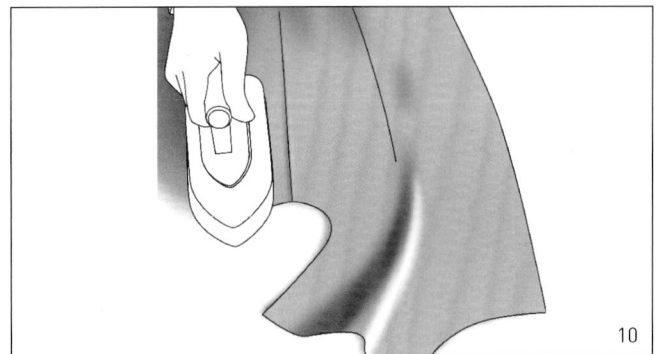

3) Stable effect: on the shoulder line, completely set the fabric, so that the gathering previously created by the left hand becomes a stable effect.

4) To eliminate the cavity, meanwhile pull the front of the dart with your left hand.

5) With the left hand, gather the fabric on the width and, stretching it, create a gap between the two sides of the dart at the waistline.

6) Continue the action upwards, moving the left hand higher up and holding the fabric taught to create a rounded effect.

7) Use the iron to reach the waist and force it to create a progressively curved effect.

8) To align the dart, use your left hand to bring the side panels together to bring the sides of the dart together, and iron over them. Note the tension of the fabric on the hip.

9) Continue with the iron to extend the fabric as desired, continuing to work on the width of the fabric.

10) Once the desired effect has been achieved, iron vertically to align the entire side panel with the dart, with the sides together, the slack removed and the underarm specified on the armscye.

IRONING THE FRONT OF THE JACKET (cont'd)

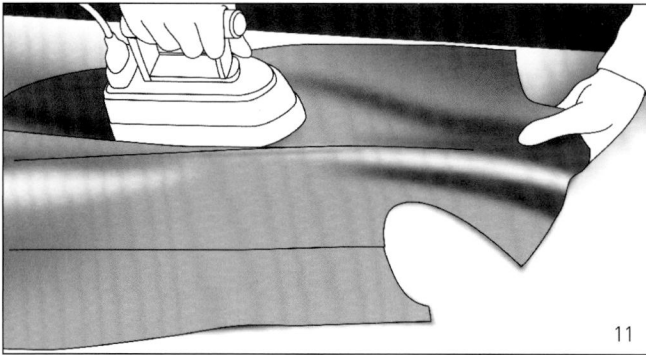

11) Trying not to interfere with the breakline of the lapel, use the iron to stress the fabric from the waistline, while the left hand makes a rotating movement.

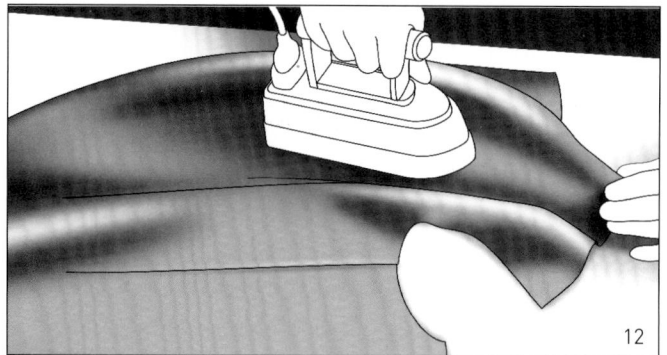

12) Advance the iron upwards, accentuating the effect.

IRONING THE BACK OF THE JACKET

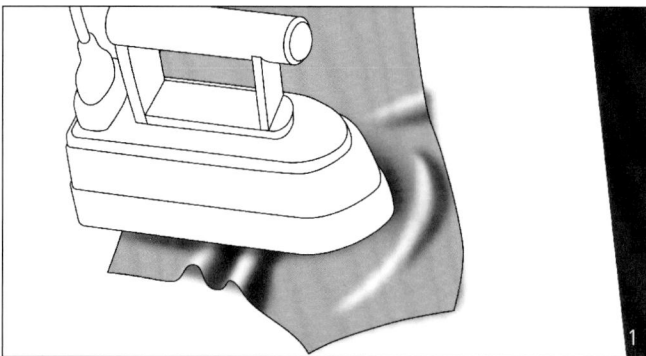

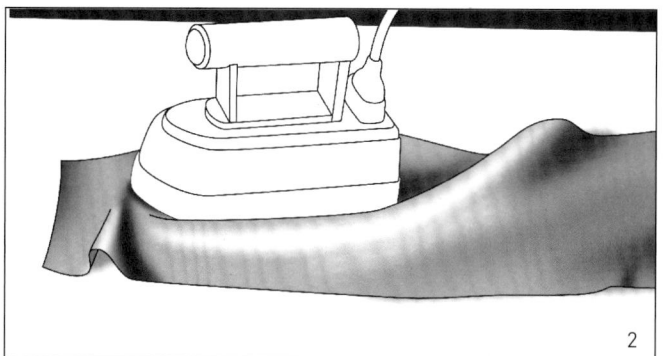

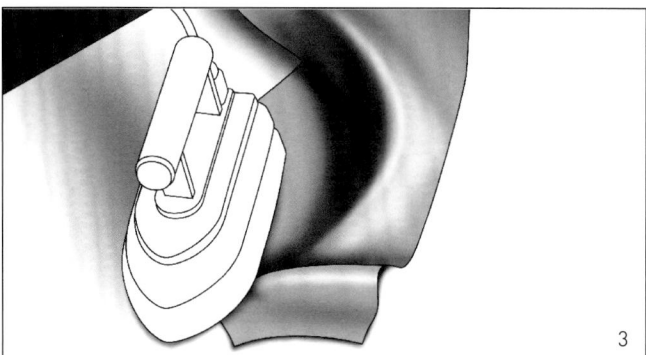

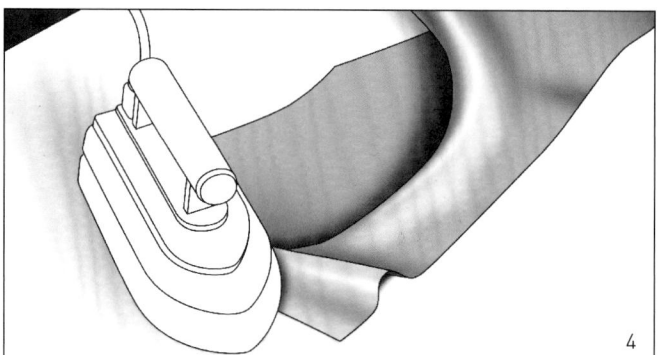

1) On the back, start ironing from the shoulder, then arrange a gathering of slack.
2) Slide the iron towards the concave part of the back, while the shoulder, held taught, is lifted from the workbench, having gathered a godet in the centre back with the hand.

3) Next, working transversally, point the iron towards the shoulder and flatten it.
4) Turn and continue towards the neckline to extend the fabric.

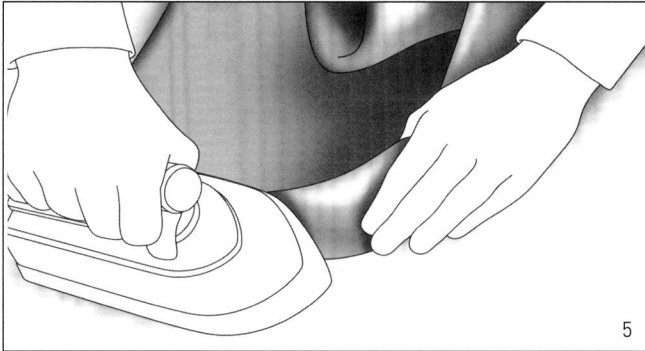

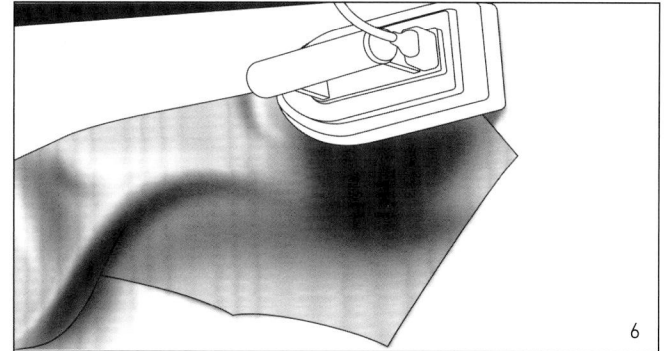

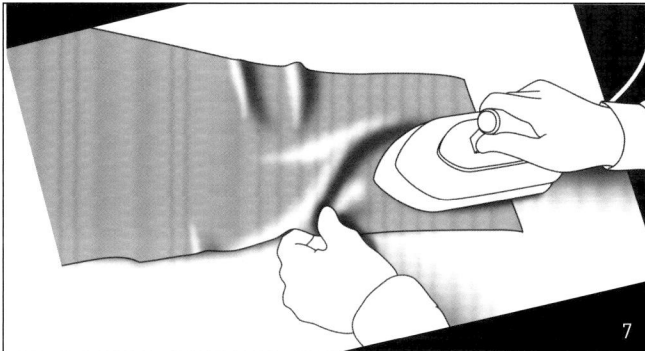

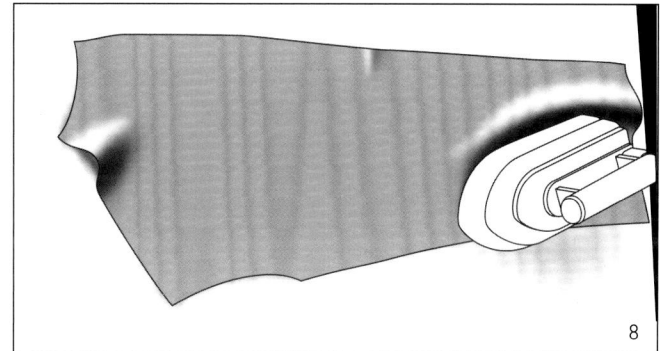

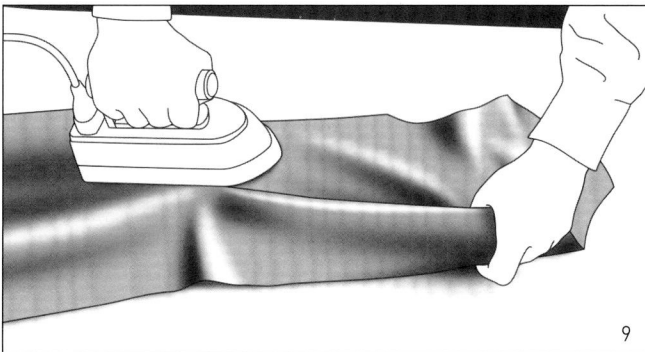

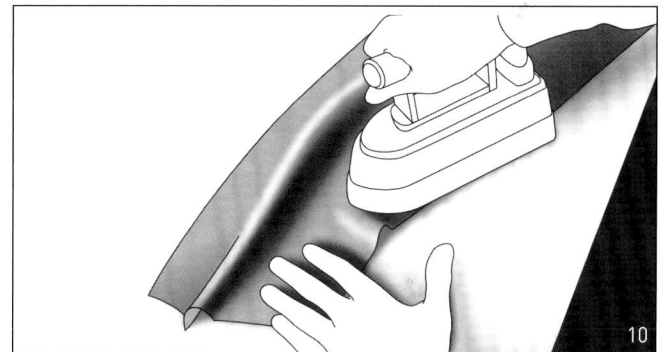

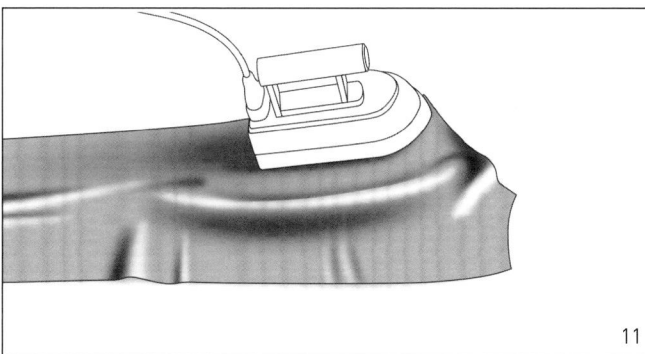

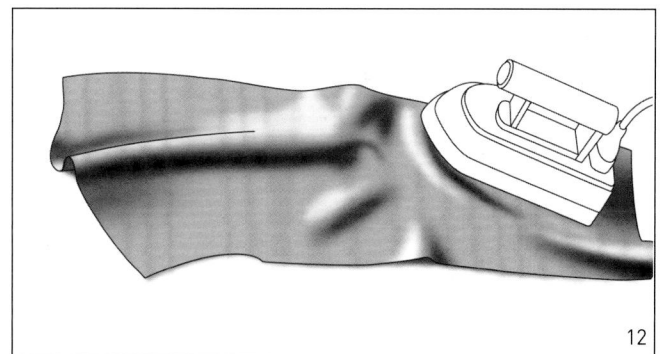

5) Work on the neckline to force the fabric. The left hand helps to subject the neckline to the exertion.

6) Immediately afterwards turn the iron onto the centre seam to iron and readjust it.

7) To remove the waist curve, slide the iron from the bottom of the hip towards the waist, while the left hand brings the fabric outwards to gather the ridge.

8) At this point, the desired effect has been achieved, in fact you can see the ridge obtained for the hip.

9) To straighten the hip, iron starting from the waist, while the left hand holds the fabric taught and moves it outwards.

10) Continue ironing above the waist to prepare for an indentation.

11) Once the desired effect has been achieved, continue ironing only to set and flatten the fabric.

12) From the bottom, run the iron along the centre seam, always working crosswise, to reach the waist curve.

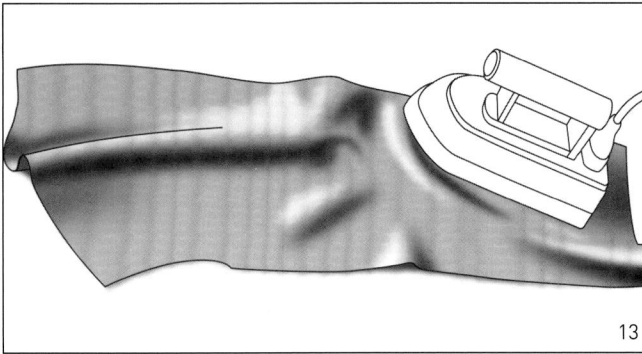

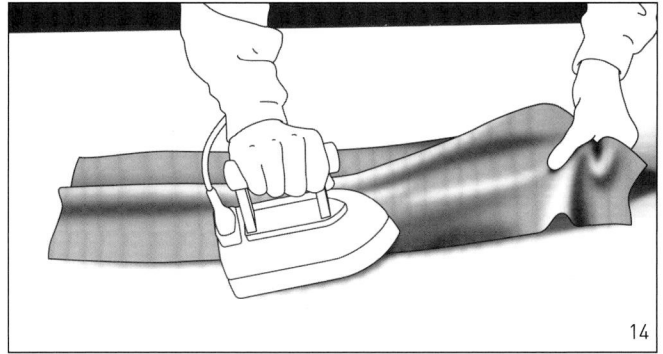

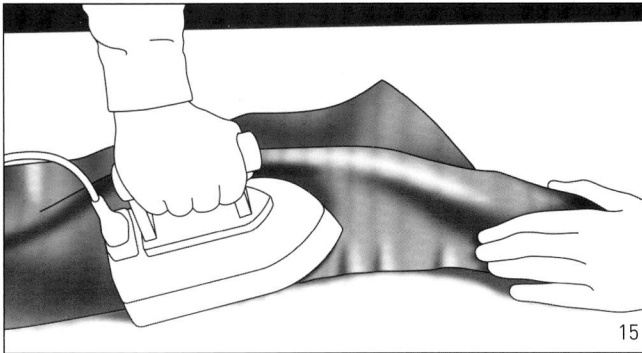

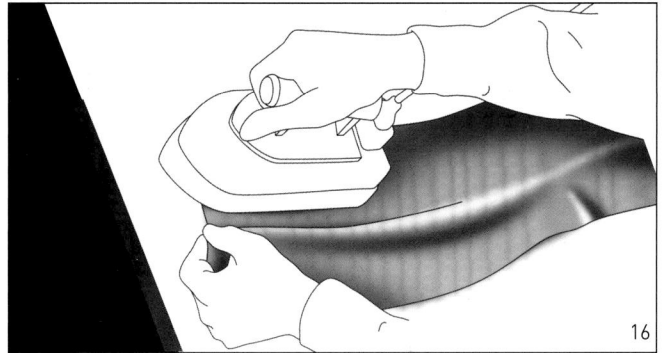

13) Holding the fabric taut, from the waist iron working crosswise while the left hand, from the shoulder blade, moves the back.

14) From the effect reached with the iron, proceed to set and iron, while the left hand holds the neckline firmly to avoid altering the centre seam.

15-16) With the iron, iron up to the middle of the neckline, while the left hand holds the edge taut to free the lateral part from the centre.

RESULTS OF IRONING

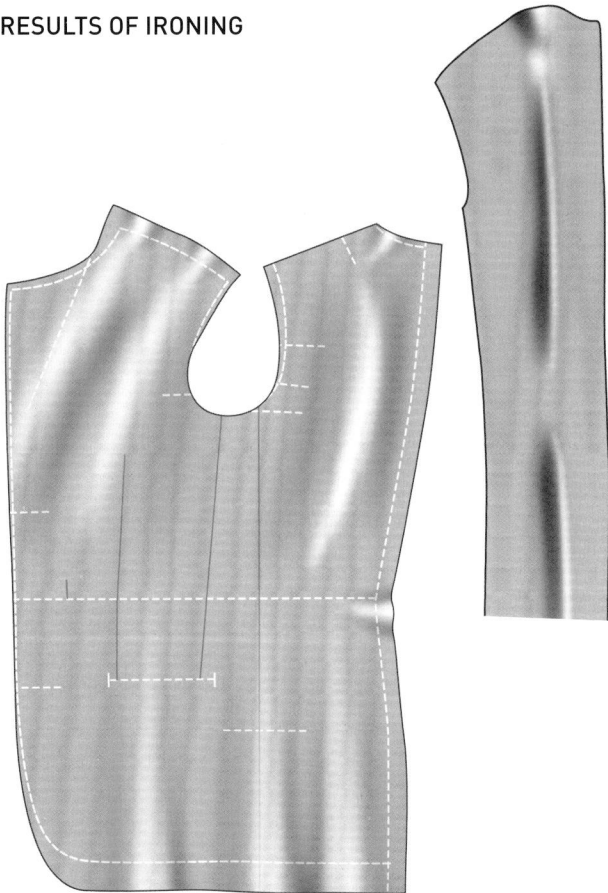

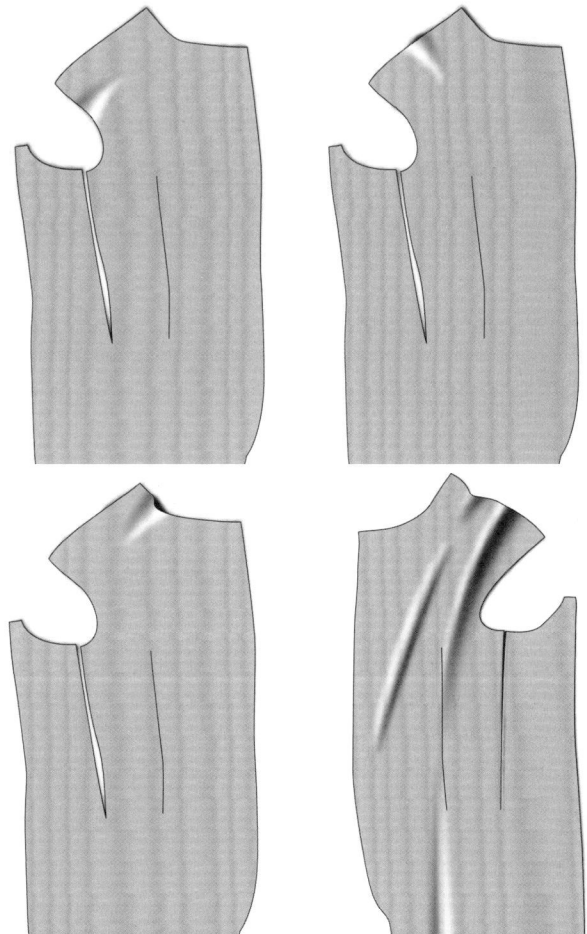

SHOULDER ASSEMBLY

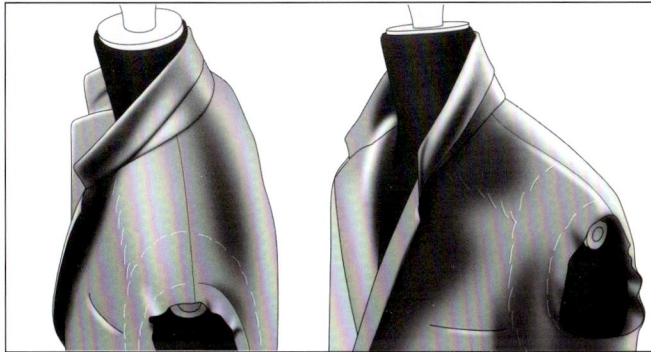

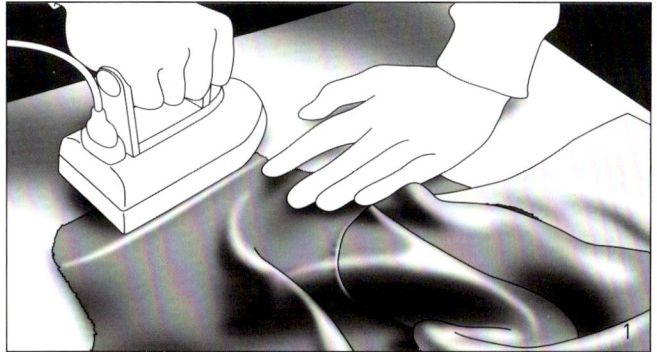

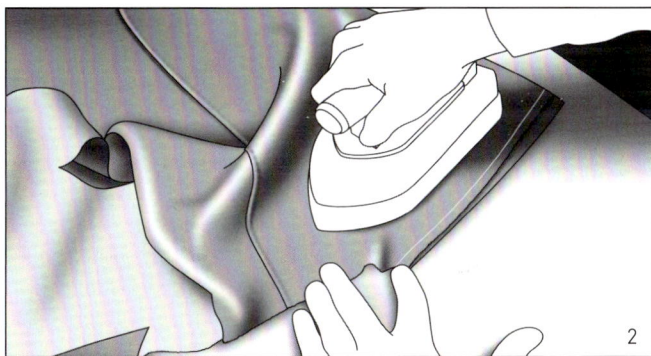

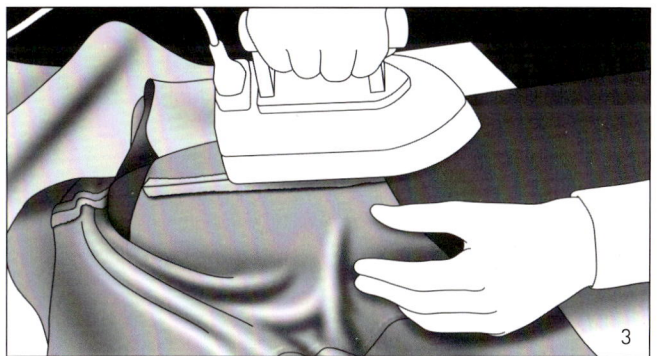

IRONING TECHNIQUE

1) Place the iron parallel to the tacking line and press, keeping the seam straight. Simultaneously, with the other hand, move the neckline so as not to lose the effects of the previous ironing efforts.

2) Slide the iron inwards to even out the parts, always keeping the seam straight. With the other hand, join the rippled effect. Sew the shoulder, taking care not to shift the slack and make a straight seam, ideally by hand to prevent the shoulder from becoming stiff or misshapen. Then move on and iron the seam.

3) After placing the shoulder on the flat tool, position the iron parallel to the seam, checking that it is set in a straight line (with the other hand, move the neckline to safeguard the concave effect). Iron, not by sliding the iron over the fabric, but by raising and lowering it to prevent the shoulder from stretching.

PLACING THE FABRIC ON THE INTERFACING

Having completed the previous steps, move on to the interfacing. The interfacing must have curvatures corresponding to the fabric, even being rather prevalent. Before proceeding, you will need to carry out a check in this regard. You will also need to seek out the vertical placement by hand, as follows: place the shoulder on the hollow of the palm and temporarily find a point of comparison similar to the one it will cover. The design of the fabric must maintain the straight of grain and the interfacing must sit well in the hollow of the hand, so that the fabric follows it effortlessly. After having completed these checks, baste by following the straight line of the design; during this step, ironing with a light upwards movement. Next, imagining the basting as the ideal centre from which the effects radiate, gently wipe towards both the elbow and the neckline.

It is very important to seek out a stretching action towards the neckline, always wiping in two directions, i.e. both outwards and upwards. This is a delicate movement that must be performed with the utmost care.

Once the shoulders have been set and placed, move on to the application of the facing and reinforcements, the adjustment of the interiors and their levelling.

LINING

The lining is an integral part of the jacket: in addition to covering the inside, it constitutes a refined, sophisticated element. It is cut and sewn along the same seam lines as the jacket, but some prudent details make it more comfortable: for example, a fold in the centre back makes it easier for the shoulders and upper back to move. Another fold is usually found between the lining and the hems of the garment: this is called folded-edge lining and allows the jacket to move comfortably when worn without straining the seams. It can be executed using the same pattern as the jacket, and all the effects applied to the fabric itself can be realised on the lining, depending on the type of fibre it is made from: dry ironing, pleats, addition of slack, etc.

The lining must be cut 1.5 cm / 0.59" higher at the armscye. This allows it to rest above the seams of the jacket armhole

MANUAL PROCESS

1) Start with a supporting seam on the edges of the neck and shoulders of the lining cut to size. Complete and iron the longitudinal seams of the bodice and sleeves, including any darts. Fold the front lining seam allowances under, iron them and make small cuts to flatten them.

2) Baste in the centre back and iron the fold towards the left back, then sew the fold with a catch stitch or cross stitch, taking up all the layers. Use the iron to create a covering pleat and a reserve pleat, iron it, and prepare the side and shoulder re-entry by ironing.

3) Baste any darts at the waist, sew them with cross stitches or catch stitches with 5 cm / 2" at the centre of the dart, then remove the basting.

4) Use long stitches to sew the lateral margins of the lining together with those of the garment fabric, up to 10 cm / 3.94" from the lower edge.

5) Make small cuts at the seam allowances of the back neckline, turn it inside out and pin it. Pin the lining around the armhole, from the underarm to the shoulder seam. Fold the edge of the rear shoulder downwards, set it on top of the front one and pin it. Baste the rear neckline and shoulder seams.

6) Overlap the front edges of the lining on the inner facing along the seam line and pin it by taking only the lining and placket facing up to 10 cm / 3.94" above the hem fold. To gather the curves, place the garment on an ironing pad. Tack by hand.

7) Hand-sew the lining around the armholes about 1.5 cm / 0.59" from the edge and use loose stitches to fasten the lining to the shoulder padding and to the sleeve seam allowance. Trim the lining in the underarm between the notches, so that it lines up with the fabric of the garment.

8) Test the garment to check if the lining falls well and is soft enough. If it is too tight, create gatherings and/or creases in the garment fabric, remove the basting as needed to adjust the lining, and baste again. At this point, the edges of the lining can be sewn with small blind stitches done by hand. Finally, remove the basting and iron if necessary.

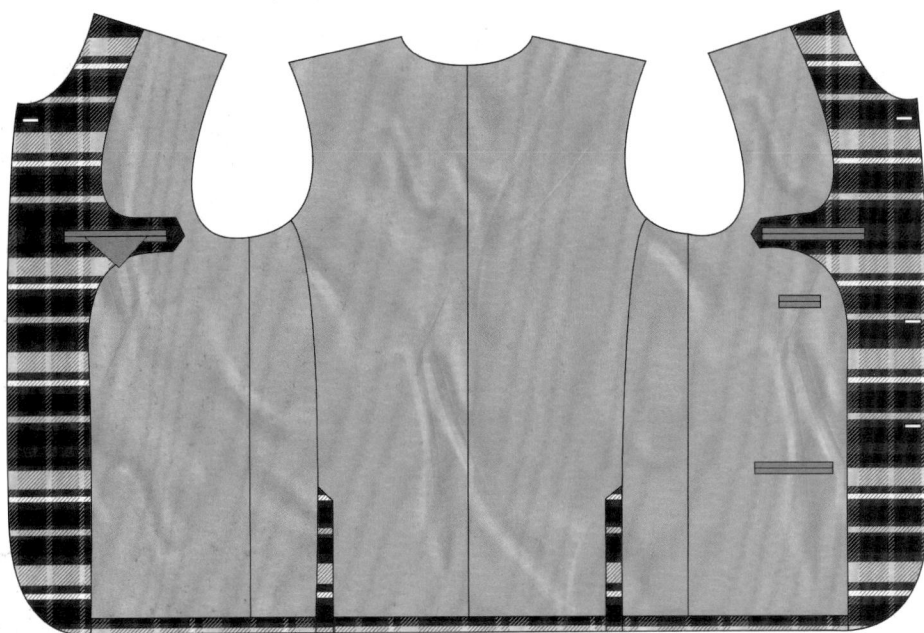

and avoids folds in this area. If, on the other hand, the pattern for the sleeve lining is made separately, check that it is correct by overlapping the sleeve pattern pieces with those of the lining, matching the stitching lines of the armscye. Cut the lining of the jacket and sleeves 1.5 cm / 0.59" longer than the length of the garment, with the hem completed. When the lining has been applied, the finished edges of the lining will fall below the mid-point of the jacket and sleeve hems. If the jacket or its sleeves need to be lengthened or shortened, adjust the length of the lining accordingly.

In order to apply the lining, the various parts of the lining are first sewn together, and then it is attached by hand or by spot-stitching on the inside of the garment: for the latter, the lining on the armholes must still be sewn by hand for an optimized fit.

SLEEVE LINING ASSEMBLY

To assemble the sleeve lining, proceed as follows:

1) Create thread gathering approximately 1 cm / 0.39" from the edge of the sleeve crown between the two notches.

2) Insert the lining into the sleeve, wrong side against wrong side. Fold down approximately 5 mm / 0.20" in the underarm between the notches and pin to the armhole seam line.

3) Pull the threads of the gathering to adapt the lining to the sleeve and fold down the edges of the lining. Pin and then sew the sleeve lining to the armhole lining with a small slip-stitch, using two lengths of waxed thread, but do not sew the garment fabric as well.

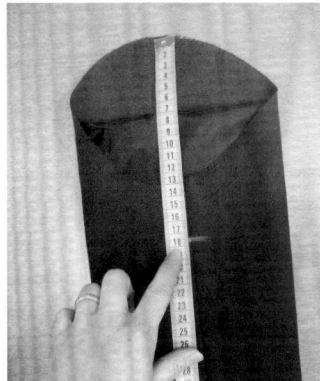

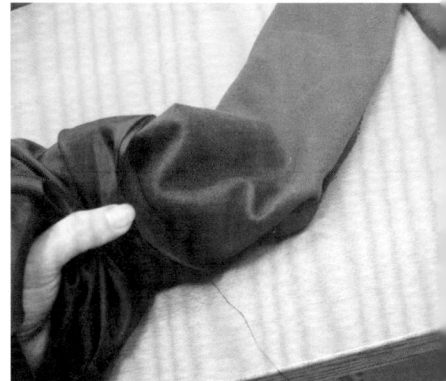

HEM THE LINING

To hem the jacket lining:

1) Pin the lining about 7 cm / 2.76" from the hem and cut the lining about 1.5 cm / 0.59" longer than the finished jacket. Then fold down the edge of the lining by about 1.5 cm / 0.59", pin it so that it just covers the hem margin and secure the lining with a slip stitch. Remove the pins.

2) Let the hem of the lining fall, which will form a crease along the lower edge of the jacket, creating the necessary ease. Now affix the front edge of the lining to the placket facing along the lower edge and iron the hem.

3) An alternative method is to hem the lining so that it is 2 cm / 0.79" shorter than the finished garment and fasten the front edge of the lining to the placket facing with a slip stitch along the lower edge. If desired, a loose bar tack can be sewn on the seams, with 3-4 stitches measuring 5 cm / 2" long reinforced with a thick blanket stitch, for extra security.

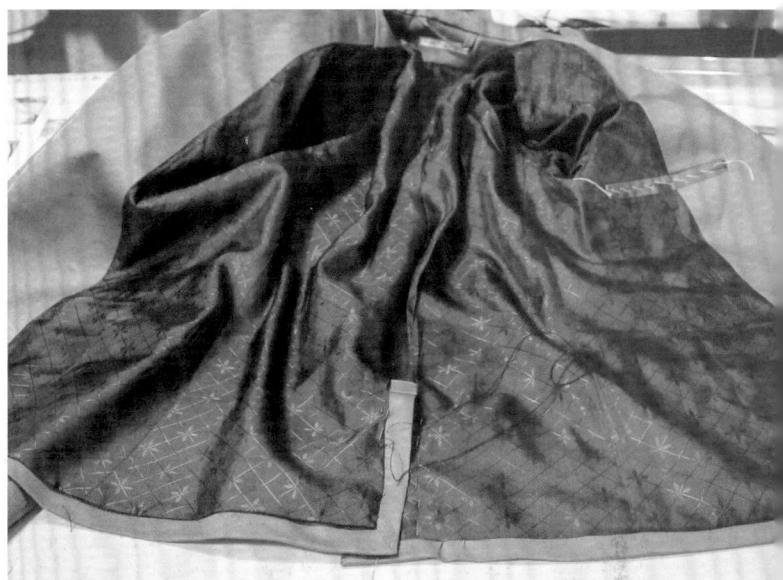

LINING WITH TRIM

1) Prepare a strip of bias lining approx. 4 cm / 1.57" wide and with a length equal to that of the front placket facing and back neckline (if any) plus 7.5 cm / 2.95". Fold over the strip and insert a thin cord or coarse cotton thread in it. Sew close to the cord using the zip presser foot.

2) Pin the trim along the right side of the placket facing up to the finished edge of the jacket. Machine tack along the seam line to the upper edge of the jacket hem.

3) Machine sew the placket facing to the lining, right sides together, keeping the cording close. Then hem the lining, fold the cord so that it is even with the lining and sew them together with a slip stitch. Iron the seam allowances.

4) For garments without facing on the back neckline, pin the lining to the armholes and back neckline, turn the seam allowance of the back shoulder underneath, and overlap it at the front. Baste and slip stitch along the neckline and shoulders.

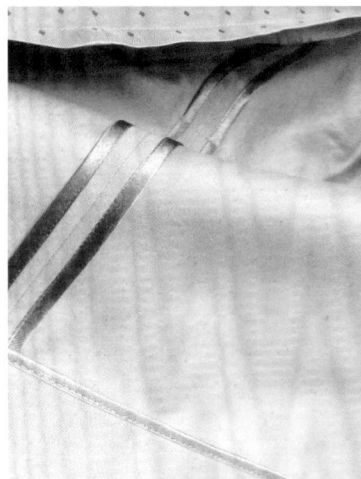

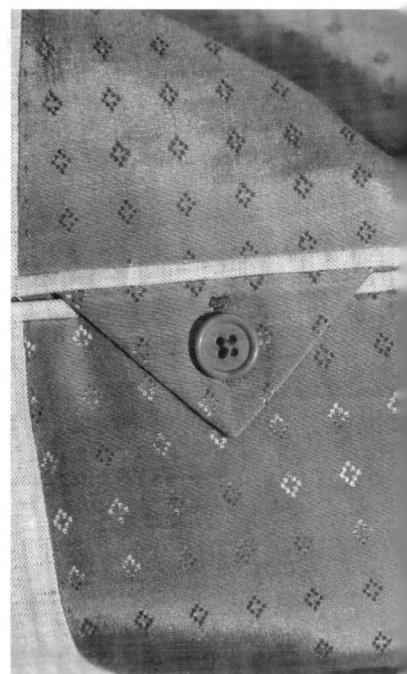

JACKET DETAIL CONSTRUCTION

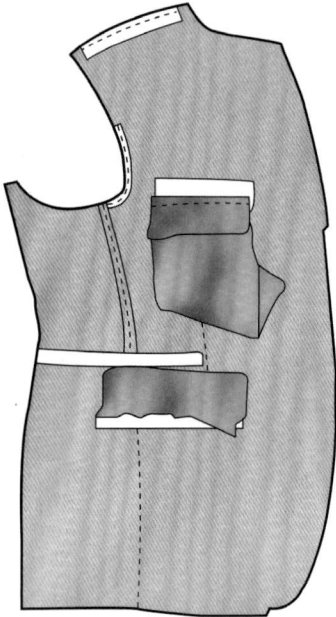

- Sew the front darts.
- Apply tape to the armhole.
- Iron the seams and darts.
- Apply fusible reinforcements along the pocket cut line and at hip height.
- Apply all pockets.

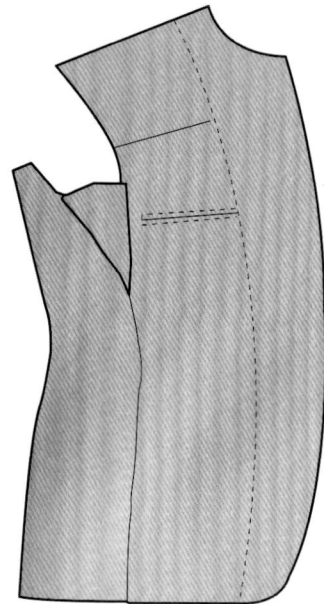

- Construct the besom pockets with edging.
- Joining seam of lining to the facing.

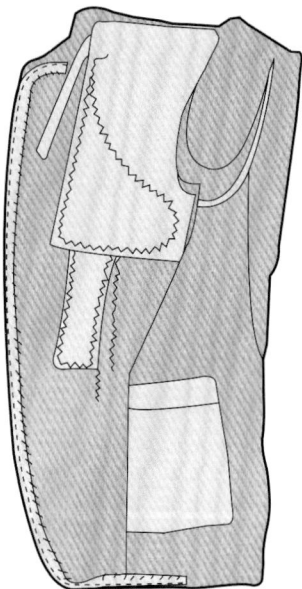

- Baste the canvassing on the inside-out front.
- Apply tape to the armscyes.
- Apply tape to the margins of the front.

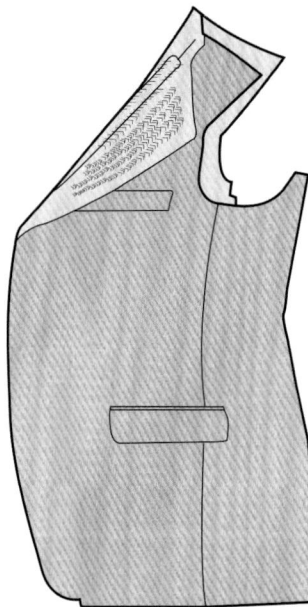

- Tailor stitch the lapels by hand or with a special sewing machine for blind stitching.

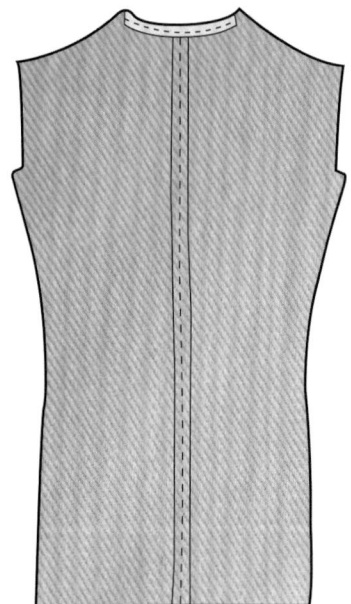

- Centre-back stitching with the application of tape to the neckline.

JACKET COLLAR AND SLEEVE CONSTRUCTION

Collar

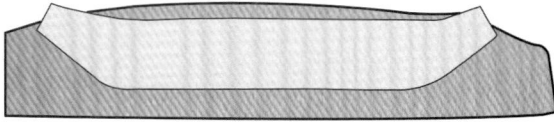

1) Trim neck and undercollar lining.

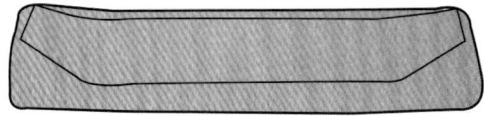

2) Apply the undercollar to the top part through reinforcement T-stitching done by hand or on a sewing machine.

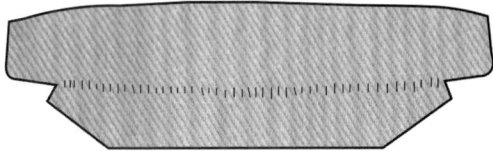

3) Stitch the corners of the undercollar with a normal sewing machine.

4) Turn collar inside out and baste by hand or by machine using a chain stitch; finish the lining and iron to smooth out the collar.

Collar assembly

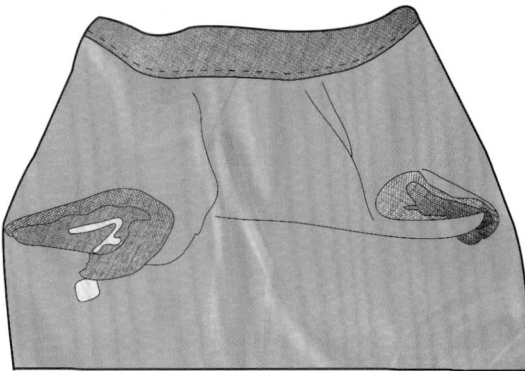

1) Baste the undercollar by hand or with a needle basting machine.

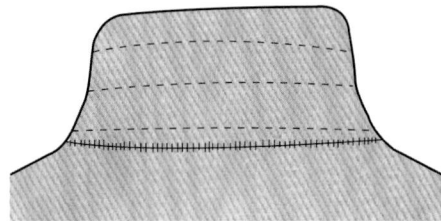

2) Reinforce the undercollar with a T-stitch by hand or with a sewing machine.

Sleeve

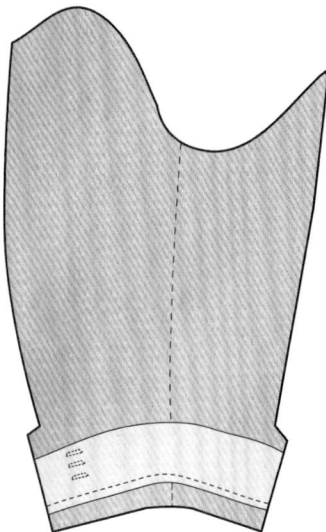

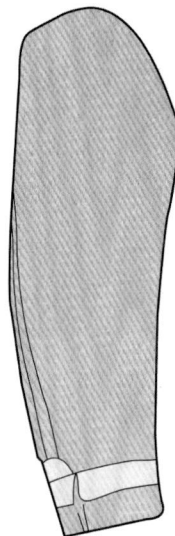

- Apply the reinforcement at the sleeve cuffs with chain stitch basting.
- Create the eyelets at the bottom of the sleeve.

WORKING STAGES OF THE CLASSIC JACKET

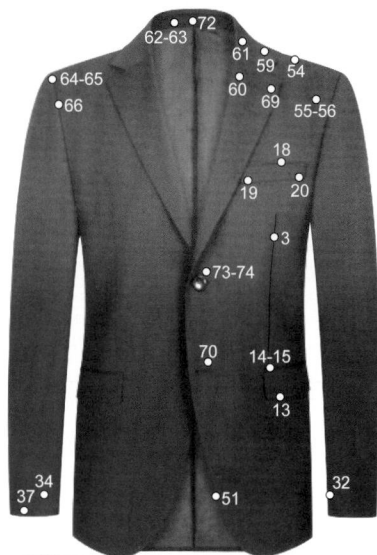

FRONT BODICE
1-2. Side seams
3. Chest and hip dart closure
4. Tape attachment around the armhole and shoulder
5. Inner basting
6. Shaping the front
7. Edge tacking
8. Fixing pocket corners on the inside

BACK BODICE
9. Creation of the centre seam
10. Tape application at the back, at the armscye and around the collar

SIDE POCKETS
11. Preparation of the small inner pocket in the side pocket
12. Finishing of the inner pocket in the side pocket
13. Pocket flap construction
14. Attachment of upper trim to the flaps
15. First seam and contemporary cutting of the side pockets
16. Finishing of the side pockets
17. Bar-tacking of the side pockets

BREAST POCKET
18. Sew and turn breast pocket trim inside out
19. Fasten breast pocket
20. Fasten breast pocket trim
21. Fasten breast pocket trim internally
22. Finish breast pocket

INNER (BESOM) POCKETS
23. Make inner pocket welting
24. First seam and simultaneous cut of inner pocket
25. Closure inner pocket
26. Bar-tacking inner pocket corners

INTERIOR (canvas)
27. Dart closure on the canvas
28. Canvas quilting

UNDERCOLLAR
29. Stitch and at the same time trim the undercollar

SLEEVES
30. Make buttonholes on sleeves
31. Sew cuff pleats
32. Sew sleeve fronts
33. Sewing of the front lining of the sleeves
34. Sew sleeve lining hems
35. Sew sleeve backs
36. Sew back sleeve lining
37. Attach the lining opening of the sleeves
38. Baste sleeve hems
39. Fasten sleeve lining to the back part
40. Baste the upper lining of the sleeves
41. Sew sleeve buttons

INNER LINING WITH FACING
42. Lining: dart closure at the chest and sides
43. Join lining to the facing
44. Close lining at sides

ASSEMBLY
45. Close sides
46. Stitch inner lining to hem
47. Sew and reinforce stitch the corners of the facing
48. Baste the facing
49. Stitching and temporary trimming of the front edges
50. Baste folded lining along hem
51. Baste profiling and edges

ASSEMBLY CYCLES
52. Baste lining to the facing
53. Baste the upper lining on the inside
54. Sew shoulder seams
55. Baste padding inside shoulder
56. Baste shoulder
57. Close shoulder seam in lining

COLLAR ASSEMBLY
58. Join undercollar
59. Join collar
60. Baste underside of collar
61. Baste collar
62. Baste collar leaf and stand
63. Sew on collar leaf and stand

SLEEVE ASSEMBLY
64. Sew on sleeves
65. Sew sleeve roll
66. Shoulder pad/epaulette to the armscye of the sleeves
67. Sewing of the lining to the armscye on the lower 3/4

FINISHING
68. Mark buttonholes
69. Make lapel buttonholes
70. Make front buttonholes
71. Bar tack buttonholes
72. Sew tab for hanging jacket
73. Sew on buttons
74. Ironing and final cleaning

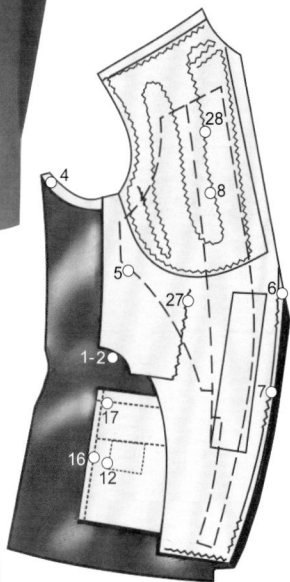

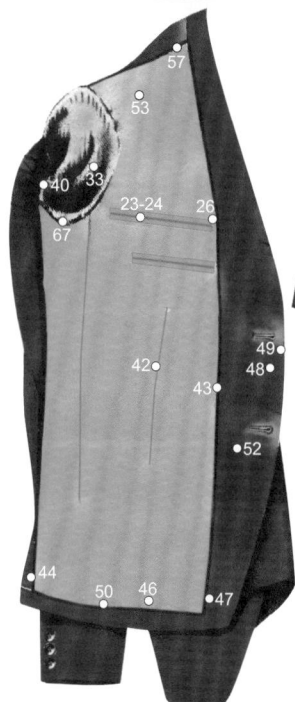

ADAPTING THE GARMENT TO DIFFERENT BODY SHAPES

Patterns made with our bases are designed for an 'average-size' man with standard measurements, illustrated in the table in the previous chapters.

The measurements and ease values taken into account are those of a size 16 UK (chest cir. of 38") used in industrial construction, which often do not correspond to the true conformation of the person to be dressed. In fact, while in the industry the measurements and values for the realisation of base patterns and size development are standardized, in bespoke tailoring the pattern must have the true measurements corresponding to each part of the body. Hence the need to properly adapt the base pattern of the bodice, if we want the final garment to fit well and look professional.

CONFORMATION OF SHOULDER WIDTH

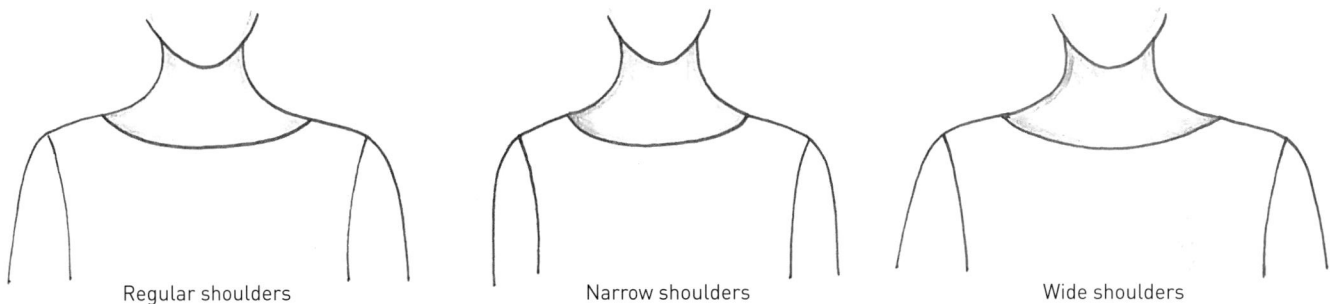

Regular shoulders   Narrow shoulders   Wide shoulders

NARROW SHOULDERS

For subjects with narrow shoulders, the shoulder point of the base pattern should be reduced by the necessary amount. Moreover, the armscye must also be corrected by raising it to compensate for the shift of the shoulder point.

SUITABLE PATTERNS

The most suitable garment patterns are those that add volume to the shoulders for a more balanced look: garments with broad, padded shoulders.

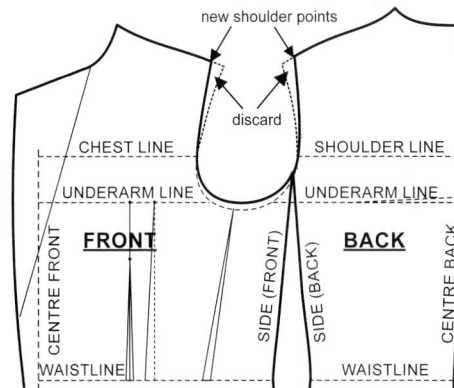

Narrow shoulders: narrow and adjust the sleeve.

WIDE SHOULDERS

For clients with wide shoulders, the shoulder point and the underarm point should be extended by the necessary amount. The armhole should be adjusted, always checking that it is appropriate to the size of the sleeve crown.

SUITABLE PATTERNS

Unstructured and unpadded garments, without yokes or cuts at the top of the shoulders.

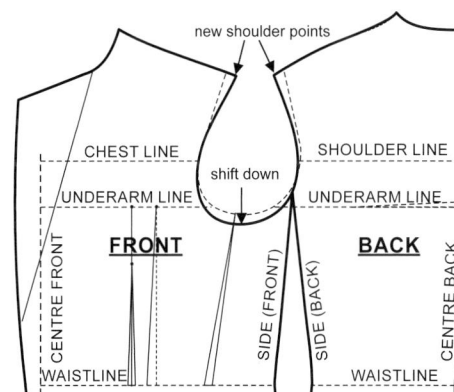

Wide shoulders: widen and adjust the sleeve.

CONFORMATION OF SHOULDER SLOPE

Regularly shaped shoulders protrude about 4-4.5 cm / 1.57-1.77", measuring from the base of the neck to the outer edge of the shoulder, as shown in the figure. Sloping or low shoulders descend more than 4.5-5 cm / 1.58-1.77" from the base of the neck. Those with a square or high conformation have shoulders that descend less than 4-5 cm / 1.58-1.77" from the base of the neck.

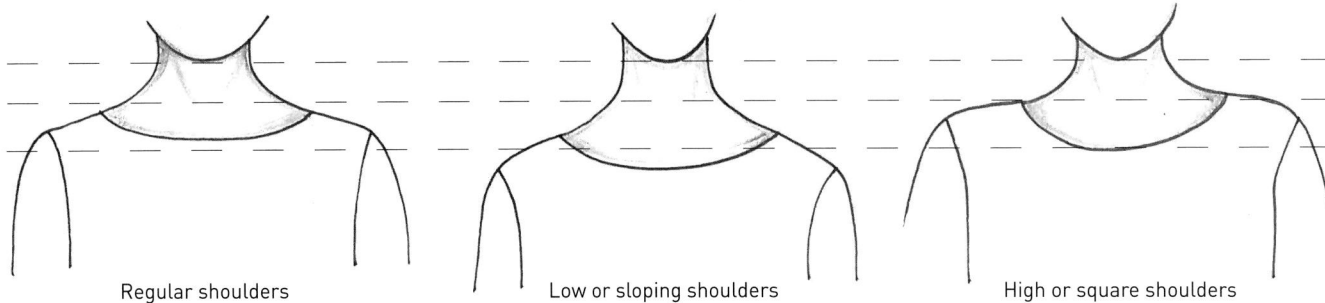

Regular shoulders

Low or sloping shoulders

High or square shoulders

Low shoulders - solution 1

In order to adapt the basic pattern to someone with sloping shoulders, lower the shoulder and underarm points by the necessary amount, or add shoulder pads, maintaining the original slope of the base, but adjusting the armhole.

SUITABLE PATTERNS

Slightly broader or padded shoulders; yoke or seams on the shoulders.

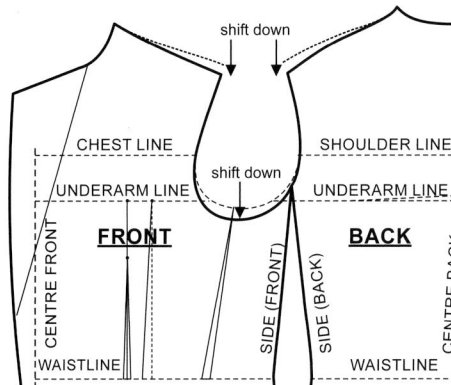

High shoulders - solution 1

For clients with square shoulders, the shoulder point and the underarm point should be raised by the necessary amount.

SUITABLE PATTERNS

Raglan sleeves and those without shoulder pads, dropped shoulders. Avoid jackets with padded shoulders.

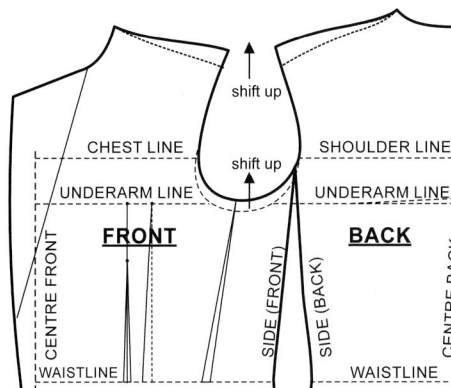

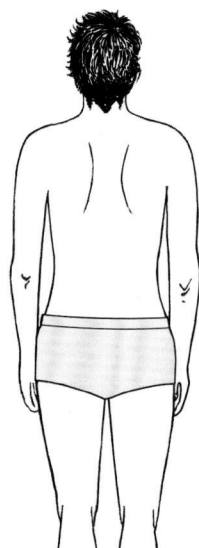

High shoulders - solution 2

Subjects with this conformation, especially when it is actually a matter of posture or habit, may also have poorly developed chest muscles.

Characteristics:
- Shoulder height 1.5-2 cm / 0.59-0.79".
- Chest deficit 1.5 cm / 0.59".

- Raise the front armscye sector Z1-S3-Q1-Q4 by 1.5-2 cm / 0.59-0.79".
- Raise the rear sector by the same amount, as shown in the figure.
- Reshape the armscye and shoulders.

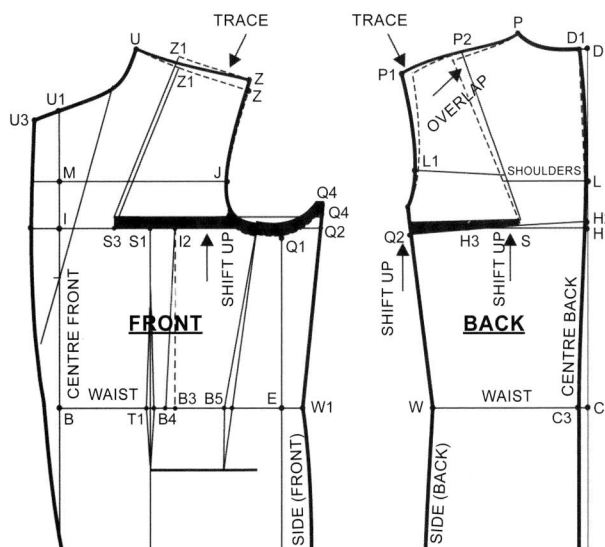

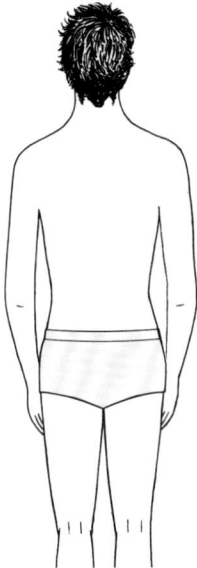

Low shoulders - solution 2

Those with this conformation may also have an underdeveloped chest and waist and protruding shoulder blades.

Characteristics:
- Low shoulders 1-1.5 cm / 0.39-0.59".
- Chest deficiency for low shoulders 1.5-2 cm / 0.59-2".
- Excess for protruding scapula 0.5 cm / 0.20".
- Waist deficit for low shoulders 1-1.5 cm / 0.39-0.59".
- Point I4 and Q2 overlap of 1-1.5 cm / 0.39-0.59".
- Point P2 opening 3 cm / 1.18".
- Stitch P3 opening 1 cm / 0.39".
- Point O consequential overlap.

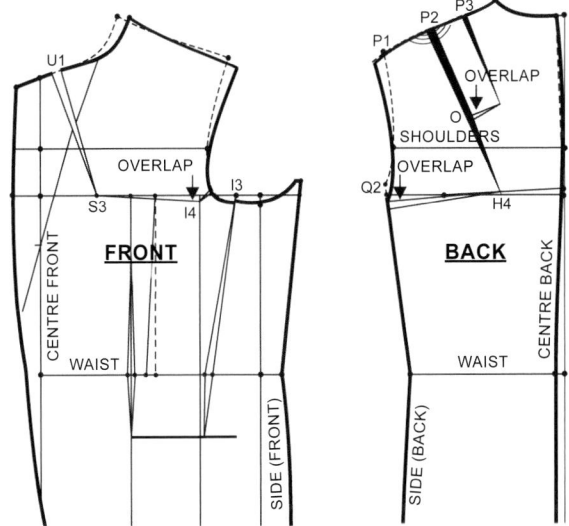

POSTURE WITH SHOULDERS AND ARMS TOO FAR BACK

Posture with the elbows and arms too far back produces an increase in the centre back cavity, decreases the posterior thoracic sector, increases the anterior thoracic sector, decreases the dorsal curve and increases the ridge of the chest.

Example measurements: posterior thorax sector 18.2 cm / instead of 19.6 cm; dorsal curve 4.3 cm / instead of 4.8 cm; shoulder slope 4.3 cm / instead of 4.8 cm; centre back dip 1.5 cm / instead of 1 cm.

Modification of the base:
- Points I3-T3 = shift 1 cm / 0.39" and join at point Z2 as shown.
- Points E4-Q3 = shift 1 cm / 0.39" and join at point P1 as shown.
- Point P3 = open 0.5 cm / 0.20"; point P4 fold.
- Points P and D1 = lower 0.5 cm / 0.20".

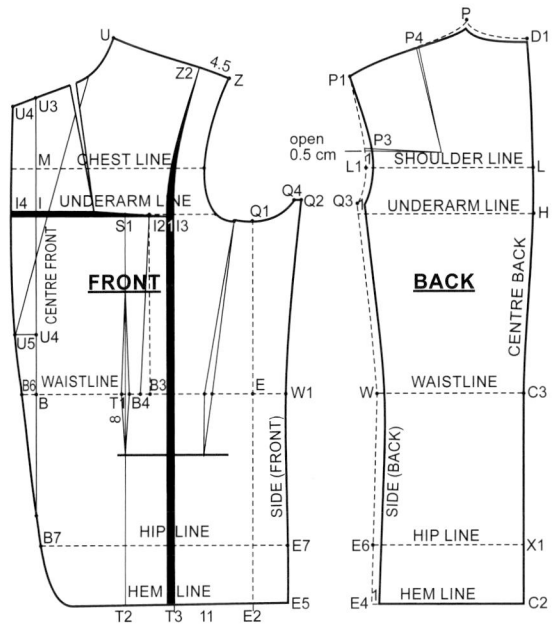

POSTURE WITH SHOULDERS AND ARMS TOO FAR FORWARD

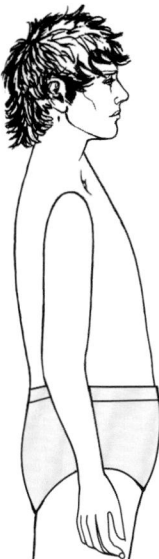

This posture causes the shoulder blades to shift forward and increases the width and convexity of the posterior sector, leading to the contraction and a flattening of the anterior sector. The scapula is less prominent.

Abnormal measurements: upper back torso 20.2 cm / instead of 19.6 cm; dorsal curve 5.3 cm / instead of 4.8 cm; shoulder angle 4.3 cm; humerus protrusion 1.5 cm.

Modification of the base:
- Cut L3-P3 and open P3 by 0.5 cm / 0.20" and create the fold in L3; cut P2-Q5 and open P2 by 1 cm / 0.39" and make the fold in Q5; points E4-Q3: shift by 1 cm / 0.39" and join to point P1 as in the figure; E4-C2 lowered by the measurement of fold Q5; W1-E5 optional indentation 1 cm / 0.39" from waist to hem (armhole advancement); point Z1: open by 0.5 cm / 0.20" and fold accordingly in U5; point J2: open 0.5 cm / 0.20" and fold accordingly in U6; point Z2 open 0.5 cm / 0.20".

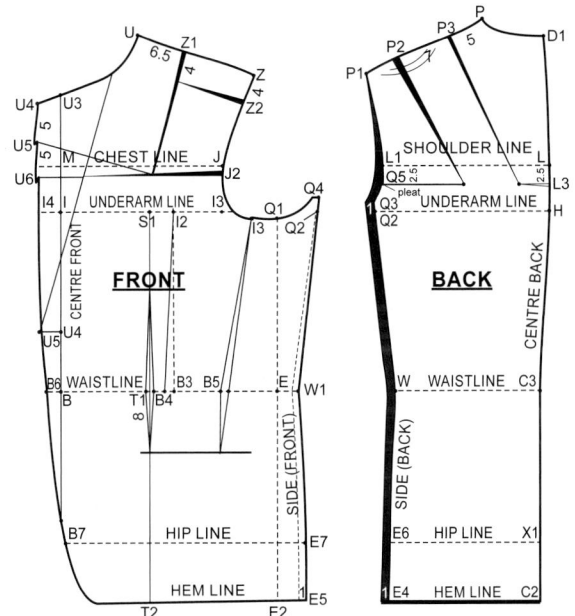

CURVED BACK

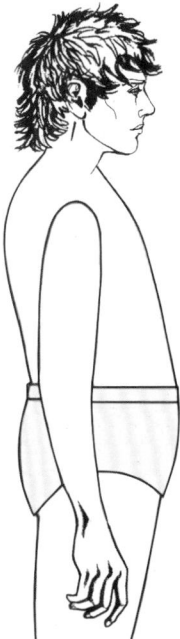

Characteristics:
- Back curve: 2 cm / 0.79".
- Arm shift: 0.5 cm / 0.20".

This conformation is the most common of all imbalances, and is characteristic of the elderly.

The centre of this 'bend' is located on the spinal column, which causes the curve of the back to increase and the chest to contract, resulting in arm advancement, expansion of the upper back and contraction of the chest.

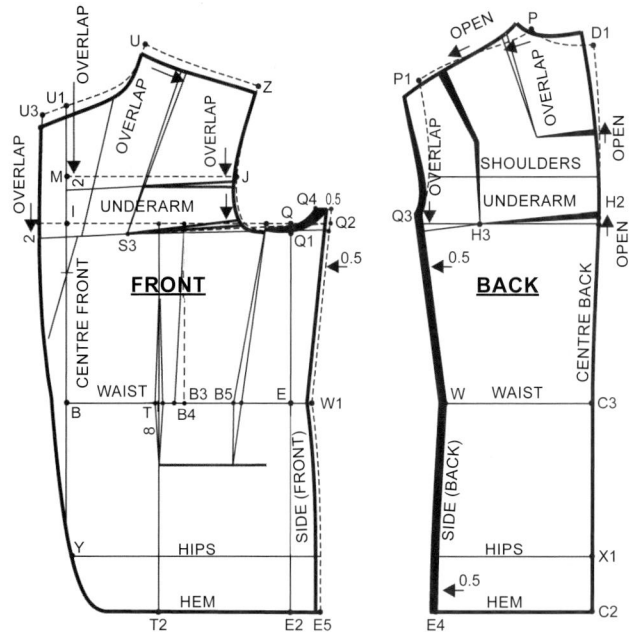

SWAY BACK

Characteristics:
- Waist drop of 2 cm / 0.79".
- Chest excess: 0.5 cm / 0.20".
- Arm shift: 1 cm / 0.39".
- Belly peak increase: 2 cm / 0.79".

This conformation is typical of overweight people, who assume this posture to better support their abdominal weight, increasing the prominence of the belly.

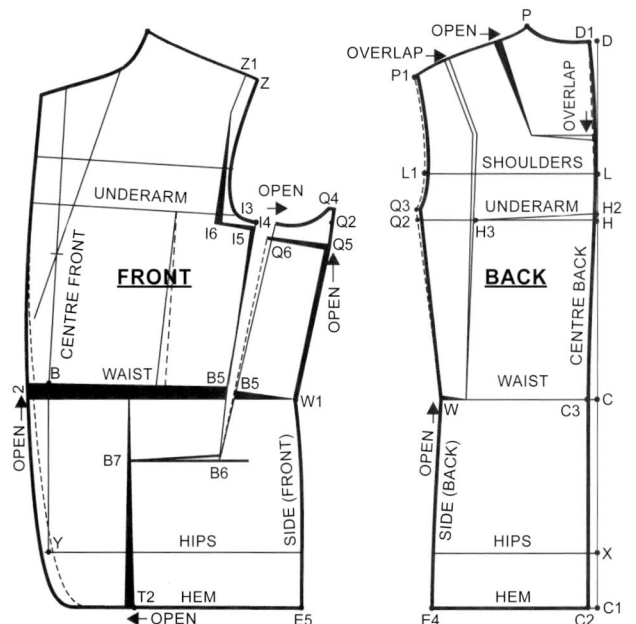

ROBUST WAISTLINE

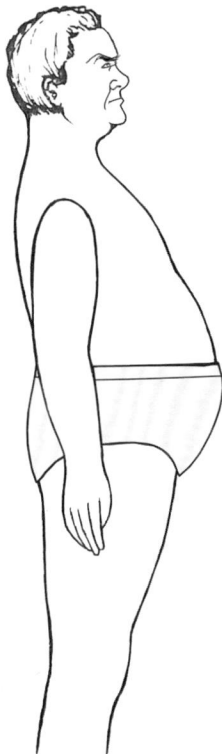

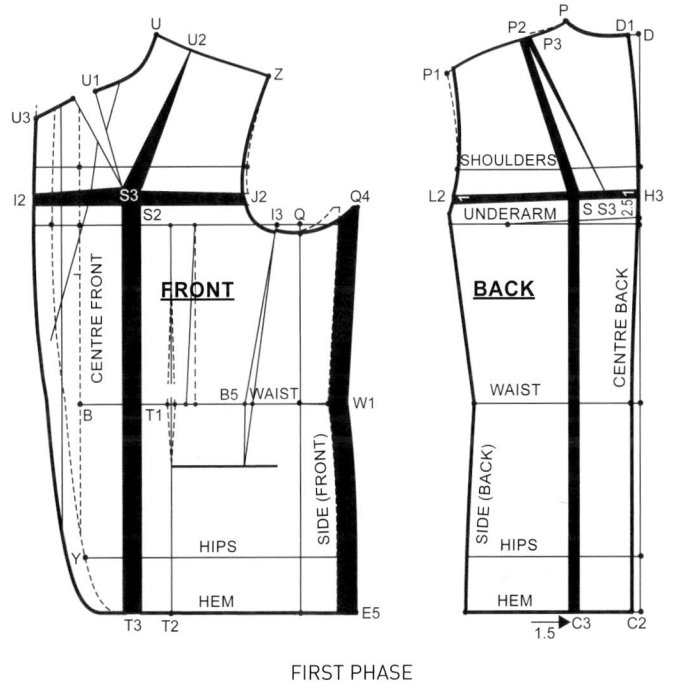

FIRST PHASE

Characteristics:
- Chest overage: 7 cm / 2.76".
- Hip overage: 7 cm / 2.76".
- Waist overage: 13 cm / 5.12".
- Neck overage: 1 cm / 0.39".
- Arm overage: 7 cm / 2.76".
- Excess arm diameter: 2.5 cm / 1".

Back
- Raise the top of H3-L2-D1-P1 by 1 cm / 0.39".
- Shift the centre back S-C3-C2-H3 by 1.5 cm / 0.59".
- Shift P2-P-D1-H3-S by 1 cm / 0.39".
- Rotate S by 0.5 cm / 0.20".
- Point P3 levelling.

Front, first phase
- Shift the side line by 2.5 cm / 1".
- Raise the top of I2-J2-Z-U-U3 by 1.5 cm / 0.59".
- Shift the centre-front part of S2-T3 by 2.5 cm / 1".
- Rotate part U2-S3-I3 and create a dart.
- Restore point U3, plumb.

Front, second phase
- Cut T3-S2 and open 2 cm / 0.79".
- Cut E3-I3 and open 1 cm / 0.39" at the bottom and reshape.
- Increase point B3 by 1.5 cm / 0.59".
- Retrace the contours.

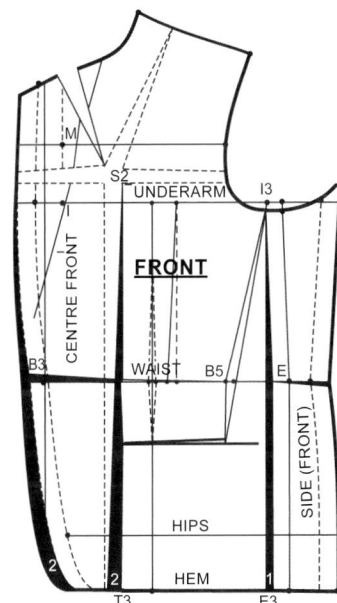

SECOND PHASE

185

TALL AND SLIM

Tall and slim people generally have circumference measurements that are smaller than average.

In this example we have used the following measures:
- Chest circumference: minus 4 cm / 1.57".
- Waist circumference: minus 3.7 cm / 1.46".
- Hip circumference: minus 4.2 cm / 1.65".
- Neck circumference: minus 1.8 cm / 0.71".
- Arm diameter: minus 1.8 cm / 0.71".

PROTRUDING SHOULDER BLADES

Winged scapulae are seen when the vertebral edge of the scapula rises away from the plane of the torso, becoming more prominent. It can be one-sided or bilateral.

As a result:
- the centre back dip increases in proportion to the extent of the scapular ridge.
- The posterior thoracic sector increases.
- The total circumference of the torso increases, again in proportion to the scapular ridge.

BASE CORRECTION
- Cut P3-L3-L4, pivot on L3 and shift P3 1-1.5 cm / 0.39-0.59" (depending on the shoulder blades).
- Cut P2-P4, pivot on P3 and shift P4 by 0.5-1 cm / 0.20-0.39" (depending on the shoulder blades).
- Cut W-C3, pivot on W and shift point C3 by 0.5 cm / 0.20".
- L4-L5 = 0.5-1 cm / 0.20-0.39".
- Lower E4-C2 by 0.5 cm / 0.20".

STOCKY OR SQUAT

Stocky subjects have a robust build that isn't proportionate to their height.
In our example, we've used the following measurements:
- Height 1.70 m / 5'7".
- The neck with an upper measurement of 1.8 cm / 0.71".
- The chest is 4 cm larger (1.57").
- The waist with an upper measurement of 3.7 cm / 1.46".
- The hips with an upper measurement of 4.2 cm / 1.65".
- The sector of the back chest is 0.8 cm / 0.31" larger.
- The sector of the front chest is 1.6 cm / 0.63" larger.

BASE CORRECTION
- M-B7 = shift the front 1.6 cm / 0.63".
- U4-M = shift the front by 0.8 cm / 0.31".
- Q4-E5 = shift the front side by 1.6 cm / 0.63".
- M1 = raise by 1.6 cm / 0.63".
- B6-W = fold 0.4 cm / 0.16".
- L3-L4 = cut and raise 0.4 cm / 0.16".
- W-C3 = fold of 0.4 cm / 0.16".
- P1-E4 = shift the back side by 0.8 cm / 0.31".

PHYSICAL ASYMMETRY

In this example, the measurements on the right side of the body are different from those on the left side.

LEFT SIDE
- Height 1.70 m / 5'7".
- 1/2 chest circumference 21 cm / 8.27".
- 1/2 waist circumference 44 cm / 17.32".
- 1/2 hips: 50 cm / 19.69".
- 1/2 neck circumference 21 cm / 8.27".
- Sector of the upper back is 19.2 cm / 7.56" larger.

RIGHT SIDE
- Height 1.70 m / 5'7".
- 1/2 chest circumference 23 cm / 9.06" (+ 2 / 0.79").
- 1/2 waist circumference 46 cm / 18.11" (+ 2 / 0.79").
- 1/2 hips: 52 cm / 20.47" (+ 2 / 0.79").
- 1/2 neck circumference 21 cm / 8.27".
- Sector of the rear torso with a measurement increased by 19.7 cm / 7.75" (+ 0.5 / 0.20").
- Sector of the front torso with a measurement increased by 18.7 cm / 7.36 (+ 0.5 / 0.20").
- Result: right shoulder is higher by 0.5 cm / 0.20".

MODIFICATION OF THE BASE
- P-P1 and U-Z = raise by 0.5 cm / 0.20".
- Q4-E5 = shift by 1.5 cm / 0.59".
- Cut W-C3 and pivot 0.3 cm / 0.12" on W.
- Cut P4-L4-L3 and pivot 0.3 cm / 0.12" on L4.
- Cut M2-J1 and pivot 0.3 cm / 0.12" on M2.
- U-Z = raise by 0.5 cm / 0.20".

ATHLETIC SHOULDERS

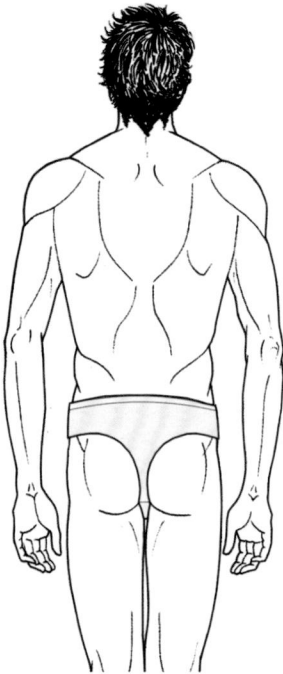

Characteristics
- Shoulder 1-1.5 cm / 0.39-0.59" high.
- Chest excess: 2 -2.5 cm / 0.79-1".
- Excess neck diameter 1.5-2 cm / 0.59-0.79".
- Excess shoulder width 1-1.5 cm / 0.39-0.59".
- Point D1 = opening of 0.8 cm / 0.31".
- Point D2 = resulting overlap.
- Point D3 = opening of 0.6 cm / 0.24".
- Point P2 = resulting overlap
- Point Q4 = increase by 1 cm / 0.39".
- Point Q5 = raise by 1 cm / 0.39".
- Point P1 = resulting shift.
- Point P = increase by 0.4 cm / 0.16".
- Point U4 = opening of 0.6 cm / 0.24".
- Point U5 = resulting overlap.
- Point I3 = opening of 1 cm / 0.39".
- Point W1 = resulting overlap.
- Point Q2 = raise armscye by 1 cm / 0.39".
- Point Z = resulting shift.
- Point U5 = resulting overlap.

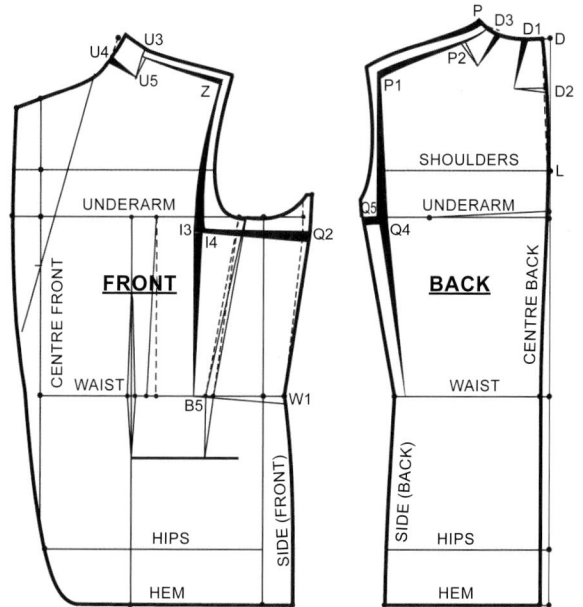

WIDER WAIST AND HIPS

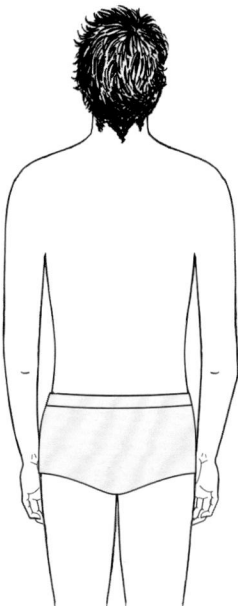

Characteristics
- Waist excess: 3 cm / 1.18".
- Hip excess: 3 cm / 1.18".
- Belly peak increase: 1-1.5 cm / 0.39-0.59".
- Point C2 = increase by 0.5 cm / 0.20".
- Point C3 and C4 = increase 1 cm / 0.39" (1/3 hip surplus).
- Point L1 = resulting overlap.
- Point E5 = increase 0.75 cm / 0.30" (1/4 hip surplus).
- Point E = increase 0.75 cm / 0.30" (1/4 waist surplus).
- Point E3 = increase 0.75 cm / 0.30" (1/4 hip surplus).
- Point W1 = increase by 0.4 cm / 0.16".
- Point B6 = opening of 0.5 cm / 0.20".
- Point Y1= overlap of 0.5 cm / 0.20".
- Point B = opening of 1 cm / 0.39".
- Point B2 = increase by 0.5 cm / 0.20".

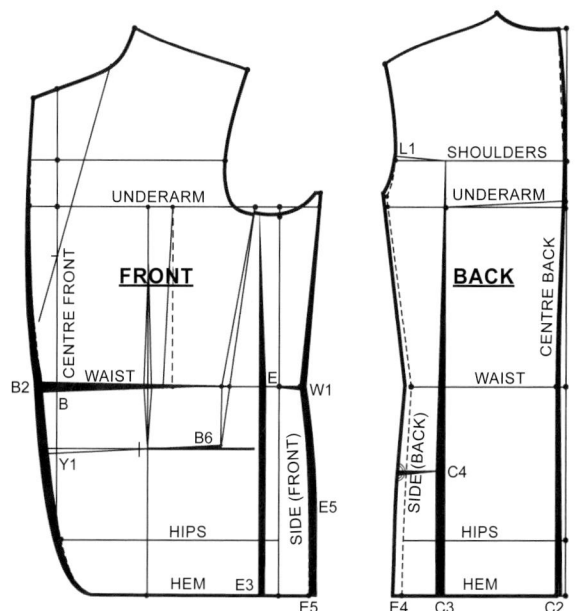

WAISTCOATS AND CASUAL JACKETS

INTRODUCTION TO WAISTCOAT

Most waistcoats, though not all, are single-breasted. As the name implies, the front of this garment should cover the waist: for this reason, it isn't worn with a belt, but braces, which are more comfortable and less bulky. The sides and the back, on the other hand, can also be a little shorter.

It's always best to choose a waistcoat that has at least one more button than the jacket it is to be worn with. Generally, single-breasted waistcoats have no lapels and, like the jacket, should be worn with the last button undone for comfort.

Double-breasted waistcoats, on the other hand, are worn on more formal occasions. They generally have 6 buttons, though 4-button and 8-button versions do exist. These waistcoats are the most formal and suitable for ceremonies and white-tie events, and they usually also have lapels, which may be shawl or more rarely peak or notched.

In general, it is best to avoid waistcoats that are too long: by shifting the centre of gravity, they risk creating an unbalanced silhouette. It should fit close to the body, but still leave room for movement.

The shoulders should be flat and lay below the points of the shirt collar, if wearing a suit, the V-neckline of the waistcoat should be narrower than that of the jacket, so that it can be seen.

HOW AND WHEN TO WEAR IT

When it comes to choosing the colour to match the waistcoat to the suit, there are mainly two palettes available: you can either create a three-piece suit all in the same fabric, or you can decide to wear a waistcoat in a contrast hue.

The waistcoat should always be worn with a fairly close-fitting shirt with a button-down collar; this also requires a matching or coordinated tie. A bow tie is not recommended, as it does not go well with three-piece suits, stylistically speaking.

The only situation in which perhaps a waistcoat really shouldn't be worn is with a double-breasted suit. Not only can it unnecessarily widen the silhouette, but with the jacket buttoned, the waistcoat wouldn't be visible.

Today's waistcoats are an evergreen item in men's fashion, to be combined with many different suits: those worn to the office, graduation ceremonies, or formal events.

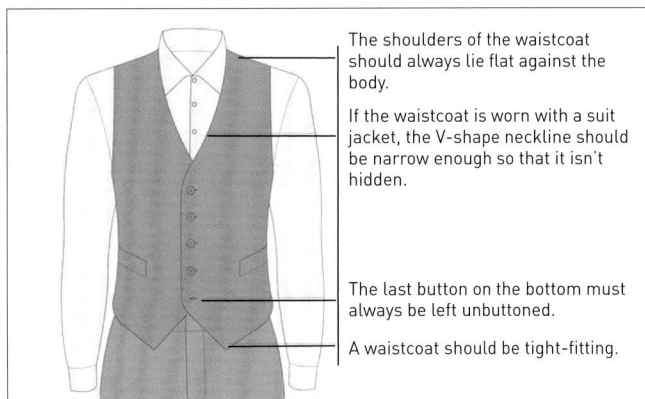

The shoulders of the waistcoat should always lie flat against the body.

If the waistcoat is worn with a suit jacket, the V-shape neckline should be narrow enough so that it isn't hidden.

The last button on the bottom must always be left unbuttoned.

A waistcoat should be tight-fitting.

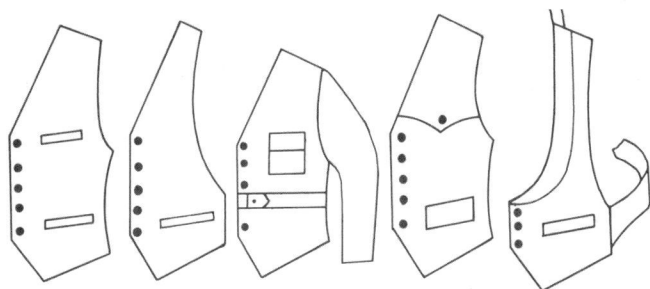

Single-breasted waistcoat

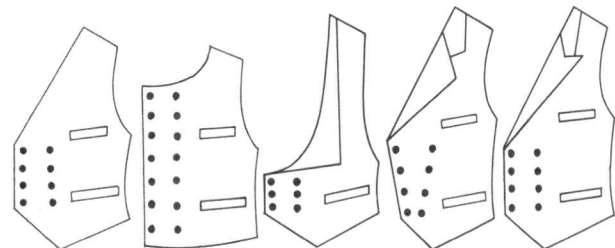

Double-breasted waistcoat

Too wide   Too narrow

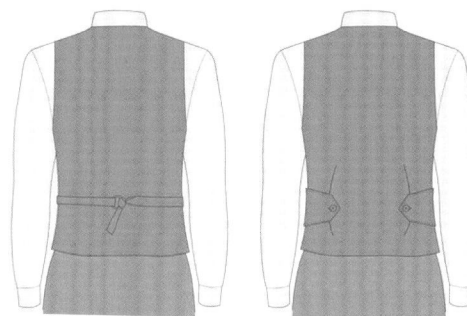

Rear cinch   Lateral cinches

Too long   Too narrow

THE BACK OF THE WAISTCOAT

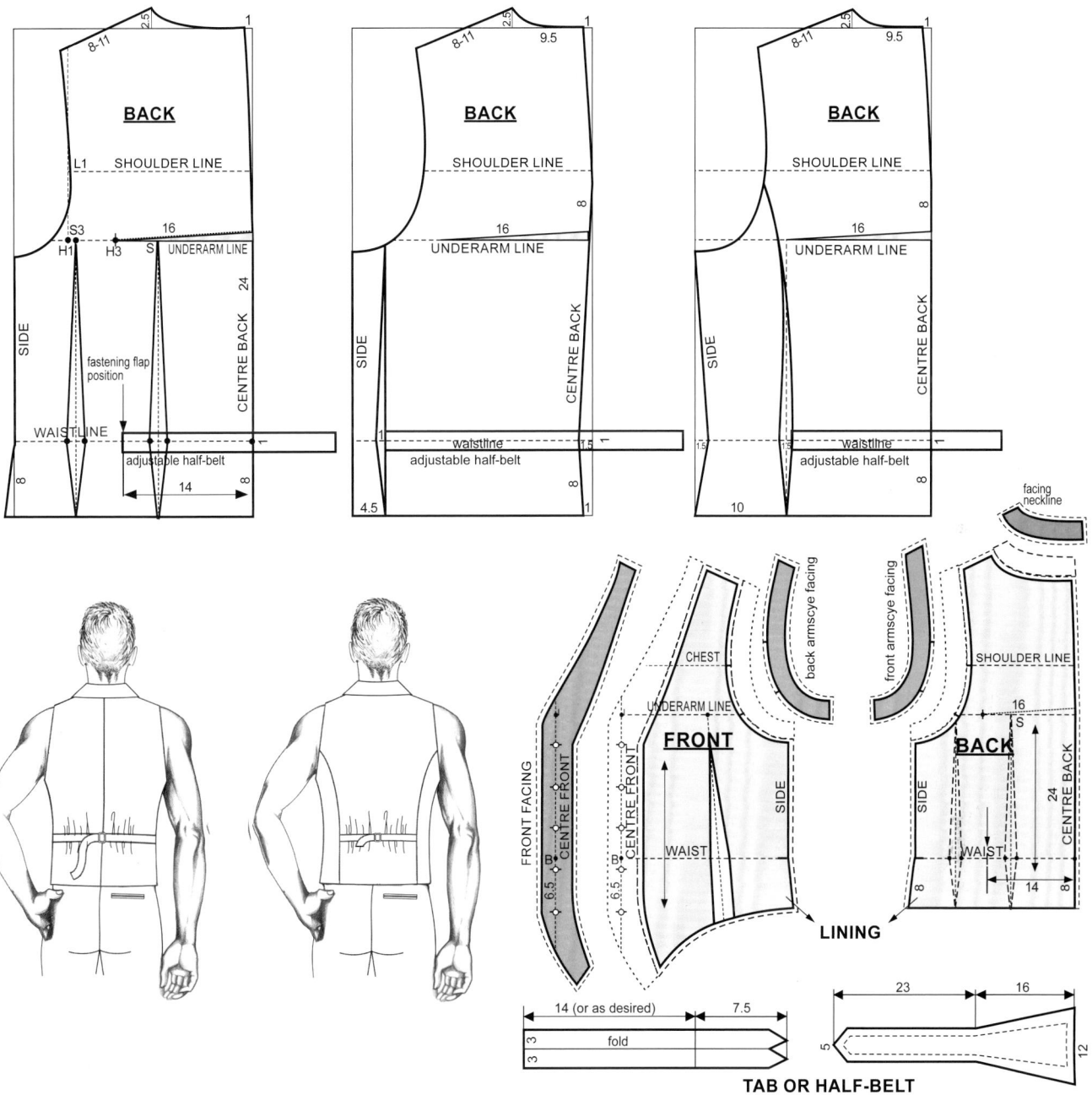

The back of the waistcoat, like other garments, can be shaped in various ways: straight without darts; with one or two darts and shorter than the front; with a side panel; with a yoke; etc. After constructing the waistcoat pattern with the required measurements, copy the back by inserting the notches at the waist, shoulder and underarm levels, as well as marking the straight of grain and adding the seam allowances.

FACING AND LINING BLOCK
- Draw the desired waistcoat pattern.
- Add the seam allowances.
- Measure the facing pieces at the front, the front and back armscyes, and the neckline (two pieces per type).

- Add seam allowances to the edges as in the figure (not on those already added on the initial base block).
- Position the notches and arrows of the straight of grain.
- The pattern parts without facing must be cut out of the lining fabric, two pieces per type.

THE STRAP
The waistcoat strap usually consists of two strips of lining fabric, joined with a buckle to adjust the fit of the waist.
The straps can be sewn in different positions on the back, remaining on the waistline: on the side seam, the side panels or the darts, equally spaced, in specially made slits on the back.

WAISTCOAT BASE BLOCK

Size 16 UK measurements

- Height 175 cm / 5'9".
- Waistcoat ease 8 cm / 3.15".
- Chest semi circumference 96 + 8 = 104 ÷ 2 = 52 cm / 20.47"
- Waist semi circumference 88 + 8 = 96 ÷ 2 = 48 cm / 18.90"
- Hip semi circumference 96 + 8 = 104 ÷ 2 = 52 cm / 20.47"
- Neck semi circumference 42 ÷ 2 = 21 cm / 8.27"
- 1/2 shoulder width 42 ÷ 2 = 21 cm / 8.27"
- Front neck to waist 46.5 cm / 18.31".
- Rear neck to waist 45.6 cm / 17.95".

Basic block construction

- Draw right angle A-B-C, with:
- B-C equal to the chest circumference + waistcoat ease = 8 m / 3.15" (e.g.: 96 + 8 = 104 ÷ 2 = 52 cm / 20.47")
- C-D rear neck-to-waist (e.g.: 45.6 cm / 17.95").
- B-E half of B-C (e.g.: 52 ÷ 2 = 26 cm / 10.24").
- A-F like B-E. Draw E-F (side line).
- A-B equal to the front neck-to-waist (e.g.: 46.5 cm / 18.31").
- D-H half of C-D (e.g.: 46.5 ÷ 2 = 23.25 cm / 9.15").
- Draw H-I (underarm level)
- D-G = 1/2 shoulder width - 2 cm / 0.79" (e.g.: 42 ÷ 2 = 21 - 2 = 19 cm / 7.49").
- H-H1 like D-G (20 cm / 7.87"). Draw H1-G.
- I-I1 like H-H1 minus 1 cm / 0.39" (20 - 1 = 19 cm / 7.49".
- H1-I1 = H-I minus (H-H1 + I-I1) e.g.: 52 - (20 + 19) = 13 cm / 5.12" (underarm sector).
- Draw I1-J1 parallel to H1-G.
- H-L = 1/3 of D-H (e.g.: 23.25 ÷ 3 = 7.75 cm / 3.05").
- Draw L-M parallel to H-I.
- B-Y and C-X = waist to hip (e.g.: 20 cm / 7.87").
- Draw Y-X (hip line).
- D-X waistcoat total front length (e.g. : 66 cm / 25.98").
- Draw X-Y1 parallel to B-C

Back

- H-H3 = 16 cm / 6.30"; H-H2 = 0.6 cm / 0.24".
- Create the right angle H3-H2-D1.
- Draw H2-D1 like H-D with a curve.
- G-O = 2.5 cm / 1".
- D1-N = 1/3 of D-G + 1.5 cm / 0.59" (e.g.: 19 ÷ 3 = 6.3 + 1.5 = 7.8 cm / 3.07").
- P-P1 like U-U2 (in this case 2 cm / 0.79").
- N-P = 2.3 cm / 0.91".
- Draw the curved line D1-P1.
- P1-P2 = desired shoulder length + 0.5 cm / 0.20" (e.g.: 8-11 cm / 3.15-4.33").
- Draw the outline P-P1 passing through O.
- Q-Q1 = 2 cm / 0.79" or as desired.
- Smoothly draw the armhole P2-L1-Q1.
- C-X1 = 8 cm / 3.15". Draw X1-E1 parallel to X-E2.
- E2-E4 = 2 cm / 0.79". Draw E-E4.
- E-Y4 = back side.
- H-S and X-X2 = 11.5 cm / 4.53".
- S-S3 and X2-X3 = 9 cm / 3.54".
- Draw the two waist darts with the appropriate measurements in relation to the waist tapering and the type of pattern.

Front

- A-U = 1/2 of A-J1-1.5 cm / 0.59" (e.g.: 19 ÷ 2 = 9.5 - 1.5 = 8 cm / 3.15").
- A-U1 like A-U.
- U-U2 and U1-U4 = 2 cm / 0.79".
- Y-Y1 = 2 cm / 0.79". Draw Y1-U3 (overlap).
- Y-Y2 = 3 cm / 1.18".
- Y1-Y3 = 12 cm / 4.72".
- U3-U5 = 18-20 cm / 7.09-7.87". Draw the line U2-U5.
- I-S1 and Y2-T = 13 cm / 5.12" Draw S1-T.
- S1-S2 = 5 cm / 2".
- Create a chest dart of 3-3.5 cm / 1.18-1.38".
- J1-V = 2.5-4 cm / 1-1.57".
- U2-Z like P1-P2 at the back (e.g.: 8-11 cm / 3.15-4.33").
- Draw the outline U2-Z passing through V.
- Smoothly draw the armhole Z-J-Q1.
- E2-E3 = 2 cm / 0.79". Draw E-E3; E-X4 = Front side.

SIX-BUTTON WAISTCOAT WITH LAPELS

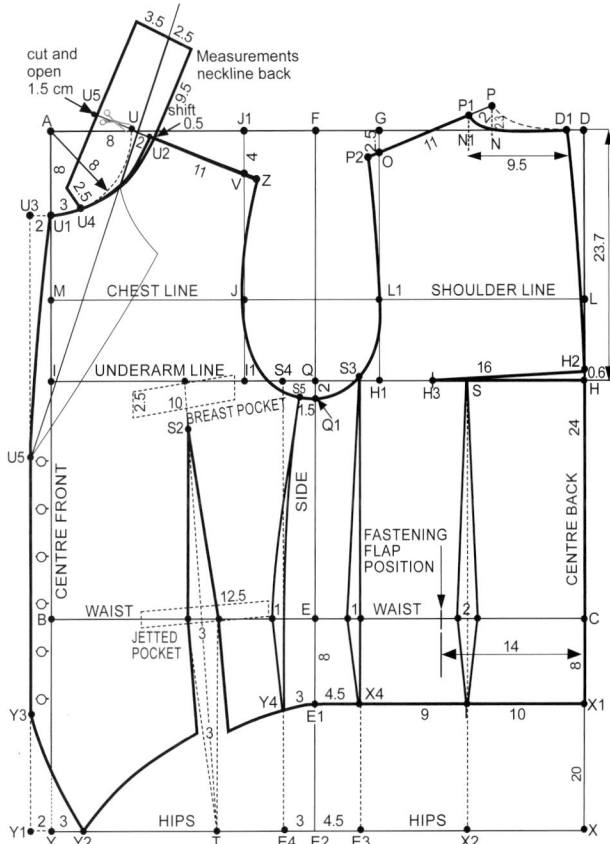

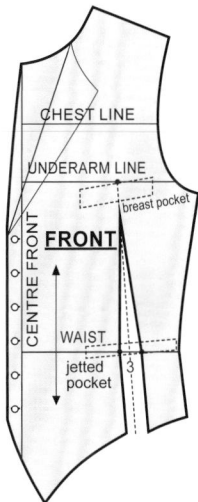

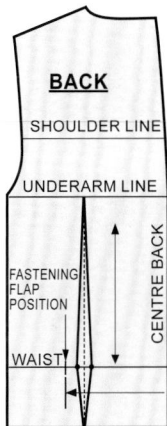

SIDE PANEL

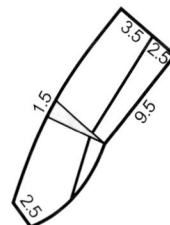

COLLAR

Size 16 UK measurements
- Height 175 cm / 5'9".
- Waistcoat ease 8 cm / 3.15".
- Chest semi-circumference 96 + 8 = 104 ÷ 2 = 52 cm / 20.47".
- Waist semi-circumference 88 + 8 = 96 ÷ 2 = 48 cm / 18.90".
- Hip semi-circumference 96 + 8 = 104 ÷ 2 = 52 cm / 20.47".
- Neck semi-circumference 42 ÷ 2 = 21 cm / 8.27"
- 1/2 shoulder width 44 + 1 = 45 ÷ 2 = 22.5 cm / 8.86".
- Rear neck to waist 46.2 cm / 18.19".
- Front neck to waist 45.6 cm / 17.95".

Create the 5-button waistcoat block and make the following changes.
- Draw the lines E3-S3 and E4-S4.
- Q1-S5 = 1.5 cm / 0.59".
- Make the side panel S3-X4-Y4-S5 as in the figure.
- Draw the extension for the fastening U1-U5-Y3-Y2.
- Draw the breakline up to the desired height (e.g.: 7 cm / 2.76" below the underarm line).
- Draw the collar as illustrated in the figure, closely following the line of the neckline and continuing along the breakline for a measurement equal to that of the neckline at the back (e.g.: 9.5 cm / 3.74") and shifting from the shoulder point by 0.5 cm / 0.20".

WAISTCOAT WITH A DEEP-V NECKLINE

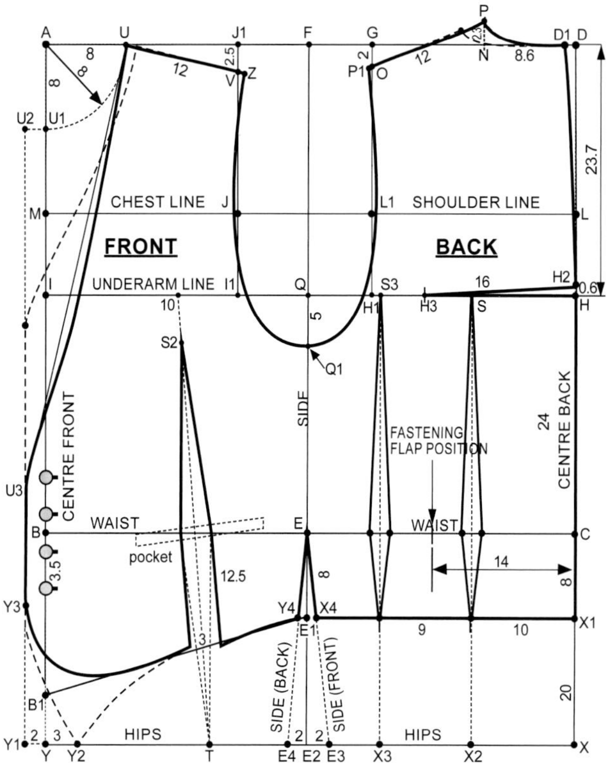

Draw the waistcoat base block with appropriate measurements and ease.

- U2-U3 = 32 cm / 12.60" or as desired.
- Draw the outline U-U3 as in the figure.
- B-B1 = 15.5 cm / 6.10".
- Draw B1-E1.
- U3-Y3 = 12.5 cm / 4.92"
- Draw the curved line Y3-E1.
- J1-V = 2.5 cm / 1".
- G-O = 2 cm / 0.79".
- U-Z= 12 cm / 4.72".
- P-P1 like U-Z.
- Q-Q1 = 4-6 cm / 1.57-2.36".
Connect the armscye.

SINGLE-BREASTED WAISTCOAT WITH A SHAWL COLLAR

Draw the waistcoat base block with the desired measurements and ease.

- U2-U3 = 30 cm / 11.81" (or as desired).
- Draw U-U3 as in the figure.
- U-U4 = 5.5 cm / 2.17". Draw U4-U3 as shown.
- Z-Z1 and P1-P2 = 3-4 cm / 1.18-17".
- Q-Q1 = 2.5 cm / 1".
- Connect the armscye.
- Lengthen the collar by the measurement of the neckline: U4-U6 like P1-D1.
- Continue as illustrated in the pattern shown here.

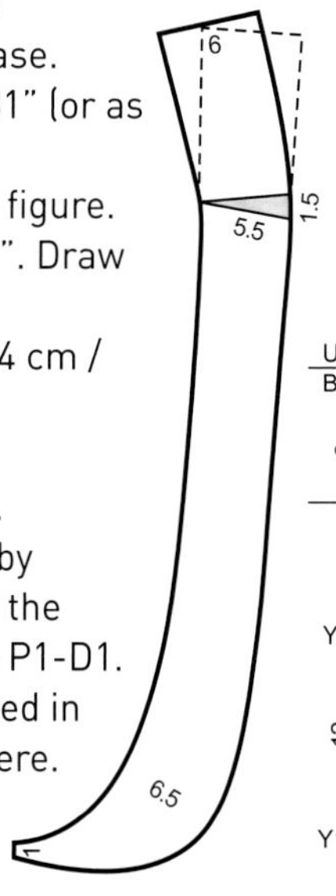

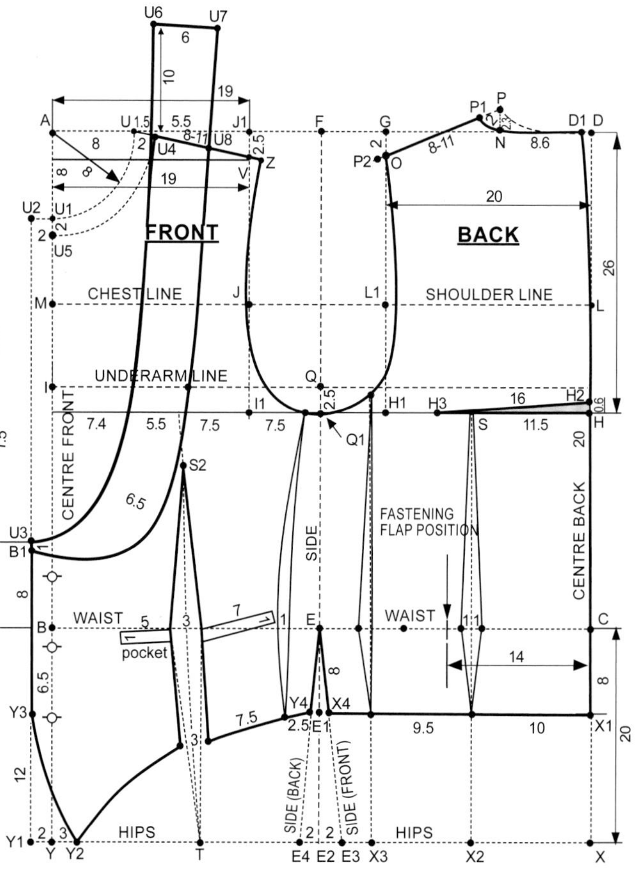

MINIMAL WAISTCOAT

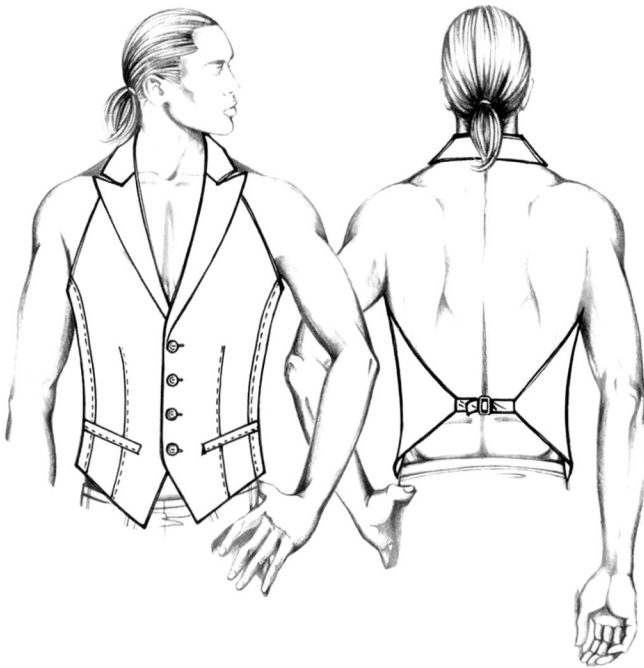

- Draw the base block of the waistcoat with suitable measurements and ease (8 cm / 3.15")
- Transform as illustrated in the figure.

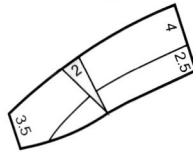

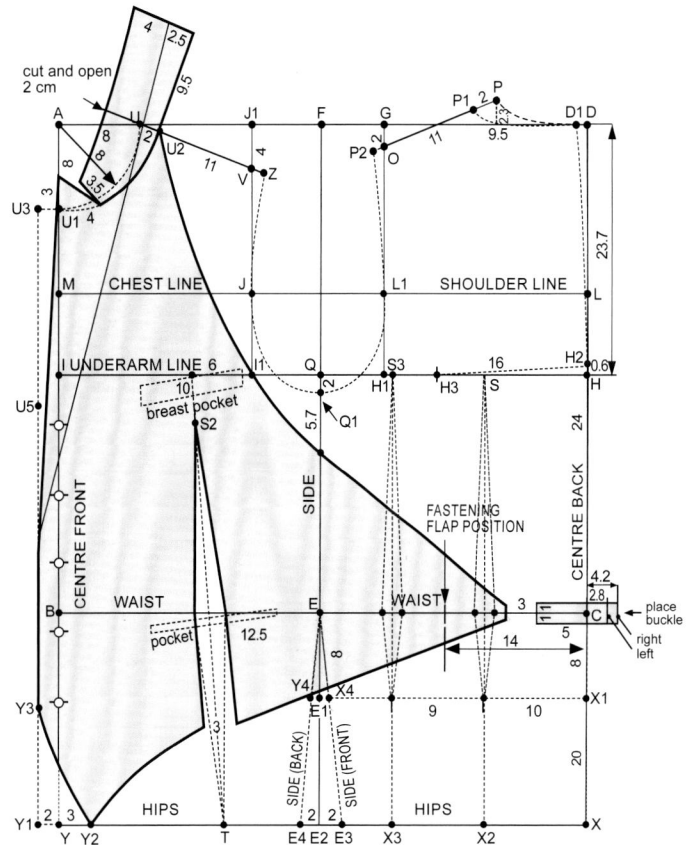

BACKLESS WAISTCOAT

- Draw the waistcoat base pattern.
- U1-U2 and Y-Y1 = 7-8 cm / 2.76-3.15".
- Draw U2-Y1.
- U3 at 2-2.5 (0.79-1" cm from the waistline.
- B-B1 = 5-5.5 cm / 1.97-2.17".
- Draw B1-Y2.
- U3-U4 = 13-13.5 cm / 5.12-5.31".
- Y1-Y3 = 4-4.5 cm / 1.57-1.77".
- Draw Y3-U3.
- U3-U5 = 10-10.5 cm / 3.94-4.13"
- Draw U3-U5-Y2.
- Connect the lower edge with a curved line.
- U-Z1 and P-P2 = 3.5-4 cm / 1.38-1.57".
- Q-Q1 = 14-15 cm / 5.51-5.91".
- Connect the armscye.

Note:
The back is limited to the collar and the rear strap.

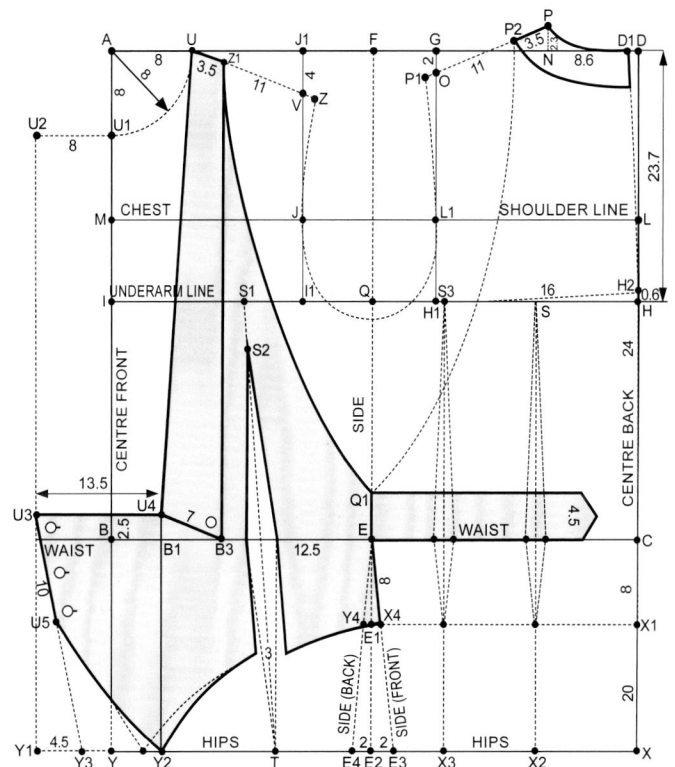

SINGLE-BREASTED WAISTCOAT

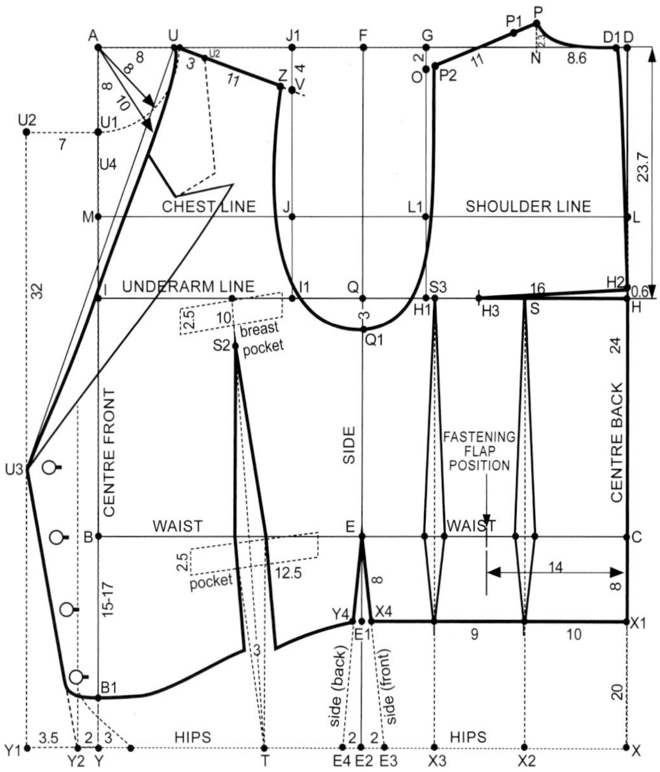

- Draw the waistcoat base pattern.
- U1-U2 and Y-Y1 = 7 cm / 2.76"
- U2-U3 = 32 cm / 12.60".
- Draw U-U3 (breakline).
- Shape the lapel line.
- Y1-Y2 = 3 cm / 1.18".
- Draw Y2-U3.
- B-B1 = 15-17 cm / 5.91-6.69".
- Draw the outline B1-E1.
- J1-V = 3-4 cm / 1.18-1.57".
- G-O = 2 cm / 0.79".
- P-P2 = 11 cm / 4.33".
- U-Z like P-P2.
- Q-Q1 = 3 cm / 1.18".

OVERLAP WAISTCOAT

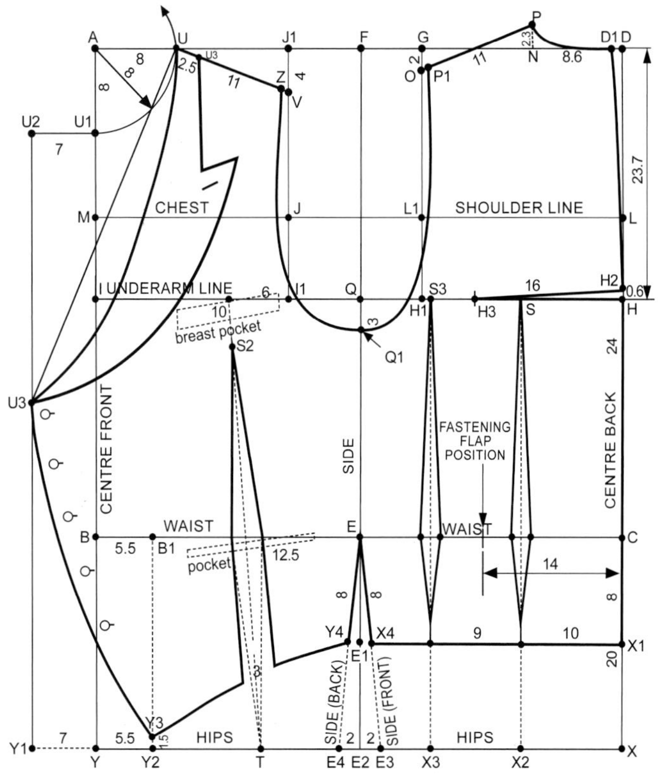

- Draw the waistcoat base pattern.
- U1-U2 and Y-Y1 = 6.5-7 cm / 2.56-2.76".
- U2-U3 = 25.5 cm / 10.04".
- Draw the breakline U-U3, then the rounded line as in the figure.
- B-B1 = 5.5 cm / 2.17".
- Draw B1-Y2.
- Y2-Y3 = 1.5 cm / 0.59".
- Draw the curved line Y3-U3.
- Connect the lower edge with a curved line.
- U-Z and P-P = 11 cm / 4.33".
- Q-Q1 = 3 cm / 1.18".
- Connect the armscye.

WAISTCOAT SEAM ALLOWANCES
MARKS FOR IRONING

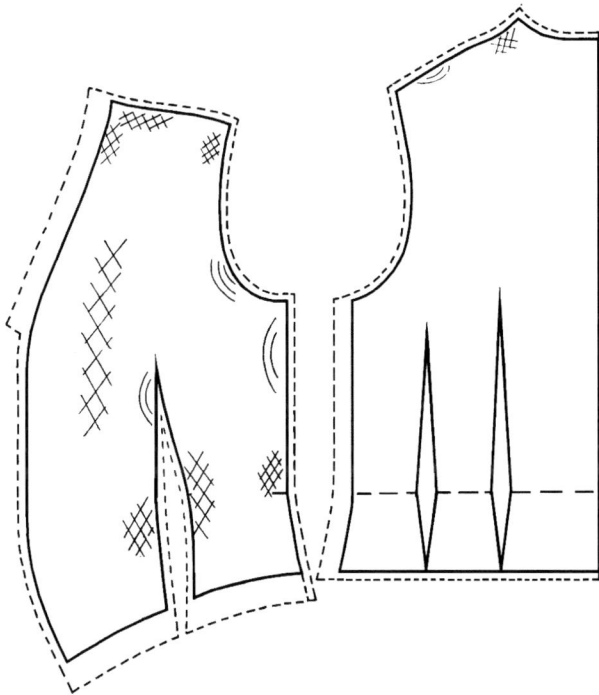

)) REDUCE

XX SLACKEN

SEAM ALLOWANCES
The seam allowances run parallel to the seam lines.

IRONING
As with jackets, the ironing process is very important to achieve a perfect fit.

With the iron, the shoulder line must be straightened from the collar to the humerus; the slack must be picked up; the dart must be flattened and adjusted, and the sides and armholes must be given the right shape.

BOMBER JACKET

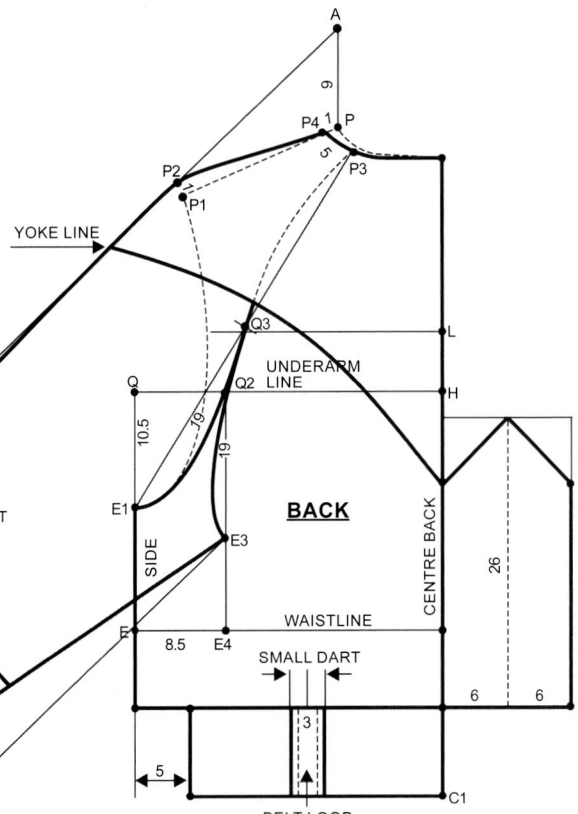

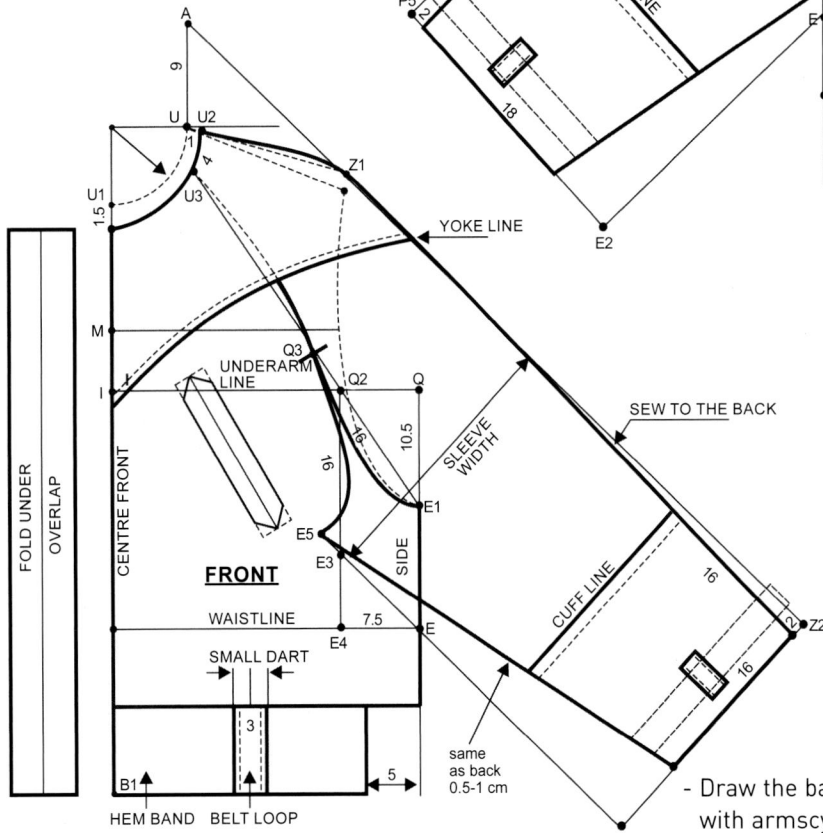

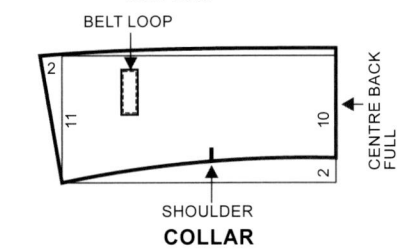

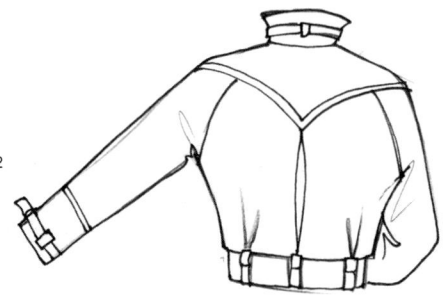

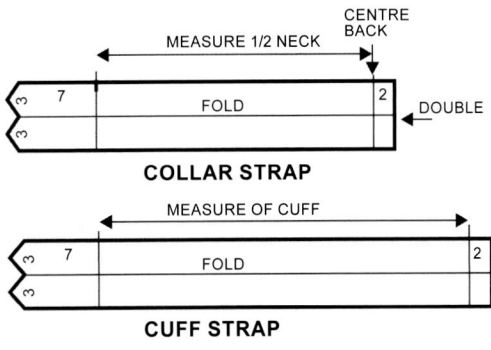

YOKE LINE

SEW TO THE FRONT

CUFF LINE

16

18

A

9

P4 1 P

5

P2

P1

P3

YOKE LINE

Q3 L

UNDERARM LINE

Q Q2 H

10.5

19

E1

SIDE

BACK

E3

CENTRE BACK

26

E

WAISTLINE

8.5 E4

SMALL DART

6 6

5

3

C1

BELT LOOP

BELT LOOP

2

11

CENTRE BACK FULL

10

2

SHOULDER

COLLAR

P5

2

A

9

U U2

1

4

Z1

U1

U3

1.5

M

I

Q3

UNDERARM LINE

Q2 Q

CENTRE FRONT

16

10.5

SLEEVE WIDTH

E1

E5

E3

SIDE

SEW TO THE BACK

CUFF LINE

16

2 Z2

FRONT

WAISTLINE

7.5 E

E4

SMALL DART

3

16

FOLD UNDER

OVERLAP

B1

HEM BAND BELT LOOP

5

same as back 0.5-1 cm

E2

E2

MEASURE 1/2 NECK

CENTRE BACK

3

7

FOLD

2

DOUBLE

3

COLLAR STRAP

MEASURE OF CUFF

3

7

FOLD

2

3

CUFF STRAP

- Draw the base block of the jacket with raglan sleeves, with armscye ease of 18-24 cm / 7.09-9.45", according to the amount of padding to be used.
- Lower the neckline for the collar.
- Lower the armscye as required (10.5 cm / 4.13").
- Create the length desired and draw the waistband, based on the waist circumference.
- Draw the front and back yoke.
- Draw the cuffs.
- Draw the overlap for the fastening.
- Draw the straps for the collar and sleeves.
- Draw the loops of the waistband, collar and cuffs.
- Draw the collar, as shown in the figure.

LOOSE-FITTING JACKET BASE BLOCK

Size 16 UK measurements

- Height 175 cm / 5'9".
- Ease of 28 cm / 11.02" (or as required for the amount of padding to be used).
- Chest semi-cir. = 96 + 28 = 124 ÷ 2 = 62 cm / 24.41"
- Hip semi-cir. = 100 + 28 = 128 ÷ 2 = 64 cm / 25.20"
- Neck semi-cir. = 42 ÷ 2 = 24.5 cm / 9.65"
- 1/2 shoulder width = 42 + 4 for ease = 46 ÷ 2 = 23 cm / 9.06"
- Rear neck to waist = 48.2 cm + 2 = 48.2 cm / 18.98".
- Front neck to waist = 45.6+ 2= 47.6 cm / 18.74".

Basic block construction

- Draw right angle A-B-C, with:
- A-B = front neck-to-waist + ease of 2 cm / 0.79" e.g.: 45.6 + 2 = 47.6 cm / 18.74".
- B-C equal to the semi-circumference of the chest + jacket ease of 28 cm / 11.02" (e.g.: 96 + 28 = 124 ÷ 2 = 62 cm / 24.41")
- C-D rear neck-to-waist + 2 cm / 0.79" ease (e.g.: 46.2 + 2 = 48.2 cm / 18.98").
- B-E half of B-C (e.g.: 62 ÷ 2 = 31 cm / 12.20").
- A-F like B-E= 31 cm / 12.20".
- Draw E-F (side line).
- D-H half of C-D (e.g.: 48.2 ÷ 2 = 24.1 cm / 9.49").
- H-I like B-C = 62 cm / 24.41" (underarm line).
- D-G = 1/2 shoulder width + 2 cm / 0.79" (e.g.: 42 ÷ 2 = 21 + 2 = 23 cm / 9.06").
- H-H1 = like D-G (23 cm / 9.06"). Draw H1-G.
- I-I1 like H-H1 minus 1 cm / 0.39" (23 - 1 = 22 cm / 8.66").
- H1-I1 = H-I minus (H-H1 + I-I1) = 15 cm / 5.91" (e.g.: 62 - (23 + 22) = 62 - 45 = 17 cm / 6.69" (underarm sector).
- Draw I1-J1 parallel to H1-G.
- H-L = 1/3 of D-H (e.g.: 24.1 ÷ 3 = 8.03 cm / 3.16").
- Draw L-M parallel to H-I.
- B-Y and C-X = waist to hip (e.g.: 20-21.5 cm / 7.87-8.46").
- Draw Y-X (Hip Line).
- D-C1 total for the length at the back (e.g.: 78 cm / 30.71").
- Y-B1 as X-C1.
- Draw C1-B1 (lower hemline).

Back

- G-O = 3.2 cm / 1.26".
- D-N = 1/3 of D-G + 1 cm / 0.20" (e.g.: 23 ÷ 3 = 7.66 + 1 = 8.66 cm / 3.41").
- N-P = 2.3 cm / 0.91".
- Draw the outline D-P.
- P-P1 = shoulder length (e.g.: 16 cm / 6.30").
- Draw P-P1 passing through O.
- L1-P1 = 15 cm / 5.91" (measurement for sleeve crown height).
- Q-Q1 = 2-3 cm / 0.79-1.18".
- Smoothly draw the armhole Z1-P1-L1-Q1.
- E1-W = 0.75 cm / 0.30".
- E1-E3 = 1 cm / 0.39". Draw the lines of side back Q1-W-E3.

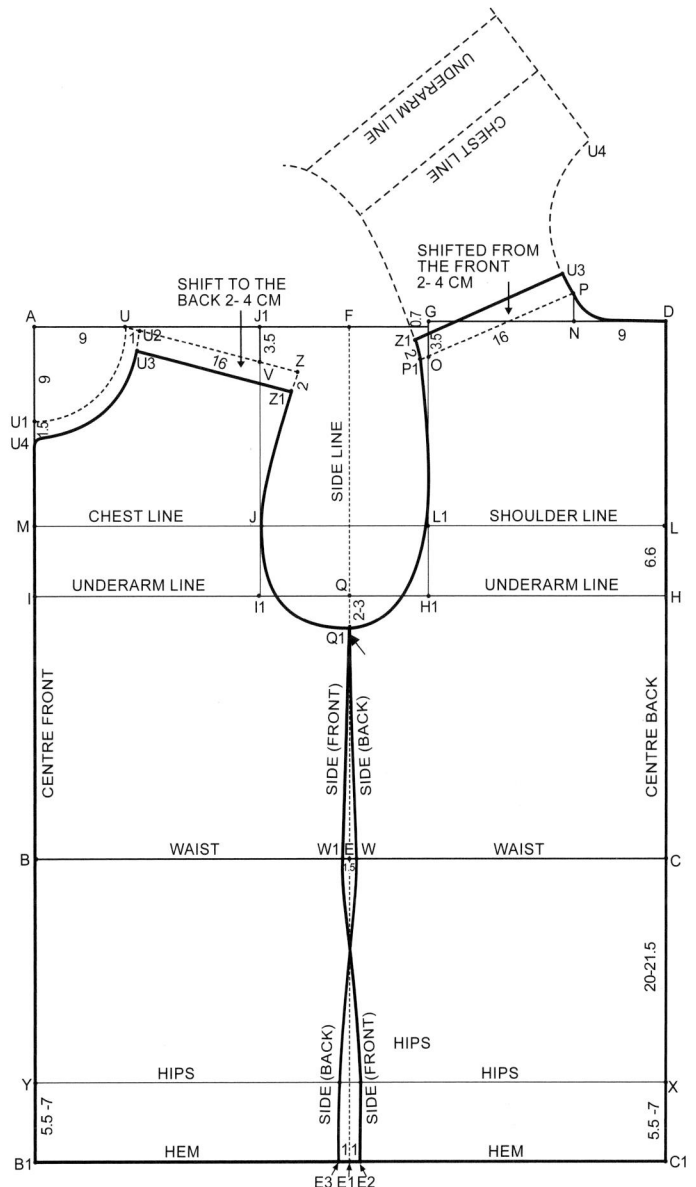

Front

- A-U half of A-J1 minus 2 cm / 0.79" (e.g.: 22 ÷ 2 = 11- 2 = 9 cm / 3.54").
- U1-U4; A-U1 like A-U; draw the arc U-U1.
- U-U2 = 1 cm / 0.39"; U1-U4 = 1.5 cm / 0.59".
- J1-V = 3.5 cm / 1.38"; draw U-U2-V-Z.
- U2-Z as P-P1 at the back (16 cm / 6.30").
- Draw U-Z passing through V; Q-Q1= 2-3 cm / 0.79-1.18".
- Smoothly draw the armhole Z-J-Q1.
- E-W1 = 1.5 cm / 0.59".
- Draw the side line Q1-W1-E3.

SLEEVE AND COLLAR BASE BLOCK FOR THE LOOSE-FITTING JACKET

MEASURE OF CUFF

FOLD

WITH ELASTIC BAND

35

CUFF

COLLAR

OVERLAP TAB

5.5

SQUARED

CENTRE FRONT | CENTRE SHOULDER | CENTRE BACK

FRONT   **BACK**

LINE FRONT

LINE BACK

CENTRE SHOULDER

ELBOW LINE

HEM

DISCARD FOR THE CUFF

Sleeve

- Draw the rectangle A-B-E-F with:
- A-B = sleeve length + 3 cm / 1.18" ease (e.g.: 61 + 3 = 64 cm / 25.20").
- A-E as the measurement of the bodice sector + 1/2 of the same sector + 2.5 cm / 1" (e.g: 17 + 8.5 = 25.5 + 2.5 = 28 cm / 11.02").
- A-G as L1-P1 on the bodice + 1 cm / 0.39"(16 cm / 6.30").
- Draw G-X. Join G-E with a diagonal line.
- A-N half of A-B + 2 cm / 0.79". Join N-P.
- A- L half of A- E. Draw L-L1.
- L2 half of G-E; E1 half of E-L2; E1 half of G1.
- Draw E-L2-G with a curved line as in the figure.
- Draw E-G1-G with a curved line as in the figure.
- Take up the front and back sleeve and draw the full sleeve as in the picture.
- B1-C1 sleeve width.
- B1-B2 and C1-C2 excess for wrist height.*

Collar

Draw a right angle A-B-C with:
- A-B = desired collar height (9 cm / 3.54").
- B-C = total length of the collar, front and back of the base block.
- B-D = collar measurement from centre back to centre shoulder.
- E-C fastening overlap measurement (5.5 cm / 2.17").
- E-E1 = 3 cm / 1.18" Draw B-D-C1-E1 with a curved line.
- E1-F like A-B square with C1-E1.
- Connect A-F.**

CHEST LINE | SHOULDER LINE | SHOULDER LINE
UNDERARM LINE | UNDERARM LINE | UNDERARM LINE

CENTRE FRONT | SIDE (FRONT) | SIDE (BACK)

FRONT   **BACK**   **BACK**

WAIST

HIPS

HEM

20-21.5

* Check that the sleeve crown measurement is 1-2 cm / 0.39-0.79" larger than the bodice armscye measurement.

** In order to ensure the sleeve falls correctly, the centre of the shoulder must be adjusted, which can be shifted towards the front or back by a few millimetres, depending on the body conformation and posture of the wearer.

JACKET WITH DROPPED SHOULDERS

- Draw the base of the loose-fitting jacket with chest circumference ease of 14-18 cm / 5.11-7.09", according to the fabric. Create the desired length and draw the high collar.
- Draw the base of the sleeve for the loose-fitting jacket, adapted as necessary.
- Draw line L-L1 on the sleeve and shape it as desired (points L-X-L1).
- Carry over the measurement of the section of sleeve crown G-L to the front armhole (points Q1-J2); position the part of the front sleeve crown L-X-E on the front shoulder and connect as shown in the figure.
- Carry over the measurement of the section of sleeve crown G1- L1 to the back armhole (points Q1-L2); position the part of the sleeve crown L1-X-E on the back shoulder and connect.
- Extend the sleeve for the inverted pleat.
- Draw the cuff and waistband.

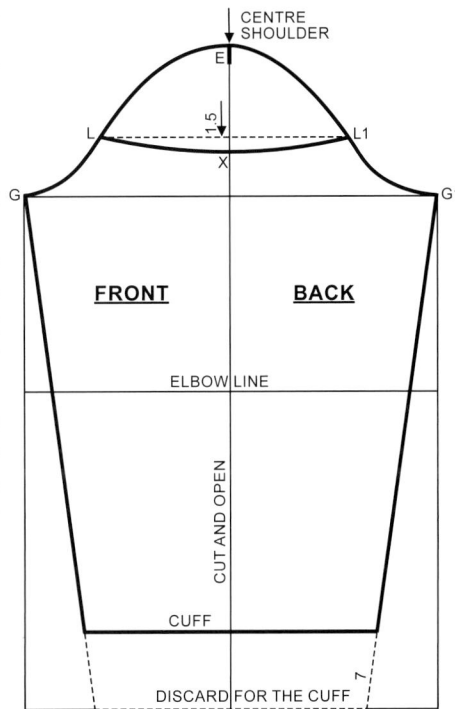

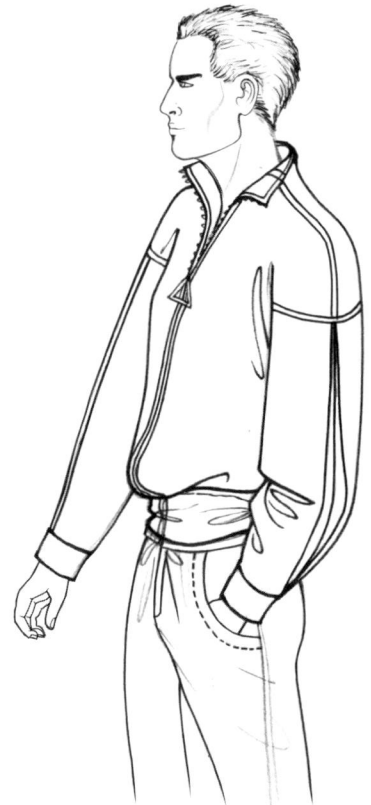

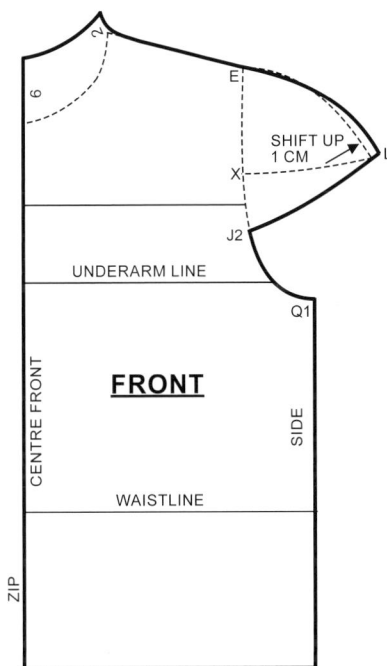

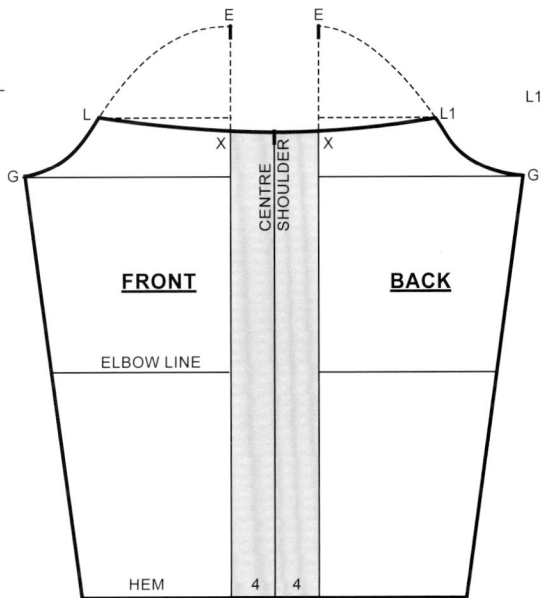

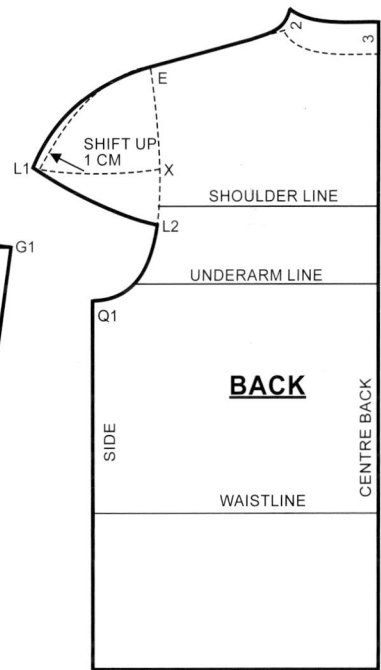

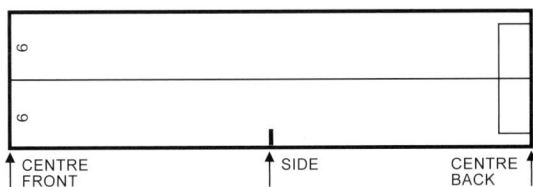

CENTRE SHOULDER

E

1.5

L   L1

X

G   G1

FRONT   **BACK**

ELBOW LINE

CUT AND OPEN

CUFF

7

DISCARD FOR THE CUFF

2

6

E

SHIFT UP 1 CM

L

X

J2

UNDERARM LINE

Q1

CENTRE FRONT

FRONT

SIDE

WAISTLINE

ZIP

E   E

L   L1

X   X

G   G1

CENTRE SHOULDER

FRONT   **BACK**

ELBOW LINE

WAISTLINE

HEM   4   4

2   3

E

SHIFT UP 1 CM

X

L1

L2

SHOULDER LINE

UNDERARM LINE

Q1

SIDE

BACK

CENTRE BACK

WAISTLINE

6

6

CENTRE FRONT   SIDE   CENTRE BACK

WAISTBAND

OVERLAP LINE

2.5   7   FOLD LINE   2.5

7

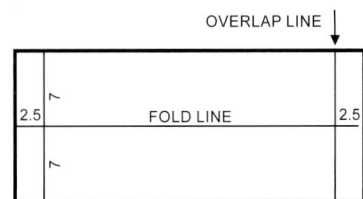

ONE-PIECE CUFF

201

LIGHTLY PADDED JACKET - BASE BLOCK

**Size 16 UK measurements - 34 cm / 13.39"
ease (or according to the padding)**
- Height 175 cm / 5'9".
- Chest semi-cir. = 96 + 34 = 130 ÷ 2 = 65 cm / 25.59"
- Waist semi-cir. = 88 + 28 = 116 ÷ 2 = 58 cm / 22.83"
- Hip semi-cir. = 96 + 34 = 130 ÷ 2 = 65 cm / 25.59"
- Neck semi-cir. = 42 ÷ 2 = 21 cm / 8.27"
- 1/2 shoulder width = 42 + 5.5 = 47.5 ÷ 2 = 23.75 cm / 9.35"
- Front neck-to-waist = 45.6 + 3 = 48.1 cm / 18.94"
- Rear neck-to-waist = 46.2 cm + 3 = 49.2 cm / 19.37"

Construct the base block
Draw the right angle A-B-C with:
- A-B equal to the front neck-to-waist + 3 cm / 1.18" for the ease (e.g.: 45.6 + 3 = 48.6 cm / 19.13").
- B-C = chest semi-circumference + ease (34-36 cm / 13.39-14.17"), (e.g.: 96 + 34 = 130 ÷ 2 = 65 cm / 25.59" waistline).
- C-D rear neck-to-waist + 3 cm / 1.18" ease (e.g.: 46.2 + 3 = 49.2 cm / 19.37").
- D-C1 rear jacket length (e.g.: 78 cm / 30.71").
- Join D-C1 and write 'Centre back'.
- C-C1 = D-C1 minus C-D = 78 - 49.2 = 28.8 cm / 11.34"
- B-B1 as C-C1 (28.8 cm / 11.34").
- B1-B2 = 0.5 cm / 0.20". Join A-B2 and write 'centre front'.
- Join B2-C1 (lower hemline).
- B-E half of B-C; B2-E1 like B-E.
- A-F as B-E. Draw F-E-E1 (centre side).
- D-H half of D-C (24.6 cm / 9.69").
- Draw H-I (underarm level).
- D-G = 1/2 rear shoulder width + 5.5 cm / 2.17" (e.g.: 42 + 5.5 = 47.5 ÷ 2 = 23.75 cm / 9.35")
- H-L = 1/4 of D-H (24.6 ÷ 4 = 6.15 cm / 2.42").
- Draw L-M (front chest and rear shoulders).
- H-H1 like D-G = 23.75 cm / 9.35".
- Draw G-L1-H1.

- I-I1 like H-H1 minus 1 cm / 0.39" (e.g.: 23.75 - 1 = 22.75 cm / 8.96").
- A-J1 like I-I1 = 22.75 cm / 8.96".
- I1-H1 = H-I minus (I-I1 + H-H1), (e.g.: 65 - (22.75 + 23.75) = 65 - 46.5 = 18.5 cm / 7.28" armscye sector.
- Draw I1-J-J1.
- B-Y and C-X = waist to hip (e.g.: 20-21.5 cm / 7.87-8.46").
- Draw Y-X and write 'Hip line'.

Back
- G-O = 3.5 cm / 1.38"; G-G1 = 0.6 cm / 4.17"; H-H2 = 0.6 cm / 0.24".
- H-H3 = 18.5 cm / 7.28". Cut and open H-H3-H2.
- D1-N = 1/3 D-G + 1 cm / 0.39" (23.75 ÷ 3 = 7.9 + 1 = 8.9 cm / 3.50").
- P-P2 = 1-1.5 cm / 0.39-0.59".
- N-P = 2.5 cm / 1". Draw P-P1 passing through O.
- P-P1 shoulder length + ease = 18-21 cm / 7.09-8.27" (based on the shoulder padding).
- L1-P1 = 21 cm / 8.27" (measurement for sleeve construction).
- Q-Q1 = 11.5 cm / 4.53". Draw the armhole P1-L1-Q1.

Front
- A-U half A-J1+ 1 cm / 0.79" (e.g.: 22.75 ÷ 2 = 11.37 + 1 = 12.37 cm / 4.87").
- U-U2 and U1-U3 = 1-1.5 cm / 0.39-0.59".
- J1-V = 3.5 cm / 1.38"; U2-Z like P-P1.
- Q-Q1 = 11.5 cm / 4.53". Connect the points as in the figure.
- Draw F-E-E1 (centre side).
- Take up the front and back, the flap for the fastening, the collar, and pockets, and add all markings.

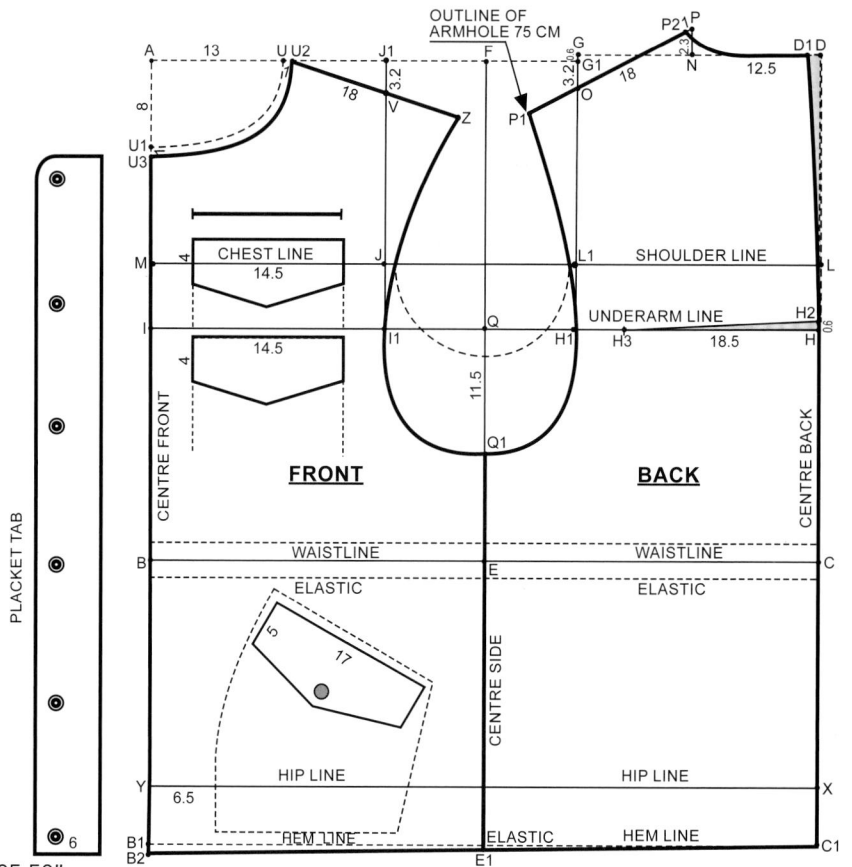

LIGHTLY PADDED JACKET - BASE SLEEVE

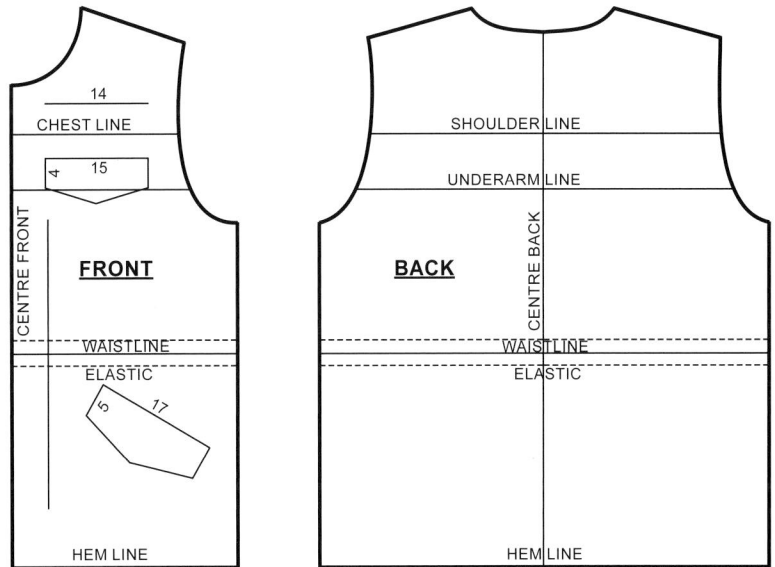

Construction

Draw the rectangle A-B-E-F with:

- A-B = sleeve length + 3 cm / 1.18" ease (e.g.: 62 + 3 = 65 cm / 25.60").
- A-E as the measurement of the bodice sector + 1/2 of the same sector + 2.5 cm / 1" (e.g.: 15.5 + 7.75 = 23.25 + 2.5 = 25.75 cm / 10.14").
- A-G as L1-P1 on the bodice + 1 cm / 0.39" (20.5 cm / 8.07").
- Draw G-X.
- Join G-E with a diagonal line.
- A-N half of A-B + 2 cm / 0.79". Join N-P.
- A- L half of A- E. Draw L-L1.
- L2 half G-E; E1 half E-L2; G1 half G-L2.
- Draw E-L2-G with a curved line as in the figure.
- Draw E-G1-G with a curved line as in the figure.
- Take up the front and back sleeve and draw the full sleeve as in the picture.
- B1-C1 sleeve width.
- B1-B2 and C1-C2 = excess to discard based on cuff height.

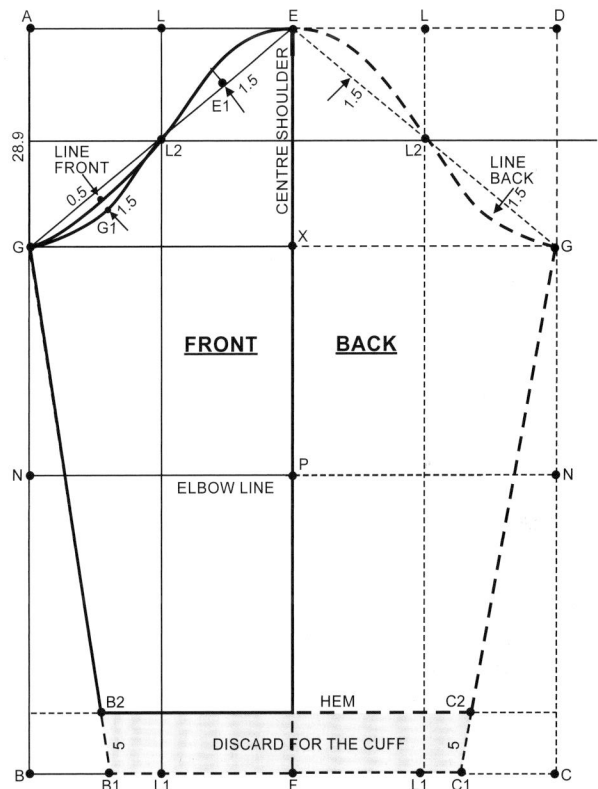

Collar

Draw a right angle A-B-C with:

- A-B = desired collar height (9 cm / 3.54").
- B-C total length of front and back collar of the base pattern.
- B-D collar measurement from centre back to centre shoulder.
- E-C fastening overlap measurement (5.5 cm / 2.17").
- E-E1 = 3 cm / 1.18". Draw B-D-C1-E1 with a curved line.
- E1-F like A-B square with C1-E1.
- Connect A-F.

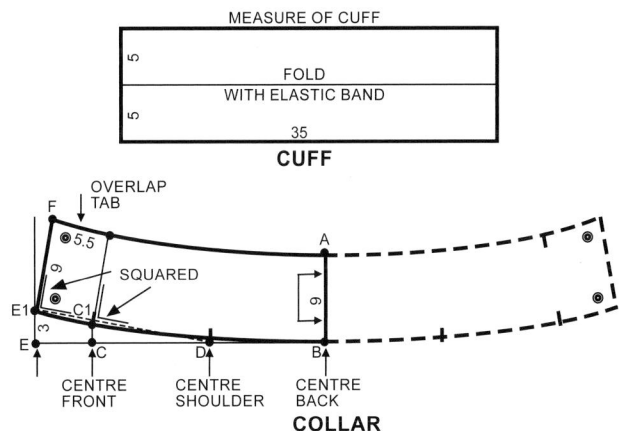

PADDED PARKA WITH RAGLAN SLEEVES

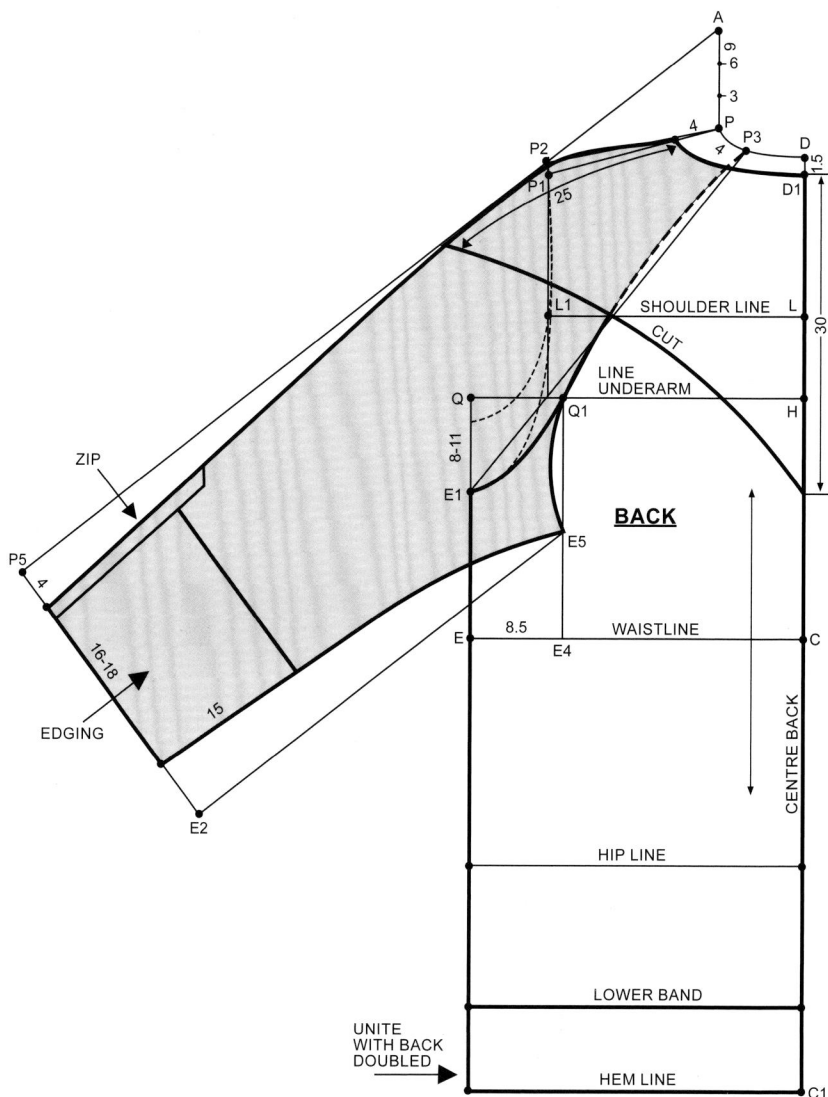

BACK

- Draw the base of the bodice with the desired measurements or size and with ease for a padded jacket.
- Separate the back half from the front half.

Back
- Draw a perpendicular line P-A in the necessary length, according to the sleeve angle chosen.
- Draw line A-P5, passing through P2 at 1 cm / 0.39" from point P1, with P2-P5 equal to the sleeve length taken from the centre of the shoulder.
- Q-E1 = 8-11 cm / 3.15-4.33" depending on the desired armscye depth.

- E-E4 = 8.5 cm / 2.56". Draw vertical line E4-Q1.
- P-P3 = 3-6 cm / 1.18-2.36" Draw guideline P3-E1.
- Draw the curved line E1-Q1-P3.
- Draw E5-Q1P3 as E1-Q1-P3.
- Draw E5-E2 parallel to P2-P5.
- Adjust the lower edge of the sleeve according to the pattern.
- Smoothly draw the outer and inner lines of the sleeve and bodice.
- Carefully copy the sleeve and bodice.

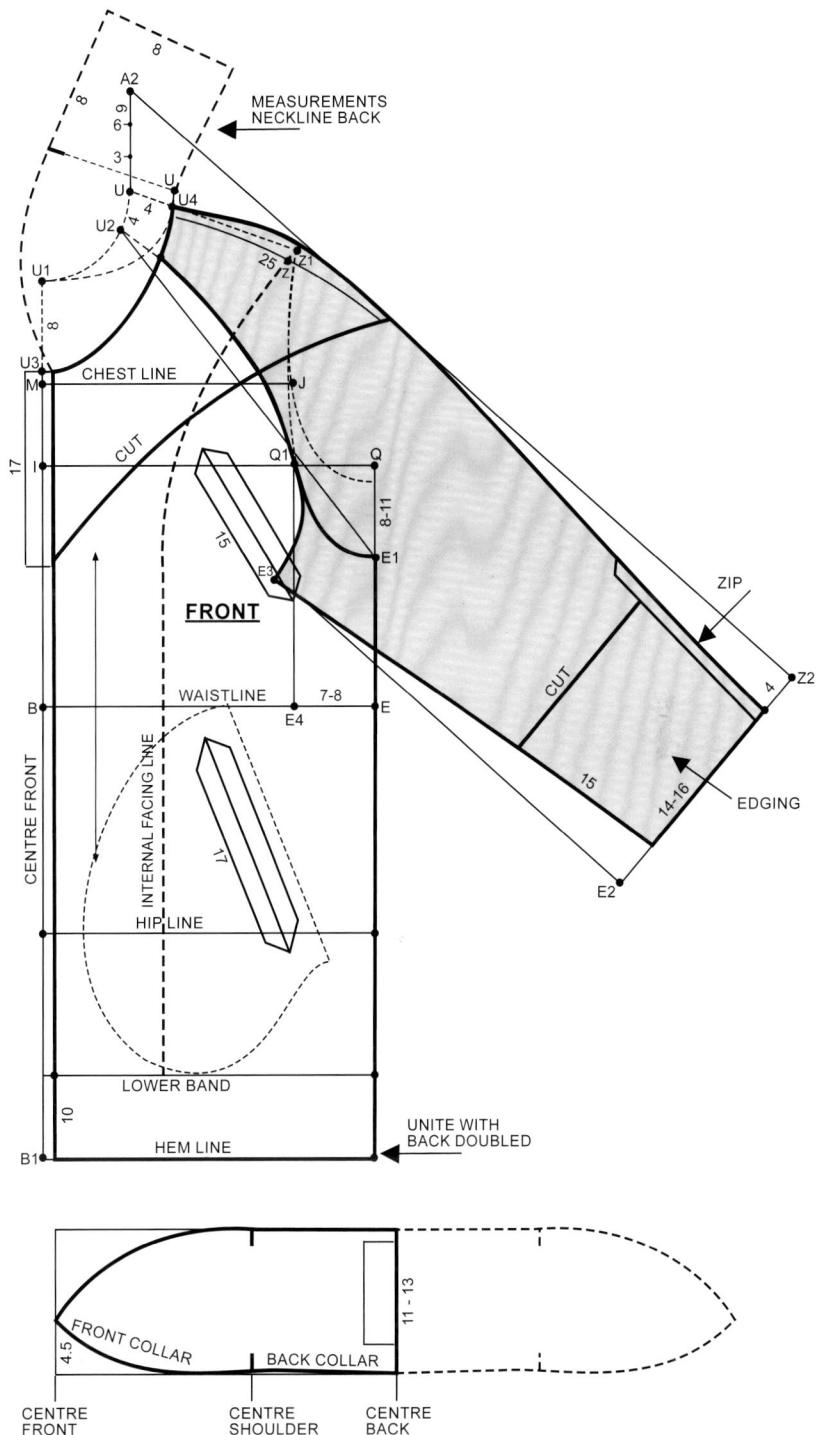

Diagram labels:

8
8
A2
9
6
3
U
U
4
U4
U2
4
U1
8
U3
M
CHEST LINE
J
17
I
CUT
Q1
Q
15
8-11
E3
E1
FRONT
CENTRE FRONT
INTERNAL FACING LINE
17
B
WAISTLINE
7-8
E4
E
HIP LINE
MEASUREMENTS
NECKLINE BACK
25
Z
Z1
ZIP
CUT
4
Z2
15
14-16
EDGING
E2
LOWER BAND
10
HEM LINE
B1
UNITE WITH
BACK DOUBLED

FRONT COLLAR
4.5
BACK COLLAR
11 - 13
CENTRE
FRONT
CENTRE
SHOULDER
CENTRE
BACK

FRONT

Front

- Draw perpendicular line U-A2 in the necessary length, according to the sleeve angle.
- Draw line A2-Z2 passing through Z1 at 1 cm / 0.39" from point Z, with Z1-Z2 equal to the sleeve length taken from the centre shoulder, like the back.
- Q-E1 = 8-11 cm / 3.15-4.33" depending on the desired armscye depth, like the back.
- E-E4 = 7-8 cm / 2.56-2.76".
- Draw vertical line E4-Q1.

- U-U2 = 3-6 cm / 1.18-2.36". Draw guideline U2-E1.
- Draw the curved line E1-Q1-U2.
- Draw E3-Q1-U2 like E1-Q1-U2.
- Draw E2-E3 parallel to Z1-Z2, in the same length as E2-E3 at the back minus 1 cm / 0.39".
- Adjust the lower edge of the sleeve according to the pattern.
- Smoothly draw the outer and inner lines of the sleeve and bodice. Carefully transfer the sleeve and bodice on another sheet of paper.

PADDED JACKET WITH SLEEVE DETAIL

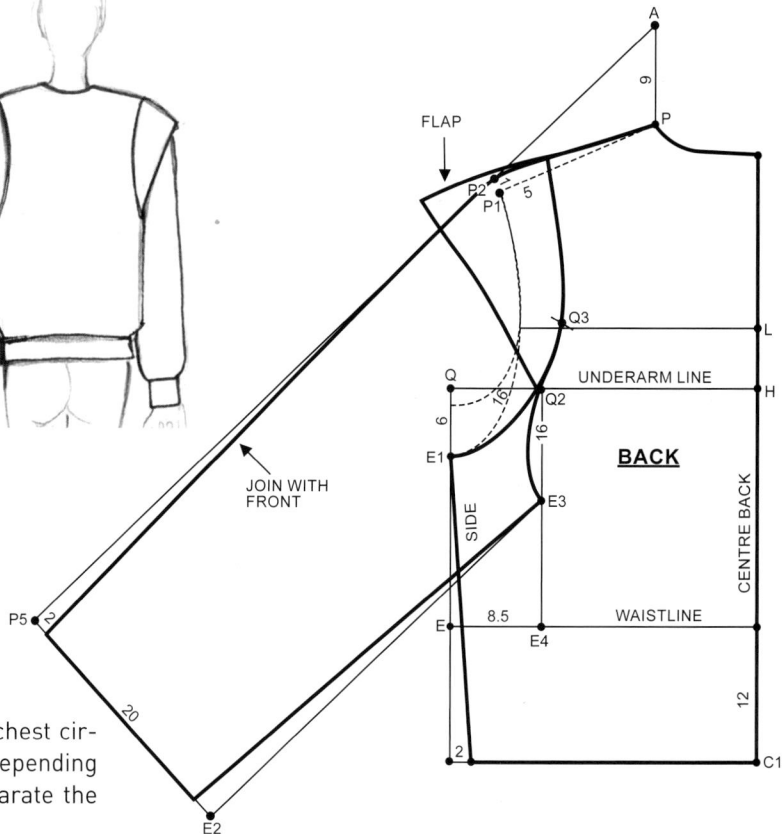

- Draw the base block of the padded jacket with chest circumference ease of 28-36 cm / 11.02-14.17", depending on the fabric. Draw the desired length and separate the front from the back.
- Reduce the shoulder of the front and back bodice by 4-6 cm / 1.57-2.36" and lower the armscye by 6 cm / 2.36", as shown in the diagram.
- Using the raglan sleeve procedure, draw the sleeve at the desired angle.
- Draw the extension of the centre front bottom for the fastening overlap.
- Draw the facing of the upper and lower front.
- Trace the front and back 'wing' in the shape and size of your choosing.

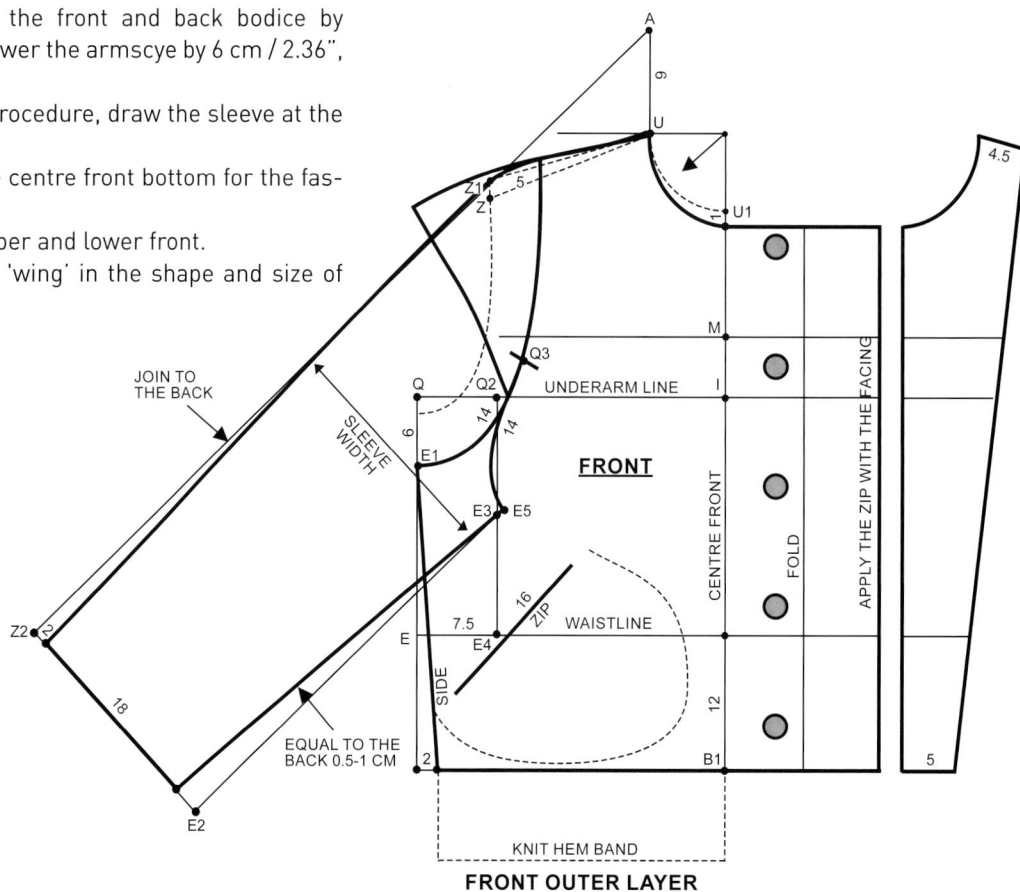

FLAP

JOIN WITH FRONT

UNDERARM LINE

BACK

SIDE

CENTRE BACK

WAISTLINE

A

P
P2
P1
5
Q3
L
Q
Q2
H
E1
E3
E
8.5
E4
2
C1

JOIN TO THE BACK

SLEEVE WIDTH

EQUAL TO THE BACK 0.5-1 CM

A
U
U1
Z1
Z
5
Q
Q2
Q3
UNDERARM LINE
M
I
E1
E3
E5
FRONT
Z2
2
E
E4
7.5
16
ZIP
WAISTLINE
SIDE
2
B1
18
E2

CENTRE FRONT
FOLD
APPLY THE ZIP WITH THE FACING
4.5
5
12

KNIT HEM BAND

FRONT OUTER LAYER

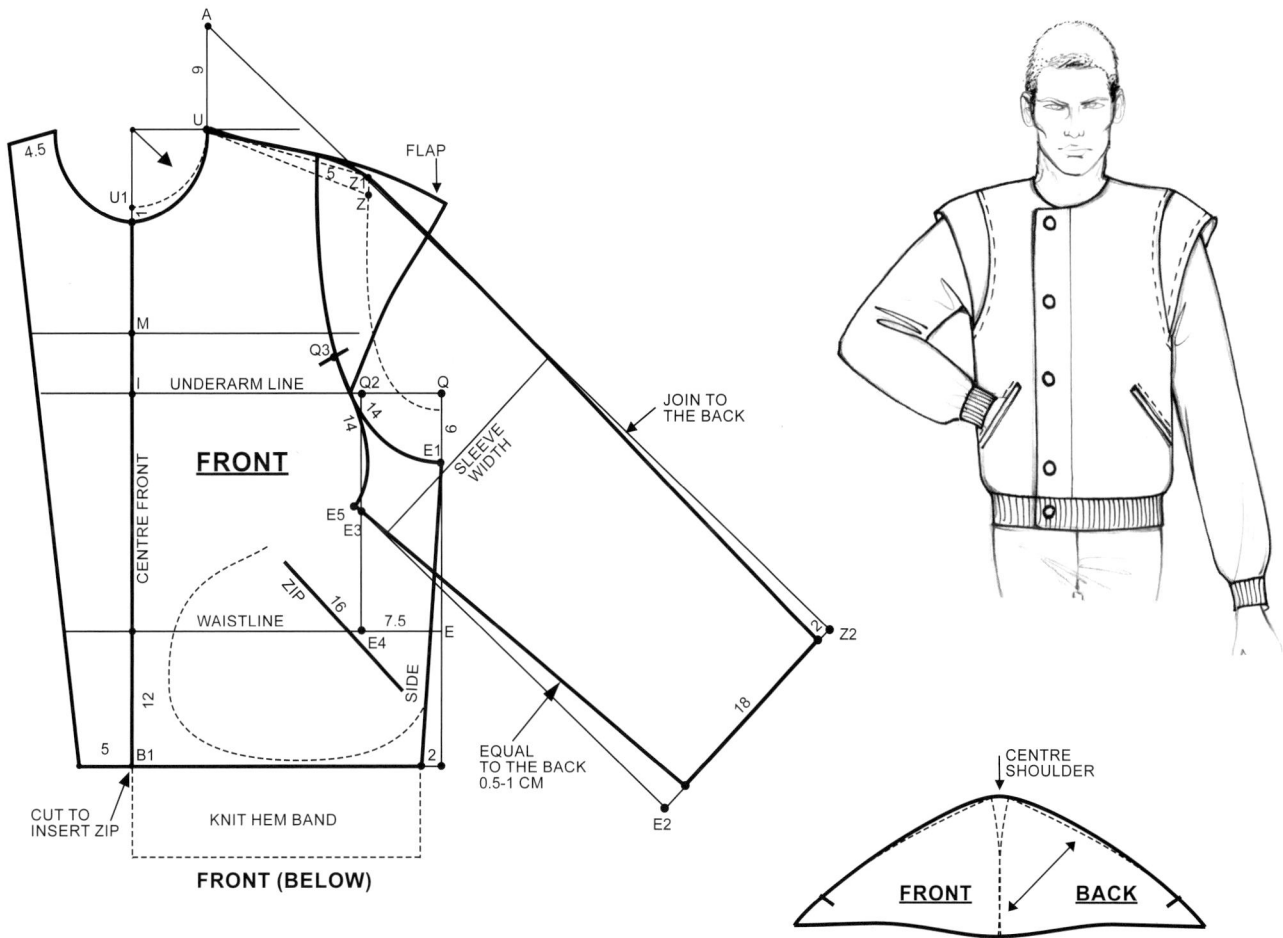

FLAP

A

9

U

U1

4.5

M

UNDERARM LINE

CENTRE FRONT

FRONT

Q3

Q2

Q

5

Z1

Z

E1

SLEEVE WIDTH

14

14

E5

E3

JOIN TO THE BACK

6

ZIP

WAISTLINE

16

7.5

E4

E

SIDE

12

EQUAL TO THE BACK 0.5-1 CM

5

B1

2

18

CUT TO INSERT ZIP

KNIT HEM BAND

Z2

E2

FRONT (BELOW)

- Draw the pattern for the rib-knit lower hem and cuffs, taking into account the elasticity of the ribbing.
- Copy the front and back sleeve blocks on another sheet of paper and connect them to the centre shoulder.
- Copy the front and back 'wings' on another sheet of paper and smoothly connect them to the centre shoulder.

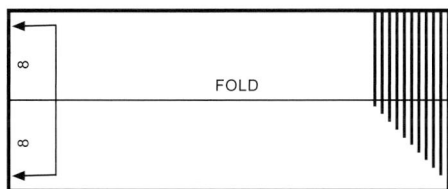

8

8

FOLD

KNIT HEM BAND

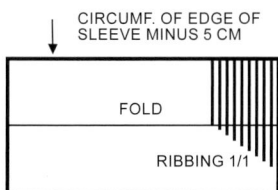

CIRCUMF. OF EDGE OF SLEEVE MINUS 5 CM

FOLD

RIBBING 1/1

KNIT CUFF

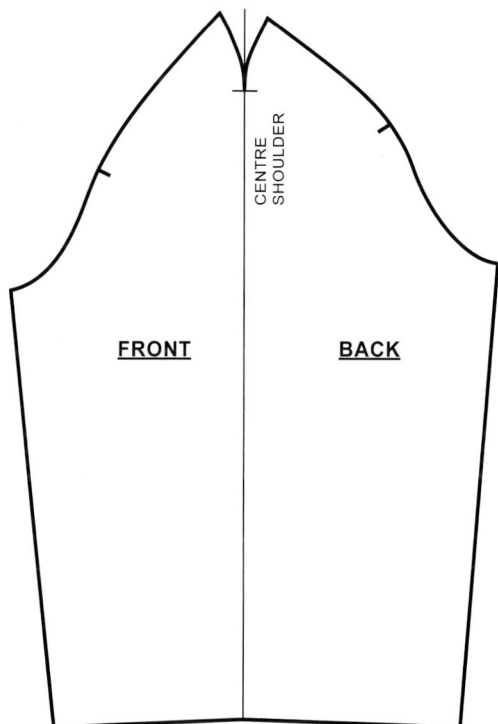

CENTRE SHOULDER

FRONT   **BACK**

CENTRE SHOULDER

FRONT   **BACK**

PADDED JACKET WITH A COVERED ZIP PLACKET

Diagram labels:

CUT AND OPEN
8
back neckline
A   U 1.5   J1   F
U2
2.5
U1
5
U3
V   Z
UNDERCOLLAR
CHEST LINE   J   L1   SHOULDER LINE   L
M
I   UNDERARM LINE   I1   Q   UNDERARM LINE   H1   H
4   17
UNDERARM LINE
Q1
CENTRE FRONT
CENTRE FRONT
FRONT   BACK
WAISTLINE   E   WAISTLINE
B   C
SIDE LINE
CENTRE BACK
5   19
CUT
6.5   HIP LINE   HIP LINE
HEM LINE   ELASTIC   HEM LINE
B1   E1   C1

G   P2 1.5 P
P1   1.5   N   D   D1
O

COLLAR
CENTRE BACK

BUTTON PLACKET
CENTRE FRONT

Bodice construction - Size 16 UK

Draw the rectangle A-B-C-D with:

- A-B equal to the front neck-to-waist + 3 cm / 1.18" for ease (44 + 3 = 47 cm / 18.50").
- B-C = (circumference of the chest + ease) ÷ 2 e.g.: 96 + 30 = 126 ÷ 2 = 63 cm / 24.80")
- B-E half of B-C.
- Draw F-E (centre side).
- B-B1 jacket extension as desired (28-35 cm / 11.02-13.78").
- Draw B1-C1 (lower hemline).
- A-U 1/6 shoulder width, including 10 cm / 3.94" for the ease (e.g.: 44 + 10 = 54 ÷ 6 = 9 cm / 3.54").
- Draw the arc U-U1 with a compass.
- C-D rear neck-to-waist + 3 cm / 1.18" ease (47 cm / 18.50").
- C-H half of C-D (21.5 cm / 8.46").
- Draw H-I (underarm level).
- H-L = 1/3 of D-H (21.5 ÷ 3 = 7.2 cm / 2.83").
- Draw L-M (chest line and shoulder line).

- D-G = rear shoulder width + 4.5-6 cm / 1.77-2.36" for ease, divided by 2 (e.g.: 44 + 4.5 = 48.5 ÷ 2 = 24.2 cm / 9.53") or 2/5 of B-C minus 1 cm / 0.39".
- H-H1 like D-G (24.2 cm / 9.53").
- Draw G-L1-H1.
- I-I1 like H-H1 minus 1.5 cm / 0.39" (e.g.: 24.2 - 1 = 23.2 cm / 9.13"). Draw I1-J-J1.
- G-O = 1.5 cm / 0.59"; D-D1 = 1 cm / 0.39".
- D-N = 1/3 D-G (9 cm / 3.54").
- N-P = 2.5 cm / 1".
- P-P1 = shoulder length + 3-4.5 cm / 1.18-1.77" depending on padding and fabric (e.g.: 15 + 4 = 19 cm / 7.48").
- P-P2 = 1.5 cm / 0.59". Draw P2-P1.
- J1-V = 5 cm / 2"; U-U2 = 1.5 cm / 0.59"; U1-U3 = 2.5 cm / 1".
- U2-Z like P2-P1. Draw U2-Z with the measurement of P2-P1.
- Q-Q1 = 8-10 cm / 3.15-3.94".

PADDED JACKET - BASE SLEEVE

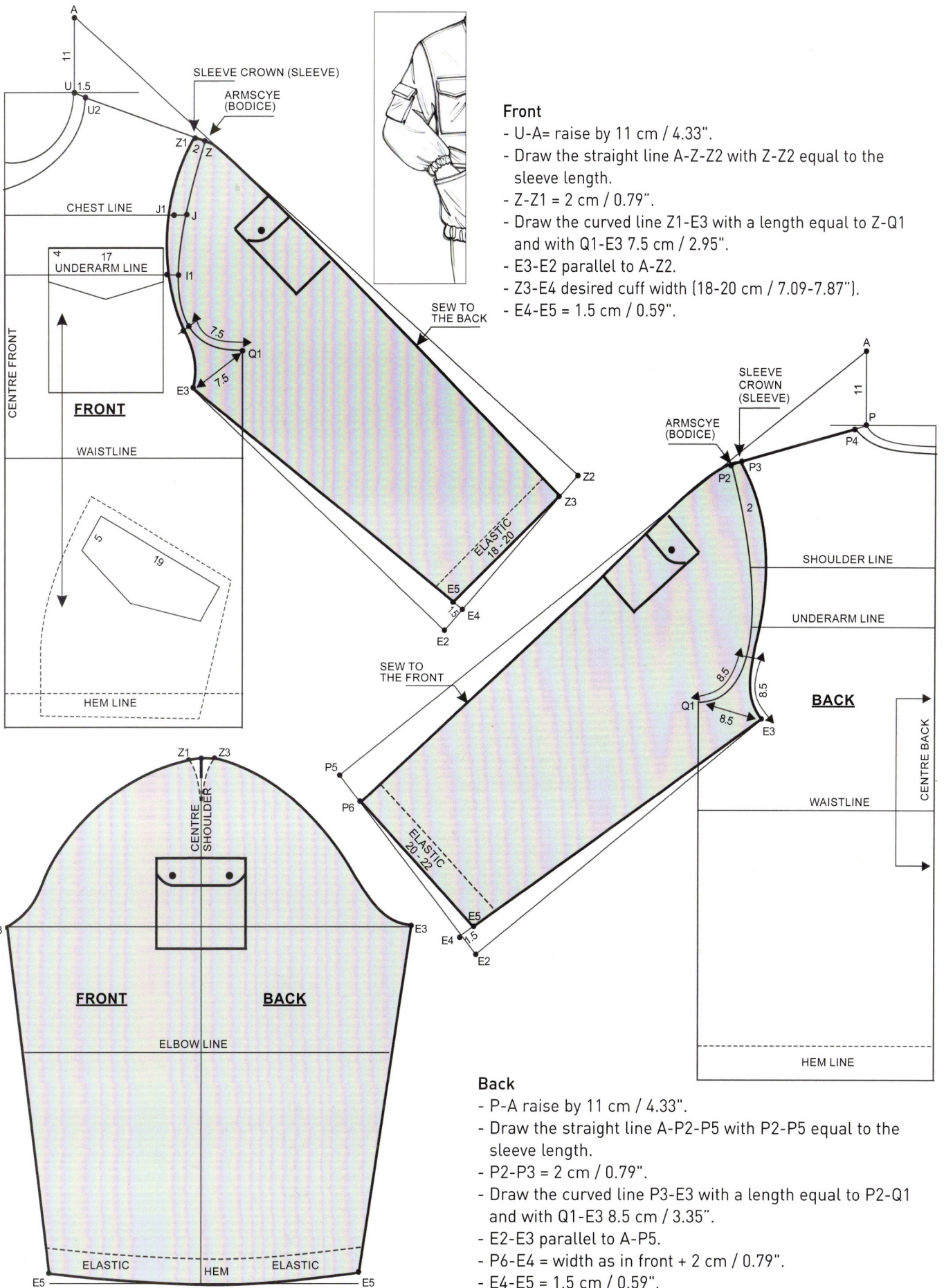

Front
- U-A= raise by 11 cm / 4.33".
- Draw the straight line A-Z-Z2 with Z-Z2 equal to the sleeve length.
- Z-Z1 = 2 cm / 0.79".
- Draw the curved line Z1-E3 with a length equal to Z-Q1 and with Q1-E3 7.5 cm / 2.95".
- E3-E2 parallel to A-Z2.
- Z3-E4 desired cuff width (18-20 cm / 7.09-7.87").
- E4-E5 = 1.5 cm / 0.59".

Back
- P-A raise by 11 cm / 4.33".
- Draw the straight line A-P2-P5 with P2-P5 equal to the sleeve length.
- P2-P3 = 2 cm / 0.79".
- Draw the curved line P3-E3 with a length equal to P2-Q1 and with Q1-E3 8.5 cm / 3.35".
- E2-E3 parallel to A-P5.
- P6-E4 = width as in front + 2 cm / 0.79".
- E4-E5 = 1.5 cm / 0.59".

LEATHER-STYLE JACKET

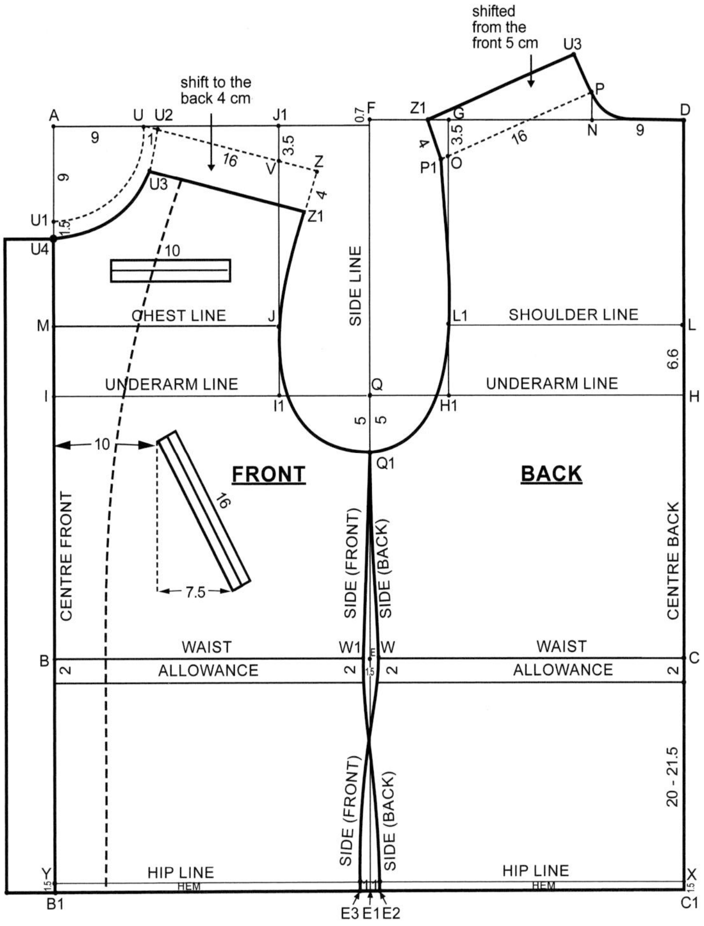

FRONT OUTER LAYER

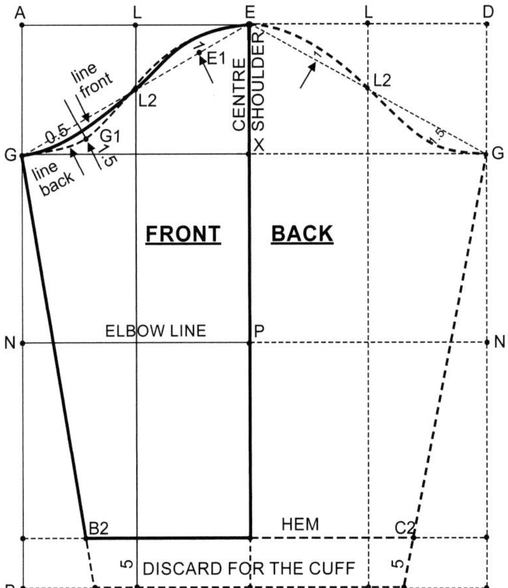

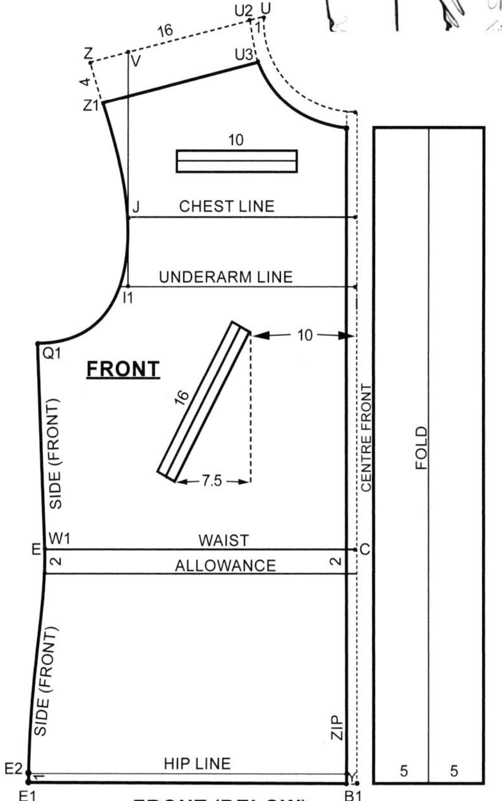

Labels in top diagram: shift to the back 4 cm · shifted from the front 5 cm · FRONT · BACK · CHEST LINE · SIDE LINE · SHOULDER LINE · UNDERARM LINE · CENTRE FRONT · CENTRE BACK · SIDE (FRONT) · SIDE (BACK) · WAIST · ALLOWANCE · HIP LINE · HEM

Sleeve diagram labels: line front · line back · CENTRE SHOULDER · FRONT · BACK · ELBOW LINE · HEM · DISCARD FOR THE CUFF

FRONT (BELOW)

Labels: CHEST LINE · UNDERARM LINE · FRONT · SIDE (FRONT) · WAIST · ALLOWANCE · HIP LINE · CENTRE FRONT · FOLD · ZIP

- Draw the base of the loose-fitting jacket with chest circumference ease of 14-18 cm (5.51-7.09"), depending on the fabric. Draw the desired length and separate the front from the back.
- Lower the armscye by 5 cm / 2", as shown in the diagram of the pattern.
- Draw the part of the front shoulder to be carried over to the back for the yoke, the part of the back sleeve to be car-

ried over to the centre front sleeve, and the rear yoke, as in the figure. Draw the extension of the lower centre front for the fastening overlap.
- Draw the facing of the upper front and the strip for the zip of the lower front. Draw the pocket and zip chest pocket.
- Create the sleeve using the procedure described for the loose-fitting jacket sleeve. Create the strap at the cuffs and the belt loops at the waist.

COATS, MACKINTOSHES, CAPES AND HOODS

COAT AND OVERCOAT LINES

The lines and lengths of coats and other outerwear also vary according to the dictates of fashion and when and where they will be worn. The fabrics used for each garment also differ according to various factors. As a rule, for more formal coats, bouclé, heavy cloth, velours, brushed cloth, winterweight wool double crêpe, camelhair cloth, Donegal wool, tweed and herringbone are ideal, while leather or other types of details can give the garment a sportier look.

Classic coat

Classic coats can be single- or double-breasted. The single-breasted closure may be smooth and without seams, and the breakpoint of the lapels at the chest or waistline. It is usually fastened by one, two or three buttons. The garment may feature seams that are cross-wise, wide or narrow at the bottom; the sleeves can be inset, raglan, kimono or with a dropped shoulder.

Double-breasted coats, on the other hand, may be six or four-button, more or less curved and with the breakpoint high on the chest or low on the waist.

The Loden overcoat

This coat gets its name from the special fabric it's made of. Originally developed as a workwear garment, it became part of everyday menswear in the 1960s in its traditional bottle-green colour. It is made of pure brushed wool and is characterised by a slightly trapezoid line, with sleeves that are attached on the shoulders and flaps to conceal the seams.

The flap is topstitched and the sleeve is attached in a way that leaves open underarm space for breathability, while also facilitating movement. At the back is a long inverted pleat secured with a hem gusset or a leather triangle.

Heavy coat

This garment is a coat with a length ranging from 3/4 (at the thigh) to 7/8 and 9/10 above the knee. It can come in any shape or cut and be made from the same fabrics as a classic coat.

Topcoat

The topcoat is a light item of outerwear made in various medium-weight fabrics to be worn mid-season.

Evolved from a surcoat, we find it as a garment as early as the 18th century, and from then until today it has undergone countless modifications and transformations.

Mackintosh or trench coat

This style of men's overcoat is made of waterproof fabric. The classic Mackintosh has a specific cut, but the name is often used to indicate different waterproof coats worn to protect against the rain. It can also be called a raincoat.

Single-breasted coat   Double-breasted coat   One-button coat

Raglan-sleeve coat   The Loden overcoat   Duffel

Chesterfield   Mackintosh or trench coat

PROPORTION ANALYSIS

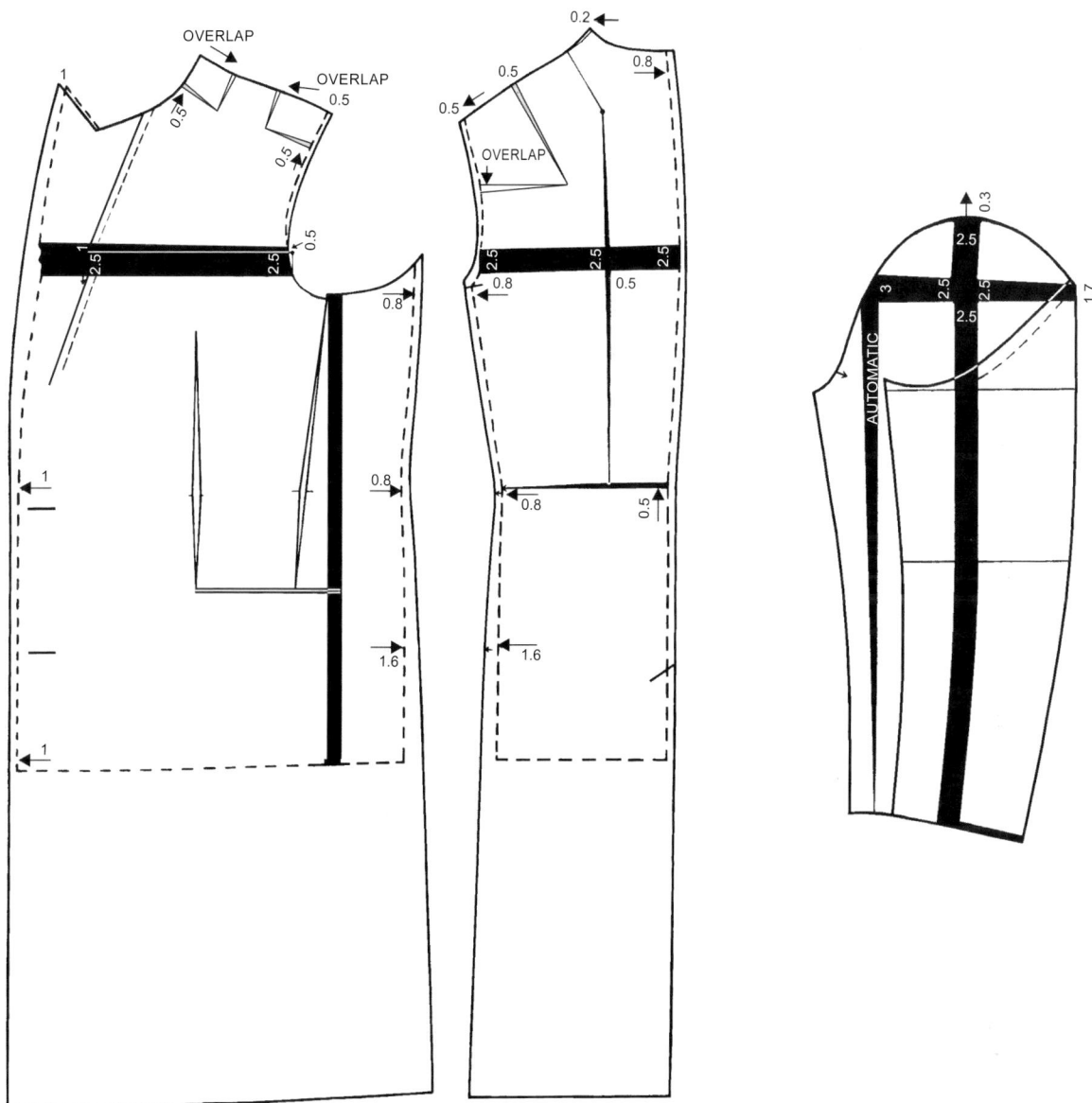

The pattern above illustrates the differences that should exist between the base of the jacket and the base of the overcoat. It highlights the fact that an overcoat does not require a purely proportional methodology.

A purely-proportioned pattern obtained only by increasing the measurement of the chest or taking the measurements directly from the jacket will not produce the correct distribution between the sectors, nor will it be correctly adapted to the wearer's shape.

Thus it is necessary to take the following into consideration:

1) Bear in mind the increased space needed for the armscye, due to the alteration in measurements caused by the jacket sleeve.

2) Consider the need to increase the curve of the shoulder due to the effect deriving from the jacket's collar.

3) The need for greater length and bulk at the lapels, to make the garment easier to wear, as well as having to overcome a kind of 'protruding' chest, caused by the doubling and overlapping of the lapels of the jacket and coat.

As such, you must analyse how exactly to create the overcoat.

Back: parallel widening of the armscye level; parallel widen-ing of the collar and hip sector; increase in the shoulder con-cavity. The back therefore increases by a total of 2.1 cm / 0.83" in width and 2.5 cm / 1" in height.

Front: in addition to lengthening the underarm level to match the back (2.5 cm / 1"), there is a total increase of 2.5 cm / 1" of the width, with a two-stage process, and also an increase of the front edge of 1 cm / 0.39" and other modifications illustrat-ed in the figure. So, in the end, the front chest width potential-ly increases 1.5 cm / 0.59"; the armscye by 2.5 cm / 1"; the back 2.1 cm / 0.83", for a total of 6.1 cm / 2.40", with a logical subdivision and rationalisation of the increases, both vertical and horizontal.

Sleeve: the increases are to be analysed by considering the two overlapping pieces, moving the pieces while respecting the horizontal aspects of the armscye and the elbow level. The central opening must be equal to the increase of the armscye on the bodice; the increase must be equal to the lowering performed on the overcoat, with two differences: the back piece turns to carry over a difference of 0.8 cm / 0.31" on the sleeve crown, while the front piece moves forward to create an interplay of length and aesthetic details on the front shoulder.

OVERCOAT BASE BLOCK

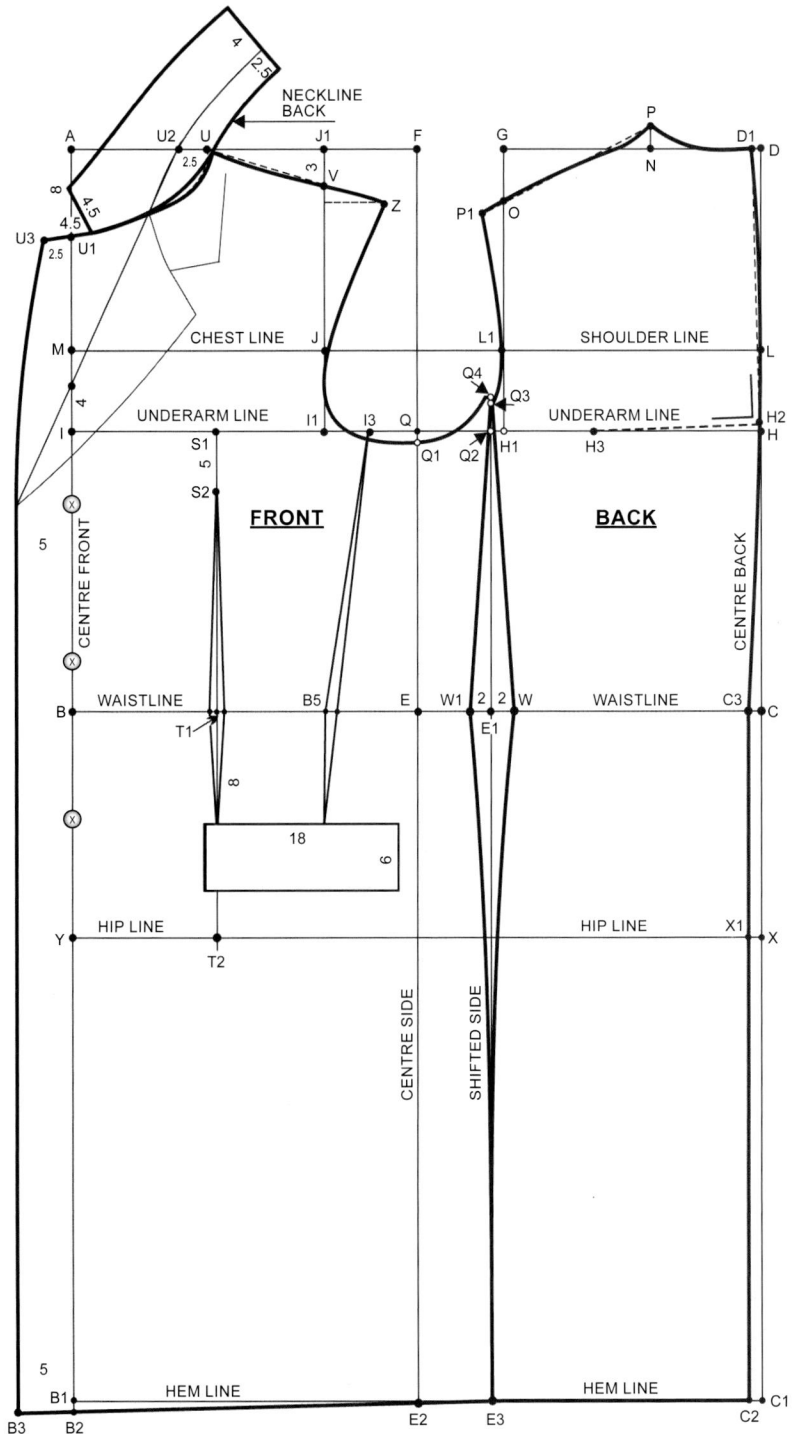

Measurements size 48 - Classic fit ease 28 cm

- Height 175 cm / 5'9".
- Chest semi-cir. = 96 + 28 = 124 ÷ 2 = 62 cm / 24.41".
- Waist semi-cir. = 88 + 28 = 116 ÷ 2 = 58 cm / 22.83".
- Hip semi-cir. = 92 + 28 = 120 ÷ 2 = 60 cm / 23.62".
- Neck semi-cir. = 42 ÷ 2 = 21 cm / 8.27".
- 1/2 shoulder width = 44 + 3 = 47 ÷ 2 = 23.5 cm / 9.25".
- Front neck-to-waist = 45.6 + 2 = 47.6 cm / 18.74".
- Rear neck to waist = 46.2 cm + 2 = 48.2 cm / 18.98".
Draw a right angle A-B-C with:
- A-B = front neck to waist + overcoat + 2 cm / 0.79" (e.g.: 45.6 + 2 = 21.5 cm / 8.46").
- B-C = chest semi-circumference + coat ease 28 cm / 11.02" (e.g.: 96 + 28 = 124 ÷ 2 = 62 cm / 24.41").
- D-C = rear neck-to-waist + ease 2 cm / 0.79" (e.g.: 46.2 + 2 = 48.2 cm / 18.97")
- D-G = 1/2 shoulder width + ease of 3 cm / 1.18" (e.g.: 44 + 3 = 47 ÷ 2 = 23.5 cm / 9.25" cm).
- D-C1 = coat length (e.g.: 112 cm / 44.10") centre back.
- Draw C1-E3-E2-B1 (lower hemline).
- B-Y and C-X = waist to hip (e.g.: 20 cm / 7.87").
- Draw Y-X (hip line).
- Y-B1 as X-C1.
- D-H half of D-C+ 0.5 cm / 0.20" (e.g.: 48.2 ÷ 2= 24.1 + 0.5 = 24.6 cm / 9.69")
- H-H1 like D-G (e.g.: 23.5 cm / 9.25").
- L-L1 like H-H1 (23.5 cm / 9.25").
- Draw G-L1-H1.
- Draw H-I parallel to B-C (UNDERARM LEVEL).
- H-I like B-C (62 cm / 24.41").
- B-E half of B-C (62 ÷ 2 = 31 cm / 12.20").

- A-F as B-E.
- Draw F-E-E2 (CENTRE SIDELINE).
- I-I1 like H-H1 minus 0.7 cm / 0.27" (e.g.: 23.5 - 0.7 = 22.8 cm / 8.98").
- Draw D-C-C1 (CENTRE BACK).
- B-B1 like C-C1.
- Draw A-B-B1 (CENTRE FRONT).
- B1-E2 like B-E. E2-E3 = 7 cm / 2.75".
- Q-Q2 like E2-E3 = 7 cm / 2.75".
- Join Q2-E3 (shifted side).
- H-L = 1/4 of D-H (e.g.: 24.6 ÷ 4 = 6.15 cm / 2.42".
- Draw L-M (L-L1 = shoulder line; M-J = CHEST LINE).
- Draw I1-J-J1 parallel to G-L1-H1.
- I1-H1 = H-I minus (I-I1 + H-H1) e.g.: 62 - (22.8 + 23.5) = 62 - 46.3 = 15.7 cm / 6.18" (ARMSCYE SECTOR).

COLLAR

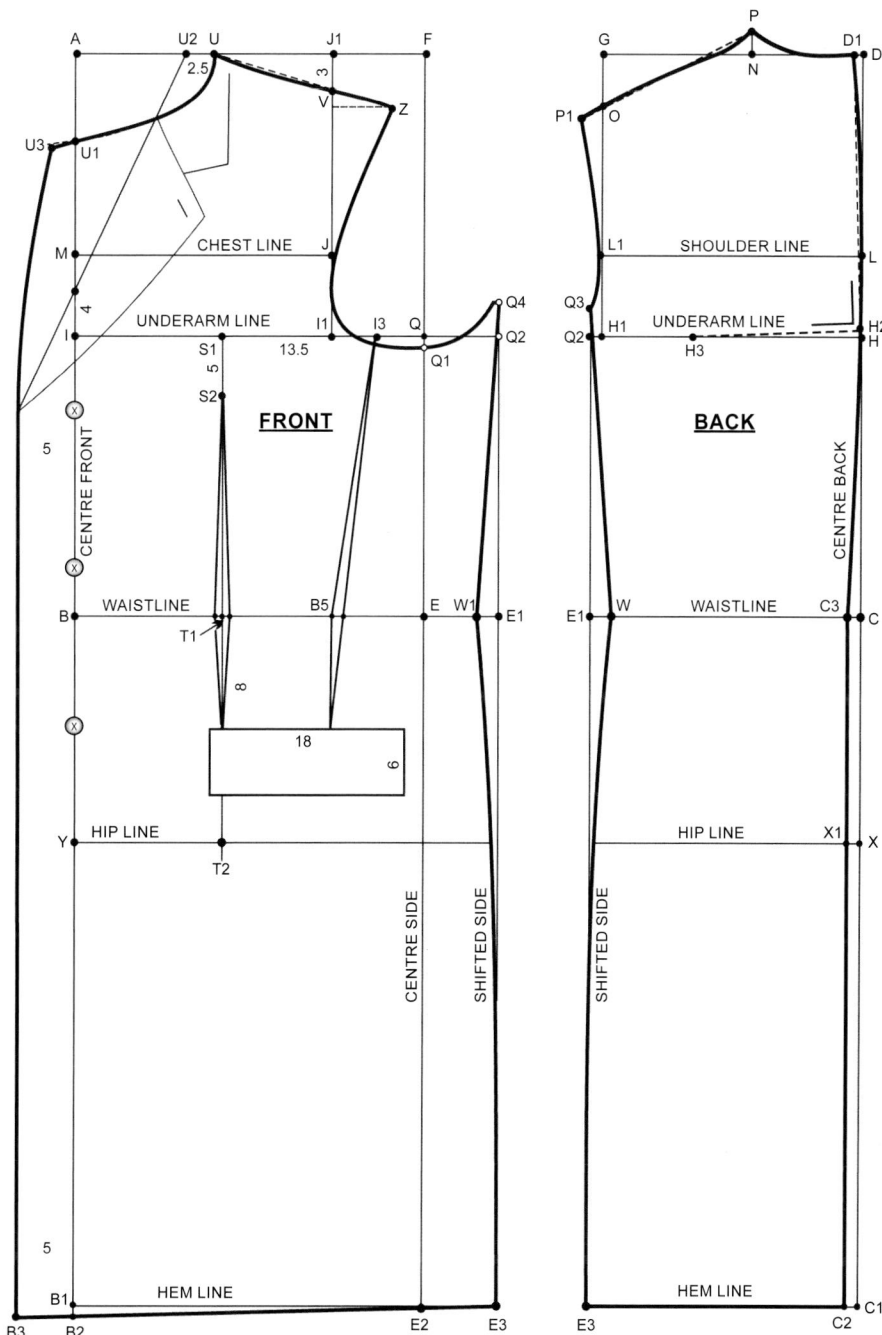

FRONT

BACK

Note:

The waist darts and the excess at the side are proportionate to the desired difference between the hips and the waist, which is to be distributed proportionally on the waist dart line and the hip line, plus the creation of a small 1.5 cm / 0.59" dart with its points on the armscye and pocket lines.

Back

- H-H3 = 16 cm / 6.30".
- H-H2 = 0.6 cm / 0.24".
- Create the angle H3-H2-D1.
- H2-D1 like H-D.
- D1-N = 1/3 of D-G + 1 cm / 0.20" (e.g.: 23.5 ÷ 3= 7.8 + 1 = 8.87 cm / 3.49")
- N-P = 2.5 cm / 1". Draw the curved line D1-P.
- G-O = 4.5 cm / 1.77".
- P-P1 = shoulder length + 2 cm / 0.79: (e.g.: 16 + 2 = 18 cm / 7.09".
- Draw the outline P-P1 passing through O.
- Q2-Q3 = 3 cm / 1.18").
- Carefully draw the armscye P1-L1-Q3.
- E1-W = 1.5-3 cm / 0.59-1.18".
- C-C3 = 1.2-1.7 cm / 0.47-0.67" .
- C1-C2 like C-C3.
- Draw the centre back line D1-L-H-C3-X1-C2.
- Draw the side line Q3-W-E3.

Front

- A-U = 11.9 cm / 4.69" (half of A-J1 + 0.5 cm / 0.20").
- A-U1 = 7.5-8 cm / 2.95-3.15".
- U-U2 = 2.5 cm / 1".

- Draw the breakline to the desired height.
- U1-U3 = 2-2.5 cm / 0.79-1".
- I-S1 = 13.5 cm / 5.31".
- I1-I3 = 4.5 cm / 1.77".
- B-B5 like I-I1 (22.8 cm / 8.98").
- Draw waist darts of 1-1.5 cm / 0.39-0.59".
- J1-V = 3.5 cm / 1.38".
- U-Z like P-P1 at the back minus 1 cm / 0.39" (17 cm / 6.69").
- Draw the outline U-Z passing through V.
- Q-Q1 = 1-2 cm / 0.39-0.79".
- Q2-Q4 = 3.5 cm / 1.38".
- Carefully draw the armscye Z-J-Q1-Q4.
- E1-W1 like E1-W.
- Draw the side line Q4-W1-E3.
- B1-B2 = 0.5-1 cm / 0.20-0.39"
- B2-B3 fastening extension = 5 cm / 2".
- Draw the curved lapel lines.
- Draw the lower hemline E3-B3.

DOUBLE-BREASTED COAT

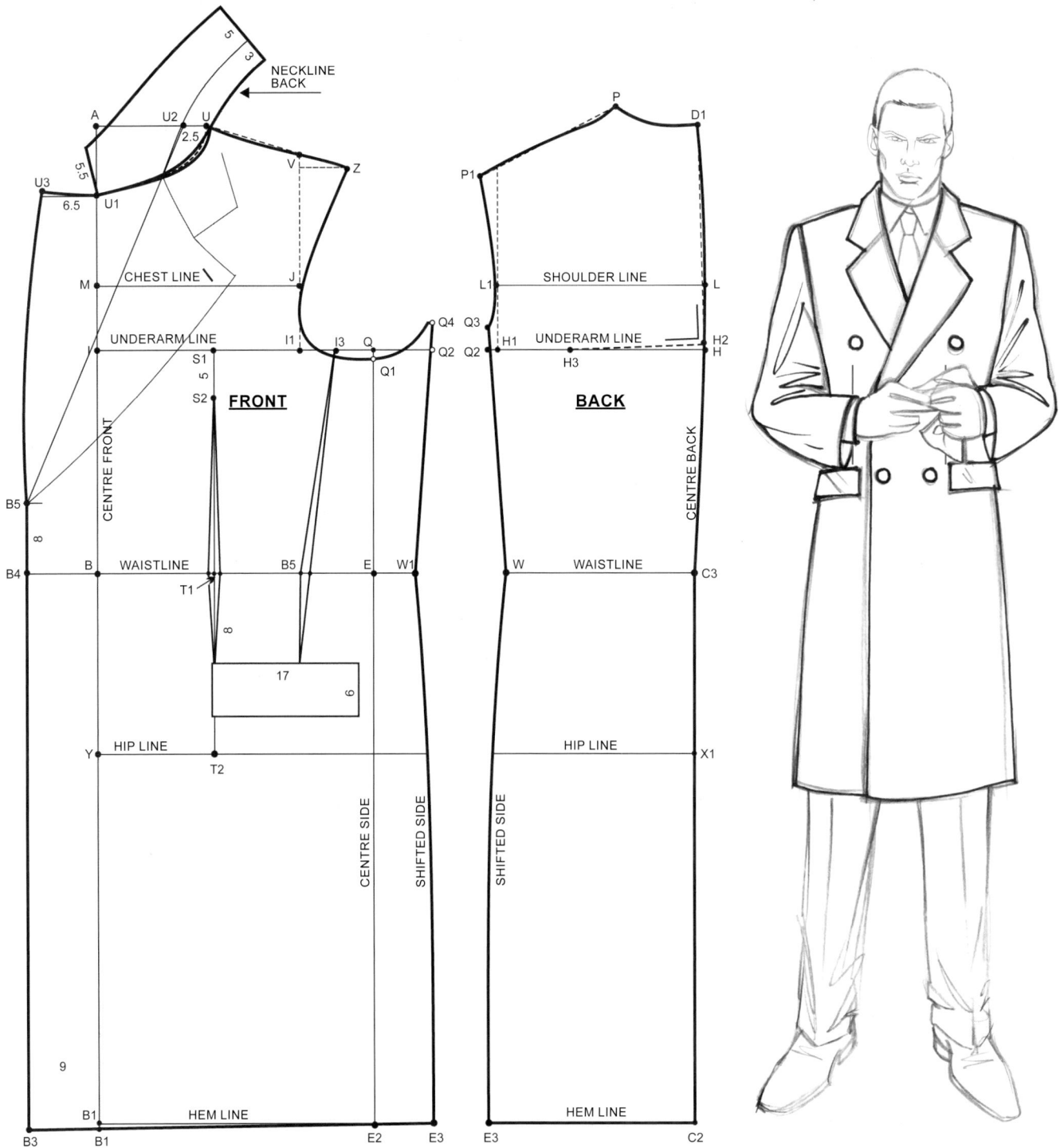

FRONT

BACK

NECKLINE BACK

CHEST LINE

SHOULDER LINE

UNDERARM LINE

UNDERARM LINE

CENTRE FRONT

CENTRE BACK

WAISTLINE

WAISTLINE

HIP LINE

HIP LINE

CENTRE SIDE

SHIFTED SIDE

SHIFTED SIDE

HEM LINE

HEM LINE

COLLAR

- Draw the coat base blocks with appropriate measurements and ease in the total length desired.
- Extend the front centre overlap B1-B3 and B-B4 by 9 cm / 3.54".
- B4-B5 = 6-8 cm / 2.36-3.15".
- Draw the breakline from U2 to B5.
- U1-U3 = 6.5-7 cm / 2.56-2.76".
- Join B3-B5-U3 as in the figure.

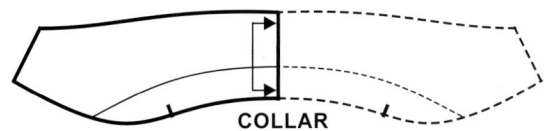

DOUBLE-BREASTED COAT WITH PEAK LAPELS

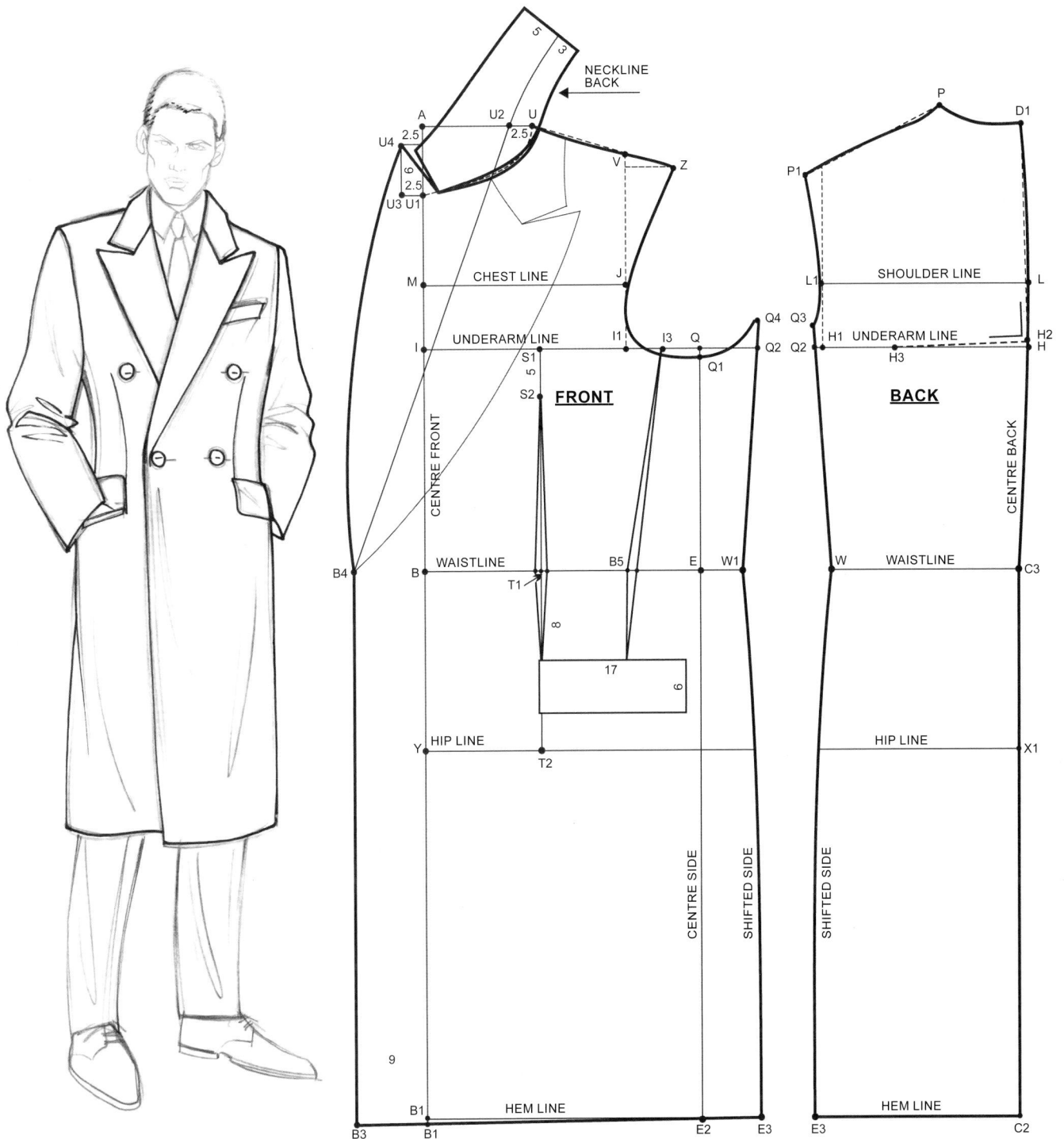

NECKLINE BACK

FRONT

BACK

CHEST LINE

SHOULDER LINE

UNDERARM LINE

UNDERARM LINE

CENTRE FRONT

WAISTLINE

WAISTLINE

CENTRE BACK

HIP LINE

HIP LINE

CENTRE SIDE

SHIFTED SIDE

SHIFTED SIDE

HEM LINE

HEM LINE

CUT & OPEN

COLLAR WITHOUT THE STAND

- Draw the base of the double-breasted overcoat with appropriate measurements and ease and in the desired overall length, with a centre front overlap of 9 cm / 3.54".
- Draw the breakline from U2 to B4 at the desired height.
- U1-U3 = 2.5-3 cm / 1-1.18".
- U3-U4 = 6 cm / 2.36" (or as desired).
- Join B3-B4-U4 as in the figure.

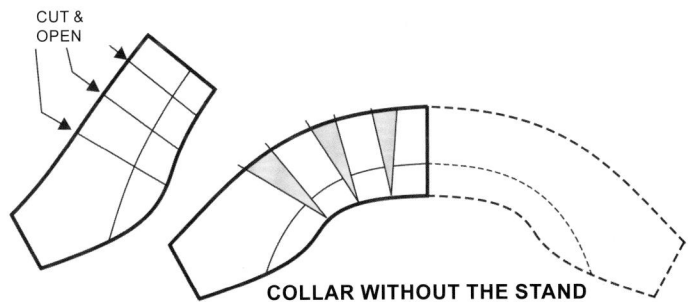

COAT ALLOWANCES

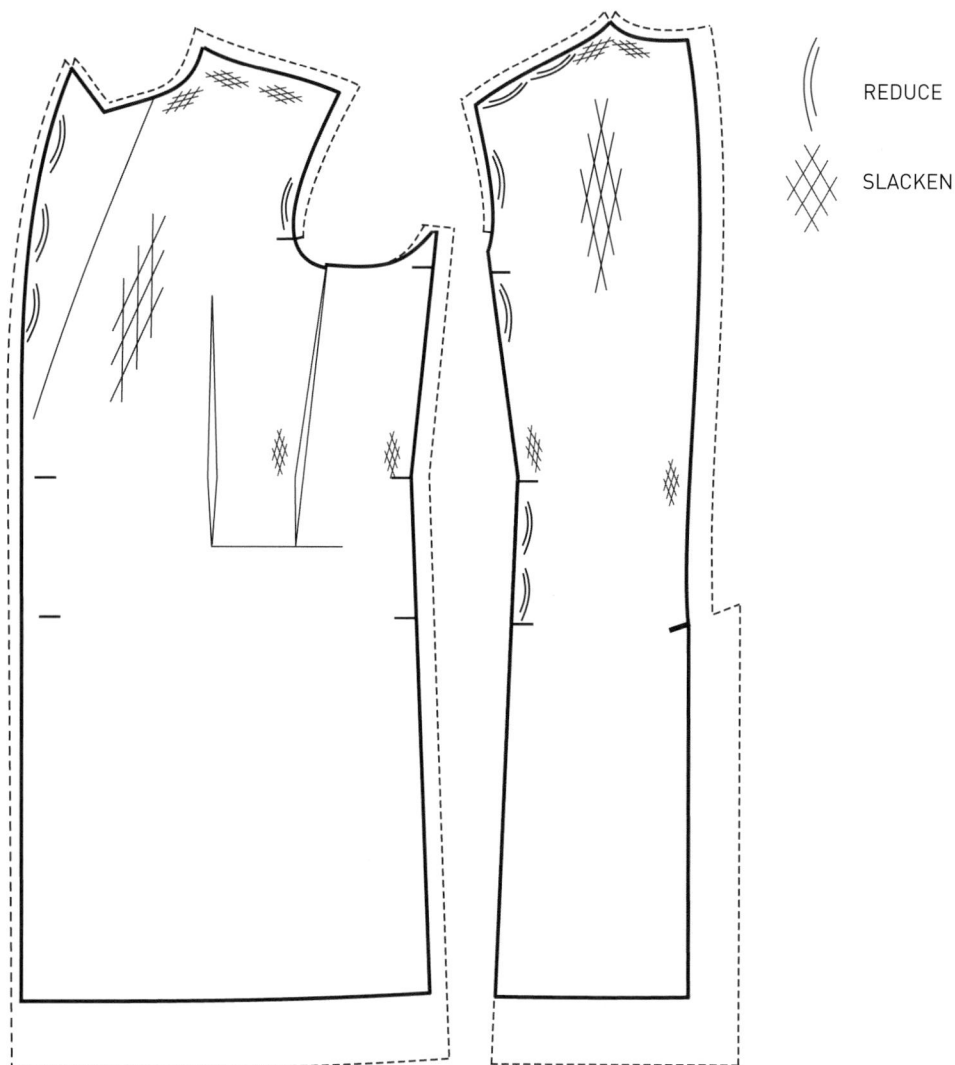

REDUCE

SLACKEN

Note for margins
Note that the margins are parallel to the seam lines; the margin on the back shoulder, which is optional, dictates that you must in any case sew below the 0.6 cm / 0.24" demarcation line.

Collar
After having temporarily placed the back of the coat over the front so that the two shoulder points meet, this collar requires that the measurements and shape are followed exactly in order to make it easier to adjust the part of the garment that surrounds the collar.

The collar will require slackening only on the back curve of the neckline and, should you wish to cut through with a break point, it may also be OK without any processing.

The break point, shifted by 2 cm / 0.79" from K to K1, will make it possible to give the part of the garment that surrounds the collar the necessary room by means of the cuts and related enlargements made, as shown in the figure.

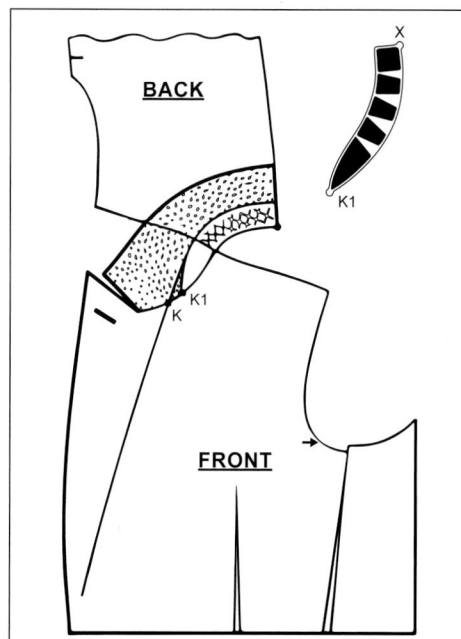

BACK

FRONT

BASE COAT SLEEVE

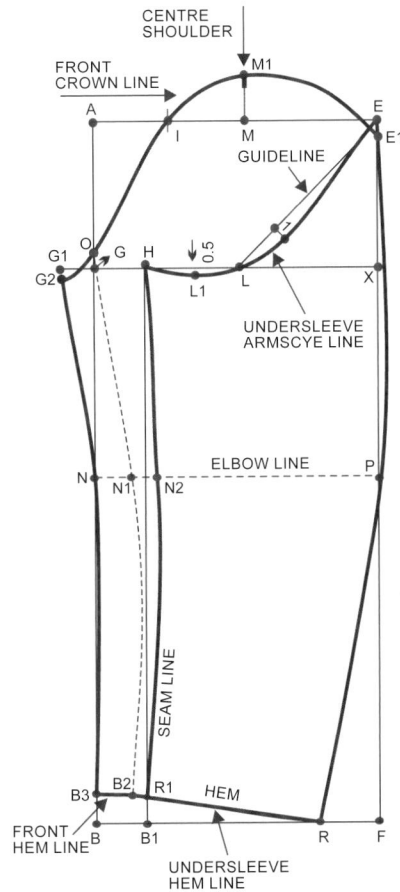

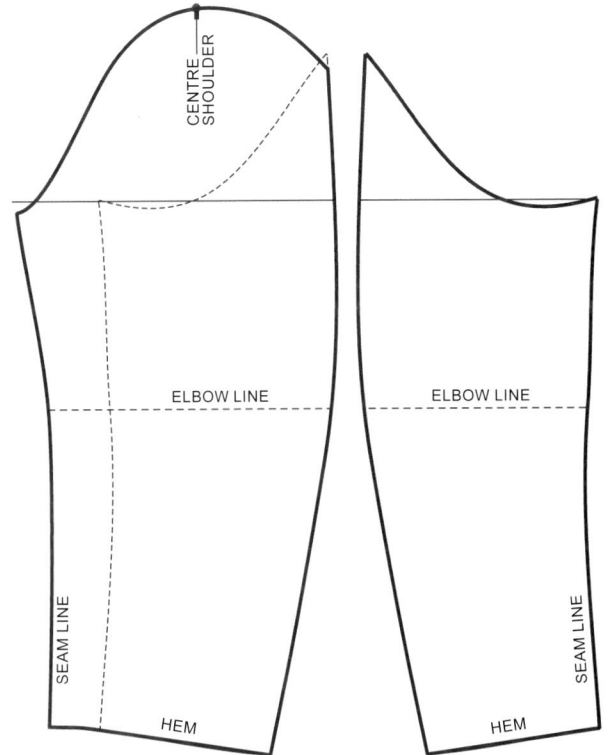

On the left side of a sheet of pattern paper, draw the rectangle A- B- E-F with:
- A-E as the bodice sector I1-H1 + 1/2 sector + 2 cm / 0.79" (e.g.: 15.8 + 7.9 = 23.7 + 2 = 25.7 cm / 10.12").
- A-B same length as the sleeve (e.g.: 62 cm / 24.41").
- A-G equal to L1-P1 + 0.5 cm / 0.39" of the rear torso base (e.g.: 12.5 + 0.5 = 13 cm / 5.12").
- Draw G-X parallel a A- E.
- A-N (elbow line) = half of A-B (e.g.: 62 ÷ 2 = 31 cm / 12.20").
- A-M (centre shoulder) = 1/2 of A-E + 1 cm / 0.39" (e.g.: 25.7 ÷ 2= 12.85 + 1 = 13.85 cm / 5.45")
- M-M1 = 1/3 of A-G (e.g.: 13 ÷ 3 = 4.35 cm / 1.71").
- A-I = 1/4 of A-E (e.g.: 25.7 ÷ 4 = 6.42 cm / 2.53").
- G-H = 3.5 cm / 1.38". G-G1 = 2.7 cm / 1.06".
- G1-G2 = 1 cm / 0.39". E-E1 = 1 cm / 0.39".
- X-L = half of G-X (e.g.: 25.7 ÷ 2 = 12.85 cm / 5.06").
- Draw guideline E-L.

- L-L1 half of H-L.
- G- O = 1.5 cm / 0.59".
- Smoothly draw the front sleeve crown E1-M1-I-O-G2.
- Smoothly draw the back sleeve crown E-L-L1-H.
- B-B1 = 4.5 cm / 1.77".
- B-B3 = 2.5 cm / 1".
- B3-B2 and N-N1 = 2.5 cm / 1".
- R-F = 5.5 cm / 2.17".
- R-R1 = 16 cm / 6.30" (depending on the desired width).
- Connect R-P-E and R1-N2-H with curved lines.
- Connect B3-N-G2 with a curved line.
- Cover the under-sleeve E-P-R-R1-N2-H-L1-L-E and position it on the E1-F line of the front part.

Always carefully double-check the total sleeve crown measurement, which must be greater than the measurement of the armscye in an amount that varies depending on the type of fabric used.

LOOSE-FITTING OVERCOAT AND SLEEVE BASE BLOCK

Measurements size 16 UK - Loose-fitting overcoat ease of 30 cm / 11.81"

- Height 175 cm / 5'9".
- Chest semi-cir. = 96 + 30 = 126 ÷ 2 = 63 cm / 24.80"
- Waist semi-cir. = 88 + 30 = 118 ÷ 2 = 59 cm / 23.22"
- Hip semi-cir. = 92 + 30 = 122 ÷ 2 = 61 cm / 24.01"
- Neck semi-cir. = 42 ÷ 2 = 21 cm / 8.27"
- 1/2 shoulder width = 44 + 4 = 48 ÷ 2 = 24 cm / 9.45"
- Front neck-to-waist = 45.6 + 2 = 47.6 cm / 18.74".
- Back neck to waist = 46.2 cm + 2 = 48.2 cm / 18.98".

Draw a right angle A-B-C with:
- A-B = front neck-to-waist + ease for a loose-fitting overcoat + 2 (e.g.: 45.6 + 2 = 47.6 cm / 18.74").
- B-C = chest semi-circumference + loose-fitting overcoat ease 30 cm (e.g. 96 + 30 = 126 : 2 = 63 cm / 24.80")
- C-D back neck-to-waist + 2 cm / 0.79" ease (e.g.: 46.2 + 2 = 48.2 cm / 18.98").
- D-G = 1/2 shoulder width + ease 4 cm (e.g.: 44 + 4 cm = 48 ÷ 2 = 24 cm / 9.44")
- D-C1 = overcoat length (e.g.: 112 cm /44.09").
- Draw D-C1 (CENTRE BACK).
- Draw C1-E3-E2-B1 (HEM LINE).
- B-Y and C-X = waist to hip (e.g.: 20 cm / 7.87").
- Draw Y-X (hip line); Y-B1 like X-C1.
- D-H half of D-C+ 0.5 cm / 0.20" (e.g.: 48.2 ÷ 2 = 24.1 + 0.5 = 24.6 cm / 9.69").
- H-H1 like D-G (e.g.: 24 cm / 9.45").

- L-L1 like H-H1 (24 cm / 9.45"). Draw G-L1-H1.
- Draw H-I parallel to B-C (underarm level)
- H-I like B-C = 62 cm / 24.41"
- B-E half of B-C (e.g.: 66 ÷ 2 = 33 cm / 13").
- A-F like B-E = 33 cm / 13".
- Draw F-E-E2 (side line).
- I-I1 like H-H1 minus 0.7 cm / 0.28" (e.g. 24 - 0.7 = 23.3 cm / 9.17").
- B-B1 like C-C1. Draw A-B-B1 (centre front).
- B1-E2 like B-E.
- H-L = 1/4 of D-H (e.g.: 25.1 ÷ 4 = 6.27 cm / 2.47").
- Draw L-M (L-L1 = shoulder line; M-J = CHEST LINE).
- Draw I1-J1 parallel to G-H1.
- I1-H1 = H-I minus (I-I1 + H-H1). E.g.: 62 - (22.8 + 23.5) = 62 - 46.3 = 15.7 cm / 6.18" (armscye sector).

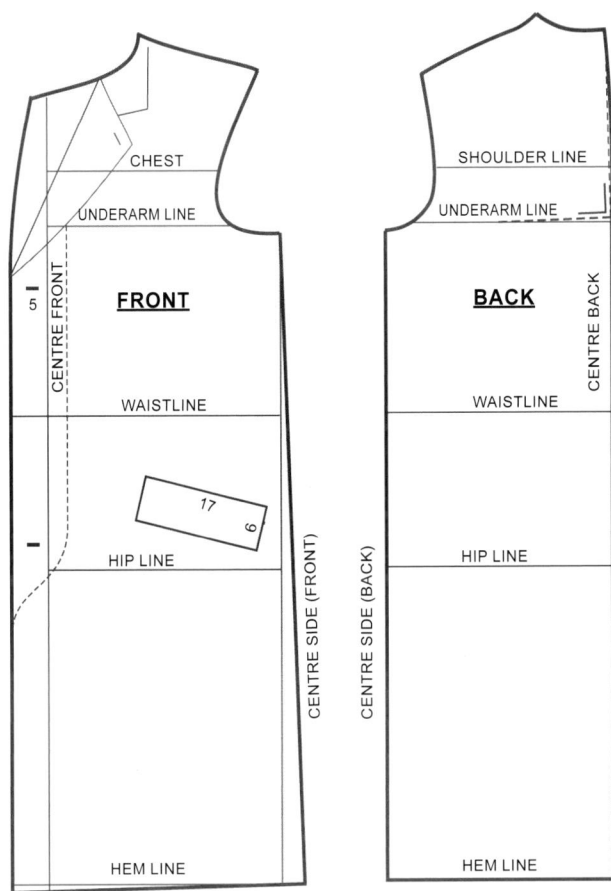

Back

- H-H3 = 16.5 cm / 6.50".
- H-H2 = 0.6 cm / 0.24".
- Create the angle H3-H2-D1.
- H2-D1 like H-D.
- D1-N = 1/3 of D-G + 1.5 cm / 0.59" (e.g.: 24 ÷ 3 = 8 +1.5 = 9.5 cm / 3.74").
- N-P = 2.7 cm / 1.06". Draw the outline D1-P.
- G-O = 4.5 cm / 1.77".
- P-P1 = shoulder length + 2 cm / 0.79" (e.g.: 16 + 2 = 18 cm / 7.09").
- Draw the curved line P-P1 passing through O.
- Q-Q1 = 1-2 cm / 0.39-0.79".
- Draw the back armscye P1-L1-Q1 smoothly.

Front

- A-U = 12.5 cm / 4.92" (half A-J1 + 0.5 cm / 0.20").
- A-U1 = 7.5-8 cm / 2.95-3.15"; U-U2 = 2.5 cm / 1".
- I-M1=3-4 cm (or at the desired height).
- Draw the breakline U3-S.
- U1-U3 = 2-2.5 cm / 0.79-1". J1-V = 3.5 cm / 1.38".
- U-Z like P-P1 at the back minus 1 cm / 0.39" (17 cm / 6.69").
- Draw the outline U-Z passing through V.
- Q-Q1 like the back (1-2 cm / 0.59-0.79").
- Draw the front armscye Z-J-Q1.
- Trace the front side Q-E2.
- B1-B2 = 0.5-1 cm / 0.20-0.39".
- B2-B3 fastening extension of 5 cm / 2".

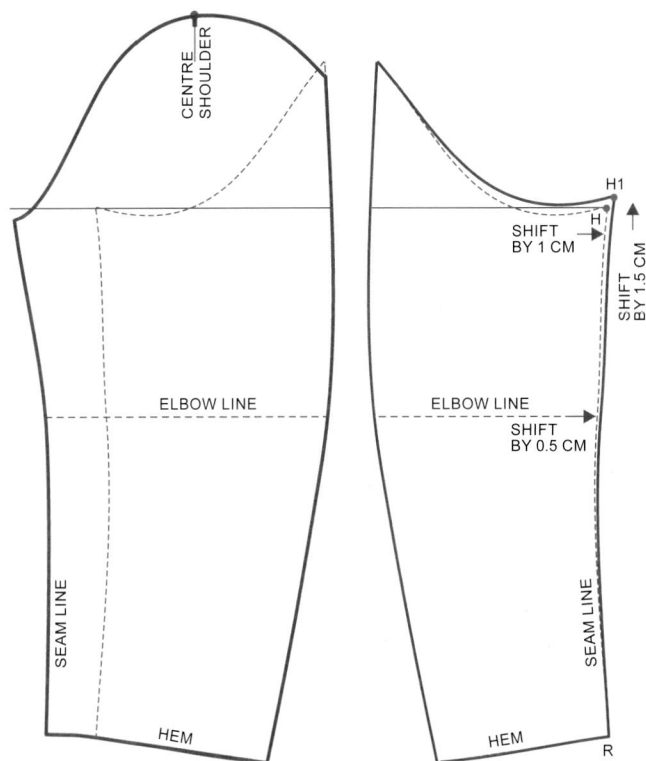

- Draw the curved lapel lines.
- Draw the hemline E3-B3.

SLEEVE

For the construction of the sleeve, the oversleeve of the classic overcoat can be used, while for the undersleeve we merely vary the position of H1, raising it by 1.5 cm / 0.59" and widening it by 1 cm / 0.39".
- Connect H1-R.

DOUBLE-BREASTED CHESTERFIELD COAT

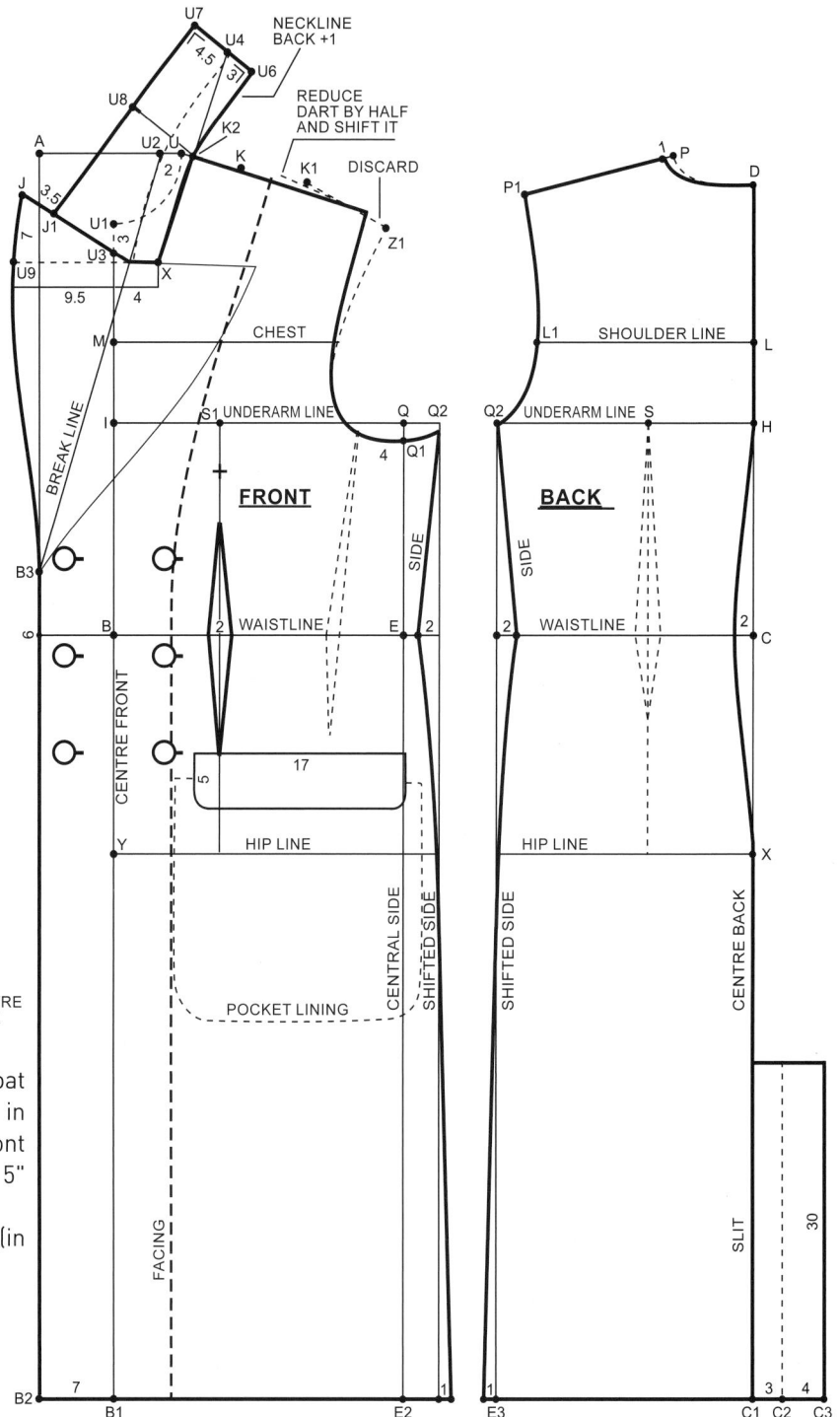

COLLAR

POINT SHOULDER | CENTRE BACK

- Draw the base of the double-breasted overcoat with appropriate measurements and ease and in the desired overall length, with the centre front overlap B1-B2 in a length of 7-8 cm / 2.76-3.15" and draw B2-A.
- Draw the breakline U2-B3 in the desired angle (in this case 6 cm / 2.36" from the waist).
- Flare at the bottom by 1-1.5 cm / 0.39-0.59".

Collar

- Draw K2-U4 with K2 shifted from U by 0.5 cm / 0.20" and with the rear neckline measurement increased by 1 cm / 0.39".
- U4-U6 = 3 cm / 1.18".
- Join U6-K2 with a curved line.
- Draw the line U6-U7 square with U6-K2, with the desired collar size (e.g.: 7 cm / 2.76").
- K2-U8 like U6-U7.
- Draw line U3-J with the angle and measurement desired (e.g.: 9.5 cm / 3.74").
- J-J1 = 3.5 cm / 1.38" or as desired; J-U9 = 7 cm / 2.76" or as desired.
- About 3 cm / 1.18" from U6, towards U7, draw a dotted line

to the breakline. This line will be the folding line of the collar, the under part must always be lower than the upper part.
- Smoothly join all the lines as in the figure and copy the collar on another sheet of paper.
- The overcollar must be 0.3-0.5 cm / 0.12-0.20" wider than the undercollar, to hide the seam.

Back

- Draw the slit on the bottom in the measurement desired.
- Taper the waist at the side like the front and centre back by the desired amount (in this case 2 cm / 0.79").

KIMONO COAT
SHAWL COLLAR WITH FUR

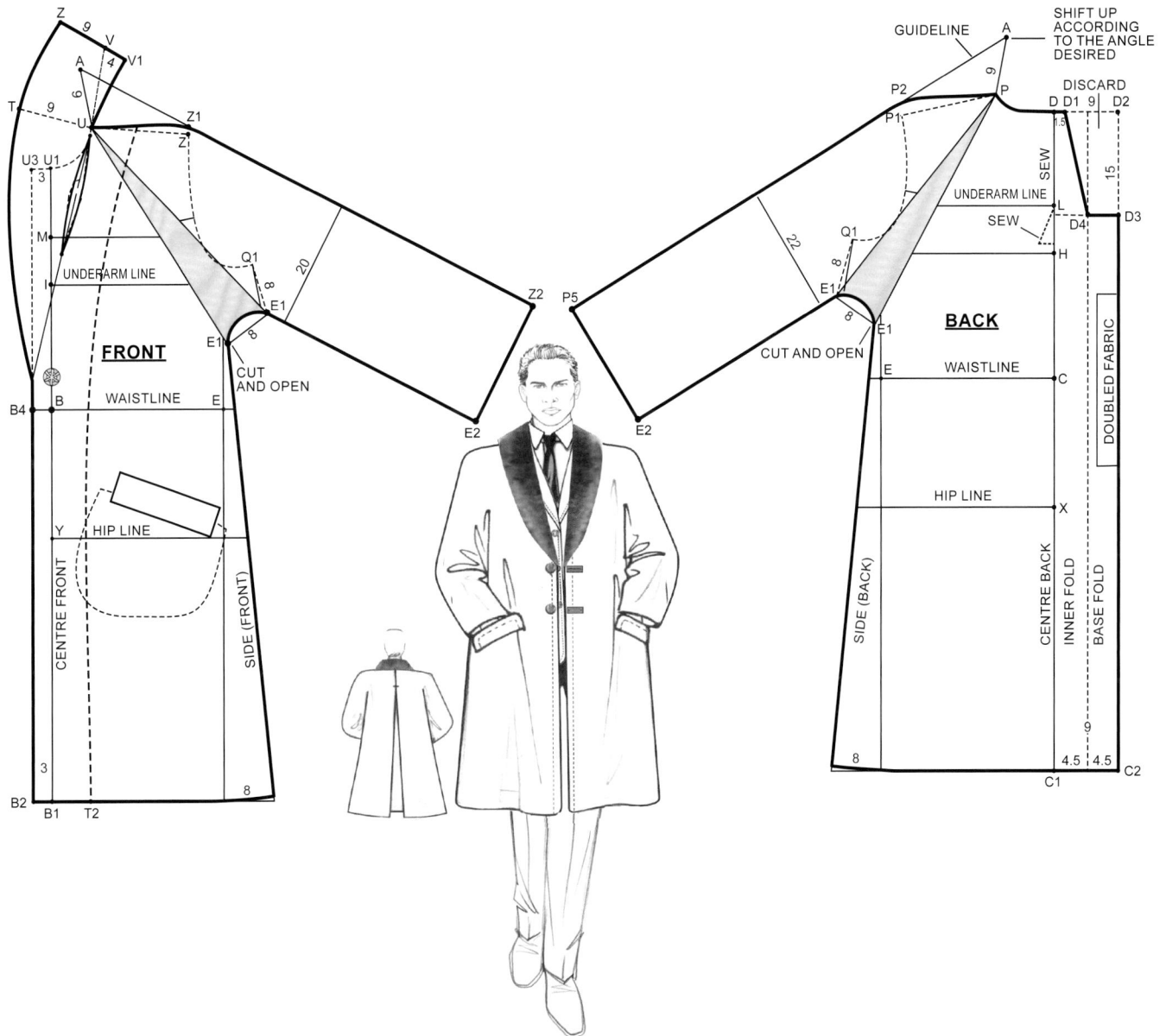

Draw the base of the coat and divide the front and back base blocks.

Back

- From point P draw a perpendicular line with its height from 9 to 12 cm / 3.54-4.72".
- From A, passing through P2 at 1-1.5 cm / 0.39-0.59" from P1, draw the straight line A-P5.
- P2-P5 in the length of the sleeve from the shoulder point.
- From point Q1, drop down 6-12 cm / 2.36-4.72" to point E1 (in this case 8 cm / 3.15").
- Draw diagonal line P-E1.
- Draw E1-E2 parallel to P2-P5.
- Draw cuff P5-E2 and adjust the width.
- Cut along diagonal line E1-P, open as required by the pattern (e.g. 8 cm / 3.15") and join the separated parts with a curved line.
- Draw the inverted pleat as in the figure.

Front

- From U, draw a perpendicular line from 9 to 12 cm / 3.54-4.72" long, like the back.
- From A, passing through Z at1 1-1.5 cm / 0.39-0.59" from Z, draw a straight line A-Z2.
- Z1-Z2 sleeve length from the shoulder point, like the back.
- From point Q1 drop down 6-12 cm / 2.36-4.72" (in this case 8 cm / 3.15" like the back) and draw point E1.
- Draw diagonal line U-E1.
- Draw E1-E2 parallel to Z1-Z2.
- Draw the cuff Z2-E2 square with Z1-Z2, adjusting the width with 2 cm / 0.79" less than the back.
- Cut along the diagonal line E1-U, open like the back according to the requirement of the pattern (e.g.: 8 cm / 3.15" like the back) and join the separated parts with a curved line.
- Check the pattern by overlapping the front on the back.
- Draw the shawl collar as shown in the figure.

RAGLAN-SLEEVE COAT

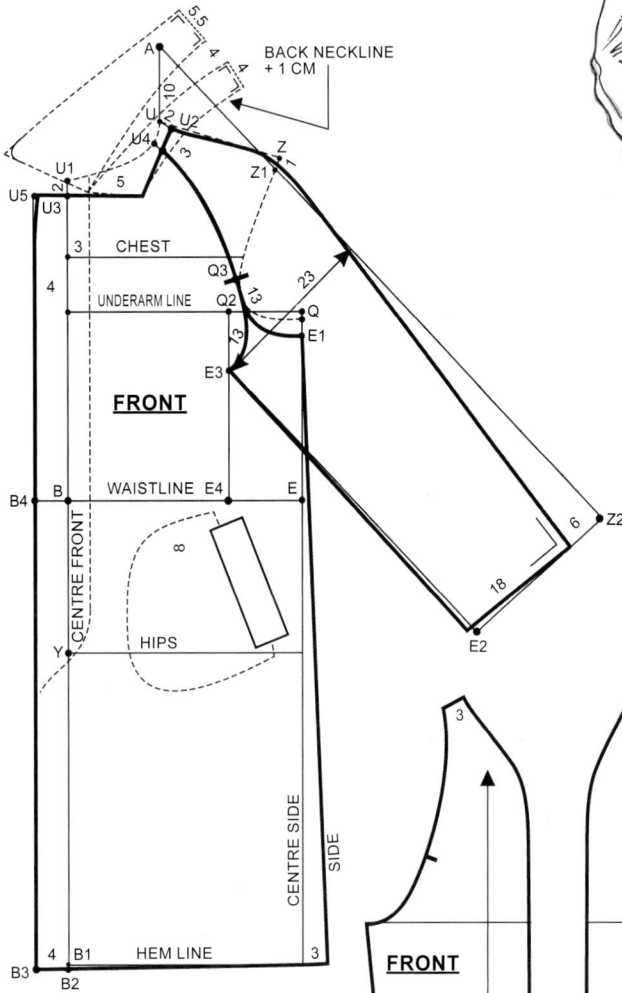

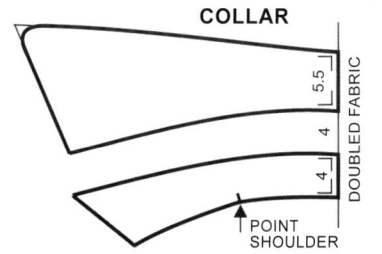

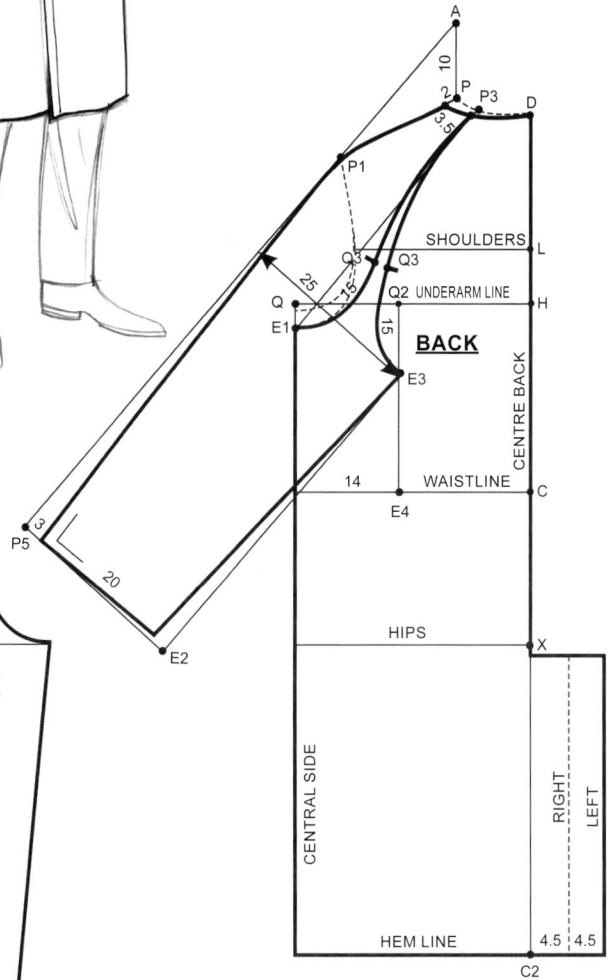

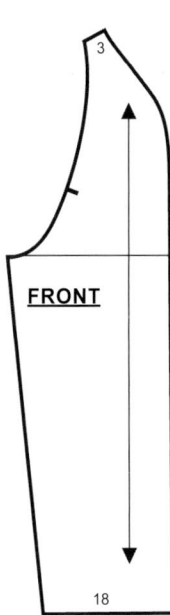

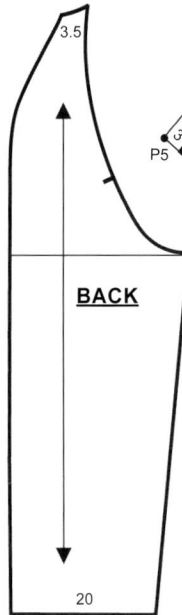

COLLAR

FRONT

BACK

FRONT **BACK**

- Draw the overcoat base pattern with appropriate ease, and with the desired neckline and length.
- Lower the armscye as desired (3-7 cm / 1.18-2.76").

FRONT

- U-A = 10 cm / 3.94" (or another measurement, depending on the desired angle).
- Z-Z1 = 1 cm / 0.39".
- Draw A-Z1-Z2.
- Z1-Z2 arm length from the shoulder point (62 cm / 24.41").
- Q-Q2 and E-E4 = 10 cm / 3.94".
- Draw Q2-E4.
- U-U4 = 3 cm / 1.18".
- E1-Q3 = 13 cm / 5.12".
- Q3-E3 like Q3-E1.
- Draw the curved lines E1-Q3-U4 and E3-Q3-E4.
- Draw the desired sleeve length and width.

BACK

- P-A like U-A. Draw A-P1-P5 like A-Z2 of the front.
- Q-Q2 = 14 cm / 5.51" (back sleeve width 2 cm / 0.79" more than the front).
- Draw Q2-E4.
- P-P3 = 3.5 cm / 1.38".
- Q3-E1 = 15 cm / 5.91".
- Q3-E3 like Q3-E1.
- Draw the curved lines P3-Q3-E1 and P3-Q3-E3.
- Draw the sleeve length like the front and the width 2 cm / 0.79" more than the front, as illustrated in the figure.
- Adjust the cuff of the sleeve.
- Copy the parts and place them on the straight of the grain.

DOUBLE-BREASTED RAGLAN-SLEEVE OVERCOAT

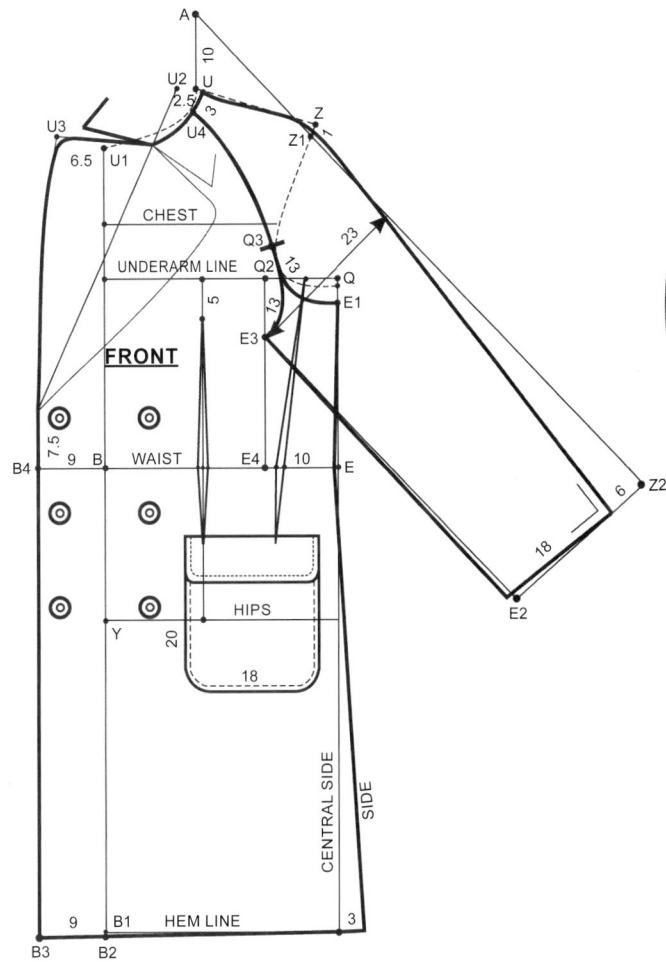

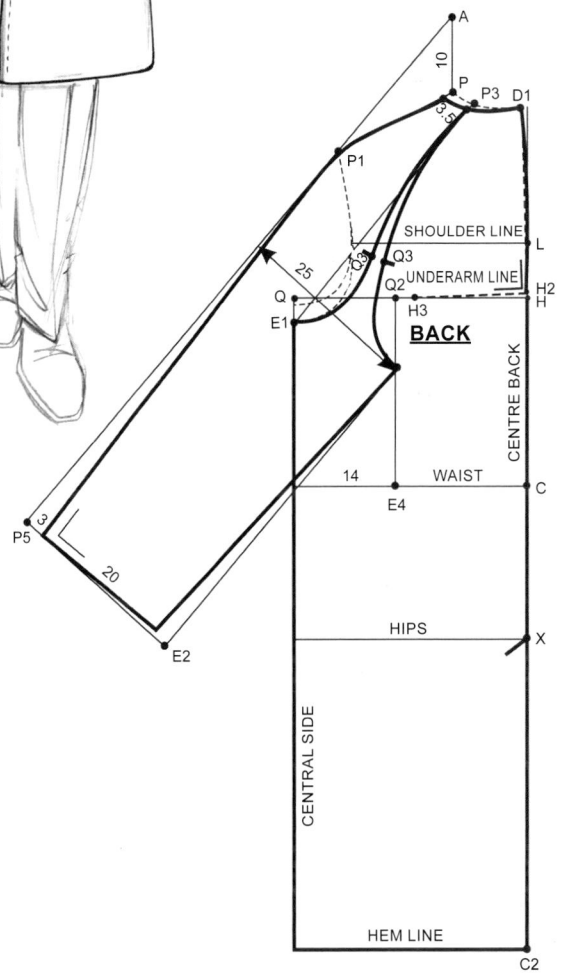

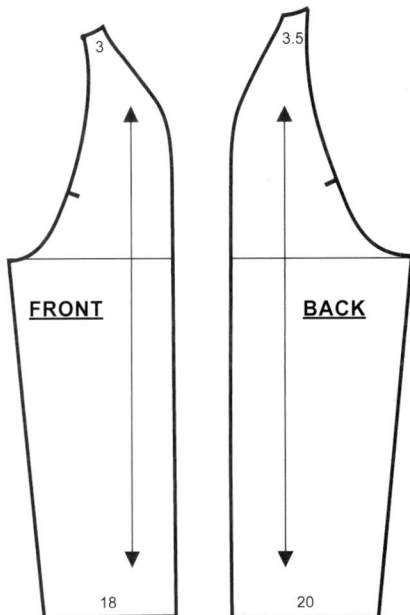

- Draw the base of the double-breasted overcoat with adequate ease and the neckline, lapels and length desired.
- Lower the armscye as required (3-7 cm / 1.18-2.76").
- Draw raglan sleeve in the desired angle and shape.

OVERCOAT WITH DEEP ARMSCYES

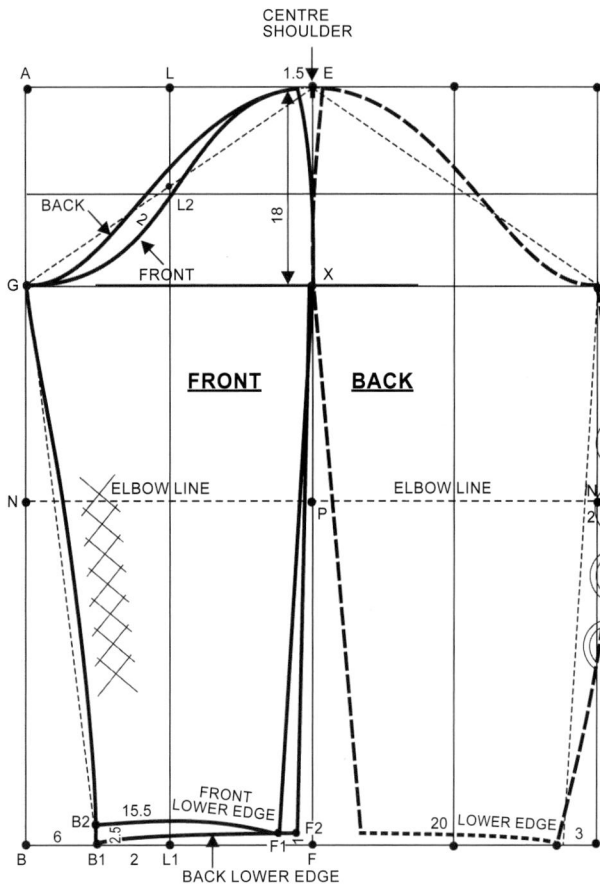

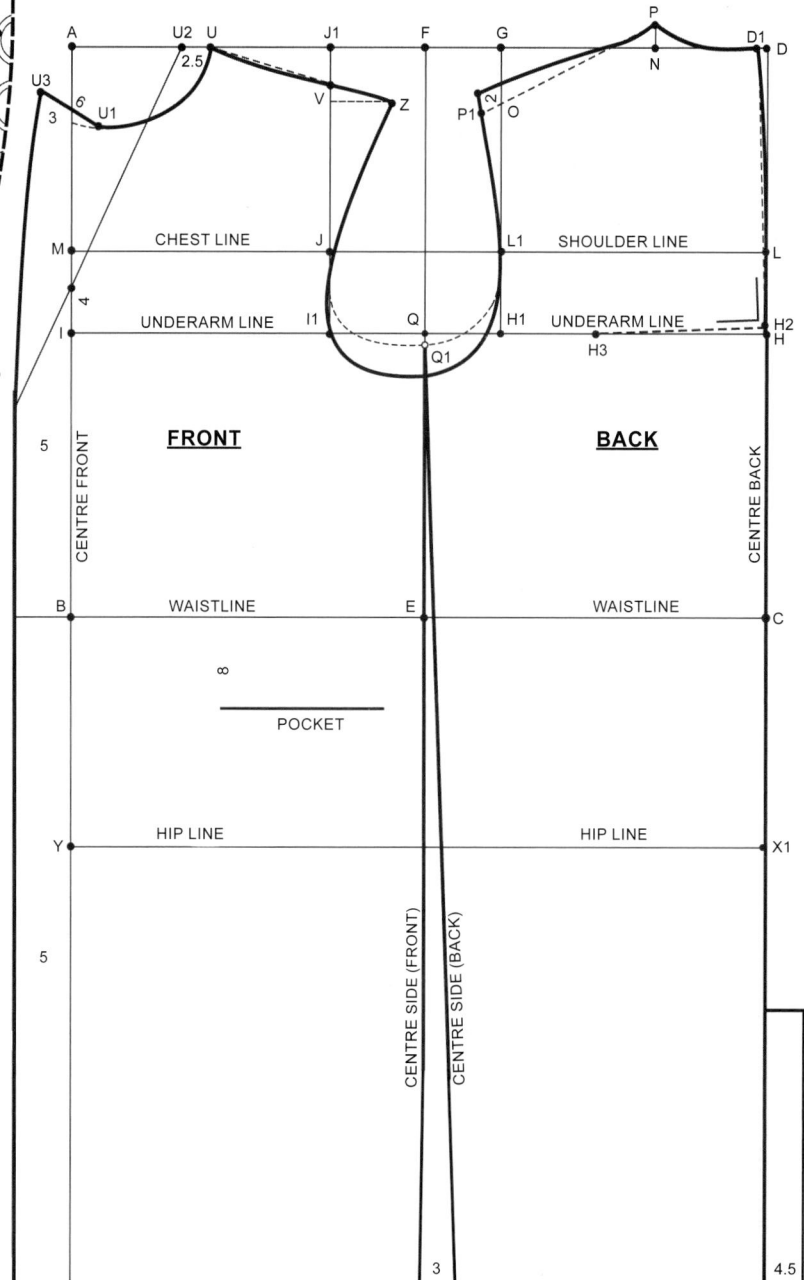

- Draw the base of the Chesterfield with suitable measurements and ease.
- Lower the underarm level as desired.
- Raise the back shoulder point by 1.5-2 cm / 0.59-0.79".

Sleeve with a central seam

- Draw the rectangle A-B-E-F with:
- A-B sleeve length + 2 cm / 0.79" (e.g.: 60 + 2 = 62 cm / 24.41").
- A-E equal to the measurement of the bodice sector + 1/2 of that same sector (e.g.: sector + 2.5 cm / 1" ease (e.g.: sector 16 + 8 = 24 + 2.5 = 26.5 cm / 10.43").
- A-G like L1-P1 on the bodice + 2 cm / 0.79" (18 cm / 7.09").
- Draw G-X. Join G-E with a diagonal line.
- A-N half of A-B + 2 cm / 0.79".
- Join N-P.
- A-L half of A-E.
- Draw L-L1.
- L2 half of G-E.
- Draw E-G at the back as in the figure.
- Draw E-G at the front as in the figure.
- B1-F2 = sleeve width.
- B2-F1 = 2-2.5 cm / 0.79-1" (adjust the bottom width).
- Copy the front and back sleeve and draw the full sleeve as in the figure.

MACKINTOSH BASE BLOCK

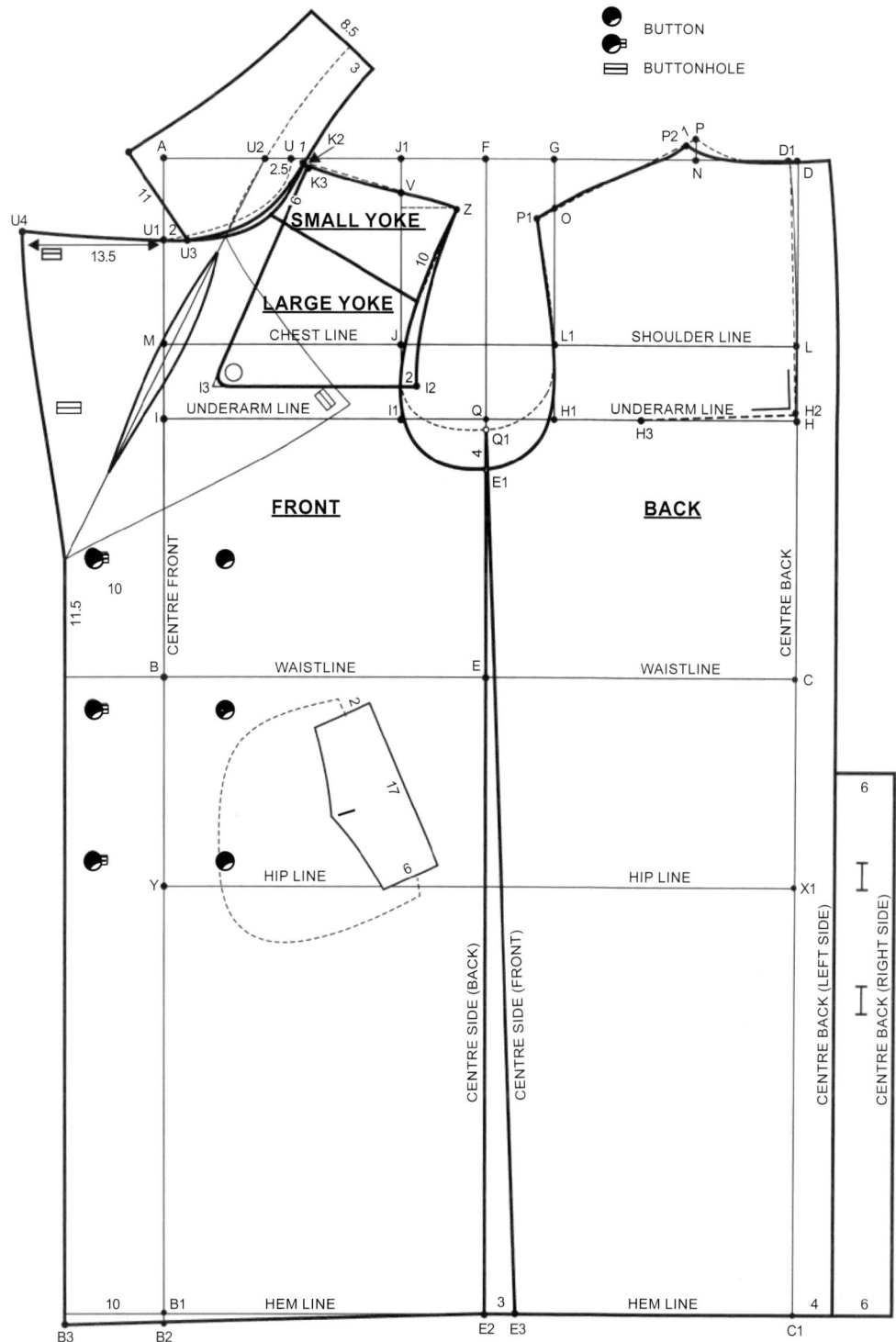

● BUTTON

▭ BUTTONHOLE

SMALL YOKE

LARGE YOKE

CHEST LINE

SHOULDER LINE

UNDERARM LINE

UNDERARM LINE

FRONT

BACK

CENTRE FRONT

CENTRE BACK

WAISTLINE

WAISTLINE

HIP LINE

HIP LINE

CENTRE SIDE (BACK)

CENTRE SIDE (FRONT)

CENTRE BACK (LEFT SIDE)

CENTRE BACK (RIGHT SIDE)

HEM LINE

HEM LINE

- Draw the base of the loose-fitting overcoat, with ease for a 'mackintosh' (see the ease chart).
- Lower the armscye by 3-4 cm / 1.18-1.57", create the desired length and flare slightly on the lower side.

Back

- For the right back, extend the Centre Back by 4 cm / 1.57" from top to bottom.
- For the left back, add another 5-6 cm / 2-2.36" for the inverted pleat, from the bottom to the hips.
- P-P2 = 1 cm / 0.39".

Front

- Extend the centre front for the fastening (double-breasted: 10 cm / 3.94").
- Draw the lapels with the desired width and depth.
- U-K2 like P-P2.
- Draw the collar in the desired shape and size.
- Draw the front yoke K3-I3-I2-Z-K3, extending it over the armscye (point I2) by 1.5-2 cm / 0.59-0.79" for freedom of movement.
- Draw the pocket according to the style of garment.

MACKINTOSH
WITH A FRONT AND BACK YOKE

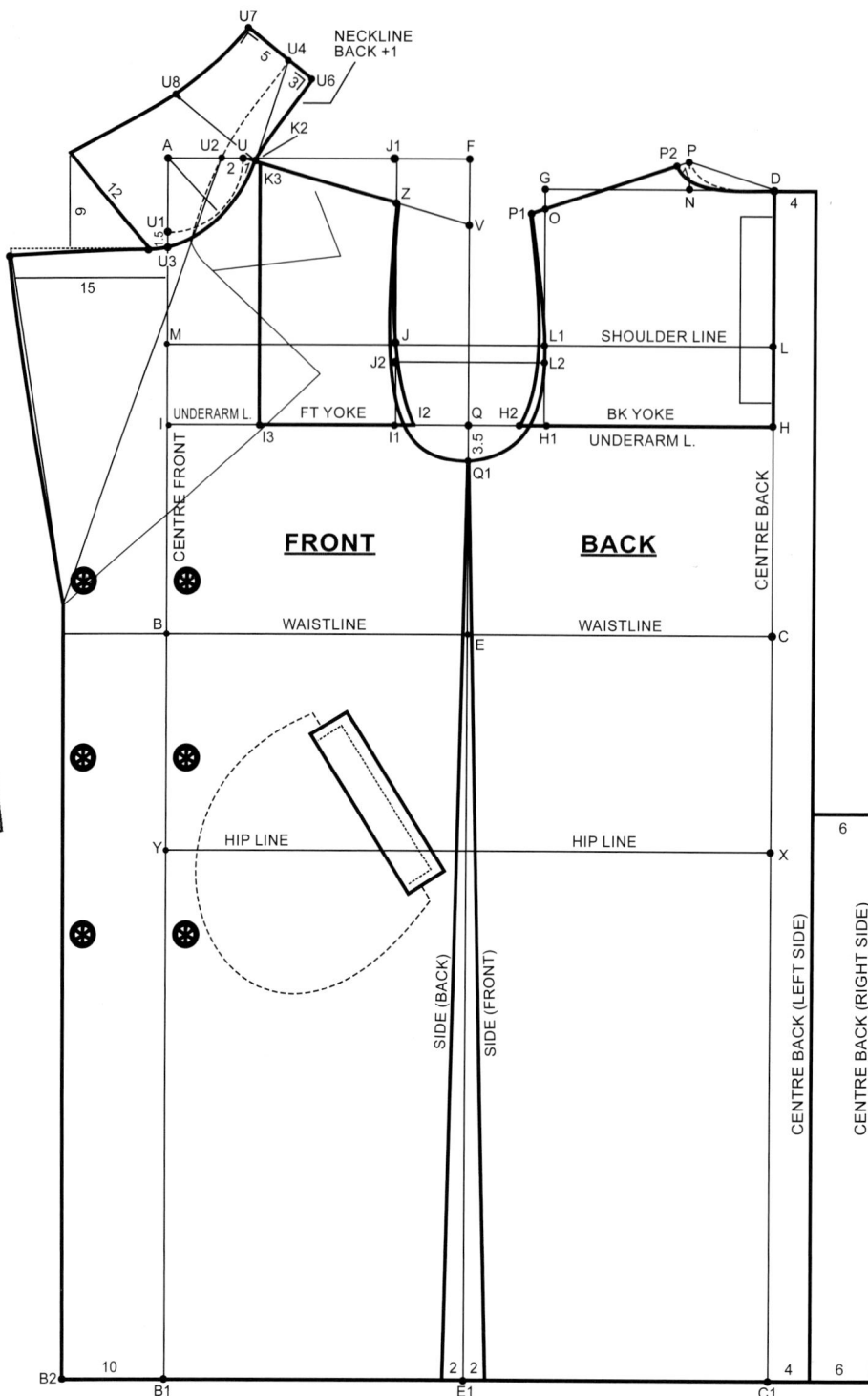

Diagram labels (front/back pattern):

NECKLINE BACK +1

FRONT · BACK

CENTRE FRONT · CENTRE BACK

UNDERARM L. · FT YOKE · BK YOKE · SHOULDER LINE · UNDERARM L.

WAISTLINE · WAISTLINE

HIP LINE · HIP LINE

SIDE (BACK) · SIDE (FRONT)

CENTRE BACK (LEFT SIDE) · CENTRE BACK (RIGHT SIDE)

- Draw the base of the loose-fitting overcoat without darts, and with the ease for a 'mackintosh' (see the ease chart). Lower the armscye by 3-3.5 cm / 1.18-1.38", create the desired length and flare slightly on the lower side.

Back
- For the left back, extend the centre back by 4 cm / 1.57" from top to bottom.
- For the back right, add another 5-6 cm / 2-2.36" for the inverted pleat, from the hem to the hips.
- P-P2 = 1 cm / 0.39".
- Create the back yoke D-H-H2-P1-P2-D, in the desired height, extending it over the armscye (point H2) by 1-1.5 cm / 0.59-0.79" for freedom of movement.

Front
- Extend the centre front for the fastening (double-breasted: 10 cm / 3.94").
- Draw the lapels with the desired width and depth.
- U-K2 like P-P2.
- Draw the collar in the desired shape and size.
- Draw the front yoke K3-I3-I2-Z-K3, extending it over the armscye (point I2) by 1-1.5 cm / 0.39-0.59" for freedom of movement.
- Draw the pocket according to the style of garment.

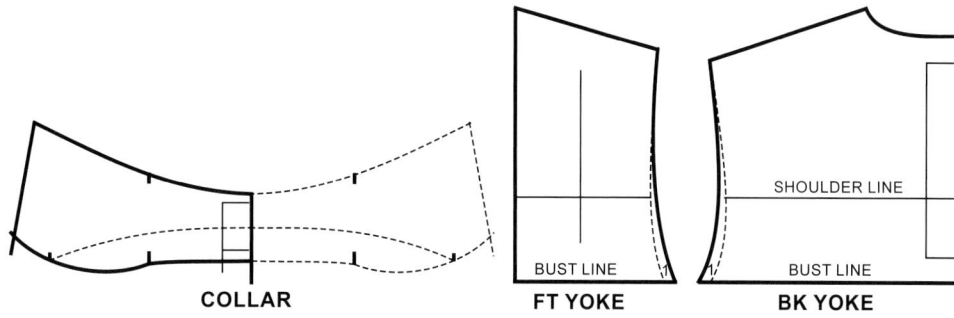

COLLAR

FT YOKE

BK YOKE

SHOULDER LINE

BUST LINE

BUST LINE

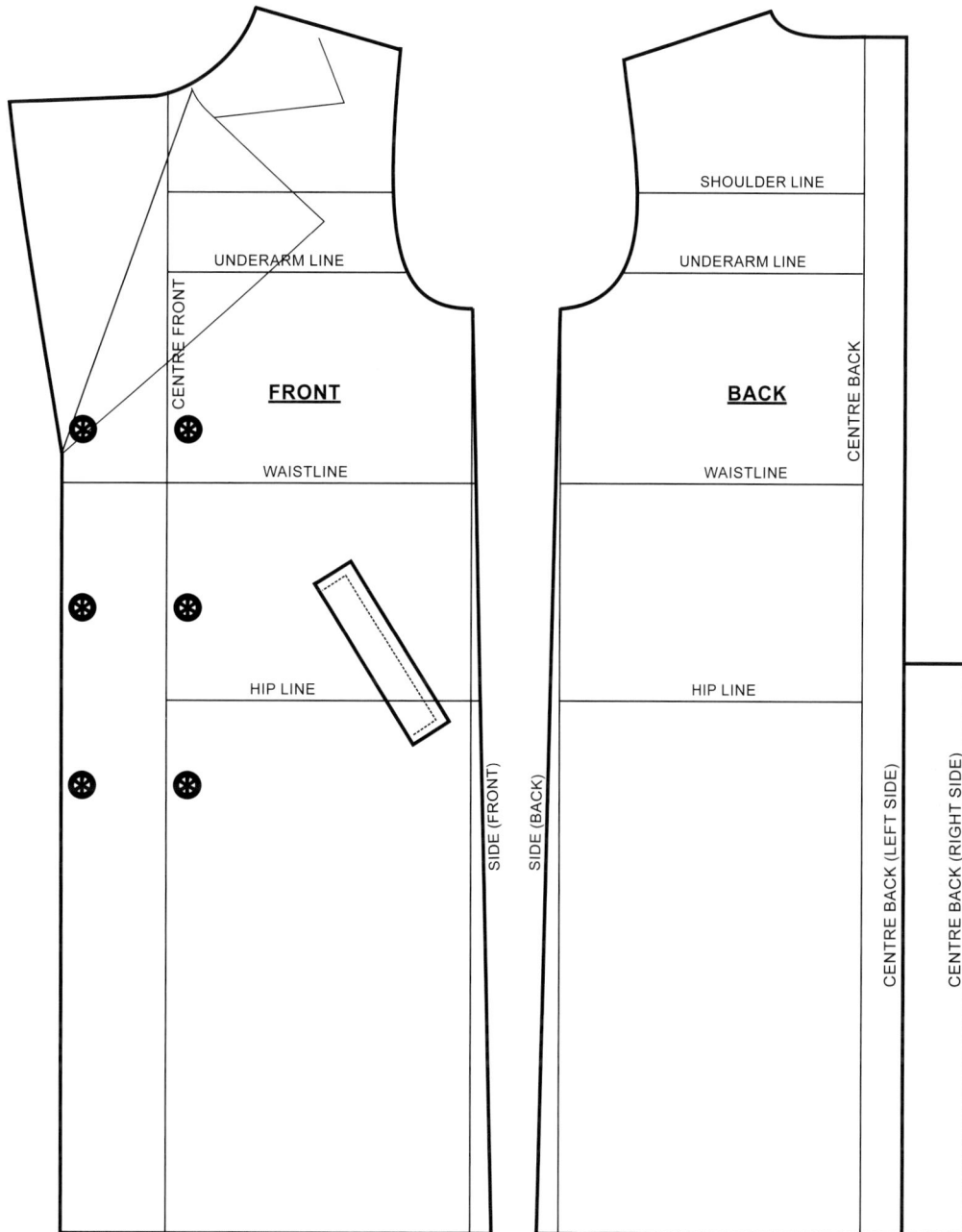

SHOULDER LINE

UNDERARM LINE

UNDERARM LINE

CENTRE FRONT

FRONT

BACK

CENTRE BACK

WAISTLINE

WAISTLINE

HIP LINE

HIP LINE

SIDE (FRONT)

SIDE (BACK)

CENTRE BACK (LEFT SIDE)

CENTRE BACK (RIGHT SIDE)

MACKINTOSH INSET SLEEVE

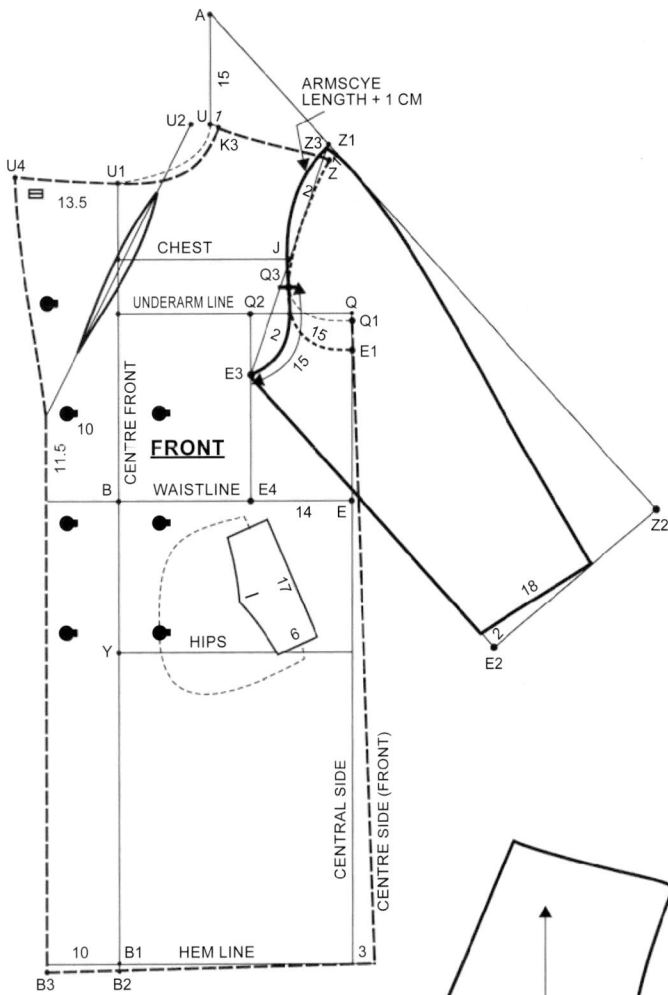

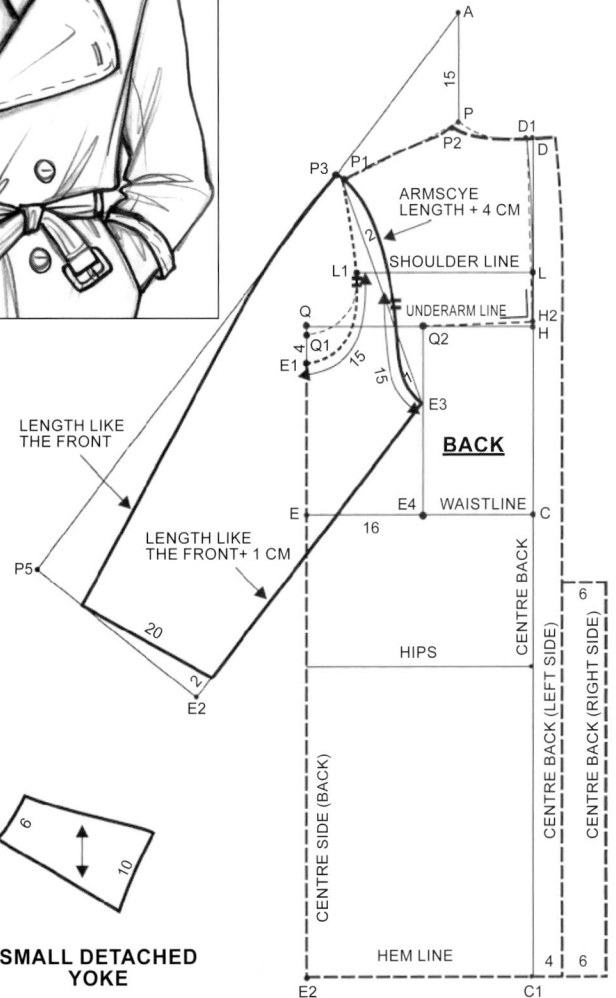

LARGE DETACHED YOKE

SMALL DETACHED YOKE

Front

- U-A= 15 cm / 5.91".
- Z-Z1 = 1 cm / 0.39".
- Draw A-Z1-Z2.
- Z1-Z3 = 1 cm / 0.39".
- Z3-Z2 equal to the arm length (62 cm / 24.41").
- Q-Q2 and E-E4 = 14 cm / 5.51"; draw Q2-E4.
- Draw the curved line Z3-E3 with a measurement equal to that of the front armscye + 1 cm / 0.39".
- E3-E2 parallel to A-Z2.
- Sleeve cuff 18 cm / 7.09" or as desired, as shown in the figure.

Back

- P-A like U-A (15 cm / 5.91"); P-P2 = 1 cm / 0.39".
- Draw A-P3-P5.
- P3-P5 like Z3-Z2.
- Q-Q2 = 16 cm / 6.30" (2 cm / 0.79" more than the front).
- Draw Q2-E4.
- Draw the curved line P3-E3, equal to the rear armscye length + 3-4 cm / 1.18-1.57".
- E3-E2 parallel to A-P5.
- Adjust the cuff to 20 cm / 7.87" (2 cm / 0.79" more than the front), as shown in the figure.

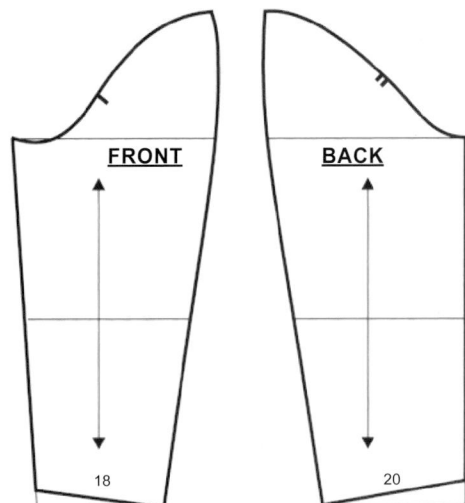

LODEN OVERCOAT

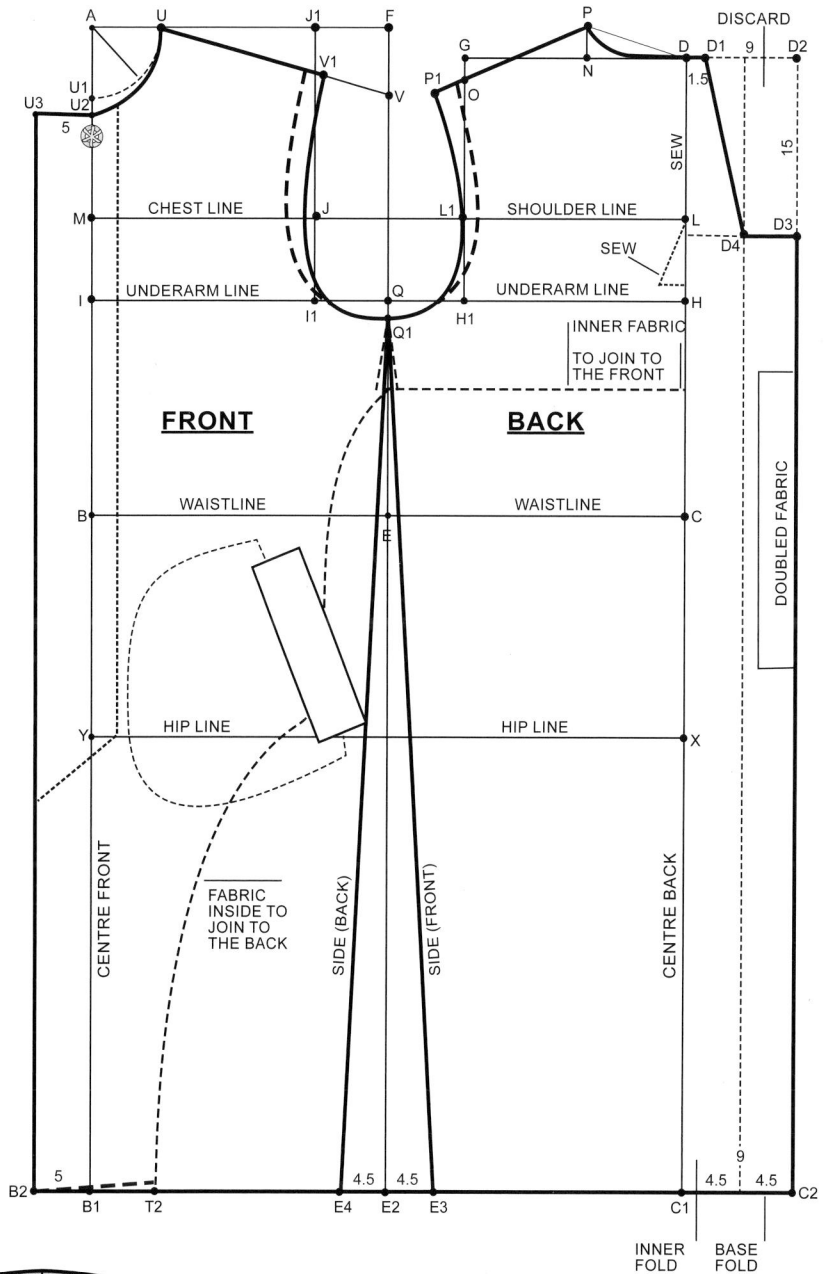

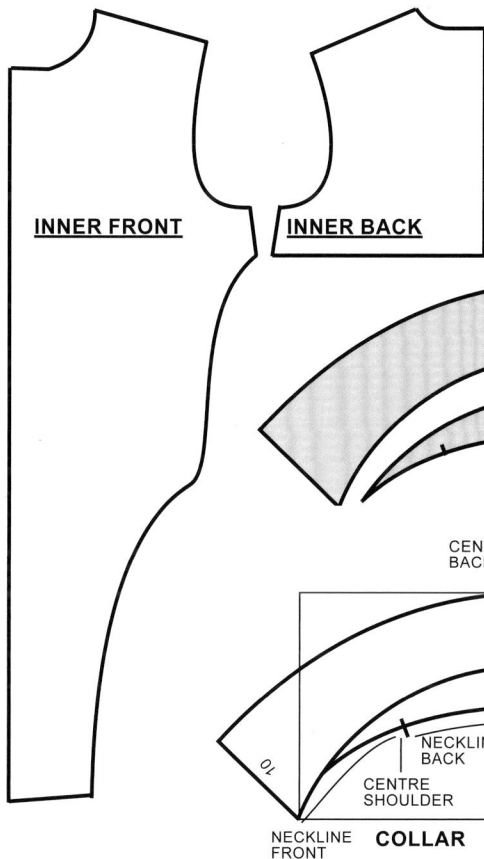

INNER FRONT **INNER BACK**

FRONT **BACK**

CHEST LINE SHOULDER LINE

UNDERARM LINE UNDERARM LINE

INNER FABRIC
TO JOIN TO
THE FRONT

WAISTLINE WAISTLINE

HIP LINE HIP LINE

CENTRE FRONT

SIDE (BACK)

SIDE (FRONT)

CENTRE BACK

DOUBLED FABRIC

DISCARD

SEW

SEW

FABRIC
INSIDE TO
JOIN TO
THE BACK

INNER
FOLD

BASE
FOLD

CENTRE
BACK

NECKLINE
BACK

CENTRE
SHOULDER

NECKLINE
FRONT

COLLAR

Measurements: size 48, as in the chart.
Loose-fitting coat ease.

- Draw the loose-fitting overcoat base pattern.
- U2-U3 = 5 cm / 2"; B1-B2 like U2-U3 (front overlap).
- D-D2 = 9 cm / 3.54"; C1-C2 like D-D2 (rear inverted pleat).
- E2-E3 = 4.5 cm / 1.77"; E2-E4 as E2-E3 (side flare).
- D2-D3 = 15 cm / 5.91"; D-D1 = 1.5 cm / 0.59".
- Sew the back piece D-L and discard D1-D4-D3-D2-D1.
- Create the patterns of the linings and facings as in the figure.

231

DUFFEL COAT

SLEEVE WITH A CENTRAL SEAM

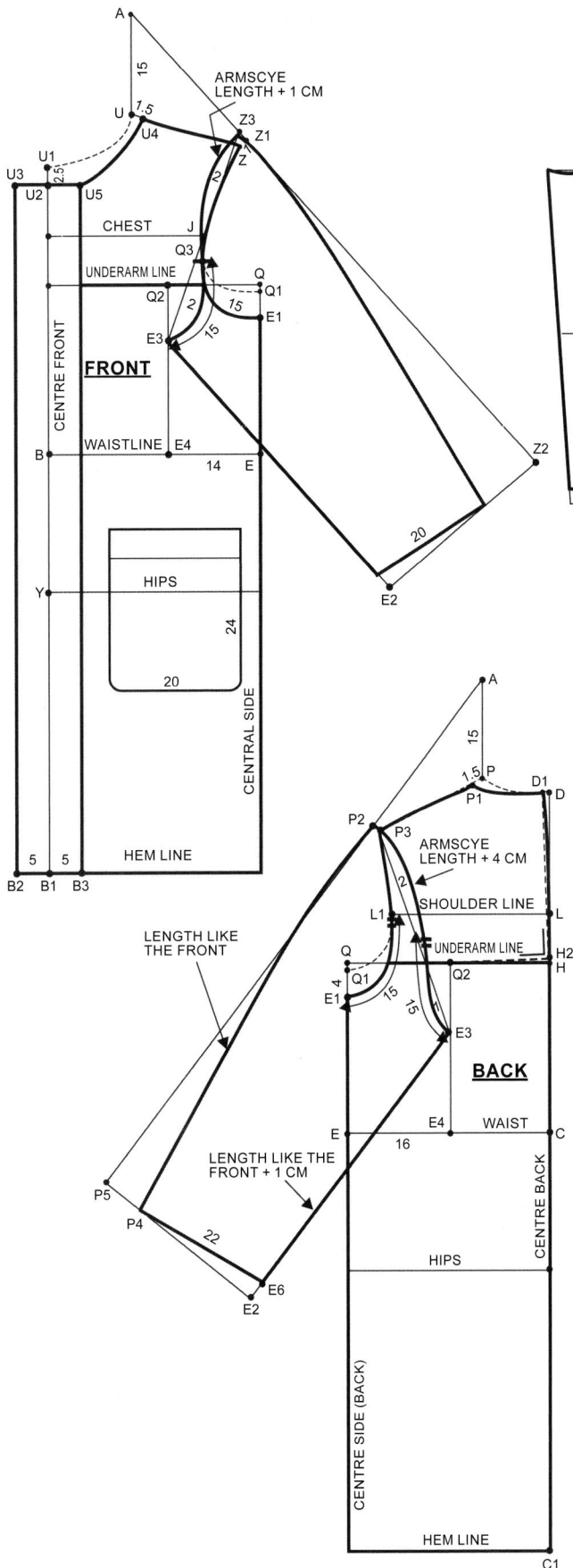

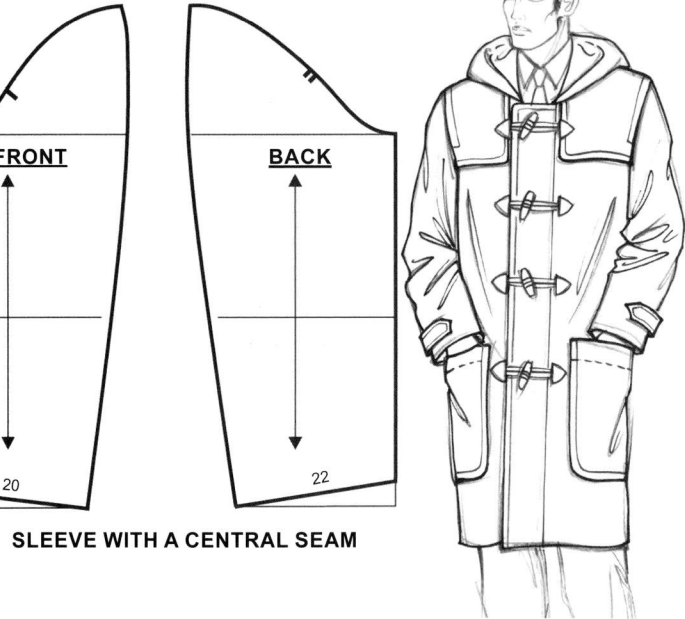

- Draw the base of the loose-fitting overcoat with 30-34 cm / 11.81-13.39" ease.
- Draw the extension of the overlap U3-B2.
- Draw the line of the yoke in the desired size and shape.
- U1-U2 = 2-2.5 cm / 0.79-1"; U2-U3 = 5 cm / 2".
- U3-U5 = 10 cm / 3.94".
- Draw U3-B2-B3-U5.
- U-U4 = 1.5 cm / 0.59".
- P-P3 at the back = 1.5 cm / 0.59".
- Draw U4-Z and P3-P2.
- Q-E1 = 4 cm / 1.57" or as desired, depending on the style of the garment.
- Draw the pocket as desired.

Front

- U-A = raise by 12-15 cm / 4.72-5.91".
- Z-Z1 = 1 cm / 0.39"; Z1-Z3 = 1 cm / 0.39".
- Draw A-Z1-Z2.
- Z3-Z2 = the length of the sleeve from the shoulder centre.
- Q-Q2 and E-E4 = 9.5 cm / 3.74". Draw Q2-E4.
- Draw the curved line Z3-E3 with a measurement equal to that of the front armscye + 1 cm / 0.39".
- E3-E2 parallel to A-Z2.
- Adjust the cuff to 20 cm / 7.87" or as desired.

Back

- P-A like U-A; P2-P1 = 1 cm / 0.39". Draw A-P2-P5.
- P2-P5 like Z1-Z2.
- Q-Q2 = 11.5 cm / 4.52" (2 cm / 0.79" more than the front).
- Draw Q2-E4.
- Draw the curved line P2-E3 with a measurement equal to that of the back armscye + 3-4 cm / 1.18-1.57".
- E3-E2 parallel to A-P5.
- Adjust the cuff P4-E6 to 22 cm /8.66" (2 cm / 0.79" more than the front, as in the figure).

232

DUFFLE SLEEVE

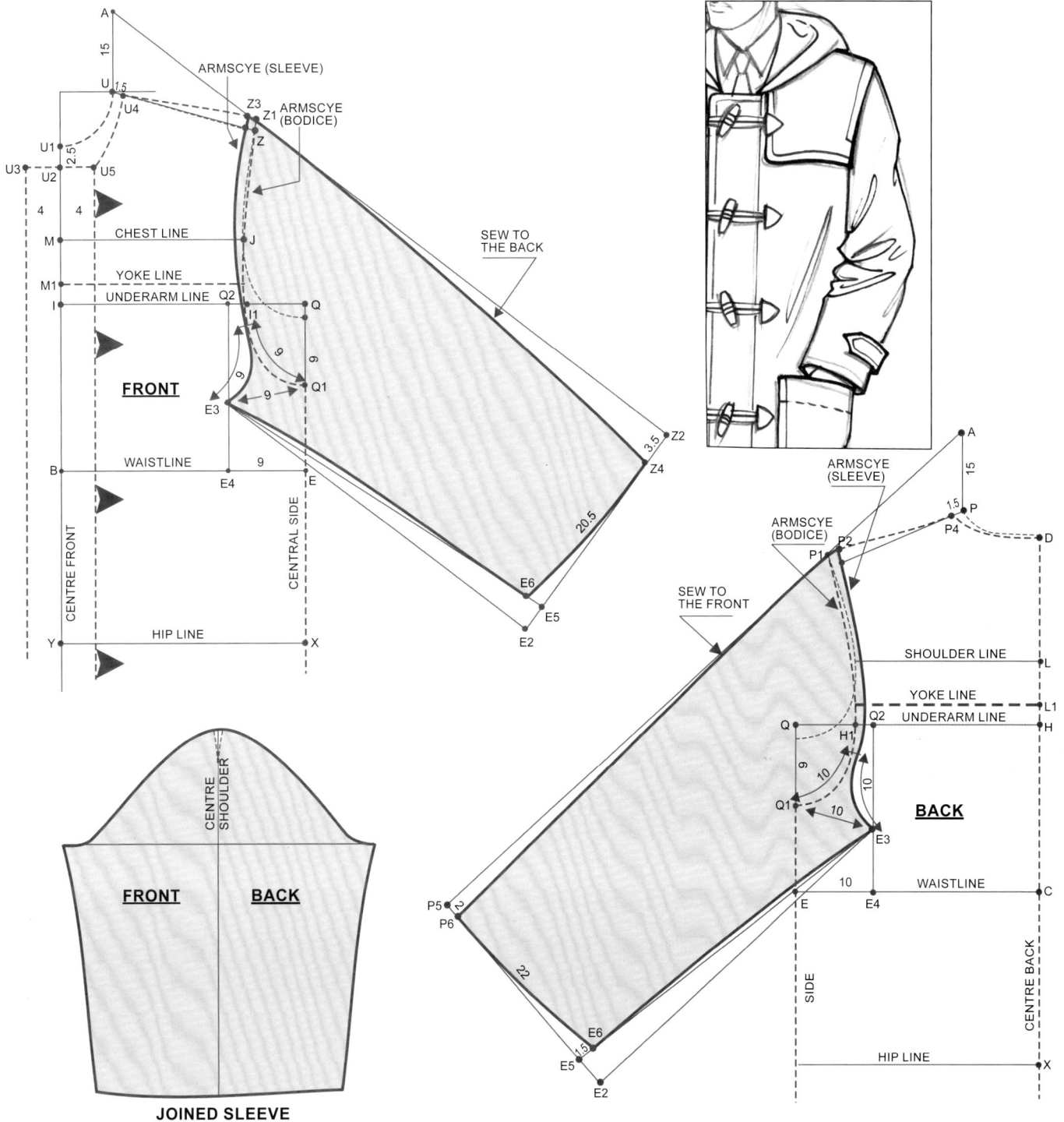

Diagram labels (Front):

A
15
ARMSCYE (SLEEVE)
U 1.5
U4 Z3 Z1 ARMSCYE (BODICE)
U1 Z
2.5
U3 U2 U5
4 4
M CHEST LINE J
M1 YOKE LINE
I UNDERARM LINE Q2 Q
I1
FRONT
9 9
9 Q1
E3 9
B WAISTLINE 9
E4 E
CENTRE FRONT
CENTRAL SIDE
SEW TO THE BACK
3.5 Z2
Z4
20.5
E6
E5
E2
Y HIP LINE X

JOINED SLEEVE
CENTRE SHOULDER
FRONT **BACK**

Diagram labels (Back):

A
15
1.5 P
ARMSCYE (SLEEVE)
ARMSCYE (BODICE)
P2 P4 D
P1
SEW TO THE FRONT
SHOULDER LINE L
YOKE LINE L1
Q Q2 UNDERARM LINE H
H1
9 10
Q1 10
E3 **BACK**
10
WAISTLINE C
P5 2
P6
E E4
22
SIDE
CENTRE BACK
E6 1.5
E5
E2
HIP LINE X

Front

- U-A = raise by 12-15 cm / 4.72-5.91".
- Draw A-ZI-Z2.
- Z-Z1 and Z1-Z3 = 1 cm / 0.39".
- Z3-Z2 equal to the sleeve length.
- Draw the curved line Z3-E3 with a length equal to Z-Q1 and with Q1-E3 = 9 cm / 3.54".
- E3-E2 parallel to A-Z2
- Z4-E5 desired cuff width (19-21 cm / 7.48-8.27").

Back

- P-A = raise by 12-15 cm / 4.72-5.91".
- Draw the straight line A-P1-P5.
- P1-P2 = 1 cm / 0.39" like the front.
- P2-P5 equal to the front sleeve length.
- Draw the curved line P2-E3 with a length equal to P1-Q1 and with Q1-E3 = 10 cm / 3.94".
- E3-E2 parallel to A-P5.
- P5-E2 width like the front + 2 cm / 0.79".
- P5-P6 = 2 cm / 0.79".
- E5-E6 = 1.5 cm / 0.59".

TECHNICAL NOTIONS

Practical three-piece sleeve construction

From a regular pattern, it is possible to create a three-piece sleeve in the following way:

Bodice
- A-A1 at the back = 1.6 cm / 0.63".
- B-B1 at the front = 1.6 cm / 0.63".

Sleeve

The sleeve, whose ideal centre is determined by point A and, precisely, by the point which normally coincides with the seam of the regular shoulder, is broken vertically up to the elbow and then, with a curved line, towards the bottom, oriented around the half-width.

- A-A1 = 1.6 cm / 0.63" (like B-B1 on the front).
- A1-A2 = 0.5 cm / 0.20".
- B-B1 = 1.6 cm / 0.63" (like A-A1 on the back).
- B1-B2 = 0.5 cm / 0.20".
- X-X1 = 2.2 cm / 0.87".
- K-K1 = 0.5 cm / 0.20" (opening).
- C-C1 = 3 cm / 1.18".
- D-D1 = 3 cm / 1.18".

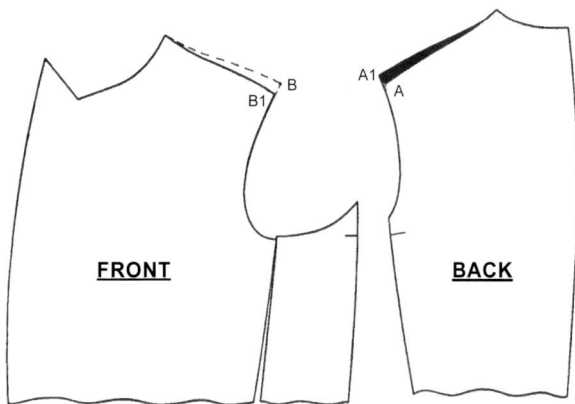

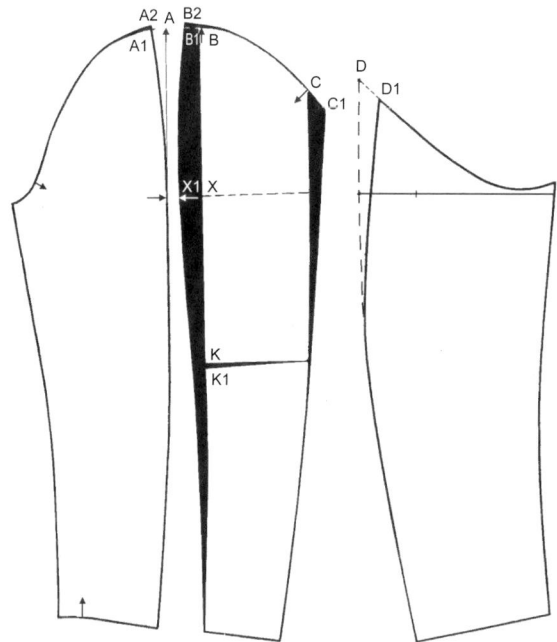

Fur collar

When a fur collar is to be fitted on a classic overcoat, it's best to adapt the pattern and garment before the try-on.

Because it is thicker than a regular collar, fur collars bulge at the neck and create notable flaws. This needs to be taken care of, first of all by establishing a larger curvature, and thus increasing the measurements.

These combined effects could also be achieved by slackening with an iron over the entire arc of the neckline. However, getting ahead of the issue and making the adjustments in the figure is the better option, as a standard neckline will already need basic slackening.

As far as the appropriate modifications are concerned, for an average fur, increase by:
- 0.3 cm / 0.12" for the opening in the centre back sector.
- 0.6 cm / 0.24" laterally.
- 0.3 cm / 0.12" on the front.

The positioning can be found below.

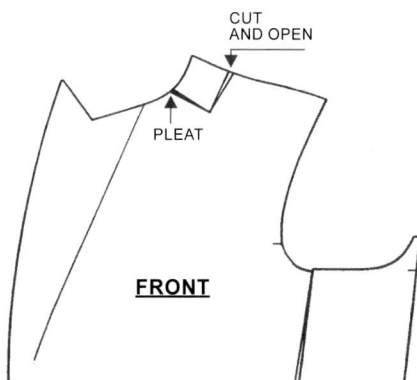

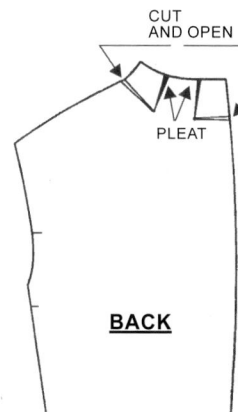

Adding a half-belt to an overcoat

Starting from a straight Chesterfield style, it is possible to easily create a classic coat with a half belt.

Logically, the result will be a pattern that, by its nature, requires special workmanship, but it will also be well equipped and functional. The transformations are clearly illustrated in the figure: the dotted lines refer to the departure (Chesterfield) pattern. In particular:

- B-B1 = 1.2 cm / 0.47". Continue parallel to the bottom. The resulting line needs to be altered from the armscye to the hem and therefore pivots on the lateral dotted line and opens at the waist as necessary.
- Then tighten by 4 cm / 1.57" parallel to the side.
- Lower the corresponding waist and hip points by 0.5 cm / 0.20".
- Elongate the lower hem by the appropriate amount. After having carefully created the two darts on the front and having enhanced the armscye detail at the underarm apex, the front will need to be extended to compensate for what was removed from the back and for that required by the seams, namely:
- P-P1 = 6.4 cm / 2.52".
- At the waist = 5.6 cm / 2.20".
- At the hip = 6.4 cm / 2.52".
- Armscye counter point shifted up by 0.7 cm / 0.28".
- From the resulting point, move up by 2.5 cm / 1" to adjust for the overlapping of the sides.

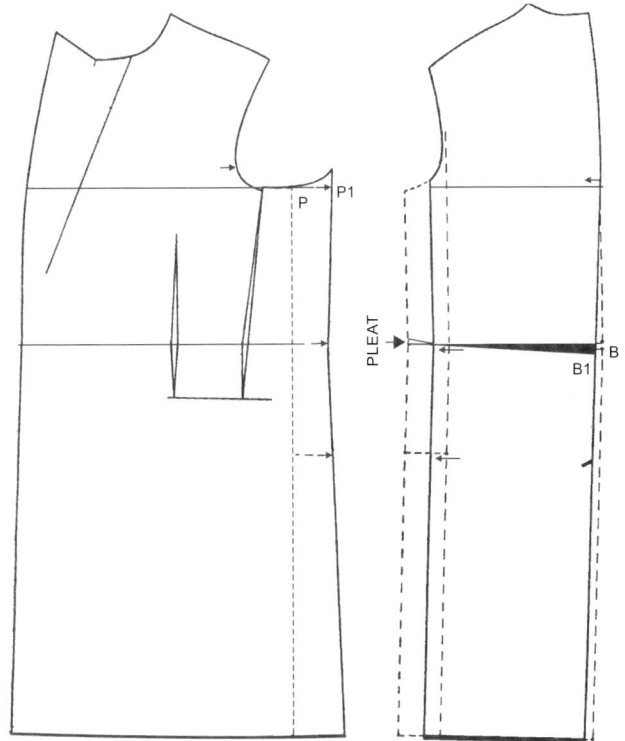

The sleeve 'tube'

Sometimes a coat may require more ease for movement on the sleeve than is normally provided.

The process shown in the figure is particularly effective because it gives the piece the harmonic movement required in this case, both for the elevation of the sleeve crown and the forward movement of the arm. The process requires two openings with pivots of equal measures, after temporarily overlapping the two parts by 1.2 cm / 0.47". The two openings allow you to raise the piece at the same time.

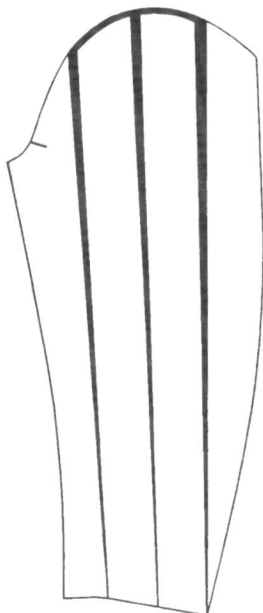

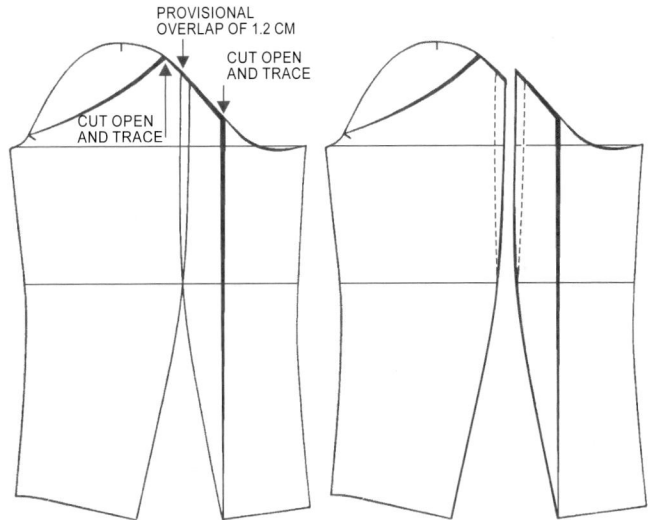

Sleeve with vertical effects

Fashion trends often feature sleeves in graceful dimensions, located on well-defined verticals, which at times are altered for stylistic reasons.

The figure depicts the details of the process and how it essentially becomes automatic, deriving from the shifting of the pieces.

The shift measurements aren't shown as they depend on the fabric. In almost all cases, however, they should be moderate. An opening of 0.5 cm / 0.20" is certainly enough, keeping in mind that you must signal the demarcation points on the fabric for every single opening. This is done so that you may then gather the greater looseness on them and re-establish the stability of the sleeve.

Increasing the arm height for raglan sleeves

This is a technical adjustment which may also be used for set-in sleeves. It corrects any possible undesired effects which may result from wearing the overcoat with a belt.

Even if not tightened excessively, a belt always gathers the width of a coat and forces it from a natural draping point to mostly converge at the waist. That means that the long, vertical lines involved (the sides for example), are effectively shortened.

A part of the length may come from the bottom, but it is obvious that one part, if we follow geometric logic, comes from the upper part - even more so if the armscye is particularly roomy.

The lengthening that comes from above acts perpendicularly and effects the sleeve. As a result, it causes a lowering and the elongation of the armscye, giving it an oval shape while blocking the movement of the sleeve.

For this reason, especially where the raglan sleeve pattern allows or requires the use of a belt, it is often necessary to modify the armscye with a riser which makes up for any possible defects.

Obviously the amount it to be shifted is calculated on a case by case basis, so not knowing exactly what the lift and the degree of tension imposed by the wearer's belt will be, we will try to be generous. In any case, the amount to be shifted must be of an equal measurement on the back and on the front.

Various widths at the bottom of split sleeves

The sleeves drop delicately from the position of the shoulders, which makes it difficult to establish the width of the cuff without respecting the movement of the meeting points of the single pieces of the sleeve.

This is true for raglan sleeves and it is true for inset sleeves with a deep armscye also.

The illustrations show the procedure for tapering the bottom in both Figure 1 and Figure 2. You will note that this variant directly involves a seam on the underarm, to which variations of the basic model are applied.

Figure 1 illustrates the procedure for tightening the bottom.
- Create a vertical cut A-B on the back and on the elbow line and overlap the bottom, opening along the underarm elbow. To aesthetically adjust the parts and balance all the effects, move the external seam, elongating the back cuff and decreasing that in the front.

Figure 2 illustrates the process which is the inverse of the elongation of the bottom.
- Create a vertical cut A-B on the back and on the elbow line. Open along the cuff, overlapping the elbow line on the under arm to increase the breadth along the hem.

In this case, the external seam does not need to be adjusted, aesthetically speaking.

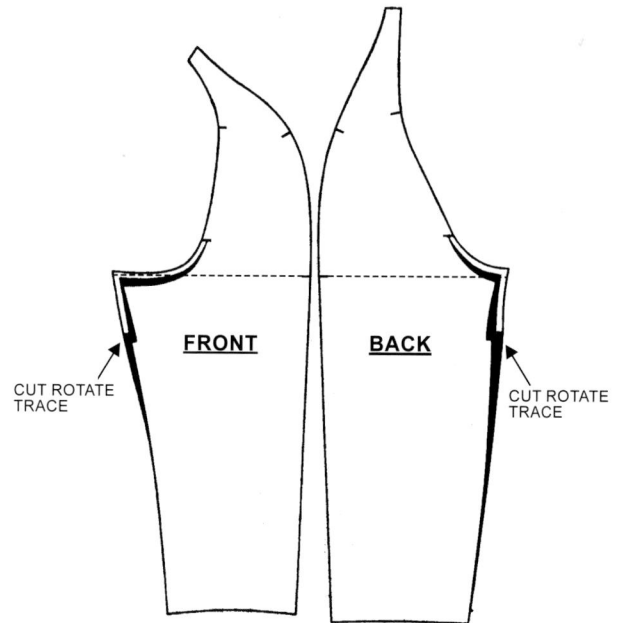

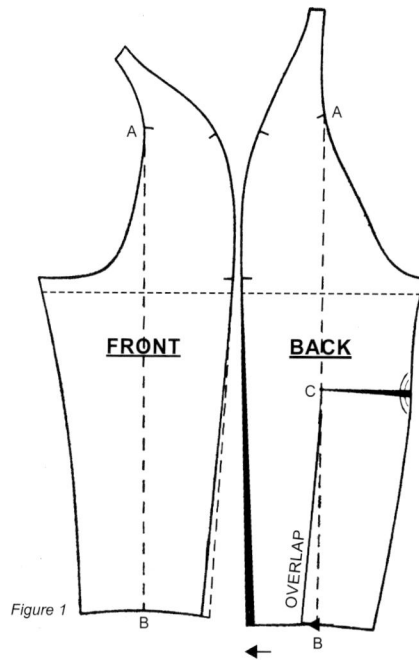

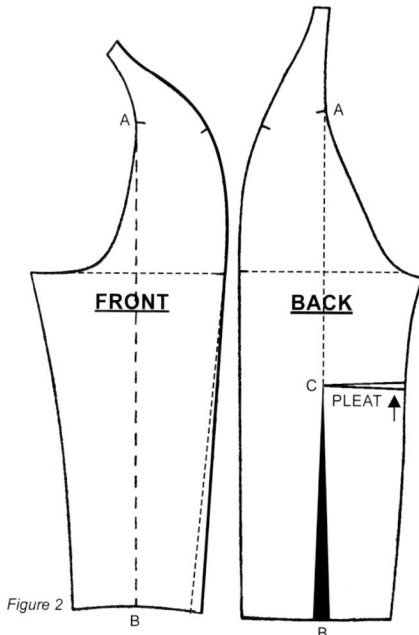

FRONT   BACK

CUT ROTATE TRACE

CUT ROTATE TRACE

Figure 1

FRONT   BACK

OVERLAP

Figure 2

FRONT   BACK

PLEAT

RAGLAN SLEEVE SEAM ALLOWANCES

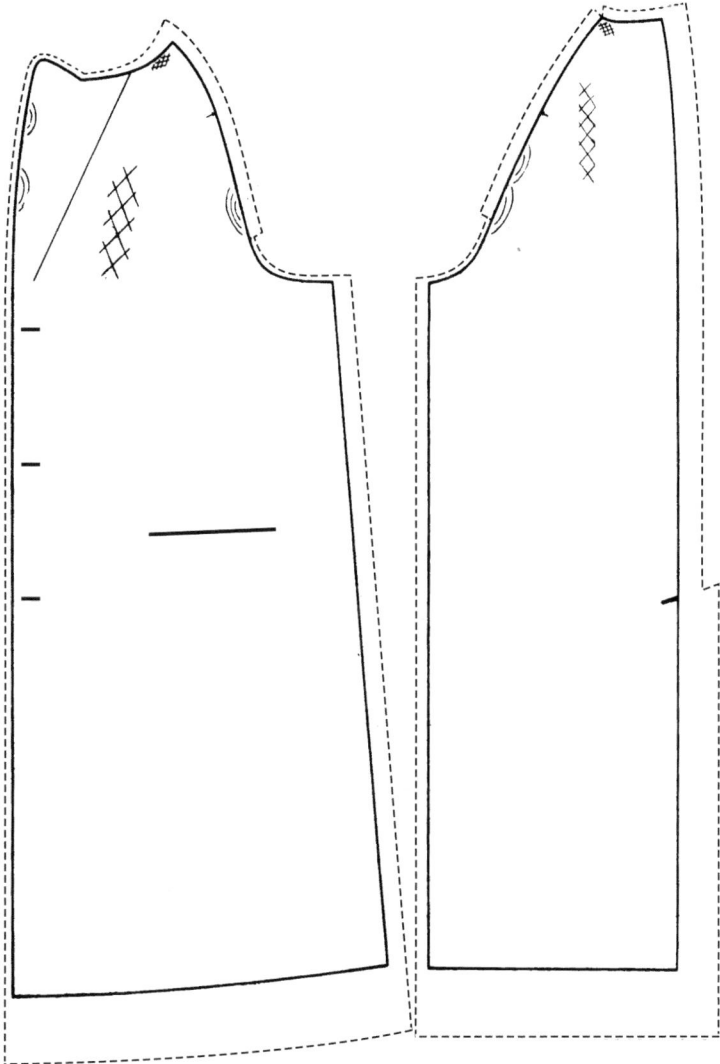

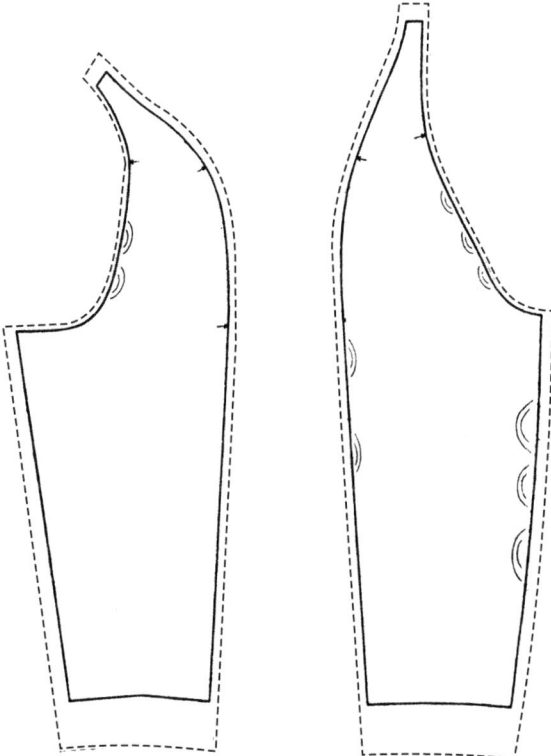

A-LINE CLOAK

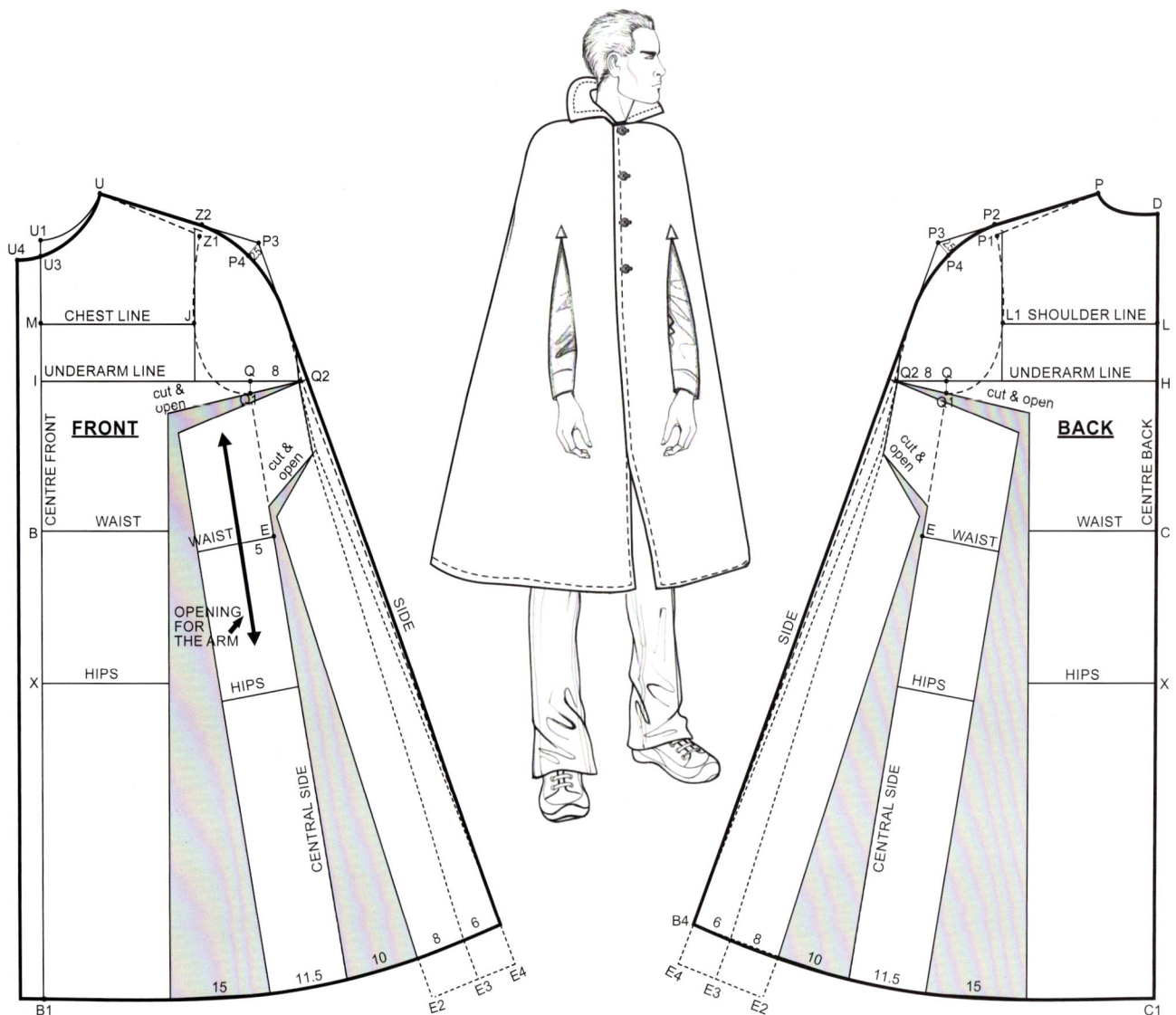

- Draw the coat base block with appropriate measurements and with the ease for a cape. Divide the back from the front on the centre-side line.

CREATE THE A-LINE SHAPE
Back
- Extend the centre-side line on the underarm level in a measurement equal to 1/4 Q-H (e.g.: 32 ÷ 4 = 8 cm / 3.15").
- Draw Q2-E3.
- Flare the bottom as desired (e.g.: 6 cm / 2.36").
- Draw Q2-E4.
- Raise point P1 by 0.5-1 cm / 0.20-0.39" (point P2).
- Extend the shoulder line P-P2.
- Extend the side line E4-Q2 until it crosses the shoulder line (point P3).
- From point P3 draw a diagonal line and mark point P4 at 4.5-5 cm / 1.77-2".
- Draw the curved line P2-P4-Q2-E4.

Front
- Q-Q2 like Q-Q2 at the back (8 cm / 3.15").
- Raise the shoulder point Z1-Z2 like at the back.
- B1-E4 like B4-C1 at the back.
- Draw the hem like the back.
- Draw the side line Z2-Q2-E4 with a curved line.
- Create the centre front extension of 3 cm / 1.18" for the fastening
- Mark the opening for the arm at 5 cm / 2" from the hip line, or as desired (e.g.: 26 cm / 10.24"), with the centre on the waistline.
- Overlap the front on the back to check that the width and curvature are equal.

A-line cloak
To add width to the lower edge, make cuts from the side line to the hem, as shown in the figure, and widen the bottom at the front and back by the same amount.

CLOAK WITH SEMI-CLOSED SLEEVES

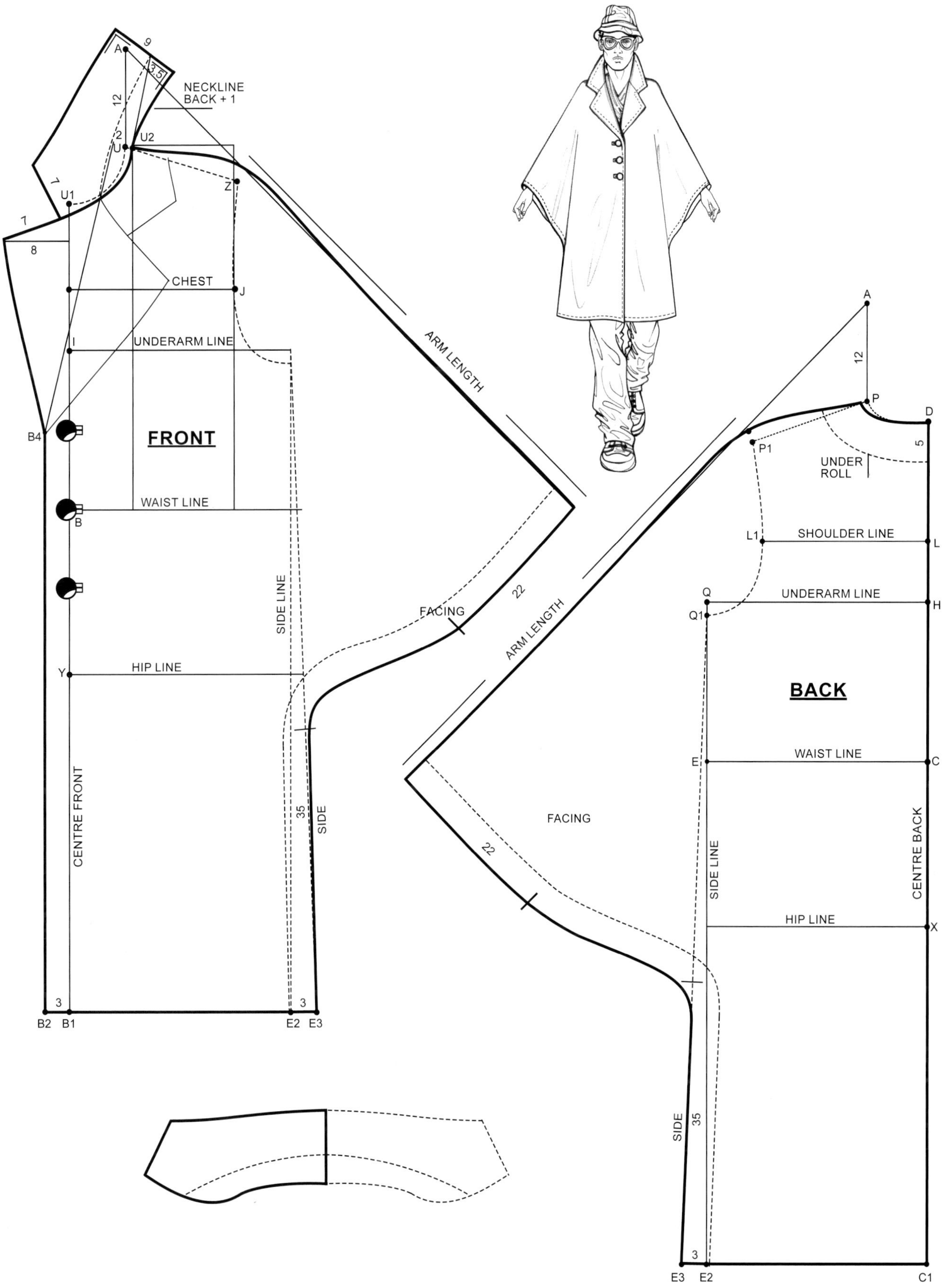

FRONT

A

9

3.5

12

NECKLINE BACK + 1

2

U U2

7

U1

7

8

Z

CHEST J

I UNDERARM LINE

B4

WAIST LINE

ARM LENGTH

SIDE LINE

FACING

22

Y HIP LINE

CENTRE FRONT

35 SIDE

3 3

B2 B1 E2 E3

BACK

A

12

P

D

5

P1

UNDER ROLL

L1 SHOULDER LINE L

Q UNDERARM LINE H

Q1

ARM LENGTH

22

E WAIST LINE C

FACING

SIDE LINE

BACK

HIP LINE X

CENTRE BACK

SIDE 35

3

E3 E2 C1

MANTLE FOR COATS

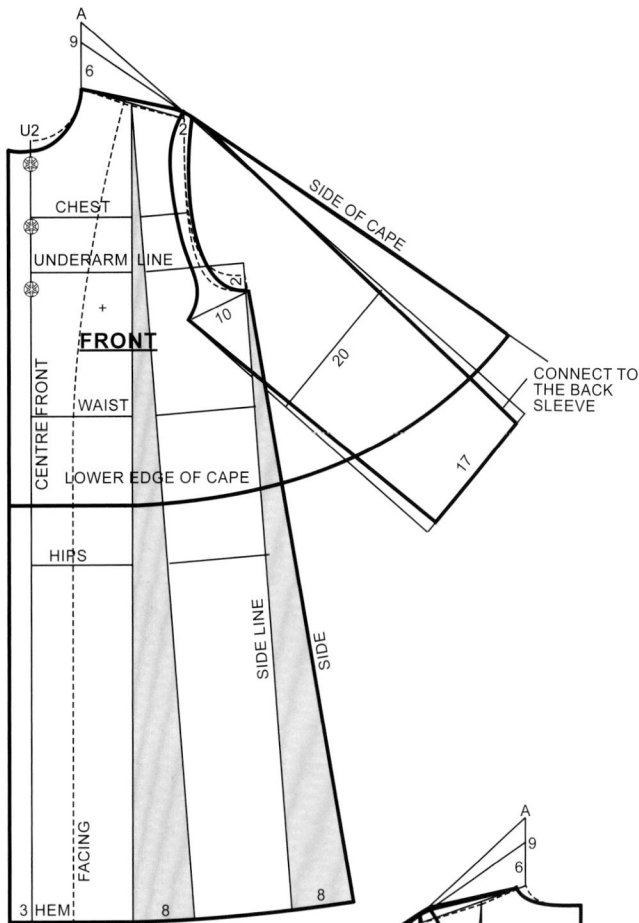

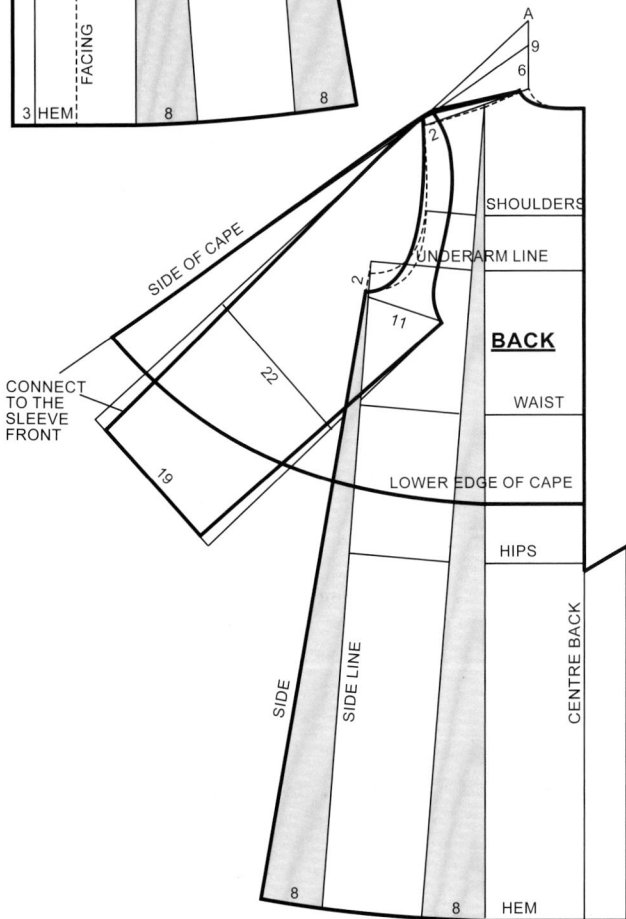

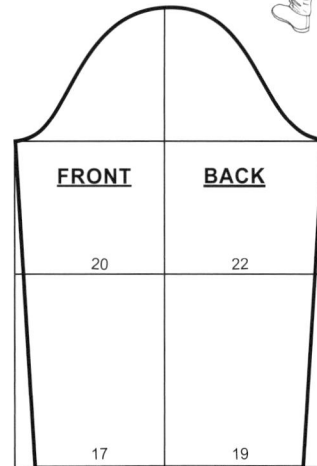

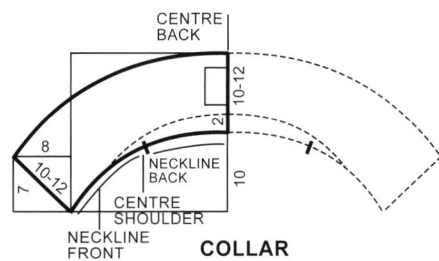

A
9
6
U2
CHEST
UNDERARM LINE
+
FRONT
CENTRE FRONT
WAIST
LOWER EDGE OF CAPE
HIPS
SIDE LINE
SIDE
FACING
3 HEM
8
8

2
SIDE OF CAPE
2
10
20
17
CONNECT TO
THE BACK
SLEEVE

A
9
6
2
SIDE OF CAPE
SHOULDERS
UNDERARM LINE
2
11
BACK
WAIST
22
CONNECT
TO THE
SLEEVE
FRONT
19
LOWER EDGE OF CAPE
HIPS
SIDE
SIDE LINE
CENTRE BACK
8
8
HEM

FRONT	**BACK**
20	22
17	19

CENTRE
BACK
10-12
2
8
10-12
7
NECKLINE
BACK
10
CENTRE
SHOULDER
NECKLINE
FRONT
COLLAR

TABARD (AND PONCHO)

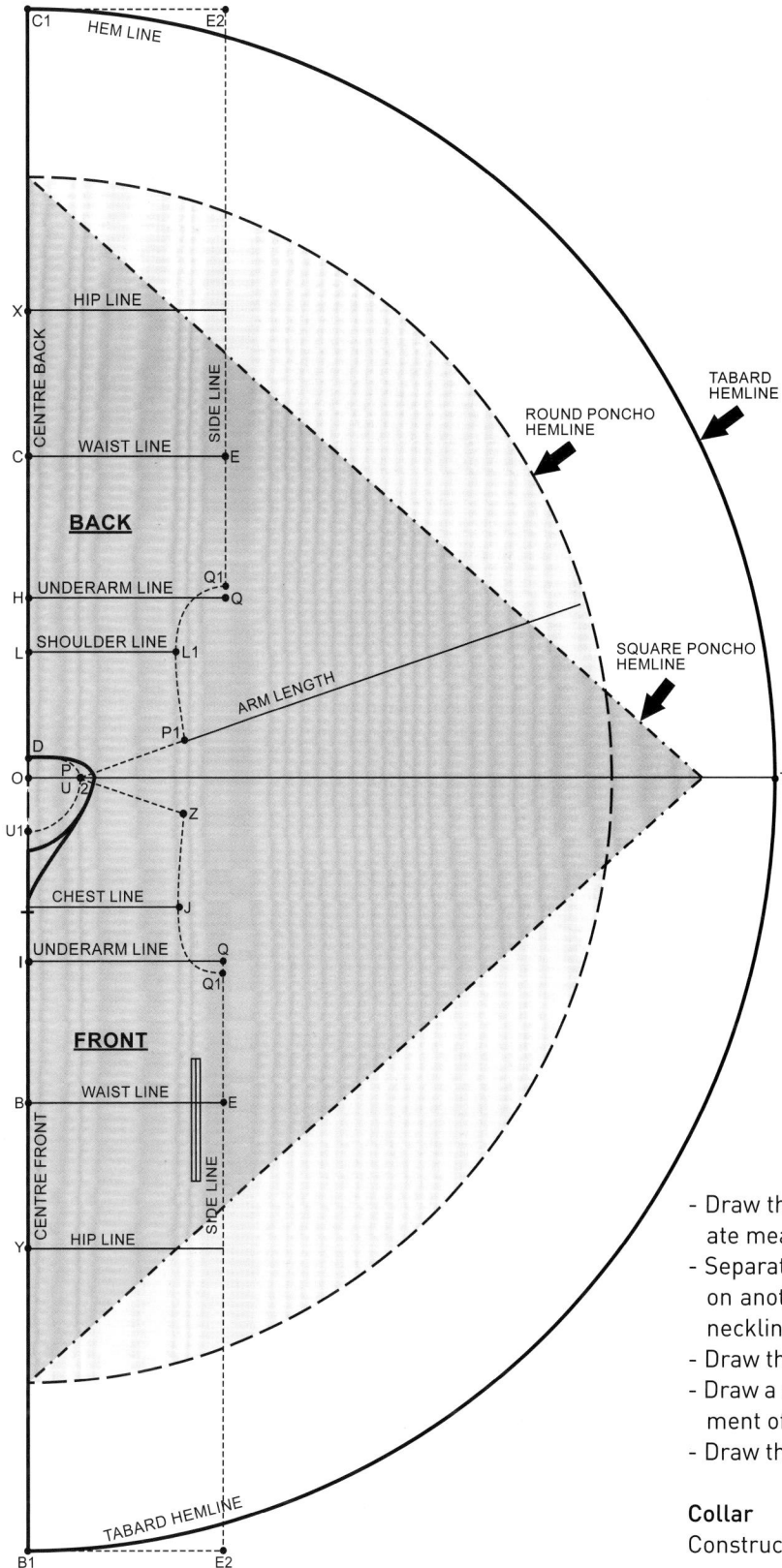

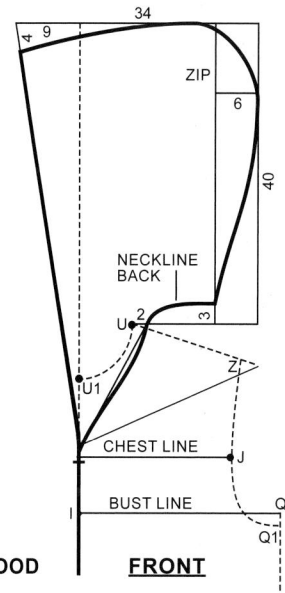

Diagram labels (large left figure)

C1 — HEM LINE — E2

HIP LINE — X

CENTRE BACK

SIDE LINE

WAIST LINE — C — E

BACK

UNDERARM LINE — H — Q1 — Q

SHOULDER LINE — L — L1

ARM LENGTH

P1

D

O — P — U — T

U1 — Z

CHEST LINE — J

UNDERARM LINE — I — Q — Q1

FRONT

WAIST LINE — B — E

CENTRE FRONT

SIDE LINE

HIP LINE — Y

TABARD HEMLINE — B1 — E2

TABARD HEMLINE

ROUND PONCHO HEMLINE

SQUARE PONCHO HEMLINE

Hood figure

34

4   9

ZIP

6

40

NECKLINE BACK

U — 2

3

U1

Z

CHEST LINE — J

BUST LINE — I — Q

Q1

OPENABLE HOOD   **FRONT**

Instructions

- Draw the base of the loose-fitting overcoat with appropriate measurements and ease.
- Separate the front from the back and place them lined up on another sheet of paper, keeping points P and U of the neckline together.
- Draw the line O-P-T, in the desired length.
- Draw a circle with centre O and the radius in the measurement of O-T.
- Draw the desired neckline.

Collar
Construct the hood neck at the front, as in the figure.

Note:
This cape can be made in one piece on doubled fabric, if the fabric permits; or with two seams on the sides, or with four seams on the hips and centre front and back.

HOODS

Hoods are head coverings with a mostly conical or rounded shape at the nape of the neck, which serves to protect the head, neck and part of the face from the rain and cold. They also can be added for stylistic reasons. A hood can be created separately or be an integral part of the garment, combined with: tracksuits, sweatshirts, anoraks, coats, capes, etc. Hoods can be:
1) fitted, with a zip;
2) regular-fit, with drawstrings;
3) roomy, with buttons;
4) embellished by a band at the back;
5) created in yet other forms.
They can come in different shapes and have various necklines, or be chin-high. The fabric used to make them is usually the same as that of the garment to which they are matched. If intended to protect from the rain, they should be in a waterproof material; made of heavy wool for jackets or capes; in other fabric for fashion garments; and finished with lining or bias strips.

1. Fitted hood with a zip   2. Roomy drawstring hood   3. Roomy hood with buttons   4. Performance hood with a rear strip

Hood measurements

The measurements to be taken for the construction of the hood are: head circumference, height and temple-to-temple.
When taking the measurements, make sure the wearer's head is in a normal position, held erect and perfectly vertical, with their hair down and free from bulky accessories.

Circumference and height

Head circumference and height are to be measured by starting with the tailor's tape at the centre of the nape of the neck and passing it around the head at the highest point.
To this measurement you will need to add the ease, which ranges from 4 cm / 1.57" for close-fitting hoods to 12 cm / 4.72" for roomy hoods (e.g.: 70+ 4 = 74 cm / 29.13").

Temple to temple

Measure one temple to the other passing around the back of the head. To this measurement you will need to add the ease, ranging from 4 to 10 cm / 1.57" to 3.94" (e.g. 42 + 4 = 46 cm / 18.11").

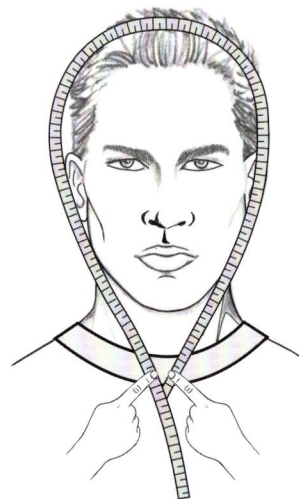

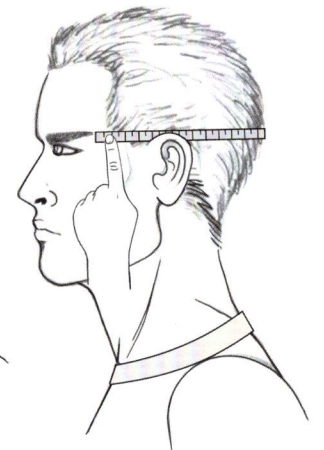

FITTED HOOD BASE BLOCK

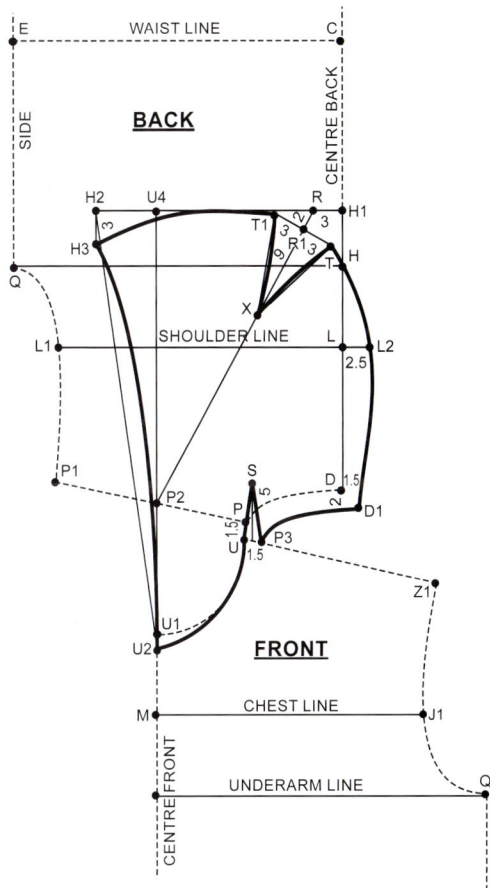

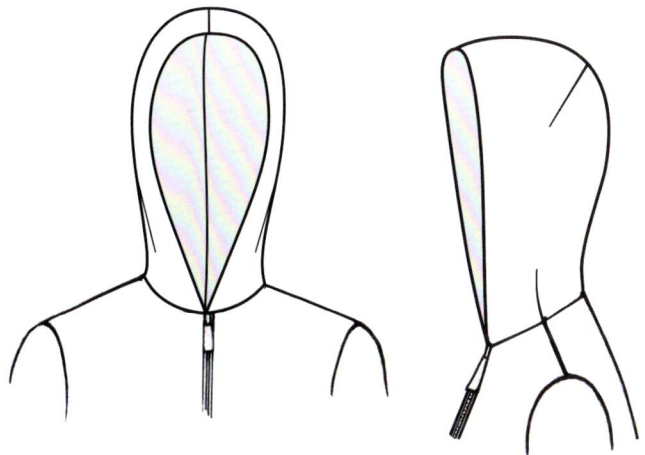

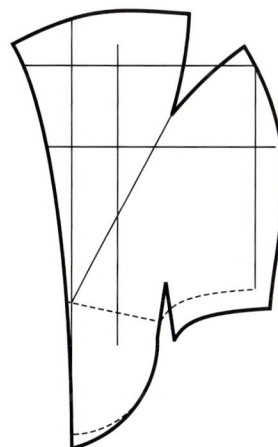

In order to create a hood that fits snug to the head, create a dart at the crown of the head and one on the neckline, at the shoulder.

Execution

- Position the back pattern of the executed garment perpendicular and opposite to that of the front, keeping the U points of the front and P points of the back 1.5 -2 cm / 0.59-0.79" apart, as in the figure.
- Extend the centre front line, from U1 to U4, by 1/2 the head height plus the ease (e.g.: 70 + 6 = 76 ÷ 2 = 38 cm / 14.96").
- Draw the horizontal line H1-U4-H2, with a length equal to 1/2 of the temple-to-temple measurement plus ease (e.g.: 42 + 4 = 46 ÷ 2 = 23 cm / 9.06").
- H2-H3 = 3 cm / 1.18".

- Draw the curved line H3-U2.
- H1-R = 3 cm / 1.18".
- Draw R-P2. R-R1 = 2 cm / 0.79".
- Draw the dart T-X-T1 with a width of 4-6 cm / 1.57-2.36" and a length 9 cm / 3.54".
- Draw the curved line H3-T1.
- Lower the back neckline D-P by 2 cm / 0.79" and shift it towards the centre back by 1.5 cm / 0.59" for the dart (points D1-P3).
- L-L2 = 2-3 cm / 0.79-1.18".
- Draw the curved line T-L2-D1.
- Draw the curved line D1-P3 equal to that of the back.
- Draw the dart U-S-P3 with a width of 1.5-2 cm / 0.59-0.79" and a depth of 5 cm / 2".

REGULAR-FIT HOOD

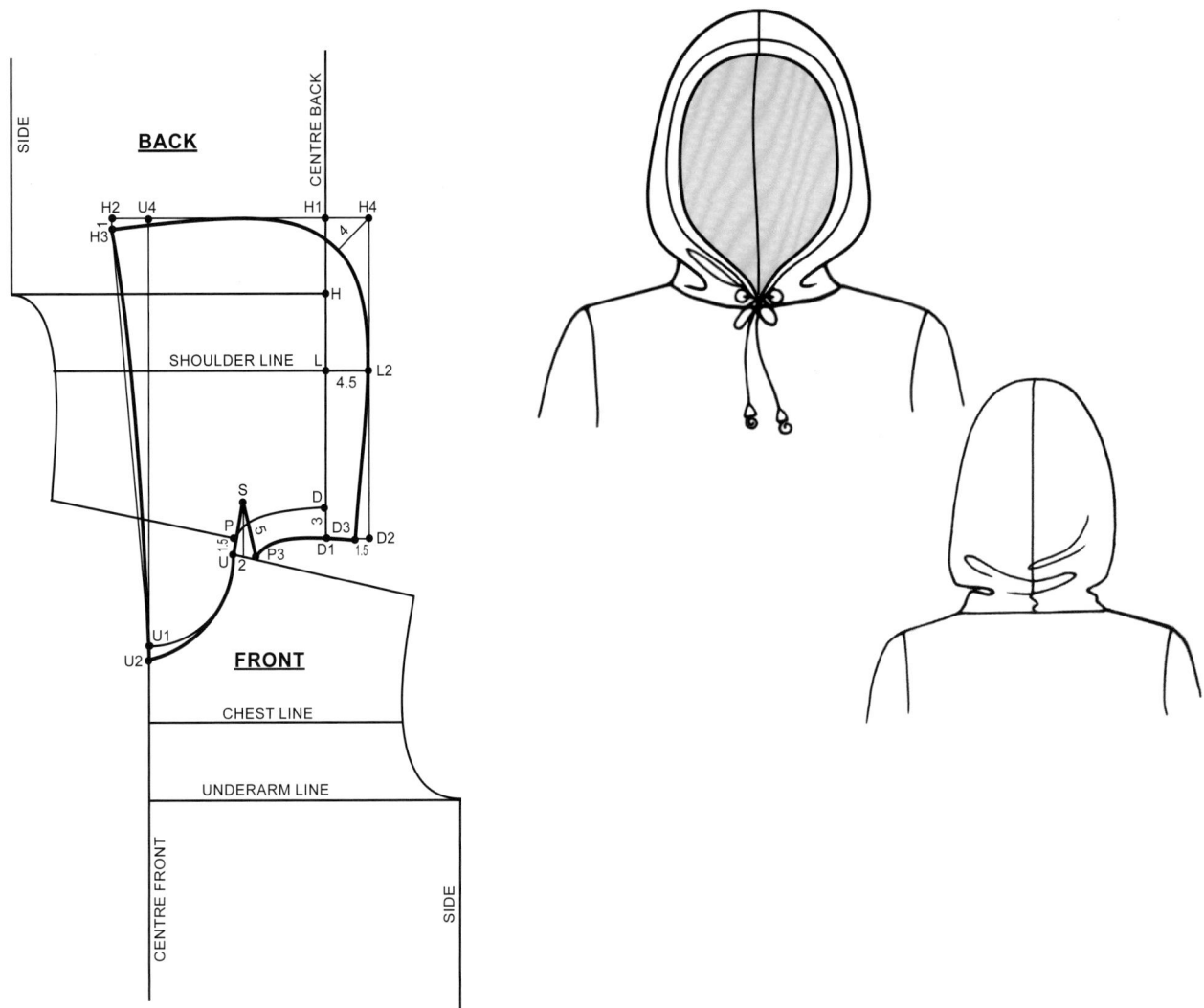

To create a loose-fitting hood, start from the base of the garment on which the hood is to be sewn, placing the front on the back at right angles on the shoulder.

Execution

- Position the back pattern of the executed garment perpendicular and opposite to that of the front, keeping the U points of the front and P points of the back 1.5-2 cm / 0.59-0.79" apart, as in the figure.
- Extend the centre front line, from U1 to U4, by 1/2 the head height plus the ease (e.g.: 70 + 10 = 80 ÷ 2 = 40 cm / 15.75")
- U4-H2 = 3-3.5 cm / 1.18-1.38".
- Draw the horizontal line H2-U4-H4 with a length equal to 1/2 of the temple-to-temple measurement plus hood ease (e.g.: 42 + 8 = 50 ÷ 2 = 25 cm / 9.84").

- D-D1 = 3 cm / 1.18".
- Draw the horizontal line D1-D2 like H1-H4.
- Draw the vertical line H4-D2.
- D2-D3 = 1.5 cm / 0.59".
- H2-H3 = 1-1.5 cm / 0.39-0.59".
- Lower the back neckline D-P by 3 cm / 1.18" and shift it towards the centre back by 1.5-2 cm / 0.59-0.79" for the dart.
- Draw the curved line D3-P3 equal to that of back neckline + 1 cm / 0.39".
- Draw the dart U-S-P3 with a width of 1.5- 2 cm / 0.59-0.79" and a depth of 5 cm / 2".
- Draw the curved centre back line H3-L2-D3.
- Draw the front line U2-H3.

LOOSE-FITTING HOOD

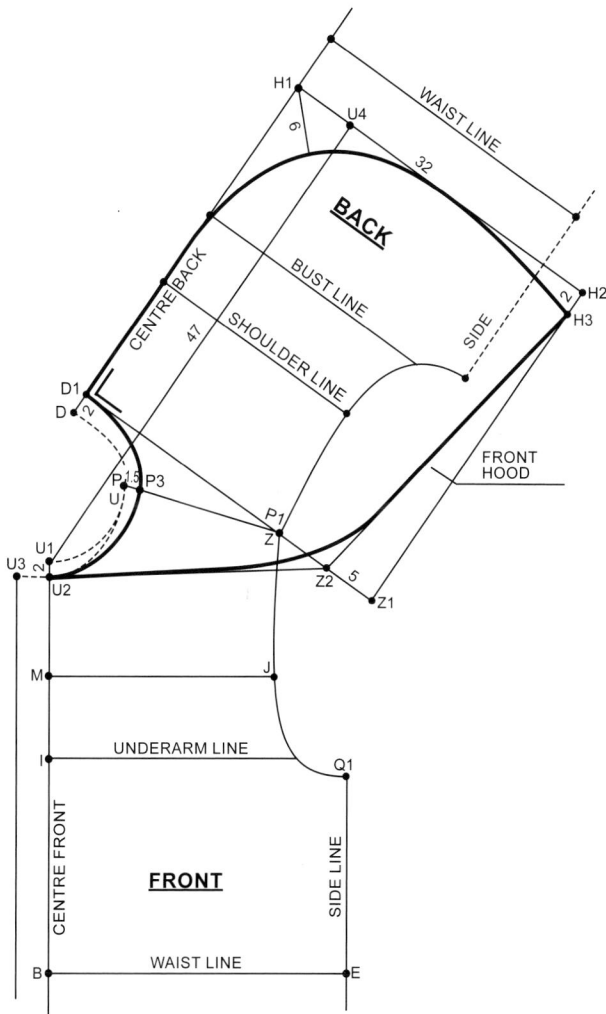

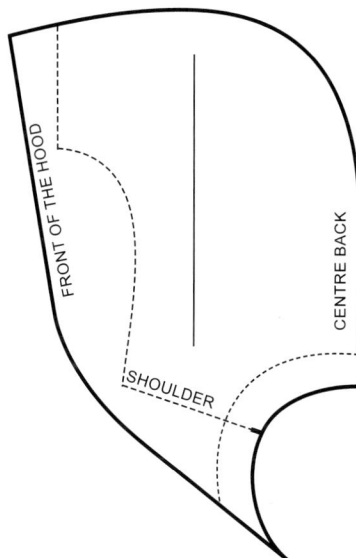

Loose-fitting hoods are constructed from the base of the garment on which it's to be sewn, whether that's a coat, cape, etc.

Execution

- Place the back bodice over the front bodice, holding them together on the shoulder line, as shown in the figure.
- Adjust the front and back neckline as required.
- Draw from point U1 to point U4, in a length that's 1/2 the height of the head from the neckline, plus the ease of 24-28 cm / 9.45-11.02" (e.g.: 70 + 24 = 94 ÷ 2 = 47 cm / 18.50").
- Draw H1-U4-H2, parallel to the waistline of the back bodice, in a length that's equal to 1/2 the temple-to-temple line of the head plus the hood ease 18-24 cm / 7.09-9.45" (e.g.: 42 + 22 = 64 ÷ 2 = 32 cm / 12.60").
- D1-Z1 like H1-H2.
- Draw H2-Z1.
- H2-H3 = 2 cm / 0.79".
- Z1-Z2 = 4-6 cm / 1.57-2.36".
- Join Z2 to U2 of the front neckline.
- Connect H3-U2 with a curved line (front hood).
- Connect D1-H3 with a curved line (rear hood).

HOOD WITH A HIGH NECK AND CENTRAL BAND

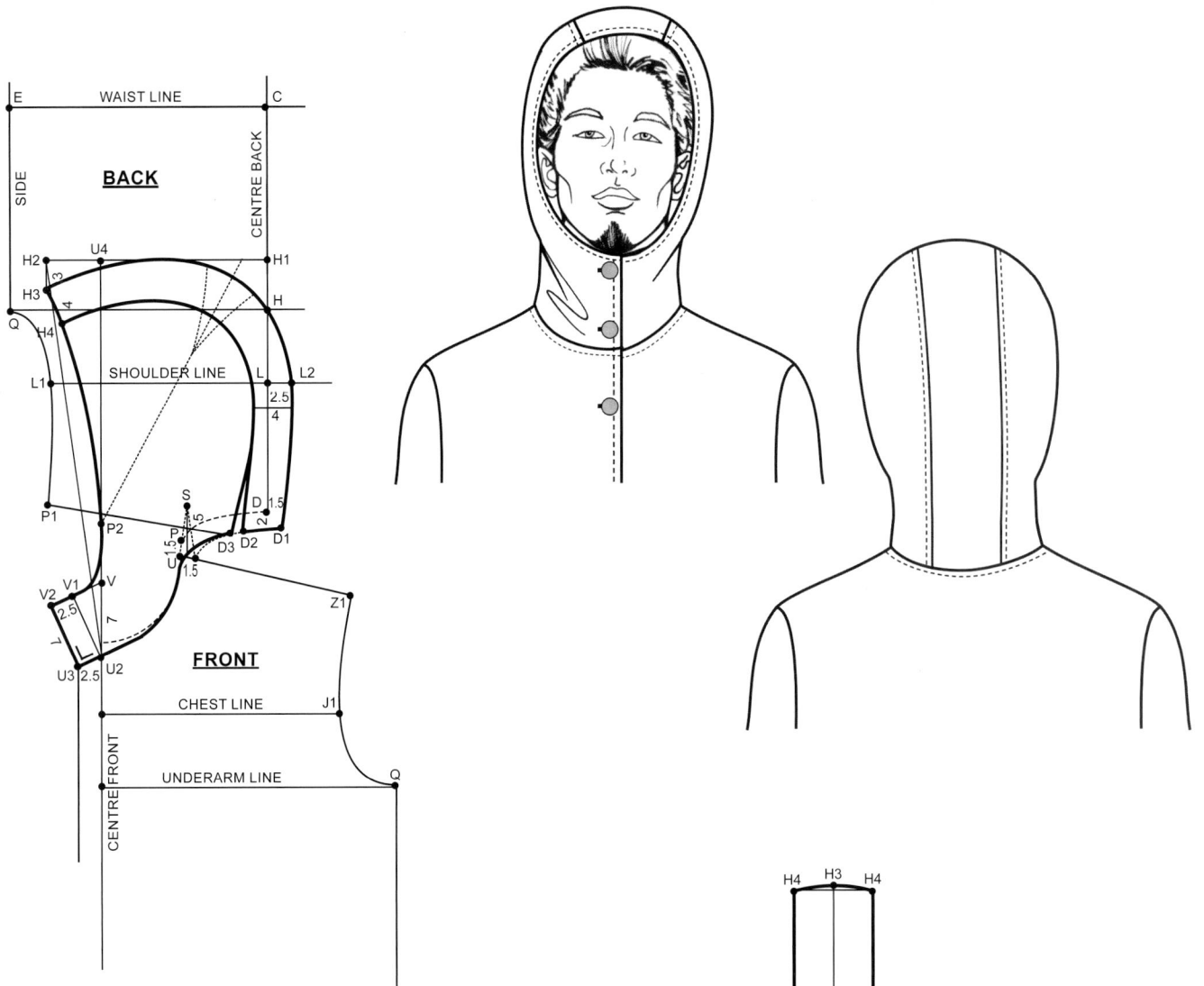

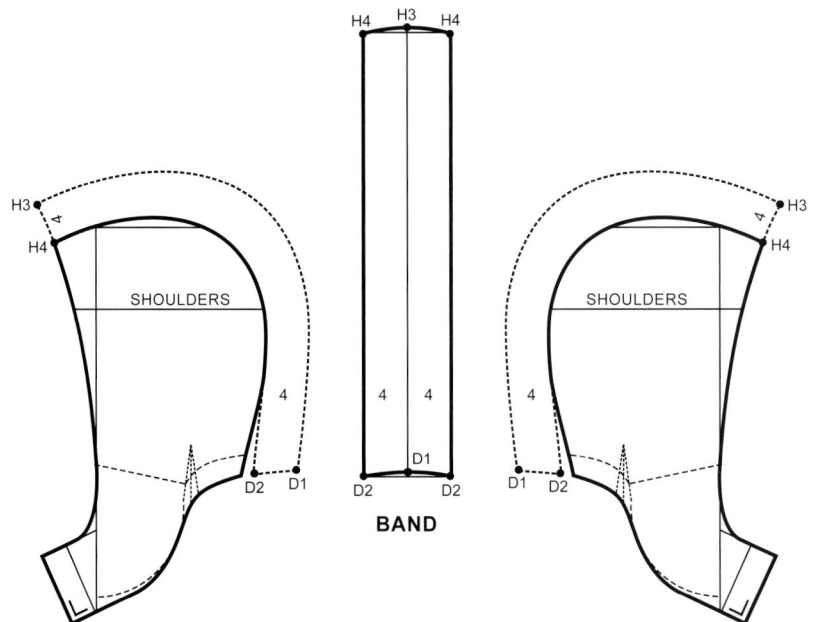

- Draw the fitted hood base pattern with appropriate size and fit, on a base with an extension for the fastening.
- H2-H3 = 3 cm / 1.18".
- H3-H4 = 4-4.5 cm / 1.57-1.77".
- D1-D2 like H3-H4.
- Draw the curved line H4-D2, parallel to H3-D1.
- Draw the neckline and merge the dart into the seam of the band (D2-D3).
- U2-V = 6.5-7.5 cm / 2.56-2.95".
- Draw V-V2 parallel to the neckline.
- U2-U3 = 2.5 cm / 1" (fastening extension).
- V1-V2 like U2-U3.
- Draw U3-V2 square with V-V2 and U2-U3.

UNDERWEAR AND KNITWEAR

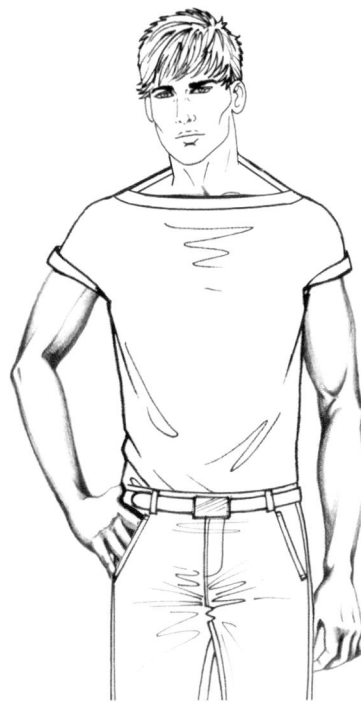

KNIT FABRICS

Knit fabrics can be made either by weft knitting, where a single strand of yarn is worked across the width of the fabric, or warp knitting, when a series of yarns are worked longitudinally in adjacent columns with respect to the fabric produced.

Weft knitting employs three principal stitches: stockinette stitch, which can be made to produce flat fabrics, also known as jersey or tubular fabric; purl stitch, and rib knit stitch.

Knit fabrics have captured a significant share of the market in the garment sector, and nearly all the stylists have a knitwear line in their collections, sportswear, casuals, and even elegant attire.

In fact, knits can be made with natural or synthetic fibres; they can be placed in collections targeted at either very high-end or very low-end markets; the knit fabric's capacity to stretch both in length and in width, and then to return to its original state, simplifies the pattern-making process with a better adaptability to the figure.

For the peculiarity of its composition, this fabric is easy to work with as it does not fray, it is comfortable to wear and it does not get rumpled.

There are various type of knit fabrics: compact and stable knits; single and light knits; structured knits; elasticized knits with two-way stretch; ribbed knits.

Compact and stable knits. This type of knit is not very elastic and should be treated like orthogonal woven fabric. This group also includes double knits characterized by longitudinal ribs on both sides. It is hard to distinguish the right side from the wrong side if there is not a decorative pattern. Raschel knits (run-resistant) use a lace-like open stitch process; they are not elastic because the longitudinal columns are blocked in some stitches of the knit. Some Raschel knits are made with thick, heavy yarns and seem like bouclé fabric or hand-knitting. Others are made with finer yarns and seem crocheted.

Single and light knits They have small longitudinal ribs on the right side and rings that run crosswise on the back. If you pull the transversal edge of a single knit, it will curl on the right side. Single knits like jersey, tricot, and interlock are not elastic in length, but they will give when pulled crosswise.

Structured knits. These can be single or double knit. This category stands out for the structured surface, usually on the right side. Terrycloth knits and velour are knit fabrics with nap that resembles their woven counterparts; in any case, they are usually very elastic widthwise. Knits for pullovers are also classified in this category. Jacquard knits for pullovers have loose threads on the wrong side; these are the coloured yarns that are shifted from one motif to another. This process limits the crosswise elasticity. Fleece knits are pleasant to wear, on the right side they seem a single knit fabric, while on the wrong side the surface is soft and napped. They are usually rather stable and not stretchy in any direction.

Two-way stretch knits. These knits have a high percentage of elastic fibres. Cotton or cotton/polyester stretch knit fabrics are ideal for sportswear like bodysuits and aerobic gym suits. Elasticized nylon knits remain stretchy even when wet, and are favoured for swimwear.

Ribbed knits. This is a very stretchy kind of knit, which can be used for tops and for edging knit apparel at the wrists, the ankles, the neckline, and the waist line. A special kind is the tubular knit, which is also sold in small pieces and can be cut open along a longitudinal rib. Another kind is the ribbed knit for borders, colour-coordinated with the knit for pullovers; one edge is finished, the other must be sewn to the garment.

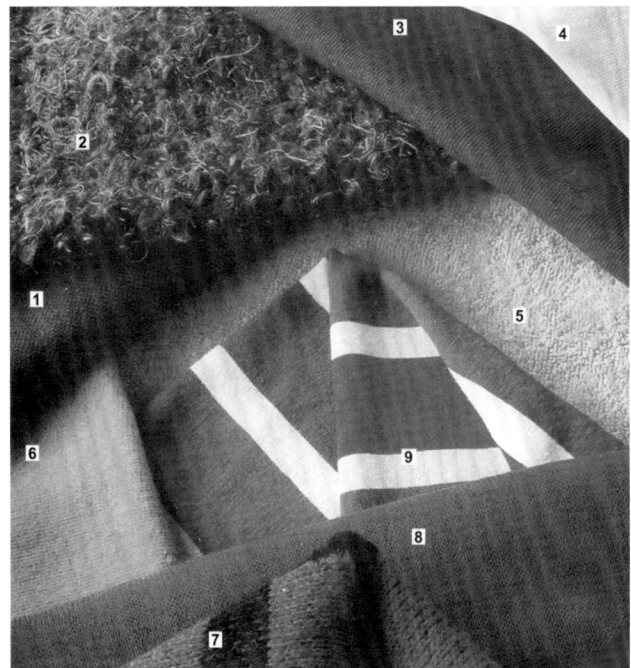

1) Double knit.
2) Raschel knit (run-resistant).
3) Jersey.
4) Tricot.
5) Terrycloth knit.
6) Velour.
7) Knit for pullovers.
8) Fleece knit.
9) Stretch knit.

THE ELASTICITY OF KNIT FABRICS

Patternmakers must be well-informed about the special qualities of knit fabrics and, in particular, about their coefficient of stretch and recovery, in order to calculate the ease to give the garment and to obtain a product suited to the requirements of comfort.

A fabric's capacity for elongation and stretch is a determinant factor for comfort, fit, stability and durability of garments.

Stretch and recovery factor

A knit fabric's stretch factor is expressed in a percentage that refers to the original length and the extension in centimetres that can be obtained under maximum tension. The extension can range from 20% to 100% of the initial length. A knit fabric's recovery factor is the degree and the capacity that it has to return to its original state after undergoing strong tension stress. A good knit should return easily to the original dimensions, otherwise the fabric will slacken and bags will form.

Resistance to traction with measurement of the extension and the recovery

Weft knit fabrics, for their high deformability, do not lend themselves to the execution of strip tests of traction resistance. Only warp knits with strong stability characteristics are subjected this kind of test. Cut five strips from the fabric, each precisely 50 mm / 0.20" in length, in the direction of both the columns and the rows, at a certain distance from the selvages. The strips are subject to traction on a dynamometer for fabrics so as to determine the load and stretch to breaking point. The average breaking point must not be inferior to the value established by the manufacturer, stated on the label.

For an immediate and simpler test for the patternmaker and garment maker, in the absence of precise indications, we can gain some knowledge about a fabric's elasticity through a manual measurement procedure, carried out as follows:

1) Fold the fabric crosswise for 8–10 cm/3.15"-3.94".
2) Insert two pins in the fold, 10 cm/3.94" apart.
3) Stretch the fabric and measure with a ruler how much longer it gets, exerting a moderate force, between the two pins.
4) The distance between the two pins after releasing the stretch can be checked to see if the fabric has become deformed.

Stretch fabrics

Fabrics made with elasticized yarns are generally classified in two main categories: high elasticity fabrics and ones with average elasticity.

Spandex-based yarns are nearly always mixed with other fibres and they are often incorporated in fabrics together with other yarns.

The primary purpose of spandex fibres is to obtain elasticity and holding power. And for this reason what type of yarn is used in the fabric and how, and in what quantity is all determined by the garment's construction, the weight of the fabric, its stretchability, and the desired holding power. Stretchiness is the main characteristic of spandex, along with holding power, and in fact spandex fibres can stretch from 400 to 700%, that is from 4 to 7 times their length at rest, before breaking. The most elastic spandex fibres are Glospan S-5 and Cleerspan, which show a 700% stretch capacity, while Lycra registers a stretch capacity ranging between 400 and 625%.

To obtain sufficient holding power to be the basis for such garments as: corsets and girdles, stretch ski pants, swimsuits, and other sportswear, a stretchabilty of 30–50% is recommended, with a loss of elastic recovery of no greater than 5-6%.

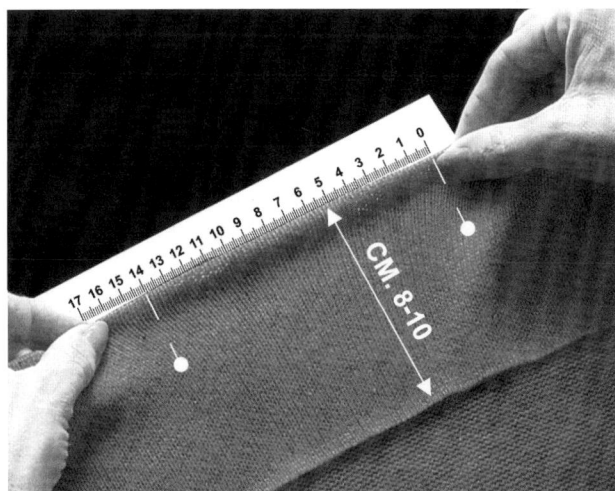

Manual test of the elasticity of a knit fabric with a stretchability of 40%. The pins are fixed 10 cm/3.94" apart with the fabric at rest.

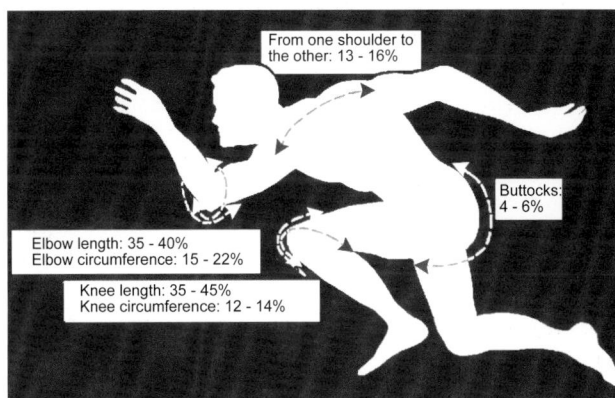

Body positions where it is necessary to stretch the fabric for freedom of movement and comfort when wearing the garment.

T-SHIRT BASE BLOCK

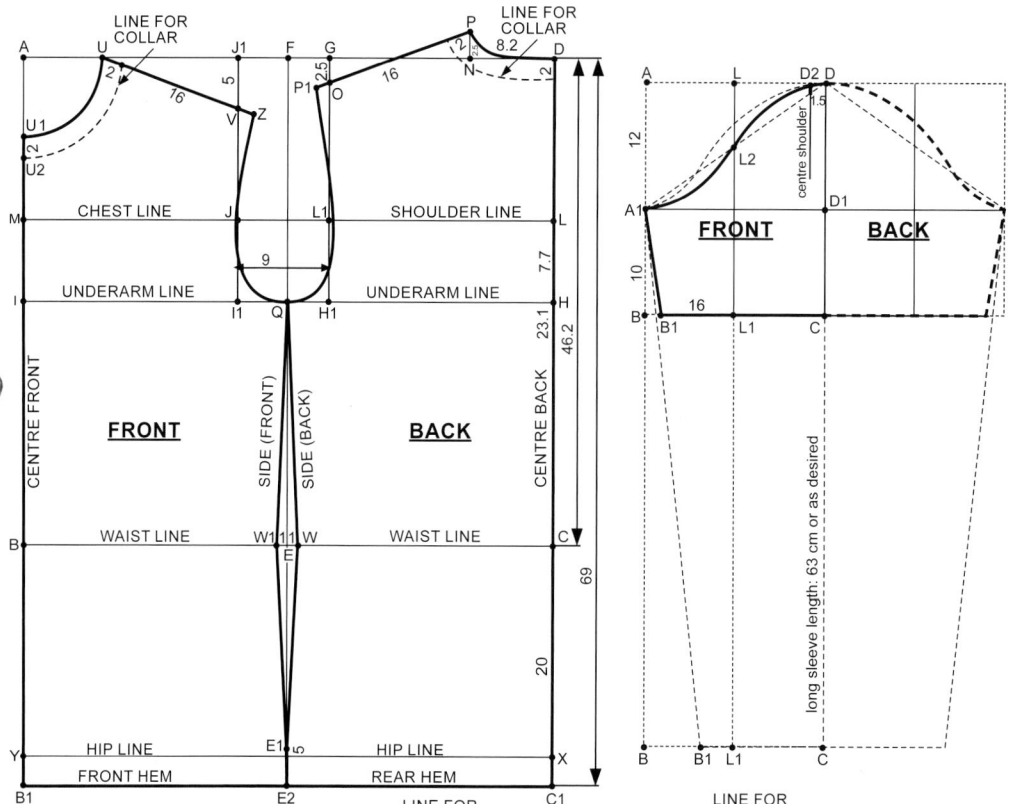

Size 16 UK measurements

- Height = 175 cm / 5'9".
- T-shirt ease = 8 cm / 3 1/8".
- Chest semi-cir. = 96 + 8 = 104 ÷ 2 = 52 cm / 20.47"
- Waist semi-cir. = 88 + 8 = 96 ÷ 2 = 48 cm / 18.90"
- Hip semi-cir. = 96 + 8 = 104 ÷ 2 = 52 cm / 20.47"
- Neck semi-circumference = 42 ÷ 2 = 21 cm / 8.27"
- 1/2 shoulder width = 44 ÷ 2 = 22 cm / 8.66"
- Back neck to waist = 46.2 cm / 18.19"; front = 45.6 cm / 17.95".

Bodice

- Draw right angle A-B-C, with:
- A-B equal to the front neck-to-waist (e.g.: 45.6 cm / 17.95").
- B-C = semi-circumference of chest + ease (6-8 cm / 2.36-3.15"), depending on the elasticity of the fabric, e.g.: 96 + 8 = 104 ÷ 2 = 52 cm / 20.47"
- C-D rear neck-to-waist (e.g.: 46.2 cm / 18.19").
- D-G = 1/2 shoulder width (e.g.: 44 ÷ 2 = 22 cm / 8.66").
- D-C1 = total length at the centre back (e.g.: 75 cm / 29.53").
- Draw Q-W-E1 and Q-W1-E1 to taper the waist (1+1 / 0.39+0.39).
- Draw C1-E2-B1 (lower hemline).
- B-B1 = extension as desired (e.g.: 18-20 cm / 7.09-7.87").
- B-Y and C-X = waist to hip (e.g.: 20 cm / 7.87").
- Draw X-Y (hip line); Y-B1 like X-C1.
- D-H half of C-D (e.g.: 46.2 ÷ 2 = 23.1 cm / 9.09").
- H-H1 like D-G (e.g.: 22 / 8.66"); draw H1-G.
- Draw H-I like B-C = 52 cm / 20.47" (underarm level).
- B-E half of B-C (26 cm / 10.24").
- A-F like B-E; draw F-E-E2 (side centre).
- I-I1 like H-H1 minus 1 cm / 0.39" (e.g.: 22 - 1 = 21 cm / 8.27").
- Draw I1-J1 parallel to H1-G.
- H-L = 1/3 of D1-H (e.g.: 23.1 ÷ 3 = 7.7 cm / 3.03").
- Draw L-M parallel to H-I.
- H1-I1 = H-I minus (H-H1 + I-I1) = 52 - (23 + 22) = 52 - 43 = 9 cm / 3.54" (armscye sector).
- M-J= chest line; L-L1 = shoulder line.
- J1-V = 5 cm / 2"; G-O = 2.5 cm / 1".
- Smoothly draw the armhole Z-J-Q-L1-P1.
- A-U = 1/6 shoulder width (e.g.: 44 + 1.5 = 45.5 ÷ 6 = 7.6 cm / 3").

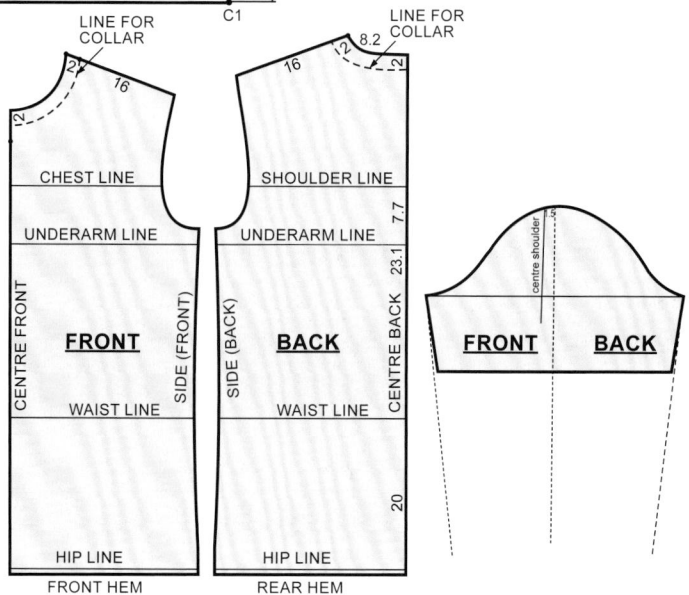

- Draw the arc U-U1 in the same length as A-U, centred on A.
- D-N like A-U + 0.6 cm = 8.2 cm / 3.23"; N-P = 2.5 cm / 1".
- Draw D-P (back neckline).
- Draw P-P1 like U-Z (rear shoulder); P1-L1 = 12.6 cm / 4.96".

Sleeve

- Draw the rectangle A-B-C-D with:
- A-B = sleeve length, as desired.
- B-C = underarm sector x 2 minus 0.5 cm / 0.20" (e.g.: 9 x 2 = 18 - 0.5 = 17.5 cm / 6.89").
- A-A1 like P1-L1 of the bodice minus 0.6 cm = 12 cm / 4.72".
- Join A1-D with a diagonal line;
- D-D1 like A-A1; D-D2 = 1.5 cm / 0.59" (centre shoulder).
- C-B1 = 16 cm / 6.30" (depending on the size of the biceps).
- Smoothly join and copy the sleeve in duplicate.
- Check the sleeve crown measurement against the armhole measurement on the bodice.

VEST

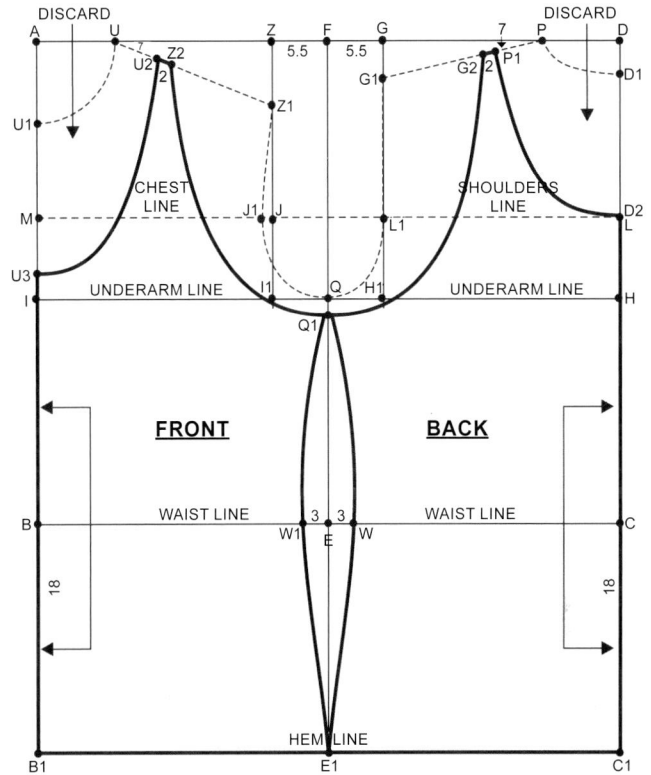

- Draw the t-shirt base block with the ease of the chest circumference from 0 to 4 cm / 1.57".

Front
- U1-U3 = 15 cm / 5.91" or as desired.
- U-U2 = 7 cm / 2.76".
- U2-Z2 = 2-4 cm / 0.79-1.57" or as desired.
- Q-Q1 = 2 cm / 0.79".
- E-W1 = 3 cm / 1.18" or according to the waist.

Back
- D1-D2 = 13 cm / 5.12" or as desired.
- P-P1 like U-U2.
- P1-G2 like U2-Z2.
- E-W like E-W1.
- Connect as in the figure.

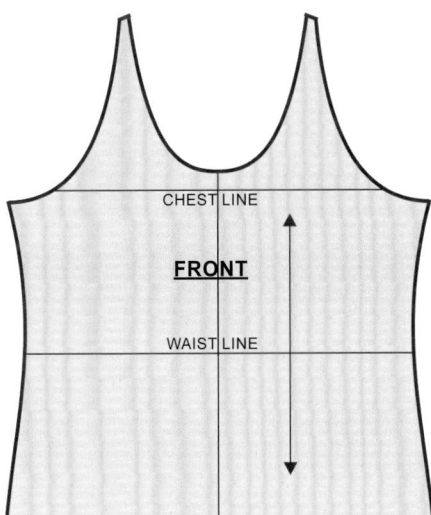

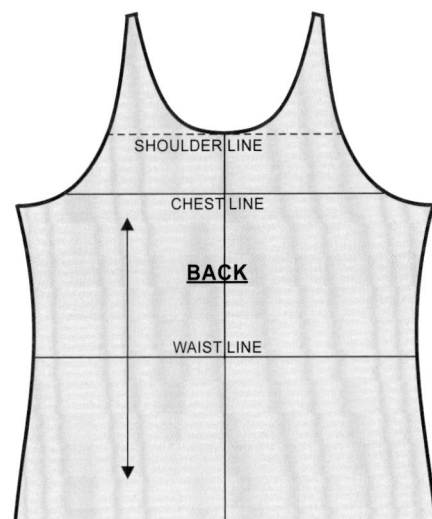

POLO SHIRT NECKLINES

A polo shirt can be worn by anyone, regardless of age or occasion. It's a garment with a fairly loose fit that gently touches upon the body's shape, not tightly. Among young men, however, a slim fit is especially popular, cut closer to the body to emphasise the muscles. In summer months, wearing a polo shirt is a good alternative to a classic shirt: it's very breathable because it is made of quality materials that are pleasant to the touch. This makes it possible to wear a garment as elegant as a shirt, but at the same time certainly less demanding and more comfortable. Originally used by polo players in India (hence the name), polo shirts are like t-shirts, but with a collar, a neckline fastened by two or three buttons and often a chest pocket. In some cases, the buttons are replaced by a zip, or are not present at all. They are usually made of Thai cotton pique knit fabric, but sometimes they're also knit from synthetic fibres.

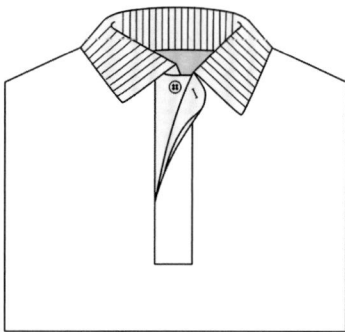
Polo shirt with a concealed placket.

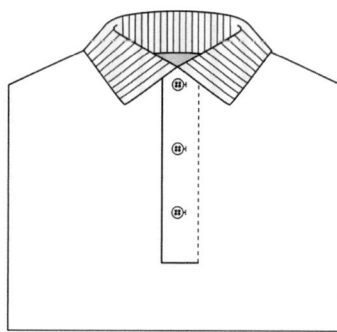
Classic three-button polo shirt.

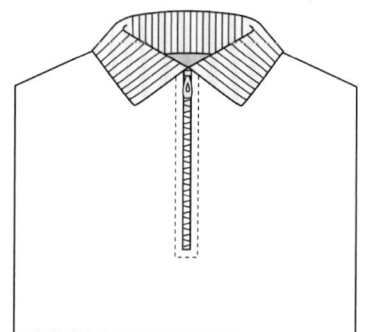
Polo shirt with a zip.

POLO SHIRT

Diagram labels (front/back pattern block):
A — U — 7.6 — J1 — F — G — 2.5 — P2 — P1 — 16 — N — 8.2 — D
P (top)
7.6 — U1 — U2 — 16 — 5 — V — Z — 2.5
15 — M — CHEST LINE — J — L1 — SHOULDER LINE — L
M1 — 1.5 — M2 — UNDERARM LINE — Q — UNDERARM LINE — H
I — I1 — H1 — H
FRONT — SIDE (FRONT) — SIDE (BACK) — BACK
CENTRE FRONT — CENTRE BACK
B — WAIST LINE — 2 — WAIST LINE — C
E
Y — HIP LINE — HIP LINE — X
B1 — 4 — FRONT HEM LINE — E1 / E3 — 5 — REAR HEM LINE — 6 — C1
E2

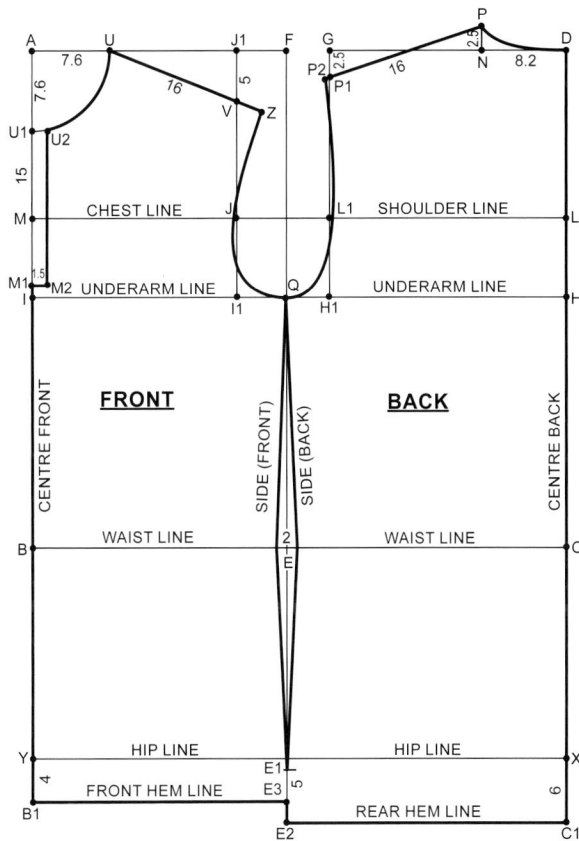

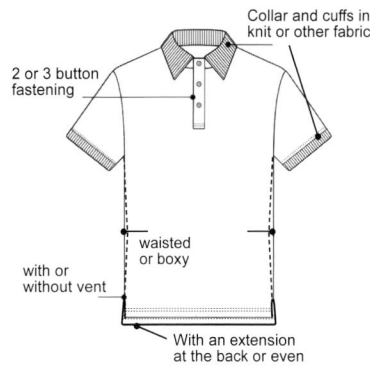

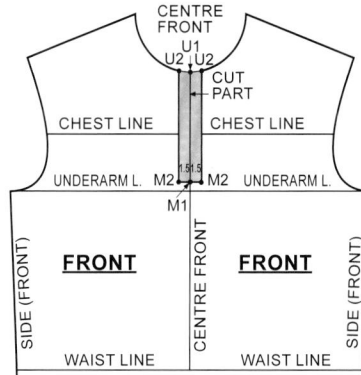

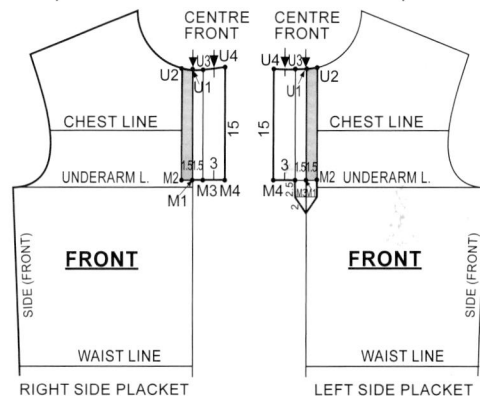

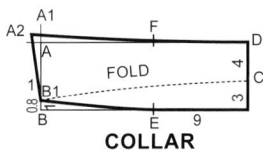

COLLAR diagram:
A1 — A2 — A — F — D — FOLD — B1 — 1 — 0.8 — B — E — 9 — 3 / 4 — C1
FOR THE COLLAR IN KNIT FABRIC DON'T MAKE THE STAND
COLLAR

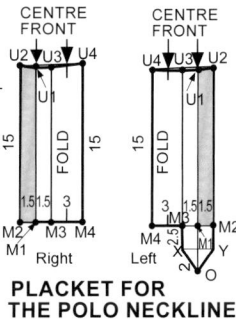

PLACKET FOR THE POLO NECKLINE
CENTRE FRONT — U2 / U3 / U4 — U1 — FOLD — 15 / 15 — 1.5 / 1.5 — 3 — M2 / M3 / M4 — M1 — Right
CENTRE FRONT — U4 / U3 / U2 — U1 — FOLD — 15 / 15 — 3 — 1.5 / 1.5 — M3 — M4 / M2 — X — 2.5 — Y — 2 — O — Left

Upper right garment sketch:
Collar and cuffs in knit or other fabric
2 or 3 button fastening
waisted or boxy
with or without vent
With an extension at the back or even

Front placket diagrams:
CENTRE FRONT — U1 / U2 — CUT PART — CHEST LINE — CHEST LINE — UNDERARM L. — M2 / 1.5 1.5 / M2 — M1 — UNDERARM L. — FRONT — FRONT — SIDE (FRONT) — CENTRE FRONT — SIDE (FRONT) — WAIST LINE — WAIST LINE

RIGHT SIDE PLACKET: CENTRE FRONT — U2 — U3 / U4 — U1 — CHEST LINE — UNDERARM L. — 15 — M2 — 1.5 1.5 — 3 — M3 M4 — M1 — FRONT — SIDE (FRONT) — WAIST LINE

LEFT SIDE PLACKET: CENTRE FRONT — U4 / U3 — U1 — U2 — CHEST LINE — 15 — 3 — 1.5 1.5 — M2 — M4 M3 — FRONT — SIDE (FRONT) — WAIST LINE

- Draw the t-shirt base block and the corresponding sleeve, with chest circumference ease of 8-10 cm / 3.15-3.94", depending on the elasticity of the knit fabric (e.g.: 96 + 8 = 104 ÷ 2 = 52 cm / 20.47")

Neckline opening
- U1-U2 = 1.5 cm / 0.59"; U2-M2 = 15-17 cm / 5.91-6.69" for 3 buttons or 10-12 cm / 3.94-4.72" for 2 buttons.
- Draw the opening U1-M1-M2-U2.

Right and left neck opening (or placket)
- Draw a rectangle U2-M2-M4-U4 with:
- U2-M2 = 15-17 cm / 5.91-6.69"; M2-M4 = 6 cm / 2.36".
- M2-M3 = half M2-M4.
- M2-M1 = half M2-M3; draw M3-U3
- Curve U2-U4 smoothly.

Left placket
- M3-X = 2.5 cm / 1"; M2-Y like M3-X.
- M1-O = 4.5 cm / 1.77"; draw M3-X-O-Y-M2.

Collar
- Take the precise measurement of the neckline at the back and front of the bodice where the collar is to be applied.
- Draw a rectangle A-B-C-D with A-B equal to the total height of the collar and B-C equal to the semi-circumference of the collar + 0.5 cm / 0.20".
- Moving from C to B, at a distance equal to 1/2 of the rear neckline (e.g.: 9 cm / 3.54"), create point E.
- Draw the perpendicular line E-F.
- From B, shift upwards by 1 cm / 0.39" (B1). Join B1-E with a curved line.
- Going from C to D, move 2.5-3 cm / 1-1.18" and create point C1.
- Join C1 with B1 via a curved line.
- From A, lengthen the line by 3 cm / 1.18" and create point A1.
- Draw the guide line A-A2 through A1, according to the desired length of the collar point.
- Connect A2-F-D with curved line or in the desired shape.

KNIT JACKET
WITH POUCH POCKETS

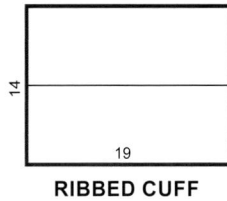

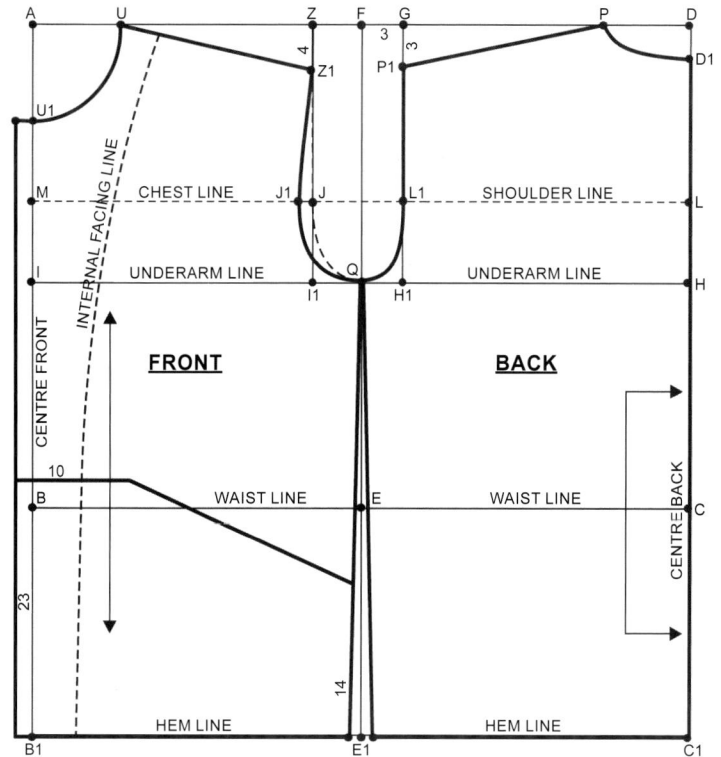

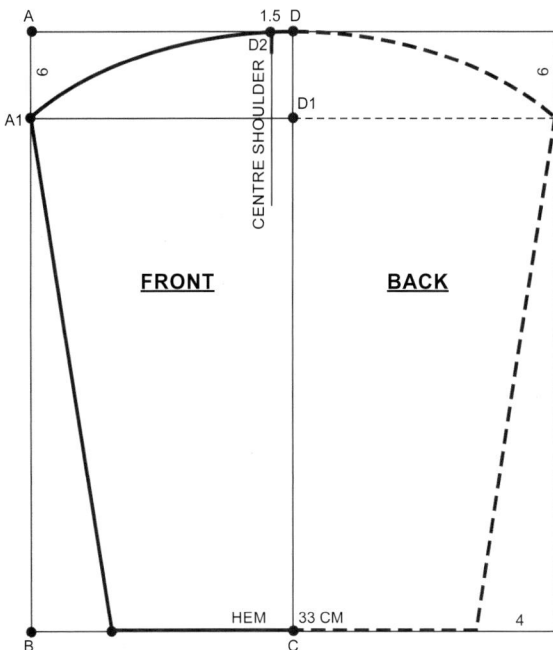

RIBBED CUFF

14

19

A U Z F G P D

U1

M CHEST LINE J1 J L1 SHOULDER LINE L

I UNDERARM LINE I1 H1 Q UNDERARM LINE H

INTERNAL FACING LINE

CENTRE FRONT

FRONT **BACK**

4 Z1

3 P1

3

Z

10

B WAIST LINE E WAIST LINE C

CENTRE BACK

23

14

HEM LINE HEM LINE

B1 E1 C1

BODICE

- Draw the rectangle A-B-C-D with:
- A-B = front neck-to-waist (e.g.: 43 cm / 16.93").
- B-C = 1/2 chest circumference + 24 cm / 9.45" ease (e.g.: 96 + 24 = 120 ÷ 2 = 60 cm / 23.62").
- C-D1 = rear neck-to-waist (e.g.: 47 cm / 18.50").
- B-E half of B-C; A-F like B-E; draw E-F.
- D1-H half of C-D1 (e.g.: 47 ÷ 2 = 23.5 cm / 9.25").
- F-G = 3 cm / 1.18"; F-Z like F-G + 1 cm / 0.39".
- H-L = 1/3 of D1-H (e.g.: 23.5 ÷ 3 = 7.8 cm / 3.07").
- Z-Z1 = 4 cm / 1.57"; G-P1 = 3 cm / 1.18".
- A-U = 1/6 shoulder width + 1.5 cm / 0.59" (e.g.: 44 ÷ 6 = 7.3 + 1.5 = 8.8 cm / 3.46").
- Draw the arc U-U1. D-P like A-U; Connect P-D1.
- B-B1 extension as desired (20-22 cm / 7.87-8.66").
- Draw the pouch pocket with the measurements and shape.
- Draw the extension for the zip.
- Taper in at the bottom on the side line by 1-2 cm / 0.39-0.79".

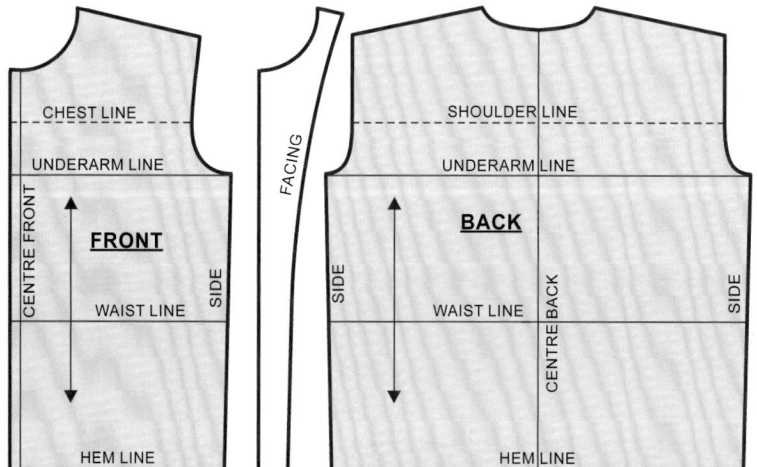

A 1.5 D

D2

CENTRE SHOULDER

6 D1 6

A1

FRONT **BACK**

HEM 33 CM 4

B C

SLEEVE

- Draw the rectangle A-B-C-D with:
- A-B equal to the sleeve length.
- B-C = underarm sector x 3 + 2 cm / 0.79" (e.g.: 8 x 3 = 24+ 2 = 26 cm / 10.24").
- A-A1 = 6 cm / 2.36".
- D-D2 = 1.5 cm / 0.59" (centre shoulder).

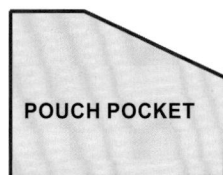

1

9 8

2.5

POUCH POCKET

CHEST LINE

UNDERARM LINE

CENTRE FRONT

FRONT

SIDE

WAIST LINE

HEM LINE

FACING

SHOULDER LINE

UNDERARM LINE

SIDE

BACK

SIDE

CENTRE BACK

WAIST LINE

HEM LINE

SWEATSHIRT WITH DROPPED SHOULDERS

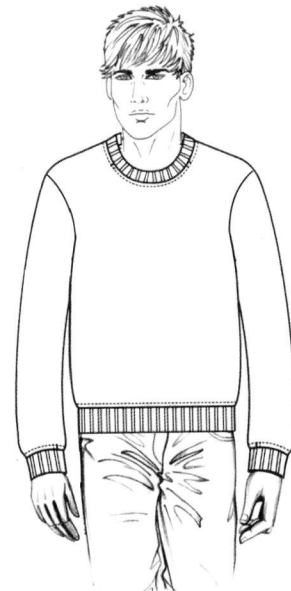

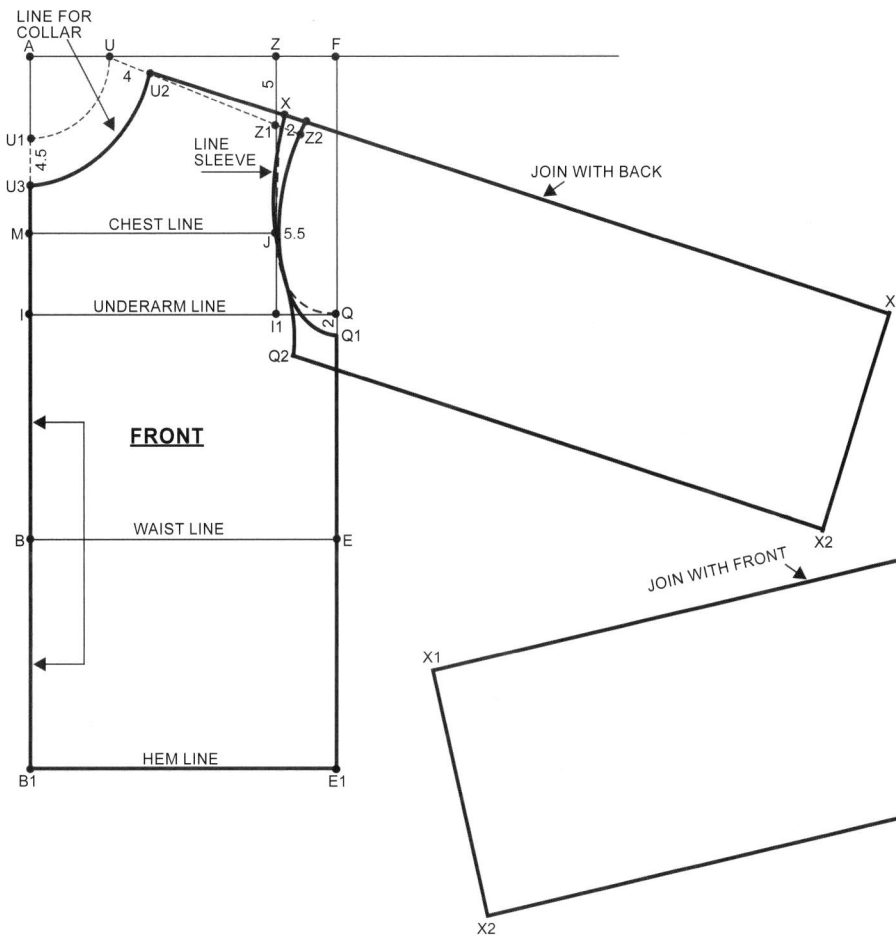

LINE FOR COLLAR

JOIN WITH BACK

LINE SLEEVE

CHEST LINE

UNDERARM LINE

FRONT

WAIST LINE

HEM LINE

X1

X2

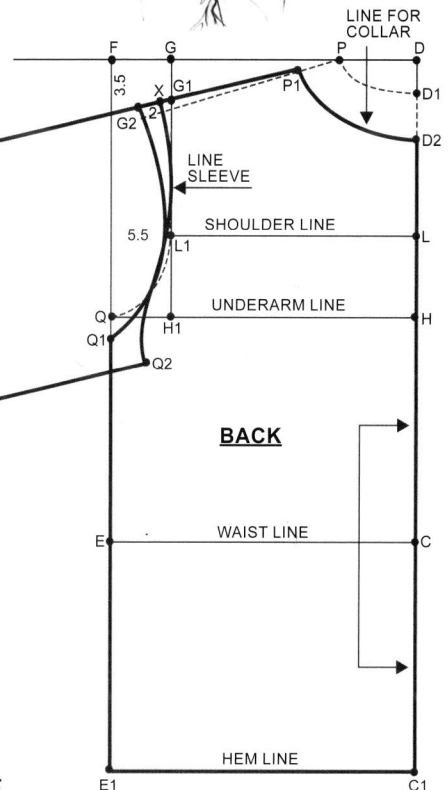

LINE FOR COLLAR

LINE SLEEVE

SHOULDER LINE

UNDERARM LINE

JOIN WITH FRONT

X1

X2

BACK

WAIST LINE

HEM LINE

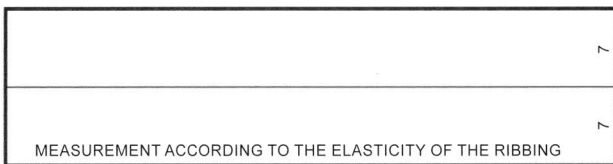

MEASUREMENT ACCORDING TO THE ELASTICITY OF THE RIBBING

RIBBED BAND

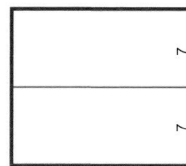

RIBBED CUFF

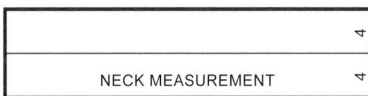

NECK MEASUREMENT

RIBBED COLLAR

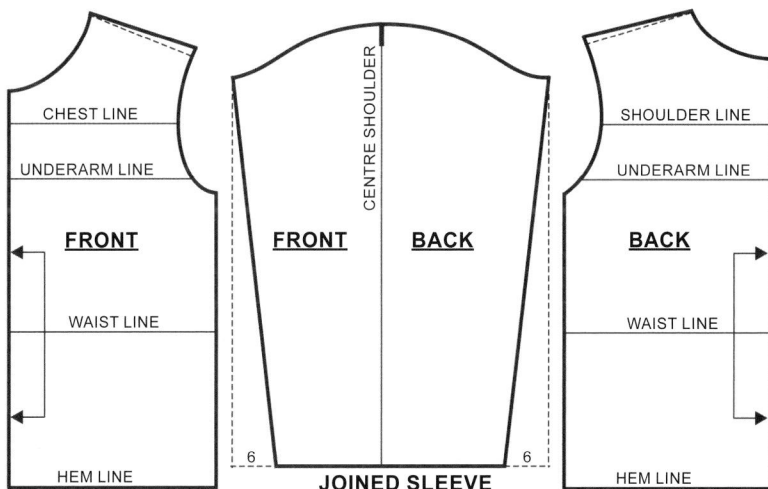

BODICE

- Draw the t-shirt base pattern with a chest circumference ease of 20 cm / 7.87" (e.g.: 96 + 20 = 116 ÷ 2 = 58 cm / 22.83").
- Lower the shoulder Z1-Z2 and G1-G2 by the desired amount (2 cm / 0.79") and raise the second shoulder point by 1 cm / 0.39".
- Lower the underarm Q-Q1 as desired (2 cm / 0.79").
- Draw the desired neck circumference.

SLEEVE

- Copy X-Q2 (the armscye), as in the raglan sleeve, indenting 2 cm / 0.79" at the shoulder.
- Extend the shoulder line by carrying over the desired sleeve length measurement X-X1. Draw Q2-X2 parallel to X-X1.
- Check that these lines are equal at the front and back.
- Join the sleeve of the front to that of the back.

CARDIGAN

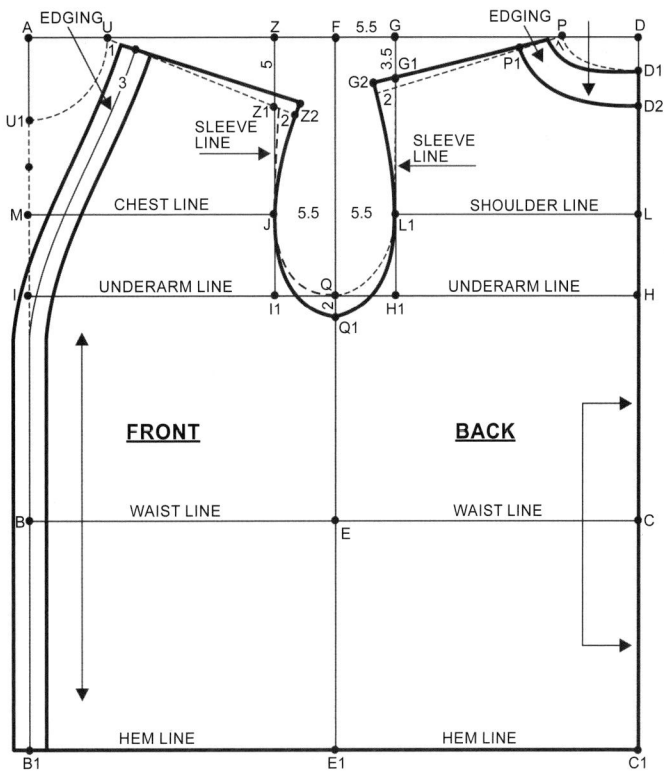

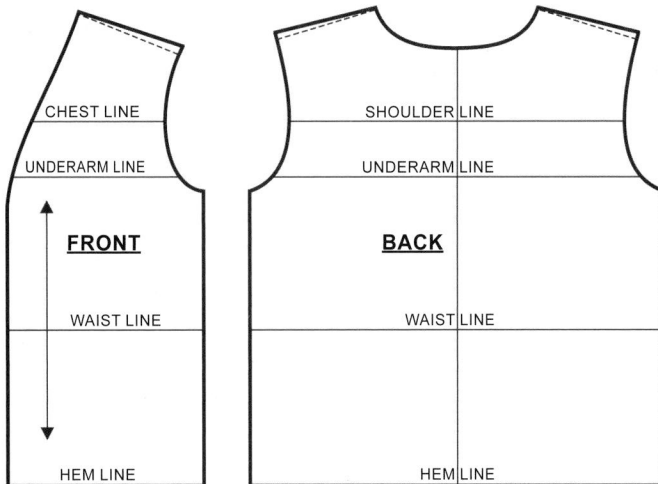

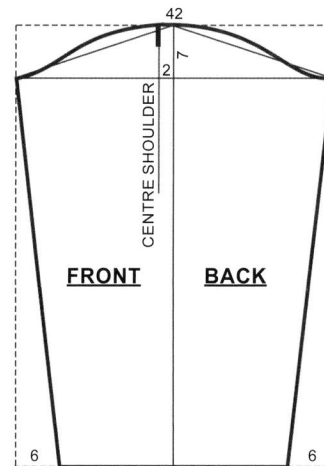

RIBBED FABRIC FOR THE TORSO

RIBBED FABRIC FOR THE CUFF

Bodice

- Draw the t-shirt base pattern with ease at the underarm level + 16 / 6.30" (e.g.: 96 + 16 = 112 ÷ 2 = 56 cm / 22.05")
- Lower the shoulder Z1-Z2 and G1-G2 by 2 cm / 0.79" and raise the second shoulder point by 1 cm / 0.39".
- Lower the underarm Q-Q1 as desired (2 cm / 0.79").
- Draw the neckline and the border on the front and back.
- Separate the parts.

Sleeve

- Draw the sleeve like that of the shirt, in the desired measurements.

Ribbed edging

- Draw the ribbed edging patterns, doubled and in a length appropriate to the elasticity of the material.

T-SHIRT WITH CAP KIMONO SLEEVES

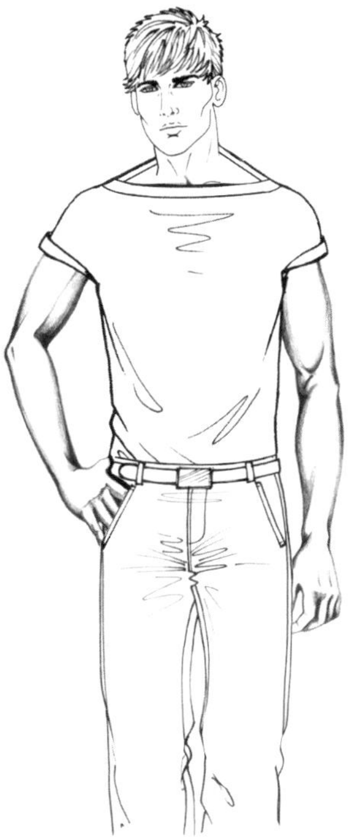

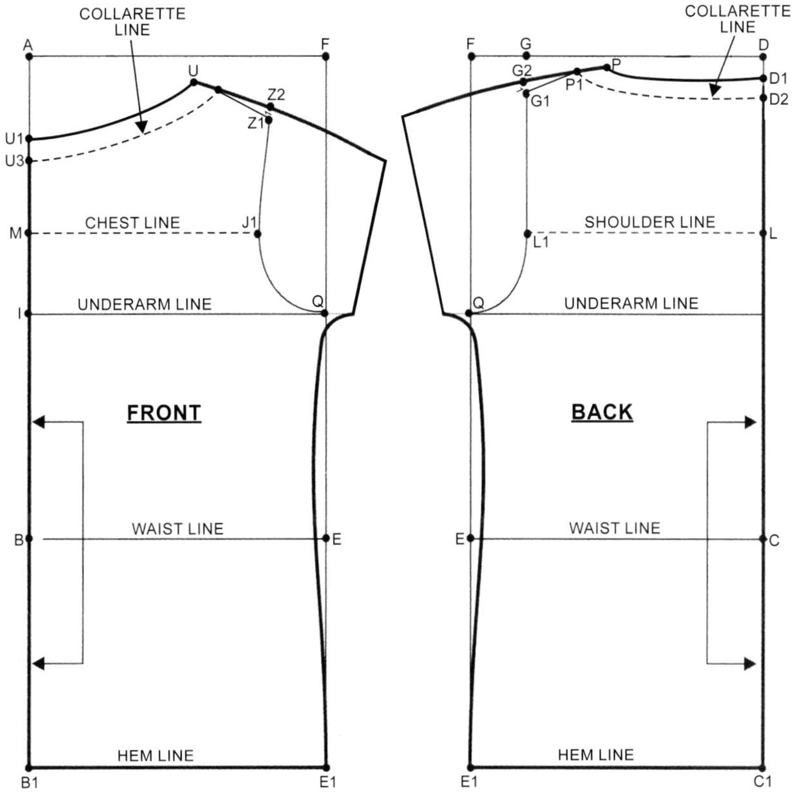

COLLARETTE LINE

COLLARETTE LINE

A · · · F

F · · G · P · · D

U

Z2

Z1

G2

G1

P1

D1

D2

U1

U3

M · · · CHEST LINE · · · J1

SHOULDER LINE · · · L

M · · · L1

I · · · UNDERARM LINE · · Q

Q · · UNDERARM LINE · · I

FRONT

BACK

B · · · WAIST LINE · · · E

E · · WAIST LINE · · · C

HEM LINE

HEM LINE

B1 · · · E1

E1 · · · C1

T-SHIRT WITH SHORT RAGLAN SLEEVES

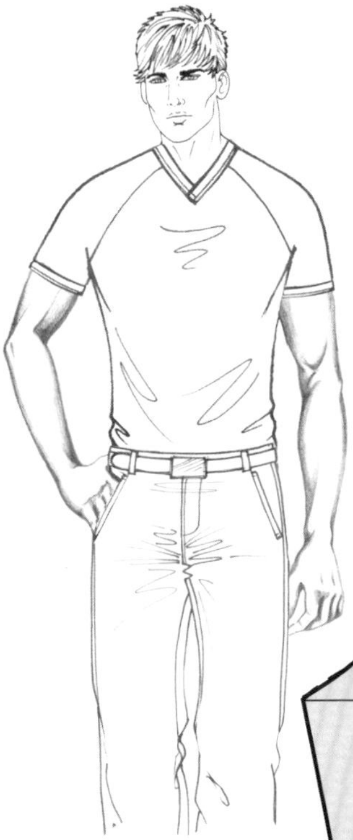

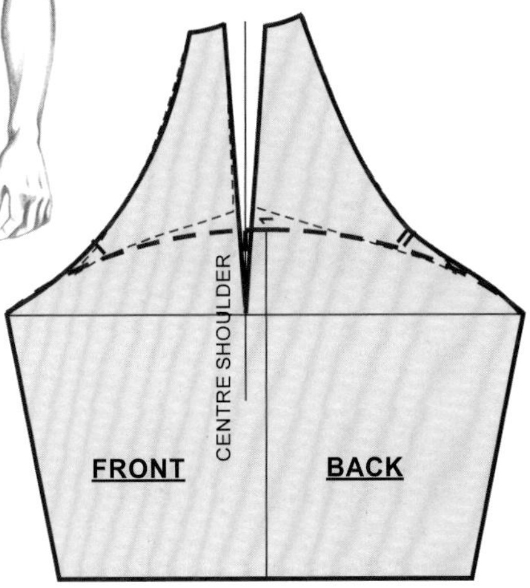

A · U · U2 · Z · F · G · P · D2

5.5 · 5.5

3

Z1

G1

P1 · 3

2

U1

U3 · 6

M · · · CHEST LINE · J1 J

L1 · SHOULDER LINE · · · L

M · · · L

I · · · UNDERARM LINE · I1

Q · H1 · UNDERARM LINE · H

FRONT

BACK

B · · · WAIST LINE

WAIST LINE · · · C

E

HEM LINE

HEM LINE

B1 · · · E1 · · · C1

CENTRE SHOULDER

FRONT · **BACK**

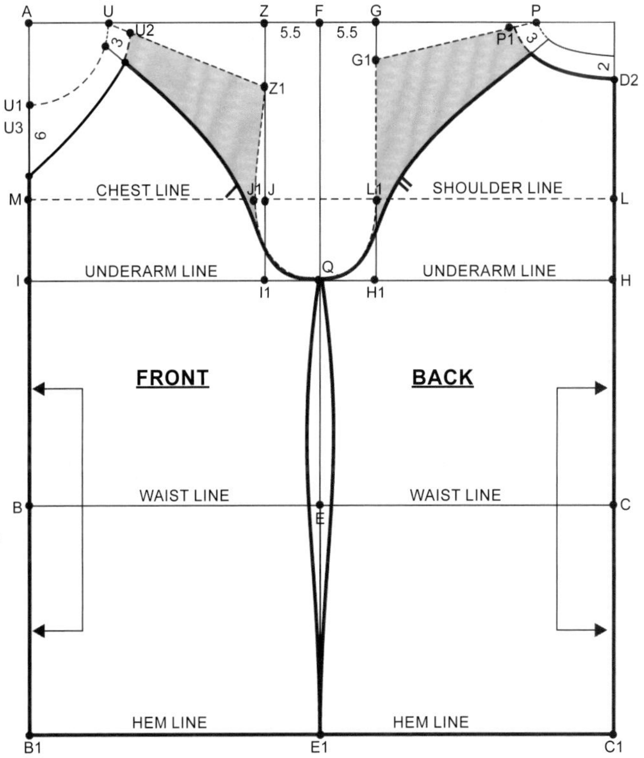

SWEATSHIRT WITH RAGLAN SLEEVES

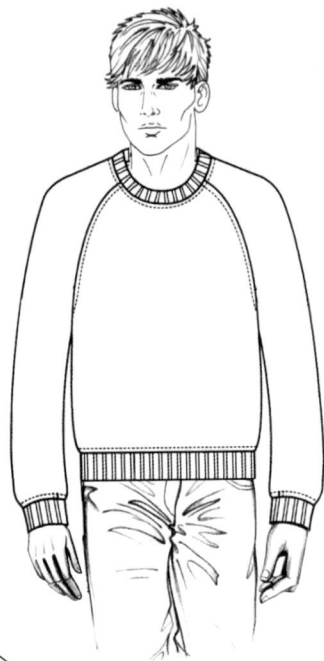

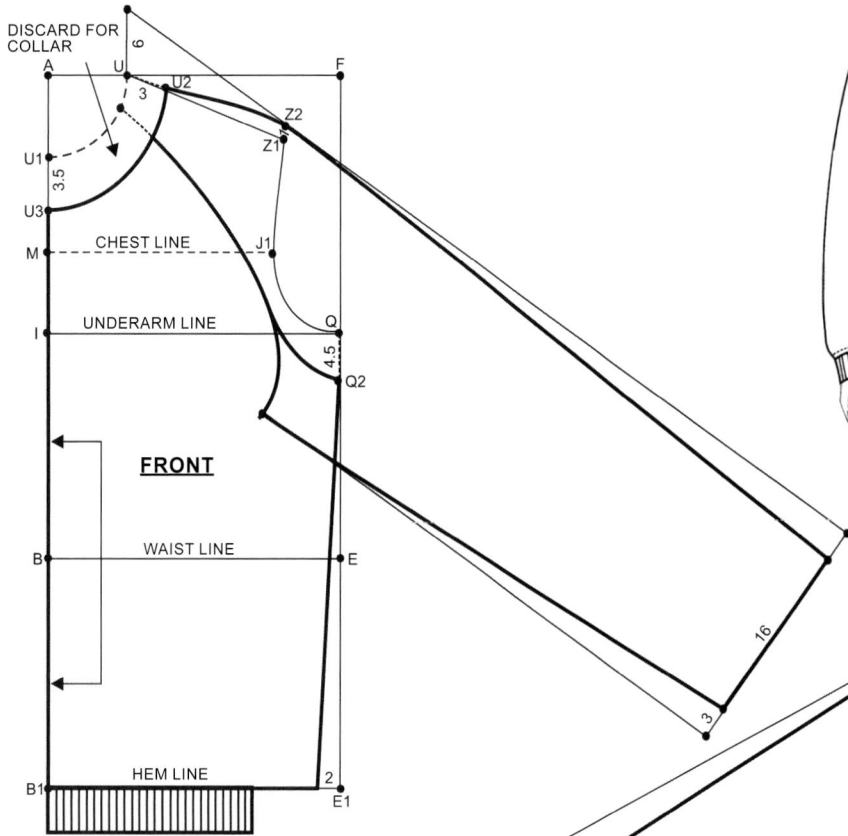

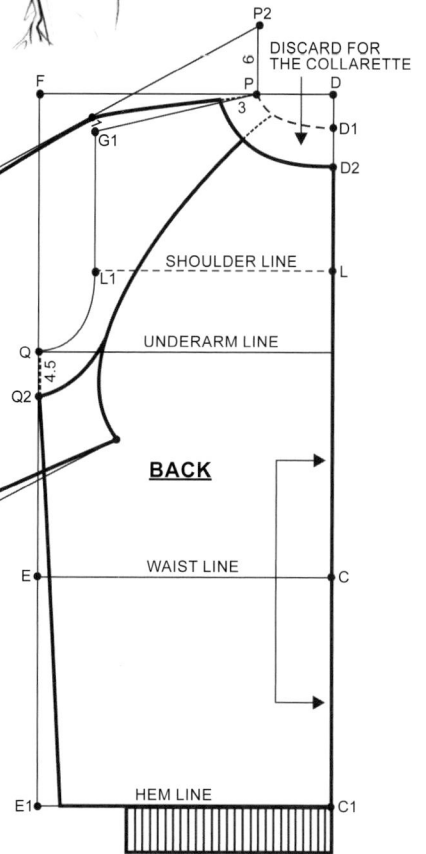

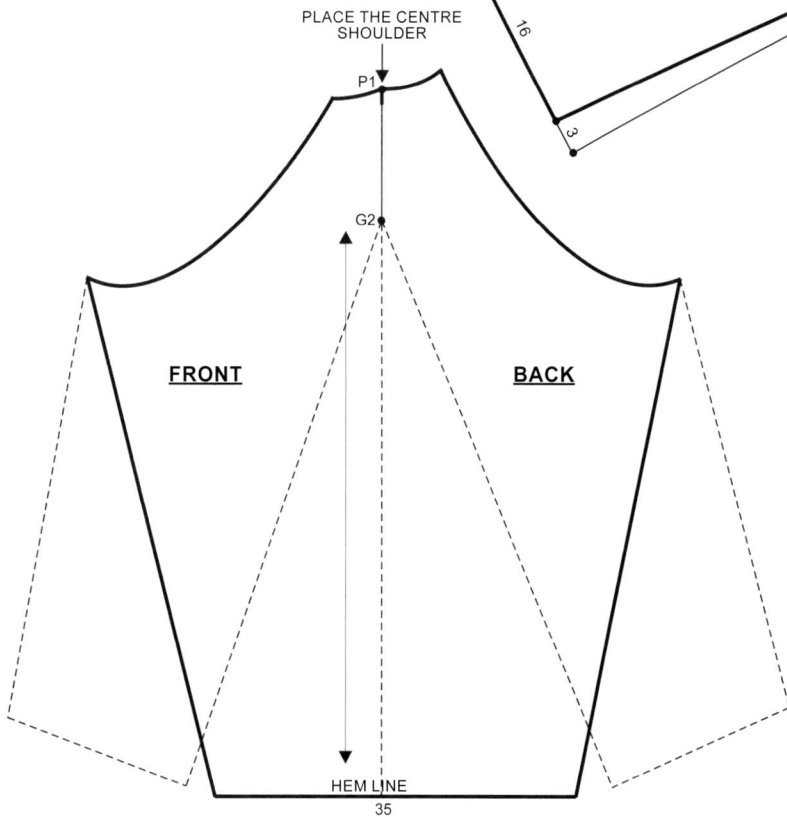

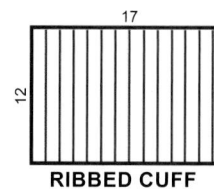

FRONT

DISCARD FOR COLLAR

A U U2 F
6
3
Z2
U1
3.5
Z1
U3
M — CHEST LINE — J1
I — UNDERARM LINE — Q
4.5
Q2

FRONT

B — WAIST LINE — E

B1 — HEM LINE — E1
2

16
3

BACK

P2
DISCARD FOR THE COLLARETTE
F P D
6
3
G1 D1
D2
L1 — SHOULDER LINE — L
Q — UNDERARM LINE
Q2
4.5

BACK

E — WAIST LINE — C

E1 — HEM LINE — C1

16
3

PLACE THE CENTRE SHOULDER

P1

G2

FRONT   **BACK**

HEM LINE
35

CHECK THE ELASTICITY OF THE RIBBED FABRIC
6

RIBBED COLLAR

17
12

RIBBED CUFF

LONG UNDERWEAR

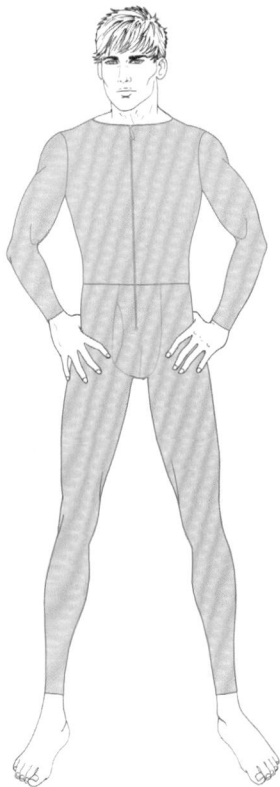

Bodice

- Draw a rectangle A-B-C-D.
- A-B = front neck to waist minus 1-3 cm / 0.39-1.18" depending on the elasticity of the material (e.g.: 50 - 3 = 47 cm / 18.50").
- B-C = semi-circumference of the chest minus 2 cm / 0.79" or more depending on the elasticity of the material (e.g.: 96 - 2 = 94 ÷ 2 = 47 cm / 18.50")
- C-D1 = rear neck-to-waist 2.5 cm / 1" (e.g.: 47 - 2.5 = 44.5 cm / 17.52").
- B-E half of B-C; A-F like B-E; draw E-F.
- D1-H half C-D1; draw H-I (underarm level).
- D-G half of shoulder width - 1.5 cm / 0.59" (e.g.: 44 - 1.5 = 42.5 ÷ 2 = 21.25 cm / 8.37")
- Draw G-H1; A-J1 like D-G; draw J1-I1.
- H-L = 7 cm / 2.76". Draw L-M (chest and shoulder line).
- G-O = 4 cm / 1.57". Draw P-P1 passing through O (shoulder width - 0.5 cm / 0.20", e.g.: 12.5 cm / 4.92").
- J1-Z like G-O. Draw U-Z1 through Z (same length as P-P1 = 12.5 cm / 4.92").
- Q-Q1 = 1 cm / 0.39". Draw the armscye or armhole Q1-J-Z1 and Q1-L1-P1 gracefully.
- A-U = 1/3 of A-J1 + 0.5 cm / 0.20" (e.g.: 21.25 ÷ 3 = 7 + 0.5 = 7.5 cm / 2.95").
- A-U1 like A-U minus 0.5 cm / 0.20".
- D-P like A-U (7.5 cm / 2.95"); D-D1 = 2.5 cm / 1"; P-N like D-D1.
- B-W = 1/4 waist circumference minus 0.5 cm / 0.20" (e.g.: 88 ÷ 4 = 22- 0.5 / 0.20 = 21.5 cm / 8.46").
- C-W1 like B-W; draw W-Q-Q1 and W1-Q-Q1.

Long underwear

- Draw the base block of the long underwear with measurements of the same size as the bodice.
- Join the base of the bodice to the base of the legs by aligning the waist line, the centre back line and the centre front line.
- Even out the waist width perfectly.

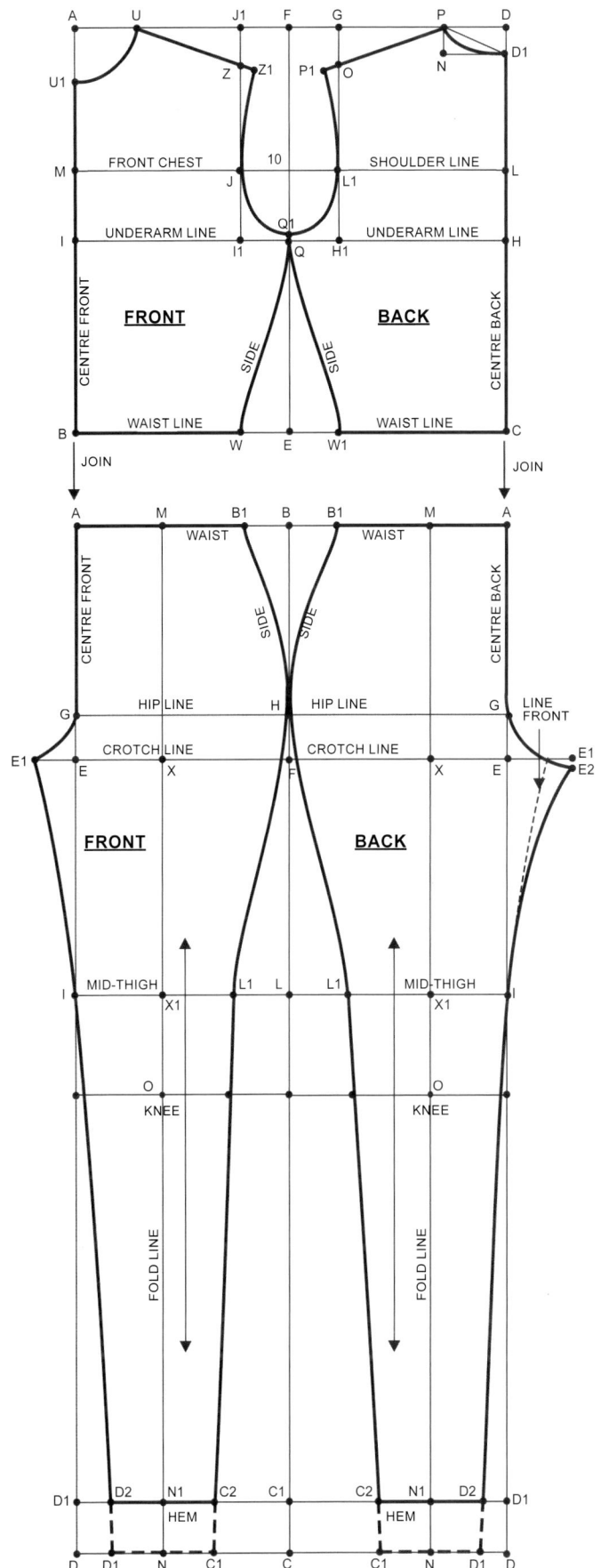

LONG UNDERWEAR SLEEVE

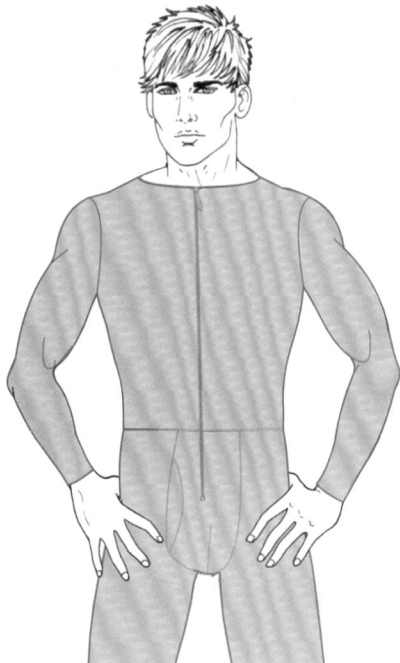

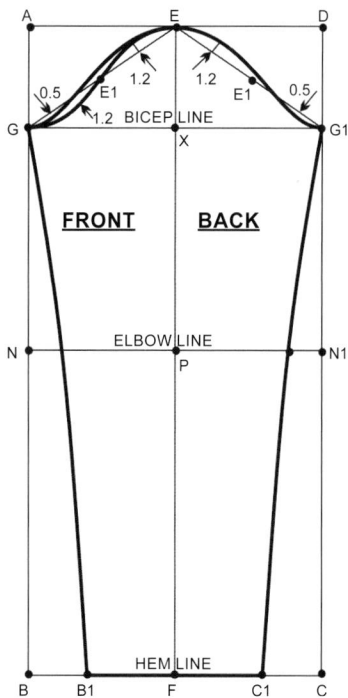

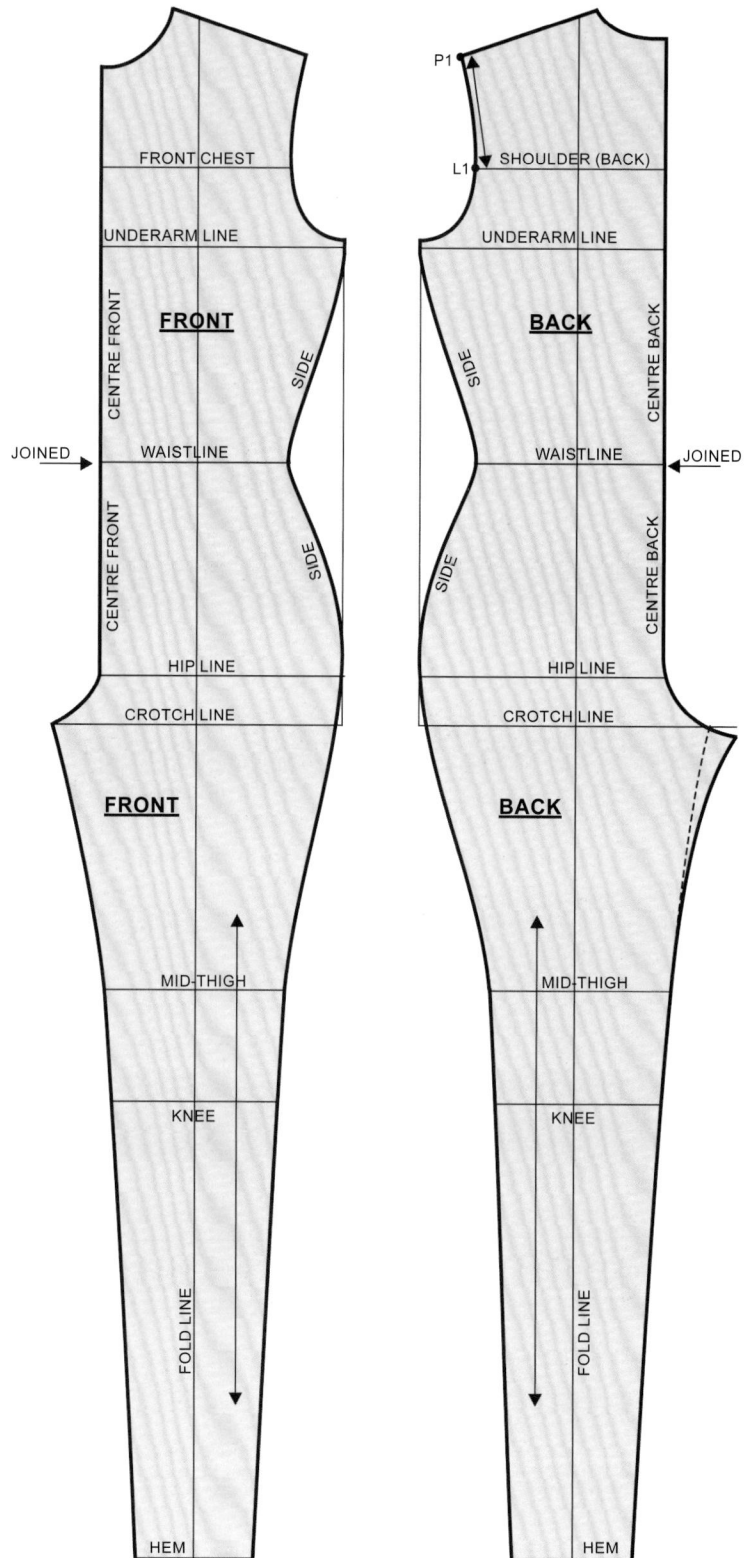

Measurements

- Arm circumference = 30.1 cm / 11.85".
- Ease for jersey fabric.
- Arm length = 60 cm / 23.62".
- On the left side of a sheet of pattern paper, draw the rectangle A-B-E-F with:
- A-E like the bodice sector + 1/2 sector (e.g.: 11 + 5.5 = 16.5 cm / 6.5").

- A-B = same length as the sleeve (e.g.: 60 cm / 23.62").
- A-G the same length as L1-P1 on the rear torso minus 1 cm / 0.39" (in this case: 11.5 - 1 = 10.5 cm / 4.13").
- Draw G-X parallel to A-E.
- A-N half of A-B (elbow line)
- E-E1 half of G-E.
- Trace the front and back sleeve crown as shown in the figure.

PREPARATION, CONSTRUCTION AND SIZING

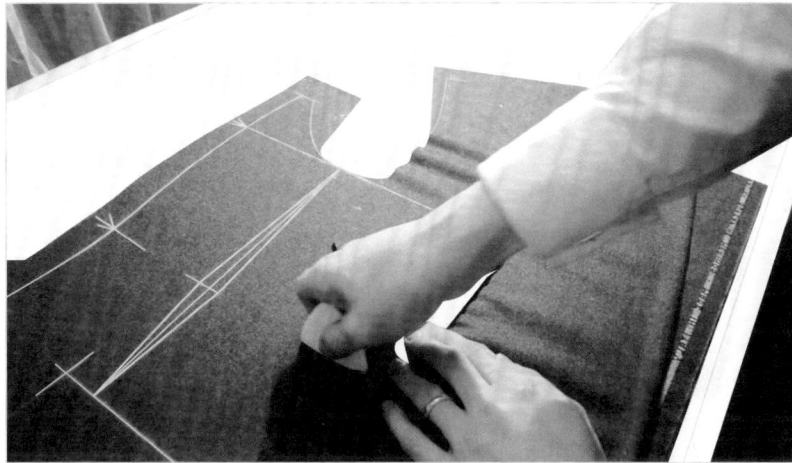

PAPER PATTERNS

Creation of a prototype paper pattern

A paper pattern is a graphic representation of the structure of a garment. It makes up the base for the subsequent phase, i.e. the assembly and construction of the garment. Working closely with the designer, the patternmaker will develop the garment's paper pattern in a standard size, usually based on the measurements of the company's pattern or the brand's measurement chart. The garment is then made in multiple versions (many of which will be discarded); after that, any defects are corrected. The final paper pattern is reworked to create the size variations determined by the company, then made as a series. Only then is the product ready to be sold.

Industrialisation of the paper pattern

Companies generally use paper patterns coming from their archive to create new collections. The base patterns are digitised and can be brought up from a computer database at any time. The end result is saved and then archived in a complete range of sizes, thus remaining available for the creation of the spreading plan.

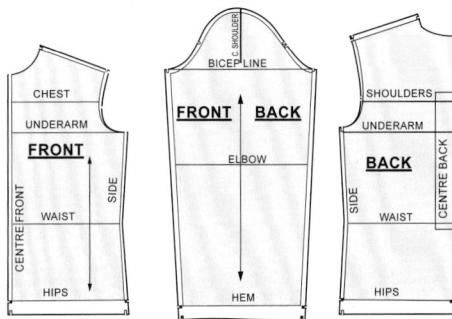

Notches

Notches are made on the edges of the pattern with special punches in different shapes and sizes, based on the intended use. They are created in various positions on the edge of the pattern, indicating:
- the distance of the seam from the edge of the fabric.
- the centre of the pattern.
- checks for pleating and slack.
- dart/pleat base.
- identification of the front (1 notch) and the back (2 notches).
- indication of the sides of the patterns to sew together.
- the position of zips, hemlines and the waistline.
- the inside of curves.
- the position of the outer point of the shoulder for kimono sleeves.
- the position of pockets and trimmings.
- the position of the centre neck on the collar.
- the sleeve crown.

Notches make it easier to line up the seams of various pieces during assembly.

Punchings or circles

These small holes are created on the pattern and then carried over to the fabric with special drill markers, or created on the garment, marking them with a special form, used to mark: the point and end of darts and pleats; dart curves; corners; the position of buttons, button holes, passementerie and pockets.

Darts

To transfer the darts from a paper pattern to fabric, it is necessary to create a different type of marking for the dart on the paper patter with the use of a tailor's scratch awl. First you will need to draw the dart as shown in the figure: add two notches to the ends and a point with a circle around it at a distance of 1.5 cm / 0.59" from the point, keeping it within the dart. At this point, to carry over the dart to the fabric, transfer the notches with a pair of scissors and make a small hole at 1.5 cm / 0.59" from the point, using the tailor's awl. Do a test run on a piece of fabric to check that the awl isn't damaging it.

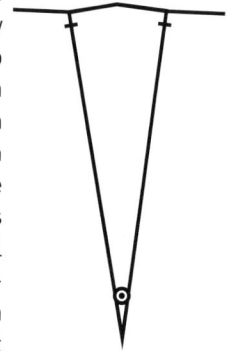

Once that's been done, draw a straight line with a ruler, connecting the two notches at the apex (which is found 1.5 cm / 0.59" from the hole made with the tailor's awl). This will make tracing the dart quick and easy. You can use a fabric marker or, just before sewing, the tracing wheel with chalk powder, which won't leave any residual marks and is ergonomic.

Seam allowances

The size of the seam margin varies according to its position, the type of garment being made, and the type of fabric. It can range from 1 to 2.5 cm / 0.39 to 1". For seams created with an overlocker, the allowances range from 0.7-1.2 cm / 0.28-0.47".

When creating the paper pattern, all the indications that can be useful to simplify the cutting and assembly processes must absolutely be marked.

The following must be marked in particular:
- the straight of grain, which should always be marked on each piece of the paper pattern with the relative arrow symbol.
- the name identifying the part of the pattern (e.g., front, back, sleeve, skirt, pocket, centre front, centre back, side, centre sleeve, etc.).
- the collection number, which is the number of the code that identifies the item.
- the size. If working with multiple sizes, the size relative to the paper pattern should be marked.
- the number of pieces to create from the same pattern.
- symbols and markings for assembly and construction, which are the circles that indicate the apex of a dart and which are used to create the holes with the drill marker on the lay during mass production.

MANUAL SIZING TOOLS

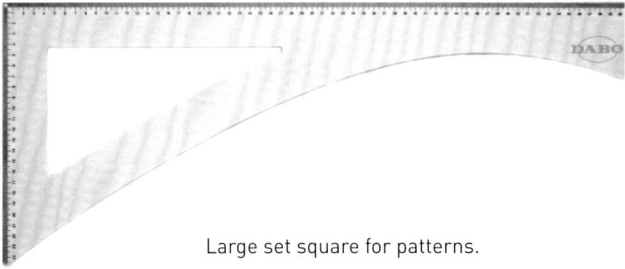

Large set square for patterns.

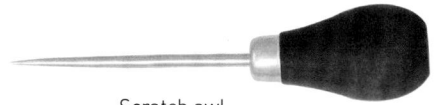

Scratch awl.

Plexiglas ruler.

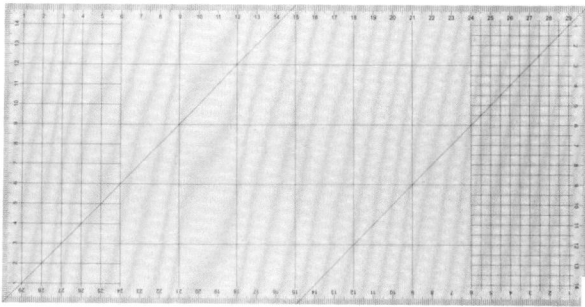

Set square for patternmakers with double grids.

Sewing machinist's scissors.

Cutter's shears.

Cardboard scissors.

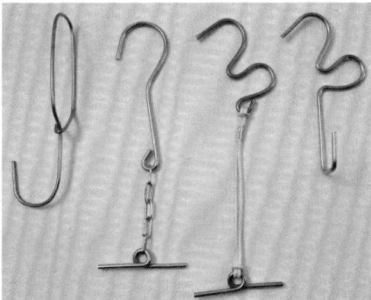

Hooks for paper patterns.

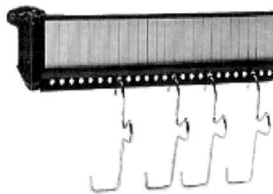

Hooks for paper patterns.

Notch punch.

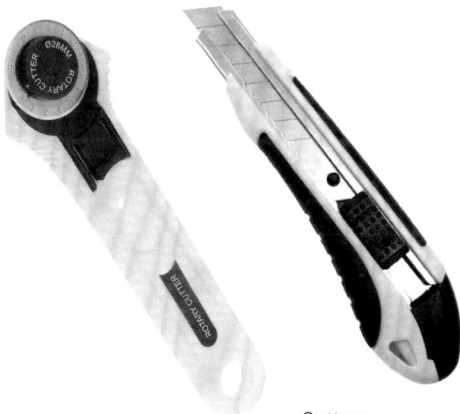

Cutters.

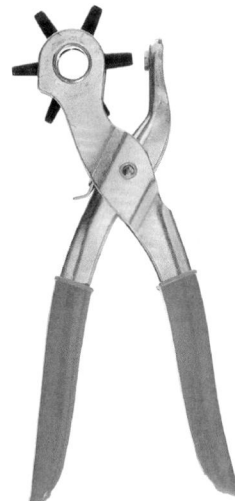

Hole punch.

SIZING (PATTERN GRADING)

Companies that want to produce and sell clothing must produce their garments in different sizes. For this reason, each garment goes through the sizing process. By sizing or pattern grading, we mean how the a pattern size can be increased or decreased with respect to the basic pattern (e.g.: size 16 in the UK) to create a range of fits. Grading factors are applied to the original measurements in length and width, to increase or decrease the size without having to create a basic pattern each time and more accurately achieving a comfortable fit. It should be mentioned that identifying a 'standard base size' is problematic in terms of measurements and sizes, due to the internationalisation of the market and the physical differences that exist between populations around the world.

MEASUREMENTS IN CM	UK tailor's dummy	Japan	USA	London fashion design	Italy
SIZE S	12	9	8	from 6 to 8	42
BUST	87	82	92	86	85-88
WAIST	64	62	74	68	67-70
HIPS	92	88	98	90	91-94
LENGTH C. BK. TORSO	40.5	37	42	41	42

COUNTRY	SIZE EQUIVALENTS							
GERMANY	34	36	38	40	42	44	46	48
SPAIN	36	38	40	42	44	46	48	50
FRANCE	36	38	40	42	44	46	48	50
ITALY	40	42	44	46	48	50	52	54
USA	6	8	10	12	14	16	18	20
UK	8	10	12	14	16	18	20	22
JAPAN	5	7	9	11	13	15	17	19

To create garments that are proportionally and aesthetically equal to the prototype, sizes must be developed: the distribution of the millimetres that distinguish one size from another with criteria analogous to those used to create base patterns. To identify these differences in millimetres, refer to the company's size and measurement chart, which has been created according to its target market. To correctly create different sizes for a pattern, a few fundamental principles need to be kept in mind: 1) the unit of measurement used to grade sizes is the millimetre; 2) the amounts that allow for variation from size to size are definite values, proportions or percentages of development; 3) each pattern is unique: you have to interpret the shapes, seams, and motifs and choose the shifting method, you need to look at the position of the points to move, ideally locating them on the person, to then refer to the relative sizing values.

Procedures

Once the garments and the relative patterns that will make up the collection have been chosen (or the single garment, for that matter), the company must decide which sizes it wants to sell. In other words, it has to define its size range. Size range examples: 12-14-16-18-20 (UK), in which the underlined size is the base pattern size.

Size grading methods

There are basically two size grading methods: manual and computer-assisted. The first method is being used less and less, even if it is still indispensable to know how to do so in order to execute other methods. Computers are being increasingly used in the fashion industry. They make it possible to automatically develop sizes, using specific mathematical formulas with specially designed CAD programs. In general, there are two size grading schools of thought: 1) that in which the incremental values are entered into a computer and applied automatically to develop other sizes, as happens with manual sizing; 2) that in which size charts are used to recalculate the measurements, for each and every size, using the same calculation method that the base size was made with. To develop sizes with a computer, you will need to either create the base pattern directly on the computer with a 1:1 scale, or upload a pre-existing paper pattern to the computer, an option which is made possible by CAD programs for patternmaking.

It is important to remember that it's best to avoid making a size range that's too broad (generally stick to 3 larger sizes

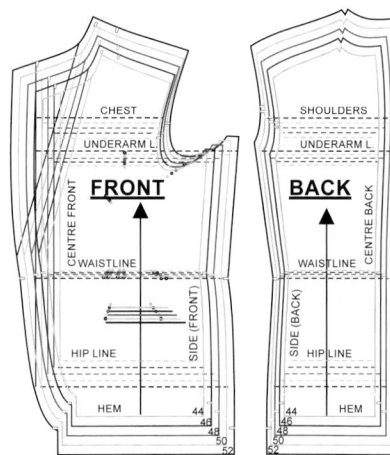

Example of sizing the front and back base of a men's jacket.

and 2 smaller ones), because it's very likely that the proportions of the base model will be distorted. For high-quality production, it's best to make a prototype in an intermediary size between that of the initial prototype and the largest size.

To start sizing a pattern, you'll need: 1) an approved pattern with the relative measurements (including the indications regarding the ease used); 2) a complete measurement chart for the sizes that need to be graded and from which to identify the grading values; 3) directly from the grading values standard, proportional or percentage measure chart (the values are in mm and refer to the total and not to 1/2 the pattern).

Manual sizing

Manually grading a pattern is done by using a base pattern which includes seams which has already been tested, with which the outline is drawn and subsequently sized. The outlines of the other sizes are marked initially with a special millimetre set square, with which the necessary measurements are applied, then connected using the base pattern as a ring ruler, in addition to the ruler and set square.

The most well-known tools for manual sizing, though used very little after the arrival of 2D CAD systems, are: the *Multi Grader* from Willcos & Gibbs, which carries out the development and cutting of patterns, and the Variator by Steiner (Switzerland), which however does not have the cutting device. These tools have command devices for horizontal and vertical movements or a combination of both types of movements, which make it possible to control the grading of the base pattern in the subsequent sizes.

Computer-assisted sizing

In the clothing industry, this process is currently carried out automatically, using computerised systems that apply specific mathematical formulas to the pattern.

The work flow is as follows: starting from the outline of the original base size pattern, created on cardboard and including seam allowances, the Cal Comp Curve Tracer or Digitiser, a tracer device that automatically outlines the edges of the pattern by pressing a button on a tracer head equipped with a cross-hairs to perfectly centre the points on the outline, or through a photographic machine connected to the CAD software.

There are two types of computerised grading methods:
1) using the incremental measurements entered beforehand in the computer, as allowed for by the program. These numbers are automatically applied to create smaller or larger sizes, reflecting the manual size grading process.
2) using the size chart, with which the calculations are redone for every single size similar to those done for the base size, ensuring the balance between size and proportion is maintained.

Grading without seams

It's good practice to apply the rules to various pieces without the seams when grading garments. The resulting pattern will be so precise that it's almost impossible for issues to arise when the garment is being constructed.

Many companies often find themselves faced with this problem: grading doesn't uphold the same precise characteristics as the base paper pattern. Essentially, the seam-free method is used to ensure control over the fit and ease, but especially over precise, meticulous assembly.

How grading is done

1) Rules are applied on each vertex of the pattern, which is a pair of measurements that is made on Cartesian axes.
2) To be able to create sizes using the seam-free method, the paper pattern has to be made by a careful, expert patternmaker, or that pattern has to be created digitally (without seams). Otherwise, it will either have to have the seams removed or be graded on the version with seams.

Grading: curves and groups

Pattern grading can be done with numerous variants, applying the rules so as to create regular sizing or irregular in some parts and regular in others, or even with certain criteria up to a certain size, and with other criteria from that size upwards. Evaluating each garment individually is best for secure, precise sizing.

Curves and sizing

When grading, the physical conformation of the person should be considered in the size being worked on:
1) if you are going up in size, remember that there are a few parts of the body that tend to increase more than others.
2) When going down in size, the proportion will change compared to when going up in size. This 'rule' isn't just a matter of intuition; it's the result of a method and a constant quest to improve the sizing services offered. It requires quite a bit of experience, because it must encapsulate the need to maintain the fit of the base garment in all other sizes.

The fit and ease start with the base paper pattern, but it should also be considered when grading. A good grader eschews the standard because they believe that each company has its own needs and each person is unique, especially if the size range is wide.

Grading groups

When there are a lot of sizes to be made, it's best to grade in size groups.

Let's see how this is done with an example. If you need to create an overcoat in a lot of different sizes (from 14 to 24 UK for example), you can't just proportionally increase the size of the pocket. If you did, size 24 would have disproportionally large pockets. In these cases, it's best to grade by size groups: 8, 10 and 12 will have one measurement, 14, 16, and 18 another, and 20, 22 and 24 yet another for the pocket. It's a matter of both aesthetics and fit.

LOOSE OVERCOAT SIZING

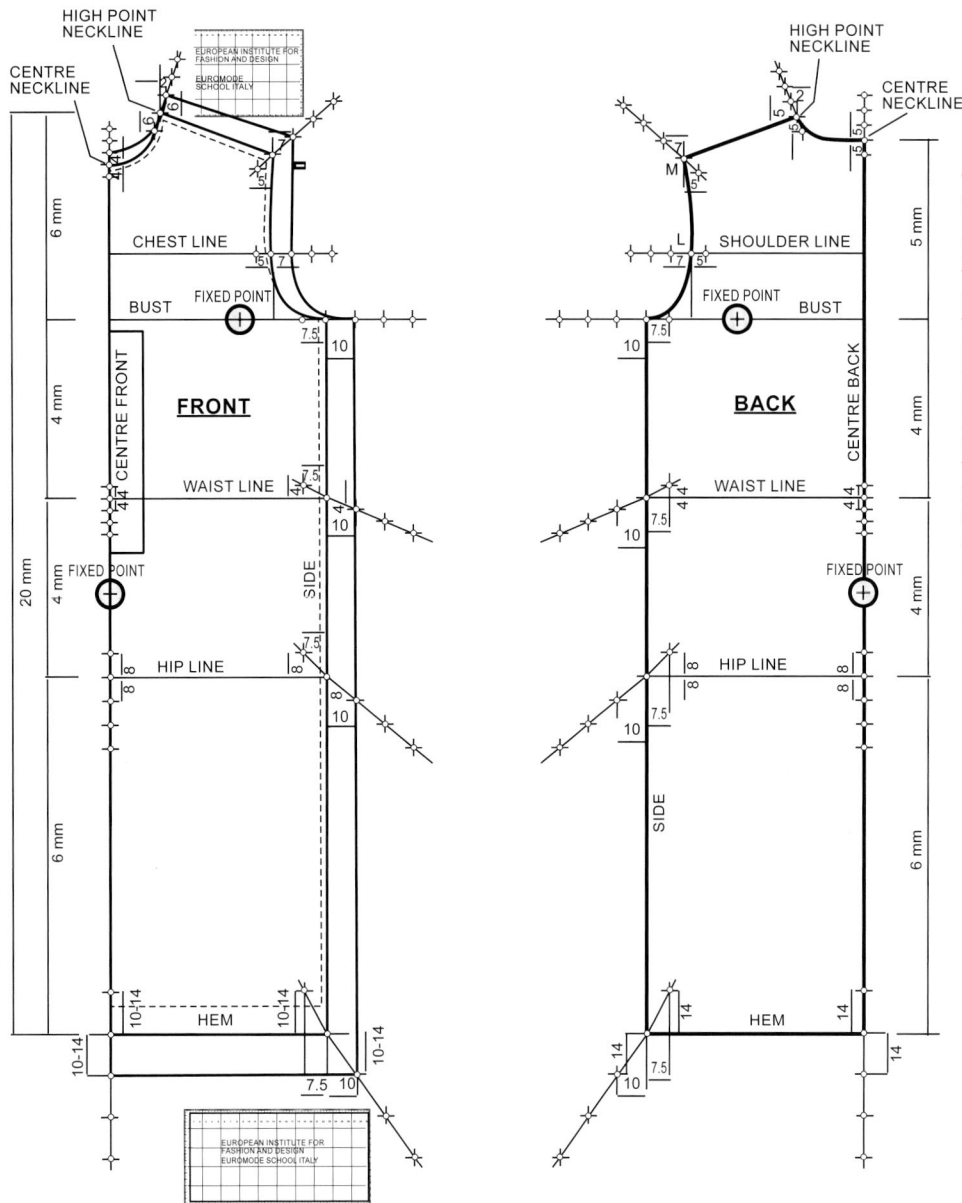

The grading of the back, in this case for both the larger and smaller sizes, is carried out by keeping the underarm line and the centre back line stable.

The grading of the front of a loose-fitting overcoat is much simpler.

To increase the values, use the same procedure as the back. The only difference is that the armscye sector increases/decreases by 6 mm / 0.24" instead of 5 mm / 0.20", with an overall increase of 20 mm / 0.79".

The length measurements at the front are lengthened/shortened by 15-20 mm / 0.59-0.79" overall, as follows:
- armscye sector, 5-6 mm / 0.20-0.24".
- waist sector, 3-4 mm / 0.12-0.16".
  hip sector, 3-4 mm / 0.12-0.16".
- hem and lower edge sector, 4-6 mm / 0.16-0.24".

Before you start:

1) make sure that the straight of grain is marked on each piece. That line is going to be used to square all the points that are to be graded.

2) Make sure that there are seam allowances.

3) Make sure that all pieces are present and that they line up.

Proceed to the grading process

- Lay out a piece of pattern paper that's suitable in terms of its consistency and size for the table you're working on.
- Place the cardboard pattern on the paper; place weights on top to ensure it doesn't move; and draw the outlines with a thin pencil.
- Draw the reference points of the straight of grain: notches, darts, etc.
- Remove the cardboard base and complete the drawing of the pattern, including the parts that were covered by the cardboard silhouette.
- Establish the overall increase/decrease measurements, in both length and width, to provide for the grading of each size, and calculate the amount for every single piece that's being graded.

This last idea is important when sizing. It makes it possible to maintain the garment's proportions, especially if there are multiple pieces in the pattern to assign the correct variation to.

For example, if we have to distribute 10 mm / 0.39" over a pattern that has two sectors, we need to first establish which of the two pieces is larger and which is smaller. Then we need to assign a greater or lesser value in length and width. Once you have mastered this mechanism of proportions, you will have overcome every challenge related to sizing. Herein we'll create sizes starting from a base size 16 (UK), with the measurements found in our size chart. The value established for the difference in length and width is shown as a double figure so that the grading diagonal can be drawn with greater precision. All the other points relative to the sizes you want to make will be plotted along this diagonal, joining the straight lines with the help of a ruler, and the curves and various contours with the original manila pattern pieces.

SIZE GRADING - INSET SLEEVES

Before starting to size grade a fitted sleeve, you need to measure by how much the armscye of the front and back bodice has increased.

To find this value, you start at the perfect drape point (point L) on the paper pattern for the back, and, moving in the direction of the new shoulder (point M), you measure the difference (in this case we found 3.5 mm / 0.14" for the back and 4 mm / 0.16" for the front). Then, keeping the pattern on the perfect drape point L, move in the direction of the graded side (point N), and measure the difference (in this case, we found 3 mm / 0.12", from point L to point N, both front and back). These values are marked on the sleeve pattern.

Now draw the sleeve and set the line R-S square with respect to the straight of grain. On the paper pattern, from the perfect drape point on the front, point A, measure 4 mm / 0.16" towards the shoulder (this is how much the sleeve is to be increased or decreased on the front) and lay this new point on the front perfect drape point; mark the new armhole on the straight grain up to the shoulder on the paper pattern.

Keeping to the paper pattern, from the shoulder moving towards the perfect drape point on the back, measure 3.5 mm / 0.14", and lay this point on the new shoulder marked S at the end of the armhole (ever respecting the straight grain) and draw the curve of the sleeve head, including the perfect drape point and the end of the armhole (point T).

From point T measure 3 mm / 0.12" and from point R on the front 3 mm / 0.12".

Finish by lengthening the sleeve by 10 mm/0.39" from points R and S, down to the cuff on the straight of grain.

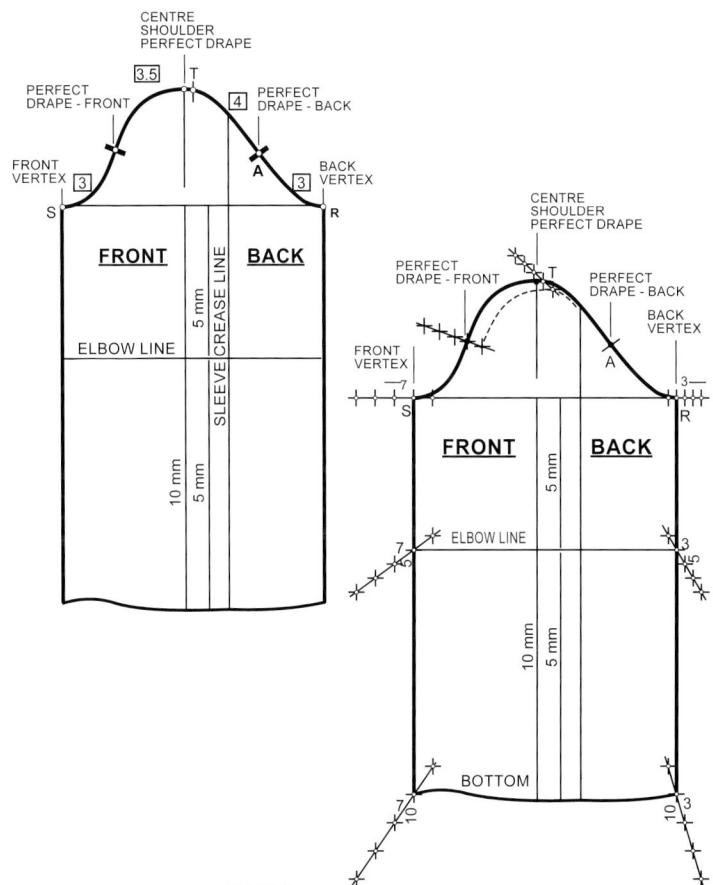

SIZE GRADING A SLEEVE WITH UNDERSLEEVE

Oversleeve

- Lay the basic bodice block over the new front perfect drape point and measure the difference between the basic block shoulder and that of the upper and lower pattern.
- Drop or raise by 3 mm / 0.12" the sleeve pattern on the shoulder drape point and, keeping it 45° to the centre shoulder line, draw the outlines as far as the front and back drape points.

Front vertex: widen and reduce 2 mm / 0.08".

Seam vertex: widen and reduce 4 mm / 0.16".

Elbow line: widen and reduce 2 mm / 0.08", raise and drop 5 mm / 0.20" on the front. Widen and reduce 4 mm / 0.16", raise and drop 5 mm / 0.20" on the seam line.

Hem point: widen and reduce 2 mm / 0.08", raise and drop 10 mm / 0.39" on the front.

- Widen and reduce 4 mm / 0.16", raise and drop 10 mm / 0.39" on the seam line.

Undersleeve

- Reduce and widen by 3 mm / 0.12" on the seam line.
- Reduce and widen 1 mm / 0.04" on the back.
- Raise and drop 5 mm / 0.20" on the elbow line.
- Extend and shorten 10 mm / 0.39" on the hem.

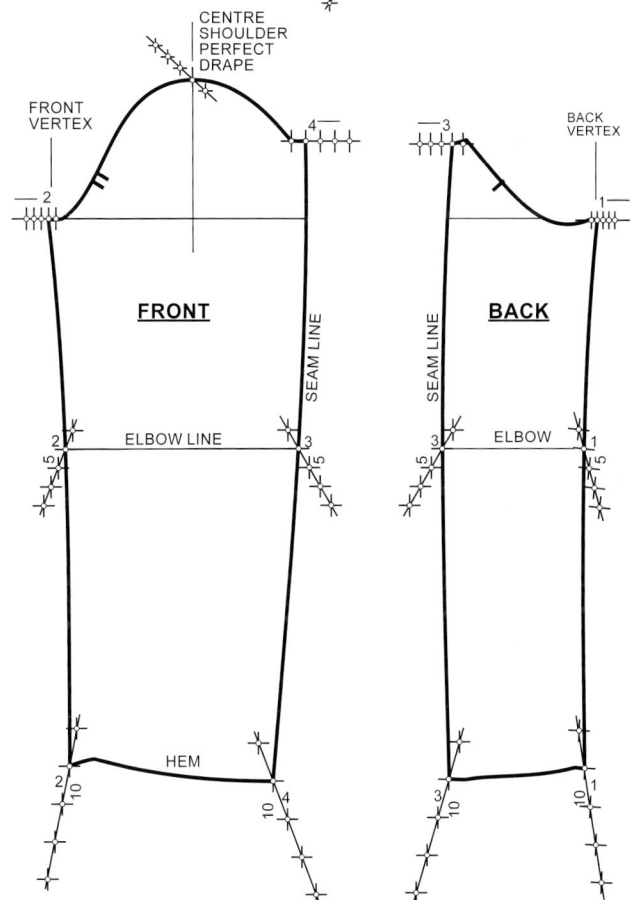

SIZING TROUSERS
KEEPING THE INSEAM AND THE DARTS FIXED

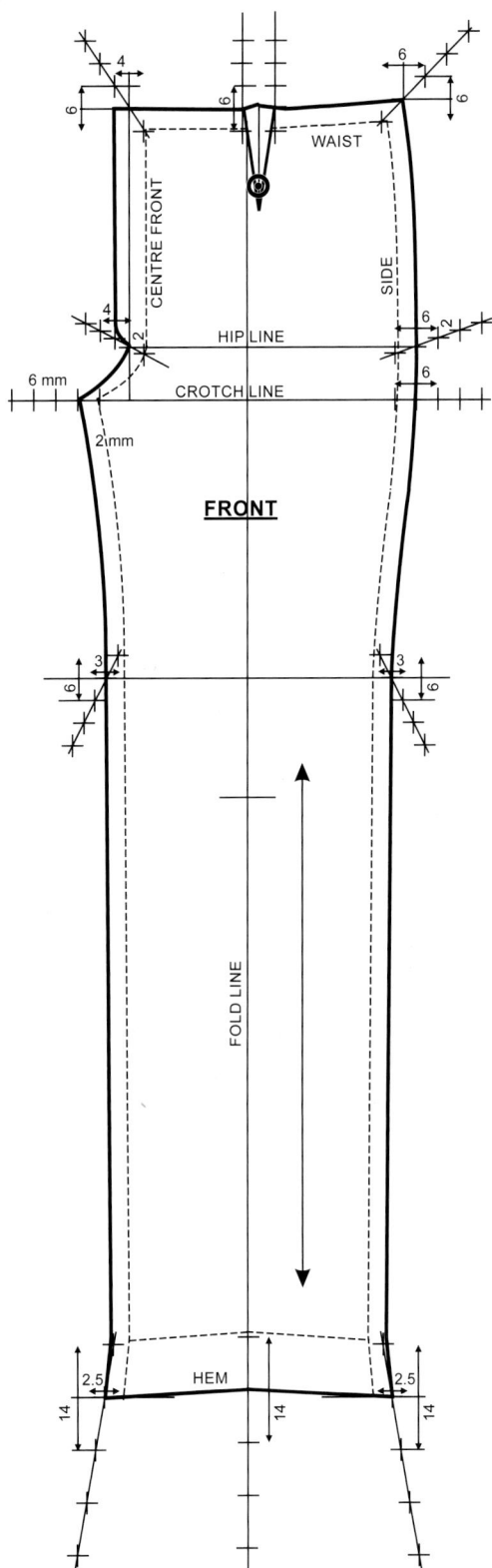

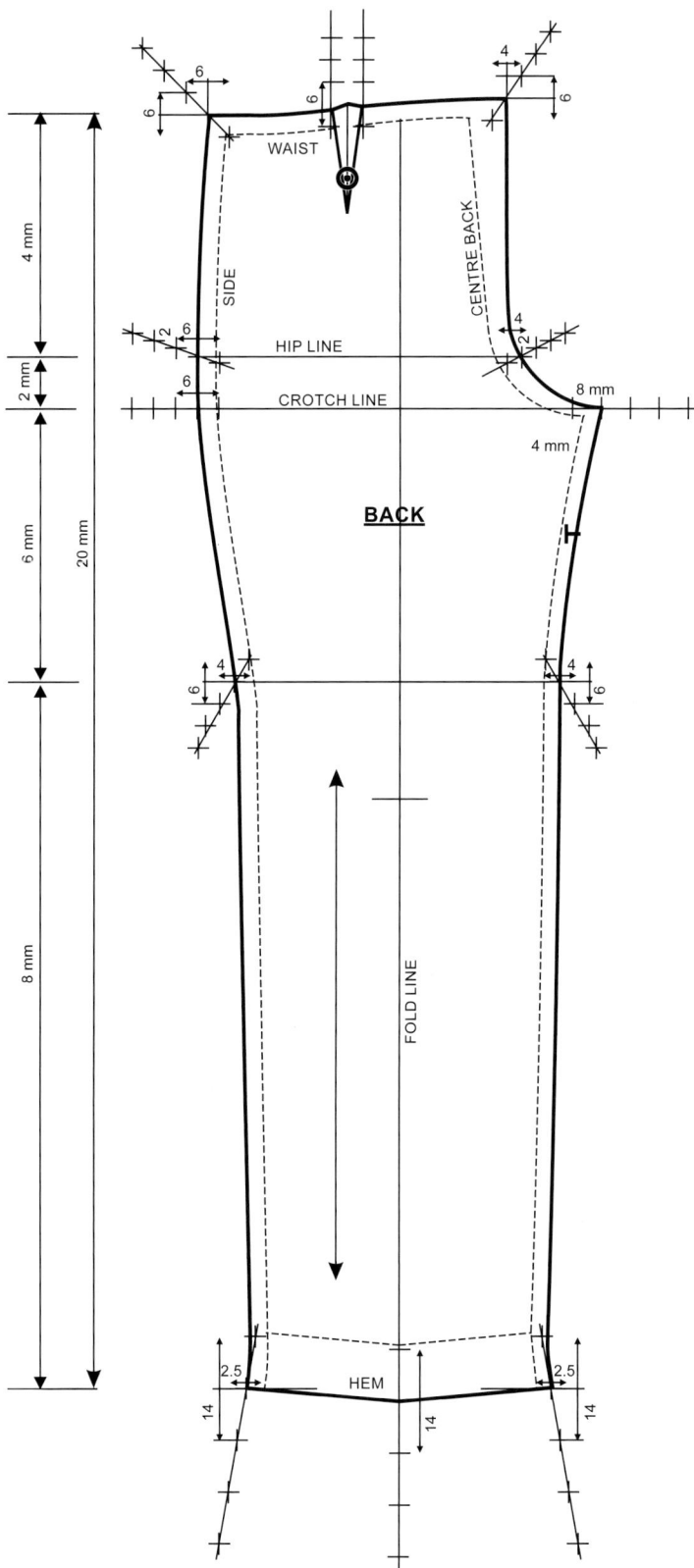

FRONT

BACK

WAIST

CENTRE FRONT

SIDE

HIP LINE

CROTCH LINE

FOLD LINE

HEM

WAIST

SIDE

CENTRE BACK

HIP LINE

CROTCH LINE

FOLD LINE

HEM

4 mm

2 mm

6 mm

8 mm

20 mm

6 mm

8 mm

2 mm

4 mm

Length
The trousers should be lengthened overall by 15-20 cm / 5.91-7.87".
The added fabric should be distributed as follows:
- Waist-side 3-4 mm / 0.12-0.16".
- Side-inseam 1.5-2 cm / 0.59-0.79".
- Crotch line/mid-thigh line 4.5-6 cm / 1.8-2.4".
- Mid-thigh line-hem 5-8 mm / 0.20-0.31".

Width
- From the centre front (or the centre back) to the side seam, narrow or widen by 10 mm / 0.39".
- Overall 4 cm / 1.57".
The front crotch line narrows or widens by 2 mm / 0.08".
The back crotch line narrows or widens by 4 mm / 0.14" because it's wider.
- Narrow the hemline by 5 mm / 0.20" both at the front and back.

SPREADING

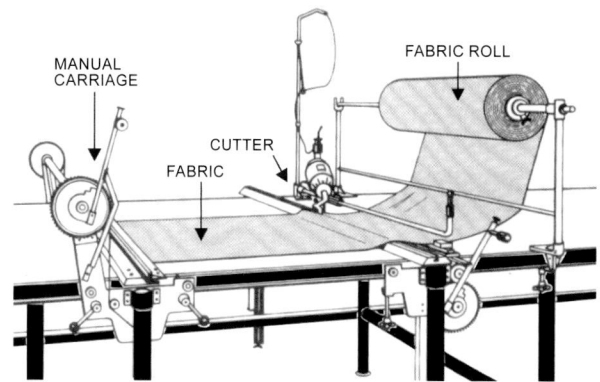

MANUAL SPREADER

The layout or spreading of the pattern on the fabric is an operation carried out when making a series of garments. The rolls of fabric are un-rolled and placed on a table made just for cutting the layers, placed one over the other, and aligned along the sides and the top. This group of layers, called a lay, makes it possible to cut multiple pieces at the same time, reducing production time and guaranteeing that all pieces are consistent.

SPREADING METHODS

You may layout or spread the fabric by hand, with a table and a manual or automated spreading machine. The latter provides continuous fabric spreading for fabric in rolls, layers, tubes or fabric that has been opened.

Hand spreading

When hand spreading, the plies are pulled manually along the cutting table, stacked, lined up and then cut as required. This system may be supported by mechanised equipment to easily unroll and cut the pieces of fabric. Hand spreading is common in small companies and is suitable for creating short plies of fabric, or when frequent changes in the colour or type of fabric are required.

Spreading with a manual spreading machine

With this method, the rolls are placed in a specifically designed holder on the spreading machine and unrolled manually by moving the machine back and forth. This type of spreader, also often used by small clothing producers, smooths each layer and aligns the fabric's edges. It is particularly useful when working with long, wide plies and when the rolls of fabric are changed less frequently.

Spreading with an automatic spreading machine

These spreading machines are fully automated and computerised, and are used by large garment production companies. They provide highly precise, rapid spreading and cutting. In their basic configuration, they can be equipped with a traditional bar to hold the roll, but also with a cradle-feeding load mechanism, thus eliminating the need for a bar. They may also have a threading device that allows the fabric to be positioned automatically through the feed rollers until the cutter; a system for layering the fabric face to face and back to back; a cutting program; a cutting program with a meter-counter; meter-counter; rotating turret; a lay counter, etc. For knitwear taken from plies of fabric with a separating thread and for small pieces of knitwear, the stacking operation isn't done by machine. Such small size pieces of fabric are usually spread by hand. In order to carry out the spreading in a logical way, guaranteeing high quality garments, the fabric should have already undergone the size stabilisation process (tentering) beforehand, as well as have been checked for defects. It is necessary to stabilise the size of the fabric so that the fabric doesn't arrive to the spreader with abnormal tension which may produce defects (which can be quite significant). All fabric has a certain amount of "springback", and it is necessary to ensure that the fabric will not shrink during the steps that come after spreading and cutting. One mustn't think that pre-existing tension in the fabric

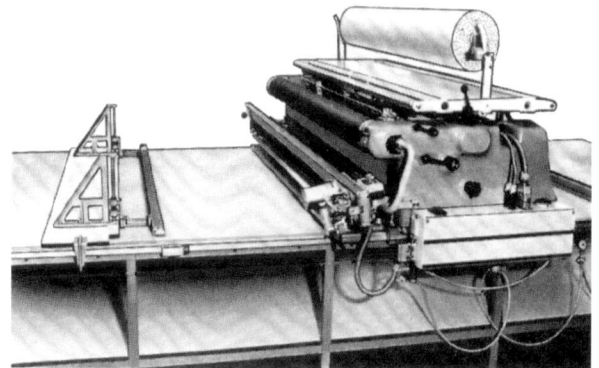

SPREADING MACHINE

COMPUTER-ASSISTED SPREADER

can be eliminated during spreading.

It's a good idea to remember that a proper spreader, that is, a machine equipped with an efficient fabric feeding mechanism, spreads the fabric with the same tension that it had before being put in the machine. For tubular fabrics, the stabilisation phase serves to guarantee that the height of the fabric is consistent along the entire piece. Checking for defects is meant to streamline the spreading operation and to avoid the possibility that a defect goes unnoticed before or during the spreading or that it passes unobserved until the final inspection of the finished garment. Checking for defects has yet another essential function: it ensures that the fabric is stored in the warehouse in the best condition possible, either rolled up or folded in layers.

The purpose of checking for defects is to streamline the folding operation and to prevent a defect not detected before or during the folding operation from going unnoticed until the final check made on the garment already packed.

SPREADING AND LAYERING TECHNIQUES

Methods for layering the fabric

The fabric may be placed in the following types of layers:
- A single ply, when only one piece of fabric is necessary (for example, to cut one pattern at a time);
- A lay: when the various plies of fabric are piled one on top of the other;
- A stepped lay: when the lay is made up of plies of fabric in various lengths, for example when there are multiple cuts in different quantities.

Spreading or layering systems

In clothing production, fabric may be spread by use of various systems, according to the characteristics of the fabric and the garment to be made: zig-zag spreading; spreading with front side against back; spreading with front to front or back to back.

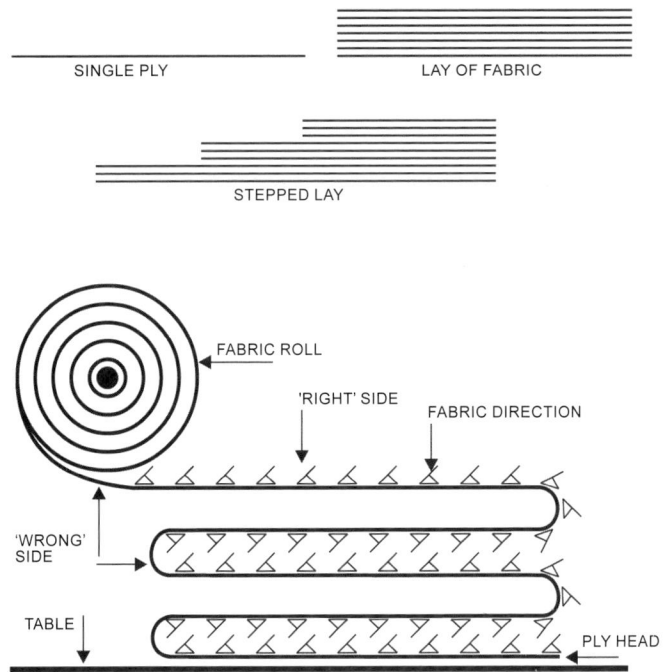

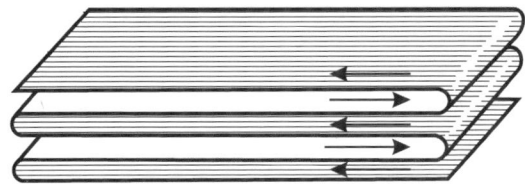

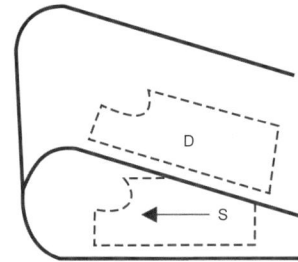

Zig-zag spreading

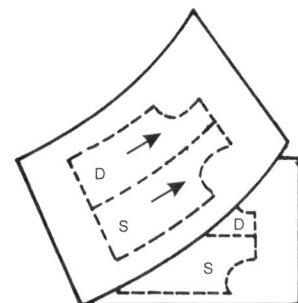

In zig-zag spreading, one layer of fabric is placed over another, without cutting to separate one layer from the next at each end of the lay. With this spreading system, the spread layers are placed 'face to face'. This means that the right side of the fabric faces the right side of the layer before it, and the knits point in opposite directions.

This spreading system is commonly used to make underwear and cut outer garments which do not require the knit or the nap of the fabric to be aligned.

Characteristics of zig-zag spreading:

1) It does not respect knit or nap orientation.

2) The right and left parts of the garment are made by superimposing the fabric in a single pack.

3) The right and left parts are perfectly equal as they are cut in a single operation.

4) Because the left and right pieces of the same garment are cut far away from each other on the strip of fabric, according to the length of the ply, it is possible that the pieces will have slight colour variations.

5) This is the quickest spreading method.

Laying fabric 'front against back'

Fabric spread with the face side against the back results in plies of fabric which are cut between one layer and the next. With this spreading system, after the separating cut is completed at the edge of the ply, the fabric is brought back to the head of the ply (where the spreading began on the previous layer) without stretching it. In this case, the knit or the top of the fabric are all facing the same direction.

This spreading system is used when it's necessary to see the top of the fabric, the nap or the knit, and to also separate the right and left parts into two distinct packs.

Characteristics of spreading with the right side against the back:

1) The head or top of the fabric, knit or nap are always facing the same direction.

2) The right and left parts are separated into two different packs.

3) The left and right parts may differ, as they are cut in two different operations.

4) The tonality and colour is generally the same, as the

SINGLE PLY   LAY OF FABRIC

STEPPED LAY

FABRIC ROLL

'RIGHT' SIDE   FABRIC DIRECTION

'WRONG' SIDE

TABLE

PLY HEAD

D

S

ZIG-ZAG SPREADING

D

S

D

S

parts of the same garment are generally located next to each other.

5) It requires almost double the time of zig-zag spreading.

Spreading fabric face-to-face

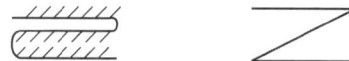

To spread fabric with the two right sides facing each other, the same process is followed as for fabric which is "face to back" (i.e., with fabric stacked with all faces pointed in the same direction), with one difference: the roll of fabric is rotated 180 degrees before each ply is spread. The coupling of the layers of fabric is analogous to the coupling of zig-zag spreading, but differs in that the direction of the nap or knit surface always has the same orientation. This spreading method is mainly chosen based on the following factors:

1) the fabric's characteristics, in terms of the orientation of the direction or the knit; 2) Manufacturing needs which require the right and left parts of the garment to be overlapped in a single parcel or separated into two different parcels.

Characteristics of spreading fabric 'face to face':

1) The head of the fabric or the knit is always facing the same direction.

2) The right and left parts are obtained from overlapping a single parcel.

3) The right and left parts are perfectly equal as they are cut in a single operation.

4) The tonality of the colours may be different as the right and left parts making up a single garment may be distant from each other depending on the length of the lay.

5) This spreading system is slower than the others.

Spreading symbols

In order to avoid errors and defects during fabric spreading and pattern layout, it is helpful to use symbols to indicate the type of layout or spreading method to adopt each time, as needed. Below you'll find the symbols used by a few companies, but this may vary by the form and type of indication.

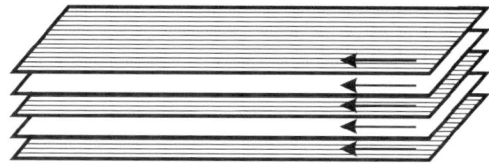

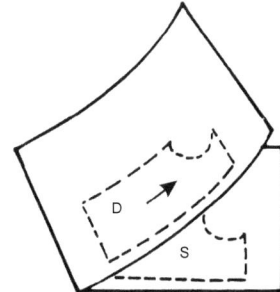

SPREADING FABRIC FACE-TO-FACE

ZIG-ZAG SPREADING

SPREADING RIGHT SIDE TO WRONG SIDE

SPREADING FABRIC FACE-TO-FACE

BASIC SPREADING SYMBOLS

SYMBOL CHART					
FABRIC	**A**	Fabric without a face (front or 'right' side), back or direction.	**SIZES**		Sizes laid out in the same direction.
	B	Fabric with a face (front) and back but without a direction.			One size laid out in one direction and the other in the opposite direction.
	C	Fabric with a semi-obligatory direction (slight nap or pile, small print).			Free layout of sizes.
	D	Fabric with an obligatory direction (velvet, prints, etc.).	**SPREADING**		**1** - ZIG-ZAG spreading with the right side in and opposite nap.
	E	Fabric with unique qualities (tartans, etc.)			**2** - Cut ply spreading with right-side in and opposite nap.
PATTERN		Matched pattern pieces.			**3** - Cut ply spreading with right side in and the same nap direction.
		Not matched pattern pieces.			**4** - Cut ply spreading, with the right side up, nap in the same direction.
		Pattern pieces laid out on the same nap.			**5** - Cut ply spreading, with the right side up and nap in opposite directions.
		Pattern pieces laid out on opposite naps.			**6** - Special spreading, with special instructions.

WIDTH OF THE FABRIC

The width of the fabric is the measurement expressed in linear centimetres of the distance between one selvedge and the other. The usable width excludes from the above measurement the two selvedges, which range from a few millimetres to a few centimetres. The width of the pattern layout is established by subtracting a few centimetres from the usable width of the fabric (usually 3-4 cm), to insure against the slippage of the layers of fabric. The width of the fabric can be single or double. It is single if less than 100 cm (usually 70-80 cm). It is double if greater than 100 cm (usually 140-150 cm). Generally speaking, summer fabrics have a single width, while wools and men's fabrics are double. Nowadays, however, textile manufacturers produce 150 cm fabric widths, regardless of the season and the fibre content, to satisfy the needs of the garment industry. There are maximum-width fabrics (from 200-300 cm), for bed linens. Fabrics made for sartorial use are wrapped on a flat cardboard core, folded double, with the right side inside the fold; those for industrial use are rolled on a cardboard or plastic cylinder, with the right side on the inside.

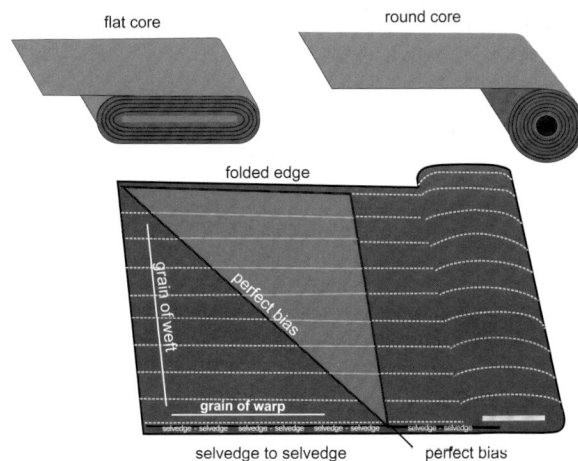

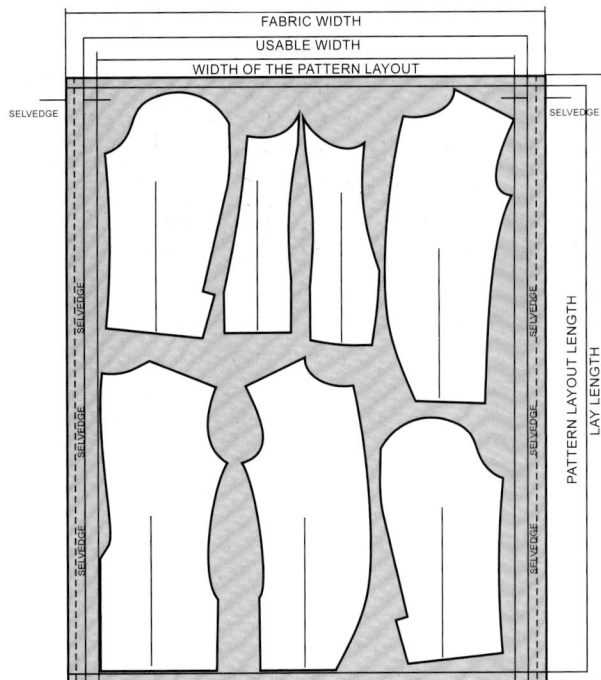

The grain of the fabric
The grain of the fabric is the same direction as the warp or the selvedge. Loom-woven fabrics are made up of longitudinal threads that intersect with the cross-threads. When these threads are perpendicular to one another, it is a straight grain fabric. It is very important to make sure that the fabric is perfectly aligned with the grain when laying out the pattern pieces to be cut. If the fabric is not cut precisely on the grain, the garment will never drape well or have a good fit.

Interlining
Facings are layers of fabric applied to the inside of garments, especially coats and jackets, between the outer layer of fabric and the lining. They help the garment keep its shape. Interlinings are established with a special process to: a) control the movement of the outer layer of fabric when washed and ironed; b) make the garment slightly more rigid, so that it holds its shape; c) create shapes and volumes, such as shoulders and necklines; d) improve the thermal insulation of the garment; e) increase the durability and resistance to wear and tear in the most delicate parts of the garment.

A lot of different types of fabric are used as interlinings, such canvas from 100% linen or 100% camel hair, or blended with other materials such as linen and viscose.

Interlinings can be made of woven or non-woven textiles or even knits, and they can be bonded to thermoplastic materials (or other materials), applying them with seams.

Woven interlinings can even be made of horsehair, be it natural or synthetic. Then there are cotton interlinings which are suitable for lightweight fabric, if stiffened with dimensional elements, such as Buckram, a sort of stiff cotton fabric with a loose weave, often muslin.

Warp-knit interlining.

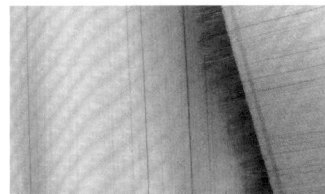

Horsehair interlining.

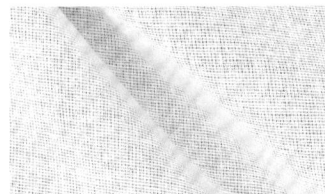

Buckram.

MANUAL LAYOUT OF THE PATTERN PIECES

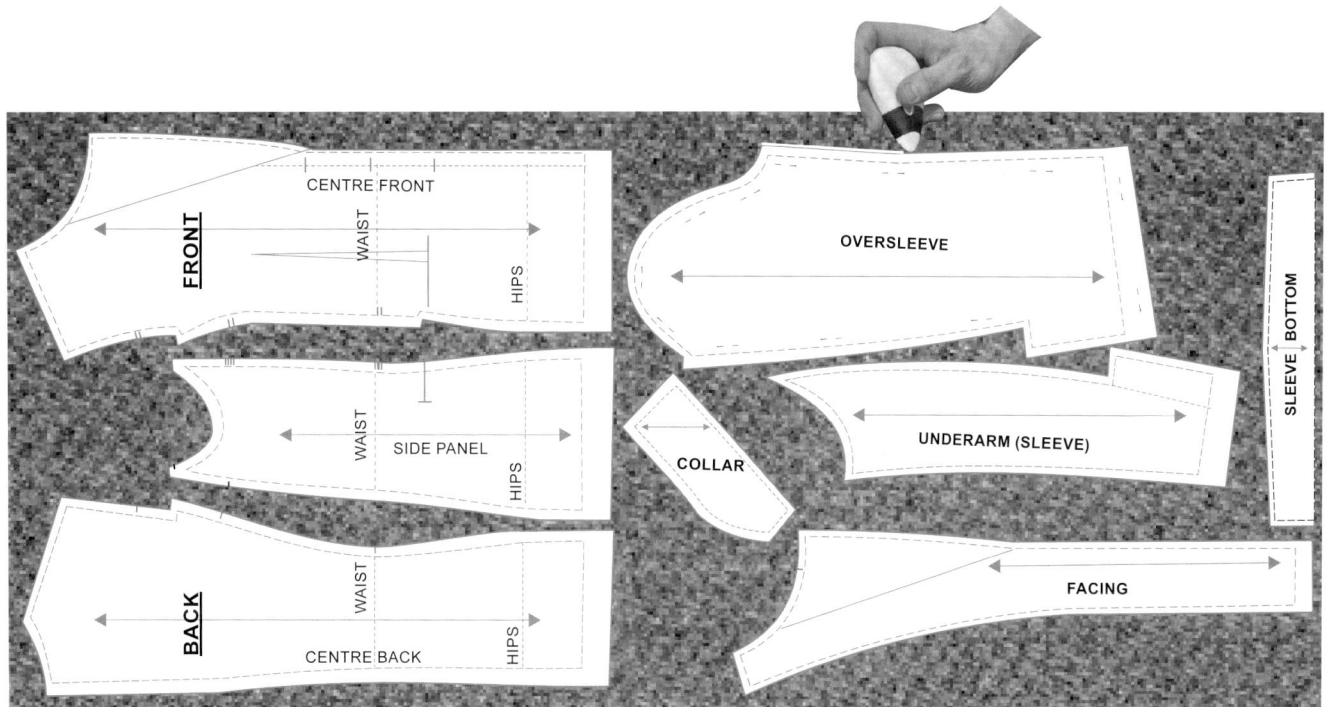

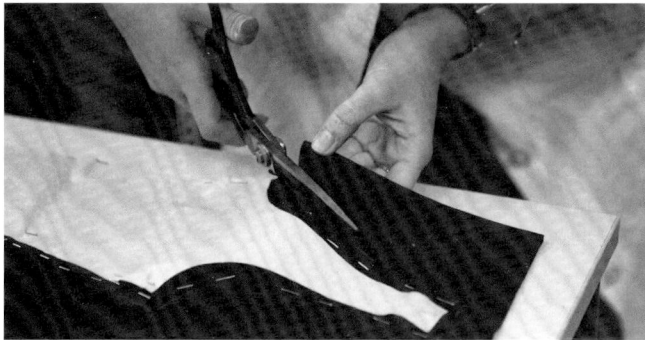

After having made the pattern and implemented any alterations, it's necessary to figure out how to best layout the pieces on the fabric that the garment will be made from. Some textiles, such as velvet, have an irregular height, so the advance study of the layout of the pieces (called nesting) makes it possible to determine how much fabric is needed. You'll need to consider a few important factors when nesting your pattern pieces. In particular: 1) does the fabric have a direction? If yes, you need to make sure that all pieces of the pattern are placed in the same direction; 2) does the fabric have a check motif? Stripes? Well then, you need to figure out the best way to nest them and make them line up; 3) Is the paper pattern to be placed on the bias? Or on the straight of grain? Grave draping defects are generally caused by the fact that they haven't been cut according to the straight of grain; 4) How many centimetres do you need to leave sartorially when you cut? Usually 2-3 cm / 0.79-1.18" are left at the sides, but if you have a shortage of fabric, you could drop down to 1.5 cm / 0.59"; 5) Is it a good idea to make a prototype out of inexpensive cloth, so that you'll be sure that the final result is perfect?

The simplest system for nesting your pattern is that of manually positioning the outlines of the pieces that make up the garment next to each other, arranging the various parts in a way that wastes as little fabric as possible while maintaining the straight of grain on each piece. Once the layout has been determined, carefully pin the pattern to the fabric. Only then should you proceed to cutting the fabric, considering the seam allowances necessary for the construction of the garment.

The patterns for the facings and linings are created by using the same paper pattern that was used for the fabric. The way in which the silhouettes are arranged will vary depending on the experience and skill of the individual tailor and/or patternmaker.

Remember that, before being nested and cut, the fabric and the inner reinforcements should be wet and steamed with the iron, or ironed with a damp cloth. This step is necessary to ensure that in the future, the fabric with which the garment is made doesn't shrink or spring back, compromising the fit after the first wash.

Also remember that the layout of the paper pattern on checked, tartan, and striped (regular or irregular) fabric is more complex as the motif has to be aligned on every part of the jacket.

SPREADING MACHINES

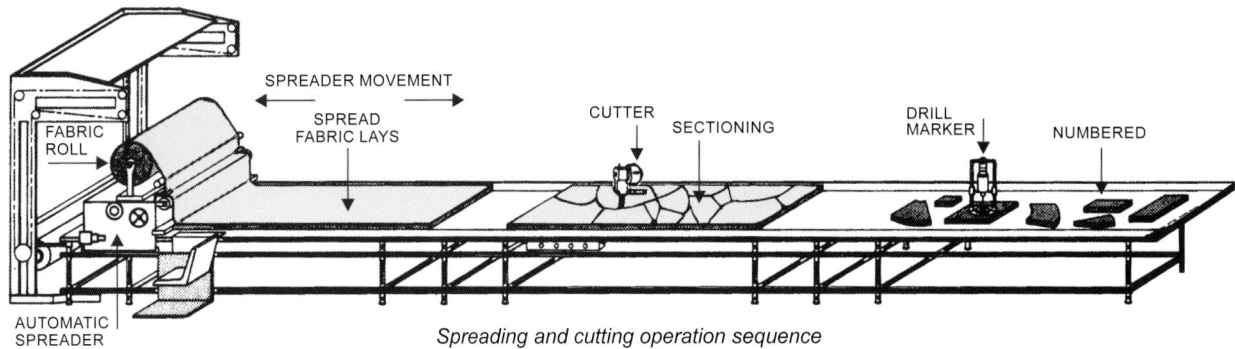

FABRIC ROLL · SPREADER MOVEMENT · SPREAD FABRIC LAYS · CUTTER · SECTIONING · DRILL MARKER · NUMBERED · AUTOMATIC SPREADER

Spreading and cutting operation sequence

Spreading machines

The use of spreading machines is important because it reduces the time and costs related to spreading.

Spreading machines are, at their base, made of a spreader carriage that runs along the table, equipped with a cradle to carry the roll of fabric that is to be spread.

After affixing the fabric on one end of the table by using the automatic gripper, the carriage is moved to the opposite end of the table, causing the fabric to be unrolled and placed on the plane of the table. Once extended for the desired length of the lay, the spreader stops and, for zig-zag spreading, the fabric is blocked by a gripping device. The machine, returning to the departure point, continues to lay the fabric across the table surface. However, in the case of 'face-to-back' spreading, a separating cut will be made before the machine returns to its departure point (of course without spreading any fabric on the return). For 'face-to-face' spreading, it is necessary to use a rotating roll cradle that so that the roll can be turned 180° after the creation of the separation cut. Again in this case, fabric is not spread on the carriage's return to the starting point.

Spreading machines are equipped with devices that facilitate and quicken spreading and which ensure that the plies are aligned, that the spreading takes place without tension on the fabric and that the separation cut is executed correctly, etc.

The various devices found on spreading machines may be engaged by hand or engaged automatically through electronically-controlled electromagnetic commands or through computer software. The former are semi-automatic spreading machines; the latter are fully automatic spreading machines.

Fabric feeding

The fabric needs to be fed so that it can move from the roll to be spread on the table without tension. Feeding may be made possible by a few counter-rotating bars covered in non-slip coating and pushed one against the other by a spring. The fabric thus passes between the two bars, which unroll the fabric by their rotation and deposit it on the table.

Device to align the fabric edges

Because of the need to pile the fabric as high as possible for the cutting phase, the edges of one layer must be perfectly aligned with the edges of the layers below it.

Automatic edge alignment device

For open fabrics or large-size tubular fabrics, for which an alignment guide may not be advised, the edges are aligned by appropriately moving the roll carried to the right or left during fabric spreading

Movement of the carriage and the feeding bars by a pair of photo-electric or laser cells. The fabric is aligned when its edge runs between the two cells during spreading.

Cutting

For 'face-against-back' and 'face-to-face' spreading, the cut is made with a circular blade cutter which runs along a transversely fixed track, placed on the rear part of the spreading machine. The cutter's electric motor, in addition to propelling the blade, provides the energy to move the cutter device parts from one side to the other of the spreading machine.

Spreading a ply of fabric

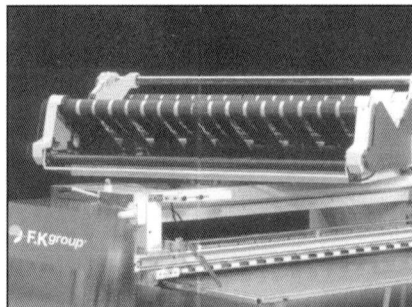

Rotating cradle for face-to-face spreading

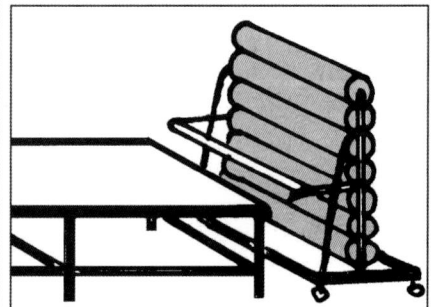

Roll stand

GRAPHIC OF THE PATTERN LAYOUT

The pattern layout graphic is the cutting path obtained with the arrangement of the pattern parts, in their various sizes made in cardboard, placing them one next to the others, spread across the width of the fabric in the best way possible, with logical schemes that ensure that fabric use is reduced to a minimum. When the layout is done using a material that allows the production of several copies, it is called a marker.

For a clothes manufacturer, the optimization of fabric use is fundamental for determining the cost of the finished garment, especially nowadays, when raw materials are so expensive.

Criteria for making the graphic

Before making the layout, it is necessary to analyse some technical factors inherent to the fabric and to the type of pattern, as well as to the garment itself. They are: 1) The height of the fabric; 2) The business classification of the fabric; 3) The symmetry of the pattern (symmetrical or asymmetrical pattern); 4) The number of sizes to lay out (one size fits all or various sizes); 5) The layout technique to use; 6) The professional skill of the operator.

The business classification of the fabric

The characteristics and the types of fabrics are numerous, so companies often draw up a classification and a codification system for internal use, for the purpose of indicating various qualities. They serve above all in the pattern layout. Fabric codification systems, using abbreviations and code names, essentially involves the following factors and characteristics:

- Fabric with no right side, wrong side or nap/direction (Class A - e.g.: facings in non-woven fabric).
- Fabric with a right side and wrong side but no nap (Class B - e.g.: fabric for linings or coated fabric).
- Fabric with a semi-obligatory cutting direction (Class C - e.g. fabric with a slight nap).
- Fabric with an obligatory cutting direction (Class D – e.g. velvet, loden, prints, etc.).
- Special fabrics to be decided individually (Class E – e.g. plaids, checks, etc.).

Class A fabrics, without a right side and wrong side and without a nap, offer the best return in terms of consumption, while as requirements and conditions grow, consumption for the same garment increases.

The fabric's structure and its pattern are elements that determine the direction in which the pattern pieces have to be laid.

Other important factors to bear in mind are:
- The straight grain of the fabric, which is any segment that runs parallel to the warp or the selvedge of the fabric.

The straight grain of the pattern, which must be clearly indicated on every pattern piece, with a line with arrows and the inscription 'straight of grain'.

When the straight of grain of the pattern coincides with the straight of grain of the fabric, the garment is said to be on the straight grain.

When the pattern is positioned with the straight grain parallel to the weft, the garment is said to be on the cross grain.

When the straight grain of the pattern is positioned on the diagonal of the fabric, it's 'on the bias'.

The straight-of-grain line drawn on the pattern should always be positioned in the direction of the warp, so the position that the pattern is given on the layout graphic is practically automatic.

NESTING CHARACTERISTICS

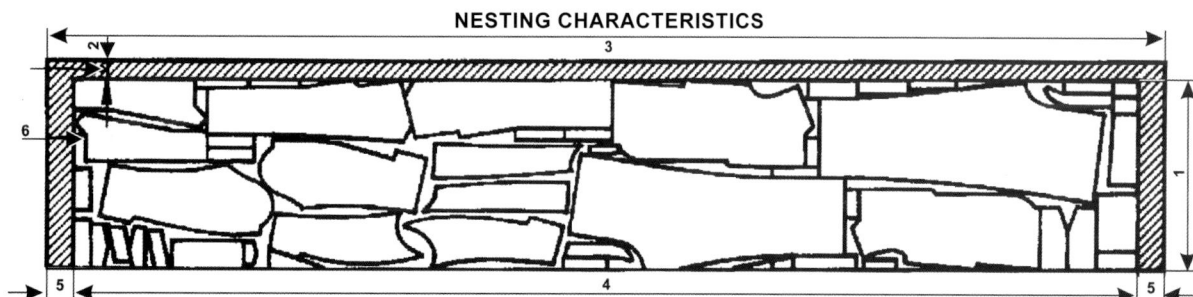

1) Usable height – width of the fabric minus the width of the selvedges.
2) Selvedge waste – Cutting waste on the width of the cloth.
3) Default length – Length of the graphic + head and foot.

4) Length of the layout graphic.
5) Cutting head and foot – Cloth remnants at the top and the bottom of the fabric.
6) Cutting waste – fabric scraps from within the pattern layout.

LAYOUT TECHNIQUES

The best-known layout techniques at the present time are as follows: 1. Direct manual layout; 2. Reduced scale layout; 3. Computer-assisted layout.

Direct manual layout

This is the simplest method and it consists in arranging the cardboard pattern pieces manually on the fabric, one next to the other, done directly by the technician, who is entrusted with maximizing the use of the fabric.

'Direct manual' layout can be performed in the following ways:

- directly on the fabric, drawing the outlines with chalk or a coloured pencil.
- directly on the fabric, drawing the outlines using dabbers or with a chalk spray pistol.
- drawing the pattern outlines in pencil on cardboard; going over them with the perforator and then dabbing the 'marker' (the diagram of the layout) with special powders.
- Laying out the pattern on the 'marker', drawing the numbered piece outlines and laying the marker on top of the layers of fabric to be cut.
- laying out the pattern on the 'marker', drawing the numbered piece outlines on carbon paper and then tracing the outlines in pencil.
- laying out the pattern, drawing the numbered piece outlines in pencil. The layout thus obtained is called a "marker" and is used to make successive copies.

Layout with reduced silhouettes

The original patterns are reduced to scale 1:30 or 1:5 using pantographic spirals and then cut. The reduced scale pattern pieces are placed on a table in the same small scale for the study of the best layout.

This method allows you to have a better overall view and therefore a better result in the least time. The marker obtained is photographed or photocopied for archiving.

To make the cut you have to enlarge the marker again, drawing it in 1:1 scale.

Layout with the use of computers

The last way to optimise the cutting layout consists in the use of computerised systems. This is carried out by an independent work unit dedicated to the study, execution and storage of layouts for the cutting room, using tables and rules and with checks and modification of the parts stored and preparation of the work sequence, style, order placement, review and restructuring files.

The layout function is made on a video graphic using 256 and more colours, from which it is also possible to access the program of control and manipulation of the digitalised pieces.

When the layout order is requested, the screen will show the area of the fabric with the height requested and a menu of the pieces required for the specific layout.

Direct manual layout.

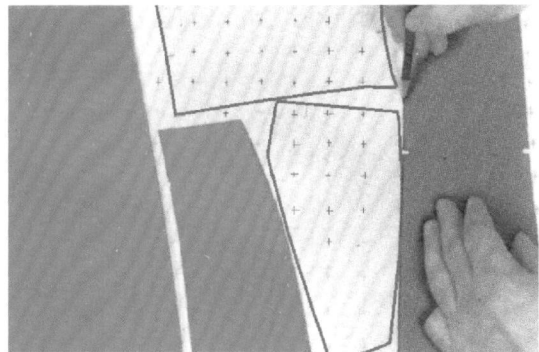

Marker made by hand-drawing the outlines.

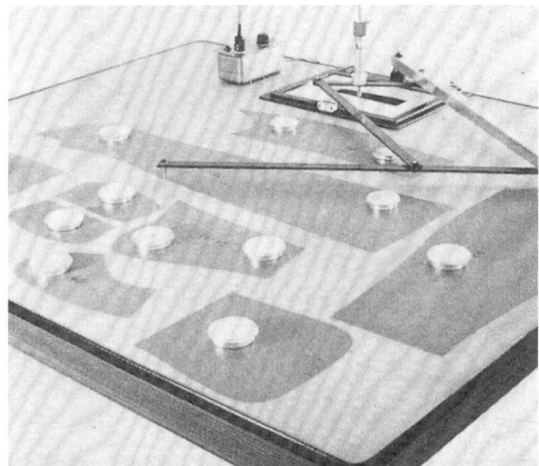

Marker made using reduced silhouettes and a pantograph.

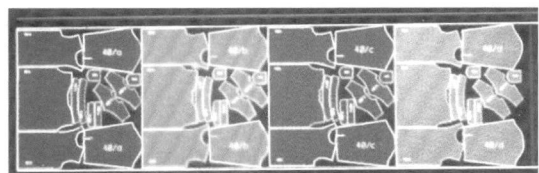

Marker made using a computer.

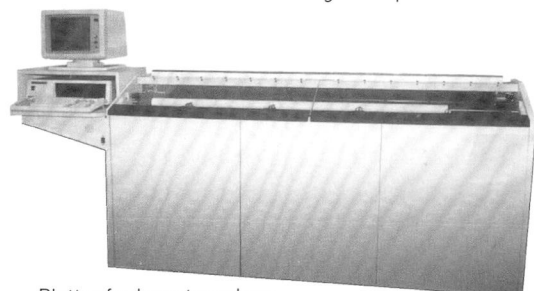

Plotter for layout markers.

LAYOUT STRATEGIES

Layout with all the pieces
The complete layout is carried out with all the pattern pieces: right and left sides, plackets and facings, collars, cuffs, etc.
This graphic is used by the industries, with fabrics laid out at full height.

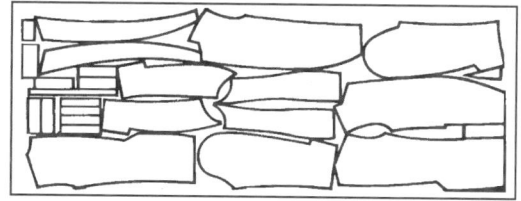
Layout with all the pieces.

Single-size layout
This is the graphic rendition of the layout using only one size pattern pieces.
This layout is quite simple and has advantages for order planning, but, compared to several-size layouts, it has the disadvantage of greater fabric consumption.

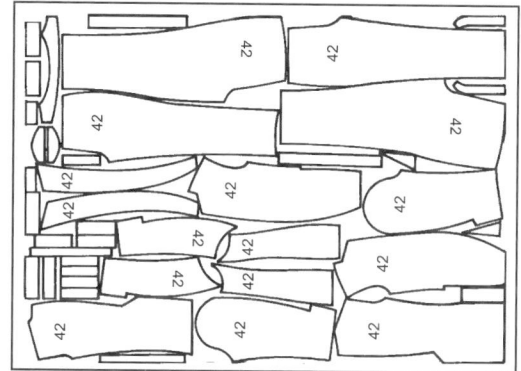
Single-size layout.

Layout with half the pieces
The layout using only half the pattern pieces (for example, with the right or the left half) is done with a double layer of fabric (face to face) or tubular fabrics.

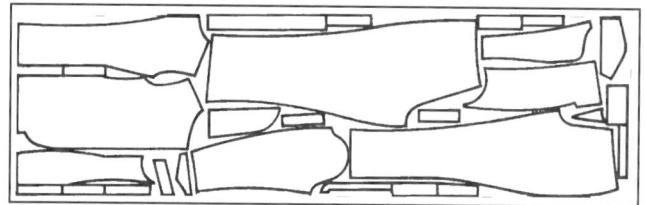
Layout with half the pieces.

Sectional nesting
This nesting style is done with two or more sizes (the same or different ones), positioned in sequence, one after the other, with the pieces arranged in a rectangular 'section'.

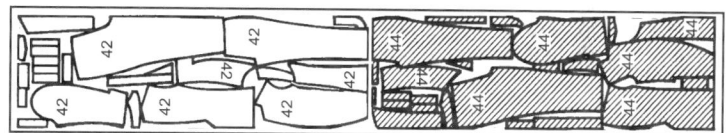
Sectional layout.

Interlocking sectional nesting
This nesting style is done with two adjacent sizes, dovetailed together.

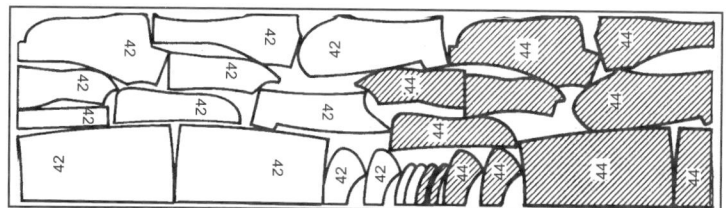
Interlocking sectional layout.

Mixed multi-size layout
This layout gets the most out the fabric as it uses pattern pieces of various dimensions, in all the available space.

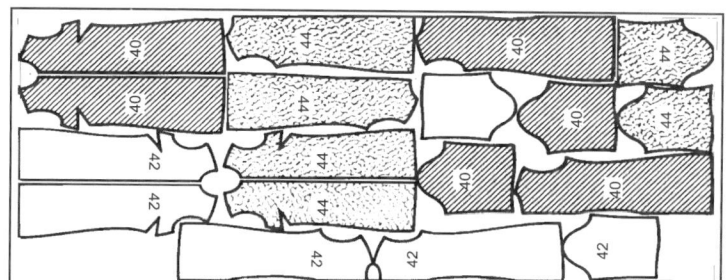
Mixed multi-size layout.

PATTERN ARRANGEMENT

Piece arrangement

The pattern arrangement can be 'matched', or 'dovetailed', when two perfectly identical pieces (e.g., the front) become a right and a left only because they are laid out facing one another on the fabric. Or it can be 'not matched', or 'in a row', but in this case the two perfectly identical pieces (e.g., the front) can be worn only on one side of the person (e.g., left), and furthermore, this arrangement is usually used for fabrics without a right side and without a nap (Class A).

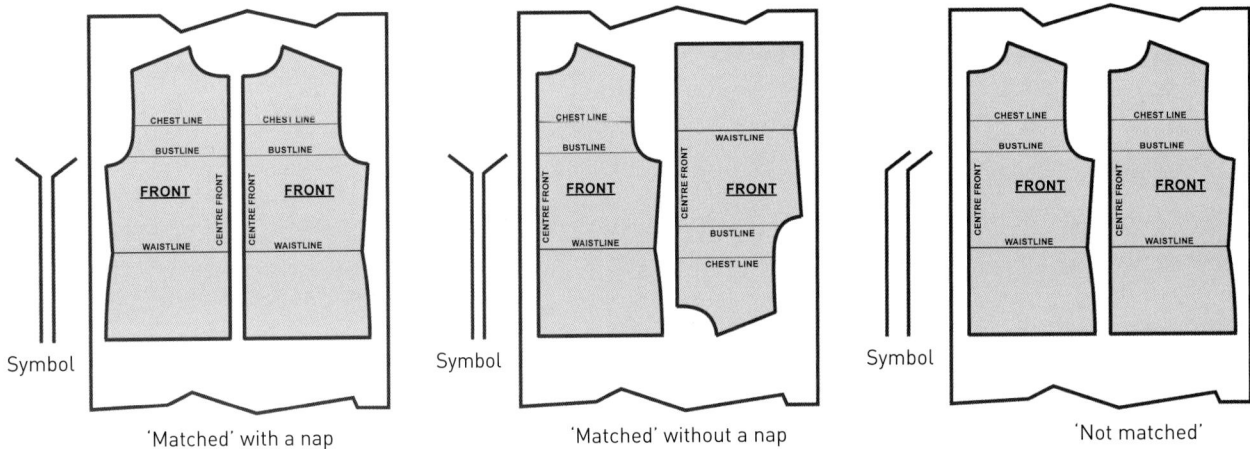

Symbol

'Matched' with a nap

Symbol

'Matched' without a nap

Symbol

'Not matched'

'Not matched' arrangement

Clothing manufacturers rarely make as many layouts as there are sizes sold: this would create a lot of scrap and greater consumption of fabric.

The most widely used solution is to keep track of sale and establish whether it is worthwhile to combine two or more sizes (or several articles of the same size) in a single layout.

Size symbols

To make the layout decided on perfectly clear, here, too, companies use a symbol code to indicate the types of pieces to lay out and the type of arrangement to use.

Examples of size symbols.

Sizes laid out in the same direction.

One size laid out in one direction and the other in the opposite direction.

Free layout of sizes.

LAYOUT NAPS

Nap of patterns of the same size

The various pattern pieces of the same size, such as, for example, the front, the back, the sleeves, etc., are laid out in different ways, depending on the nap of the fabric.

To indicate the nap of the fabric, companies use symbols, as for the layout and the sizes.

Layouts without a nap

For Class A and B fabrics, which do not have a grain, the pattern pieces are laid out any which way, as in the following example, where a back, a front, and a sleeve are laid out in one direction, while a front and another sleeve are positioned in the opposite direction.

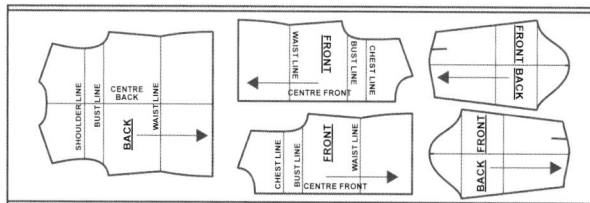

Layout with a nap

For Class C and D fabrics, which have a nap, the pattern pieces are laid out with attention to the nap, as in the following example, where the back, the front, and the sleeves are positioned all in the same direction.

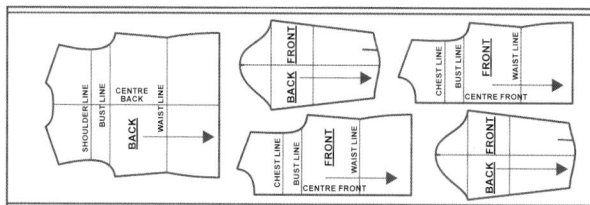

Pattern pieces laid out in the same direction.

Pattern pieces laid out on opposite naps.

Layout of pattern pieces of the same size without nap.

Layout of pattern pieces of the same size with nap.

Layout with two sizes and:	
-Fabric class	A
-Not matched pattern	
-Pattern without nap	
-Free layout of pattern pieces	
-Sizes	42 and 44

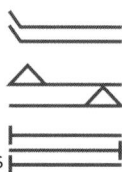

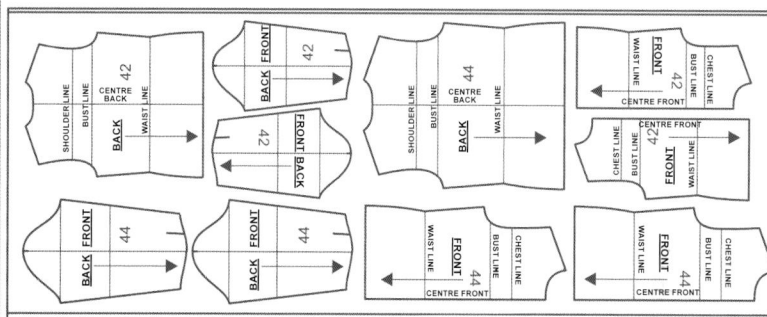

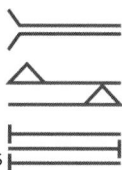

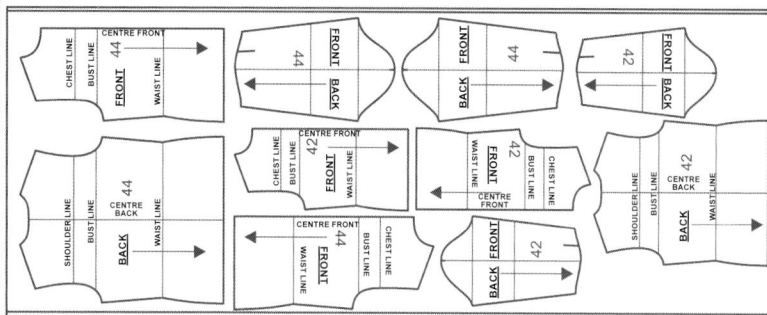

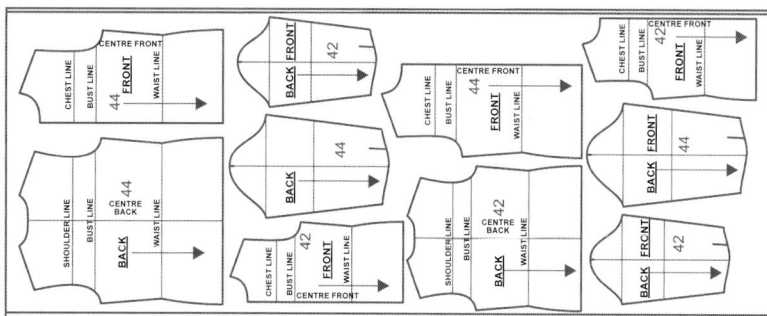

Layout with two sizes and:	
-Fabric class	B
-Matched pattern	
-Pattern without nap	
-Free layout of pattern pieces	
-Sizes	42 and 44

Layout with two sizes and:	
-Fabric class	C and E
-Matched pattern	
-Pattern with nap	
-Pattern pieces laid out on the same nap	
-Sizes	42 and 44

CUTTING

After studying the layout, the spreading of the fabric and the marker making, the lay is ready to be cut. 'Cut' is understood to mean the trimming of the pieces of the pattern as they are marked on the layout graphic, on the various layers of overlapping fabric. Usually the layout graphic, created according to various techniques (drawn, traced, sprayed, glued or sewn), is placed on the first layer of the stack.

Cutting is broken down into two operations: division, that is sub-dividing the lay into smaller, more manageable parts so that the following operation of cutting the curves into the fabric is easier; and the cutting into the precise, exact shapes of the individual pieces. Precision mainly depends on the type of equipment used for cutting. The lay is cut with electric table cutters and belt-run saw cutters if done manually, or with a cutter incorporated into the spreading machine if done automatically.

Electric table cutters are divided into two categories: circular blades and vertical blades.

- Circular blade cutters: this type of cutter is used for the division of small or medium thickness lays. They cannot be used to cut the curved portions of a pattern as it is too difficult to trace sharply arched lines and corners in particular, due to the shape and thus the footprint of the blade itself.

- Vertical blade cutters: this type of cutter is useful for the division of small, medium and thick lays as well as for cutting the curves of a piece. This is possible thanks to the reduced footprint of the blade and its alternating vertical movement which allows it to closely and precisely follow the edges of a pattern.

Belt-run saw cutters are used for ultra-precise cutting, especially for the smaller pieces of a pattern. With these cutters or saws, the pieces are easier to move and manipulate as the operator can use both hands to control the lay as they cut. This last machine may be equipped with two blade rotation speeds: the slower speed is used for cutting fabrics with a high percentage of synthetic fibres in order to avoid melting.

The cutting or the dividing of the lay may be done directly on the spreading table with technologically advanced equipment which carries out the complete operation with maximum precision and notable speed.

In this case, the next lay is spread after the first stack of fabric is moved by conveyor belt to the adjacent cutting table.

Numbering the pieces

'Numbering' is understood to mean the placing of a small label or tag on every cut piece of fabric which makes up a garment. Numbering is useful to avoid sewing pattern pieces cut from different plies of fabric, thus avoiding possible colour defects in the same garment.

The label or the tag contains certain data or numbers which, as a code, may help identify the fabric. For example: the client's name, the order number, the cut, how many garments are included in the order, the colour, the operator that created the numbering, other instructions from the company, and the layer number, etc.

The machine used for this operation is the Saobar, the maker of which is based in the UK.

Spring clamps for fabric

Pressure grip clamps for fabric

Vertical blade cutter

Circulate blade cutter

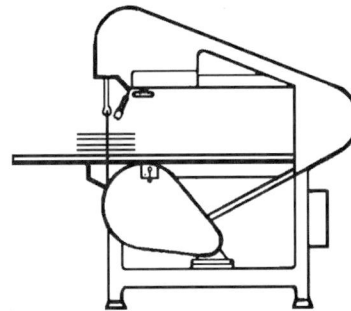
Band saw for fabric

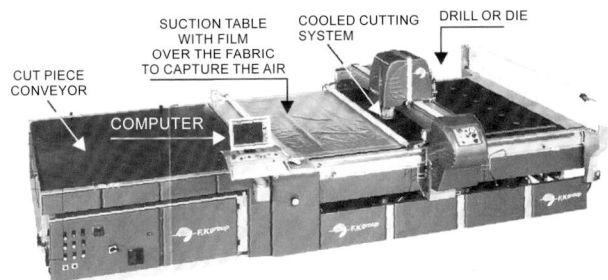
Automated cutting machine

Cutter with sharpening and flexion controls

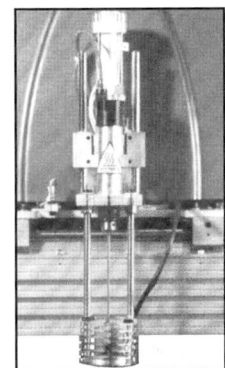
Die-cutting or punching device

PARCEL FORMATION

'Parcels' are created for greater security when cutting, so that the pieces are not confused during the production process.

You can create the parcel before or after numbering, according to the type of layout. If there is just one garment in one size on the layout, you can send it on to be numbered immediately. Otherwise, you must first subdivide the pieces and then send them for numbering.

To facilitate subdivision, each piece within the layout should have its size clearly labelled on it. If there are numerous garments to be cut, it is incredibly important that there is an additional number or letter or symbol which can identify how the pieces are to be grouped.

A possible example of the letters/numbers/symbols to be written on each piece (for example, with 3 garments all in the same size) is as follows: Sz.14/A Sz.14/B Sz.14/C

After the pieces have been numbered, you must prepare for the subdivision into many other parcels (or rolls if the parcels are small), which may be grouped:

1) by colour.
2) by the number of clients they will be sent to.
3) by the factories that will produce them.
4) by the production lines to be fed.
5) by the needs of each company.

Binding the parcels or rolls

To organise the pieces of the parcel, consider two systems:
1) Tying the smallest parts (flaps, loops, pockets, etc.) with elastic, twine or adhesive tape and eventually putting all the parcels in a single bag. This system is costlier, including during subsequent production phases, but it is more secure as the pieces are less likely to be lost.
2) Stacking the pieces. Place the largest piece at the bottom then, one by one, stack the smaller pieces on top. Roll everything together and tie with a strip of fabric, twine, adhesive tape, etc. This system costs less, but the pieces within the roll may slide out, thus increasing the chance of mixing them up or losing them.

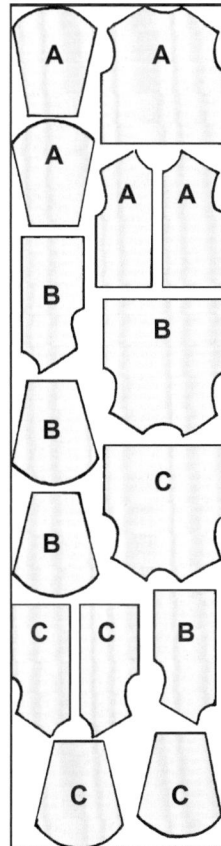

Layout of 3 garments

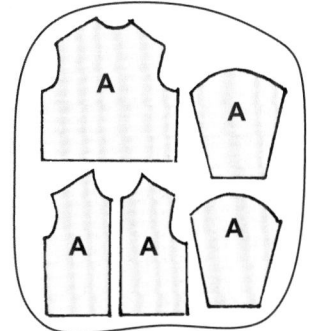

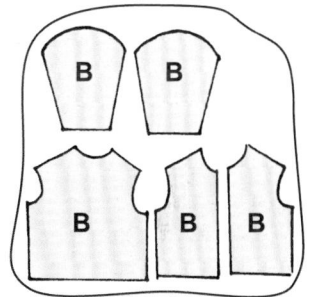

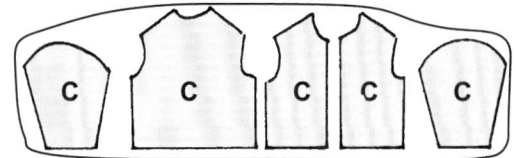

Division of pieces with the same symbol

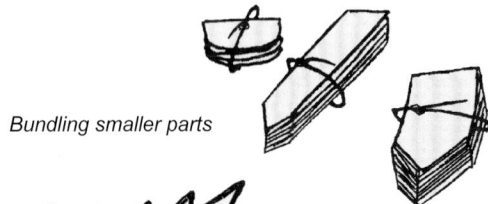

Bundling smaller parts

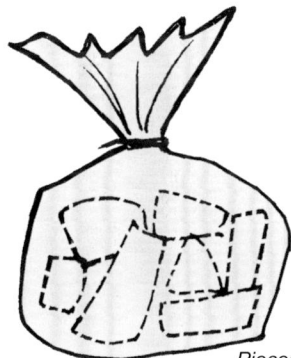

Pieces in a single bag

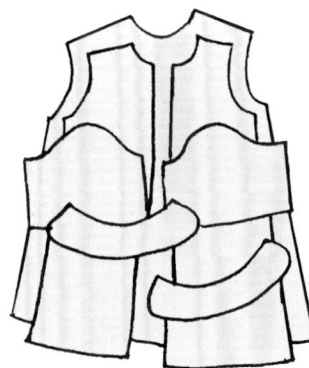

Stacking the pieces

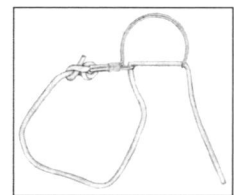

Cord with a hook

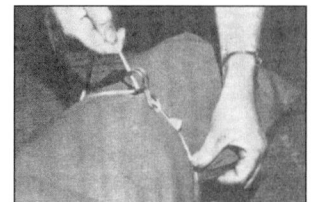

Tying the pieces

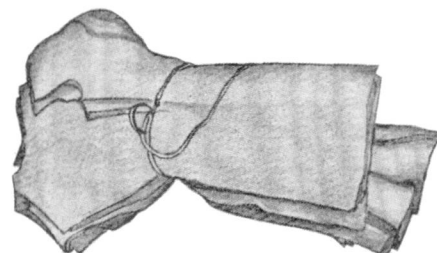

Parcel tied with elastic

PATTERN DATA SHEET

The pattern data sheet, usually drawn up by the designer along with the patternmaker, is an indispensable tool for defining and completing the description of all the details that make it up.

The data sheet should include the technical sketch of the pattern, rendered as clearly as possible and which, if necessary, should highlight all the details needed to understand every part of it. Furthermore, there should be a detailed description of any instructions concerning the layout and any accessories, the dimensions of any appliqués, the type of fabric to use, the most important measurements, and the features of the pattern.

This card must be a reliable guide for the accurate realization of the garment conceived.

GARMENT FEATURE NOTES	PATTERN	
	SIZE	
	CLASS	
	SKETCH PATTERN	

INTERIOR AND ADHESIVES

PRODUCTION INSTRUCTIONS

'DO NOT SEW THE GARMENT BEFORE GETTING APPROVAL'	BUTTONS
	BUTTONS
	ELASTIC
	EPAULETTES
	ZIP
	HOOKS
	OTHER ACCESSORIES

DETAILS

SPECIAL DETAILS

MEASURES									FABRIC	HEIGHT	TYPE

DESIGNER/PATTERNMAKER	DATE

COST ANALYSIS SHEET

The cost analysis sheet, usually put out by the production planning department, flanked by the designer and the head of purchasing, should contain all the information necessary for making the pattern for the garment; the type of fabric and its cost; the accessories that go along with the garment, and their costs; and the time needed for individual processing and the relative costs. This sheet is very useful for the production of the garment, especially to define the costs and, if these prove to be too high with respect to the target market's expectations, it provides the opportunity to intervene on the factors that determine it.

GENERAL INFORMATION			FABRIC INFORMATION		GARMENT INFORMATION	
TYPE	HEIGHT	SIZE	RESOURCES		DEPARTMENT	
			PATTERN		NAME OR N°.	
			WIDTH		PRICE	
			PRICE		SEASON	
			CONTENTS		REF. NUMBER	
			COLOURS		DATE	
			AGENT		ARTICLE	
			TEL. N°		SIZE	
			BLEND		COLOURS	
					COMPOSIT.	

1 - MATERIAL -	ESTIMATED WASTE	ACTUAL WASTE	PRICE PER METER	TOTAL PRICE	DESIGN
LINING					
INTERIOR					

TOTAL COST OF ALL THE OTHER MATERIALS USED _____

2 - ACCESSORIES -	ESTIMATED QUANTITY	ACTUAL QUANTITY	PRICE EACH	TOTAL PRICE
BUTTONS				
ZIP				
WAISTBAND				
PLEATS				

TOTAL COST OF ACCESSORIES _____

3 - LABOUR	ESTIMATED TIME	REAL TIME	TOTAL COST
CUT			
ASSEMBLY			

TOTAL COST OF LABOUR _____

TOTAL COST		
MARKUP	%	
WHOLESALE PRICE		
VAT		
TOTAL		
NOTES		

SPECIAL DETAILS

TECHNICAL OFFICE HEAD   DATE

ACKNOWLEDGEMENTS

The outlines from which the garment construction references are derived, in exact reference to the structure of the body, are more than basic expressions of a system. They are derived from rationally constructed patterns that have been duly executed and tested with the collaboration of lecturers and external consultants of Euromode School Italia - European Institute for Fashion and Design, of which I am honoured to be the General Director.
I would like to express my heartfelt thanks to them for making the garments, whose various steps and construction methods have been illustrated and explained.

In particular, I would like to mention and express my gratitude to:
- Cinzia Trovesi, lecturer in patternmaking and tailoring, for her collaboration in creating the models.
- Sartoria Cassera di Marisa Cassera - Grassobbio (BG), Euromode School Italia teacher, for the collaboration in the production and testing of the garments presented in the book.
- Studio Carissoni Indust. Clothing Consultant owned by P.I. Ezio Carissoni - Orio al Serio (Bergamo).
- Elisabetta 'Kuky' Drudi for the illustrations.
- Graphic design studio Dabo di Tarnghi Valter- Grumello del Monte (Bergamo).
- Studio Emdo di Emanuela Donnanno for the copyright.

I would also like to express my gratitude for the cooperation and support of:
- Lanieri Reda S.p.A. - Val di lana (Biella) - made-to-measure clothing production.
- Genny S.p.A. - Ancona - industrial clothing production.
- Cotonificio Albini - Albino (Bergamo).
- Rinaldo Donagemma & C. - Tailoring equipment - Cinisello Balsamo (Milan).
- Macpi Group S.p.A. - Palazzolo sull'Oglio (Brescia). Industrial ironing machines and irons.
- Bianchi-Maré - Industrial sewing machines.
- F.K. System - Dalmine (Bergamo) - Computerised systems for industry and tailoring.

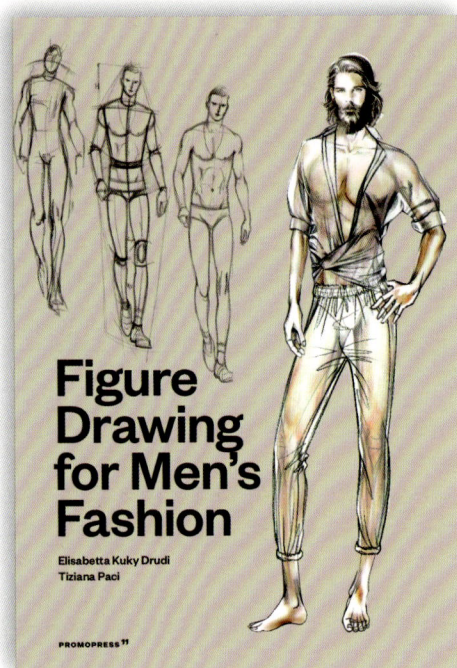

FIGURE DRAWING FOR MEN'S FASHION

Elisabetta Kuky Drudi and Tiziana Paci

ISBN: 978-84-17412-83-8
210 x 297 mm. 352 pages

This completely redesigned and updated long-selling manual, specifically dedicated to the male figure in fashion design, offers a comprehensive guide to acquiring and perfecting the skills needed to produce realistic and precise fashion drawings that accurately reflect a designer's creative vision. It covers all aspects related to the drawing of male human figure, male fashion figurines, colouring styles and techniques, as well as the design and representation of fabrics. The book also includes technical details and examples of different types of clothing and accessories. The best-selling authors, Elisabetta Kuky Drudi and Tiziana Paci, have decades of experience in the fashion industry and have created an invaluable resource for designers, design students and illustrators.

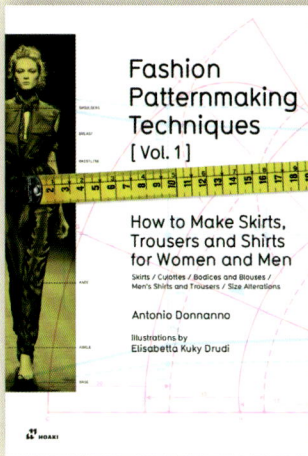

FASHION PATTERNMAKING TECHNIQUES [VOL. 1]
How to Make Skirts, Trousers and Shirts for Women and Men
Antonio Donnanno
Illustrations by
Elisabetta Kuky Drudi

ISBN: 978-84-15967-09-5
210 x 297 mm. 256 pages

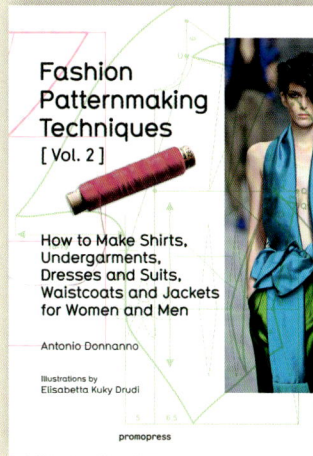

FASHION PATTERNMAKING TECHNIQUES [VOL. 2]
How to Make Shirts, Undergarments, Dresses and Suits, Waistcoats and Jackets for Women and Men
Antonio Donnanno
Illustrations by
Elisabetta Kuky Drudi

ISBN: 978-84-15967-68-2
210 x 297 mm. 256 pages

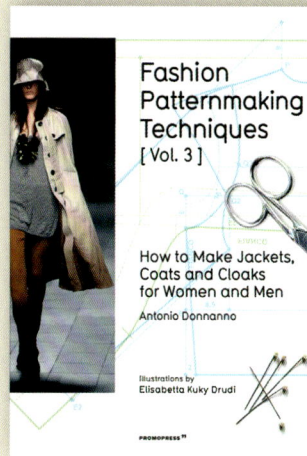

FASHION PATTERNMAKING TECHNIQUES [VOL. 3]
How to Make Jackets, Coats and Cloaks for Women and Men
Antonio Donnanno
Illustrations by
Elisabetta Kuky Drudi

ISBN: 978-84-16504-18-3
210 x 297 mm. 176 pages

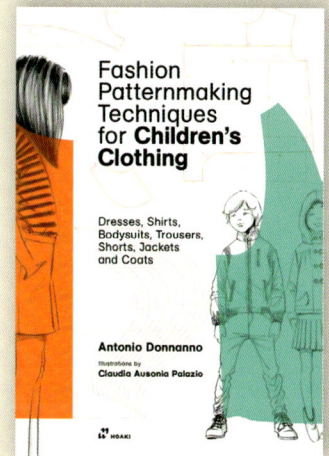

FASHION PATTERNMAKING TECHNIQUES FOR CHILDREN'S CLOTHING
Dresses, Shirts, Bodysuits, Trousers, Shorts, Jackets and Coats
Antonio Donnanno
Illustrations by
Claudia Ausonia Palazio

ISBN: 978-84-16851-14-0
210 x 297 mm. 232 pages

FASHION PATTERNMAKING TECHNIQUES HAUTE COUTURE [VOL. 1]
Haute Couture Models, Draping Techniques, Decorations
Antonio Donnanno

ISBN: 978-84-16504-66-4
210 x 297 mm. 256 pages

FASHION PATTERNMAKING TECHNIQUES HAUTE COUTURE [VOL. 2]
Creative Darts, Draping, Frills and Flounces, Collars, Necklines and Sleeves, Trousers and Shirts
Antonio Donnanno

ISBN: 978-84-17412-38-8
210 x 297 mm. 200 pages

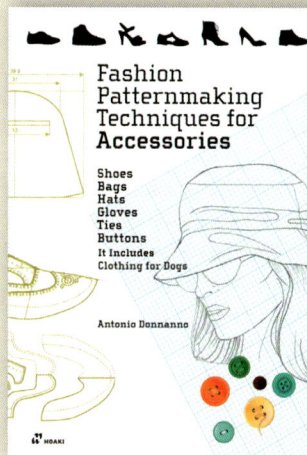

FASHION PATTERNMAKING TECHNIQUES ACCESSORIES
Shoes, Bags, Hats, Gloves, Ties, Buttons. It Includes Clothing for Dogs
Antonio Donnanno

ISBN: 978-84-16851-61-4
210 x 297 mm. 240 pages

Follow us:
www.hoaki.com
hoakibooks